Teaching Developmental Writing

Background Readings

Second Edition

Susan Naomi Bernstein

The University of Houston–Downtown

Bedford/St. Martin's   Boston   ◆   New York

For Bedford/St. Martin's
Developmental Editor: Karin Halbert
Senior Production Editor: Lori Chong Roncka
Senior Production Supervisor: Dennis Conroy
Editorial Assistant: Caryn O'Connell
Production Assistants: Kristen Merrill, Amy Derjue
Copyeditor: Jane Zanichkowsky
Text Design: Claire Seng-Niemoeller
Cover Design: Donna L. Dennison
Composition: Karla Goethe, Orchard Wind Graphics
Printing and Binding: Haddon Craftsmen, Inc., an R.R. Donnelley & Sons Company

President: Joan E. Feinberg
Editorial Director: Denise B. Wydra
Editor in Chief: Karen S. Henry
Director of Marketing: Karen Melton Soeltz
Director of Editing, Design, and Production: Marcia Cohen
Managing Editor: Elizabeth M. Schaaf

Manufactured in the United States of America.

8   6   6   5
f   e   d   c

For information, write: Bedford/St. Martin's, 75 Arlington Street, Boston, MA 02116 (617-399-4000)

ISBN: 0–312–41189–8

Acknowledgments
Linda Adler-Kassner, "Just Writing, Basically: Basic Writers on Basic Writing." Copyright © 1999 by the *Journal of Basic Writing*, The City University of New York. Reprinted from Volume 18, Number 2, by permission.
Gloria Anzaldúa, "How to Tame a Wild Tongue." From *Borderlands/La Frontera: The New Mestiza*. Copyright © 1987, 1999 by Gloria Anzaldúa. Reprinted by permission of Aunt Lute Books.
Susan Naomi Bernstein, "Instructional Note: Life Writing and Basic Writing." Originally published in *Teaching English in the Two-Year College*, May 1998. Copyright © 1998 by the National Council of Teachers of English. Reprinted with permission.
Linda Lonon Blanton, excerpt from "Classroom Instruction and Language Minority Students: On Teaching to 'Smarter' Readers and Writers." From *Generation 1.5 Meets College Composition: Issues in the Teaching of Writing to U.S.-Educated Learners of ESL*, edited by Harklau, Losey & Siegal. Lawrence Erlbaum Associates. © 1999. Reprinted by permission of the author.

Preface

Students arrive in our developmental writing classrooms with a variety of needs; perhaps the most pressing is the need to learn skills that they can immediately apply in their writing for other college courses, for work, and for everyday life. To succeed, they need to see writing as "real" and connected to their experiences and goals. *Teaching Developmental Writing: Background Readings,* Second Edition, has been designed with both students' and teachers' needs in mind. The descriptions of pedagogy and practice offered in this text show that the teaching and learning of developing writers takes place in a variety of contexts and under a variety of circumstances.

Much has changed since my work began on the initial *Background Readings* ancillaries that accompanied Anker's *Real Writing* and Kirszner and Mandell's *Writing First,* from which this book was adapted. Research and practice in the field of developmental writing continue to expand, but one critical question persists, as indicated in the thirteen new readings in this edition: What is the purpose of the developmental writing course? A lively discussion ensues about whether students ought to be learning how to write academic discourse, learning how to develop their own writing voices and styles, or learning some combination of both of these strategies. An additional issue addressed by the selections in the text is the impact that technology continues to have on our profession. The chapter on technology has been thoroughly revised to reflect the fact that computer access is not universal, as well as to offer suggestions for increasing access for developing writers. This edition also focuses on reading as a critical component of the developmental writing course, particularly for students who are nonnative speakers of English.

Another critical question raised by the selections in this book is: How do we create an environment in which a culturally diverse student body can thrive? Throughout this revision, I have sought to retain the first edition's significant focus on diversity. There are separate chapters titled "Writing and Race, Class, and Gender" and "Teaching ESL." Diversity-focused articles are also included in the chapters titled "Basic Writing: Students' Perspectives," "Writing and Adult Learners," and "Basic Writing and the Writing Center." Moreover, throughout the selections in *Teaching Developmental Writing: Background Readings,* we hear the voices of students from varying cultural backgrounds. Presenting excerpts from student writing, as well as narratives and interviews, the authors illustrate the growth of their diverse student writers. In this way, we can see the profound impact that pedagogy and practice may have on perhaps our most important goal: the development of all our students as writers and critical thinkers.

Teaching Developmental Writing: Background Readings also answers the practical questions that we ask every day in our work as teachers. How can we design courses that truly meet our students' needs? How can we accommodate students with different learning styles? How should we approach assessment at both the classroom and the institutional levels, and, perhaps most significant, how do these issues affect our day-to-day teaching? I have selected readings that can help us address these questions, both as individual teachers and as a community, and have organized them into fourteen chapters. The editorial apparatus is divided into practical sections. Chapter introductions present a context for the selections and offer a range of perspectives on the issues to be discussed, and the reading headnotes identify the most important features of the article. The "Classroom Activities" sections provide suggestions for creating classroom projects based on ideas or concepts from each reading. The "Thinking about Teaching" sections allow room for professional reflection and action, offering ideas for contributing to the professional discussions taking place in our hallways, offices, staff meetings, and elsewhere in our institutions — and in the forums of our journals, conventions, and Internet listservs. Finally, an updated end-of-book bibliography provides the reader with more sources of information for further reading and research.

As developmental writing teachers, we often find that our status seems marginal, outside the larger conversations taking place in the rhetoric and composition community. Moreover, the needs of our students, as well as the complicated nature of our working conditions, often prove more urgent and immediate than abstract theoretical arguments. How can we create a supportive working environment for students who may be under extreme economic and personal pressures that we can only begin to imagine? How can we be effective teachers if we spend our professional lives as "freeway fliers," rushing across town and across communities to our varied and different classrooms? Although *Teaching Developmental Writing: Background Readings* does not provide easy solutions to these dilemmas, it does present a range of perspectives offered by experienced teachers and emphasizes practical approaches to the everyday problems of our classrooms and our institutions. Each article invites us to examine classroom practice and to take part in professional discussions about our students and our teaching.

Acknowledgments

At Bedford/St. Martin's, I would like to thank Joan Feinberg, president; Chuck Christensen, former president; and Karen Henry, editor in chief, for their commitment to providing teachers with the best possible tools for meeting the needs of their students. I am also grateful to Denise Wydra, editorial director, who first suggested this project in the spring of 1996; Michelle Clark, who carefully nurtured and served as editor of the first version of *Background Readings;* Talvi Laev, who guided me through the second version of *Background Readings;* Amanda Bristow, editor of the 2001 edition of *Teaching Developmental Writing: Background Readings;* Beth Castrodale, for her confidence in offering me the challenge of this revision; Caryn O'Connell, who wrote the very thorough and helpful notes about the contributors, and Caitlin Kimball, who researched them; and, finally, Karin Halbert, my current editor, for critically important discussions and feedback as this new edition was shaped and reshaped.

I would also like to thank the people in my professional and personal life who have shared so much of their knowledge about writing over the years and who continue to make an extraordinary difference in their own work: Francie Blake, Linda Robinson Fellag, and Tom Ott, Community College of Philadelphia; Michael Bibby and Shari Horner, Shippensburg University; Ann E. Green, Saint Joseph's University; Bill Gilbert, Robin Davidson, Valerie Kinloch, JoAnn Pavletich, and Johanna Schmertz, University of Houston–Downtown; Michelle Gibson, University of Cincinnati; Bill Lalicker, West Chester University; Amy Winans, Susquehanna University; and my students at the University of Houston–Downtown and Saint Joseph's University, who have inspired this current edition with their energy and perseverance.

Thanks also go to my brother Aaron Bernstein, who drove me a long distance for an important meeting after I missed the train; my high school English teacher Angela W. Graham, who taught me the meaning of the words *lucid* and *succinct;* Michael Pinelli for countless discussions on writing and life; my niece Missy Starcher for her sustaining e-mails and telephone calls; James Wrable for invaluable insights on critical thinking; the memory of my mother-in-law, Elley Cormany, for her patience and strength; and all those not mentioned here who have had an impact on my thinking about teaching and writing.

Finally, thanks to Stephen Cormany, my spouse, who, when all else fails, lends courage and inspiration for all my writing moments and more. I dedicate this revision to him with love and admiration.

SUSAN NAOMI BERNSTEIN

Contents

1 Basic Writing: Teachers' Perspectives   1

Mina Shaughnessy
Some New Approaches toward Teaching   2

"A teacher must know deeply what it is he is teaching — what is arbitrary or given and what is built upon skills the student already possesses. This is his preparation."

Adrienne Rich
Teaching Language in Open Admissions   14

"What fascinates and gives hope in a time of slashed budgets, enlarging class size, and national depression is the possibility that many of these young men and women may be gaining the kind of critical perspective on their lives and the skill to bear witness that they have never before had in our country's history."

William B. Lalicker
A Basic Introduction to Basic Writing Program Structures: A Baseline and Five Alternatives   29

"A greater understanding of the alternatives will help you determine [which model is] most suited to your [basic writing] program's theories and goals, most achievable with your institution's mission and resources, and most successful for meeting the literacy challenges of your basic writing students."

4 Writing and Reading 79

Amelia E. El-Hindi

Connecting Reading and Writing:
College Learners' Metacognitive Awareness 79

"Attending to metacognitive awareness within academic support classes can benefit college learners seeking to improve their reading and writing skills. [. . .] Furthermore, as evidenced by this study, use of reading logs can help college students understand the process of reading and the process of writing as a single act of literacy."

Ilona Leki

Reciprocal Themes in ESL Reading and Writing 93

"The time seems to have come for a new reintegration of reading and writing classrooms rather than a division of language into atomized, learnable bits or skills. The fact that reading and writing processes can be isolated does not mean that teaching those isolated processes is the best way to help our students read and write with greater ease."

5 Approaches to Grammar Instruction 115

Janice Neulieb and Irene Brosnahan

Teaching Grammar to Writers 116

"When teachers do more than 'cover' grammar, writers will improve their writing by using the grammar they have learned."

Rei R. Noguchi

Teaching the Basics of a Writer's Grammar 123

"Just as students can improve paragraphs and whole essays by learning about and partaking more consciously in the process of writing, so too can they improve their sentence mechanics by learning about and partaking more consciously in the process (i.e., the operations) of sentence formation."

"GOALS: To help writers see the effectiveness of using present participle phrases, when used as free modifiers. In addition, to help writers
see that they can sometimes move such phrases for greater effectiveness, as they revise. Such lessons are most appropriate for writers who
provide few narrative and descriptive details in their writing, or writers who provide such details in separate sentences, instead of appropriately subordinating some details in modifying phrases."

"When a college, its faculty, and the learning disabled student identify
and fulfill their responsibilities, success is inevitable."

"In working with students with LD, it is important to try to create a
classroom that offers the pleasures of academic writing [. . . .] Teaching
that attempts to 'remediate' by focusing on what is wrong with the way
students are reading and writing only emphasizes their disability."

"The problem-posing process directs students to name the problem,
understand how it applies to them, determine the causes of the problem, generalize to others, and finally suggest alternatives or solutions
to the problem."

"The point of my going into such detail here is that as more and more adult women return to school, notions about the academy's role in the community, about acceptable academic discourse, and about effective teaching practices in higher education may all be challenged."

"Returning adult students can increase their odds for success in college by using their existing languages and literacies to negotiate their learning of new discourses and literacies. [. . .] All students entering college, regardless of writing placement test scores, benefit from immediate engagement with assignments that foster critical reasoning, interpretive reading, analytical as well as narrative writing, and persuasion."

"My assumption is that the more active students are in the lesson (with appropriate scaffolding, of course), the more engaged they will be in the subject matter and the better opportunity they will have to learn and apply course concepts."

"In my own teaching, [Critical Incident Questionnaires] give me good information about students' readiness for a particular learning activity. This, in turn, helps me pace the course. CIQs also help me curb my tendency to equate silence with mental inertia."

"Specifically, we will analyze a brief stretch of discourse, one in which a student's personal history and cultural background shape a somewhat unconventional reading of a section of a poem. We will note the way the mismatch plays itself out in conversation, the logic of the student's reading and the coherent things it reveals about his history, and the pedagogical implications of conducting a conversation that encourages that logic to unfold."

"In order to deal with this perplexity — that collaborative writing is at once so valuable, so important, and yet so problematic — I've come to use the collaborative collage."

"The [following] narrative, I hope, will honestly expose the errors — strategic and pedagogical — as well as ground our feelings of success. I hope, too, that this story will encourage the many four- and two-year colleges whose nonresidential campuses make learning communities seem improbable consider developing them."

"Somebody (usually somebodies) is making the choice (or not) to make available certain writing technologies (and not others) to basic writing students, teachers, and programs. Do we, as basic writing teachers and administrators, take part in these decision-making processes? If not, why not?"

"When I asked [students] to read and respond to one another's writings in class, what I mostly overheard was, 'I liked it,' 'That's really good,' 'Yeah, that same thing happened to me.' But when I began requiring them to respond asynchronously, posting their responses to our class conference, they began taking more time and thinking of more specific things to say."

"I remember being caught speaking Spanish at recess — that was good for three licks on the knuckles with a sharp ruler. I remember being sent to the corner of the classroom for 'talking back' to the Anglo teacher when all I was trying to do was tell her how to pronounce my name."

"There are three qualities of Black English — the presence of life, voice, and clarity — that testify to a distinctive Black value system that we became excited about and self-consciously tried to maintain."

"It is time for English instructors, when faced with students from radically different cultural backgrounds and whose needs differ from those of mainstream students, to stop blaming the high failure and attrition rates solely on bilingualism, substandard schooling, low self-esteem, lack of familiarity with SAE, and/or lack of motivation — it is time to look beyond these factors and work to mitigate all the barriers that all minority culture students face."

"If the goal of ESL composition instruction is to help students become proficient writers of English, it must provide a learning environment which both allows students to gain confidence in their ability as writers and transfers the ultimate responsibility for their development as writers from teachers to students."

"As indicated by the majority of these ESL students' autobiographies, the students would like their American teachers to understand their struggle with learning the new language, literacy skills, and academic content at the same time. One way of building the understanding is for teachers to learn about the students' native language and literacy backgrounds."

"Whatever else teachers do with language minority students to prepare them for academic study, we must create opportunities for them to interact with texts: Create opportunities to know that a text can function as a fulcrum to bring reader and writer together; to know that the reader has the responsibility of giving voice to the writer's argument, in the writer's absence, and then engaging in conversation with that voice."

"More than many issues within the field of composition studies, writing assessment evokes strong passions."

"Teachers in ENG 098 know that the students, by their own admission, are asking for some help to get ready for college writing. No developmental writing teacher begins class with the view that the first order of business is to prove to the student that he or she was indeed placed correctly. Our best students are the ones that ask us to help them learn, and now in no other class on campus can a teacher assume with as much confidence that this is precisely what every student in the ENG 098 class wants."

"This paper, then, explores what we now see as our failure in assessing Mica's work and speculates on how we might reconceptualize the assessment of writing, particularly the writing of culturally diverse students."

"Each week, my work in the writing center presents me with at least a couple of the dilemmas that I describe with Marcus. I have come to call them questions of autonomy and voice, since their implications go well beyond issues of 'appropriateness' or academic format."

"Rather than frequent urgings to 'talk less,' perhaps what Morgan most needed was advice to *listen more* — for the clues students like Fannie would provide, for those moments when she might best shed her teacherly persona and become once again a learner."

Basic Writing:
Teachers' Perspectives

W hat is "basic writing"? This chapter introduces you to ways in which this question has been framed by professionals in the past quarter century. We begin with Mina Shaughnessy, who defines basic writing from a teacher's perspective. Shaughnessy bases her definition on her classroom observations of urban open-admissions students in the 1970s. She is a firm believer in "buil[ding] upon the skills the student already possesses." Feminist poet and essayist Adrienne Rich, who taught under Mina Shaughnessy's direction at City College of New York, adds her own views of the joys and challenges of working with basic writers in "Teaching Language in Open Admissions."

William B. Lalicker, writing a generation after Shaughnessy and Rich, looks at basic writing from the point of view of a writing program administrator. His article describes the advantages and disadvantages of several program models. He urges readers to create a program that is "most achievable with your institution's mission and resources." Seen together, these three articles give readers a sense of the beginnings of basic writing as its own academic discipline — and of our discipline's future in the twenty-first century.

Some New Approaches toward Teaching

Mina Shaughnessy

First published in 1970 in A Guide for Teachers of College English *(and later reprinted in a 1994 edition of the* Journal of Basic Writing*), the following essay grew out of Mina Shaughnessy's experiences working with basic writing students at the City College of New York. The essay, which includes helpful examples, useful insights, and practical strategies for teaching developing writers, presents Shaughnessy's early theories on basic writing, theories on which she later expanded in her pioneering book* Errors and Expectations *(1977). Here she lays out her ideas about where to begin a course in developmental writing, and as in all her work, she bases her ideas on the belief that her students are not unskilled but rather inexperienced.*

Teaching Basic Writing

I

The term "basic writing" implies that there is a place to begin learning to write, a foundation from which the many special forms and styles of writing rise, and that a college student must control certain skills that are common to all writing before he takes on the special demands of a biology or literature or engineering class.* I am not certain this is so. Some students learn how to write in strange ways. I recall one student who knew something about hospitals because she had worked as a nurse's aide. She decided, long before her sentences were under control, to do a paper on female diseases. In some way this led her to the history of medicine and then to Egypt, where she ended up reading about embalming — which became the subject of a long paper she entitled "Postmortem Care in Ancient Egypt." The paper may not have satisfied a professor of medical history, but it produced more improvement in the student's writing than any assignments I could have devised.

Perhaps if students with strong enthusiasms in special fields were allowed to exercise themselves in those fields under the guidance of professors who felt responsible for the writing as well as the reading of students, we could shorten the period of apprenticeship. But clearly this is not the way things are, and students who need extra work in writing are therefore placed in courses called Basic Writing, which are usually taught by English teachers who, as specialists themselves, are inclined to assume that the best way to teach writing is to talk about

---

*Note that although Shaughnessy uses the referent pronoun *he* throughout the article, she herself notes that she was writing in less enlightened times. In a footnote to *Errors and Expectations,* Shaughnessy offers: "After having tried various ways of circumventing the use of the masculine pronoun in situations where women teachers and students might easily outnumber men, I have settled for the convention, but I regret that the language resists my meaning in this important respect. When the reader sees *he,* I can only hope *she* will also be there" (4).[Editor's note]

literature. If such talk will stimulate the student to write, however, then it will serve most students at least as well as mummies, for the answer to improved writing is writing. Everything else — imaginative writing texts, thoughtfully designed assignments, elaborate rationales for teaching writing this way or that — is merely part of the effort to get writing started and to keep it going.

There are many views on the best way to do this and there is some damning evidence piled up against some of the ways that once seemed right. Since English teachers are often considered both the victims and the perpetuators of these apparently mistaken approaches, it becomes important for them to try once in a while to think away everything except the facts and insights that their experiences with students as writers have given them.

The following pages are my effort to do this.

II

Writing is the act of creative reading. That is, it is the encoding of speech into lines of print or script that are in turn decoded into speech by a reader. To understand the nature of writing, and therefore the way writing can be learned, it is necessary to understand the connections and distinctions between speech, writing, and reading and to identify the skills that are implied in the ability to write.

For most people, speech is easy and writing is difficult; the one is inevitable, the other acquired, generally under conditions that seem to violate rather than use the natural learning abilities of people. Because of this violation, learning to write requires almost as much undoing as doing, whether one is involved with those skills implied in the encoding process itself (handwriting, spelling, and punctuation) or those skills that are carried over from speech to the page (making and ordering statements).

Beyond these two types of skills, there is an additional opportunity in writing that distinguishes it both as a skill and as a product: the opportunity to objectify a statement, to look at it, change it by additions, subtractions, substitutions, or inversions, the opportunity to take time for as close and economical a "fit" as possible between the writer's meaning and the record of that meaning on the page. The typescript of a taped discussion is not, therefore, writing in this sense; it is, rather, a repetition on the page of what was spoken. And the goal in writing is not simply to repeat speech but to overcome certain disadvantages that the medium of sound imposes upon speech. (In speech, time says when you are finished; in writing, you say when you are finished.)

Writing thus produces a distinctive circuitry in which the writer continually feeds back to himself (as writer and reader) and acts upon that feedback at any point and for as long a time as he wishes before his statement is finally put into circulation. This opportunity for objectifying a statement so as to "work" on it is the distinctive opportunity of writing, and the central goal of any writing class is therefore to lead the student to an awareness of his power to make choices (semantic, syntactic, organizational) that bring him closer and closer to his intended meaning. Ideally, this opportunity should free the writer because it increases his options; it should give him pleasure because it sharpens his sense of what to say and thereby his pleasure in saying it; and it should make him feel comfortable with so-called mistakes, which are simply stages in the writing process. Unfortunately, the fact that writing can by its very nature produce a more precise and lasting statement than speech has led teachers to expect (and demand) a narrow kind of perfection which they confuse with the true goal in writing, namely, the "perfect" fit of the writer's words to his meaning. Teachers, in other words, have not only ignored the distinctive circuitry of writing — which is the only source of fullness and precision — but have often shortcircuited the writing activity by imposing themselves as a feedback. Students, on the other hand, have tended to impose upon themselves (even when bluebook essays do not) the conditions of speech, making writing a kind of one-shot affair aimed at the teacher's expectations. Students are usually surprised, for example, to see the messy manuscript of pages of famous writers. "You should see how bad a writer Richard Wright was," one of my students said after seeing a manuscript page from *Native Son*. "He made more mistakes than I do!" Somehow students have to discover that the mess is *writing;* the published book is *written.*

A writing course should help the student learn how to make his own mess, for the mess is the record of a remarkable kind of interplay between the writer as creator and the writer as reader, which serves the writer in much the same way as the ear serves the infant who is teaching himself to speak. No sooner has the writer written down what he thinks he means than he is asking himself whether he understands what he said. A writing course should reinforce and broaden this interplay, not interrupt it, so that the student can use it to generate his own criteria and not depend upon a grade to know whether he has written well. The teacher can help by designing writing situations that externalize the circuitry principle. The teacher and the class together can help by telling the writer what they think he said, thereby developing an awareness of the possibilities for meaning or confusion when someone else is the reader.

But if the student is so well equipped to teach himself to write and the teacher is simply an extension of his audience, why does he need a teacher at all? The answer is, of course, that he doesn't absolutely need a teacher to learn to write, that, in fact, remarkably few people have learned to write through teachers, that many, alas, have learned to write in spite of teachers. The writing teacher has but one simple advantage to offer: he can save the student time, and time is important to students who are trying to make up for what got lost in high school and grade school.

To help in even this limited way, a teacher must know what skills are implied in the ability to write what is called basic English and he must understand the nature of the difficulties students seem to have with each of them. The following list is a move in that direction.

HANDWRITING   The student has to have enough skill at writing to take down his own dictations without getting distracted by the muscular coordination writing requires. If a student has done very little writing in high school, which is often the case, he may need to exercise his writing muscles. This is a quantitative matter — the more of anything he copies, the better the coordination. Malcolm X's exercise of copying the dictionary may not be inspiring enough for many students, but if a student keeps copying something, his handwriting will begin to belong to him. Until then, he is likely to have his problems with handwriting mistaken for problems with writing.

SPELLING AND PUNCTUATION   To write fluently, a student must feel reasonably comfortable about getting the words and punctuation down right, or he must learn to suspend his concern over correctness until he is ready to proofread. If he is a bad speller, chances are he knows it and will become so preoccupied with correctness that he will constantly lose his thought in order to find the right letters, or he will circumlocute in order to avoid words he can't spell. A number of students enter our classes every semester so handicapped by misspelling and generally so ineffectively taught by us that they are almost certain not to get out of basic writing. It is a problem neither we nor the reading teachers have willingly claimed, but it presses for a solution. The computer, which seems to hold great promise for misspellers, is still a laboratory. The Fidel chart, so successfully used by Dr. Gattegno in teaching children and illiterate adults to read, has not yet been extensively tried in college programs such as ours.[1]

Students are generally taught to think of punctuation as the scribal translation of oral phrasing and intonation. Some students have, in fact, been taught to put commas where they breathe. As a translation of voice pauses and intonations, however, punctuation is quite crude and almost impossible to learn. Commas can produce as long a pause as a period, and how much time does a semicolon occupy? Most students solve the problem by working out a private punctuation system or by memorizing a few "rules" that often get them into more trouble than they are worth (like always putting a comma before "and").

In the end, it is more economical for the student to learn to translate punctuation marks into their conventional meaning and to recognize that while there are stylistic choices in punctuating, even these choices are related to a system of signs that signal grammatical (or structural) information more accurately than vocal spacing and intonation. The marks of punctuation can in fact be studied in isolation from words, as signals that prepare a reader for certain types of constructions. Whether these constructions are given their grammatical names is not important, but it is important that a student be able to

reconstruct from a passage such as the following the types of constructions he — and other readers — would expect:

_____ . _____ :
_____ . _____ , and
_____ . _____ , _____ ,
_____ . _____ : _____ , _____ , _____ .

Sentence fragments, run-ons, and comma splices are mistranslations
of punctuation marks. They can occur only in writing and can be understood once the student understands the structures they signal. This
suggests that punctuation marks should not be studied in isolation
from the structural units they signal. For example, when the student is
experimenting with the ways in which information can be added to a
subject without creating a new sentence (adjectival functions), it is a
good time to look at the serial comma, the appositional commas, and
the comma in the nonrestrictive clause.

MAKING SENTENCES An English-speaking student is already a maker
of statements that not only sound like English but sound like him.
Because he has spoken so many more years of sentences than he has
written, however, there is a gap between what he can say and what he
can write. Sometimes the writing down of sentences is in fact such a
labor that he loses his connection with English and produces a tangle
of phrases he would never speak. Such a student does not need to learn
how to make statements but how to write them at least as well as he
speaks them. Other students with foreign-language interferences may
have to work on English sentence structure itself, but even here their
speech is doubtless ahead of their pens. Learning to write statements,
therefore, is at first a matter of getting the ear to "hear" script. Later,
when the writer wants to exploit the advantages that writing has over
speech, the advantage of polishing and perfecting, he may write things
he would not be likely to say, but this happens after his pen has caught
up with his voice. Students who have little confidence in their voice, or
at least in the teacher's response to that voice, have often gone to a
great deal of trouble to superimpose another voice upon their writing — sometimes it represents the student's version of a textbook voice;
sometimes it is Biblical; sometimes it is a business letter voice — but
almost always it seems to keep the writer from understanding clearly
what he wants to say. The following sentence, which seems to be a version of the textbook voice, illustrates the kind of entanglement that
can result:

> In a broad sense admittance to the SEEK program will serve as a basis
> of education for me in terms of enlightenment on the tedious time and
> effort which one must put into all of his endeavors.

A student will usually not abandon this acquired voice until he begins
to recognize his own voice and sees that it is safe to prefer it.

There is another skill with sentences which affects the quality of a student's theme as well as his sentences. It involves his ability to "mess" with sentences, to become sensitive to the questions that are embedded in sentences which, when answered, can produce modifications within the sentence or can expand into paragraphs or entire essays. It involves his awareness of the choices he has in casting sentences, of styles in sentences. As Francis Christensen has illustrated in *Notes toward a New Rhetoric,*[2] the sentence is the microcosm. Whatever the writer does in the sentence when he modifies is in principle what he does in paragraphs and essays. The principle of coordination and subordination can be learned there. The foundation of a paragraph, a chapter, a book is there. It is tempting to say that a student who knows his way around the sentence can get anyplace in writing. And knowing his way means working on his own sentences, not so much to polish them as to see how much of his meaning they can hold.

But for many students, putting sentences on a page seems a little like carving something on stone: an error cannot be ignored or skimmed over as it can be in speech. It is there forever. "Everything has to be exactly right," explained one of my students, "and that makes me nervous." The page disconnects the student from his product, which will appear alone, before strange eyes, or worse, before the eyes of an English teacher who is a specialist at finding mistakes. To make matters worse, most students feel highly mistake-prone about sentences. They half remember prohibitions about beginning with certain words, but they aren't certain of which words or why (probably the result of lessons on sentence fragments). In short, they feel they are about to commit a verbal sin but they aren't certain what sin it is. In such a situation, it seems safer to keep still. It is not unusual to have students at the beginning of the semester who sit through several class periods without writing a word, and when they explain that they don't know how to begin, they are not saying they don't have an idea. They are saying they are not certain which are the "safe" words to begin with.

Students who become observers of sentences and experimenters with sentences lose their fear of them. This experimentation can take many forms. Sentences can be examined as if they were separate compositions. A sentence such as the following by Richard Wright can be written on the board without reference to its context:

> Those brave ones who struggle against death are the ones who bring new life into the world, even though they die to do so, even though our hearts are broken when they die.

Students can talk about the way the sentence is built; they can try to imitate it or change it; or they can try to build a paragraph by expanding some part of it.

There is a kind of carpentry in sentence making, various ways of joining or hooking up modifying units to the base sentence. Suffixes added to make adjectives or adverbs, prepositions, "wh" words like where, when, who, which, etc., the double commas used in appositional constructions — all of these can be seen as hooking devices that preserve us from the tedium of Dick-and-Jane sentences. As a form of sentence-play, students can try to write fifty- or one-hundred-word sentences that contain only one independent clause. Once discovering they can do it, they usually lose their inhibitions about "real" sentences. Some even move from carpentry to architecture. This sentence was written by a student who was asked in an exam to add information to the predicate of the sentence: "The problem will be solved."

> The problem will be solved with the help of the Almighty, who, except for an occasional thunderstorm, reigns unmolested, high in the heavens above, when all of us, regardless of race or religious differences, can come together and study this severe problem inside out, all day and all night if necessary, and are able to come to you on that great gettin' up morning and say, "Mrs. Shaughnessy, we do know our verbs and adverbs."

ORDERING SENTENCES   Order is an arrangement of units that enables us to see them as parts of something larger. The sense of orientation that results from this arrangement creates a pleasure we call understanding. Perhaps because writing isolates a reader from everything except the page, whereas speech is supported by other gestures and by the right of the audience to query and disagree, we seem to be more tolerant of "disorder" (no clear pattern) in speech than in writing. The talker is not, therefore, committed to knowing where he is going in quite the way that a writer is although he often gets someplace in a way that turns out to have order to it. The writer, however, puts himself on the line, announcing where he is going to go before he sees how he is going to get there. He has to move in two directions at the same time — ahead, point by point toward a destination he has announced but never been to, and down, below the surface of his points to see what they are about. Sometimes, having decided on or having been given an overall arrangement (or plan) that seems a sensible route to where he is going, the writer hesitates to leave the security of this plan to explore the parts of his paper. Result: a tight, well-ordered but empty paper. At other times, the writer stops to explore one point and never gets back because he cannot get control over the generating force of sentences, which will create branches off branches off branches unless the writer cuts them off. Result: a wilderness.

The skill of organizing seems to require a kind of balance between the demand that a piece of writing get someplace along a route that is sufficiently marked for a reader to follow and the demand that there be freedom for the writer to explore his subject and follow where his questions and inventions take him. The achievement of this balance produces much of the "mess" in writing. Often, however, teachers stress the "administrative" aspects of writing (direction and procedure) over the generative or even assume that the generative is not a part of the organizing skill. This assumption in turn seems to lead to the formulation of organizational patterns in isolation from content (pyramids, upside-down pyramids, etc.) and the efforts to get students to squeeze their theme materials into these patterns. I do not mean to say that restrictions or limits in writing are necessarily inhibiting. They can be both stimulating and liberating, as the sonnet illustrates. But the restrictions I speak of here merely hint at forms they are unable to generate, leaving the reader with the feeling that there is a blank to be filled in but with no sense of how to do it.

Because of this isolation of form from content, students have come to think of organization as something special that happens in themes but not in themselves, daily, as they think or talk. They do not notice that they usually "talk" a better-organized paper than they write, that they use illustrations, anticipate questions, repeat thematic points more effectively in conversation than in writing, whereas the conscious effort to organize a theme often cuts them off from the real content of the theme, giving them all the organizational signposts but no place to go. In talking, they are evolving order; in writing, they often feel they must impose it.

This is not to say that developing a paper is as easy as talking but simply that the difficulty lies not in fitting an amount of raw content into a prefabricated frame but in evoking and controlling the generating power of statement. Every sentence bears within it a new set of possibilities. Sometimes the writer chooses to develop these possibilities; sometimes he prefers to let them lie. Sometimes he decides to develop them fully; at other times, only slightly. Thus each step in the development of a base or thesis statement must inevitably send the writer into a wilderness of possibilities, into a fecundity as dense and multiform as thought itself. One cannot be said to have had an idea until he has made his way through this maze. Order is the pattern of his choices, the path he makes going through.

The initial blocking out of a paper, the plan for it, is a kind of hypothesis which allows the writer to proceed with his investigation. Any technique of organization, however, that ignores the wilderness, that limits the freedom of the writer to see and make choices at every step, to move ahead at times without knowing for certain which is north and south, then to drop back again and pick up the old path, and finally to get where he is going, partly by conscious effort but also by some faculty of intellection that is too complex to understand — any technique that sacrifices this fullest possible play of the mind for the security of an outline or some other prefabricated frame cuts the student off from his most productive thinking. He must be allowed something of a frontier mentality, an overall commitment, perhaps, to get to California, but a readiness, all along the way, to choose alternative routes and even to sojourn at unexpected places when that seems wise or important, sometimes, even, to decide that California isn't what the writer really had in mind.

The main reason for failure in the writing proficiency test at City College, a test given to all upperclassmen, has not been grammar or mechanics but the inability to get below the surface of a topic, to treat a topic in depth. The same problem arises in bluebook essays. It is the familiar complaint of students: "I can't think of anything more to say." They are telling us that they do not have access to their thoughts when they write. A part of this difficulty may be related to the way they have learned to write. And a part of the answers may lie in our designing assignments that make the student conscious of what the exploration of an idea is and how this exploration relates to organization.

GRAMMATICAL CORRECTNESS   Correctness involves those areas of a dialect where there are no choices. (The "s" on the present tense third-person singular is correct in standard English; the use of a plural verb with the subject "none" is a choice; the comparison "more handsome" is a choice but "more intelligenter" is incorrect.) Native speakers of a dialect are not concerned with correctness; they unconsciously say things the correct way. Non-native speakers of a dialect must consciously acquire the "givens" if they want to communicate without static in that dialect. This is a linguistic fact that seems at the outset to put speakers of a nonstandard dialect at a disadvantage. But it is a strange logic that says having access to one dialect is better than having access to two, particularly when we know that every dialect or language system sets limits on the ways we can perceive and talk about the world.

Unfortunately, this is not the way speakers of other dialects have been encouraged to think about their dialects, with the result that writing classes and writing teachers seem to put them at a disadvantage, creating either an obsessive concern with correctness or a fatalistic indifference to it. The only thing that can help the student overcome such feelings is to help him gain control over the dialect. It is irresponsible to tell him that correctness is not important; it is difficult to persuade him after years of indoctrination to the contrary that "correctness" plays a subordinate role in good writing; but it is not impossible to give him the information and practice he needs to manage his own proofreading.

The information will inevitably be grammatical, whether the terminology of grammar is used or not. But it is more important to remember that the student who is not at home with standard English has most likely had several doses of grammar already and it hasn't worked. For reasons that he himself doesn't quite understand, the explanations about things like the third-person "s" or the agreement of subject and verb haven't taken. He is not deliberately trying to make mistakes but for some reason they keep happening. What he often does not realize, and what the teacher has to realize is that his difficulties arise from his *mastery* of one language or dialect, and that changing to another often involves at certain points a loss or conflict of meaning and therefore difficulty in learning, not because he is stubborn or dumb or verbally impoverished but because he expects language to make sense. (The student, for example, who finally told me he *couldn't* use "are" to mean something in the present because it was too stiff and formal and therefore faraway, and the Chinese student who could not make a plural out of sunrise because there is only one sun, were both trying to hold on to meaning, as Will James, the cowboy author, was when he continued to use "seen" for the past tense because it meant seeing farther than "saw.")

These are obviously grammatical matters, but this does not mean they require the traditional study of grammar. The question of what they do require is widely debated. Certainly it should be apparent that teachers working with students who have black dialect or Spanish or Chinese or some other language background should be familiar with the features of those languages that are influencing their students' work in Standard English. This should be part of the general equipment of us all as teachers. And the new insights that come from the linguists should also be ours. But none of this information will be of much use if we simply make pronouncements about it in class. Students cannot be expected to get more help from memorizing two grammatical systems instead of one, and the diagrams in transformational grammar are still diagrams. The acquisition of new information will not automatically make us better teachers. To make this happen, we need to develop a sharp sense of the difference between talking and teaching. We need to design lessons that highlight the grammatical characteristics of a dialect so that the student can discover them for himself. (It is one thing to tell a student about the "s" in the third-person present singular; it is another for him to discover the power of that schizophrenic letter which clings so irrationally to its last verb to mark its singularity while it attaches itself to nouns to mark their plurality, and then, confusing things further, acquires an apostrophe and marks the singular possessive.) We need to devise ways of practicing that the student enjoys because he is able to invent rather than memorize answers. We need, finally, to teach proofreading as a separate skill that uses the eye in a different way from reading and places the burden of correctness where it belongs — at the end of (rather than during) the writing process. To do things for the student that he can do himself is not generosity but impatience. It is hard work for a teacher not to talk, but we must now be very industrious if we want our students to learn what we have to teach.

III

I have been speaking about the skills that seem basic to writing, but basic writing courses that prepare students for college writing are actually concerned with a rather special kind of prose called exposition, a semiformal analytical prose in which the connections between sentences and paragraphs surface in the form of conjunctive adverbs and transitional sentences. More simply, it means the kind of writing teachers got B's and A's for in college, a style whose characteristics they have now internalized and called a standard.

Teachers of basic writing are thus responsible for helping their students learn to write in an expository style. They must also give them practice in writing to specification (i.e., on a special topic or question and in a certain form) since many assignments require it. The question of how to reach such objectives and at the same time give each student a chance to discover other things about writing and about his individual powers as a writer troubles many teachers and creates many different "positions." Where, for example, on the following list, ranging from highly controlled to free assignments, it is best to begin a course in basic writing:

1. paraphrase

2. summary

3. exegesis of a passage

4. theme in which topic sentence and organizational pattern are given

5. theme in which topic sentence is given (includes the examination question which is usually an inverted topic sentence)

6. theme in which subject is given

7. theme in which form is given — description, dialogue, argument, etc.

8. theme in which only the physical conditions for writing are given — journal, free writing, etc.

Teachers take sides on such a question, some insisting that freedom in anything, including writing, cannot exist until there is control and that this comes through the step-by-step mastery of highly structured assignments; others insist that students must begin not with controls but with materials — the things they have already seen or felt or imagined — and evolve their own controls as they try to translate experience into writing. Meanwhile students confuse the issue by learning to write and not learning to write under almost all approaches. I prefer to start around #7, with description. But then, I have to remember the student who started a research paper on mummies before she could manage her sentences. "Positions" on curriculae and methods are somehow always too neat to say much about learning, which seems to be sloppy. They tend to be generalizations about students, not about the nature of the skills that have to be mastered, and the only generalization that seems safe to make about students is the one they persistently make about themselves — that they are individuals, not types, and that the way to each student's development is a way the teacher has never taken before. Everything about the teacher-student encounter should encourage a respect for this fact of individuality even though the conditions under which we must teach in large institutions often obscure it. Books do have to be ordered and teachers do have to make plans. But perhaps the plans need not be so well laid that they cannot go awry when the signals point that way. A teacher must know deeply what it is he is teaching — what is arbitrary or given and what is built upon skills the student already possesses. This is his preparation. But he cannot know about his student until both meet in the classroom. Then teaching becomes what one student described as "simply two people learning from each other."

In the confusion of information on methods and curriculae that comes to us from publishers — and from each other — it is probably important to emphasize this single truth.

Notes

1. Caleb Gattegno, *Teaching Reading with Words in Color* (Educational Solutions, Inc., New York, 1968).
2. Francis Christensen, *Notes toward a New Rhetoric* (New York, Harper & Row, 1967).

Classroom Activities

Have students generate lists of three to five rules that they have learned about writing (this may be done individually or in small groups). Then compile the separate lists into one long list that will be distributed to the entire class. You may wish to use the following questions as a starting point for class discussion:

- Is there more than one way of stating the same rule?
- Are some rules more difficult to understand than others?
- Which of the rules seem contradictory?
- Which rules seem helpful?
- Are there writing situations in which these rules may be broken?
- What are the consequences of breaking the rules?
- What are the choices that writers can make about how to compose their writing?

Thinking about Teaching

As you read the essays in *Teaching Developmental Writing: Background Readings,* you are encouraged to keep a journal to record your reactions to the readings and to write down student responses to class activities. Think about sharing your journal entries with other teachers —

and especially with your students. The pedagogy that Shaughnessy advocates implies engaged involvement between students and teacher. Journaling with your students can be an important means of creating an engaged classroom.

Record your impressions of your students' responses to the above activity. Were you surprised by their lists or by the discussion of rules? What ideas from the lists or from the discussion can you use in class?

Shaughnessy, writing in the mid-1970s, lists the following skills as critical for "the ability to write what is called basic English": spelling and punctuation, making sentences, ordering sentences, and grammatical correctness. Can you think of any others (some examples might be keyboarding and awareness of audience and purpose)? Are there any skills that you would eliminate or revise from Shaughnessy's list? What has changed since Shaughnessy first wrote this article?

Shaughnessy suggests that one way of answering the question of where it "is best to begin a course in basic writing" may be for teachers to evolve a working metaphor of their own practice. "There is a kind of carpentry in sentence making," Shaughnessy writes, "various ways of joining or hooking up modifying units to the base sentence." What metaphors would you use for your own practice of writing and of teaching writing? Why do you find those metaphors particularly helpful or descriptive?

Teaching Language in Open Admissions

Adrienne Rich

First published in 1972 and informed by the political struggles of its era, feminist poet and essayist Adrienne Rich's article "Teaching Language in Open Admissions" is a testimony to the necessities and possibilities of teaching students in basic writing. With a nod toward the liberatory philosophies of Paulo Freire and Jean-Paul Sartre, Rich analyzes both the philosophical and the practical issues of teaching open-admissions students at the City College of New York in the late 1960s and early 1970s — the same time and place in which Mina Shaughnessy began the inquiry that would lead to Errors and Expectations. *"Teaching Language in Open Admissions," dedicated to Shaughnessy, stands as a companion piece to the foundational work of* Errors and Expectations.*

---

*See Halasek and Highberg (xvi), who provide a similar context for "Teaching Language in Open Admissions." Halasek, Kay, and Nels P. Highberg. Introduction: Locality and Basic Writing. *Landmark Essays on Basic Writing.* Landmark Essays Vol. 18. Ed. Kay Halasek and Nels P. Highberg. Mahwah, New Jersey: Lawrence Erlbaum Associates, 2001. xi–xxix.

To the memory of Mina Shaughnessy, 1924–1978

I stand to this day behind the major ideas about literature, writing, and teaching that I expressed in this essay. Several things strike me in rereading it, however. Given the free rein allowed by the SEEK program (described in the text of the essay) when I first began teaching at the City College of New York, it is interesting to me to note the books I was choosing for classes: Orwell, Wright, LeRoi Jones, Lawrence, Baldwin, Plato's *Republic*. It is true that few books by black women writers were available; the bookstores of the late sixties were crowded with paperbacks by Frederick Douglass, Malcolm X, Frantz Fanon, Langston Hughes, Eldridge Cleaver, W. E. B. Du Bois, and by anthologies of mostly male black writers. Ann Petry, Gwendolyn Brooks, June Jordan, Audre Lorde, I came to know and put on my reading lists or copied for classes; but the real crescendo of black women's writing was yet to come, and writers like Zora Neale Hurston and Margaret Walker were out of print. It is obvious now, as it was not then (except to black women writers, undoubtedly) that integral to the struggle against racism in the literary canon there was another, as yet unarticulated, struggle, against the sexism of black and white male editors, anthologists, critics, and publishers.

For awhile I have thought of going back to City College to ask some of my former colleagues, still teaching there, what could be said of the past decade, what is left there of what was, for a brief time, a profound if often naively optimistic experiment in education. (Naively optimistic because I think the white faculty at least, those of us who were most committed to the students, vastly underestimated the psychic depth and economic function of racism in the city and the nation, the power of the political machinery that could be "permissive" for a handful of years only to retrench, break promises, and betray, pitting black youth against Puerto Rican and Asian, poor ethnic students against students of color, in an absurd and tragic competition for resources which should have been open to all.) But it has seemed to me that such interviews could be fragmentary at best. I lived through some of that history, the enlarging of classes, the heavy increase of teaching loads, the firing of junior faculty and of many of the best and most dedicated teachers I had known, the efforts of City College to reclaim its "prestige" in the media; I know also that dedicated teachers still remain, who teach Basic Writing not as a white man's — or woman's — burden but because they choose to do so. And, on the corner of Broadway near where I live, I see young people whose like I knew ten years ago as college students "hanging-out", brown-bagging, standing in short skirts and high-heeled boots in doorways waiting for a trick, or being dragged into the car of a plumed and sequined pimp.

Finally: in reprinting this essay I would like to acknowledge my debt to Mina Shaughnessy, who was director of the Basic Writing Program at City when I taught there, and from whom, in many direct and indirect ways, I learned — in a time and place where pedagogic romanticism and histrionics were not uncommon — a great deal about the ethics and integrity of teaching.

This essay was first published in *The Uses of Literature*, edited by Monroe Engel (Cambridge, Mass.: Harvard University, 1973).

M y first romantic notion of teaching came, I think, from reading Emlyn Williams's play *The Corn Is Green*, sometime in my teens. As I reconstruct it now, a schoolteacher in a Welsh mining village is reading her pupils' essays one night and comes upon a paper which, for all its misspellings and dialect constructions, seems to be the work of a nascent poet. Turning up in the midst of the undistinguished efforts of her other pupils, this essay startles the teacher. She calls in the boy who wrote it, goes over it with him, talks with him about his life, his hopes, and offers to tutor him privately, without fees. Together, as the play goes on, they work their way through rhetoric, mathematics, Shakespeare, Latin, Greek. The boy gets turned on by the classics, is clearly intended to be, if not a poet, at least a scholar. Birth and family background had destined him for a life in the coal mines; but now another path opens up. Toward the end of the play we see him being coached for the entrance examinations for Oxford. I believe crisis strikes when it looks as if he has gotten one of the village girls pregnant and may have to marry her, thus cutting short a career of dazzling promise before it has begun. I don't recall the outcome, but I suspect that the unwed mother is hushed up and packed away (I would be more interested to see the play rewritten today as *her* story) and the boy goes off to Oxford, with every hope of making it to donhood within the decade.

Perhaps this represents a secret fantasy of many teachers: the ill-scrawled essay, turned up among so many others, which has the mark of genius. And looking at the first batch of freshman papers every semester can be like a trip to the mailbox — there is always the possibility of something turning up that will illuminate the weeks ahead. But behind the larger fantasy lie assumptions which I have only gradually come to recognize; and the recognition has to do with a profound change in my conceptions of teaching and learning.

Before I started teaching at City College I had known only elitist institutions: Harvard and Radcliffe as an undergraduate, Swarthmore as a visiting poet, Columbia as teacher in a graduate poetry workshop that included some of the best young poets in the city. I applied for the job at City in 1968 because Robert Cumming had described the SEEK program to me after Martin Luther King was shot, and my motivation was complex. It had to do with white liberal guilt, of course; and a political decision to use my energies in work with "disadvantaged" (black and Puerto Rican) students. But it also had to do with a need to involve myself with the real life of the city, which had arrested me from the first weeks I began living here.

In 1966 Mayor John Lindsay had been able, however obtusely, to coin the phrase "Fun City" without actually intending it as a sick joke. By 1968, the uncollected garbage lay bulging in plastic sacks on the north side of Washington Square, as it had lain longer north of 110th Street; the city had learned to endure subway strikes, sanitation strikes, cab strikes, power and water shortages; the policeman on the corner had become a threatening figure to many whites as he had long been to blacks; the public school teachers and the parents of their pupils had been in pitched battle. On the Upper West Side poor people were being evicted from tenements which were then tinned-up and left empty, awaiting unscheduled demolition to make room for middle-income housing, for which funds were as yet unavailable; and a squatter movement of considerable political consciousness was emerging in defiance of this uprooting.

There seemed to be three ways in which the white middle class could live in New York: the paranoiac, the solipsistic, and a third, which I am more hesitant to define. By the mid-sixties paranoia was visible and audible: streets of brownstones whose occupants had hired an armed guard for the block and posted notices accordingly; conversations on park benches in which public safety had replaced private health as a topic of concern; conversion of all personal anxieties into fear of the mugger (and the mugger was real, no doubt about it). Paranoia could become a life-style, a science, an art, with the active collaboration of reality. Solipsism I encountered first and most concretely in a conversation with an older European intellectual who told me he liked living in New York (on the East Side) because Madison Avenue reminded him of Paris. It was, and still is, possible to live, if you can afford it, on one of those small islands where the streets are kept clean and the pushers and nodders invisible, to travel by cab, deplore the state of the rest of the city, but remain essentially aloof from its causes and effects. It seems about as boring as most forms of solipsism, since to maintain itself it must remain thick-skinned and ignorant.

But there was, and is, another relationship with the city which I can only begin by calling love. The city as object of love, a love not unmixed with horror and anger, the city as Baudelaire and Rilke had previsioned it, or William Blake for that matter, death in life, but a death emblematic of the death that is epidemic in modern society, and a life more edged, more costly, more charged with knowledge, than life elsewhere. Love as one knows it sometimes with a person with whom one is locked in struggle, energy draining but also energy replenishing, as when one is fighting for life, in oneself or someone else. Here was this damaged, self-destructive organism, preying and preyed upon. The streets were rich with human possibility and vicious with human denial (it is breathtaking to walk through a street in East Harlem, passing among the lithe, alert, childish bodies and attuned, observant, childish faces, playing in the spray of a hydrant, and to know that addiction awaits every brain and body in that block as a potential killer). In all its historic, overcrowded, and sweated poverty, the Lower East Side at the turn of the century had never known this: the odds for the poor, today, are weighted by heroin, a fact which the middle classes ignored until it breathed on their own children's lives as well.

In order to live in the city, I needed to ally myself, in some concrete, practical, if limited way, with the possibilities. So I went up to Convent Avenue and 133rd Street and was interviewed for a teaching job, hired as a poet-teacher. At that time a number of writers, including Toni Cade

Bambara, the late Paul Blackburn, Robert Cumming, David Henderson, June Jordan, were being hired to teach writing in the SEEK program to black and Puerto Rican freshmen entering from substandard ghetto high schools, where the prevailing assumption had been that they were of inferior intelligence. (More of these schools later.) Many dropped out (a lower percentage than the national college dropout rate, however); many stuck it out through several semesters of remedial English, math, reading, to enter the mainstream of the college. (As of 1972, 208 SEEK students — or 35 to 40 percent — have since graduated from City College; twenty-four are now in graduate school. *None* of these students would have come near higher education under the regular admissions programs of the City University; high-school guidance counselors have traditionally written off such students as incapable of academic work. Most could not survive economically in college without the stipends which the SEEK program provides.)

My job, that first year, was to "turn the students on" to writing by whatever means I wanted — poetry, free association, music, politics, drama, fiction — to acclimate them to the act of writing, while a grammar teacher, with whom I worked closely outside of class, taught sentence structure, the necessary mechanics. A year later this course was given up as too expensive, since it involved two teachers. My choice was to enlarge my scope to include grammar and mechanics or to find a niche elsewhere and teach verse writing. I stayed on to teach, and learn, grammar — among other things.

The early experience in SEEK was, as I look back on it, both unnerving and seductive. Even those who were (unlike me) experienced teachers of remedial English were working on new frontiers, trying new methods. Some of the most rudimentary questions we confronted were: How do you make standard English verb endings available to a dialect-speaker? How do you teach English prepositional forms to a Spanish-language student? What are the arguments for and against "Black English"? The English of academic papers and theses? Is standard English simply a weapon of colonization? Many of our students wrote in the vernacular with force and wit; others were unable to say what they wanted on paper in or out of the vernacular. We were dealing not simply with dialect and syntax but with the imagery of lives, the anger and flare of urban youth — how could this be *used*, strengthened, without the lies of artificial polish? How does one teach order, coherence, the structure of ideas while respecting the student's experience of his or her thinking and perceiving? Some students who could barely sweat out a paragraph delivered (and sometimes conned us with) dazzling raps in the classroom: How could we help this oral gift transfer itself onto paper? The classes were small — fifteen at most; the staff, at that time, likewise; we spent hours in conference with individual students, hours meeting together and with counselors, trying to teach ourselves how to teach and asking ourselves what we ought to be teaching.

So these were classes, not simply in writing, not simply in literature, certainly not just in the correction of sentence fragments or the
redemptive power of the semicolon; though we did, and do, work on all
these. One teacher gave a minicourse in genres; one in drama as literature; teachers have used their favorite books from *Alice in Wonderland*
to Martin Buber's *The Knowledge of Man*; I myself have wandered all
over the map of my own reading: D. H. Lawrence, W. E. B. Du Bois,
LeRoi Jones, Plato, Orwell, Ibsen, poets from W. C. Williams to Audre
Lorde. Sometimes books are used as a way of learning to look at literature, sometimes as a provocation for the students' own writing, sometimes both. At City College all Basic Writing teachers have been free to
choose the books they would assign (always keeping within the limits
of the SEEK book allowance and considering the fact that non-SEEK
students have no book allowance at all, though their financial need
may be as acute.) There has never been a set curriculum or a required
reading list; we have poached off each others' booklists, methods, essay
topics, grammar-teaching exercises, and anything else that we hoped
would "work" for us.[1]

Most of us felt that students learn to write by discovering the validity and variety of their own experience; and in the late 1960s, as the
black classics began to flood the bookstores, we drew on the black novelists, poets, and polemicists as the natural path to this discovery for
SEEK students. Black teachers were, of course, a path; and there were
some who combined the work of consciousness-raising with the study
of Sophocles, Kafka, and other pillars of the discipline oddly enough
known as "English." For many white teachers, the black writers were a
relatively new discovery: the clear, translucent prose of Douglass, the
sonorities of *The Souls of Black Folk*, the melancholy sensuousness of
Toomer's poem-novel *Cane*. In this discovery of a previously submerged
culture we were learning from and with our students as rarely happens in the university, though it is happening anew in the area of
women's studies. We were not merely exploring a literature and a history which had gone virtually unmentioned in our white educations
(particularly true for those over thirty); we were not merely having to
confront in talk with our students and in their writings, as well as the
books we read, the bitter reality of Western racism: we also found ourselves reading almost any piece of Western literature through our students' eyes, imagining how this voice, these assumptions, would sound
to us if we were they. "We learned from the students" — banal cliché,

---

[1]What I have found deadly and defeating is the anthology designed for multiethnic
classes in freshman English. I once ordered one because the book stipends had been cut
out and I was trying to save the students money. I ended up using one Allen Ginsberg
poem, two by LeRoi Jones, and asking the students to write essays provoked by the
photographs in the anthology. The college anthology, in general, as nonbook, with its
exhaustive and painfully literal notes, directives, questions, and "guides for study," is
like TV showing of a film — cut, chopped up, and interspersed with commercials: a
flagrant mutilation by mass technological culture.

one that sounds pious and patronizing by now; yet the fact remains that our white liberal assumptions *were* shaken, our vision of both the city and the university changed, our relationship to language itself made both deeper and more painful.

Of course the students responded to black literature; I heard searching and acute discussions of Jones's poem "The Liar" or Wright's "The Man Who Lived Underground" from young men and women who were in college on sufferance in the eyes of the educational establishment; I've heard similar discussions of *Sons and Lovers* or the *Republic*. Writing this, I am conscious of how obvious it all seems and how unnecessary it now might appear to demonstrate by little anecdotes that ghetto students can handle sophisticated literature and ideas. But in 1968, 1969, we were still trying to prove this — we and our students felt that the burden of proof was on us. When the Black and Puerto Rican Student Community seized the South Campus of C.C.N.Y. in April 1969, and a team of students sat down with the president of the college and a team of faculty members to negotiate, one heard much about the faculty group's surprised respect for the students' articulateness, reasoning power, and skill in handling statistics — for the students were negotiating in exchange for withdrawal from South Campus an admissions policy which would go far beyond SEEK in its inclusiveness.

Those of us who had been involved earlier with ghetto students felt that we had known their strength all along: an impatient cutting through of the phony, a capacity for tenacious struggle with language and syntax and difficult ideas, a growing capacity for political analysis which helped counter the low expectations their teachers had always had of them and which many had had of themselves; and more, their knowledge of the naked facts of society, which academia has always, even in its public urban form, managed to veil in ivy or fantasy. Some were indeed chronologically older than the average college student; many, though eighteen or twenty years old, had had responsibility for themselves and their families for years. They came to college with a greater insight into the actual workings of the city and of American racial oppression than most of their teachers or their elite contemporaries. They had held dirty jobs, borne children, negotiated for Spanish-speaking parents with an English-speaking world of clinics, agencies, lawyers, and landlords, had their sixth senses nurtured in the streets, or had made the transition from southern sharehold or Puerto Rican countryside to Bedford-Stuyvesant or the *barrio* and knew the ways of two worlds. And they were becoming, each new wave of them, more lucidly conscious of the politics of their situation, the context within which their lives were being led.

It is tempting to romanticize, at the distance of midsummer 1972, what the experience of SEEK — and by extension, of all remedial freshman programs under Open Admissions — was (and is) for the students themselves. The Coleman Report and the Moynihan Report have left echoes and vibrations of stereotypical thinking which perhaps only a first-hand knowledge of the New York City schools can really silence. Teaching at City I came to know the intellectual poverty and human waste of the public school system through the marks it had left on students — and not on black and Puerto Rican students only, as the advent of Open Admissions was to show. For a plain look at the politics and practices of this system, I recommend Ellen Lurie's *How to Change the Schools*, a handbook for parent activists which enumerates the conditions she and other parents, black, Puerto Rican, and white, came to know intimately in their struggles to secure their children's right to learn and to be treated with dignity. The book is a photograph of the decay, racism, and abusiveness they confronted, written not as muckraking journalism but as a practical tool for others like themselves. I have read little else, including the most lyrically indignant prose of radical educators, that gives so precise and devastating a picture of the life that New York's children are expected to lead in the name of schooling. She writes of "bewildered angry teen-agers, who have discovered that they are in classes for mentally retarded students, simply because they cannot speak English," of teachers and principals who "behaved as though every white middle-class child was gifted and was college material, and every black and Puerto Rican (and sometimes Irish and Italian) working-class child was slow, disadvantaged, and unable to learn anything but the most rudimentary facts." She notes that "81 elementary schools in the state (out of a total of 3,634) had more than 70 percent of their students below minimum competence, and 65 *of these were New York City public schools!*" Her findings and statistics make it clear that tracking begins at kindergarten (chiefly on the basis of skin color and language) and that nonwhite and working-class children are assumed to have a maximum potential which fits them only for the so-called general diploma, hence are not taught, as are their middle-class contemporaries, the math or languages or writing skills needed to pass college entrance examinations or even to do academic-diploma high-school work.[2] I have singled out these particular points for citation because they have to do directly with our students' self-expectations and the enforced limitation of their horizons years before they come to college. But much else has colored their educational past: the drug pushers at the school gates, the obsolete texts, the punitive conception of the teacher's role, the ugliness, filth, and decay of the buildings, the demoralization even of good teachers working under such conditions. (Add to this the use of tranquilizing drugs on children who are considered hyperactive or who present "behavior problems" at an early age.)

To come out of scenes like these schools and be offered "a chance" to compete as an equal in the world of academic credentials, the white-collar world, the world beyond the minimum wage or welfare, is less romantic for the student than for those who view the process from a distance. The student who leaves the campus at three or four o'clock

---

[2]Ellen Lurie, *How to Change the Schools* (New York: Random House, 1970). See pp. 31, 32, 40–48.

after a day of classes, goes to work as a waitress, or clerk, or hash-slinger, or guard, comes home at ten or eleven o'clock to a crowded apartment with TV audible in every corner — what does it feel like to this student to be reading, say, Byron's "Don Juan" or Jane Austen for a class the next day? Our students may spend two or three hours in the subway going to and from college and jobs, longer if the subway system is more deplorable than usual. To read in the New York subway at rush hour is impossible; it is virtually impossible to think.

How does one compare this experience of college with that of the Columbia students down at 116th Street in their quadrangle of gray stone dormitories, marble steps, flowered borders, wide spaces of time and architecture in which to talk and think? Or that of Berkeley students with their eucalyptus grove and tree-lined streets of bookstores and cafés? The Princeton or Vassar students devoting four years to the life of the mind in Gothic serenity? Do "motivation" and "intellectual competency" mean the same for those students as for City College undergraduates on that overcrowded campus where in winter there is often no place to sit between classes, with two inadequate bookstores largely filled with required texts, two cafeterias and a snack bar that are overpriced, dreary, and unconducive to lingering, with the incessant pressure of time and money driving at them to rush, to get through, to amass the needed credits somehow, to drop out, to stay on with gritted teeth? Out of a graduating class at Swarthmore or Oberlin and one at C.C.N.Y., which students have demonstrated their ability and commitment, and how do we assume we can measure such things?

Sometimes as I walk up 133rd Street, past the glass-strewn doorways of P.S. 161, the graffiti-sprayed walls of tenements, the uncollected garbage, through the iron gates of South Campus and up the driveway to the prefab hut which houses the English department, I think wryly of John Donne's pronouncement that "the University is a Paradise; rivers of Knowledge are there; Arts and Sciences flow from thence." I think that few of our students have this Athenian notion of what college is going to be for them; their first introduction to it is a many hours' wait in line at registration, which only reveals that the courses they have been advised or wanted to take are filled, or conflict in hours with a needed job; then more hours at the cramped, heavily guarded bookstore; then perhaps, a semester in courses which they never chose, or in which the pace and allusions of a lecturer are daunting or which may meet at opposite ends of an elongated campus stretching for six city blocks and spilling over into a former warehouse on Broadway. Many have written of their first days at C.C.N.Y.: "I only knew it was different from high school." What was different, perhaps, was the green grass of early September with groups of young people in dashikis and gelés, jeans and tie-dye, moving about with the unquenchable animation of the first days of the fall semester; the encounter with some teachers who seem to respect them as individuals; something at any rate less bleak, less violent, less mean-spirited, than the halls of Benjamin Franklin or Evander Childs or some other school with the line painted down the center of the corridor and a penalty for taking the short-cut across that line. In all that my students have written about their high schools, I have found bitterness, resentment, satire, black humor; never any word of nostalgia for the school, though sometimes a word of affection for a teacher "who really tried."

The point is that, as Mina Shaughnessy, the director of the Basic Writing Program at City, has written: "the first stage of Open Admissions involves *openly admitting* that education has failed for too many students."[3] Professor Shaughnessy writes in her most recent report of the increase in remedial courses of white, ethnic students (about two-thirds of the Open Admissions freshmen who have below-80 high school averages) and of the discernible fact, a revelation to many, that these white students "have experienced the failure of the public schools in different ways from the black and Puerto Rican students." Another City College colleague, Leonard Kriegel, writes of this newest population: "Like most blue-collar children, they had lived within the confines of an educational system without ever having questioned that system. They were used to being stamped and categorized. Rating systems, grades, obligations to improve, these had beset them all their lives. . . . They had few expectations from the world-at-large. When they were depressed, they had no real idea of what was getting them down, and they would have dismissed as absurd the idea that they could make demands. They accepted the myths of America as those myths had been presented to them."[4]

Meeting some of the so-called ethnic students in class for the first time in September 1970, I began to realize that: there *are* still poor Jews in New York City; they teach English better to native speakers of Greek on the island of Cyprus than they do to native speakers of Spanish on the island of Manhattan; the Chinese student with acute English-language difficulties is stereotyped as "nonexpressive" and channeled into the physical sciences before anyone has a chance to find out whether he or she is a potential historian, political theorist, or psychologist; and (an intuition, more difficult to prove) white, ethnic working-class young women seem to have problems of self-reliance and of taking their lives seriously that young black women students as a group do not seem to share.

There is also a danger that, paradoxically or not, the white middle-class teacher may find it easier to identify with the strongly motivated, obviously oppressed, politically conscious black student than with the students of whom Kriegel has written. Perhaps a different set of preju-

---

[3]Mina P. Shaughnessy, "Open Admissions — A Second Report," in *The City College Department of English Newsletter,* vol. II, no. 1., January 1972. *A. R., 1978:* See also Shaughnessy's *Errors and Expectations: A Guide for the Teacher of Basic Writing* (New York: Oxford, 1977), a remarkable study in the methodology of teaching language.

[4]"When Blue-Collar Students Go to College," in *Saturday Review,* July 22, 1972. The article is excerpted from the book *Working Through: A Teacher's Journal in the Urban University* (New York: Saturday Review Press, 1972). Kriegel is describing students at Long Island University of a decade ago; but much that he says is descriptive of students who are now entering colleges like C.C.N.Y. under Open Admissions.

dices exists: if you're white, why aren't you more hip, more achieving, why are you bored and alienated, why don't you *care* more? Again, one has to keep clearly in mind the real lessons of the schools — both public and parochial — which reward conformity, passivity, and correct answers and penalize, as Ellen Lurie says, the troublesome question "as trouble-making," the lively, independent, active child as "disruptive," curiosity as misbehavior. (Because of the reinforcement in passivity received all around them in society and at home, white women students seem particularly vulnerable to these judgments.) In many ways the damage is more insidious because the white students have as yet no real political analysis going for them; only the knowledge that they have not been as successful in school as white students are supposed to be.

Confronted with these individuals, this city, these life situations, these strengths, these damages, there are some harsh questions that have to be raised about the uses of literature. I think of myself as a teacher of language: that is, as someone for whom language has implied freedom, who is trying to aid others to free themselves through the written word, and above all through learning to write it for themselves. I cannot know for them what it is they need to free, or what words they need to write; I can only try with them to get an approximation of the story they want to tell. I have always assumed, and I do still assume, that people come into the freedom of language through reading, before writing; that the differences of tone, rhythm, vocabulary, intention, encountered over years of reading are, whatever else they may be, suggestive of many different possible modes of being. But my daily life as a teacher confronts me with young men and women who have had language and literature *used against* them, to keep them in their place, to mystify, to bully, to make them feel powerless. Courses in great books or speed-reading are not an answer when it is the meaning of literature itself that is in question. Sartre says: "the literary object has no other substance than the reader's subjectivity; Raskolnikov's waiting is *my* waiting which I lend him. . . . His hatred of the police magistrate who questions him is my hatred, which has been solicited and wheedled out of me by signs. . . . Thus, the writer appeals to the reader's freedom to collaborate in the production of his work."[5] But what if it is these very signs, or ones like them, that have been used to limit the reader's freedom or to convince the reader of his or her unworthiness to "collaborate in the production of the work"?

I have no illuminating answers to such questions. I am sure we must revise, and are revising, our notion of the "classic," which has come to be used as a term of unquestioning idolatry instead of in the meaning which Sartre gives it: a book written by someone who "did not have to decide with each work what the meaning and value of litera-

---

[5]Jean-Paul Sartre, *What Is Literature?* (New York: Harper Colophon Books, 1965), pp. 39–40.

ture were, since its meaning and value were fixed by tradition."[6] And I know that the action from the other side, of becoming that person who puts signs on paper and invokes the collaboration of a reader, encounters a corresponding check: in order to write I have to believe that there is someone willing to collaborate subjectively, as opposed to a grading machine out to get me for mistakes in spelling and grammar. (Perhaps for this reason, many students first show the writing they are actually capable of in an uncorrected journal rather than in a "theme" written "for class.") The whole question of *trust* as a basis for the act of reading or writing has only opened up since we began trying to educate those who have every reason to mistrust literary culture. For young adults trying to write seriously for the first time in their lives, the question "Whom can I trust?" must be an underlying boundary to be crossed before real writing can occur. We who are part of literary culture come up against such a question only when we find ourselves writing on some frontier of self-determination, as when writers from an oppressed group *within* literary culture, such as black intellectuals, or, most recently, women, begin to describe and analyze themselves as they cease to identify with the dominant culture. Those who fall into this category ought to be able to draw on it in entering into the experience of the young adult for whom writing itself — as reading — has been part of the not-me rather than one of the natural activities of the self.

At this point the question of method legitimately arises: How to do it? How to develop a working situation in the classroom where trust becomes a reality, where the students are writing with belief in their own validity, and reading with belief that what they read has validity for them? The question is legitimate — How to do it? — but I am not sure that a description of strategies and exercises, readings, and writing topics can be, however successful they have proven for one teacher. When I read such material, I may find it stimulating and heartening as it indicates the varieties of concern and struggle going on in other classrooms, but I end by feeling it is useless to me. X is not myself and X's students are not my students, nor are my students of this fall the same as my students of last spring. A couple of years ago I decided to teach *Sons and Lovers*, because of my sense that the novel touched on facts of existence crucial to people in their late teens, and my belief that it dealt with certain aspects of family life, sexuality, work, anger, and jealousy which carried over to many cultures. Before the students began to read, I started talking about the time and place of the novel, the life of the mines, the process of industrialization and pollution visible in the slag heaps; and I gave the students (this was an almost all-black class) a few examples of the dialect they would encounter in the early chapters. Several students challenged the novel sight unseen: it had nothing to do with them, it was about English people in another era, why should they expect to find it meaningful to them, and so forth.

[6]Ibid., p. 85.

I told them I had asked them to read it because I believed it was meaningful for them; if it was not, we could talk and write about why not and how not. The following week I reached the classroom door to find several students already there, energetically arguing about the Morels, who was to blame in the marriage, Mrs. Morel's snobbery, Morel's drinking and violence — taking sides, justifying, attacking. The class never began; it simply continued as other students arrived. Many had not yet read the novel, or had barely looked at it; these became curious and interested in the conversation and did go back and read it because they felt it must have something to have generated so much heat. That time, I felt some essential connections had been made, which carried us through several weeks of talking and writing about and out of *Sons and Lovers*, trying to define our relationships to its people and theirs to each other. A year or so later I enthusiastically started working with *Sons and Lovers* again, with a class of largely ethnic students — Jewish, Greek, Chinese, Italian, German, with a few Puerto Ricans and blacks. No one initially challenged the novel, but no one was particularly interested — or, perhaps, as I told myself, it impinged too dangerously on materials that this group was not about to deal with, such as violence in the family, nascent sexual feelings, conflicting feelings about a parent. Was this really true? I don't know; it is easy to play sociologist and make generalizations. Perhaps, simply, a different chemistry was at work, in me and in the students. The point is that for the first class, or for many of them, I think a trust came to be established in the novel genre as a possible means of finding out more about themselves; for the second class, the novel was an assignment, to be done under duress, read superficially, its connections with themselves avoided wherever possible.

Finally, as to trust: I think that, simple as it may seem, it is worth saying: a fundamental belief in the students is more important than anything else. We all know of those studies in education where the teacher's previously induced expectations dramatically affect the learning that goes on during the semester. This fundamental belief is not a sentimental matter: it is a very demanding matter of realistically conceiving the student where he or she is, and at the same time never losing sight of where he or she *can* be. Conditions at a huge, urban, overcrowded, noisy, and pollution-soaked institution can become almost physically overwhelming at times, for the students and for the staff: sometimes apathy, accidia, anomie seem to stare from the faces in an overheated basement classroom, like the faces in a subway car, and I sympathize with the rush to get out the moment the bell rings. This, too, is our context — not merely the students' past and my past, but this present moment we share. I (and I don't think I am alone in this) become angry with myself for my ineffectualness, angry at the students for their apparent resistance or their acceptance of mediocrity, angriest at the political conditions which dictate that we have to try to repair and extend the fabric of language under conditions which tend to coarsen our apprehensions of everything. Often, however, this anger, if not driven in on ourselves, or converted to despair, can become an illuminating force: the terms of the struggle for equal opportunity are chalked on the blackboard: this is what the students have been up against all their lives.

I wrote at the beginning of this article that my early assumptions about teaching had changed. I think that what has held me at City is not the one or two students in a class whose eyes meet mine with a look of knowing they were born for this struggle with words and meanings; not the poet who has turned up more than once; though such encounters are a privilege in the classroom as anywhere. What has held me, and what I think holds many who teach basic writing, are the hidden veins of possibility running through students who don't know (and strongly doubt) that this is what they were born for, but who may find it out to their own amazement, students who, grim with self-depreciation and prophecies of their own failure or tight with a fear they cannot express, can be lured into sticking it out to some moment of breakthrough, when they discover that they have ideas that are valuable, even original, and can express those ideas on paper. What fascinates and gives hope in a time of slashed budgets, enlarging class size, and national depression is the possibility that many of these young men and women may be gaining the kind of critical perspective on their lives and the skill to bear witness that they have never before had in our country's history.

At the bedrock level of my thinking about this is the sense that language is power, and that, as Simone Weil says, those who suffer from injustice most are the least able to articulate their suffering; and that the silent majority, if released into language, would not be content with a perpetuation of the conditions which have betrayed them. But this notion hangs on a special conception of what it means to be released into language: not simply learning the jargon of an elite, fitting unexceptionably into the status quo, but learning that language can be used as a means of changing reality.[7] What interests me in teaching is less the emergence of the occasional genius than the overall finding of language by those who did not have it and by those who have been used and abused to the extent that they lacked it.

The question can be validly raised: Is the existing public (or private) educational system, school, or university the place where such a relationship to language can be developed? Aren't those structures already too determined, haven't they too great a stake in keeping things as they are? My response would be, yes, but this is where the *students* are. On the one hand, we need alternate education; on the other, we need to reach those students for whom unorthodox education simply

---

[7]Compare Paulo Freire: "Only beings who can reflect upon the fact that they are determined are capable of freeing themselves." *Cultural Action for Freedom,* Monograph Series No. 1 (Cambridge, Mass.: Harvard Educational Review and Center for the Study of Development and Social Change, 1970).

means too much risk. In a disintegrating society, the orthodox educational system reflects disintegration. However, I believe it is more than simply reformist to try to use that system — while it still exists in all its flagrant deficiencies — to use it to provide essential tools and weapons for those who may live on into a new integration. Language is such a weapon, and what goes with language: reflection, criticism, renaming, creation. The fact that our language itself is tainted by the quality of our society means that in teaching we need to be acutely conscious of the kind of tool we want our students to have available, to understand how it has been used against them, and to do all we can to insure that language will not someday be used by them to keep others silent and powerless.

Classroom Activities

Rich discusses the readings that her open-admissions students often found meaningful, including literary works by Richard Wright, William Carlos Williams, Henrik Ibsen, and Audre Lorde. She also mentions authors whose works she wishes had been available to her students, such as Zora Neale Hurston and Margaret Walker. Consider bringing excerpts from these writers' works (as well as your own favorite texts — and works recommended by the students) to class to facilitate reading and writing opportunities for students. As an extended assignment, students can choose to read an entire text (such as Margaret Walker's *For My People* or Henrik Ibsen's *A Doll's House*) and respond with analytic and/or creative writing of their own.

Thinking about Teaching

The problems that Rich poses in her essay are still as much a part of the discussion of teaching basic writing today as they were in the late 1960s and early 1970s. Rich lists questions that grew out of her early experience in teaching basic writing, an experience that she found both "unnerving and seductive":

- How do you make standard verb endings available to a dialect speaker?

- How do you teach English prepositional forms to a Spanish-language student?

- How does one teach order, coherence, the structure of ideas while respecting the student's experience of his or her thinking or perceiving?

- How do you develop a working situation in the classroom where trust becomes a reality, where students are writing with belief in their own validity, and reading with belief that what they read has validity for them?

In your teaching journal, respond to some of these questions. Do they continue to hold relevance today for your own classroom? You may want to share the approaches you use to address the needs and desires of today's generation of basic writing students with colleagues. What impact has the composition theory and practice of the past thirty years had on your own methods? What similarities and differences do you find between your own classrooms and the ones that Rich describes? How do you deal with new issues (such as the decline of equal-access education and open-admissions universities and the rise of standardized testing) not addressed in Rich's essay? How would you update Rich's essay to address contemporary concerns of students in basic writing?

A Basic Introduction to Basic Writing Program Structures: A Baseline and Five Alternatives

William B. Lalicker

In 1999, William B. Lalicker conducted a survey on the Writing Program Administrators' listserv in order to determine the different kinds of basic writing program models at a variety of institutions. From these results, he was able to describe a "baseline" model of a basic writing program and five "alternative" models. In the following article, first published in 2000 in Conference on Basic Writing: Basic Writing e-Journal, *he lists the advantages and disadvantages of each model, as well as such important features as credit status, placement, and grading. These descriptions give us a sense of the variety and scope of the programs in place and the program options available at various institutions.*

In January 1999, I conducted a brief survey of writing program administrators to determine the alternative structures for basic writing programs. My query on the Writing Program Administrators listserv asked respondents to identify their basic writing program structures according to five models I'd identified from a general search of scholarship on the subject. Respondents not only described their basic writing programs as variants of the five models; they provided useful insights concerning the advantages and disadvantages of each model in their specific institutional contexts. (Examples of basic writing programs herein, when not otherwise cited, are taken from that listserv survey.)

The following is a summary, a kind of primer, about those models and their features.

Although the appropriateness of each model relies strongly on a combination of site-specific conditions such as the institution's mission, its demographics, and its resources, no pattern emerged linked to the generic type of college or university in question. Institutions of every type have developmental writing programs. One might expect research universities, comprehensive state universities, liberal arts colleges, and community colleges to favor particular models according to institutional type, but such seemed not to be the case. Individual institutional needs — and, possibly, the theoretical or epistemological assumptions driving the writing program — seemed to be a stronger determinant.

Basic writing program directors, then, should be able to borrow from a range of structural alternatives in designing the best possible program for their students. The introduction below will begin by describing a baseline approach — the "prerequisite" model. (Since critiques of this model, especially of its placement and grading systems, are prolific in basic writing journals, I will refrain from extensive analysis and will simply describe this system in order to provide a starting point for comparing the alternatives.) I will use a parallel descriptive structure to sketch the key features of alternative approaches.

Baseline: The Prerequisite Model

- *Description:* This is the "current-traditional" approach to basic writing. This model assumes that basic writers are provisionally allowed to enter college despite literacy abilities that are sub-college-level. Writers may earn their way into the college-worthy elite (signified by admission to standard composition) by successfully completing the basic writing course; the course frequently focuses more on grammatical conformity than on rhetorical sophistication. Many institutions have used this model for decades. Some examples of this model still rely on grammar-drill workbooks and limit the scope of student writing to the paragraph level; others attempt to apply more progressive rhetorical theory within a structure unchangeable due to local political or budgetary limitations.

- *Credit status:* The prerequisite model carries with it the assumption that basic writing isn't really "college-level" writing. Although this assumption seldom if ever prevents the college or university from collecting tuition for the course, it usually prevents the institution from awarding college credit. Typically, the three credit hours of the basic writing course are allowed to count toward full-time enrollment status for a student's financial aid qualification, but do not count toward the number of credit hours required for a degree, and do not count as part of the general education core.

- *Placement:* Initial placement is usually determined by locally decided threshold scores on a standardized national examination (ACT-English, SAT Verbal, or infrequently the Nelson-Denny test). A locally developed writing examination — usually a short, timed, impromptu, no-revision-allowed essay — administered near the start of classes may influence placement. Although the timed impromptu essay has its champions (see White), most in the field find alternatives preferable (see Harrington). More rarely, a portfolio of writing solicited as part of the admissions application, or high school grades, may also be used. (For two useful surveys of the most common approaches to placement, see Huot, and Murphy et al.)

- *Grading:* Students may earn a grade on the regular A-through-F four-point scale, or may take the course pass-fail. Grading may be affected by a heavily weighted exit examination, sometimes a test of isolated grammatical questions. Additionally, a number of institutions dictate a higher minimum passing grade: if D is the minimum passing grade in most (that is, "college-level") courses, a C may be the minimum grade for a student to complete the basic writing prerequisite and continue to standard general-education composition.

- *Advantages:* This system can be simple to administer and staff, due to its compatibility with standardized placement, mechanical grammar drill, and Scantron-ready exit exams. Depending on the degree of mechanical standardization in the placement and exit exam practices, this system may be inexpensive to provide. Moreover, it powerfully refutes accusations of grade inflation and general mollycoddling of underprepared students. (Some educators and politicians apparently see this as a "tough love" system: applying this basic writing hazing, we'll have done our students the good service of preparing them for the rigors of academic discourse.)

- *Disadvantages:* Stigmatizing elements of system, and arbitrary-appearing placement and exit exams, can raise resentment in students and parents. Lack of graduation and general education credit raises similar resentments. Outcomes of this approach to basic writing may not be theoretically or epistemologically compatible with outcomes being assessed for the composition program as a whole, especially if the composition program is driven by progressive rhetorical theory.

Alternative 1: The Stretch Model

- *Description:* "Stretch" programs serve basic writers by allowing them to complete a typical introductory standard composition course over two semesters instead of one. After taking this two-semester version of English 101, students take other general-education writing courses as required by the institution's standard curriculum. The stretch program might be numbered as, for instance, ENG 100 and ENG 101, retaining the standard composition course number but adding a prerequisite for some students (the system at Arizona State University, a prominent stretch model). Alternatively, it might be numbered, for example, ENG 99 and ENG 100, with the two courses together carrying general education credit equal to (and substituting for) ENG 101. Some stretch models structure the course as a truly integrated one-year version of introductory composition; others make the basic writing course a discrete prerequisite for standard composition, but allow that prerequisite to carry general-education, elective, or graduation credit.

- *Credit status:* A stretch sequence typically carries general-education credit — but requires students to have three additional composition credit hours compared to students not in the developmental sequence.

- *Placement:* Standard placement methods (SAT Verbal score, writing exam, entrance portfolio, or sometimes pre-enrollment writing sample or high school grade).

- *Grading:* Standard options — may be regular grade; may be pass-fail; or first course in sequence may be pass-fail, with second course being regular grade (to keep number of regular-grade general education credit hours equal for basic writers and nonbasic writers).

- *Advantages:* Number of credit hours and resources devoted to composition remains essentially unchanged from system in which some students are required to take a basic writing prerequisite to standard composition. Faculty roles, number of faculty credit hours taught, and general logistics remain the same as in the baseline programs. Moreover, more faculty may be willing to teach the basic writing course once it's declared 100-level and credit-bearing, since some faculty (like some students) bring a sense of stigma or fear to any course called 0-level. Placement methods are flexible; options are essentially the same as for any other model. Not only students and faculty, but also parents, may find less stigma when starting with general-education credit-bearing, 100-level courses. In the stretch model, all students begin English Comp as university students — members of the academic community — rather than as nonqualifying, 0-level, pre-college-level outsiders. Yet basic writing students get the extra practice they need. Basic writing students begin work on the same general-education objectives as standard comp students, but have more time to reach those outcomes.

- *Disadvantages:* Simply renaming ENG 099 as ENG 100, and then requiring basic writing students to take ENG 101, doesn't necessarily change the substance and perception of a course that is often ghettoized and stigmatized. Also, students are required to earn three additional credit hours to graduate, compared with students not in the basic writing sequence. Although additional required credit hours are a feature of almost any basic writing model, the promotion of basic writing to credit-bearing status in the stretch (or any) model doesn't prevent basic writers (or their parents) from resenting that requirement, especially if it means extra tuition to pay. And a credit-bearing basic writing course may be illegal in states where legislators (or in institutions where administrators) mandate an absolute requirement that students with low SAT, ACT, or Nelson-Denny scores take 0-level courses.

Alternative 2: The Studio Model

- *Description:* A "studio" program typically allows all students to begin their general-education English Composition in the standard comp course, but places certain students in small required group sessions to supplement the work in that standard course. The studio course runs concurrently with the standard comp course and may have the same instructor, a different instructor, or may use teaching assistants or Writing Center tutors. Studio sessions, consisting of six or eight students, discuss grammatical and rhetorical issues from the composition course and do writing workshops to improve the essay drafts assigned in the standard course.

- *Credit status:* Regular general-education credit, although typically the course earns only one credit hour. May be analogous to a science "lab section" — a fourth credit hour added to a three-hour course.

- *Placement:* At the institution that initiated the studio model (the University of South Carolina), students are placed by recommendation of their composition instructors during the second week of the standard comp course. Instructors use two student writing assignments, plus portfolios of writing submitted upon university admission, to decide whether students are assigned to a studio. Some students self-select the studio to improve their skills. However, students might be placed in the studio course by any of the standard methods (SAT Verbal score, or locally designed writing examination, for instance).

- *Grading:* Studio sections are usually (but not necessarily) pass-fail; work in the studio section is assumed to influence the comp course grade indirectly (work in studio section leads to better work and a higher grade in the comp course).

- *Advantages:* Studio sections can mitigate stigma by allowing students to get general-education credit and take standard composition concurrently with raising ability levels for basic writers; many parents and students currently complain that taking basic writing before standard comp (the prerequisite approach) puts them "behind schedule" toward graduation. The studio model unites the curriculum of basic and standard comp: the writing outcomes of basic writers and standard comp are the same, with assessment in the comp section only. This enforces the notion that basic and standard composition students are all working equally and collaboratively toward fluency in academic discourse and critical discourse consciousness (rather than segregating basic writers in a simplistic linguistic world where grammatical conformity dominates). According to Grego and Thompson of the University of South Carolina, "the Studio program gives body and voice to a part of the academic institution which is working to see the personal and interpersonal aspects of learning as part of the 'thinking' that constitutes academic discourse" (81).

- *Disadvantages:* At some institutions, it could be logistically tricky for the registrar to allow students to enroll in a class two weeks into a semester. (Presemester placement, as in the intensive model described below, would solve this problem, albeit with the reintroduction of some stigma and stress for parents and students.) If the studio course is one credit hour, this will significantly reduce (by two-thirds) the number of credit hours generated now by basic writing (reducing course-generated income that supports faculty and programs — an issue in some departments). Studio sections might cost more than the three-hour-requirement system on a per-student basis if the three-hour basic writing course section is larger than eighteen. (An instructor in the studio model teaches only eighteen students if there are six students per studio; but if an instructor teaches three eight-student studio sections, the total of twenty-four students is larger than most basic writing three-credit sections.) The studio system places heavy responsibility for placement on instructors, if the South Carolina placement system is adopted. (This isn't necessarily bad; as Susanmarie Harrington notes concerning placement, "The newer models rely on teacher expertise to sort students into appropriate courses" [53]; William Smith defends this approach based on his experience at the University of Pittsburgh [142–205]. But I tend to share the view of Richard Haswell and Susan Wyche-Smith, whose work with the system at Washington State University leads them to emphasize the care and training such instructor-reliant placement requires [204–07].) finally, the studio model may not be an option where non-credit-bearing "remedial" writing is required based on entrance test score or other placement measures.

Alternative 3: The Directed Self-Placement Model

- *Description:* "Directed Self-Placement" might be called "Basic Optional": advisors and the writing program administrator (or basic writing director) suggest or persuade, rather than require, designated students to start with basic writing rather than standard English Comp. In fact, directed self-placement isn't really a model in the structural sense: it can be used with a wide variety of course and credit arrangements. But the attitudinal change it seeks to foster in students — that basic writing is something students choose because they know they need it, rather than something forced upon them — may make a number of creative and effective course structure alternatives politically possible, even palatable, in the eyes of some constituencies (students, parents, faculty, administrators). (See Royer and Gilles for a complete description of the model and its effects at Grand Valley State University.)

- *Credit status:* At Grand Valley State University (Michigan), which has pioneered this model, students may choose to take ENG 098, a three-credit-hour, non-general-education-credit course. Programs have the option of using this model with 100-level elective basic writing courses offering general-education credit.

- *Placement:* The writing program administrator at Grand Valley State addresses an assembly of all incoming students during orientation, directing them to respond for themselves on key statements defining their literacy levels. Students consider statements such as "I read newspapers and magazines regularly." "In high school, I wrote several essays per year," and "My ACT-English score was above 20" (analogous to "My SAT Verbal score was above 490"). Then, for students who answer "No" to the questions, he makes the case for ENG 098 instead of standard comp, and students sign up for the course in which they believe they belong.

- *Grading:* The basic writing course may be traditionally graded or pass-fail.

- *Advantages:* Students take responsibility for their own literacy — and for their own placement in English Composition. This may lead students to resent their placement less, and to motivate themselves more energetically in whatever writing course they choose. Placement is less expensive and time-consuming: no local testing systems or portfolio assessment necessary. As the subtitle of the Royer and Gilles article concludes, "Directed Self-Placement Pleases Everyone Involved" (65).

- *Disadvantages:* Although Grand Valley State's conclusion is that the students who should have been taking developmental comp all along tended to place themselves in it, there is the possibility that some students who would benefit from the developmental course would avoid basic writing. Some students may self-place inaccurately, be overwhelmed by early academic expectations, and perform more poorly in standard comp and other university writing tasks. If self-directed placement leads to significantly fewer basic writing sections, a loss of income-generating credit hours or critical program mass may lead to a marginalized program without resources to serve its constituency. Directed self-placement may depend upon an enhanced Writing Center (and a commitment to an enhanced Writing Center budget) to provide support to students who might receive extra instruction through basic writing but are placed in standard comp. Finally, the "optional" quality of self-directed placement may not be legal in states where legislators (or campus administrators) mandate placement in "pre-college-level" writing based on test scores or other standardized measures.

Alternative 4: The Intensive Model

- *Description:* The "intensive" model offers two kinds of standard composition sections: the regular sections, plus "intensive" sections that include additional instruction time or writing activities tailored for basic writers. To some degree, the intensive model is a variation on the studio model, usually differing from the standard studio model in two ways. First, in intensive-model basic writing, students start in special intensive composition sections from the first day of classes, based on common placement methods such as test scores or portfolio ratings. Second, in the intensive model, students usually are part of one five-credit class group, while in the studio model, students from several different sections of standard composition come together at random in the studio lab sections; each structure leads to different pedagogical possibilities.

- *Credit hours:* Intensive sections of comp generally offer five credit hours for the course, rather than the standard three-credit-hour sections. All sections — intensive and standard — carry general-education credit.

- *Placement:* Any placement system may be used; institutions presently using the intensive system tend to use SAT Verbal scores for placement.

- *Grading:* Students in intensive sections get regular grades, counting for five credit hours for the initial general-education composition course, rather than the standard three credit hours.

- *Advantages:* Writing program administrators at two of the noted programs using this system (Illinois State University and Quinnipiac College) endorse the intensive model; Mary T. Segall says that the intensive model has removed the basic-writing stigma and increased motivation (38–47). The system also may remove the complaint about prerequisite basic writing delaying the start of general-education comp, may integrate students into mainstream academic writing situations more quickly, and may help unify basic writing and English Comp writing standards and assessment outcomes. Students who are part of a unified classroom group for all of the work that five credit hours implies may find it easier to collaborate with the stable community of student-colleagues. The two-credit-hours' worth of added work in each intensive section is focused on the tasks of one course section (unlike in the studio system, where studio work may include students comparing perspectives from slightly differing course sections).

- *Disadvantages:* In a five-credit-hour system, one-third fewer credit hours would be generated by basic writing than are generated in a prerequisite basic writing system (with possible budgetary consequences). Five-credit courses might be logistically tricky to work into instructors' nine- or twelve-credit-hour loads (and adjunct faculty at many institutions are paid by three-credit-hour course), necessitating some special prorated pay arrangements or overtime salary. If credit is awarded for intensive courses, this policy may violate state or institutional mandates that low-performing entrants take non-credit-bearing "remedial" writing.

Alternative 5: The Mainstreaming Model

- *Description:* "Mainstreaming" essentially eliminates basic writing classes and puts all students, no matter what their apparent writing ability, into standard comp classes. Students address deficiencies in their writing through their own initiative in the Writing Center or use other tutoring options (including increased one-on-one help from professors in conferences).

- *Credit:* Regular general-education credit — basic writers take standard composition.

- *Placement:* No placement into basic writing necessary.

- *Grading:* Same as in standard composition.

- *Advantages:* "Mainstreaming" — teaching special needs students (in this case, basic writers) in standard classes — has been championed in many levels of education for social reasons, mainly the elimination of the "outsider" status of a segment of the student population. Some mainstreaming schools (such as the City College of New York) adopted mainstreaming for the philosophical view that all students should be part of a united community without stigmatized segments (before the CCNY trustees eliminated basic writing in an anti-remedial-education move). In practical terms, there is some evidence that mainstreamed students improve their writing faster when immersed in the higher-level academic discourse of the standard comp class. Some institutions (such as Essex Community College in Maryland) claim that basic writers placed in basic writing classes are ultimately less successful in college writing tasks than basic writers who skip basic writing and go into standard comp (Adams 22–36) (although this may be an argument for "directed self-placement" rather than mainstreaming). Mainstreaming eliminates costs of basic writing placement.

• *Disadvantages:* Some basic writing students might find themselves overtaxed in standard comp classes, with possible consequences ranging from poorer overall student writing performance to decreased retention and graduation. Instructors in standard comp classes would need to be prepared to do more diagnostic work and one-on-one tutoring. Mary Soliday and Barbara Gleason at CCNY warn that mainstreaming requires increased tutoring support and faculty development to meet the needs of basic writers (22–36). Inadequately supported Writing Centers would likely be overwhelmed by demand for service, and might need increased and sustained resources. Alternatively, the regular general-education comp courses might have to lower established standards and expected outcomes, or be revised with an eye toward what has been basic writing instruction (possibly serving basic writers adequately, but more prepared writers less appropriately than under the status quo). Mainstreaming would mean the elimination of basic writing; in some cases, this may mean the elimination of basic writers, especially in jurisdictions where basic writing is mandated for low-scoring students — a violation of many institutions' missions to serve disadvantaged populations or broad regional needs. In some systems, mainstreaming means the loss of budgetary dollars generated by basic writing credit hours (erstwhile basic writing students would be taking three fewer credit hours).

Which model should you adopt? Should you copy the key features of a typical system as described here, or design a variant by playing mix-and-match? A greater understanding of the alternatives will help you determine the answer most suited to your program's theories and goals, most achievable with your institution's mission and resources, and most successful for meeting the literacy challenges of your basic writing students.

Works Cited

Adams, Peter Dow. "Basic Writing Reconsidered." *Journal of Basic Writing* 12.1 (Spring 1993): 22–36.

Grego, Rhonda, and Nancy Thompson. "Repositioning Remediation: Renegotiating Composition's Work in the Academy." *CCC* 47.1 (Feb. 1996): 62–84.

Harrington, Susanmarie. "New Visions of Authority in Placement Test Rating." *WPA: Writing Program Administration* 22.1/2 (Fall/Winter 1998): 53–84.

Haswell, Richard, and Susan Wyche-Smith. "A Two-Tiered Rating Procedure for Placement Essays." *Assessment in Practice: Putting Principles to Work on College Campuses.* Ed. Trudy Banta. San Francisco: Jossey-Bass, 1995. 204–07.

Huot, Brian. "A Survey of College and University Writing Placement Practices." *WPA: Writing Program Administration* 17.3 (Spring 1994): 49–65.

Murphy, Sandra, et al. Report to the CCCC Executive Committee: Survey of Postsecondary Writing Assessment Practices. 1993.

Royer, Daniel J., and Roger Gilles. "Directed Self-Placement: An Attitude of Orientation." *CCC* 50.1 (Sept. 1998): 58–70.

Segall, Mary T. "Embracing a Porcupine: Redesigning a Writing Program." *Journal of Basic Writing* 14.2 (Fall 1995): 38–47.

Smith, William. "Assessing the Reliability and Adequacy of Using Holistic Scoring of Essays as a College Composition Placement Technique." *Validating Holistic Scoring for Writing Assessment: Theoretical and Empirical Foundations.* Ed. Michael M. Williamson and Brian Huot. Cresskill, NJ: Hampton, 1993. 142–205.

Soliday, Mary, and Barbara Gleason. "From Remediation to Enrichment: Evaluating a Mainstreaming Project." *Journal of Basic Writing* 16.1 (Spring 1997): 64–78.

White, Edward M. "An Apologia for the Timed Impromptu Essay." *CCC* 46.1 (Feb. 1995): 30–45.

Classroom Activities

Encourage students to reflect on their own education by thinking about the six models for basic writing that Lalicker presents. In order to offer a more relevant approach to the idea of an educational model for students, you might ask them to respond to the following prompts:

- Describe your experiences with studying writing and reading in grade school, high school, or GED or ABE programs. What was the best experience you ever had with writing? What was the worst? What made these experiences memorable?

- Compare your previous experiences with writing to your basic writing course(s) in college. What differences do you see? What similarities? Are the expectations for writing in college similar or different than in your previous education? Why or why not?

- How does your education in writing compare or contrast to your education in some other discipline(s) (math, science, social studies, and so forth)? What similarities do you see in how these disciplines are taught? What differences? How are these similarities and differences important to your education as a whole?

Thinking about Teaching

In your teaching journal, reflect on your students' responses to the above questions. What surprised you or otherwise jogged your thinking? How can you use your insights about this discussion to help shape activities in your classroom?

Examine the baseline model and the alternative models represented in Lalicker's article. Which model(s) seem to be used in the institution(s) in which you teach? Does this model seem to be appropriate for the student population and the mission of the institution? Why or why not? Do you have questions about how the model came to be used in your institution?

Can you conceptualize another kind of model, one not described in Lalicker's essay? What would that model look like? How would a new model benefit students? How would it facilitate teaching? Are there any details that Lalicker left out of his descriptions of the models? What are they?

As appropriate, share your reflections and questions on the above issues with students, faculty, and administrators. What kinds of questions does your institution need to ask about basic writing? Why?

2

Basic Writing: Students' Perspectives

Who are basic writing students? Whether you are a first-year or a veteran teacher, this chapter will help you think through your own response to this question. We already know that, for a variety of reasons, basic writing students arrive in our classrooms underprepared to write for first-year composition courses. Some students, for instance, may have graduated from underfunded inner-city or rural high schools; other students may be returning to school after several years away and need extra support as they begin college. Still other students come to college from GED or ABE programs; and a growing number of students claim English as their second language. Whatever the reasons, as Linda Adler-Kassner argues, the voices of basic writing students need to be heard if we want to better understand their needs as writers. Adler-Kassner presents interviews with basic writing students at the University of Michigan–Dearborn as a primary form of research.

Ann E. Green, in "My Uncle's Guns," creates the voice of a fictional basic writing student who lives, works, and writes in a white, working-class farming community in Pennsylvania. The main character writes as a "personal narrator" much like one assigned in many basic writing courses. The narrator comments on her own writing process throughout her story. Green presents critical issues of social class and region that affect the interactions of basic writing teachers and students. Her short story urges the reader to consider how social class is constructed and represented in basic writing classrooms — and in the writing process itself.

Just Writing, Basically:
Basic Writers on Basic Writing

Linda Adler-Kassner

In the following excerpt from a longer article first published in 1999 in the Journal of Basic Writing, *Linda Adler-Kassner continues the work begun in "The Dilemma That Still Counts" (a 1998* JBW *article coauthored with Susanmarie Harrington). In seeking to answer the question "Who are basic writers?" Adler-Kassner includes the self-descriptions of student writers. The voices of students "Tom" and "Susan" inform her analysis throughout the article.*

Back to Basics: Defining Basic Writers

Who are basic writers? In "The Dilemma That Still Counts," we examined the ways in which basic writers (and basic writing) have been defined through twenty-odd years of basic writing research. We argued that while "basic writing" remains an essential concept in the academy, we must work to clarify what the term means in order to act upon it, particularly in light of political actions like those recently taken within the CUNY system. Among the issues we posed for further investigation in our article was learning more about how basic writers (or, more appropriately, students labeled basic writers within particular institutions) defined themselves. How do they understand their experiences with writing and reading? Do they find particular features in their writing to be problematic? Do they contest their labeling as "basic writers"? Do they perceive their skills and challenges differently than the university does?

In order to find out how basic writers at my institution answered these questions, my colleague Randy Woodland and I interviewed sixteen students chosen randomly from the eighty who placed into our basic writing course during the fall semester of 1998. The questions that we asked students in our interviews reflected the two approaches which Susanmarie and I presented as widely prevalent in basic writing research in "The Dilemma That Still Counts." Cognitively based studies, we wrote, were concerned with writers' individual processes as they wrote and read. The processes which writers bring to producing or decoding texts are the subjects of study. Thus, in designing this current study Randy and I asked students to bring in examples of past writing that they particularly liked and to talk with us about them, and asked questions that prompted students to reflect on their composing processes. Susanmarie and I also suggested that a later trend in basic writing scholarship is toward culturally based studies, which examine the writer in relationship to larger cultures (like the academy). In this light, a writer is seen as within a broader matrix of literate processes, some or all of which might come into play during their encounters with academic texts. This approach is reflected in questions directed to University of Michigan–Dearborn (UM–D) students about their writing and reading histories and those about their perceptions of writing and reading requirements that they will encounter in college.[1] The interview protocol was divided into four basic areas . . . :

I. *Existing writing.* In the letter inviting students to talk with us, we asked if they had a paper (or several papers) that they particularly liked, and if they would bring those with them to the interview so that we could talk with them about the essays.

II. *Experiences with and ideas about writing and reading.* These included questions about students' families and family histories with writing and reading; students' histories with writing and reading inside and outside of school; students' present writing and reading habits; students' experiences with writing and reading in school; about connections between writing and reading outside and inside of the classroom; and about how students defined key terms related to writing and reading.

III. *Expectations for college.* Here, we asked students if they had a planned major and, if they did, what it was. Additionally, if they had a major in mind, we asked what they expected would be required of them in courses in their major.

IV. *Conceptualizations of and expectations for writing.* Questions here fell into two general areas: those related to the basic writing course (including "what is a basic writer?"), and the specific writing and reading expectations in their proposed or prospective majors.

Students' responses to these questions have helped us develop a better understanding about how they approach postsecondary education, how they imagine the role of writing in that education, and how they see themselves in relation to what they imagine the academy to be. They also provide the foundation for a compelling argument about the responsibilities that institutions (and the teachers who are a part of them) have toward students who are identified as basic writers. Helping students to contest and, ideally, to overcome their status as basic writers is an implied goal of most basic writing courses.[2] But these interviews suggest that to really help students develop a sense of that definition and the means to overcome it, we need to do more than imply. In fact, we need to explicitly help students understand and act on what all of this means in *our specific institutional contexts*. We might even make the questions "what does it mean to be a basic writer *here*, and what does it take to not be one?" part of the "subject" of our basic writing courses.

To illustrate these findings, I'll ground the discussion in portions of interviews with two writers, Tom and Susan.[3] In some ways, these two writers are typical of UM–D's basic writing population. Like most of our students, they came from inner-ring suburbs of Detroit and commuted to UM–D from homes where they lived with two parents or guardians. Both came from homes where some writing and reading took place, although writing and reading was not a main focus in either home. Tom was unusual in that neither of his parents had completed a two- or four-year degree, but was typical in that at least one of his parents had attended (if not completed) community college.[4] Both described themselves as fairly good students.[5] Neither writer professed a great love of writing or reading outside of the classroom (although Tom said he enjoyed science fiction novels); in this respect, they were also quite representative of the other students whom we interviewed.

After taking the UM–Dearborn placement exam, both Tom and Susan received two scores of 2 (out of a possible score of 6) on the exam. According to the scoring guidelines, a "2" essay

> has significant weakness of one or more kinds: Development of ideas may be weak with few specific details to support main ideas. Paragraphs may be relatively short and loosely organized with inadequate transitions. The overall organizational pattern may be loose or not apparent. There may be a pattern of major grammatical errors or numerous misspellings.

Most writers who take basic writing at UM–D receive scores of 2 on their exams, and in this light Tom and Susan were also fairly representative. Their responses to questions about writing in college were also fairly typical of the basic writers whom we interviewed, and they nicely foreground some of the most interesting findings to emerge from our discussions with basic writing students.

Tom's and Susan's Interviews

Tom

Like the vast majority of students on our commuter campus, Tom still lived at home. His father was recently retired from "Ford's";[6] his mother worked at the Kmart Headquarters in Troy, Michigan. Tom said neither he nor anyone in his family did a lot of writing or reading outside of school, although he did enjoy "making up a story and writing about it" and he liked science fiction. Once, in school, he got to write a science-fiction story as a paper, which he enjoyed. But most of his high school writing and reading he found tedious — reading a book and writing reports, and doing "analyzing." Tom could name only one book he enjoyed reading in high school, *To Kill a Mockingbird*.

At UM–D, Tom planned to major in Computer Information Systems, a major housed in the College of Engineering and Computer Science. When I asked Tom if he thought he'd have to do a lot of writing or reading for his major, he said, "I don't believe so," although he hadn't talked to anyone to get a sense of whether his impression was correct. He did think he'd have to do a lot of math, "and . . . research with the books and the computer books and stuff," but since he was "into computers," he didn't think he would be "handed a book and [told,] 'Here, read this.'"

When I asked him to describe his writing, Tom said, "I can get creative, but it's mostly just like science fiction stuff that I like to come up with." As a writer, he said, "I'm only doing it 'cause I have to, and I have to get a good grade on it." Tom thought he would learn "how to write essays, you know, essays, papers," in basic writing. Additionally, he thought he'd learn to

> try to keep focus on certain points and use proper grammar, which I was never really good with anyways, but . . . actually, it's the grammar that I don't really care for. I learned a lot of it, but I just can't remember.

Susan

Susan also graduated from an inner-ring suburban high school. Susan's dad was "kind of self-employed," and her mother was a nurse. She said her family did some reading and writing — her mom "[wrote] e-mails a lot and read magazines a lot," and her stepfather read the newspaper. She didn't do a lot of writing or reading. She had a creative writing class in school that she liked, but they didn't do a lot of writing the first semester, and had "a journal" in the second. "It wasn't really a writing class. It ended up being a relationship class." She liked her ninth grade English teacher, who "really pushed you, and made you understand [reading in the class]."

Susan thought she would major in business at UM–D, but wasn't really sure. Susan expected to write papers in college, and that those papers would be "so much different [from high school] . . . everything [in college] is just more intellectual and you have to think more and go, you know, deeper into things and explain yourself . . . and just have things to back it up."

When I asked her if she thought of herself as a good student she didn't answer directly. Instead, she said, "I know what I want to do and I know what I have to do, so. . . ." As a writer, Susan said, "I think I have a lot to say . . . but I don't know how to write it. I don't know how to put my words together and write it down and make it flow good and make it sound right. I can't do that." She said her writing now was

> really shaky . . . 'cause I'll have to sit there and I'll have to write something over and over again 'cause it just doesn't flow right and it doesn't make any sense the first time I write it, so I have to sit there and I have to really work at it.

I asked her if it came out, but it wasn't what she was thinking, and she said,

> Exactly. . . . Afterwards, when I look at it . . . I'm, like, that wasn't what I was trying to say at all. And I try to put it in different words or I'll just

try to rewrite it out later on and it just doesn't work and I'll have to sit there and I'll have to work at it for a while.

Sometimes she continued to work at it; sometimes, she gave up because she found it frustrating. "Being a writer," Susan said, was "being creative about what you say and being able to write it down; having it make sense and come together and having people read it and understand it and know what you're talking about. . . . The thoughts [in your head] come out right." "Learning to write" meant "just developing the skills that you need to get all your words down, all your thoughts out and get them out properly, and just brainstorming and putting it all together and writing it down." In the basic writing course, Susan hoped to learn "better writing techniques, how to get everything out properly, and how to write it down and make everything flow."

Included in Tom's and Susan's responses are three compelling issues that came up with most of the writers whom we interviewed: their understanding of the term "basic writing," their expectations for writing and reading in other college courses, and their conceptualizations of writing. For those who have worked in basic writing for any length of time and/or those versed with basic writing literature, these issues may sound familiar. However, hearing them expressed from students' perspectives led me to think carefully about the responsibilities that we have toward basic writers as teachers and as representatives of the institutions where we teach.

Issue #1

Basic Writers on "Basic Writers": What's in a Name?

> Teachers often label students "remedial," "marginal," "at risk," "basic," or "illiterate": labels given by the judges, not the judged.
> — Alan Purves, "Clothing the Emperor"

What do the words "basic writer" mean to you?

> Just writing simple. Just well, yeah, that's important for jobs and communicating with other people, that's the same thing there.
> — Tom

> Basic writer. I guess just a person who writes, probably someone who just, you know, writes things just . . . like their given assignment and they'll just write it down. But I think a writer is actually somebody who does writing and writes a lot.
> — Susan

Among the questions that Susanmarie and I raised in "The Dilemma That Still Counts" is whether basic writers contest the label that had been attached to them as a result of their performance on some kind of assessment measure (like our composition placement exam). But Tom and Susan, like every other writer we interviewed for this study, don't know what "basic writer" means. I don't mean that they don't know what it means to *be* a basic writer — they certainly know that they're not taking first-year composition. But they don't know that they are *called* basic writers, or that the course they're in (ours is called "Writing Techniques") is spoken of in the field as a "basic" (or "developmental") writing course.

I think that this is a dilemma for several reasons. In a recent essay, Peter Mortenson raised questions about the ethics of using subjects anonymously in our research. I see this as an extension of that problem — here, the issue of "basic writing" itself is anonymous, at least (as Tom, Susan, and Alan Purves suggest) to the people who are labeled that way. In fact, many basic writing researchers and teachers have worked long and hard to help erase the stigma that we think students must feel when they are placed in basic writing courses. Some researchers, for instance, attempt to identify the ways in which basic writers are multiply literate, despite the labels that have been affixed to them based on performance on a measure like a placement exam. Their positions are clear: these writers have abilities outside of the classroom; their performance in the classroom is affected by the ways that they approach their work (and those approaches, in turn, are affected by any number of internal and external circumstances).

We have taken these more complex labels into the classroom, as well. Many basic writing instructors (and I include myself here) have been shaped by the ideas of Mina Shaughnessy and her intellectual descendants (Perl, Hull, Rose, Bartholomae, and so on). We have developed a number of skillful ways to talk about literacy (or literacies) so that students don't feel they are failures, don't see their experiences as isolated, and don't feel that the literacies that they bring to the academy are "bad." In the mythic story of basic writing, we say that this different way of talking about basic writers and their abilities works against the deficit model that has framed writing instruction since the end of the nineteenth century, pointing to the creation of English A at Harvard University while gnashing our teeth and wringing our hands.

Sometimes, as in some of my own classes, we use texts (like *Lives on the Boundary*) with which we hope basic writers will identify — that they will read and say, "Aha! That person's experience is like mine!" Because the texts are always carefully chosen (again, like *Lives*), the hope is that students will then understand that they bring something different — not bad, but different — to their learning, and need to find ways to fit that "difference" into writing in this context. But this approach, which certainly isn't one that only I use, still elides the question of what it means to be a basic writer in the specific context in which these writers find themselves. In a sense, it asks students to participate in a system of values that surrounds a particular "reading" of *Lives on the Boundary*. Yet one of the tenets of recent culturally based approaches to basic writing work is the notion that these writers do not share (some) of the same values reflected in academic discourse.

Thus, the logic here is inconsistent: Shared interpretation, to some degree, is based on shared culture. And basic writing scholarship has suggested that these writers do not participate in this culture. Therefore, they might not share interpretations held by members of this culture.[7] (Additionally, imagine the dizzying connections between these things! Is one academic institution like another? Yes, in some ways. Is UM–Dearborn in 1999 like Loyola or UCLA in the mid-1960s and early 1970s? In some ways yes, and in some no. But why should we expect students to make the rather abstract connections that we might see between that circumstance and theirs?) Since we — since *I* — sometimes don't tell basic writers *exactly* what it means to be a basic writer (in this time and place), these students are left to their own devices to figure out what basic writing is, and what makes them basic writers.

Meanwhile, while we talk with students about their multiple literacies inside the classroom, we're talking about them as "basic writers" outside of it, as in this article. I'm a member of the Conference on Basic Writing. I subscribe to the *Journal of Basic Writing*. But the idea of the "basic writer" and all of the characteristics associated with it are invisible to the students themselves.

One could make the argument that I'm quibbling over issues of mere semantics, but I don't think I am. After all, how can basic writers contest their labeling *as* basic writers (and then refute it as well) if they don't know that this is what they're called? Certainly, they can tell us that they know more than they have been labeled as knowing; they might say that they're better at writing in different contexts — they can say a lot of things. But if language is power (and I believe that it is), not giving students the language to talk about themselves (or, at least, their labels) and their situations seems to me an act of withholding power. . . .

Notes

1. These questions were also shaped, in part, by Deborah Mutnick's outstanding study of basic writers described in *Writing in an Alien World*. Questions asking writers to define some terms ("basic writer," "learning to write," "being a writer") were asked by Mutnick, and were used in our study with her permission.

2. This notion of basic writing and basic writer is in some ways reflected in (and is a reflection of) the research in basic writing. Often, the pedagogy in basic writing courses is influenced by research which focuses on helping students work through issues that have resulted in their placement in basic writing courses. While the analysis in that research probably stems from specific institutional contexts (like this article's does), the ideas in it are meant to be generalizable (as the ideas in this article are). But we must ask ourselves: Does the need to construct "basic writers" and "basic writing" as semihomogenous categories lend credence to an avoidance of specifically defining those categories? While this issue is outside the scope of this article, it will be taken up by the larger study of which this research is a part.

3. These names, along with all other student names in this article, have been changed.

4. While we did not ask specifically about parents' education levels, most students told us something about their parents' educational backgrounds. Two students had at least one parent with an advanced degree; five had at least one parent with a four-year degree; four had at least one parent with a two-year degree; three had parents with no higher education. Among those who didn't specifically identify higher education experiences of their parents, three had at least one parent in what might typically be considered a "blue-collar" job (e.g., working on the line in a stamping plant); three had at least one parent who worked in what might be considered a "white-collar" job (e.g., nursing).

5. Admission to UM–Dearborn is quite competitive — generally, students are in the top 10 percent of their high school classes. For this reason, it is not surprising that Tom and Susan described themselves as fairly good students.

6. Typically, blue-collar workers at Ford Motor Company (or those related to them) refer to the company as "Ford's"; employees in more "professional" positions (e.g., managers or engineers) refer to it as "Ford."

7. Of course, this is a point raised in Glynda Hull and Mike Rose's article "'This Wooden Shack Place': The Logic of an Unconventional Reading" as well.

Classroom Activities

Create a "literacy narrative" assignment for students. Invite them to reflect on the topics that Adler-Kassner asked her own basic writing students to reflect on in their interviews. Have students consider how their own family and educational histories of reading and writing affect their position as basic writing students. Questions based on Adler-Kassner's research could include the following:

- Existing writing: Is there a paper you have written that you particularly like? What do you especially like about it?

- Describe your family background and your family's history and experiences with reading and writing.

- What is your own history with reading and writing, inside and outside of the classroom?

- What are your present reading and writing habits?

- How do you define key terms related to reading and writing?

- What are your expectations for college? Do you have a planned major, and if so, what is it? What expectations do you have of the requirements of your major?

- What are your conceptualizations and expectations for writing in college?

- What is a basic writer?

- What are the specific writing and reading expectations in your proposed or prospective majors?

- How do you understand your experiences with reading and writing? Do you find particular features in your writing to be problematic? Do you contest your labeling as "basic writer"? Do you perceive your skills and challenges differently than the university does?

Thinking about Teaching

Conduct your own research with students based on the above questions. What similarities do the students seem to share? What differences? Write your reflections in your journal and consider revising them for publication. Share the results with your students in class.

Push your research one step further. What assumptions underlie the above questions? Can you think of questions that you would add or eliminate in your own research project?

Consider how your institution defines basic writers. How is the basic writing program set up? How many courses does it include? Are there separate courses for ESL and native speakers? How does placement work? How are the courses set up? Does each teacher use a common syllabus or common textbooks? What assumptions does your institution seem to make about basic writers? Do you believe these assumptions to be correct? Why or why not? As appropriate, share your reflections and questions on the above issues with students, faculty, and administrators.

My Uncle's Guns

Ann E. Green

In her short story "My Uncle's Guns," Ann E. Green creates a first-person narrative from the point of view of a basic writing student from a working-class and poor white community in rural Pennsylvania. As the narrator tells this story, she includes metacognitive comments that demonstrate the frequently ignored impact of social class differences on students and teachers. The story was first published in 1997 in Writing on the Edge.

My uncle, who is not really my uncle but my father's best friend since grade school, bought an antique gun from the First World War. We saw it when we went over to my uncle's house to visit. Dad and T.J. were talking, having conversations with long pauses, while I watched out the living room window.

I'm not sure how these essays are supposed to start. You said in class that a narrative should tell a story. How much of the story do I have to tell? Should I put in a reflection now? Should I tell you about smoking? Growing up, I watched men have conversations with each other filled with these long moments of silence where they smoked. One of them would light another cigarette or refill his pipe or, on a special occasion, smoke a cigar. If they didn't smoke, they chewed, either wintergreen Skoal or a pipe stem or a long piece of hay. Dad smoked a pipe with Old Hickory Tobacco until he quit farming. T.J., according to Dad, used to have every vice imaginable and then some, but he had quit smoking both cigarettes and cigars, almost entirely stopped chewing tobacco, and even cut back on his drinking since his heart attack. Every time I watch Dad talk, I remember how he smoked. Should this be part of the story?

While I was looking out the window, two deer appeared from the woods and strolled out into the yard. Although T.J. and Dad hunted together every year, T.J. fed wild animals, birds and rabbits, deer and even stray dogs in his back yard. The two deer went to pick at the food that had fallen from the bird feeders. One was a good-size doe, the other a late-born fawn with spots on its rump yet. When I walked up to the window to get a closer look, the deer spooked and leaped over the stone wall separating the lawn from the woods. Dad said, "Damn it, T.J., where's your camera?"

"Don't own one. If I shoot something, it ain't going to be for a god damn picture, anyway." He paused and slowly stood up from his recliner. "Come here, I'll show you what I'll shoot it with come December."

Dad and I went into T.J.'s spare bedroom to his gun cabinet, and he pulled out the WW I gun, a rifle whose stock had been cut off and refinished, evidently as a deer hunting gun. T.J. said, "It's my gun from the First World War." And then he laughed long and hard at his own joke. His laugh, as usual, drowned out any other sound and ended with a couple of snorts after which he laughed again. T.J. hadn't seen any combat after he enlisted. His ROTC scholarship paid for Penn State, but instead of sending him to Korea where the fighting was, the Army sent him to West Germany as a stretcher carrier in a medical unit. For the Army, it hadn't been bad, T.J. said. They spent most of their time moving the mobile medical unit along the East German border, to practice in case of a communist attack.

My father took the gun from T.J.'s hands. "Nice job cutting it back. Craig .340."

The gun didn't look any different to me than the dozens of other guns I'd seen and handled. I didn't hunt, or at least I didn't shoot, but I occasionally had gone out for turkey with Dad in the spring. We'd never even seen one, but it was beautiful in the woods at dawn.

At twelve, my first date was a picnic on roast woodchuck in a field near home; the gun that shot the chuck was a bolt-action 30.30. Everyone in my class took the Hunter Safety course in sixth grade, before it was legal for us to hunt at twelve. All of my boyfriends and a good many of my girlfriends owned guns for shooting or hunting purposes, and school was canceled for the first day of buck season in December. In the fall, I was late home from dates because any boy I was with would use the drive home as a good opportunity to spotlight deer, to see how many there were before hunting season.

> Are these the kinds of details that you mean when we talk in class about significant details? How am I supposed to know which details are important to you?
> I feel like I have to tell you all the details about deer hunting so you won't think we're simple or backward or country, getting all excited about looking at somebody's gun. Even though you assign us those Tim O'Brien stories with lists, you really don't think we'll write like that do you? And you would tell us we were too repetitive if we did. You're not from around here, and I can see you don't like us sometimes when we go outside on break from class and smoke and talk too loud about how we hate our jobs.
> You look at us and think that we don't know anything. You think that teaching us how to write can't help us cause we're not going to change our lives by reading some essays. But we all want to do well in this class. Can't you just tell us what you want us to write about?

As Dad looked the Craig .340 over, peering down the barrel, checking to see if it was loaded, he said, "Let's try the son-of-a-bitch out in November at the fireman's shoot-in and pig roast." We left then, in our pickup, complete with spotlight and gun rack in the cab. Dad had to get home to go work as a janitor at 7 A.M. , while I had to make it in early to run the drive-by window at the bank. We saw twelve deer in a field on the way home, and nothing was unusual.

In fact, the night that it happened I had gone to the fair with Dad and his new woman, Louise. It was about time Dad found somebody else, and I was glad it was Louise, who was younger than Dad but older than me by quite a bit. I'd seen what other kinds of women men found after their first wives.

> I'll cut Louise out of this paper later, because I know that you'll think she's extra, just one more person who's not really in the rising action of this story, but right now it's important to me that she stay in here. Most of the time I'm too busy trying to figure out how I'll pay for my next class and my car insurance to sit around and think about how I feel about somebody who's important in my life, but not a pain in my ass in some way. Louise has just been a fixture, a nice addition to Dad's life that makes him leave me alone more.

I rode down to the fair that night with Dad and Louise, knowing that I'd most certainly see somebody I knew and come home with whoever was there. T.J.'s volunteer fire company had beer at its fair, so it was a big event. It was high school reunion week, but nobody had called me to go as a date. I guess after this long, everybody brought their wives. What I didn't expect at the fair was that Mike would show up, looking better than the last I'd seen him, appearing between the clam and the beer tents while Dad brought Louise and me beers. He wasn't wearing anything Army. Evidently he no longer needed to show his pride in the uniform by wearing it to public events. He came over and asked Dad how he was and what he was doing since he wasn't farming. Mike nodded to Louise, but he was looking me up and down, checking to see if I had a wedding band, if weight had settled on my legs or on my ass, trying to see if the rumor about me taking college classes could be true. Dad said, "Mike, are you staying with your folks? Could you run Maria home on your way?"

I was mad that Dad was passing me off on Mike, even if I did plan on staying later. I could find my own way home and always had.

"I'll take her home. No problem," Mike said, grinning at me. "Does she have to be home at any particular time these days?"

We all laughed, because even when there were particular times, I had often missed them. Mike and I had another good long look at each other. No beer belly. No visible scars. Lines around his eyes. Teeth still straight and white. The Army has good dental.

The good dental is an important detail, and you probably don't know that. If you're on welfare, you get dental, same if you're in the Army, but if you work loading potato chips on tractor trailers you don't get dental, the bank gets some dental (because otherwise who'd deposit their paycheck with a teller-girl minus a front tooth?) but if you're self-employed or working in a stone quarry, you don't get dental. First thing that goes on people round here, makes them look older than they are, are teeth. That's why kids in Head Start are fluoridated almost to death. Mary, from our class, her kid is in Head Start, and she says they make those kids brush their teeth twice in the three hours they're there. It's like that Head Start teacher believes Mary's teeth are bad because she doesn't brush them, not because her Mom raised her on potato chips and soda. If those kids don't look poor, if they have good teeth, a decent set, they might just make it.

"How's the babies doing?"

"Fine. Growing like weeds. They're still in Texas. This is a short trip, just me seeing Mom and Dad and going to the reunion. Karen's pregnant again, and she don't travel too good."

I remembered the one time I'd seen Karen, she was a dishwater blond with circles under her eyes and a crooked, white smile. Mike had met her at basic training in Oklahoma. Mike just came back from that last ten day brutal basic training hike in the desert and proposed. They were married before he was shipped to Germany, and they were in Germany when Mike got shipped to Saudi. She had stayed in Germany, praying that what was at first a conflict wouldn't last too long, and then praying that the war wouldn't kill him before their first child was born.

We decided to go get a drink at our favorite bar, the Tea Kettle, because it had been a good place to skip an afternoon of school when we were growing up. It seemed like a perfect place to fill Mike in on the local gossip.

Mike was driving a familiar car, his Dad's ancient, rust and white colored Ford Fairlane, the passenger seat littered with the usual collection of empty cigarette packages, a partially filled bottle of oil left over from a previous oil change, and an oil filter wrench. Mike threw the junk into the back seat on top of a light-weight fluorescent orange hunting vest with the license pinned in the back and an ancient red hunting cap. I smiled because the clutter in the back seat was so familiar. The extra flannel shirts and jumper cables didn't seem to have moved in the years since I'd ridden with him.

You said something in class about Tim O'Brien and parataxis. Is that a list or something? Does this description of Mike's back seat count? Should I describe the flannel shirts? Do you even know what an oil filter wrench looks like?

At the Tea Kettle, we started drinking shots and went through our high school classmates, listing births, deaths, marriages, divorces, and affairs. We'd each graduated with about seventy people, most we'd known all our lives, and we had talked about almost everybody when I started asking him about his time in the Gulf.

"It was lots of sand and way too hot," he said. "But in that way it was like Oklahoma and basic all over again. MREs and sweat. No black widow spiders, though. Did I tell you about that?"

"No. Don't we have black widow spiders around here? The males have the red hour glass on their backs?"

"No, the females. They bite their mates after they have sex and kill them."

"But what about the Gulf? Your Mom told Dad that you were in the actual fighting and some of the digging of the bodies out of the bunkers after stuff was over."

"It wasn't that big a deal. The hardest thing was losing the barracks to the Scud. I knew those people to speak to. . . . They were Pennsylvanians, reserve, not career military. Stupid loss, shouldn't have been there.

"But anyway, I was on maneuvers in the Oklahoma desert," Mike continued. "Last ten day stretch of basic. The Army has convinced you, you can't brush your teeth unless somebody else says it's O.K. and shows you how, and we're supposed to be out surviving in combat conditions. I'm in my tent putting on socks . . ."

"Putting on socks?"

"Yeah. We had to march ten miles back and my feet are blistered, so I'm putting on a pair of these stupid army issue socks. I'm pulling the left sock on and I feel this sharp pain, and I look down and there's a god damn black widow spider stuck to my leg. And we'd been told

there are no black widow spiders in the Oklahoma desert, no dangerous spiders at all."

"Wait a second. No bad spiders. How in the hell did it end up on you
then?"

"Christ, I don't know. But this drill sergeant has been giving me
shit since the beginning, saying that it don't matter if my father was in
Asia, that I'm such a smart ass that I'm not going to make it through
basic. And since I think I'm so god damn intelligent, I should try for an
ROTC scholarship in the Air Force, and just look at war on a computer
screen, like Space Invaders. He's been busting on me for weeks, and
now he's not going to let me finish basic. Or he's not going to believe
me, and by the time he does I could be dead."

"Why are they such sons-of-bitches?"

"Right now you can only be career Army if they keep moving you
up the chain of command. Career Army means retirement at thirty-
eight and a new life. This weekend warrior shit means dying whenever
somebody who's been away for a while forgets the rules and has an
accident and you're in the line of fire or in the tank that he mistakes
for the enemy."

I don't know if this is the kind of dialogue that you say "reveals character." We said "fuck" a lot more than I'm writing down now, but you
probably don't want that in a paper. It's probably one of those things
that a professional author can use, but that we can't yet. Like we have
to get good at knowing how to use big words first, before we can write
like we talk. See, for me the spider symbolizes what Mike's life has been
like, something always biting him on the ass at a crucial moment and
screwing things up, but I don't know if you'll get the spider comparison.
It doesn't seem "realistic," but it's what he said really happened, so it
must be true.

Is this the language of "the oppressed" that you've been talking about
in class? Like that guy who taught those peasants, those peasants
probably said "fuck" in Spanish a lot, too, but that probably wasn't
included in their essays, right?

"So, anyway, you're still in the Army," I said, motioning the bar-
tender to give me another chaser. "So what did you do about the spider?"

"Well, the Army gives you this stuff that freezes on contact. Why
not just a bottle of bug spray, I don't know. So I'm hopping up and down
and grabbing the can from my kit, dumping stuff all over, and the
spider's trying to beat a hasty retreat and I'm hopping after it, knock-
ing the tent down, till I finally freeze the sucker. I'm trying to figure
out . . ."

*The door to the Tea Kettle slams, and Candy Dimock, now married
to a Brown, bursts in, talking before she's in the door.*

*"There's bodies in the road. Please come help. They're dead. We think
they're dead, but we're not sure. Bodies . . ."*

"What bodies, Candy?" I ask, but people are already standing up and pushing forward. "What road, where?"

"Up the hill," she says. I had seen her from a distance at the fair grounds earlier with her husband. They must have been driving home and seen something. "Danny went to call the state cops, the ambulance."

"Run over?" I ask. Candy says, "Blood in the road. I don't know . . ."

Mike grabs Candy by the arm. "Come show us where you saw them," he says. "We'll see if we can help. Maria, you know CPR, right?" He pulls Candy toward the Ford and throws open the back seat door for her. Reaches around and pulls a thirty-thirty out from underneath the hunting clothes. "Get in," he says, and pushes Candy inside, handing me the rifle. "There are shells in the glove box." Other people are getting into their cars, some still holding their beers. Some are unpacking knives and deer rifles from beneath their back seats. They are waiting to follow us. I fasten my seat belt and open the glove compartment while Mike gets in the car. When I open the glove box, Mike's grandpa's service issue revolver tumbles out with boxes of shells, pink registration information, and their Family Farm insurance card. Mike backs up fast, while I start slipping long yellow-colored bullets into the chamber of the thirty-thirty, load it and put the safety on. Candy says, "Maria, do you remember two-man CPR in case we need it? I can't remember how many breaths per second . . ."

"How far," Mike asks, voice calm. He doesn't wait for an answer before he says, "Load the Colt, too."

I am already filling the Colt from the other box of bullets. The only gun I have shot on a regular basis. Friday nights shooting bottles filled with water and watching them explode. Saturday nights shooting mailboxes at midnight driving too fast, throwing beer bottles at the mailboxes if it wasn't your turn with the gun.

"Here," Candy says, but at first we see nothing. Then we spot the white in the ditch, the unmoving white in the ditch.

I remember (from first aid class):
   — gun shot wounds are to be treated as puncture wounds;
   — knife wounds also puncture (don't remove the knife);
   — cover and try and prevent bleeding with direct pressure.

Mike gets out of the car with the thirty-thirty, metal glinting, catching the light from a car pulling up behind us. Others pull up behind us, also get out. Slowly. Moments drag on and on. I hold the forty-five. The bodies are end to end in a ditch by the road side. Blood has run from the man's chest onto the road and pools on the asphalt. In the headlights, it's not clear whether the woman's sweatshirt is gray or white. She lies on her side, and I can see that she was shot from the front because the exit wound on her back is big enough for me to put one of my hands in.

"Two," Mike says, his hand gently lifting the man's dark hair from his neck as he feels for the carotid pulse.

My fingers probe the woman's neck for the artery, any sign of life. Their clothes are red and maroon, fresh and bright, partly dried blood. Her eyes are wide open, but she is dead. It is silent as we gather around the bodies, not moving them. Sticking the guns back in the vehicles, finishing the beers, lighting cigarettes, waiting for the cops. No one recognizes the two dead.

We found out later it was a lover's triangle involving newcomers. The guy who did the killing went to the fair with his ex-girlfriend. She wanted to be friends and invited him to come with her to meet her new boyfriend. The old boyfriend was in the back seat of the car, pulled out a gun, shot through the seat and killed the boyfriend. She stopped the car, turned around, and said, "What the hell is going on?" and was shot in the chest. He panicked, threw the bodies in the ditch and drove off. Threw the revolver and its clip out at different places on his way out of town, but was caught before he hit the interstate because a cop stopped him and noticed the blood and rips on the passenger seat. The cops found the clip the first day, on the five mile strip of two lane that was most likely, but they couldn't find the gun. T.J.'s fire company cleaned up from the fair and then helped hunt for the gun. T.J. found the weapon three days later, ten yards from the road, in the rain. He knocked over some strands of purple and white vetch with a branch when the stick hit the gun. It was his sixtieth birthday, and after he found the gun, all the state cops shook his hand. His picture, holding his walking stick and grinning, was in the local paper.

That night, after we'd talked to the cops, Mike drove me home and finished telling me about the Gulf.

"Since I'm in for twenty years and already served almost half, they stuck me in a tank with more firepower than you'd ever imagine, guarding some West Point son-of-a-bitch commander who'd never even sweated in a desert. He was trained in jungle warfare, a kind of leftover. It was just miles and miles of tunnels, sand, and oil. And we were going to suffocate them in their bunkers anyway."

As I sit here trying to write this story, I try and remember what was said about a good narrative, what a good narrative consists of, but I don't have a conclusion in this story, just more fragments: Dad and T.J. hunted deer and came back empty-handed; Mike's mother sent over a venison roast from one of their deer; we ate the venison roast today at noon, with potatoes. And I don't have any questions for peer reviewers, because now that I'm in these night classes with these eighteen-year-olds, they don't understand my life anyway. At least in the continuing ed classes we had a variety of experiences, like shitty jobs or boyfriends, and shared ideas about good writing, like no comma splices and clear words. These girls can't even tell the difference between a Honda and a Ford, a double barrel shot gun and a pellet gun, or even, a buck and a doe. Some of them aren't even sure what their major is, while I'm trying to get enough algebra in my head to pass chemistry, qualify for the nursing program.

The assignment sheet said that this narrative should contain reflections, reveal something about ourselves and how we were changed by an event. But how should I be changed by finding a couple of bodies on a strip of two lane a couple of miles from home? Should I have a moral about how guns are dangerous and bad and nobody should have them anymore? Should I lie and tell you that I'll never be around guns anymore, that I'll be a good girl now and stay away from violent people and places?

How can I explain to you or to the other people in class that I finally decided that the noise I'm hearing outside the window as I write this isn't firecrackers, but gunfire. And that the phone just rang, and I talked to my neighbor who apologized for shooting his gun off, although it's ten on a Sunday night. I told him no big deal and he said, "I'm sorry for what I done, but I needed to do that, or I'd have to go somewhere and hit somebody." I don't tell him that Dad's not here, and that I'm trying to finish writing an essay.

And that he scared me.

And that while I've been listening to the shooting, I've propped the twelve-gauge at the front door and the thirty-thirty at the back.

Classroom Activities

Ann E. Green's short story resembles a "think-aloud protocol" in that the narrator includes metacognitive comments about her writing process, her teacher and the other students, and her story itself. Invite students to include their own metacognitive comments in a draft of their next essay or short story. What were they thinking about as they were writing? How might that thinking be included as part of a revised version of their text?

"My Uncle's Guns" is a story that foregrounds differences in social class and cultural and regional origin between teachers and students. Have students write an essay or short story that highlights social class, race, gender, region, and/or other cultural differences in the lives of the characters. Students can also try writing their essay or story first from their own perspective, and then from the perspective of a teacher or other authority figure.

Give students "My Uncle's Guns" as a reading assignment and ask them to respond to what seems interesting about the form and content of the story. Do the narrator's comments on her own story seem appropriate? Are cultural differences important to an understanding of the story? What else seems striking about the story?

Thinking about Teaching

Record your students' responses to any of the above classroom activities. What issues seemed to be important for the students in discussing the structure of the narrative? What concerns do students have in discussing cultural differences? What insights did students provide on the relationships between students and teachers in a basic writing classroom? Share your reflections with students. In your journal, or in discussion with other teachers, disclose your own assumptions about your relationships with your students, and about cultural differences. Which issues are easy for you to discuss, and which are difficult? How do you account for this difference? For instance, how do you interpret the following statement by Green's narrator: "You look at us and you think that we don't know anything. You think that teaching us how to write can't help us cause we're not going to change our lives by reading some essays. But we all want to do well in this class. Can't you just tell us what you want us to write about?"

Write a short story or personal narrative about a classroom incident from your perspective as a teacher. Then write about the same incident from the point of view of a student. What differences do you notice? How can those differences help inform your classroom practices? As appropriate, share your reflections and questions on the above issues with students, faculty, and administrators.

3

Adapting the
Writing Process

Sometimes the most difficult part of teaching developing writers is convincing them that good writing is the result of a process — that there is nothing magical about it. Good writing comes from the writer continually asking the following questions: Why am I writing? For whom am I writing? What do I want to say? How can I clarify my meaning? How can I identify and avoid errors that confuse my meaning? The articles in this section invite students to consider the writing process in forms that require a strong sense of audience and purpose: personal letters and life writing. As writers directly engage their readers, they are encouraged to slow down and focus on each step of the process.

To demonstrate his own approach to writing as a process, Gregory Shafer discusses how he wrote his assignments with his students. Shafer's students critiqued his writing — and thus came to understand that revision includes more than simply proofreading for errors. Susan Naomi Bernstein includes a sample of student writing in her description of her life writing assignment. As part of the writing process, students reflected on the criteria for evaluating life writing and suggested how the teacher might evaluate writing that is extremely personal. To understand how life writing may be contextualized in larger social and cultural issues, the students read widely for this assignment.

Using Letters for Process and Change in the Basic Writing Classroom

Gregory Shafer

In the following article, first published in Teaching English in the Two-Year College *in 1999, Gregory Shafer describes how his students learned about the writing process by writing letters to both personal and public audiences. Shafer also participated in this process of letter writing, and the results were significant for both students and teacher. Letters from colleagues follow this article, illustrating once again the potential for using letter writing to teach various aspects of the writing process.*

> The curriculum in Developmental English breeds a deep social and intellectual isolation from print.
> — Mike Rose (211)

> Basic writing, alias remedial, developmental, pre-baccalaureate, or even handicapped English, is commonly thought of as a writing course for young men and women who have many things wrong with them.
> — Mina Shaughnessy (289)

Introduction

I never truly understood the discontent of the developmental writing student until I had the chance to teach a remedial writing class designed for students who have "significant weakness in basic sentence structure." It was during the opening day that I began to sense the isolation and alienation to which Rose and Shaughnessy refer. As a class, the students were unlike the frenetic and rather optimistic group that filled my college-level composition classes. Rather than walking in with smiles and eager anticipation, there was resignation and sober resolve — an atmosphere reminiscent of children waiting to be disciplined. It was the first time I had entered a class devoid of casual banter, and I sensed an almost tangible foreboding as I greeted students who sat stoically, eyes focused on books or the desks below.

Later, after collecting their writing samples, I began to further understand the unique and anxious perspective many of these "remedial students" have. "I never liked english," wrote one student, in response to a questionnaire. "It was always to prove what I couldn't do," she said. Added a second respondent, "I hated the workbook exercises. I couldn't get the hang of it."

Helping such students to "get the hang of it" — to feel that they had a voice worthy of respect — was my main goal as I prepared for a first foray into this basic writing course. From the start, I was convinced that the class would only be successful if it could transcend the deluge of skills exercises that remove these students from what Stephen

Judy calls "writing for the here and now" (101). While acknowledging the acute lack of formal writing experience the students brought to the class, I also had to recognize the wealth of personal experiences, the sophisticated linguistic abilities they wield and have possessed since childhood. I was determined to allow these students to join what Frank Smith has called the "Literacy Club" — a place where language instruction is inclusive, personal, and predicated upon relevance. Of course, we all want our students to enjoy a democratic environment, but the idea of Smith's "Literacy Club" begins with the premise — like a club — that participants will be allowed a certain acceptance and autonomy as members. Indeed, both children and adults appreciate clubs because they can join with others to engage in fun and meaningful activities — activities where each member is respected as an active voice, where each individual parades certain abilities while collaborating with more experienced members to enhance specific skills. Thus, Smith asserts, learning in a club is almost invariably "collaborative," "effortless," and "no-risk" (21). It is a celebration of communal engagement and sharing, whether people share their love of cards, plants, or in this case, reading and writing.

Letters

The question was what to do with the developmental students — students who seemed scarred from years of failure and apathy. Writing would have to be the foundation of the course, but it would have to be a writing that was neither intimidating nor too lengthy — a writing that was accessible, that assured students an opportunity for success. It had to entice while still working on a practical level, something that made sense to a class of mostly working-class pupils.

I decided to begin with a class-wide engagement in letter writing. Because it is short and yet a complete unit of discourse — and because it has a place in the real world of most students — writing letters seemed an auspicious way to introduce students to writing that transcended skills instruction. Most of the class indicated that they had experience in writing short letters and felt a certain comfort in exploring the various ways the medium could become a theme of the course.

With the general concept of letter writing established, the class began with personal letters as an introductory assignment. In describing the possibilities, I was adamant about stressing the choices writers had and the latitude available to explore both personal and fictitious topics. Many wanted to compose personal letters to loved ones who were either dead or who had moved away, while others contemplated the idea of penning a series of letters that would become chapters of a fiction story. What was most edifying for me as an instructor was the ebullience, the alacrity, that permeated the class not long after I suggested topics and presented a sample. Within minutes, I could feel an effusive energy, as faces became illuminated with potential for writing. Clearly, these were students who were both ready and willing to compose. Much of the second half of class would find me stepping aside, facilitating the flurry of ideas as they whirled from student to student.

From the introductory moments of that day, I continued to act as catalyst, providing ideas, personal examples, and encouragement. Day two, then, became established as a workshop session, a chance for students to continue brainstorming and planning so that each could present a detailed plan or proposal for the letters they would compose. As with the opening day, students worked assiduously, methodically, honing their topics and grafting new ideas onto their original plans. Shantel, who was a single parent of five, planned to write a letter to the father of her children, a man she had not seen in almost five years. Malique, in contrast, had decided to write a letter that was "long overdue" to the woman he had been dating for the past two years. Jackie, in a third contrast, decided to write some very personal words to her deceased grandfather, a man she had loved like a father until his death at sixty-eight.

As class concluded for the week, I could see the dramatic change in atmosphere, a fulminating sense of enthusiasm pervading the discussions. Many students were beginning to write opening paragraphs, asking about going to the writing center to "get started," or about the specific length for the first draft. Next week, the rough draft would be due, and many were ready to write. Indeed, as I reviewed the class for the week, I thought of Mike Rose and his contention that developmental writers "know more than their tests reveal but haven't been taught how to weave their knowledge into coherent patterns" (8).

The Rigors of the Process

The process of moving from idea to rough draft is perhaps one of the most chaotic and exciting stages in composition — especially as it relates to basic or developmental writers. Suddenly, sentences are taking their place on paper, interacting with other sentences, forming paragraphs, changing plans, and acting as catalysts for new directions. Process. Journey. As we joined to share our rough drafts, I continued to reiterate these words. Many students were frustrated, finding the transition from idea to draft a very daunting and messy endeavor. "It's not coming out the way I planned, and I get new ideas I don't know what to do with," lamented one student. Others found the idyllic prose they had in their heads failing to make its way neatly onto their papers. "This isn't as good as I thought," said another. Many were frustrated as they confronted the fact that writing is not a linear, step-by-step process. Now came the process of revision, of working with the organic and unwieldy character of creating prose.

We devoted the beginning moments of the rough draft session to forming small groups, reading each other's papers, and offering suggestions for possible revision. For many, it was the first time an essay of theirs had ever been revised or critiqued. Many were discouraged and found their peers focusing on annoying spelling errors rather than the development of ideas. All of the old memories associated with red ink and derisive comments were resurfacing and creating a contentious atmosphere. Thus, after about fifteen minutes of small group work, I told the class to form a circle with their desks, so we could share our work as an entire class.

Writing with One's Students

It was during this time that I recognized the significance of Donald Murray's admonition that "writing begins when teachers give their students silence and paper — then sit down to write themselves." With most of the class in a rather irritated and frustrated mood, it was an ideal time to use my own letter as an introduction to the plans and questions I had for my own writing — and to the role they could play in helping me to revise. The key, I thought, was moving the class beyond cosmetic changes. The students were devoting too much of the session to discussing surface errors and spending too little time on the solid but incipient ideas in their letters. It was a special opportunity to read and discuss my composition and invite students to discuss the ways I could reach my goal for the letter.

This whole class critique involving my letter was perhaps the turning point in the way the class thought about writing. While many of the students still harbored a reductive view of writing as a process of finding errors, the class discussion of my letter — to my recently deceased father — helped highlight the more compelling reasons one has to write. At the same time, the movement toward content helped show participants the importance of transcending errors and focusing instead on the evolution and improvement of message or substance.

Because of the emotional content, many distanced themselves from petty arguments over subject/verb agreement and were motivated instead by the message I had for my father. At the same time, I was beginning to understand what Frank Smith meant when he argued that anyone who hopes to teach writing must first "demonstrate what writing does and demonstrate how to do it" (31). To this, I would add, teachers must take risks with their students and illustrate the way emotion and writing coalesce to serve very personal needs. Thus, as I began to read the letter, I was learning as well as teaching, opening up and changing the way students perceived writing.

This experience also reminded me of the importance of risk taking and the role teachers play in making it possible. As I read my letter and asked students for suggestions about revising, I recognized the sensitive position I was in as a writer and how protective I felt about the letter in front of me. How, I wondered, would I react if students negated the essence of the letter, focusing instead on comma splices or apostrophe use? Would I become a bit alienated, a bit disconcerted, if the gist of the discussion was about rules rather than the passion that emanated from the prose? Would such an approach tend to make writing irrelevant? Would it truncate the creative process? Such questions enhanced my ability to teach these developmental students from a more empathetic position. At the same time, it brought me back to the theme of the writing club and the idea that one must participate in a writing club if one is to lead it.

The critique session involving my letter lasted for twenty minutes and again placed the spotlight on the need for process and revision. Students who earlier were ready to edit rough drafts for spelling and then prepare them for submission were now aware of the way one can use writing for expression and to clarify questions about life and death dilemmas. As they pored over my two-page letter, pensively evaluating the message, I sensed that they better appreciated their roles as companion writers in a process rather than as editors who search feverishly to expunge error. Like any good reader, they were sensitive to my endeavors and seemed to thrive in their new, more holistic approach. As the discussion moved from observations to questions about specific parts of my paper, we began to better demonstrate the goal of any good writing conference: improvement of one's whole draft.

"Did you really feel that angry toward your father?" From the first questions, students were focused on content, on the message and its efficacy in communicating my true feelings. "I like the realism of the letter," suggested Kaleb. "You can tell that this is real. People just don't make this stuff up." Part of the reason why students transcended issues of surface structure was a set of questions I gave them before we started. Based on the idea that writing conferences should be a sharing of perceptions and constructive suggestions, the questions asked students to identify the best qualities in the writing, the questions they had about the writing, and any suggestions for improvement. "Don't you want to communicate your love for him too?" asked a student in making a suggestion for improvement. "I don't know if you want it to be this cold," added another. Clearly, as we continued to read and discuss the letter, the students were demonstrating an understanding of process and change in writing. We had taken a step forward.

Thus, as we concluded class, we agreed as a group to read and revise our papers for the next session, placing special emphasis on the specific objectives we had for our letters and the way those objectives could be best accomplished. After doing a short class critique on my paper, students better understood the need to set aside questions of spelling and focus instead on the substance of the work — on the use of organization, style, and diction to enliven the personal feelings held by the author. We left class that day with what clearly seemed to be the active, collaborative, inclusive spirit that epitomizes the idea of Smith's "Literacy Club."

Process and Change

The next class session demonstrated further evidence of this spirit when most of the students entered with revised, completed drafts as well as a renewed sense of the writing process. Shantel, who had grappled with her letter to the estranged father of her children, had made great strides in putting aside entanglements concerning grammar and spelling, to compose a very moving two-page letter.

"I just want you to know," she wrote in this second draft, "that your kids are still your kids no matter how far you distance yourself from them. Time and space can't change some things," she added. Later, she concluded with a very moving and poignant effluence of feeling, telling her estranged lover that "I still think about you and tell good things to our children. I remember the good times [. . .] ."

Other drafts seemed to highlight the same kind of clear, dramatic direction. Gina's letter, which had gone through three revisions since the opening discussion, was transformed into an incisive, moving missive to her deceased mother. As with Shantel, Gina had extricated herself from nettlesome questions involving usage and mechanics, and had, in the process, composed a letter that captured the loneliness and loss she felt.

"You always be special," she wrote. "I'll always speak to you, when I go to sleep, when I deal with problems, when I feel wonder about my life."

Both revisions, it is important to note, were the result of a vigorous, recursive, unencumbered writing process — one that allowed students to see themselves as authors in a community or club of writers, rather than as patients in a clinic for the syntactically or mechanically impaired. Where Rose laments the stultifying effects of reducing writing to questions of correctness, these students felt liberated to put expression first, treating their letters as serious drafts rather than objects for correction. For once, ideas and expression — passion and memories — took precedence over the conspicuous inexperience they demonstrated in generating polished prose. And as we engaged in small group critiques, adhering to the set of questions they answered for my letter earlier, we continued to learn about writing by doing it, by perceiving ourselves as writers, and collaborating in its evolutionary process.

Punctuation and usage, it is instructive to note, become more comprehensible and relevant when associated with holistic writing. Thus, as we formed groups of three and began to read and discuss the letters in small groups, we could consider the context in which errors were made. Deneitha's letter had frequent errors in spelling, but with her work flowering into a complex story about two estranged lovers, the misspellings seemed ancillary and insignificant. Of course, she would have to consult a dictionary and proofread more carefully, but such editing concerns were being handled after the essence of her piece had been written — after she had the chance to immerse herself in the empowering experience of creating a story and perceive herself as a writer.

Sondra Perl has suggested that even inexperienced writers bring a sophisticated knowledge of the writing process to the composition experience. During her study of remedial writers, she found that all students "displayed consistent composing processes; that is, the behavioral subsequences prewriting, writing, editing appeared in sequential patterns that were recognizable across writing sessions and across students" (31). In fact, as I observed students reading and critiquing in small groups, I noticed an assiduous attention to the evolutionary character of writing. Shantel's paper had problems with syntax as well as organization and spelling. And yet, her readers focused on her message and how it could be made more coherent as well as correct. Their efforts at keeping the focus on Shantel's goals allowed the process to continue while errors were eliminated. "You need to be more specific as to what he did and why he left," wrote one reader. "And you also need to reread your first two sentences. It wasn't clear to me, cause a word might have been missing."

A second reader agreed, highlighting the interesting ideas as well as the lack of clarity in certain spots. "This is going to be good. It's getting better too. But you have to watch for the fragments. Some of your ideas are still kind of fragmented and so it's not understandable."

From that second critique session came a final revision which was done on a computer. Later the next week, selected students made copies of their letters for the entire class to read and evaluate. For some, the final draft represented up to six revisions of work.

Marcus's final paper was perhaps most emblematic of the development that occurs when one is allowed to write and revise without the cumbersome drone of the grammar guardian filling the air. His letter to his deceased friends from a gang war evolved from clumsy, indelicate writing, to a forceful series of letters that blended the dialect of the street with terse and even opulent prose: "You went in a lightning strike of gun fire, and I miss you all cause you're no longer at my back. The streets are still frigid with the feel of your deaths, but that don't mean, I can't warm up to the memory of your friendship. Good bye."

Wrote Andre, another student who was also a veteran of the streets and the problems and temptations they represent: "I'm writing to you, Ma, because you were there to keep me in the house and far from the 'boys' that wanted me for their 'family.' I can't thank God for the past or future till I give you this letter for being my best friend forever."

Such is the kind of vigor and passion that I found in these developmental writers after several revisions and a thorough journey through the writing process. With mechanics put in perspective, and with each student free to experiment and take risks, correctness seemed to coalesce with clarity.

New Visions of Developmental Writers

Again, it is important to return to the concept of the writing club and the medical metaphor that has traditionally pervaded the teaching of developmental students. "Teachers and administrators," argues Mina Shaughnessy, "tend to discuss basic-writing students much as doctors tend to discuss their patients [. . .]" (289). With the sick, there must be a prescription, but for those who are well, there is guidance, encouragement, and an invitation to succeed through the writing process. In the same spirit, there is a concomitant need to envision a writing club, one that makes composition a group activity rather than a mandate from teacher to student. As my students completed their first letter, replete with rough draft and critique sheets, I realized that their abilities far transcended my expectations and that my role was as catalyst, not only in helping them to read and edit, but also to use the stages of writing, so that editing was postponed until ideas had been formulated and writers began to believe in their work.

Letter writing, I should note, is invaluable not only for its short, holistic character but also for the many political and liberating opportunities it offers. Not long after the class completed the introductory letters to friends and family, it began an exploration of the newspaper and the possibility of writing letters to editors and selected columnists. Many, lamentably, did not know what an editorial was, while even fewer understood the difference between an opinion and a fact. For many, there was confusion as to how one could question the newspaper, since it only printed the "truth." In this case, I found it helpful to refer to Nietzsche's famous quotation that "there are no truths, only interpretations" (25). At the same time, I read and explored the newspaper with the students and discussed the idea of political agendas, power, and the place students have in shaping them. In the end, I found this type of letter writing, with work, can also transcend the academic and awaken the fledgling iconoclast.

As we moved on to other writing endeavors, students became increasingly more familiar and confident with their writing and the stages it entailed. Working within the recursive stages of the writing process — allowing for mistakes and learning from them — facilitates a meaning-first approach, one that permits students to work through their weaknesses as they compose. "Writing," contends Peter Elbow, "is like trying to ride a horse which is constantly changing beneath you" (25). As with college-level writers, my developmental students learned to write by mounting the horse, grappling with the problems, and constructing short but holistic letters. And while their weaknesses far exceeded the average student, their engagement in writing helped them to recognize why clarity is needed and how the process works to make that clarity a reality.

Works Cited

Elbow, Peter. *Writing without Teachers*. New York: Oxford UP, 1973.
Judy, Stephen. *Explorations in the Teaching of English*. New York: Dodd, 1974.
Murray, Donald. "First Silence, Then Paper." *FForum*. Ed. Patricia Stock. Upper Montclair: Boynton, 1983. 227–33.
Nietzsche, Friedrich. *The Use and Abuse of History*. New York: Bobbs, 1949.
Perl, Sondra. "The Composing Processes of Unskilled College Writers." *Cross Talk in Comp Theory: A Reader*. Ed. Victor Villanueva. Urbana: NCTE, 1997. 17–42.

Rose, Mike. *Lives on the Boundary: A Moving Account of the Struggles and Achievements of America's Educationally Underprepared*. New York: Penguin, 1989.

Shaughnessy, Mina. "Diving In: An Introduction to Basic Writing." *Cross Talk in Comp Theory: A Reader*. Ed. Victor Villanueva. Urbana: NCTE, 1997, 289–96.

——. *Errors and Expectations: A Guide for the Teacher of Basic Writing*. New York: Oxford UP, 1977.

Smith, Frank. *Joining the Literacy Club*. Portsmouth: Heinemann, 1988.

Responses

Response to "Using Letters for Process and Change in the Basic Writing Class" by Gregory Shafer

Dear Greg:

Your article pleased me immensely by supporting my belief that classroom letter writing is good pedagogy. My own article gives a brief history of letter writing in the classroom and highlights a number of recent studies on its usage in first-year composition courses, but it lacks the specificity of your account of experiences with basic writers.

Whereas I concentrated mainly on letters that actually get sent, I like your idea of letter writing as personal expression of, for example, feelings about a missing partner or deceased parent. This reminds me of the ancient teachers' use of *progymnasmata*, or rhetorical exercises, where students wrote according to a formula in order to practice style. Many of the exercises stressed *copia*, or copiousness. That is, they served as a means to get students to write a lot, assuming that more writing meant more practice which led to better writing fluency. Certainly with basic students, this makes sense. When teachers assign an essay, students tend to ask, How long do you want this to be? This contrasts sharply with the effusive energy you report among your students whose emotions dictate how much they will write.

You describe how your students discover the way emotion and writing coalesce to serve very personal needs and the move they make to writing editorials or letters to editors. This seems appropriate to me because it replicates the move from personal to academic that is so important for college writers — and so vital to their success. You also emphasize content over correctness, an approach that many theoreticians applaud. I agree that letter writing provides motivation for self-correction. Students recognize from the start that letters have audiences (even, surprisingly, letters that never get mailed). Awareness of a reading other, a recipient, stimulates them to write clearly and correctly. If a classmate says, I don't get this part, the student willingly makes changes. I wish young writers felt this way about all their writing tasks.

Recent interest in reflection, stirred by Kathleen Yancey and others, suggests the next logical step you might take with your students.

After their initial epistolary exercise (or exercises), they could compose a letter of reflection which they actually send to the teacher. This letter would be a place for students to consider what happened to them as they wrote and revised the earlier assignment. Can they talk about the change of focus? Can they articulate the benefits of revision? What did they learn from the exercise? Is their work finished? Will they mail the letters? Why or why not? When the teacher reads and responds to their reflections, a dialogue ensues which extends the classroom discussion into written form, thus providing both a strong sense of audience and additional writing practice. It also reinforces the rapport already established in the classroom.

I really like the idea of reflection and a responding voice. Your article gave me opportunity for both, and I thank you.

Sincerely,

Elaine Fredericksen
The University of Texas
El Paso, Texas

Response to "Letter Writing in the College Classroom"
by Elaine Fredericksen

Dear Elaine:

The research is convincing and copious. Students bring rich and imaginative linguistic skills to our writing classes, whether they are labeled advanced or developmental. Too often, however, we fail to acknowledge this linguistic acumen, choosing instead to treat students as if they are sick and in need of our prescription. Thus, Mina Shaughnessy reminds us, medical metaphors dominate the language while "teachers and administrators tend to discuss basic writing students much as doctors tend to discuss their patients [. . .]" (289). They are remedial and in need of diagnosis or a trip to the clinic. Only recently have we begun to speak of the amazing ability they bring to the writing process.

That's what is so valuable and illuminating about your essay, "Letter Writing in the College Classroom." Rather than listing the ways letters can promote better skills exercises in isolation, it begins with the premise that all students are ready to write — that they bring linguistic knowledge to the writing context. And as a result, you invite students to join an activity that is rife with pleasure, both aesthetic and social. They are told, implicitly through the approach, that composition is about self-actualization and authentic communication. In short, you treat them as competent language users, people who have something important to say.

Why is this important? Frank Smith suggests that all learning is predicated upon the context in which we learn and those people with whom we are studying. Thus, if we are immersed in a setting that tells us that writing is an arcane, irrelevant activity — one filled with cumbersome prewriting exercises — we are likely to eschew it as one would anything that is unpleasant. In the same way, if we are led to believe that composition is not personally empowering but simply an act of academic imitation, we are again likely to venture elsewhere for life affirming experiences. All learning, contends Smith, pivots on who we think we are and who we see ourselves as capable of becoming (11). We learn, he continues, from the individuals or groups with whom we identify (10).

What is exciting, Elaine, about your letter writing use is its efficacy in creating a nurturing environment. True social exchange, you argue, stimulates students and their readers. Hence, your assignments revolve around what students can do in a setting that is based upon the worlds they inhabit. Because choices emanate from class population and student interest, relevance is virtually assured. In the process, so is true, active, thoughtful participation. The writer is made an active agent. Writing and existence converge.

Along the way, students acquire a variety of lessons about learning. Perhaps the most important of these is the value of the students' voice and personal perspective. With letter writing, composition becomes an extension of one's life. One of the most useful aspects of your essay is the divisions you create for different writers in various contexts. Letters can be used not only for business communication but as a way to express one's feelings or pose questions about a grade. In short, students become major players in a class that is decidedly bottom-up in its approach. The impetus for the letter — whether it is a reflective self-assessment or a fictitious missive to an author — radiates from the students and serves their needs. Relevance is assured.

Of the many interesting ideas you present, none is more helpful than the reflective pieces you assign. In asking your pupils to ponder and assess their progress and performance, you are again emphasizing the need for student engagement. In those contexts, the students are perceived as writers who are in control of their work and cognizant of its strengths and weaknesses. Such involvement is essential in designing a class that fosters student autonomy and creativity. With each letter representing a significant part of the grade, the students learn not only to take responsibility for their work but to appreciate the chaotic, capricious character of the writing process. Rules and injunctions are replaced with introspection and assessment. I especially enjoyed the first piece you include from one of your students. It's reminiscent of Peter Elbow and reveals the kind of progress that can be made when students are extricated from stifling mandates for correct writing:

> I forced myself to write professionally during the first draft. That's always a mistake; it came out lifeless and stilted. But fortunately, good prose isn't written. It's rewritten.
> The essay became my own when I stopped trying to write a good English 101 paper. I let myself have fun and put all my bizarre and

seemingly unconnected ideas onto the page. This free-writing process gave me a clear theme that I could expand into an actual essay (9–10).

Such student autonomy is invaluable. In many ways, it represents a break with the paradigm that tells instructors that their duty is to initiate students into the world of academic discourse. Such an approach relegates students to the job of imitation and follower. Instead of creating and developing new prose through a personal journey, the writer becomes a scribe, a disciple of the instructor, who in his omniscient role is the purveyor of truths. In this setting, little is really learned because the pupil is never allowed to invent and learn through the process of trial and error. No voice is ever forged because the entire goal of the class is not personal voice but academic allegiance.

"[. . .] teachers," you write toward the end of your essay, "can at least help students recognize that they each have a distinct voice and some truths worth communicating" (p. 283). Yes, they can, but only if the assignments — whether they are letters or five-paragraph essays — emanate from the student and include that student in the production of the piece. This approach begins with a view of writers that is inclusive and aware of their linguistic abilities. Once we acknowledge the wealth of language that is brought to the college classroom — and respect the universal need to use language for self-empowerment and discovery — we can begin to design classes that have the kind of success that you experienced.

What is especially good about letter writing is its departure from the impersonal world of the academy. With students practicing a form of discourse that is familiar and nonthreatening, writing becomes an activity that is fun and enriching — something worth exploring. From that point, as you so eloquently suggest, assignments can develop and diverge into letters to authors, to literary characters, and to other writers. They can, in short, serve the higher level thinking skills while remaining accessible to the writers in our classrooms — a goal that is progressive and still very practical.

Sincerely,

Gregory Shafer
Mott Community College
Flint, Michigan

WORKS CITED

Shaughnessy, Mina. "Diving In: An Introduction to Basic Writing." Villanueva. 289–296.
Smith, Frank. *The Book of Learning and Forgetting*. New York: Columbia UP, 1998.
Villanueva, Victor, ed. *Cross Talk in Comp Theory: A Reader*. Urbana: NCTE, 1997.

Classroom Activities

Invite students to follow the steps in Shafer's assignment for writing personal letters. As Shafer describes, try giving students time to write rough drafts in class and to then share their drafts with the whole group in order to work on revision. Be sure to share drafts at each stage of the process, including a reading of final copies on the day that the last revised version of the letters is due.

Once students are comfortable with writing personal letters and sharing them with peers, consider extending the assignment to include letters to the editors of local newspapers. Students will need to see copies of such letters, as Shafer suggests, to gain a sense of the genre. Be sure to workshop several drafts of the letters to take students through the writing process and to sharpen their sense of audience and purpose.

Consider beginning a lengthy correspondence with another group of students, either by using the method Shafer suggests or via e-mail. Students can correspond with each other, across classrooms at the same institution, across classrooms at different institutions, and so forth. The letters can discuss reading or writing assignments that students may have in common, college survival strategies, or other issues of personal, academic, or political interest.

Thinking about Teaching

Consider following Shafer's model: Write the assignment with your students and follow each step of the process, including writing and workshopping rough drafts. Try writing personal letters, letters to the editor, and letters to colleagues so that students can observe the differences and similarities in your writing process for different audiences and purposes.

Read the responses at the end of the article. Invite colleagues to correspond with you throughout an entire semester. You might want to trade observations of your students' progress, compare assignments, or discuss pedagogy. At the end of the semester, review the letters to see how critical issues were addressed and what ideas could be implemented in a subsequent semester. As appropriate, share your reflections with students, faculty, and administrators — and consider coauthoring an article with a colleague.

Instructional Note:
Life Writing and Basic Writing

Susan Naomi Bernstein

In the following article, first published in 1998 in Teaching English in the Two-Year College, *Susan Naomi Bernstein examines the transformative nature of life writing for students of basic writing and suggests how the writing process might be enacted in a sample assignment. In response to reading about issues of oppression and social justice, students write their own autobiographies, biographies, or fictional narratives about themselves, friends, relatives, or others in the community. Students address several aspects of the writing process as they work toward completed essays.*

A basic writing student from Cambodia writes about an essay which she is composing:

> This essay is about my parents during the Civil War. At last I finally was able to write about how they survive. And also one of the essays that brought me tears, anger, and frustration. And for that I learned something . . . .

The student writes these reflections as part of an ongoing correspondence to a student enrolled in another basic writing class at her community college. Both students are engaged in learning to write as non-native speakers of English and use the correspondence as an opportunity to reflect on cultural and historical issues related to events and observations in their own lives. Because the students understand that I am engaged in "research as a systematic reflection of [my] teaching . . . in an attempt to become a more effective" instructor (Blake 5), they know that I am also an audience for this correspondence. From this work, all of us learn that life writing takes on different forms in different contexts.

As the students and I study life writing in basic writing courses, we experiment with composing in a variety of genres; we also read literary autobiographies. Our criteria for choosing these autobiographical texts is as follows. First of all, the rhetorical situation must be clear; audience, purpose, and occasion for writing must be apparent. Also the sense of the writer's involvement with historical, cultural, and social issues should be of primary importance. The text itself must be persuasive — motivating the reader to take action or to be convinced of a particular point of view. Moreover, there needs to be a sense that the writer is still in process, much as society is still in process. There should be a strong indication of the need to continue to work on social problems beyond the historical moment when the text ends. Such life writing includes Maya Angelou's *I Know Why the Caged Bird Sings;* the anonymous *Go Ask Alice,* the diary of a teen-age drug user; *The Autobiogra-*

phy of Malcolm X; Anne Moody's *Coming of Age in Mississippi;* and Elie Wiesel's *Night.*

Life writing, in order to be persuasive, needs to be socially and rhetorically conscious rather than nostalgic or rooted in idealistic interpretations of an ahistorical past. Writing assignments that are generated from such readings are rhetorically driven, as students are urged to consider the needs of their readers as they tell their stories. Yet, since no one should have to confess her past in order to succeed in a basic writing course, I invite the students to consider the following three options as they begin one particular aspect of life writing, the narrative assignment:

1. Autobiography: For the autobiography, write a personal story about a significant event (or series of events) in your own life. Select an event that holds importance for you. Moreover, choose an event that will communicate the significance of your experience to the reader.

2. Biography: For the biography, write a story about an event (or series of events) in the life of a friend, relative, or acquaintance with an interesting experience to relate. You will need to interview this person to collect the necessary details. You also may think of this option as a kind of oral history. In the past, students have written successful essays by interviewing Vietnam veterans; recent immigrants to the United States; parents, grandparents, or others who remember historical events and/or life in your community in past decades.

3. Fiction: Invent your own story — fiction, science fiction, fables, fairy tales, and so forth would all be appropriate for this option.

But what if students confronted with such an assignment still choose to disclose events so intensely autobiographical that the reader cannot help being moved or disconcerted by them? How is a teacher to evaluate such potentially critical self-disclosures? I decided to ask students to write to me about this issue. Might I grade life writing without grading lives? After reading their responses, I wrote back to the students as follows:

> Your suggestions for evaluating Essay #1 closely parallel the established grading criteria: structure, organization, grammar, punctuation, spelling, length, understanding of audience, communication of message and/or point of view. I was urged not to grade essays on the writers' opinions or on their life stories — but on how the ideas themselves are expressed. Everyone has lived through something difficult, I was reminded, but it matters most how the writer portrays his/her experiences. As you revise the final copy of Essay #1, keep these criteria clearly in mind.

In a recent semester, basic writing students in my course read Elie Wiesel's *Night* and reflected on how oppression had figured in their own lives or the lives of family or acquaintances. The student cited in the introduction created a particularly memorable essay, recounting her family's experiences in a Cambodian concentration camp in the late 1970s:

> Soon my father was able to build a small hut for the three of us. Soon he was force to live separated from my mother and I at another camp. At this time I was almost three years old, left to the care of the elderly while my mother left home at early dawn to work at the rice plantation. There she was to excavate dirt with a hoe to make a water canal for rice or sometimes the soldiers would put a limit for her. For days she had to be able to dig up at least 6 to 8 tree trunks that were about two or three times her size. If she couldn't finish, tomorrow she would be forced to work with higher limitations. At this point she was also pregnant. At noon she was allowed to come back in the camp at the mess to feed me and herself. Unfortunately there nothing to eat but porridge (rice soup), porridge that mostly filled with water and vegetable and a few seeds of rice in a bowl. At the rice plantation, every chance she got, my mother tried to find any small animal such as apple snail, frog, or fish etc . . . just satisfied our hunger at night.

When the student read this paragraph aloud to her classmates and me, time seemed to stand still. "Is something wrong?" the student asked in response to the silence that greeted her reading. This question at last moved us to language. We noted the way in which the writer selected details, so that the reader felt at once a part of the scene. Moreover, we praised how such pointed description allowed the reader to gain empathy with the characters of the narrative, to begin to understand this experience of a Cambodian concentration camp.

On hearing this piece, some students were persuaded to continue working on oral histories of oppression. In particular, one student chose to interview his grandfather who, as an American soldier near the end of World War II, participated in the liberation of Buchenwald. His grandfather, the student related, had not spoken much of his wartime experiences, and the student looked forward to this project as a way of setting down his grandfather's memories:

> The orders then came in to take the concentration camp of Buchenwald. That was one of the first times I was afraid for my life, stated [my grandfather.] This was because the entire place smelled of death, and when he went into the barracks he pulled out a cigarette to calm himself down, every man in the room rushed him trying to get a smoke. Out of fear he threw the pack into air to let them fight it out. He's not sure but he thinks one or two might have died in the fighting.

Again, students reacted powerfully to this piece in light of their new-found knowledge of Cambodia, as well as their reading of Wiesel's *Night*. This particular class of urban community college students included people from a variety of cultural backgrounds, from students in their late teens who had recently graduated from high school, to returning adult women in their forties and fifties who had earned the GED. A broad range of life and educational experiences was represented, several audiences within one heterogeneous grouping. The students responded to these stories of oppression and survival with not only the shock of discovering histories previously unexamined, but also with empathic recognition: These are important stories, the students expressed over and over again. We need to know about them in order to understand our own life histories and our own experiences with racism and oppression, in order to understand the positions of cultures other than our own living in the United States and in our communities. Such understanding deepened the category of life writing beyond the usual narratives of "prom night" or "what I did on my summer vacation," allowing students to make connections between seemingly unrelated historical events and their own lives.

Often as instructors, we avoid assigning life writing because we fear the results may be too "personal" to assess objectively. Yet we run the risk of shutting down an important opportunity for facilitating potentially transformative writing experiences for students in basic writing classrooms. The self, in these shifting contexts, continually refigured in terms of reading and writing, becomes an identity that moves and changes with the demands of the course and the needs of the audience — and the writer — and which is immersed in the material conditions of social life. By these means, life writing becomes persuasive, as the students and I have the opportunity to challenge our thinking regarding the nature of "personal" experience. According to Francie Blake, such work allows "students to claim their own education" by actively reclaiming their own histories (Blake 6). As we examine the exigencies for engaged learning in basic writing classrooms, life writing can become a crucial part of this process.

Work Cited

Blake, Francie. "Identity, Community, and the Curriculum: A Call for Multiculturalism in the Classroom." *The Journal of Developmental Education: A Publication of the ESS Division of the Community College of Philadelphia* 2.2 (1997): 3–7.

Classroom Activities

Present students with the options suggested by Bernstein in the narrative assignment. Be sure to carefully explain the differences among autobiography, fiction, and nonfiction. Read examples of each genre in class and have students discuss the important points of each approach. Why might writers choose to fictionalize their lives? Why might they wish to write autobiography or to write the biography of someone else? Include this discussion as part of the prewriting process for writing a narrative assignment. You might also wish to have students write in imitation of one of the writers that they read for the course.

Discuss grading criteria for personal narratives. Have the students read samples of exemplary narratives and invite them to discuss the qualities of a good narrative. At each step of the writing process, have students identify those qualities in their own and peers' papers. Invite students to join you in creating a list of grading criteria for their narrative assignment based on principles of sound rhetorical structure and on the qualities they identified as critical throughout each step of the writing process.

Invite students, if they are willing, to hand in duplicate copies of their narrative assignment. If facilities exist, compile the narratives into a booklet that can then be copied and used later in the course and in subsequent semesters. The booklet will allow students to see their own and others' work in the final stage of the writing process and will suggest possibilities for writing a narrative in subsequent semesters.

Thinking about Teaching

Write a series of entries in your teaching journal that document each stage of the students' writing process for the narrative assignment. What steps of the process seemed to go particularly well? Which steps were difficult? Did students seem to make important discoveries along the way? As appropriate, share this entry with students, teachers and administrators.

Based on students' discussion of grading criteria, write a journal entry or initiate a discussion with other teachers on how to grade a personal narrative. How should teachers respond when students write about difficult personal experiences? What kinds of suggestions can teachers make for revision that will honor those experiences and foster growth in student writing? Perhaps start an online discussion on a listserv to see how other instructors have dealt with this difficult issue.

Writing and Reading

R ecent research on basic writing and reading highlights the connections between the two activities, treating reading and writing as
similar meaning-making composing processes. Drawing on such
research, the articles in this section persuasively make the case that
reading should not be taught in isolation from writing, and that developmental students can usefully and successfully engage the interconnections and similarities between these processes. Amelia E. El-Hindi
demonstrates the positive results that "at-risk" students can achieve
by gaining metacognitive awareness of their reading and writing processes. Similarly, Ilona Leki shows how an understanding of the connections between these processes can be beneficial for students whose
home language is not English (as well as for developmental writers
and readers from other backgrounds). In addition to providing helpful
research in the processes of writing and reading, El-Hindi and Leki
also offer practical classroom applications of their ideas.

Connecting Reading and Writing: College Learners' Metacognitive Awareness

Amelia E. El-Hindi

First published in 1997 in the Journal of Developmental Education, *this
article centers on students' awareness of their processes of reading and
writing, as well the connections between these processes. Focusing on a
summer bridge program for a group of "at-risk" students from
underrepresented populations, Amelia E. El-Hindi shows how a combination of reflective reading journals, instruction in metacognitive strategies,*

and questionnaires to assess metacognitive growth can help foster in
students a more critical engagement with text. As illustrations of the
types of metacognitive strategies that students learned to use, the essay
includes reading log excerpts. El-Hindi also offers an analysis of stu-
dents' questionnaire responses in order to create a strong argument that
"for college learners, metacognitive awareness for both reading and
writing can be enhanced by providing direct instruction."

First-year college students are faced with many pressures. College
life is a difficult adjustment at best and the transition from high
school is overwhelming. Of the many pressures faced by this special
population is the demand to integrate information from vast amounts
of text. For perhaps the first time in their lives, these students must
complete large amounts of reading and rapidly synthesize and communicate ideas from text. However, between 30 percent and 40 percent of
first-year college students have deficiencies in the reading and writing
skills necessary for college performance (Moore & Carpenter, 1985).
This trend coincides with disturbing evidence cited by Brozo and
Simpson (1995) which indicates that, although junior and senior high
students can handle basic literacy skills, very few junior high and senior high students are gaining advanced literacy skills. Such trends
pose disturbing implications for the future of first-year college students.
Students who lack the sophistication to rapidly digest text could be set
up for failure in reading-intensive courses. First-year students need to
develop these skills early in their college careers and can do so with
the help of developmental educators. This is particularly important for
college students from underrepresented populations who may be considered at risk for completing their programs. Such a population is the
focus of this study.

Purpose

This paper reports on a study of first-year college students who received instruction in metacognitive awareness for reading and writing.
Metacognition or "thinking about thinking" involves the awareness and
regulation of thinking processes. Metacognitive strategies are those
strategies that require students to think about their own thinking as
they engage in academic tasks. Within this study, students were taught
specific metacognitive strategies for both reading and writing as part
of a six-week residential summer program. Students' use of a reflective
reading journal or "reading log" was integral to the strategy instruction. The students used the reading logs to reflect on their own thinking processes as they engaged in reading and writing tasks. The focus
of this article is on the students' increase in metacognitive awareness
revealed by analyses of their metacognitive awareness questionnaires
and their reading log entries.

Related Literature

Skilled learners tend to be active learners who are aware of their own learning processes. The use of metacognitive strategies, the awareness and regulation of cognitive activity (Baker & Brown, 1984; Flavell, 1976, 1978, 1993; Flavell & Wellman, 1977), characterizes an active learner who exercises control over the learning process (Mayo, 1993). Empirical studies show that metacognition is linked to both reading ability (Balajthy, 1986; Brown & Day, 1983; Brozo, Stahl, & Gordon, 1985; Gambrell & Heathington, 1981; Hare & Pulliam, 1980; Paris, Cross, & Lipson, 1984; Paris & Jacobs, 1984) and writing ability (Englert, Raphael, Fear, & Anderson, 1988; Raphael, Englert, & Kirscher, 1989). Empirical research also suggests that, for college learners, metacognitive awareness for both reading and writing can be enhanced by providing direct instruction (El-Hindi, 1996).

The increased attention on metacognition coincides with current definitions of literacy which suggest that reading and writing are interconnected. Brozo and Simpson (1995) indicate that reading and writing are "parallel processes" students use to gain meaning from text. Mulcahy-Ernt and Stewart (1994) appeal to a constructivist view of literacy, indicating that "writing and reading processes provide a student with the communicative tools for independent learning, the mark of a mature student" (p. 107). Today's vision of reading and writing processes suggests that they are interconnected, recursive processes used by metacognitively aware learners to actively create meaning through text. Shanahan (1990) recommends teaching reading and writing in conjunction with each other because exposing learners to both sides of the literacy process provides an understanding of the social and communicative nature of literacy. These theoretical perspectives about reading and writing form the foundation for the study reported here in which students are exposed to the interconnections between reading and writing processes through metacognitive instruction.

Methodology

Participants

Participants were volunteers from a six-week residential academic program in Summer of 1993 for prefreshmen from a major Northern university. The program targeted incoming first-year students from underrepresented populations who were considered at risk for completing their programs. The residential program also solicited students with learning disabilities and students interested in math, science, or technology. The majority of the students were either required or encouraged to participate in the program by their academic departments. All students who enrolled in the program completed an intensive reading-writing class. Four sections of the reading-writing class were designated to receive the instruction in metacognitive awareness. Students in these sections completed reading logs as an integral part of

the metacognitive instruction. The mean age of the thirty-four participants (thirteen male, twenty-one female) was 17.53 with a standard
deviation of .56. The majority of the student participants were African
American (73.53 percent), whereas a minority were either Hispanic
(11.76 percent), Caucasian (11.76 percent), or Asian (2.94 percent).

Metacognitive Strategy Instruction

Metacognitive instruction for reading and writing processes was provided during the six-week course by the researcher who worked in conjunction with two instructors. A model for the instruction (see El-Hindi,
1996) was developed based on scholarship on metacognitive processes
for reading (Baker & Brown, 1984; Paris, Wasik, & Turner, 1991) and
on metacognitive processes for writing (Englert et al., 1988; Raphael et
al., 1989).

One important assumption of this model is that reading and writing are interactive processes linked to one another. Reading lends itself to writing and writing lends itself to reading. Another assumption
of the model is that reading and writing involve three recursive phases:
planning (before the process), drafting (during the process), and responding (after the process) (see Figure 1).

The metacognitive instruction involved teaching students specific
strategies which corresponded to each of the three phases. As seen in
Figure 1, metacognitive strategies corresponding to the planning stage
for reading included identifying a purpose for reading, activating prior
knowledge, previewing text, and making predictions about text. Planning strategies for writing included identifying a purpose for writing,
activating prior knowledge of a writing topic, and organizing ideas.
Drafting strategies for reading included comprehension monitoring and
self-questioning, strategies cited by Baker and Brown (1984) as important to effective reading. Self-questioning and monitoring were also
taught as strategies which facilitated the drafting stage of writing.
Learners were taught to self-question as they produced their own texts
and to monitor their progress at completing a writing task.

Figure 1 also illustrates the responding phase of both reading and
writing as involving evaluating, reacting, and relating. In the context
of reading, students were taught to evaluate their understanding, react to the text they were reading, and relate the text to their prior
experience. Within the context of writing, students were taught to evaluate their success as writers, react to their written texts as readers, and
examine their texts holistically to see connections among different parts
of their texts. Englert et al. (1988) identified self-evaluation of a paper's
completeness as an important metacognitive activity for writing.

The model was developed and used to organize specific lessons in
metacognitive awareness for reading and writing. Each metacognitive
strategy was explained and demonstrated, and students practiced use
of the strategies in conjunction with course reading and writing assignments.

Figure 1. The interaction of various phases of the reading and writing processes.

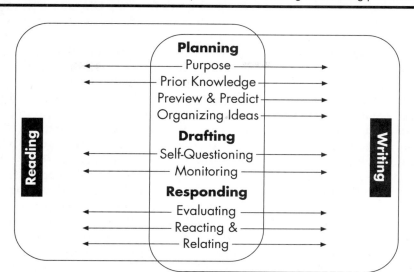

Students completed weekly reading assignments which included chapters from the course text, *Writing with Power* (Elbow, 1981), and articles written by contemporary professional writers. Students were instructed to use their reading logs to comment on their thoughts and actions as they completed their readings for the course. For example, students would write down thoughts that came to mind when they first read the title or would use the reading log to comment on actions, such as referencing a dictionary, they would take when they encountered a word or phrase that was confusing. Students were asked to write in their reading logs each week.

Reading logs were collected and reviewed each week by the instructors. At the end of the course, reading logs were collected and photocopied for analysis. The instructors provided feedback on the reading logs by writing comments and questions in the margins. Students were given feedback and prompted to write critical commentaries on what they read, synthesize the ideas presented by the authors, and indicate how the text related to their own experience.

Assessment of Metacognitive Awareness

Metacognitive awareness was assessed by examining two sources of data: results from questionnaires designed to assess metacognitive awareness for both reading and writing, and the reading log entries generated by each student. A discussion of each data source follows.

Questionnaires for metacognitive awareness included two thirty-six-item instruments developed as part of a larger study (El-Hindi,

1996) and used to assess students' metacognitive awareness both prior to and after the metacognitive strategy instruction. One questionnaire assessed metacognitive knowledge for reading, and the other assessed metacognitive knowledge for writing.

Each questionnaire was composed of four sets of questions. For each set of questions students responded to a specific reading or writing scenario. For example, the first scenario described a hypothetical student who was about to read an assignment for a class. After reading the scenario, students responded to the prompt, "if you were in this situation would you . . . " for nine specific activities by checking "yes" or "no" for each activity. Each activity was classified as either an activity which involved metacognition (i.e., writing down a reason for doing the reading) or an activity which did not (i.e., just starting to read without doing anything). Each response received a specific score. A yes response to a metacognitive activity was scored as a 1 and a yes response to a nonmetacognitive activity was scored as a 0. A no response to a nonmetacognitive activity was scored as a 1 and a no response to a metacognitive activity was scored as a 0. For each questionnaire, the scores on all the items were added to provide an overall score of metacognitive knowledge for reading and an overall score of metacognitive knowledge for writing.

Reading log entries were requested from students as they completed their reading assignments for each week. Entries ranged in length from two to five pages. Each student generated six reading log entries which were photocopied for analysis. The "constant comparative method of analysis" was used for analysis of the reading log entries (Glaser & Strauss, 1967). The researcher completed an initial reading of all the reading log entries. Then the entries were broken down into paragraphs and each paragraph was transcribed onto an index card. The paragraphs were then sorted by the researcher according to categories which emerged from the initial reading of the full entries and were refined during the sorting process (Strauss & Corbin, 1990). According to Bogdan and Biklen (1992) data analyzed in this way provides a descriptive theory around which to organize phenomena.

The constant comparative analysis for the study's reading logs identified three major categories: (a) excerpts which showed a student's use of a particular metacognitive strategy; (b) excerpts which showed a change in the student's metacognitive awareness; and, (c) excerpts which showed the students' awareness of the connection between reading and writing. Often an excerpt would fall into more than one category and this was noted by the researcher. Still, the major categories which emerged from the data provided the means for organizing the excerpts from the reading log entries. This method of analysis allowed specific themes to emerge which captured the students' developing sophistication as readers and writers. Representative samples of entries are presented in the "Results" section. The students' identities are protected with the use of pseudonyms.

Results: Use of Metacognitive Strategies

Questionnaire Results

Results from the responses on the questionnaires indicated a significant increase in students' metacognitive awareness of reading. Prior to instruction students' mean score for metacognitive awareness of reading was 36.79 with a standard deviation of 11.11. By the end of instruction, the comparable mean score was 44.85 with a standard deviation of 9.29. A paired *t*-test indicated a significant gain in metacognitive awareness for reading ($t(32) = 4.66, p = .00005$).

Although scores on metacognitive awareness for reading increased significantly, scores for metacognitive awareness of writing increased but not at a statistically significant level. The mean score for metacognitive awareness of writing prior to instruction was 44.84 with a standard deviation of 8.85, and the corresponding mean score after instruction was 48.18 with a standard deviation of 6.84.

Reading Log Results

As evidenced by the entries, the students engaged in highly strategic activity as they interacted with their texts. Often the reading log entry would reveal the student's use of a particular metacognitive strategy. Strategies most frequently illustrated by the entries included: (a) relating the text to previous experience, (b) visualizing oneself in the text, (c) talking with classmates about the reading, and (d) examining the title to make predictions about the text.

The following example from a second reading log entry shows how one student, Cathy, engages in metacognitive processes. In writing this entry, Cathy activated her own previous experience and used visualization to make sense of the text as she reacted to an author's description of a Kentucky Fried Chicken restaurant in an inner city neighborhood:

> As I read this passage I was shocked. I, too, had walked down the same street, lined with foreigners peddling their wares. I visualized myself standing at the corner near KFC staring straight towards the Apollo. Orlean encourages me to read on in this way.

Cathy's reading log entry shows her active engagement with the text. She can relate to the experience discussed by the author and actually comments on how the author would want her to read the text while visualizing herself in that neighborhood.

Another student, Marsha, demonstrated similar engagement as evidenced by the following entry from her fourth reading log in which she responded to an article about children growing up in ghetto neighborhoods:

> When I spoke to a classmate about the article he understood Freddie Brown's situation "for Freddie, poverty was not only a dearth of material comforts and opportunities; even more crippling, he wrestled with a poverty of hope." My classmate told me that he was luck [sic] to go home from school without getting harassed by a drug dealer for money, or the police thinking he's a dealer.

The excerpt shows the overall trend on the part of the students to share insights about the text with other classmates. It also shows the sense of active engagement of relating the text to previous experience and making connections between the text and their personal lives.

Another student, Nimi, articulated a detailed process for analyzing the title of one of her readings:

> I spent a lot of time analyzing this article and I began with the title. I had no idea what, "In these girls, hope is a muscle meant." First I decided to break down the title so I can decipher it. I knew what "In these girls," meant but I had a harder time with "hope is a muscle."
>
> A muscle is a part of your body that helps you move so I wrote out the sentence, Hope is a part of you that helps you move. I had an idea about the title but it was too general. So the next thing I did was look up the word muscle in my dictionary. I came up with the meanings "Power or influence especially when based on force or threats" and "To make one's way or take control by sheer strength or force or threats or force or control."
>
> Now I made up a new sentence. Hope is to make one's way to take control by sheer strength or force or threats of force or control. This sentence made a lot more sense to me than the first one and made me understand the title.

This critical examination of the title demonstrates Nimi's increased metacognitive awareness for reading and her heightened engagement with text. By the end of writing her entry, Nimi had increased her understanding of the hidden meaning of the title and how the title fit with the remainder of the article.

Changes in metacognitive awareness were evidenced by analysis of the reading log entries. As students progressed through the six-week class, they became more critical in examining text. Early reading log entries tended to show more summarizing of text, whereas later reading log entries tended to show more critical reflection and commentary. Use of metacognitive strategies became more apparent as the students wrote in their logs over time.

Sample entries from one student, Robert, illustrated this increased metacognitive sophistication. The following series of entries, which focus on Robert's making sense of the titles of the various articles he read, were representative of the type of metacognitive growth revealed by the reading log entries of the students overall.

In his first reading log entry Robert wrote: "The title, 'Making yourself at home: The baby boom generation yearns to settle down,' threw me off a bit. I knew he was going to talk about staying home but the baby boom part, I didn't understand it until I read the whole article." This excerpt showed Robert's use of examining the title in order to make some predictions about the text he was about to read. Robert continued in this vein in his third entry which showed a greater sophistication in use of this metacognitive strategy:

> The first time I read the title "In these girls hope is a muscle" I was looking for the reading assignment on the sheet. I read the title and didn't know what to think. I thought that these girls were using hope to get them moving. Like a muscle is able to make you move, hope gets you motivated. I had a feeling that the article was going to be about a sport but I didn't think it would be about basketball.

In Robert's final reading log entry, he again commented on a title and showed a greater understanding of how a title can communicate:

> When I first read the title "A Crowded Writer on the Lonely Prairie," I was stumped. I didn't know what to think, but while reading the passage, it came to me. The title is really sarcastic. If someone read the title alone that person may think that the writer is crowded but it's lonely on a prairie. That's not what it means at all. The writer is really alone because there aren't many writers that tell the story of small rural towns in the Dakotas.

This series of excerpts shows Robert's developing sophistication as a reader. He is metacognitively aware in using the title to gain insights and make predictions about the text. The excerpts also show how he refined his use of the strategy of examining the title to make predictions about the text.

Reading and writing connections were strengthened through the reading logs in addition to their allowing students to articulate metacognitive processes while reading. The logs also served as a vehicle for many participants to realize the connection between their metacognitive processes as readers and their metacognitive processes as writers.

Students' developing awareness of the reading and writing connection was a compelling insight revealed by the entries. Later reading log entries illustrated that the students reacted to the text by referring to their own experiences as writers. Jamal wrote the following in response to an essay by Robert Hass:

> While reading this essay . . . it reminded me of the last paper I wrote on a meaningful place. The way Hass described the house where one of his babysitters lived was very similar to the way I described my grandmother's house in my paper where I wrote about the face of the house being filled with lilacs and a big tree in the front.

Consider how Jamal reflected on his own writing as he tried to make sense of the essay. This showed growing metacognitive awareness of Jamal's stance as a writer. Like Jamal, Cathy, too, reflected on her role as a writer in the following excerpt from her fifth reading log entry in response to an article by Kathleen Norris:

> As I read on, I noticed that Kathleen Norris spoke of many of the same problems I had encountered in writing my paper. One of the obvious parallels was when she quoted a North Dakota Ranch woman saying, "I'd like to write about my relatives, but I'm no good at disgusting things." In writing my memoir, there were many places where I avoided telling the truth about my family.

This excerpt showed Cathy's comparison of the author she was reading with herself as an emerging writer. Another student, Robert, also demonstrated metacognitive awareness for reading-writing connections in the following excerpt in which he wrestled with his struggle to write about himself:

> The article by Jill Johnston, "Fictions of the Self" helped me to understand that anyone can write an autobiography. I'm the type of person that hates writing about myself but from this text Johnston explains that it isn't really that hard to do. Jill Johnston used a lot of sources and I think that was a good move. She would start by saying, "I've read somewhere that . . ." and then write about the way she feels about certain statements from the sources she picked. She also describes the way she has changed after writing an article or a book. In a way I think she is trying to find herself through her writing. She wants to know who she is and what she's about. Through her writing she's finding a way to identify herself.

In writing this entry, Robert looked to the author he was reading for insights on his own writing. In later reading log entries, Robert came to grips with writing about himself and looked to the authors he read for additional clues. He demonstrated his developing awareness of himself as a reader and as a writer.

This connection between reading and writing was also expressed by Nancy, who wrote the following in her fifth reading log in responding to an article by a memoirist:

> I was surprised that the opening anecdote was not altogether true. To me, as a reader, it seemed very believable. He stated "but no memoirist writes for long without experiencing an unsettling disbelief about the reliability of memory, a hunch that memory is not, after all, just memory." I find this to be the case in my own writing. Because I had not been to Jamaica in so long, my memory of the place may not be completely accurate. I was not sure about the name of the housekeeper and at first I attempted to put it in, but after realizing that the name was not real I left it out.

In reading the opening anecdote, Nancy struggled with the underlying issue of the author's stretching the truth to make a point about writing from memory. She not only reflected this struggle in her analysis of the text, but she also reflected on this struggle as she thought about her own experience as a writer in the class. This reflective analysis showed metacognition of both reading and writing processes. Moreover, it demonstrated Nancy's developing awareness of the connections between reading and writing.

Nancy's example serves to illustrate how participants realized the connection between their roles as readers and their roles as writers. As they critically reflect on the processes used to understand reading text, they also reflect on their own experiences as developing writers: both examples of self-regulation of thinking processes or strategic metacognitive activity.

Reading log entries provided students with a vehicle for articulating their metacognitive processes. As analysis of the entries showed, students gained metacognitive awareness for reading and writing and also demonstrated understanding of the connections between being good readers and being good writers.

Discussion

Journals have been shown to be effective for documenting and observing metacognitive development (Newton, 1991). Analyses of the reading log entries written by the participants for this study as well as results of the questionnaire to assess metacognitive growth have indicated that such journals can assist students in articulating their metacognitive processes. In teaching college students about metacognitive processes for reading, part of the challenge is in the very articulation of processes. Students tend to read on "automatic pilot," and not realize when they have trouble comprehending or truly digesting text. Within this class, the use of the reading log caused students to actively engage in thought processes as they were completing reading for the course. By completing the reading log entries, students were required to stop, slow down, and actively think about what they were reading as opposed to simply reading text from start to finish. This slowing down proved to be beneficial to their developing awareness of reading and writing processes.

Excerpts from the reading logs also provide evidence of students' critical engagement with text. Sample excerpts illustrate students' reflections on past experience and prior knowledge to make sense of their reading. This notion is supported by the transactional view of reading which posits that meaning resides within the transaction between reader and text instead of within the text alone (Rosenblatt, 1978). This view of reading promotes the idea that students move beyond literal recall of text and into the realm of higher order thinking as they react to what they read (Kelly & Farnan, 1991).

The reading logs provided a forum for students to articulate their metacognitive processes while engaging in both reading and writing tasks. Journals, therefore, can be justified as a tool to promote metacognitive awareness on the part of college learners. Use of such journals can also assist students with realizing the connection between their roles as critical readers and their roles as critical writers.

The very words expressed by the students themselves as they struggled with their emerging voices as writers provides testimony of the power in using reading logs as a tool for teaching reading and writing skills to college learners. Consider Maurice's words in his fifth reading log entry as he reflects on how he has changed as a reader:

> When I first began to read essays, I never focused on anything that could warm me up for the reading. In other words, I would go right into the reading without thinking about the essay I was going to read. I didn't set a purpose for myself. As I began to read my final essay in this course, Memory and Imagination, I realized that I was doing things that I didn't do before.

Maurice's words give testimony to the growth he experienced as a learner throughout the course. Such awareness is, in itself, a powerful key to obtaining success in college environments. Developmental educators set out to equip their students with the tools necessary to become proficient in college. Metacognitive awareness is one such tool. Skilled learners who are metacognitively aware tend to succeed at academic tasks. This study demonstrates the effectiveness of using journals to enhance metacognitive instruction. Use of such journals also can help students realize the connection between reading and writing.

At the very least, college learning demands sophistication in gaining information from text and being able to communicate through writing. Metacognitive awareness is a key ingredient to such sophisticated literacy processes. However, too often metacognitive instruction is sacrificed to isolated skill instruction within academic support classes. Attending to metacognitive awareness within academic support classes can benefit college learners seeking to improve their reading and writing skills. Use of a reflective journal, such as a reading log, can allow students the vehicle for becoming more metacognitively aware as they approach the reading and writing demands of college courses. Furthermore, as evidenced by this study, use of reading logs can help college students understand the process of reading and the process of writing as a single act of literacy. Such an integrative view of literacy will help at-risk learners cope with the demands of college learning.

References

Baker, L., & Brown, A. (1984). Metacognitive skills and reading. In D. Pearson, R. Barr, M. Kamil, & P. Mosenthal (Eds.), *Handbook of reading research* (pp. 353–394). New York: Longman.

Balajthy, E. (1986). The relation of training self-generated questioning with passage difficulty and immediate and delayed retention. In J. Niles & R. Lalik (Eds.), *Solving problems in literacy: Learner teachers, and researcher* (pp. 41–46). Rochester, NY: National Reading Conference.

Bogdan, R. C., & Biklen, S. K. (1992). *Qualitative research for education: An introduction to theory and methods*. Boston: Allyn and Bacon.

Brozo, W. G., & Simpson, M. L. (1995). *Readers, teachers, learners: Expanding literacy in secondary schools* (2nd ed.). Englewood Cliffs, NJ: Prentice-Hall.

Brozo, W. G., Stahl, N. A., & Gordon, B. (1985). Training effects of summarizing, item writing, and knowledge of information sources on reading test performance. In J. Niles & R. Lalik (Eds.), *Issues in literacy: A research perspective* (pp. 48–54). Rochester, NY: National Reading Conference.

Brown, A. L., & Day, J. D. (1983). Macrorules for summarizing tests: The development of expertise. *Journal of Verbal Learning and Verbal Behavior* 22(1), 1–14.

Elbow, P. (1981). *Writing with power.* New York: Oxford University Press.

El-Hindi, A. (1996). Enhancing metacognitive awareness of college learners. *Reading Horizons,* 36(3), 214–230.

Englert, C. S., Raphael, T. E., Fear, K. L., & Anderson, L. M. (1988). Students' metacognitive knowledge about how to write informational texts. *Learning Disability Quarterly,* 11(1), 18–46.

Flavell, J. H. (1976). Metacognitive aspects of problem solving. In L. Resnick (Ed.), *The nature of intelligence* (pp. 231–235). Hillsdale, NJ: Lawrence Erlbaum Associates.

Flavell, J. H. (1978). Metacognitive development. In J. M. Scandura & C. J. Brainerd (Eds.), *Structural / process models of complex human behavior* (pp. 213–245). Alphen aan den Rijn, The Netherlands: Sijthoff & Noordhoff.

Flavell, J. H. (1993). *Cognitive development* (3rd ed.). Englewood Cliffs, NJ: Simon & Schuster Company.

Flavell, J. H., & Wellman, H. M. (1977). Metamemory. In R. V. Kail, Jr. & W. Hagen (Eds.), *Perspectives on the development of memory and cognition* (pp. 3–33). Hillsdale, NJ: Erlbaum.

Gambrell, L. B., & Heathington, B. S. (1981). Adult disabled readers' metacognitive awareness about reading tasks and strategies. *Journal of Reading Behavior,* 13(3), 215–222.

Glaser, B., & Strauss, A. (1967). *The discovery of grounded theory.* Chicago: Aldine.

Hare, V., & Pulliam, C. (1980). College students' metacognitive awareness of reading behaviors. In M. L. Kamil & A. J. Moe (Eds.), *Perspectives on reading research and instruction. Twenty-ninth yearbook of the National Reading Conference* (pp. 226–231). Washington, DC: The National Reading Conference, Inc.

Kelly, P. R., & Farnan, N. (1991). Promoting critical thinking through response logs: A reader-response approach with fourth graders. In P. Zutell & S. McCormick (Eds.), *Learner factors / teacher factors: Issues in literacy research and instruction. Fortieth yearbook of the National Reading Conference* (pp. 277–284). Rochester, NY: National Reading Conference.

Mayo, K. E. (1993). Learning strategy instruction: Exploring the potential of metacognition. *Reading Improvement,* 30(3), 130–133.

Moore, W., & Carpenter, L. C. (1985). Academically underprepared students. In U. Delworth & G. R. Hanson (Eds.), *Increasing student retention* (pp. 95–115). San Francisco: Jossey-Bass.

Mulcahy-Ernt, P., & Stewart, J. P. (1994). Reading and writing in the integrated language arts. In L. M. Morrow, J. K. Smith, & L. C. Wilkinson (Eds.), *Integrated language arts: Controversy to consensus* (pp. 105–132). Boston, MA: Allyn & Bacon.

Newton, E. V. (1991). Developing metacognitive awareness: The response journal in college composition. *Journal of Reading,* 34(5), 477–479.

Paris, S. G., Cross, D. R., & Lipson, M. Y. (1984). Informed strategies for learning: A program to improve children's reading awareness and comprehension. *Journal of Educational Psychology,* 76(6), 1239–1252.

Paris, S. G., Lipson, M. Y., & Wixson, K. K. (1983). Becoming a strategic reader. *Contemporary Educational Psychology,* 8(3), 293–316.

Paris, S. G., & Jacobs, J. E. (1984). The benefits of informed instruction for children's awareness and comprehension skills. *Child Development,* 55, 2083–2093.

Paris, S. G., Wasik, B. A., & Turner, J. C. (1991). The development of strategic readers. In D. Pearson, R. Barr, M. Kamil, & P. Mosenthal (Eds.), *Handbook of reading research* (pp. 609–640). New York: Longman.

Raphael, T. E., Englert, C. S., & Kirscher, B. W. (1989). Students' metacognitive knowledge about writing. *Research in the Teaching of English,* 23(4), 343–379.

Rosenblatt, L. (1978). *The reader, the text, the poem.* Carbondale: Southern Illinois University Press.

Shanahan, T. (1990). Reading and writing together: What does it really mean? In T. Shanahan (Ed.), *Reading and writing together: New perspectives for the classroom* (pp. 1–21). Norwood, MA: Christopher Gordon Publishers, Inc.

Strauss, A., & Corbin, J. (1990). *The basics of qualitative research.* Newbury Park: Sage.

Classroom Activities

Copy and distribute to students the illustration depicted in Figure 1. Early in the semester, discuss the model with the class, and have students create their own map of the metacognitive processes they used while reading or writing a particular assignment for the course. Ask students to keep a reading log in which they track their metacognitive awareness of the connections between writing and reading throughout the semester. As the semester progresses, invite students to note the changes in their awareness of the interactions of these processes.

Thinking about Teaching

El-Hindi suggests that reading logs can "assist students with realizing their roles as critical readers and their roles as critical writers." To test this assumption, consider creating your own reflective practice based on El-Hindi's research. Collect the students' journals periodically and note the metacognitive connections, if any, that students find between writing and reading. You might also want to develop your own questionnaire that assesses students' growth in metacognitive awareness. Share your research with your students and invite them to examine what they are learning through this process. You can then investigate for yourself El-Hindi's conclusion that presenting the connections between writing and reading is more effective than "isolated skill instruction within academic support classes."

Reciprocal Themes in ESL Reading and Writing

Ilona Leki

Originally published in 1993 in Reading in the Composition Classroom: Second Language Perspectives,* *Ilona Leki's essay presents a particularly effective analysis of how changes in our understanding of ESL students' writing processes have "reciprocal themes" in studies of reading processes. She suggests, for example, that the notion of writing for specific purposes correlates to the idea of reading for specific purposes. Leki argues that focusing simply on reading for "the main idea" or for answers to post-reading questions in a textbook is unhelpful for students because such skills are often presented in isolation from "making meaning" from the text itself. In the same vein, Leki suggests that "we are preventing the very grappling with meaning that would allow students to develop their own strategies for rapid and accurate text processing," including discovering internal motivation for reading. Although Leki emphasizes the importance of such processes for ESL students, her findings are also relevant for other developmental reading students who are often enrolled in our basic writing classes.*

> Reading, like writing, begins in confusion, anxiety and uncertainty . . . it is driven by chance and intuition as well as by deliberate strategy and conscious intent . . . certainty and authority are postures, features of a performance that is achieved through an act of writing, not qualities of vision that precede such a performance. (Bartholomae & Petrosky, 1986, p. 21)

O ver the last ten to twenty years, research in L2 reading and writing has progressed almost entirely independently, yet their findings echo each other. Relying heavily on insights from L1 research and on psycholinguistic studies of reading and composing processes, L2 researchers have made extensive use of miscue, protocol, and think-aloud analyses of the reading and writing of proficient and less skilled L2 readers and writers. As a result of these studies, we have some idea of where L2 readers focus their attention as they try to make sense of a text — to what extent they predict upcoming text and relate it to what they have already read (Carrell, 1983b; Clarke, 1979; Cziko, 1978; Devine, 1988; Hudson, 1982; Rigg, 1977). We also have an idea of what goes on in the minds of experienced and inexperienced L2 writers as they compose — how much they plan, how much they translate from their L1, where they focus their attention, how they handle vocabulary problems (see Krapels, 1990 for an overview of L2 writing research; Arndt, 1987; Cumming, 1989; Hall, 1990; Jones & Tetroe, 1987; Raimes, 1985; Zamel, 1983).

*Throughout her essay, Leki's references to "this volume" pertain to *Reading in the Composition Classroom: Second Language Perspectives,* ed. Joan Carson and Ilona Leki (Boston: Heinle, 1993).

Often (but not always — see Raimes, 1985) these studies reveal that less skilled readers and writers both appear to attend to the same thing, to the text on the page rather than to the meaning potential of that text, to the forms of the letters and words rather than to the overarching connections between them. Inefficient L2 readers read too locally (Cohen et al., 1979), failing to link incoming text with previous text, and because they are unskilled in rapid text processing in L2, depend too heavily on bottom-up strategies to decode or extract the message assumed to exist in the text (Carrell, 1988b; Hosenfeld, 1984; McLaughlin, 1987; Stanovich, 1980).[1] Poor L2 writers focus excessively on word- and sentence-level grammatical and print code concerns (Arndt, 1987; Hatch, Polin, & Part, 1970; Silva, 1990).[2] All of this is to the detriment of meaning. Good readers and writers, on the other hand, are better able to focus on broader concerns related to communication.

Further parallels between cognitive research in reading and in writing indicate that proficient L2 readers and writers use strategies not hierarchically or linearly, but interactively in reading and recursively in writing (Carrell, 1983b; Zamel, 1983). The unifying characteristic of good readers and good writers seems to be flexibility, the ability to use and reuse different strategies as the moment calls for them.

The implications of this research have generally discouraged teachers from our previous focus on subskills of reading and writing, such as grammar and vocabulary, and encouraged us to focus on cognitive strategies that imitate those of proficient L1 readers and writers. Classrooms have turned toward teaching the processes of reading and writing.

Yet, oddly enough, until recently little in the L2 research literature has addressed reading and writing together, and despite the parallels between research findings in these domains and despite commonsense views that reading and writing have a reciprocal effect on each other, including the notion that good writers learn to write well in part by reading a great deal (see, however, Flahive & Bailey, this volume), adult ESL classrooms are only beginning to consider how to effectively integrate both reading and writing. We know that reading builds knowledge of various kinds to use in writing and that writing consolidates knowledge in a way that builds schemata to read with (Bereiter & Scardamalia, 1987; Sternglass, 1988). We also know that, for example, biology professors learn to write articles the way biology professors do by reading articles that biology professors have written. We do not have courses that teach biology professors to write like biology professors. Yet we continue to separate ESL reading courses from ESL writing courses.

This anomaly probably results from several causes. First, reading researchers themselves have urged that reading be taught in its own right and not be thought of as merely a skill in support of other language skills (Grabe, 1986). That is, reading should be thought of as more than merely a prompt for discussion or writing.

Second, writing pedagogy of the 1980s has also made the role of reading material in the ESL classroom unclear. In the past, readings that appeared in ESL writing textbooks were used as model texts; classes analyzed the structure of these texts, and students were instructed to pattern their own writing after those model structures (Raimes, 1986; Reid, this volume). Influenced by process approaches to writing instruction, teachers became reluctant to continue the use of texts as models because of the implication that form pre-exists content, that to write well students needed only to pour their content into the model forms exemplified in the reading passages. The role of reading in the writing classroom became somewhat uncertain. Were readings to be used as source material for student writing, as stimulus for ideas? How were writing teachers to treat those reading texts? Were writing teachers being asked to teach reading at the same time as writing? (See Kroll, this volume, for the argument that L2 writing teachers must also be reading teachers.) No systematic approach or consensus on how to use nonfiction readings in ESL writing classrooms has yet emerged. Up to now, discussion in the literature on using reading in writing classrooms has primarily revolved around making a case for teaching fiction (Gajdusek, 1988; Mlynarczyk, 1992; Spack, 1985).

A third reason functioning to keep reading instruction out of the advanced ESL writing classroom is related to the structure of higher education in this country. Although native English speakers take courses in freshman composition (often without readings in support of writing), reading courses are considered remedial for native students (Bartholomae & Petrosky, 1986) and as a result are typically also unavailable for nonnatives except in language institutes.[3] It is assumed that ESL students at advanced levels are already reading well independently. (See Blanton, this volume, on the error of this view.) After all, these students are reading a great deal in other content-area classes. But difficulty and inefficiency in reading are easily dissimulated. This effort is hidden from us and from our content-area colleagues. While we see and hear about our students' problems in writing, their reading problems may remain invisible, implying no problem exists.

Finally, however problematic, exit exams in writing are quite common in colleges and universities, prompting the development of writing courses to prepare students for them; this is not the case in reading.[4] As a result, we have advanced ESL writing courses but do not typically teach reading beyond the level of language institutes despite the fact that ESL students report a greater need for proficiency in reading than in any other English language skill at the university level (Carrell, 1988a; Christison & Krahnke, 1986).

The unfortunate separation of reading and writing has impoverished instruction in both domains. Without readings in ESL writing classrooms, teachers tend to rely heavily on expressivist writing assignments based on personal experience or previous knowledge (Bazerman, 1980; Horowitz, 1986b; Spack, 1988). While this form of writing is valuable, it is limited and not the type of writing typically required from ESL students in higher education (Horowitz, 1986a; Johns, 1981; Reid, 1987). Reading, a major source of new knowledge, is ignored, and students are not called upon to develop the ability to se-lect and integrate new knowledge with knowledge and information they already possess and with their analyses and reactions to that new knowledge and information. It is this ability to integrate or internalize new information in writing that undergirds the notions both of knowl-edge-transforming (Bereiter and Scardamalia, 1987) and of critical lit-eracy (Flower et al., 1990) and may in fact be what we actually mean when we speak of comprehension of a text.

Writing pedagogy in the 1980s and 1990s has remained fairly closely in line with writing research, having undergone an enormous change in the 1980s, a virtual paradigm shift, as teachers abandoned remedial models of writing instruction and incorporated research insights into the classroom. While L2 reading research has produced insights as far-reaching as those of writing research, its impact on textbooks and class-rooms has been less noticeable (Grabe, 1986). Schema theory and the notion of top-down processing of text did inspire the successful incor-poration of pre-reading activities into many reading classrooms (Ander-son & Pearson, 1984; Carrell & Eisterhold, 1983; Goodman, 1976). But to judge by textbooks and pedagogical articles on reading in the 1980s, researchers' exploration of the notion of the interactive nature of read-ing (Rummelhart, 1977; Stanovich, 1980) has had an almost negligible impact (Grabe, 1986). As a result, the unfortunate effect of teaching reading and writing in separate courses has had dramatic consequences on reading instruction, robbing reading of its natural purpose and ig-noring its social dimensions. The rest of this chapter will explore the implications of this situation, touching on a number of themes that will be taken up again more specifically in the subsequent chapters of this book.

Isolated Reading Classes: Reading for No Real Reason

The research literature in L2 emphasizes the importance of purpose in both writing and reading (Eskey, 1986; Kroll, 1991). In recent writing instruction, purpose for writing has become a central focus. Many class-rooms now include, for example, unevaluated writing journals in which students can freely explore topics of personal interest to them and from which they may select entries to develop into full essays (Blanton, 1987; Spack & Sadow, 1983). Writing on topics selected in this manner goes a long way toward ensuring the kind of internal motivation for writing which presumably results in the commitment to task which, in turn, is thought to help writing and language improve. But the immediate pur-pose for writing about a particular subject is neither language nor even writing improvement. It is, rather, a more natural purpose, i.e., com-munication with a reader about something of personal significance to the writer. The emphasis on publishing student writing grows from the same belief in the importance of purpose; if a piece is to be published, a student has far more reason to feel intellectually committed to the writing, to both the content and form of the text. Finally, the entire thrust of writing instruction within an English for Specific Purposes context rests on the belief that students should learn to write what they will need to write and in the way they will need to write within the academic disciplines they have chosen (Horowitz, 1986a; Reid, 1987).

The literature on reading has also pointed out that readers read for different purposes and that those purposes affect what is attended to and with what intensity (Eskey, 1986). This concern with purpose has emerged in the L2 reading classroom most clearly in pre-reading questions intended to lend direction to reading by giving students something to read for. But this understanding of purpose is extremely narrow. Certainly, having a purpose for reading a text should make that text easier to read, but that avoids the real question: Why is this text being read in the first place? While it is axiomatic that our L2 students learn to read by reading, it appears that in L2 reading classes this axiom has been inappropriately reversed: the reason for reading a text is to learn to read. Yet as Flower et al. (1990) point out,

> Literacy, as Richardson, Vygotsky, and others have defined it, is not synonymous with the ability to read (decode) or write (transcribe) per se. Rather it is a "goal-directed, context-specific" behavior, which means that a literate person is able to use reading and writing in a transactional sense to achieve some purpose in the world at hand. . . . (p. 4)

The failure to provide real purposes for reading suggests that in isolated L2 reading classes (i.e., ones in which students are not reading to write), students are not reading but merely practicing reading. This "reading practice" is evident in reading selections and in pedagogical focuses in L2 reading classrooms.

Text Selection

The reading material used in many ESL reading classes both reveals and furthers the distortion of the reading class into the reading practice class. Since isolated reading classes serve no other purpose than to teach reading, there is no particular reason to read one text rather than another. In line with that reasoning, then, most readings in L2 reading classes are short texts on a variety of topics that are thought to be of high interest to our students: pollution, friendship, language, cultural differences, education, the role of women in various cultures.[5]

Short texts are selected because they conveniently fit into our class periods better than long texts, they take less time to read, and they are thought to be easier to read than longer texts. But short texts are, in fact, likely to be more difficult to read since students never read enough about the subject to build the knowledge about it that would allow them to read with ease and pleasure. (See Sternglass, 1988 on the issue of knowledge building for the purpose of knowledge making.) Like our students, we allow our intuitions to lead us astray — when our students have trouble reading, they slow down and try to decode the text word for word, operating locally, microscopically, and hoping that by simplifying and separating, they will later be able to add up all the pieces and understand. When confronted with students having difficulties reading, we have the same reaction: to break up the reading, go microscopic, and give students shorter, "easier" texts to read (Bartholomae & Petrosky, 1986).

Furthermore, we select a variety of subject matters to maintain student interest and motivation and, ostensibly, to focus attention on content. We hope that by using a shotgun approach to subject matter we will eventually hit upon at least one subject of interest to each of our students. That may or may not happen, but the result of constant shifts in subject matter is once again the same: The texts are harder to read because the students must gear up for a new subject with each reading selection. This approach to reading material also denies our students the eye-opening experience readers have when they return to a text read earlier with new knowledge structures born of reading other texts on the same subject (see Spack, this volume). The original text now literally means something new to the reader; the meaning of sections of text previously blurred by misunderstanding is clarified through the lens of new knowledge. But the possibility for such growth is eliminated by asking students to switch their attention from pollution to animal behavior to education with each new chapter.

Finally, there is the question of high interest. It is possible to argue that the subjects typically covered in ESL readers are of high interest to teachers and textbook writers, but not particularly to L2 students. The topics *might* be of high interest if these students could already read them as easily as *we* read them. But L2 reading is a struggle, and these subjects are unlikely to be of high enough personal interest to our students to compensate for the burden created by asking students to read a hodge-podge of subjects for no particular reason except to learn to read English better. (See Kroll, this volume, for a glimpse into a classroom using such an approach.) This approach to teaching reading resembles writing classes of ten years ago, when teachers struggled to divine what might be interesting, motivating topics for students to write on and came up with such assignments as "Describe your most embarrassing moment." Even if we locate high interest readings, as Bartholomae & Petrosky (1990) maintain, the issue is less what students read (i.e., the discovery of the perfect text) than what they then *do* with what they read, how we ask them to engage that text.

Pedagogical Practices

One source of the problems in isolated reading classes is confusion about what we can accomplish. If we are convinced by evidence that pleasure reading contributes to L2 reading and writing proficiency (Elley & Mangubhai, 1983; Hafiz & Tudor, 1989; Krashen, 1988, 1984; van Naerssen, 1985), one goal of a reading class might be to promote pleasure reading. Unfortunately, this goal is unrealistic; for all but the most proficient of our students, L2 reading is too difficult a chore to be engaged in simply for pleasure (Janopoulos, 1986), and to build proficiency in reading strictly through pleasure reading takes time our ESL students may not have.

Our goal then becomes to attempt to preempt reading difficulties by teaching generic strategies for reading *any* text. Our teaching strategy has been to examine the cognitive processes of proficient readers, those who presumably do read a great deal for pleasure, to isolate the strategies they use, and to teach these strategies to our students. We find that proficient readers do not read all texts in an invariable, plodding pace from word to word, dictionary in hand, as some of our less proficient students do. Instead, they skim some texts or sections of text, they scan, they read in chunks rather than word for word, they note cohesion markers, they guess vocabulary meaning from context, and they read fast (Grabe, 1986). So we direct our students to imitate these behaviors and practice skimming, scanning, guessing, and chunking texts; we tell them not to use dictionaries; we give them practice recognizing cohesion markers; and we push them to read fast (Eskey & Grabe, 1988).

The problem with teaching these cognitive strategies is that even if our students accomplish these goals, they are still not learning reading; they are learning strategies for reading, which can at best be only imitations of reading behaviors, like children turning the pages of books they cannot yet read. We seem to have assumed that these strategies are the causes of proficiency in reading. But these strategies are the *result* not the cause of reading proficiency; good readers read fast because they can. They are able to comprehend incoming text quickly. If our students use dictionaries and read slowly with an even amount of attention to every word, they do this because this is all they *can* do. They do *not* comprehend; they do not know which words are essential to meaning and which may be passed over.[6] If proficient readers skim some texts, they do so because the text, as they themselves judge it for their own internally motivated purposes, merits no more careful reading. The answer to the question of which texts should be skimmed, which scanned, which words looked up in the dictionary, or which texts abandoned altogether is determined by the reader's purpose in reading. If the purpose in reading is only to practice reading, there can be no internally motivated answers to these questions. With no purpose for reading, then skimming, scanning, or any of the other strategies we teach all become no more than artificial exercises. By taking over control of their reading through post-reading exercises and telling our students which texts to skim, which information to scan for, and how fast to read, we are preventing the very grappling with meaning that would allow students to develop their own strategies for rapid and accurate text processing. (See Devine, this volume, for discussion of the interaction between goal setting, or purpose, and metacognition.)

The problems inherent in teaching strategies to improve reading devoid of any true purpose for reading are exacerbated by textbooks that direct students to practice these techniques thoroughly, that is, with every, or nearly every, text in the book. Despite the research findings that good readers read for varying purposes and with varying degrees of attention, isolated reading courses tend in fact to direct students to do the opposite, to regard each reading selection addressed in class as equally important and eligible for similar analysis. Again we see clear parallels with the kinds of discredited writing instruction practices in which every text students write is taken to be a final draft and then corrected and evaluated.

Another nearly universal pedagogical practice in L2 reading classrooms is post-reading comprehension checks, often aimed, like standardized reading tests, at checking comprehension by asking students to identify the main idea of a text or passage. But this enterprise is problematic. First, knowing the main idea of a text does not mean understanding the text. Second, questioning students about the main idea does absolutely nothing to *show* students how to achieve comprehension, whether or not they can successfully spot the same main idea we spot. Finally, pointing out that our students' version of the main idea is or is not the same as ours, far from helping our students achieve understanding, does not even help our students identify the main idea! It is not clear that we even know exactly how we determine what the main idea of a text is. (See Parry, 1987 for an interesting discussion of factors that may have influenced a group of West African students in their construction of the meaning of a text.) If we do not know how we ourselves recognize the main idea of a text, we cannot teach it to our students and end by merely mystifying them. Yet there seems to be almost an obsession with main ideas in reading pedagogy and testing that is reminiscent of the previous exaggerated interest in topic sentences in writing and that represents a reductionist view of reading. By relying so heavily and confidently on comprehension and main idea questions, we seem to be defining — and encourage our students to define — text comprehension as correct responses to comprehension questions. Yet, many would argue that

> the only way to demonstrate comprehension is through extended discourse where readers become writers who articulate their understandings of and connections to the text in their responses. Response is, then, an expression and explanation of comprehension; and comprehension means using writing to explicate the connections between our models of reality — our prior knowledge — and the texts we recreate in light of them. (Petrosky, 1982, pp. 24–25, discussing David Bleich)

Typical comprehension checks also imply that the meaning of a text resides in the text and that the students' goal is to ferret out the meaning the author put there. This implication is out of tune with the notions, so pervasive in current reading research, of reading as the construction, not the deciphering, of meaning and of reading as interaction between reader and text, in which meaning depends as much on what the reader brings to the text as what the text brings to the reader. The usual comprehension check denies the role of the reader in constructing meaning. Yet Tierney & Pearson (1983) assert that "there is no meaning on the page until a reader decides there is" (p. 569).

Furthermore, exactly what do our students gain by correctly identifying the main idea in an ESL textbook article on dreams or friendship? What difference does it make if the student correctly or incorrectly identifies the same main idea as the teacher? In natural reading contexts, proficient and even less skilled readers reading for a real-world purpose not only skim, scan, or chunk for their own purposes, but they also choose to privilege either main ideas or details of a text, again depending on their purpose in reading. In a given text read by a specific reader in a real-world context, the main idea may or may not be significant. The reader may retain only a striking image or line of reasoning, or even, as is often the case with academic readers, only a citation or reference to another text. But if the purpose for reading a text is to practice reading, then students have no basis on which to privilege main ideas or details. By persistently imposing a check for comprehension of main ideas, we may in fact be training our students to read in ways characteristic of poor readers, bound to the text and lacking the purpose that would allow them to skip over information they themselves judge uninteresting or unnecessary.

Thus on one hand, a leveling process takes place such that all the texts read are given equal attention and therefore equal weight, and on the other hand, a selection process occurs whereby someone besides the reader decides what should be salient to the reader. If that which resonates for the student does not match the main idea of the text, the importance of the student's encounter with the text is undermined and the student's reading is dismissed as a failure to understand.

Attempting to Teach What Cannot Be Taught

Perhaps one difficulty with the entire enterprise of teaching the construction of meaning, whether in reading or in writing, is that although it can be learned, in some important, very real sense, it cannot be taught (see Eskey, 1986). Perhaps we are unwilling to believe this. Perhaps it is because we feel we need to teach *something* in isolated reading classes that we have typically turned to teaching not reading, not text comprehension or meaning construction, but reading strategies and study skills.

One of the complaints in the early 1980s against traditional approaches to teaching L2 writing was that students were not really writing but rather manipulating language, not using language to communicate but rather to practice grammar or to practice larger components of written texts, such as rhetorical patterns (Kroll, 1991). In traditional approaches to teaching writing, we assumed that by teaching students to write a topic sentence, to select and explain three examples, and to write a conclusion, we had given students all the building blocks necessary to create virtually any expository text (Kroll, 1991).

Don't we see the same kinds of narrowly focused aims in current traditional reading courses, aims of learning vocabulary by studying prefixing and suffixing, aims of identifying main idea and supporting details, aims of recognizing discourse features? Certainly, the ability to recognize discourse features and a large number of vocabulary items helps make reading easier, but if these abilities are set as the goals for the course rather than as a means of facilitating the reading of specific texts selected for a real purpose, we are back to teaching skills. More sophisticated ones, to be sure, but for all their sophistication, they still do not get to the heart of the question of how to help L2 students read.

Ironically, it may be that both proficient and less skilled L2 readers already have and can make use of the entire gamut of skills that we teach in reading classes but use these skills to different degrees in L2 reading (Sarig, 1987). L2 reading classes may not even *need* to teach skills, which L2 readers may already possess, but could provide the opportunity for L2 readers to discover *through meaningful contact with L2 texts* which combination of skills works best for them in L2.

In the 1980s, we recognized that if the purpose of writing in a writing class is to practice writing in order to get ready for "real" assignments, students were being seriously handicapped in the development of their ability to decide what to write and how to write it. As long as reading classes have no other purpose than to develop skills, to practice reading, or to learn language, attempts to get students to read with real direction are similarly doomed. The reading class becomes a hothouse, self-referential and solipsistic, in which students spend all their time rehearsing and never performing, getting ready to read while real reading is deferred. (See Blanton, this volume, on reading as performance.) When we teach a reading or writing course as a skills course, we act as though real reading and writing will come later, once our students know where to look for the main idea of a text or how to write a topic sentence. But it makes no sense to defer real reading and writing until students are adequately prepared, because adequate preparation is itself a result of a purposeful plunge into the struggle with meaning.

Reading researchers, paralleling writing researchers, have for years indicated that reading instruction must be more concerned with meaning and less with skills. For over twenty years in the literature on teaching reading to native speakers, researchers have been calling for a focus on meaning (Goodman, 1976; Smith, 1971); for ten years in the L2 literature (Carrell, 1983a; Hudson, 1982), researchers have emphasized the importance of text content over reading skills. Yet as lately as the December 1989 *TESOL Quarterly*, Carrell, Pharis, & Liberto must again call for approaches to teaching reading, including semantic mapping and ETR, which will aid students not in developing skills and strategies with which to confront *any* text, but in comprehending specific texts.[7] Hudson (1991) makes a similar plea for ESL reading. Isolated L2 reading classes seem to have allowed us to get lost in details, not of decoding skills as in the past, but of main idea hunting and learning word suffixes and prefixes, and to lose sight of reading as a purposeful, real-world activity.

The benefits of integrating L2 reading and writing in the same classroom thus seem undeniable and, since reading and writing draw upon the same cognitive text world (Carson, this volume; Kucer, 1985), reciprocal. The chapters of this book detail the ways in which reading in the composition classroom sustains writing.

But writing, even beyond providing a purpose for reading, clearly also enhances reading. Anticipating in writing the content of a text, i.e., writing before reading (Spack, 1990), primes schemata and thereby facilitates reading a text. Interacting with the content of a text by annotating and engaging the text in dialogue brings home more clearly the reader's own understanding of the text, for it is often through the pressure of new or opposing ideas that our own ideas may become clear to us, just as it is often by expressing the ideas of others in our own words (in effect, translating them), that these other or new ideas begin to have meaning. Writing is a way of reading better "because it requires the learner to reconstruct the structure and meaning of ideas expressed by another writer. To possess an idea that one is reading about requires competence in regenerating the idea, competence in learning how to write the ideas of another" (Squire, 1983, cited in Sternglass, 1986, p. 2). (See Zamel, 1992, for a further discussion of writing to read.) Furthermore, as a student engages a reading text by responding or reacting to it in writing, in effect communicating with the writer through text, the essentially social nature of literacy becomes unmistakable.

Social Acts of Reading and Writing

Research on cognitive processes has had tremendous influence on reading and writing theory, on writing pedagogy, and to some degree on reading classroom practice. But writing classrooms have counterbalanced this emphasis on cognitive processes with an awareness of the social dimension of writing. Writing classrooms have, for example, been much concerned with audience, the discourse communities into which we hope to initiate our students as writers. The recognition of the social dimension of writing has also become commonplace in writing classrooms in the form of peer responding, which has helped to break down the isolation of the individual author and to work against the very notion of individual authorship (Allaei & Connor, 1990; Leki, 1990b; Mittan, 1989).

Like writing, reading is not only a cognitive process. It is intricately bound up in a social, historical, and cultural network, one we are only beginning to explore (Carson, 1992). As readers, we are members of discourse communities formed primarily through reading the same texts. It is this broad social dimension of reading that allows us teachers and textbook writers to agree on the main idea of a text, for example, and to make assertions about textual misinterpretations we think our students make. If we agree on the main idea of a text, it is not because the main idea mechanically signals itself in the text (it is obviously not always the last sentence of the introduction or the first sentence of some fixed paragraph), but because we share the writer's discourse community. An important key to helping our students read better may also lie in clearer classroom recognition of this social dimension of reading.

But reading is also an essentially social activity in the more immediate sense that the text is where a specific reader and writer meet. Reader response theory describes text as the locus of struggle over meaning, suggesting the importance not of the text (where meaning does *not* reside) but of the encounter between individual human beings mediated through the text (Dasenbrock, 1991; Fish, 1980; Nystrand, 1989; Robinson, 1991; Rubin, 1988). L2 reading research, particularly in an interactive view of reading, also does not locate meaning in the text and has shown us repeatedly that the meaning of a given text depends on who is reading it (Anderson et al., 1977; Carrell, 1983a; Parry, 1987; Steffenson & Joag-Dev, 1984). Each reader's reading of a text is somewhat different. Different readings are created not only by different readers but also over time. Thus the Shakespeare we read today is not and cannot be the same work that people read in Shakespeare's time. (See Dasenbrock, 1991 for the L1 debate about the ontological status of historical texts.) In fact, we count on that very fluidity of meaning over time when we advise students to leave a draft aside for a few days before rereading it for revision.

Yet despite this recognition of the instability of meaning, we often seem to entertain only in theory the idea that meaning does not reside in the text. In practice, our insistent privileging of cognitive strategies betrays our view of the text as a puzzle. If meaning did reside in the text, then well-honed cognitive strategies would be sufficient to unravel meaning. But a text is not a puzzle or a dictator; it is a partner in a dialogue, in a negotiation. Yet little is done to give students practice in negotiating meaning mediated by text or to foster the notion that meaning is created by the interaction of a specific reader and a text. In our reading classes a single, privileged interpretation of a text dominates, as is made clear by post-reading comprehension checks with their predetermined answers, ones that the teacher knows and the students must guess.

Ironically, this cognitive bias may be increased by reading theory's current view of reading as interactive, locating meaning in the interaction between the reader and the text, but with no clear role for the writer. The interactive view does, however, leave room for a social dimension in terms of the individual reader's formation as a social being. Schema theory, on which interactive views of reading are based, clearly views schema formation as the result of individual experience *within* a social context. (See, for instance, Anderson et al., 1977; Flynn, 1983; Kintsch & Greene, 1978; and Steffenson & Joag-Dev, 1984 for descriptions of different stances taken before texts by different genders and sociocultural groups.)

Nevertheless, we seem consistently to ignore the social dimension of reading. The usual practice in our reading classrooms, for example, has worked against the idea of the classroom as an interpretive community and instead often sends our students home to read, alone, already published texts, by authors they do not know, writing about settings with which they are not familiar. Significantly, it is only when they return to class that they learn, from the teacher, how well their personal struggle with the text went. Certainly, the struggle with meaning is internal, and cognitive, but this struggle can also be made external, public, and social. By so doing, we can balance the action of individual cognition with the power of social interaction to shape and restructure meaning.

On the Brink of a Change: The Transactional Reading/Writing Classroom

While the attitudes and activities described above persist in reading classes, we seem now to be on the brink of a shift in reading pedagogy similar to the one that occurred in writing over the last ten years and at least partly occasioned by the growing interest, of which this volume is evidence, in bringing reading systematically into writing classrooms. If we use reading and writing reciprocally in L2 classrooms, focusing less on teaching language, reading, or writing and more on allowing students to engage intellectually with text, this engagement with text fosters a view of reading and writing as active construction of meaning. The text can now legitimately be read with varying degrees of attention since the text has peaks and valleys of importance for the reader; comprehension of each section of the text is no longer necessary; the significance of main ideas and details becomes clearer as the student determines which ones further his or her purposes; structures of knowledge are built that can be used to read/write other texts on the same subject; and the student reader/writer must come to terms with the transformation of old knowledge and incorporation of new knowledge into existing schemata (Bereiter & Scardamalia, 1987). Most importantly, teaching reading in the composition classroom no longer defers real reading until the future; reading is done for present, legitimate purposes.

Reading in composition classrooms may also give reading a social dimension that we have ignored by operating as though reading can only be individual and by directing our students to read at home alone and then answer questions about the text. Our students' facility in reading need not improve only through reading published texts. By reading each other's texts in a reading/writing class, students directly confront the elusive, slippery nature of meaning. A writer intends a meaning; a reader perceives something else. When the reader and writer are face to face (especially with the support of a teacher's expert guidance), a real negotiation over meaning can take place.

If we are convinced by an interactive view of reading, we need to permit and encourage our students to become more active in reading — not merely to be led by the text, but to make it their own by responding to whatever is salient *to them* rather than merely pursuing the writer's meaning. This means that for some texts, the author's main idea may be entirely irrelevant to the reader's purpose and will play no role in the reader's use of the text. In this way we might see the metaphor of interactive as extending beyond its cognitive dimension, i.e., beyond the idea that both top-down and bottom-up strategies interact in reading. In a reading/writing class, interactive takes on a transactional meaning, implying an essential interface of reading and writing (Sternglass, 1986), by which we understand (1) that reading and writing interact, or function reciprocally; (2) that the reader can interact more actively with the text by viewing reading as dialogic and by writing to the text (responding to it, for example, with notes in the margin or in a reading journal); and (3) that in reading, the reader is also interacting with a writer who wrote for genuine purposes of communication.

In many writing classrooms these days, students read each other's writing and respond to it to help the writer improve that draft. In a reading/writing classroom, this activity can take on a new role, not only the one of various kinds of text repair or editing but of students using each other's writing as sources for their own writing, considering and addressing their classmates' points of view, and citing each other, not only published work, in their bibliographies.

Even with published texts, by reading them together in groups and interpreting as they go, students witness competing meanings and clarify their own understandings through discussion, debate, and the need to translate their understandings into their own words. By ultimately forming joint interpretations of their readings rather than learning from the teacher what the meaning of a text is, students experience the social dimension inherent in communicating through a text, a dimension too long neglected in ESL reading instruction. By making reading social, we externalize the process and demonstrate, or allow students to demonstrate to each other, that reading is meaning construction, that competing meanings are generated by texts read by different people or even by the same people at different times. (See Section III of this volume, on Social Perspectives, for further examples of ESL reading instruction that aims at these goals.)

The notion of meaning as negotiation and text as the locus of struggle suggests another insight that current views on writing may have to offer reading specialists. In post-reading comprehension questions, reading classrooms maintain an emphasis on error that many writing classrooms have chosen to downplay. Writing research has emphasized the futility and the negative, stifling effect of marking all the errors L2 students make in writing (Leki, 1990a; Zamel, 1985). As writing specialists tried to come to terms with the problem of errors in L2 students' writing, it became increasingly clear that it makes more sense to focus on what students can do well, rather than constantly reminding them of what they know they cannot do well, and to intervene in their writing process to help them do what they cannot do. In many writing classes these days, students show their drafts to others, including the teacher, as the drafts are developing in order to get guidance and feedback on their writing. Most writing teachers are convinced of the value of that kind of intervention. How might such an attitude be adopted in reading instruction in order to promote the goals of helping L2 students learn to read with ease, pleasure, and understanding? How can we intervene in our students' reading processes?

In a first step, again by analogy to procedures in writing classes in which teachers refuse to appropriate their students' writing, reading teachers might consider refraining from appropriating the meaning of the texts their students read. In other words, in helping students read, the question should not be "What is the author saying here? What is the author's main idea?" but rather "What did you get out of this? What do you make of this part? How does it happen that different class members understand this text differently?" While students lose little by not getting the main idea of an ESL reading passage about dreams or animal behavior, they gain a great deal if they are able to make some portion of that text their own, linguistically, rhetorically, or conceptually.

A de-emphasis of error also implies our acceptance of the idea that our students cannot understand everything they read and that they do not need to. They need to read actively and selectively, picking out what they can use to advance their own agendas. Furthermore, since any individual act of understanding is a reconstruction and in that sense necessarily a misreading (see Bartholomae, 1986), we must also accept that our students will not interpret texts the same way we do.[8] But negotiating through their understandings of a text with other students requires the struggle with meaning that leads to the ability to engage in constructing meaning with power and confidence.

We can also make our struggle with meaning visible by letting students see our reading processes. Many writing teachers write with their students and share their drafts to demonstrate their writing processes (Spack, 1984). In teaching reading we might consider doing more reading out loud in our classes and doing so in a way that demonstrates our reading processes, thinking aloud as we read, as subjects are asked to do in protocol analyses (Davey, 1983). Rather than only giving individual students individual exercises in chunking, we might show them by reading out loud how we ourselves chunk groups of words together, how we use intonation to gets us through heavy embedding, how we backtrack when we have lost the thread of the text, how we ignore incongruities or puzzling words for as long as possible before interrupting the flow of our reading, and, most importantly, how we work to tie the incoming text to patterns of information we already know. To help our students read faster, instead of timing them and pushing them to read faster individually, by reading out loud we keep them to a brisker pace than they might normally adopt when reading silently, and yet through intonation, pauses, and backtracking we also give them additional cues on how we are interpreting a text. By the same token, like writing conferences, reading conferences in which individual students reveal and demonstrate their reading processes to us may also uncover unproductive or self-defeating approaches to reading and allow us to intervene directly in the students' construction of meaning from a text.

Conclusion

While the research findings in reading and writing echo each other, teaching practices have not kept pace with each other, especially not in helping advanced ESL students read. The separation of reading from writing may be the result of our natural inclination to divide things up in order to deal with them, or it may be that the inclination to divide language up is a legacy of the ALM days, but, as this volume demonstrates, the time seems to have come for a new reintegration of reading and writing classrooms rather than a division of language into atomized, learnable bits or skills. The fact that reading and writing processes can be isolated does not mean that teaching those isolated processes is the best way to help our students read and write with greater ease. The construction of meaning, whether through reading or writing, is a messy, organic, and holistic task, perhaps less amenable to generic attempts to preempt problems than we once thought. Bringing the world of text together in one classroom gives every promise of enhancing our ESL students' ability to both read and write English through the cross-fertilization of reading and writing pedagogy, research, and theory.

Notes

1. Evidence from studies of inefficient L1 readers also shows the opposite tendency, excessive and inaccurate guessing about the meaning of a text without enough bottom-up information (Kimmel & MacGinitie, 1984).
2. The picture is actually more complex than this. L1 studies consistently show this pattern of allotting attention (Bereiter & Scardamalia, 1987; Perl, 1979), but at least one L2 study shows that even less-proficient writers also attend to meaning (Raimes, 1985).
3. Among the odd historical divisions within higher education in this country, we might also mention the division in English departments between literature and writing instruction, in certain ways analogous to the division between writing and reading courses: the first in each pair considered more prestigious and more appropriately a concern of higher education.
4. This is not to suggest in any way that there should be exit exams in reading. The wisdom of exit exams in writing is already questionable enough.
5. ESP, adjunct, and sheltered writing courses are the exceptions to this pattern.
6. In the same way, excessive attention to details in inexperienced writers is the symptom, not the cause, of difficulty with the task.
7. These techniques have been used for some time to teach reading to native

English-speaking children. For more information on these techniques, see Heimlich & Pittelman (1986), Stahl & Vancil (1986), and Au (1979).

8. It is interesting to note that in certain domains, such as in reading literature, idiosyncratic readings are often prized as more illuminating than pedestrian interpretations of a text. What we admire in the best literary critics and the best scientists is not that they understand texts well but that they extend our understanding of the meaning of a text by moving beyond the standard interpretation rendered by the discourse community for which it is intended.

Works Cited

Allaei, S.K. & Connor, U.M. (1990). Exploring the dynamics of cross-cultural collaboration in writing classrooms. *The Writing Instructor, 10,* 19–28.

Anderson, R.C. & Pearson, P.D. (1984). A schema-theoretic view of basic processes in reading comprehension. In P.D. Pearson (Ed.), *Handbook of reading research* (pp. 255–287). New York: Longman.

Anderson, R.C., Reynolds, R.E., Schallert, D.L., & Goetz, E.T. (1977). Frameworks for comprehending discourse. *American Educational Research Journal, 14,* 367–381.

Arndt, V. (1987). Six writers in search of texts: A protocol-based study of L1 and L2 writing. *ELT Journal, 41,* 257–267.

Au, K. H.-P. (1979). Using the experience-text-relationship method with minority children. *The Reading Teacher, 32,* 677–679.

Bartholomae, D. (1986). Wanderings: Misreadings, miswritings, misunderstandings. In T. Newkirk (Ed.), *Only connect: Uniting reading and writing* (pp. 89–118). Upper Montclair, NJ: Boynton/Cook.

Bartholomae, D. & Petrosky, A. (1990). *Ways of reading.* New York: Bedford/St. Martin's.

Bartholomae, D. & Petrosky, A. (1986). *Facts, artifacts, and counterfacts: A reading and writing course.* Upper Montclair, NJ: Boynton/Cook.

Bazerman, C. (1980). A relationship between reading and writing: The conversational model. *College English, 41,* 656–661.

Bereiter, C. & Scardamalia, M. (1987). *The psychology of written composition.* Hillsdale, NJ: Erlbaum.

Blanton, L. (1987). Reshaping students' perceptions of writing. *ELT Journal, 41,* 112–118.

Carrell, P.L. (1988a). Introduction. In P.L. Carrell, J. Devine, & D. Eskey (Eds.), *Interactive approaches to second language reading* (pp. 1–7). New York: Cambridge University Press.

Carrell, P.L. (1988b). Some causes of text-boundedness and schema interference in ESL reading. In P.L. Carrell, J. Devine, & D. Eskey (Eds.), *Interactive approaches to second language reading* (pp. 101–113). New York: Cambridge University Press.

Carrell, P.L. (1983a). Some issues in studying the role of schemata, or background knowledge, in L2 comprehension. *Reading in a Foreign Language, 1,* 81–92.

Carrell, P.L. (1983b). Three components of background knowledge in reading comprehension. *Language Learning, 33,* 183–205.

Carrell, P.L., Devine, J., & Eskey, D. E. (Eds.). (1988). *Interactive approaches to second language reading.* New York: Cambridge University Press.

Carrell, P.L. & Eisterhold, J.C. (1983). Schema theory and ESL reading pedagogy. *TESOL Quarterly, 17,* 553–573.

Carrell, P.L., Pharis, B.G., & Liberto, J.C. (1989). Metacognitive training for ESL reading. *TESOL Quarterly, 23*, 657–678.

Carson, J.G. (1992). Becoming biliterate: First language influences. *Journal of Second Language Writing, 1*, 53–76.

Christison, M.A. & Krahnke, K. (1986). Student perceptions of academic language study. *TESOL Quarterly, 20*, 61–81.

Clarke, M. (1979). Reading in English and Spanish: Evidence from adult ESL students. *Language Learning, 29*, 121–150.

Cohen, A., Glasman, H., Rosenbaum-Cohen, P.R., Ferrara, J., & Fine, J. (1979). Reading for specialized purposes: Discourse analysis and the use of student informants. *TESOL Quarterly, 13*, 551–564.

Cumming, A. (1989). Writing expertise and second language proficiency. *Language Learning, 39*, 83–141.

Cziko, G. (1978). Differences in first- and second-language reading: The use of syntactic, semantic and discourse constraints. *Canadian Modern Language Journal, 34*, 473–489.

Dasenbrock, R.W. (1991). Do we write the text we read? *College English, 53*, 7–18.

Davey, B. (1983). Think-aloud: Modeling the cognitive processes of reading comprehension. *Journal of Reading, 27*, 219–224.

Devine J. (1988). A case study of two readers: Models of reading and reading performance. In P. Carrell, J. Devine, & D. Eskey (Eds.), *Interactive approaches to second language reading* (pp. 127–139). New York: Cambridge University Press.

Devine, J., Carrell, P.L., & Eskey, D.E. (Eds.). (1987). *Research in reading in English as a second language*. Washington, DC: TESOL.

Dubin, F., Eskey, D.E., & Grabe, W. (Eds.). (1986). *Teaching second language reading for academic purposes*. Reading, MA: Addison-Wesley.

Elley, W.B. & Mangubhai, F. (1983). The effect of reading on second language learning. *Reading Research Quarterly, 19*, 53–67.

Eskey, D.E. (1986). Theoretical foundations. In F. Dubin, D.E. Eskey, & W. Grabe (Eds.), *Teaching second language reading for academic purposes* (pp. 3–21). Reading, MA: Addison-Wesley.

Eskey, D.E. & Grabe, W. (1988). Interactive models of second language reading: Perspectives on instruction. In P.L. Carrell, J. Devine, and D. Eskey (Eds.), *Interactive approaches to second language reading* (pp. 223–238). New York: Cambridge University Press.

Fish, S. (1980). *Is there a text in this class? The authority of interpretive communities*. Cambridge: Harvard University Press.

Flower, L., Stein, V., Ackerman, J., Kantz, M.J., McCormick, K., & Peck, W.C. (1990). *Reading to write: Exploring a cognitive and social process*. New York: Oxford University Press.

Flynn, E.A. (1983). Gender and reading. *College English, 45*, 236–253.

Gajdusek, L. (1988). Toward wider use of literature in ESL: Why and how. *TESOL Quarterly, 22*, 227–257.

Goodman, K. (1976). Reading: A psycholinguistic guessing game. In H. Singer & R. Ruddell (Eds.), *Theoretical models and processes of reading* (2nd ed.) (pp. 497–505). Newark, DE: International Reading Association.

Grabe, W. (1986). The transition from theory to practice in teaching reading. In F. Dubin, D.E. Eskey, & W. Grabe (Eds.), *Teaching second language reading for academic purposes* (pp. 25–48). Reading, MA: Addison-Wesley.

Hafiz, F.M. & Tudor, I. (1989). Extensive reading and the development of language skills. *ELT Journal, 43*, 1–13.

Hall, C. (1990). Managing the complexity of revising across languages. *TESOL Quarterly, 24*, 43–60.

Hatch, E., Polin, P., & Part, S. (1970). Acoustic scanning or syntactic processing. Paper presented at the meeting of the Western Psychological Association, San Francisco.

Heimlich, J.E. & Pittelman, S.D. (1986). *Semantic mapping: Classroom applications.* Newark, DE: International Reading Association.

Horowitz, D. (1986a). Essay examination prompts and the teaching of academic writing. *English for Specific Purposes, 5*, 107–120.

Horowitz, D. (1986b). Process, not product: Less than meets the eye. *TESOL Quarterly, 20*, 141–144.

Hosenfeld, C. (1984). Case studies of ninth grade readers. In J.C. Alderson & A.H. Urquhart (Eds.), *Reading in a foreign language* (pp. 231–244). New York: Longman.

Hudson, T. (1991). A content comprehension approach to reading English for science and technology. *TESOL Quarterly, 24(1)*, 77–104.

Hudson, T. (1982). The effect of induced schemata on the "shortcircuit" in L2 reading: Non-decoding factors in L2 reading performance. *Language Learning, 32*, 1–31.

Janopoulos, M. (1986). The relationship of pleasure of reading and second language writing proficiency. *TESOL Quarterly, 20*, 763–768.

Johns, A. (1981). Necessary English: A faculty survey. *TESOL Quarterly, 15*, 51–57.

Johnson, D.M. & Roen, D.H. (Eds.). (1989). *Richness in writing: Empowering ESL students.* New York: Longman.

Jones, S. & Tetroe, J. (1987). Composing in a second language. In A. Matsuhashi (Ed.), *Writing in real time* (pp. 34–57). New York: Longman.

Kimmel, S. & MacGinitie, W.H. (1984). Identifying children who use a preservative text processing strategy. *Reading Research Quarterly, 19*, 162–172.

Kintsch, W. & Greene, E. (1978). The role of culture-specific schemata in the comprehension and recall of stories. *Discourse Processes, 1*, 1–13.

Krapels, A. (1990). An overview of second language writing process research. In B. Kroll (Ed.), *Second language writing* (pp. 37–56). New York: Cambridge University Press.

Krashen, S.D. (1988). Do we learn to read by reading? The relationship between free reading and reading ability. In D. Tannen (Ed.), *Linguistics in context: Connecting observation and understanding* (pp. 269–298). Norwood, NJ: Ablex.

Krashen, S.D. (1984). *Writing: Research, theory, and applications.* Oxford: Pergamon.

Kroll, B. (1991). Teaching writing in the ESL context. In M. Celce-Murcia (Ed.), *Teaching English as a second or foreign language* (2nd ed.) (pp. 245–263). New York: Newbury House.

Kroll, B. (Ed.). (1990). *Second language writing.* New York: Cambridge University Press.

Kucer, S. (1985). The making of meaning: Reading and writing as processes. *Written Communication, 2*, 317–336.

Leki, I. (1990a). Coaching from the margins: Issues in written response. In B. Kroll (Ed.), *Second language writing* (pp. 57–68). New York: Cambridge University Press.

Leki, I. (1990b). Potential problems with peer responding in ESL writing classes. *CATESOL Journal, 3*, 5–19.

McLaughlin, B. (1987). Reading in a second language: Studies of adult and child learners. In S.R. Goldman & H.T. Trueba (Eds.), *Becoming literate in English as a second language* (pp. 57–70). Norwood, NJ: Ablex.

Mittan, R. (1989). The peer review process: Harnessing students' communicative power. In D.M. Johnson & D.H. Roen (Eds.), *Richness in writing: Empowering ESL students* (pp. 207–219). New York: Longman.

Mlynarczyk, R. (1992). Student choice: An alternative to teacher-selected reading material. *College ESL, 1*(2), 1–8.

Nystrand, M. (1989). A social-interactive model of writing. *Written Communication, 6*, 66–85.

Parry, K.J. (1987). Reading in a second culture. In J. Devine, P.L. Carrell, & D.E. Eskey (Eds.), *Research in reading in English as a second language* (pp. 59–70). Washington, DC: TESOL.

Perl, S. (1979). The composing processes of unskilled college writers. *Research in the Teaching of English, 13*, 317–336.

Petrosky, A. (1982). From story to essay: Reading and writing. *College Composition and Communication, 33*, 19–37.

Radecki, P.M. & Swales, J.M. (1988). ESL students' reaction to written comments on their written work. *System, 16*, 355–365.

Raimes, A. (1986). Teaching ESL writing: Fitting what we do to what we know. *The Writing Instructor, 5*, 153–166.

Raimes, A. (1985). What unskilled writers do as they write: A classroom study. *TESOL Quarterly, 19*, 229–258.

Reid, J. (1987). ESL Composition: The expectations of the academic audience. *TESOL Newsletter, 21*, 34.

Rigg, P. (1977). The miscue-ESL project. In H.D. Brown, C.A. Yorio, & R.H. Crymes (Eds.), *Teaching and learning ESL: Trends in research and practice. On TESOL '77* (pp. 106–118). Washington, DC: TESOL.

Robinson, D. (1991). Henry James and euphemism. *College English, 53*, 403–427.

Rubin, D.L. (1988). Introduction: Four dimensions of social construction in written communication. In B.A. Rafoth and D.L. Rubin (Eds.), *The social construction of written communication* (pp. 1–33). Norwood, NJ: Ablex.

Rummelhart, D. (1977). Toward an interactive model of reading. In S. Dornic (Ed.), *Attention and performance*, vol. 6 (pp. 573–603). New York: Academic Press.

Sarig, G. (1987). High-level reading and the first and foreign language: Some comparative process data. In J. Devine, P.L. Carrell, & D.E. Eskey (Eds.), *Research in reading in English as a second language* (pp. 105–120). Washington, DC: TESOL.

Silva, T. (1990). ESL composition instruction: Developments, issues and directions. In B. Kroll (Ed.), *Second language writing* (pp. 11–23). New York: Cambridge University Press.

Smith, F. (1971). *Understanding reading: A psycholinguistic analysis of reading and learning to read*, 1st ed. New York: Holt, Rinehart, and Winston.

Spack, R. (1990). *Guidelines: A cross-cultural reading/writing text*. New York: St. Martin's.

Spack, R. (1988). Initiating ESL students into the academic discourse community: How far should we go? *TESOL Quarterly, 22*, 29–51.

Spack, R. (1985). Literature, reading, writing, and ESL: Bridging the gaps. *TESOL Quarterly, 19*, 703–726.

Spack, R. (1984). Invention strategies and the ESL college composition student. *TESOL Quarterly, 18*, 649–670.

Spack, R. & Sadow, C. (1983). Student-teacher working journals in ESL freshman composition. *TESOL Quarterly, 17*, 575–594.

Stahl, S.A. & Vancil, S.J. (1986). Discussion is what makes semantic maps work in vocabulary instruction. *The Reading Teacher, 40*, 62–67.

Stanovich, K.E. (1980). Toward an interactive-compensatory model of individual differences in the development of reading fluency. *Reading Research Quarterly, 16*, 32–71.

Steffensen, M.S. & Joag-Dev, C. (1984). Cultural knowledge and reading. In J.C. Alderson & A.H. Urquhart (Eds.), *Reading in a foreign language* (pp. 48–61). New York: Longman.

Sternglass, M. (1988). *The presence of thought: Introspective accounts of reading and writing.* Norwood, NJ: Ablex.

Sternglass, M. (1986). Introduction. In B. Petersen (Ed.), *Convergences: Transactions in reading and writing* (pp. 1–11). Urbana, IL: NCTE.

Tierney, R.J. & Pearson, P.D. (1983). Toward a composing model of reading. *Language Arts, 60*, 568–569.

Van Naerssen, M. (1985). Relaxed reading in ESP. *TESOL Newsletter, 19*, 2.

Zamel, V. (1992). Writing one's way into reading. *TESOL Quarterly, 26*, 463–485.

Zamel, V. (1985). Responding to student writing. *TESOL Quarterly, 19*, 79–101.

Zamel, V. (1983). The composing processes of advanced ESL students: Six case studies. *TESOL Quarterly, 17*, 165–187.

Classroom Activities

One of the most critical "reciprocal themes" that Leki draws from ESL reading and writing is the social nature of these processes and the importance of small-group work for reading as well as for writing. As she suggests, "By making reading social, we externalize the process and demonstrate, or allow students to demonstrate to each other, that reading is meaning construction, that competing meanings are generated by texts read by different people or even by the same people at different times." With this in mind, invite students to read and interpret together a text that they choose as a group (perhaps a reading from a newspaper, a textbook, or a section from a longer book). Students can develop their own purposes for reading this text together (to gain inspiration for writing a paper, perhaps, or to develop their understanding of a current event or other relevant topic), and then work together on reaching their own interpretations of the text ("making meaning"). If students already collaborate in peer response groups for writing, it would be helpful for them to note the similarities and differences in working in peer response groups for reading as well.

You can also foster students' involvement in text by having them read their peers' work. Leki points out, "By reading each other's texts in a reading/writing class, students directly confront the elusive, slippery nature of meaning. [. . .] When a reader and writer are face to face (especially with the support of a teacher's expert guidance), a real negotiation can take place." You may want to go a step beyond peer response and ask students to use each other's writing as source material for their own essays (making sure to use proper citation, of course). When students respond to and build on each other's ideas, they will better understand the concept of reading and writing as a purposeful means of communication between a writer and an audience.

Thinking about Teaching

Leki notes that many teachers already share their writing processes with students and suggests that a similar strategy would be appropriate for demonstrating reading processes. If you decide to engage in this activity, keep track of your own reading processes in your teaching journal. What do you notice about yourself as a reader? How do you create meaning from words on the page? Then demonstrate your reading processes to students by reading aloud to the class. Provide them with a copy of the text or project it onto a screen using a computer or an overhead projector. Think aloud as you read, and give students the opportunity to take notes on the processes you use to construct meaning from the text. Then have students read to each other and think aloud in pairs, taking notes on one another's processes. Students can share these notes with each other, and then share their work in a whole-class discussion that emphasizes the importance of reading purposefully and of making meaning from language in order to engage their own internal motivations for reading.

5

Approaches to Grammar Instruction

Teaching grammar remains a contentious issue in many college and university English departments. Though a number of studies have addressed the question of whether grammar instruction leads to improved writing, there has been little consensus, and teachers of composition still find themselves embroiled in debate as they define their programs and plan their courses. The debate is particularly relevant to the teaching of developmental writers, who some argue suffer simply from a lack of foundation in grammar, usage, and mechanics. The writers in this chapter acknowledge the politicization of the issue. They move, however, to a middle ground: Grammar instruction should be an effective transfer of the rules to students' own writing; in this way, students become more aware of their options as writers. "Practice of forms improves usage," Janice Neuleib and Irene Brosnahan suggest, citing Henry Meckel, "whereas memorization of the rules does not." Rei R. Noguchi agrees that teaching grammatical categories in a way that is more accessible and "operational" can make grammar "a more efficient and effective tool for writing improvement." Constance Weaver, meanwhile, suggests directed activities for teaching grammar in the context of students' own writing.

Teaching Grammar to Writers

Janice Neuleib and Irene Brosnahan

Janice Neuleib and Irene Brosnahan situate their ideas within contemporary arguments about whether or not to teach grammar. In this article, first published in 1987 in the Journal of Basic Writing, *they examine findings from research and address the need to teach grammar to undergraduate students, especially those who are studying to be writing teachers. In their classrooms, Neuleib and Brosnahan have observed the ineffectiveness of having students simply memorize grammar concepts, especially students' "inability to apply grammar to editing problems." To ameliorate such difficulties, they believe it is important to teach students to recognize patterns of errors, "to understand how language works."*

At a recent workshop for high school and community college teachers, an earnest young high school teacher explained forcefully to an experienced community college teacher that grammar was of no use in teaching writing. The high school teacher cited the now-famous Braddock, Lloyd-Jones, and Schoer quotation. She said that knowing grammar had no effect on writing ability, insisting that "all the research" counterbalanced any intuitive and experiential evidence the older teacher might have to offer. The young teacher had, however, misquoted the passage; it says: "the teaching of *formal* [emphasis ours] grammar has a negligible or, because it usually displaces some instruction and practice in composition, even a harmful effect on the improvement of writing" (37–38).

Taking the words *teaching of formal grammar* to mean *knowing grammar* is a serious mistake. What the research cited by Braddock et al. indicates is that instruction in traditional grammar over a limited period of time (a semester or less in the research studies being discussed) showed no positive effect on students' writing. In fact, several research studies and much language and composition theory argue for certain types of grammar instruction, when effective methods are used for clearly defined purposes. When writers learn grammar, as opposed to teachers merely "covering" it, the newly acquired knowledge contributes to writing ability.

In separate essays on grammar, both Kolln (139) and Neuleib (148) point out that the often-quoted passage in Braddock et al. was preceded by "Uncommon, however, is carefully conducted research which studies composition over an extended period of time" (37). Few people seem to pay attention to the qualification, however. Also, another 1963 study, one that Kolln reviews, has attracted much less notice than *Research in Written Composition*. Yet that other study, by Meckel, is more extensive and thorough in its conclusions and recommendations than is the Braddock work. Meckel's work shows that major questions still existed in 1963 about the teaching of grammar.[1]

Meckel points to three crucial issues (981): First, none of the grammar studies up to 1963 extended beyond one semester — "a time span much too short to permit development of the degree of conceptualization necessary for transfer to take place." Second, none of the studies had to do with editing or revising, that is "with situations in which pupils are recasting the structure of a sentence or a paragraph." Finally, none of the studies makes comparisons between students who had demonstrated knowledge of grammar and those of equal intelligence who had none.

Meckel's recommendations indicate that studies with systematic grammatical instruction ran too short a time or that the research involved presentation of rules without assured student comprehension. Meckel offers several important conclusions (981): (1) Although grammar has not been shown to improve writing skills, "there is no conclusive evidence, however, that grammar has *no* transfer value in developing composition skill." (2) More research is needed to be done on "the kind of grammatical knowledge that may reasonably be expected to transfer to writing."[2] (3) Sometimes *formal grammar* has meant grammar without application; grammar should be taught systematically with applications. (4) "There are more efficient methods of securing *immediate* [Meckel's emphasis] improvement in the writing of pupils, both in sentence structure and usage, than systematic grammatical instruction." (5) Practice of forms improves usage whereas memorization of rules does not.

In spite of Meckel's work being little known, trends in the profession were confirming his conclusions. The years following 1963 were filled with sentence-combining research that showed statistically significant results on methods that relied on practice with forms (e.g., Mellon; O'Hare). This research culminated in the 1979 study by Daiker, Kerek, and Morenberg in which college students made significant progress in writing, including surface structure and punctuation, without any kind of instruction except in sentence-combining exercises and essay writing. Sentence combining, a method of teaching grammar without explicit grammar instruction, fits with Meckel's earlier conclusion on the effectiveness of practice of forms as opposed to the learning of rules.

Shaughnessy in her 1977 *Errors and Expectations* developed a new method of helping students with writing by using grammar. Working with open-admissions students, she developed a form of grammar instruction that has since been called error analysis. Error analysis fits with Meckel's recommendation that students work only on the errors in their own writing and not on rules external to that writing. Teachers gear instruction only to the needs of the students. Shaughnessy shows many error patterns which teachers can use to understand each student's needs. Shaughnessy offers an approach to error excluding formal grammar instruction, but including grammar at every step.

D'Eloia in the *Journal of Basic Writing* explained the reason for the grammatical approach to basic writing instruction introduced by

Shaughnessy: ". . . something was radically wrong with the research design [of earlier studies which rejected grammar instruction] or with the instruction in grammar itself. . . . They [basic writing teachers] cannot bring themselves to believe that units combining the analysis of a grammatical principle with well-structured proofreading, imitation, paraphrase, and sentence consolidation exercises, and with directed writing assignments could fail to produce more significant results in both fluency and error control" (2). D'Eloia then offers applied grammar activities effective with basic writers similar to those in Shaughnessy's book.

More recently, Bartholomae in "The Study of Error" shows how instructors can discover error-producing language patterns in student writing. He shows that correcting these patterns requires special insight on the part of teachers. Says Bartholomae, "An error . . . can only be understood as evidence of intention. . . . A writer's activity is linguistic and rhetorical activity; it can be different but never random. The task for both teacher and researcher, then, is to discover the grammar of *that* [Bartholomae's emphasis] coherence. . . ." (255).

Harris demonstrates this error-analysis approach to a specific problem. She shows that the fragmented free modifier can indicate linguistic growth. Rather than being a case for the red pencil, the fragmented free modifier is often a chance for a teacher to encourage growing linguistic strength. Being able, however, to recognize such indication of growth and using it to help a student develop requires sophisticated grammatical knowledge on the part of the teacher.

Student-centered approaches similar to those illustrated by Harris and Bartholomae demonstrate how grammar can be effectively used in teaching. Of course, merely covering grammar from a workbook would detract from student achievement. Teaching grammar from a traditional grammar text would be worse. DeBeaugrande explains why grammar texts do not teach students either grammar or writing. He argues that teachers need to understand grammar if they are to help improve students' writing. He attacks grammar textbooks, though, saying that they are written for and by grammarians who find the concepts easy since they "know what the terms mean" (358). He calls for a "learner's grammar" taught by techniques that are accurate, workable, economical, compact, operational, and immediate (364). He illustrates some of the techniques, many of which expand and extend Shaughnessy's and D'Eloia's patterns.

Shaughnessy, D'Eloia, Bartholomae, Harris, and DeBeaugrande all illustrate how grammar instruction improves writing skills. Teachers, however, need grammatical knowledge to use the methods illustrated. To analyze errors and to discover language patterns, teachers need to do more than "cover" grammar. They need to be able to work out exercises of the types illustrated by Shaughnessy and D'Eloia, exercises patterned to students' individual language problems.

Yet, received knowledge in the profession seems to legislate in another direction. A few years ago, every time we did a workshop in the schools, teachers were shocked when we said that studies showed that teaching traditional grammar would not improve students' abilities as writers. More recently we have found many teachers too ready to assume that they can omit grammar instruction because it will not help students to write better. These assumptions are reinforced by journal articles which reject formal grammar instruction.[3]

This dismissal of grammar teaching is unfortunate not only because practice has shown that teachers must know grammar to analyze student errors but also because many questions regarding grammar instruction are worth studying. Fundamental questions concern what kind of grammar is being taught, how it is being taught, and what the rationale for that teaching is. Finally, we as a profession need to ask if we understand grammar and the nature of language.

In our opinion, the preparation of teachers is the crucial issue in teaching effectiveness. A confused teacher increases student perplexity. Arguing against the teaching of grammar in the lower grades, Sanborn tells of a teacher who was confused about the difference between a participle and a gerund: The teacher said "being" in "Being accused of something I didn't do made me mad" was a participle (73). Of course, traditional grammar is replete with ambiguities in its terminology. The term *participle* is ambiguous in that it is both a form term (for a verb) and a function term (modifying a noun, another ambiguity), and the term *gerund* is a function term (functioning in a nominal position) with an implied form (a verb form ending in *-ing*). If our profession had prepared the teacher well, she would have been aware of the ambiguities in the grammar. If some teachers want to teach eight parts of speech in English, for instance, they need to know that the parts of speech are defined neatly, sensibly, and logically by inflectional forms in Latin but that they are defined inconsistently and illogically by mixing form and function in English. Unless teachers are informed about the imperfections of traditional grammar, students will fail to understand it and thereby to learn and retain it.

Superficial retention became painfully obvious to us in a recent survey we conducted in an English grammar course required of upperclass students seeking teacher certification in English. At the beginning of the course, the prospective teachers filled out a questionnaire and took a test in grammar. The questionnaire asked when the prospective teachers had been taught grammar, what kind of grammatical activities they had had, and how they rated themselves on various types of grammatical knowledge. Of the twenty-four participants in the study, twenty-three reported having studied grammar at two or more levels of schooling (elementary school, junior high, high school, college), and fifteen at three or more levels. All reported having learned grammar through a variety of activities such as diagramming sentences, memorizing grammatical terms and labeling parts of speech, identifying and correcting grammatical errors, writing sentences and paragraphs with grammatical forms indicated, and so on. They also rated themselves rather high (mostly 3 or above on a scale of 1 to 5) in most grammatical skills listed, particularly in knowing names of and identifying parts of speech and parts of sentences, standard grammatical usage, and correct punctuation rules and applications.

The results of the grammar test, given with the questionnaire, however, indicated little retention of formal grammatical knowledge and an inability to apply grammar to editing problems. Only three out of twenty-four prospective teachers could accurately name the eight parts of speech — most of them could name four or five (usually noun, verb, adjective, adverb), but function terms like subject and object were mixed in. Most participants could name the two important parts of a sentence and count the number of sentences in a given passage taken from Warriner (58), but no one could accurately count the number of clauses in the paragraph. Some participants even counted fewer clauses than sentences. Although most of these prospective teachers knew what a verb was, only half the group could pick out a transitive verb, and no one could identify an intransitive verb. Only six could find the solitary passive verb in the passage. A prepositional phrase was easily identified, but only two participants correctly picked out an adverbial clause, and only four found an adjective clause. Quite a few people labeled phrases as clauses, apparently not knowing the difference between phrases, clauses, and sentences. Thus, an obvious discrepancy existed between the prospective teachers' perceptions of their formal grammar knowledge and their demonstrated knowledge.

The grammar test also contained two sentences which the participants were to punctuate. They also had to explain their reasons for using each punctuation mark as they did:

1. Please turn off the light its much too bright

2. I was anxious to go shopping but my mother who is usually so organized was taking her time today.

Only seven participants, less than a third of the group, could punctuate sentence 1 correctly; many either used a comma to separate the two clauses and/or neglected the apostrophe for *its*. With sentence 2, almost everyone separated the nonrestrictive clause with a pair of commas, and thirteen of them put a comma before *but*. As for providing the rules of punctuation, only three participants could explain the punctuation in sentence 1 in appropriate grammatical terms, and only one participant could do so for sentence 2. A number of the participants offered explanations involving pauses and meaning, while others misused grammatical terms. For the majority of these prospective teachers, therefore, punctuation rules had not been learned at the conscious operational level. Of course, we realize that the performance of this group of prospective teachers cannot be generalized to all students who have studied grammar, but having taught grammar to similar upperclass students in the last fifteen years, we can say that their lack of formal grammatical knowledge is typical.

We would like to suggest that the first step in increasing teachers' understanding of grammar is to develop a clear definition of the term. Theorists as disparate as Kolln and Hartwell stress the confusion in the definition of grammar. Kolln points out that the Braddock et al. report did not define "formal grammar," so conclusions could not be confirmed (292–293). In addressing this need for definition, Hartwell builds upon W. Nelson Francis's 1954 "Revolution in Grammar" to define five grammars: Grammar 1 is intrinsic knowledge of language rules and patterns that people use without knowing they use them; Grammar 2 is the linguistic science that studies the system of Grammar 1; Grammar 3 merely involves linguistic etiquette, such as calling "he ain't" bad grammar; Grammar 4 is "school grammar," the system that is oversimplified in traditional handbooks and workbooks; Grammar 5, stylistic grammar, uses grammatical terms to teach prose style, in the manner of Lanham, Williams, Christensen, and Strunk and White (Hartwell 109–110). Hartwell stresses that these five grammars often do not match. They are pieces of puzzles that fit into different pictures or that overlap untidily in the same picture. Without being aware of the mismatch between Grammar 4, "school grammar," and Grammar 1, intuitive grammar, many teachers teach Grammar 4 as if it made perfect sense.

We strongly feel that writing teachers need to study the historical background of grammar, be well-acquainted with better descriptions of language (that is, with Grammar 2, linguistic studies, as well as Grammar 5, stylistic grammar), and appreciate relations among different grammars. Still, teachers should not begin to teach linguistics in their writing classes. College level linguistics is not the solution for junior and senior high school students. Rather, when teachers understand how language works, they can make the description of the language accessible to students.

The challenge now is in the area of teacher training and retraining. At the end of the semester, the prospective teachers described in the study above had been exposed to the history of language study and to many of the concepts reviewed here. They went on to learn that to work with basic writers at any level, teachers have to do the hard part. They have to understand stylistic choices, and they have to analyze errors so that they can show students how language works. When teachers do more than "cover" grammar, writers will improve their writing by using the grammar they have learned.

Notes

1. For a thorough review of the research, see Meckel; for a summary of Meckel's findings, see Kolln.
2. Sentence-combining research represents at least one kind of grammatical knowledge that has proved to be transferable to writing. See Neuleib for a summary of sentence-combining research through that date.

3. Hartwell's "Grammar, Grammars, and the Teaching of Grammar" illustrates the sort of dismissal of grammar that encourages this attitude in teachers. Hartwell does mention error analysis, but in his conclusion he calls for a halt to all grammar research. The message teachers often carry from such an article is to abandon grammar instruction of any type.

Works Cited

Braddock, Richard, Richard Lloyd-Jones, and Lowell Schoer. *Research in Written Composition.* Urbana, IL: National Council of Teachers of English, 1963.

Bartholomae, David. "The Study of Error." *College Composition and Communication* 31 (1980): 253–269.

Christensen, Francis. "A Generative Rhetoric of the Sentence." *College Composition and Communication* 14 (1963): 155–161.

Daiker, Donald, Andrew Kerek, and Max Morenberg. "Sentence-Combining and Syntactic Maturity in Freshman English." *College Composition and Communication* 29 (1978): 36–41.

DeBeaugrande, Robert. "Forward to the Basics: Getting Down to Grammar." *College Composition and Communication* 35 (1984): 358–367.

D'Eloia, Sarah. "The Uses — and Limits — of Grammar." *Journal of Basic Writing* 1 (1977): 1–48.

Francis, W. Nelson. "Revolution in Grammar." *Quarterly Journal of Speech* 40 (1954): 299–312.

Harris, Muriel. "Mending the Fragmented Free Modifier." *College Composition and Communication* 32 (1981): 175–182.

Hartwell, Patrick. "Grammar, Grammars, and the Teaching of Grammar." *College English* 47 (1985): 105–127.

Kolln, Martha. "Closing the Book on Alchemy." *College Composition and Communication* 32 (1981): 139–151.

Lanham, Richard. *Revising Prose.* New York: Scribner's, 1979.

Meckel, Henry. "Research on Teaching Composition and Literature." *Handbook of Research on Teaching.* Ed. Nathaniel L. Gage. Chicago: Rand, 1963.

Mellon, John. *Transformational Sentence Combining: A Method for Enhancing the Development of Fluency in English Composition.* Urbana, IL: National Council of Teachers of English, 1966.

Neuleib, Janice. "The Relation of Formal Grammar to Composition." *College Composition and Communication* 23 (1977): 247–250.

O'Hare, Frank. *Sentence-Combining: Improving Student Writing Without Formal Grammar Instruction.* Urbana, IL: National Council of Teachers of English, 1971.

Sanborn, Jean. "Grammar: Good Wine Before Its Time." *English Journal* 75 (1986): 72–80.

Shaughnessy, Mina. *Errors and Expectations.* New York: Oxford UP, 1977.

Strunk, William, and E. B. White. *The Elements of Style,* 3rd ed. New York: Macmillan, 1979.

Warriner, John E., John H. Treanor, and Sheila Y. Laws. *English Grammar and Composition 8.* Rev. ed. New York: Harcourt, 1965.

Williams, Joseph. *Style: Ten Lessons in Clarity and Grace.* Glenview, IL: Scott, 1981.

Classroom Activities

Develop a questionnaire for basic writing students similar to the one that Neuleib and Brosnahan provided for their own students (preservice student teachers). The purpose of the questionnaire is for students to reflect not only on how much grammar knowledge they have retained, but also on how they have studied grammar throughout their schooling. A similar questionnaire for developing writers would provide interesting results for both students and teachers. Students could describe their experiences with the study of grammar or list rules they have learned over the years. You may approach class discussion of the results of these self-assessments by comparing your own experiences with grammar instruction to those described by students.

Thinking about Teaching

Neuleib and Brosnahan suggest error analysis as an appropriate means of teaching grammar to basic writers. If students are able to recognize patterns of error, they will become more adept at editing their work. In this context, it may be useful to collaborate with colleagues to determine which errors are the most common among your population of students. Create a rubric based on categories suggested by Neuleib and Brosnahan. Then exchange student papers and diagnostic tests and proofread for categories of error that seem most prevalent. After this exchange, discuss the kinds of errors that predominate and the best ways to approach such editing difficulties with your students.

Teaching the Basics of a Writer's Grammar

Rei R. Noguchi

The following selection comes from Rei R. Noguchi's National Council of Teachers of English monograph Grammar and the Teaching of Writing *(1991) in which he argues that basic writing students learn to edit more effectively not by memorizing grammar rules but by becoming more aware of how grammar functions in their own writing. Accordingly, Noguchi suggests that we move toward teaching the "operational definitions" of grammar terms, as opposed to the "compositional definitions." Noguchi argues that students need to acquire "underlying knowledge" of several major areas of language usage in order to "crack 'the grammar code.'" Those areas include pronoun usage, understanding the sentence as a whole, and the use of presentence elements. Noguchi's strategies can help you teach developing writers to identify and correct "status marking" and "stigmatized" error, which often have significant consequences in real-world written communication.*

Cracking the Grammar Code

How can students crack the "grammar code"? How can they gain a working knowledge of basic grammatical categories such as sentence, subject, verb, etc., if such categories are defined in terms of other categories? Isn't it much like looking up the word *structure* in a dictionary and finding the definition "form" and under the entry for *form* finding the definition "structure"? I believe students can crack the grammar code but not by the time-consuming and frustrating methods of the past. The solution lies not in presenting semantic or compositional definitions, which inevitably entail either opaque or interlinking definitions of the categories, but rather in operational definitions. By an operational definition here, I mean a definition which defines by means of what an entity does or can have done to it rather than what comprises the entity. To cite a mundane example outside of grammar, one definition of *water* would be an aqueous chemical compound composed of two atoms of hydrogen and one atom of oxygen. This definition focuses on the composition of the entity and thus resembles many of the problematic definitions found in the study of grammar (e.g., "A sentence is composed of a subject and a predicate"). In contrast, an operational definition of *water* would be a liquid ingested by plants and animals to sustain life, or, perhaps, a liquid used to wash and rinse cars, dishes, etc. Granted, operational definitions are not as impressive or as delimiting as nonoperational definitions. The important point here is that they do not have to be. All that is required of operational definitions is that they work in actual use and that they avoid interlinking technical terms, something which the nonoperational definition of *water* does not do.

The Underlying Knowledge of "Pronoun"

As startling as it may sound at first, all students who have acquired English as a native language (as well as many who have acquired it non-natively) already possess an immense knowledge of the operations (i.e., descriptive rules) of English, including its syntax. This must be so, or they would not be able to produce grammatical sentences in everyday conversation. This knowledge, however, is largely unconscious. Students normally cannot explain the operations, or rules, but the knowledge is nonetheless there and waiting to be tapped. Consider pronouns. Most grammar books state explicitly that a pronoun is a word that "substitutes for a noun." Yet this traditional definition of pronoun is clearly incorrect, or at least incomplete, since a pronoun can substitute not just for a noun (e.g., *boys* → *they*) but also, among other things, a noun phrase (e.g., *the noisy boys in the back of the room* → *they*) or any construction that functions as a noun or noun phrase, including other pronouns (e.g., *he and she* → *they*). Indeed, if students dutifully mastered and meticulously applied the grammar-book definition of a pronoun and only that, they would be unable to identify many pronoun substitutions in the language. Whether grammar books state the definition of a pronoun correctly or completely, fortunately, does not really matter in the end. Native students already unconsciously know the correct version of the pronoun substitution rule; otherwise they could not use pronouns in everyday conversation.

If given the following sentences and personal pronouns, students who are native speakers of English would find little difficulty in substituting the pronoun for the appropriate word or words in the sentence:

1. Jane and Bob bought a book during the trip to San Francisco. (*she*)

2. He and she live in New York City. (*they*)

3. It was the Beatles who first made British rock music popular. (*they* or *them*)

4. That Mary studied hard was very clear to John. (*it*)

5. Most people believe that the world is round. (*it*)

6. Sometimes, exercising can be relaxing. (*it*)

Items 1–6 above illustrate two important facts concerning personal pronouns. First, personal pronouns do, indeed, substitute for a variety of constructions in English. In (1), *she* substitutes for the noun *Jane;* in (2), *they*, for the compound pronoun *he and she;* in (3), *they,* for the noun phrase *the Beatles;* in (4), *it,* for the noun clause *that Mary studied hard;* in (5), *it,* for the noun clause *that the world is round* or, alternatively, for the noun phrase *the world;* in (6), *it,* for the gerund *exercising.* Second, errors involving prescriptive rules (i.e., usage errors) may often occur but errors involving descriptive rules rarely occur. For example, in (3), students may substitute the pronoun *them* for *the Beatles* instead of the more formal *they.* However, this is a very different type of error from substituting a personal pronoun for *made* (a verb) or for *popular* (an adjective). Stated more generally, though students may substitute the incorrect form of a personal pronoun, they will never substitute a personal pronoun for any grammatical category other than a noun, a noun phrase, or a construction that serves as such.

The above exercise with personal pronouns helps point out some significant advantages of operational definitions in the teaching of grammar. If students can substitute pronouns for the appropriate word or words in exercises like (1–6) above and in utterances of daily speech — in ignorance of or, perhaps, despite the inaccuracy or incompleteness of the common textbook definition — then teachers do not really have to teach the definition of pronoun, not even the operational one. Students already have that knowledge. Put in a more general way, teachers cannot teach students what they already know. Although students probably cannot state the operation of pronoun substitution in the metalanguage of grammar, they must already possess the tacit knowledge that a personal pronoun, at the least, is a word that can take the place of a noun, noun phrase, or something that functions as either. (The foregoing is a rough operational definition of a personal pronoun.) Again, without this kind of unconscious linguistic knowledge, students would be unable to make pronoun substitutions for the appropriate words in daily speech.

The fact that students already have such knowledge can also help teachers clarify some facts about English grammar. If students already unconsciously know that a personal pronoun can substitute for a noun, noun phrase, or some construction that functions as either, then they must also know that these elements which accept pronoun substitution are all syntactically (though not necessarily semantically) similar. That is, despite the various forms and lengths which these units take, students already unconsciously know that they function as one category, namely, that of noun. Indeed, precisely because the noun clauses *that Mary studied hard* and *that the world is round* in (4) and (5) above allow the personal pronoun *it* as a proper substitution, teachers can plausibly argue that these constructions, while not having the form of nouns, are functioning as nouns. That is, even though the shapes are different, the function is the same. This fact is important since it means teachers can use pronoun substitution as an operational test for nouns (and vice versa). If a personal pronoun can appropriately substitute for a word or group of words, then the word or group of words is functioning as a noun, regardless of its form. This, in turn, obviates the need to teach formally the definitions of noun, noun phrase, and the other constructions which substitute for nouns. If such constructions allow personal pronouns as substitutions in a sentence, then, operationally, they are nouns.

Reliance on this kind of unconscious underlying knowledge of the language, of course, has always been implicit — and crucial — in the development of transformational/generative grammar and its derivative applications for the classroom. It should come as no surprise that the basic design and the general success of sentence-combining exercises rest greatly on this kind of intuitive knowledge. Indeed, without such knowledge, students would be unable to carry out the instructions (i.e., perform the operations) required of such exercises. Yet, with the exception of a small number of studies (D'Eloia 1977; DeBeaugrande 1984; Noguchi 1987), little has been done to exploit this powerful resource to define grammatical categories for writers, even though the very same resource has been used fruitfully by linguists in their syntactic analyses for the past thirty or so years.

The Underlying Knowledge of "Subject"

An approach capitalizing on intuitive linguistic knowledge can be used to define, for example, the notion of "subject of a sentence." For students, being able to locate the subject of a sentence easily is a valuable skill since several kinds of common stylistic problems require the identification of subjects — for example, errors in subject-verb agreement, unnecessary shifts in person, overuse of nonagent subjects. Locating subjects can most easily be handled by exploiting some descriptive rules of grammar which operate on or interact with subjects. Consider the following declarative sentences and their corresponding tag and yes-no questions:

7. a. Jim and Sue can dance the tango.
   b. Jim and Sue can dance the tango, can't they?
   c. Can Jim and Sue dance the tango?
8. a. The company, which employed many workers and made many different kinds of products, went out of business.
   b. The company, which employed many workers and made many different kinds of products, went out of business, didn't it?
   c. Did the company, which employed many workers and made many different kinds of products, go out of business?
9. a. The cost of the three typewriters and the four clocks will be raised.
   b. The cost of the three typewriters and the four clocks will be raised, won't it?
   c. Will the cost of the three typewriters and the four clocks be raised?
10. a. Tom ate some bad spaghetti and had a stomachache all day.
    b. Tom ate some bad spaghetti and had a stomachache all day, didn't he?
    c. Did Tom eat some bad spaghetti and have a stomachache all day?
11. a. Doing math problems isn't one of Billy's favorite activities.
    b. Doing math problems isn't one of Billy's favorite activities, is it?
    c. Isn't doing math problems one of Billy's favorite activities?
12. a. Whether Sam likes it or not, Janet should telephone David again.
    b. Whether Sam likes it or not, Janet should telephone David again, shouldn't she?
    c. Whether Sam likes it or not, should Janet telephone David again?

Forming the corresponding tag and yes-no questions from the original declarative sentences offers a way of identifying subjects operationally. With tag questions (all the (b) sentences above), the pronoun copied at the end of the tag question refers to the subject of the sentence. Stated more simply, the last word of the tag question stands for the subject. For example, in (7b), the last word *they* stands for *Jim and Sue*, the subject of the sentence; in (8b), the last word *it* stands for *the company*; in (9b), *it* stands for *the cost;* in (11b), *it* stands for the whole sequence *doing math problems* (not just *math*), and, hence, the whole sequence is the subject of the sentence. With yes-no questions (all the (c) sentences above), an auxiliary, or "helping," verb has been moved leftward to occupy a new position. If no auxiliary verb occurs in the original declarative sentence, as in (8a) and (10a), an appropriate form of the *do* auxiliary verb (*do, does,* or *did*) is added instead. The subject of the sentence can be identified relative to the new position of the moved or added auxiliary. More specifically, the (simple) subject is the first noun or noun substitute that stands to the immediate right of the moved or added auxiliary verb. Stated more in everyday English, the subject is the first noun or noun substitute that stands to the nearest right of the moved (or added *do*) word. Thus, in (7c), the noun phrase *Jim and Sue* stands to the nearest right of the moved word *can* and, hence, is the subject of the sentence; in (8c), the noun or noun substitute standing to the nearest right of the moved word *did* is *company;* in (9c), the noun or noun substitute standing to the nearest right of the moved word *will* is *cost.*

Handling Some Exceptions

As with any method dealing with the complexities of English grammar, real or apparent exceptions may occur. The key is to explain them as clearly as possible. For example, sentences like (13a) and (14a) will yield a proper corresponding tag question but not a proper corresponding yes-no question:

13. a. For Tommy to pass now isn't going to be easy.
    b. For Tommy to pass now isn't going to be easy, is it?
    c. *Isn't for Tommy to pass now going to be easy?[1]

14. a. That Jane is a genius is obvious to everyone.
    b. That Jane is a genius is obvious to everyone, isn't it?
    c. *Is that Jane is a genius obvious to everyone?

Conversely, a sentence like (15a) will yield a proper corresponding yes-no question but sometimes a noncorresponding (yet proper) tag question:

15. a. I believe that a good education makes a big difference in life.
    b. *I believe that a good education makes a big difference in life, doesn't it? (instead of the syntactically corresponding "I believe that a good education makes a big difference in life, don't I?")
    c. Don't I believe that a good education makes a big difference in life?

The general problem in (13–15) is that the tag question and the yes-no question give conflicting indications of what is the subject of the original sentence. For example, in (13b), the *it* in the tag question refers to or stands for the infinitive phrase *for Tommy to pass now*, and, hence, the whole infinitive phrase is the subject of the sentence. In (13c), however, the yes-no question is corresponding but ungrammatical. To make matters worse, the first noun or noun substitute occurring to the nearest right of the moved word is *Tommy* and, thus, students may incorrectly identify *Tommy,* rather than the whole infinitive phrase *for Tommy to pass now,* as the subject of the sentence.

Rather than merely viewing the results in (13–15) as contradictory or unrevealing, teachers can exploit such situations not only to sharpen but also to expand their students' skills in employing operational definitions. For example, if in (13b) the last word *it* truly represents a pronominal copy of the subject (i.e., *for Tommy to pass now*), then we ought to be able to substitute *it* for the subject without changing the essential meaning of the sentence. This we can do in both (13a) and (13b) to get *It's not going to be easy* and *It's not going to be easy, is it?,* respectively, thus providing strong evidence that *for Tommy to pass now* is, indeed, the actual subject. Significantly, we can also substitute *it* for the same group of words in the problematic (13c) to get *Isn't it going to be easy?,* again giving strong evidence that *for Tommy to pass now* is the subject of the sentence. (Note that if *Tommy* alone were the subject of the sentence, the corresponding tag question would be the ungrammatical **For Tommy to pass now isn't going to be easy, is he?*) Further analysis, then, shows that the subject of the sentences in (13) is, indeed, the whole infinitive phrase *For Tommy to pass now* rather than just *Tommy* or any other portion of the infinitive phrase. The same line of argument can also be used to explain the discrepancy in identifying the subject in (14).

The discrepancy in (15) can also be explained in a revealing way for students. In (15c), the moved word in the yes-no question correctly indicates that *I* is the subject of the sentence; in (15b), however, the copied pronoun *it* in the tag question refers to *a good education,* and, thus, erroneously indicates that *a good education* is the subject. The cause of the discrepancy here lies more in the *use* of tag questions than in their formation. For example, the tag question that syntactically corresponds to *I believe that a good education makes a big difference in life* is *I believe that a good education makes a big difference in life, don't I?* (If this is offered as a possible tag question to (15a), most, if not all, students will agree.) However, though this is a syntactically correct tag question, we normally do not utter it for reasons having to do with the semantics (i.e., meaning) and pragmatics (i.e., use) of such questions. In contrast to yes-no questions, which seek from the addressee a neutral *yes* or *no* response, tag questions seek a confirmation of whatever the addresser asserts. Put in another way, yes-no questions roughly mean something like, "My utterance here offers you a free choice. I ask you to indicate the choice with a *yes* or *no.*" Tag questions roughly mean something like, "My utterance here asserts something. I ask you to confirm or deny the assertion." In the tag question *I believe that a good education makes a big difference in life, don't I?,* the addresser asserts his or her belief about the importance of a good education in life. However, the meaning of the sentence is strange in that the addresser explicitly affirms his or her own belief (with *I believe*) and then denies or casts doubt on it (with *don't I?*). Because of this conflict between self-affirmation and self-doubt, students often prefer the syntactically noncorresponding tag question *I believe that a good education makes a big difference in life, doesn't it?* We can check this explanation against a comparable tag question, such as *Maria believes that a good education makes a big difference in life, doesn't she?*, which lacks the conflicting beliefs of the addresser and, hence, is more acceptable than **Maria believes that a good education makes a big difference in life, doesn't it?* (Teachers can encourage further exploration of this phenomenon by asking students to substitute other nouns and personal pronouns for the pronoun *I*.) The reason that sentences like (15b) sometimes occur as the tag-question counterparts for sentences like (15a) then is not that students do not know the syntax of tag questions (they do) but rather that they also know something about the semantics and pragmatics (or the meaning and use) of tag questions.

The Importance of Tag-Question and Yes-No Question Formation

What the preceding examples with tag questions and yes-no questions indicate is that students also unconsciously know a great deal more about the categories of English grammar than teachers realize. The very ability to perform the operations of tag-question formation and yes-no question formation presupposes that students already have an underlying knowledge of not only the concept of "subject" but also those of "auxiliary verb," "negative," and "personal pronoun" (and, as we shall see later, also "sentence" and "presentence modifier"). That students have already acquired the concept of personal pronoun (along with the associated concepts of case, number, and gender) is evident in their ability to add the correct noun-equivalent pronoun (with matching case, number, and gender) at the end of the tag question. That students have already acquired the concept of auxiliary verb is evident in their uncanny ability to select, among numerous possibilities within a sentence, the correct word to copy in the tag part of the tag question or the correct word to move leftward in the yes-no question. (The ability to identify auxiliary verbs is further verified when students insert a form of *do* in sentences containing no auxiliary verb. How can they tell that a sentence lacks a movable or copiable auxiliary verb unless they know first what constitutes an auxiliary verb?) That students have already acquired the concept of negative is evident in their ability to add and contract *not* in the tag (or in their ability to negate any positive sentence of English). If students did not possess an underlying knowledge of such categories, they would be unable to produce grammatical tag questions and yes-no questions in everyday conversation.

The Underlying Knowledge of "Main Verb"

The underlying knowledge of native speakers also includes knowledge of the category "main verb." The ability to locate main verbs is important because some highly frequent stylistic errors concern main verbs. These errors involve not only the choice of main verbs (as suggested by the oft-quoted advice, "Write with action verbs") but also their form (incorrect tense, lack of subject-verb agreement, improper tense shifting, nonstandard dialectical forms). Locating the main verb of a sentence, however, is not always easy for students, even when they know the subject of the sentence. Simply asking students, "What is the subject doing?" will not work when, for example, the sentence is passive or the main verb is some form of *be*. Students do, nonetheless, have an underlying knowledge of main verbs. After students have learned how to identify both the subject of a declarative sentence and the correct pronominal form of the subject operationally, teachers can tap their underlying knowledge of main verbs by having students work with sentence frames like A and B below. Frame A isolates the predicate of a sentence in the second slot. If that predicate contains the verb *be,* frame B is then used to separate the linking verb *be* from the passive *be.* In fact, frame B works only with passive sentences and serves to isolate the "real" main verb.

A. They somehow got _____ to _____.

B. But it wasn't me who did the _____-ing.

To locate main verbs with sentence frames A and B, students start with any (declarative) sentence and then use that sentence to fill in the blanks of A and B. The operational test here requires two basic steps:

1. Insert in the first slot of A the subject of the (declarative) sentence in the appropriate pronoun form and insert in the second slot whatever remains of the sentence.

2. If (and only if) the second slot in A has *be* as the first word, try to fill the slot in B with the appropriate word from the original sentence (this word also has to appear in the second slot in A). If this can't be done, don't worry.

To simplify matters here, sentence negatives may be ignored. Although the sentences produced from following the steps above may sometimes be strange, they will, nonetheless, be sentences (keep in mind that, even in real life, people sometimes utter strange but syntactically correct sentences). More important, the resulting sentences will isolate the main verb in the second slot in A or, if the original sentence is passive, the main verb will appear in the slot in B. The previous declarative sentences in (7–12), repeated for convenience below as (16–

21) illustrate the isolation of the main verb. The (a) versions are the original sentences, the (b) versions are the results of using frame A, and the (c) versions show the results of using frame B.

16. a. Jim and Sue can dance the tango.
    b. They somehow got *them* to *dance the tango*. (Hence, *dance* is the main verb.)

17. a. The company, which employed many workers and made many different kinds of products, went out of business.
    b. They somehow got *it* to *go out of business*. (*Go* is the main verb.)

18. a. The cost of the three typewriters and the four clocks will be raised.
    b. They somehow got *it* to *be raised*.
    c. But it wasn't me who did the *raise*-ing. (*Raise* is the main verb.)

19. a. Tom ate some bad spaghetti and had a stomachache all day.
    b. They somehow got *him* to *eat some bad spaghetti and (to) have a stomachache all day*. (Two main verbs here: *eat* and *have*.)

20. a. Doing math problems isn't one of Billy's favorite activities.
    b. They somehow got *it* to *be one of Billy's favorite activities*.
    c. But it wasn't me who did the _____?_____-ing. (Since frame B does not work here, *be* is the main verb.)

21. a. Whether Sam likes it or not, Janet should telephone David again.
    b. They somehow got *her* to *telephone David again, whether Sam likes it or not*. (*Telephone* is the main verb.)

Even the troublesome declarative sentences in (13–15), repeated here as (22–24), yield their main verbs, as indicated below:

22. a. For Tommy to pass now isn't going to be easy.
    b. They somehow got *it* to *be easy*.
    c. But it wasn't me who did the_____?_____-ing. (Hence, *be* is the main verb.)

23. a. That Jane is a genius is obvious to everyone.
    b. They somehow got *it* to *be obvious to everyone*.
    c. But it wasn't me who did the _____?_____-ing. (Hence, *be* is the main verb.)

24. a. I believe that a good education makes a big difference in life.
    b. They somehow got *me* to *believe that a good education makes a big difference in life*. (*Believe* is the main verb.)

As shown by the examples above, sentence frames A and B work together to isolate main verbs from declarative sentences. Sentence frame A isolates transitive and intransitive main verbs from the sentence, while sentence frame B separates the main verb *be* from a passivized main verb (i.e., a main verb which occurs in passive form and which occurs after the auxiliary verb *be*). Working in tandem, sentence frames A and B make the isolation of main verbs considerably easier because they operationally remove distracting auxiliary verbs from consideration as main verbs. For example, the active sentence *Bill could have been taking care of his tired feet* becomes in sentence frame A, *They somehow got him to take care of his tired feet,* while the passive sentence *Mary might have been chosen* becomes in sentence frames A and B, *They somehow got her to be chosen* and *But it wasn't me who did the choosing.*

The Underlying Knowledge of "Sentence"

Being able to identify main verbs, main subjects, and auxiliary verbs can, of course, aid students in identifying sentences and defining the all-important notion of "sentence." However, to piece together these elements with others to define a sentence is wasteful of time and effort because native speakers of English already know what a sentence is. That this knowledge already exists, tacit though it may be, is evidenced in the very ability to form grammatical tag questions and yes-no questions. Regardless of the vast numbers of sentences that can be transformed into tag questions or yes-no questions, the key point to keep in mind here is that the operations that form tag questions and yes-no questions work properly only on genuine sentences. While students will have no difficulty in transforming the (a) sentences in (7–12) into tag questions and yes-no questions, they will find the task impossible with such nonsentences as the following:

25. Enjoyed the baseball game on Saturday.

26. Whatever you could do to help my sister.

27. The wind howling through the trees last night.

28. If you came tomorrow afternoon at one o'clock.

29. In order to find a job he liked.

Try as they may, students will find it impossible to form either the corresponding tag question or the corresponding yes-no question for the sequences in (25–29). If forced to write or utter a "corresponding" tag or yes-no question for the sentence in, say, (25), students might come up with one of these constructions:

30. Didn't he enjoy the baseball game on Saturday?

31. Enjoyed the baseball game on Saturday, didn't you?

32. You enjoyed the baseball game on Saturday, didn't you?

Yet even these forced and noncorresponding questions are highly instructive, for they reveal some of the elements which might be added to (25) to make it into a complete sentence. The yes-no question in (30) reveals that (25) lacks a possible *he* subject; the tag questions in (31) and (32) implicitly and explicitly reveal that (25) lacks a possible *you* subject. That is, the very attempt to force a tag question or a yes-no question from a nonsentence offers evidence not only of the existence of a student's underlying knowledge of a (complete) sentence but also the strength of this knowledge.

What ultimately makes tag questions and yes-no questions so useful in differentiating sentences from nonsentences is their ability to mark sentence boundaries. Every sentence, no matter how complex, has two boundaries, one that marks the beginning of the sentence and one that marks its end. (In writing, we can call these two boundaries the left and right boundary, respectively.) Differentiating a sentence from a nonsentence — or, in our terms, defining a sentence operationally — crucially depends upon identifying the two boundaries, since what lies in between them is the sentence. Indeed, one major advantage of using tag-question formation and yes-no question formation as a test for "sentencehood" is that the operations involved visually mark the boundaries of a sentence. Tag-question formation visually marks the right boundary by placing the appropriate tag there (e.g., *isn't he, aren't they*); the yes-no question formation visually marks the left boundary by moving the auxiliary (or adding a *do* form) there. If both boundaries cannot be so marked, then the original sequence falls short of being a sentence.

The following sequences help illustrate the marking of boundaries ("//" indicates a sentence or independent clause boundary):

33. a. //It's a great party//
    b. It's a great party//isn't it?
    c. Is//it _____ a great party?
34. a. //Whatever you say will be okay with Mary//
    b. Whatever you say will be okay with Mary//won't it?
    c. Will//whatever you say _____ be okay with Mary?
35. a. //The man and the woman, neither of whom Ted knows, came from a place called Hamburg//
    b. The man and the woman, neither of whom Ted knows, came from a place called Hamburg//didn't they?
    c. Did//the man and the woman, neither of whom Ted knows, come from a place called Hamburg?

With tag questions, the right sentence boundary is marked even if, for semantic and pragmatic reasons, the wrong subject is copied as the pronoun in the tag, as in (36b) and (37b), or even if the auxiliary verb lacks an accepted negative contracted form, as in (38b) and (39b):[2]

36. a. //I think Bob is going to Sally's Halloween party in a Dracula costume//
    b. *I think Bob is going to Sally's Halloween party in a Dracula costume//isn't he?
    c. Do//I think Bob is going to Sally's Halloween party in a Dracula costume?

37. a. //We are certain that Janice and her two friends will not get an A in history//
    b. *We are certain that Janice and her two friends will not get an A in history//will they?
    c. Are//we _____ certain that Janice and her two friends will not get an A in history?

38. a. //Dave might finish the assignment over the weekend//
    b. *Dave might finish the assignment over the weekend//mightn't he? (This one is acceptable in certain dialects.)
    c. Might//Dave _____ finish the assignment over the weekend?

39. a. //I'm just being stubborn//
    b. *I'm just being stubborn//am't/ain't I?
    c. Am//I _____ just being stubborn?

With yes-no questions, the left boundary is marked even if the moved element creates an awkward or, to some, an ungrammatical sentence, as in (40c) or (41c):

40. a. //That the rock singer may cut his hair could be a problem//
    b. That the rock singer may cut his hair could be a problem// couldn't it?
    c. Could//that the rock singer may cut his hair _____ be a problem?

41. a. //To be a famous movie star can mean a life without privacy//
    b. To be a famous movie star can mean a life without privacy// can't it?
    c. Can//to be a famous movie star _____ mean a life without privacy?

As one final verification of sentencehood, teachers might enlist students to try a simple operation that is independent of both tag- and yes-no question formation. As all native speakers of English implicitly know (just as all teachers who have used sentence combining as a teaching device explicitly know), sentences can be embedded, or nested, within another. One such embedding environment, or slot, for declarative sentences occurs in (42):

42. They refused to believe the idea that _____.

Although many word sequences will properly fit in the above slot, whatever these sequences are, most of them take the form of a (declarative) sentence. Thus, the (a) sentences in (7–12) can be embedded in (42), as the complex sentences in (43–48) below show:

43. They refused to believe the idea that Jim and Sue can dance the tango.

44. They refused to believe the idea that the company, which employed many workers and made many different kinds of products, went out of business.

45. They refused to believe the idea that the cost of the three typewriters and the four clocks will be raised.

46. They refused to believe the idea that Tom ate some bad spaghetti and had a stomachache all day.

47. They refused to believe the idea that doing math problems isn't one of Billy's favorite activities.

48. They refused to believe the idea that, whether Sam likes it or not, Janet should telephone David again.

In contrast, nonsentence sequences, such as those in (25–29), cannot be embedded in the same environment:

49. *They refused to believe the idea that enjoyed the baseball game on Saturday.

50. *They refused to believe the idea that whatever you could do to help my sister.

51. *They refused to believe the idea that the wind howling through the trees last night.

52. *They refused to believe the idea that if you came tomorrow afternoon at one o'clock.

53. *They refused to believe the idea that in order to find a job he liked.

In most cases, the above method proves easy to use because it provides a controlled syntactic context in which to judge sentence completeness.

The Underlying Knowledge of "Presentence Modifier"

In addition to marking the left boundary of a sentence, yes-no question formation is helpful in identifying presentence modifiers. Being able to identify these modifiers proves useful in writing since a comma is sometimes required to set off the presentence modifier from the rest of the sentence.[3] Although appearing in various forms and lengths, all presentence modifiers share two syntactic characteristics: they occur, as the grammatical terminology suggests, at the beginning of the sentence, and they are movable to some other location in the sentence, whether it be the end or somewhere in the middle (the exact position is unimportant here). The basic problem of identifying presentence modifiers, or really separating them from the rest of the sentence, lies in the variety of forms they take. They can be a word, a phrase, or a clause. The value of yes-no question formation lies in its ability to treat them all alike syntactically. If a presentence modifier occurs in a declarative sentence, yes-no question formation will either place the moved auxiliary to its right or displace the modifier to some other location in the sentence. (The displacement of the modifier occurs because of stylistic reasons and is not a part of the yes-no question rule itself.) In either case, the presentence modifier becomes easily identifiable. The presentence modifier is either everything in the sentence that stands to the left of the moved auxiliary verb (or added *do* form) or everything that moves rightward to some other position in the sentence. The following sentences, containing a variety of presentence modifiers, illustrate the point (the modifiers under consideration are in italics for easy reference):

54. a. *Frankly,* everyone says that my fifth-grade teacher is mean.
    b. *Frankly,* does everyone say that my fifth-grade teacher is mean?
    c. Does everyone say, *frankly,* that my fifth-grade teacher is mean?

55. a. *Consequently,* the whole street was destroyed by the tornado.
    b. *Consequently,* was the whole street destroyed by the tornado?
    c. Was the whole street, *consequently,* destroyed by the tornado?

56. a. *In Los Angeles about this time,* Janine claimed that she saw a flying saucer zoom over her house.
    b. *In Los Angeles about this time*, did Janine claim that she saw a flying saucer zoom over her house?
    c. Did Janine claim that *in Los Angeles about this time* she saw a flying saucer zoom over her house?

57. a. *Things being what they are,* Jerry's mother is very angry at him.
    b. *Things being what they are,* is Jerry's mother very angry at him?
    c. Is Jerry's mother very angry at him, *things being what they are?*

58. a. *Although he has never hit a home run in his life,* Jeremy still loves to play baseball.
    b. *Although he has never hit a home run in his life,* does Jeremy still love to play baseball?
    c. Does Jeremy still love to play baseball, *although he has never hit a home run in his life?*

59. a. *When the food arrives,* we'll start with the pepperoni pizza first.
    b. *When the food arrives,* will we start with the pepperoni pizza first?
    c. Will we start with the pepperoni pizza first *when the food arrives?*

Pedagogically, the main benefit of using the yes-no question to identify presentence modifiers lies in avoiding the laborious and time-consuming chore of presenting all the various types of presentence modifiers. Teachers need not introduce individually such modifiers as adverbial disjuncts, conjunctive adverbs, prepositional phrases, nominative absolutes, and adverbial clauses; nor need teachers differentiate between one-word, phrasal, or clausal modifiers. Syntactically blind to such distinctions, yes-no question formation operationally defines presentence modifiers in one general and easily perceptible way: they either occur to the left of the moved auxiliary or added *do* form or else they get moved from the presentence position.

The Applicability of the Basic Categories

We have now operationally defined a set of basic categories — subject, verb (both main and auxiliary), (presentence) modifier, and sentence (or independent clause). If we take into account other categories that become transparent in tag-question formation, we may supplement the basic set with (personal) pronoun, noun, noun phrase and noun substitute, and negative. While the foregoing categories are by no means all the categories that we might define operationally, they comprise a fundamental set for identifying and correcting many highly frequent and sometimes highly stigmatized kinds of errors. In reducing these errors, some of these categories constitute a starting point; for others, they constitute the crucial category (or categories). The importance and potential utility of these categories become clearer if we distribute them in relation to Connors and Lunsford's (1988) list of the twenty most frequent formal errors:

1. No comma after introductory element (presentence modifier, sentence)

2. Vague pronoun reference (pronoun, noun, noun phrase, noun substitute)

3. No comma in compound sentence (independent clause)

4. Wrong word

5. No comma in nonrestrictive element

6. Wrong/missing inflected endings (verb, noun)

7. Wrong or missing preposition

8. Comma splice (sentence or independent clause)

9. Possessive apostrophe error

10. Tense shift (main verb, auxiliary verb)

11. Unnecessary shift in person (possibly subject or pronoun)

12. Sentence fragment (sentence or independent clause)

13. Wrong tense or verb form (main verb, auxiliary verb)

14. Subject-verb agreement (subject, auxiliary verb, main verb)

15. Lack of comma in series

16. Pronoun agreement error (pronoun, subject, main verb, auxiliary verb)

17. Unnecessary comma with restrictive element

18. Run-on or fused sentence (sentence or independent clause)

19. Dangling or misplaced modifier (presentence modifier, sentence)

20. Its/it's error

The importance and potential utility of these categories also become more apparent when they are placed in relation to Hairston's (1981) "status marking" and "very serious" errors, the two most stigmatized kinds of stylistic errors:

Status Marking

nonstandard verb forms in past or past participle (verb)

lack of subject-verb agreement: *We was* instead of *We were; Jones don't think it's acceptable* instead of *Jones doesn't think it's acceptable* (subject, main verb, auxiliary verb)

double negatives (negative)

objective pronoun as subject (pronoun, subject)

Very Serious

sentence fragments (sentence or independent clause)

run-on sentences (sentence or independent clause)

noncapitalization of proper nouns (noun)

would of instead of *would have* (possibly auxiliary verb)

lack of subject-verb agreement, non-status marking (subject, auxiliary verb, main verb)

insertion of comma between the verb and its complement (main verb) nonparallelism

faulty adverb forms

use of transitive verb *set* for intransitive *sit* (verb)

The Practical Benefits

Isolating basic categories of grammar in the manner demonstrated here, then, produces practical benefits. Aside from its relevance to correcting some highly frequent and stigmatized errors, the method reduces significantly the time expended on grammar instruction.[4] Teachers need not present to students all the customary grammatical categories, only a small set of them. Second, and as a direct result of the first benefit, it creates more time to devote to other matters of writing. While unconventional features of style need attention at some point in writing instruction, they should not be the sole nor the primary area of attention. Third, because the method demonstrated here relies on a body of already acquired knowledge, it requires less effort to present the basic categories. Teachers present — and students apply — what they already unconsciously know. Fourth, the method ties in nicely with a process approach to writing. Just as students can improve paragraphs and whole essays by learning about and partaking more consciously in the process of writing, so too can they improve their sentence mechanics by learning about and partaking more consciously in the process (i.e., the operations) of sentence formation.

Notes

1. The asterisk here denotes an ungrammatical sentence, that is, one which violates the descriptive rules of English grammar.
2. When working with tag-question formation, instructors will sooner or later encounter word sequences which are genuine sentences but which, on first try, cannot be transformed into grammatical tag questions (at least not in all regional or social varieties of English). These cases involve sentences containing modal verbs (a subclass of auxiliary verbs) like *may, might, ought,* and *shall,* which, if contracted with *not,* produce in some dialects or styles the unacceptable **mayn't, *mightn't, *oughtn't,* and **shalln't* (*shalln't* [or *shan't*], for example, being unacceptable in many non-British dialects), or the main or auxiliary verb form *am* (which, if contracted with *not,* results in the unacceptable *amn't*). Although such verbs may not contract with *not* to form grammatical tag questions, in some varieties of English they do appear in *uncontracted* form in tag questions. Thus, for example, *He might come tomorrow* can be transformed into *He might come tomorrow, might he not?* (or, possibly, *He might come tomorrow, might not he?*). Although the resulting tag question is formal in style, it is, nonetheless, in some varieties of English, a grammatical — and corresponding — tag question. To keep matters simple, instructors should, whenever appropriate, inform students that, if the inability to contract the verb is the *only* problem in forming the proper tag question, then the proper tag question is a formal one (i.e., one with an uncontracted verb in the tag part of the question). One other point

needs mentioning. Even though verb forms like *may, might, ought, shall,* and *am* may not be contracted with the negative in some varieties of English, so strong is the pattern to have a contracted verb in tag questions (assuming, of course, the original sentence is positive) that native speakers of English will often substitute for an uncontractable verb a contractable one and usually one that's similar in meaning or time reference. Thus, in informal styles, the following changes will occur: *may, might → won't; ought → shouldn't; shall → won't; am → aren't, ain't.* Teachers and students should view such changes solely as efforts of English speakers to get around the uncontractability problem mentioned above.

3. Some handbooks state that the comma should be inserted only if the introductory phrase or clause is a "long" one, usually set arbitrarily at five or more words; however, students who add a comma even for "short" introductory phrases and clauses can hardly go wrong, given the arbitrariness of what constitutes "long." If students realize that all presentence modifiers are also fragments, then a more general and more acceptable rule is possible: "When a fragment immediately precedes a (genuine) sentence and both are intended to be read as one unit, the fragment is set off from the sentence by a comma." The greatest advantage of this rule is that instructors do not need to define the various kinds of phrases (e.g., prepositional, participial, infinitive) or the various kinds of dependent clauses (e.g., adverbial). When a fragment immediately *follows* a (genuine) sentence and both are intended to be read as one unit, the fragment is often (not always) set off by a comma.

4. Using the same underlying principles but slightly different operational syntactic tests than the ones outlined in this study, DeBeaugrande (1984) reports impressive results in getting college students to identify subjects, number-carrying verbs, verb tenses, and fragments. For example, he states that, with respect to identifying subjects and predicates, posttest scores showed an improvement of approximately five hundred percent over pretest scores (363); the same study found that forty-five students who had been taught an operational test for identifying number-carrying verbs and verb tenses made less than half as many errors in recognition than before treatment (365).

My own work with the approach based on underlying syntactic knowledge shows less spectacular gains but highly favorable responses from teachers who use the approach. In the fall of 1988, I conducted a study which differed significantly from DeBeaugrande's insofar as it contrasted two approaches (i.e., a traditional or conventional approach versus the approach based on underlying syntactic knowledge) and covered a wider range of students with greater variability in writing skills, specifically, one sixth-grade elementary school class, three ninth-grade junior high classes, and two freshman-level and two developmental-writing college classes. As a means of identifying fragments, run-ons, and comma splices, the participating teachers (all of whom taught multiple classes or sections) taught a traditional (usually a traditional grammar) approach to one set of students and the approach based on underlying syntactic knowledge to another set of students.

On the basis of pretests and posttests, the experimental groups (i.e., students taught the approach based on underlying syntactic knowledge) showed about the same positive gains in identifying fragments, run-ons, and comma splices as the control groups (i.e., students taught a traditional approach). At the least, the results indicated that students generally do benefit from exposure to some grammar instruction, whether formal or informal, in identifying the three kinds of sentencing errors. In all likelihood, the lack of differentiation in the results of the two approaches lay in two substantial factors: (1) because the experimental and control groups in the study generally could not be equalized with respect to academic ability without severely disrupting the teachers' normal conduct of classes, the higher-achieving class was always assigned as the control group and the lower-achieving class (or classes) as the experimental group, and (2) because most students in the study reported that they had studied traditional grammar for many years, the control groups (both students and teachers) generally had much more exposure and practice with the traditional method than the experimental groups had with the new approach. Yet, despite the probable influence of these two factors, many students in the experimental groups made significant gains, some comparable to those reported by DeBeaugrande. The most impressive findings, however, lay in teachers' responses to the approach based on underlying syntactic knowledge. An attitudinal questionnaire completed by the five teachers who participated in the study and by three other teachers who had also used the approach during the same period generally showed favorable or highly favorable responses with respect to ease of presentation, economy of time, and overall impression. Further, all believed strongly or very strongly that they could get better results with more practice, and all strongly or very strongly indicated that they planned to use the approach in future writing classes (the latter item on the questionnaire, in fact, received the highest positive score of all, with seven out of eight teachers indicating "very strongly"). Lastly and somewhat strangely, a majority of instructors (five out of seven) perceived the experimental method as bringing better results than traditional methods, even though their students, on the average, made about the same gains with the experimental method as with the conventional method. In light of the other responses to the questionnaire, a likely explanation here is that these instructors interpreted "better results" in the questionnaire item "Did the USK [i.e., the Underlying Syntactic Knowledge] method bring better results than the method(s) you normally use?" to mean better results with respect to time and effort spent. (I wish to thank Jeffrie Ahmad, Linda Beauregard-Vasquez, Pamela Grove, Lynn McDonie, John Peters, Mary Riggs, Ilene Rubenstein, and Anne Lise Schofield for their aid in completing this study.)

Positive responses to the underlying-syntactic-knowledge method also came from students themselves. In a study of developmental writers conducted at Antelope Valley College, Beauregard-Vasquez (1989) found that students who were taught the underlying-syntactic-knowledge method not only made 40.5 percent fewer errors in identifying fragments and 37.9 percent fewer errors in identifying run-ons and comma splices but also, with much less classroom instruction, made greater average gains than a control group taught only traditional grammar. Just as important, students greatly preferred the underlying-syntactic-knowledge method over traditional grammar instruction. On the basis of narrative student evaluations of the method, Beauregard-Vasquez states that students found the underlying-syntactic-knowledge method to be a "fun" and "easy" way to "fix" their papers and that students wished that they had learned the method earlier, or in the words of one student:

> I have gone to many English classes all through my years of school, and I have been taught the same type of skills. . . . But the tag and yes-no question method is by far the most unique and simplified method I have ever been taught. . . . I like the method because it is something new and exciting. It is far better than anything else they tried to teach me. (16)

Beauregard-Vasquez notes that the method seems to give students a greater sense of confidence and helps reduce the "excessive blame they tend to place on themselves for not already knowing grammar," or as stated by another student:

> I'm very excited about this new way of learning grammar. I've always felt that I was the problem when it came to learning; however, I thought that it was a lack of attention or just being unable to soak up the material. But now I know it's not; in fact, it was never me. It was the way the material was presented. (15)

Works Cited

Beauregard-Vasquez, Linda. "The USK Alternative to Traditional Grammar Instruction: A Case Study of Student Writers at A.V.C." Unpublished ms. 1989.

Connors, Robert J., and Andrea A. Lunsford. "Frequency of Formal Errors in Current College Writing, or Ma and Pa Kettle Do Research." *College Composition and Communication* 39 (1988): 388–93.

DeBeaugrande, Robert. "Forward to the Basics: Getting Down to Grammar." *College Compositon and Communication* 35 (1984): 358–67.

D'Eloia, Sarah. "The Uses — and Limits — of Grammar." *Journal of Basic Writing* 1.3 (1977): 1–48.

Hairston, Maxine. *Successful Writing: A Rhetoric for Advanced Composition.* New York: Norton, 1981.

Noguchi, Rei R. "Transformation-Generative Syntax and the Teachings of Sentence Mechanics." *Journal of Basic Writing* 6.2 (1987): 26–36.

Classroom Activities

Have students work together in pairs or small groups to try Noguchi's operational approach. Ask them to bring a draft to the group; you should provide copies of some of the exercises Noguchi lists in this article. First, have students identify the sentence-level errors in each other's drafts; next, working on their own drafts, students can use Noguchi's rubrics (tag questions, yes-no questions marking sentence boundaries, and so forth) to improve their own sentences. As Noguchi suggests, these rubrics enable students to conceptualize different choices for correcting errors as well as to internalize the operational definitions of sentence structure. Finally, as a whole group, students can compare sentences before and after editing, writing original and revised sentences on the board to become more aware of this important aspect of the writing process.

Thinking about Teaching

Reflect on your own notions of "socially approved" grammar in your teaching journal. Noguchi suggests that "violations of the prescriptive rules still result in English sentences, even though the sentences may not be socially approved." The rules of standard written English have been presented as a kind of canonical grammar; not following the "rules" in this sense may be equated with transgressing the social order, which carries political implications. Language usage is often understood as a class marker within and outside of our classrooms. What to teach as "standard" thus becomes a dilemma.

Discussing the concept of "social approval" with other teachers is one way to examine this problem. Also included in this category may be the politically charged issues of the back-to-basics movement and the teaching of Ebonics. To emphasize the rhetorical differences in language usage, teachers may at some point wish to share their insights on these divisive subjects with developing writers. In this context, teachers can present *determining audience and purpose* and *editing* as equally crucial parts of the writing process, thereby demystifying the notion of "perfect" or "correct" grammar.

Teaching Style through Sentence Combining and Sentence Generating

Constance Weaver

In Teaching Grammar in Context *(1996), Constance Weaver argues that the most effective form of grammar instruction does not have students memorize rules. Instead, it teaches grammar in connection with real writing, which includes material written by students themselves. The following selection, taken from that book, presents several creative strategies that will help students add variety to their sentences and develop a more sophisticated writing style. Throughout the mini-lessons presented here, Weaver emphasizes the potential for creativity in grammar instruction and demonstrates her enthusiasm for playing with language and ideas.*

Teachers who need more background in grammar to adapt and expand [the following] lessons or develop their own might find Diana Hacker's *A Writer's Reference* (1995) particularly useful. More realistic in its assessment of how the language is really used by educated people is *The Right Handbook: Grammar and Usage in Context,* by Belanoff, Rorschach, and Oberlink (1993). Both of these would also be excellent references for students at the high school and college levels.

Usually, it works well for the teacher to make transparencies for the concepts being taught, and to use different colored transparency pens to clarify particular constructions, marks of punctuation, and so forth. I prefer to use examples from students' own writing or examples from literature, such as the many published examples in Scott Rice's *Right Words, Right Places* (1993); in practice, though, I all too often find myself concocting short examples that can easily be printed by hand on a transparency. All these lessons can be taught to the entire class or to a smaller group of students, but follow-up application commonly needs to be guided individually. Or to put it bluntly, without further guidance, such lessons will not necessarily transfer to students' own writing any better than traditional grammar book exercises have done; they simply reflect a more efficient use of time than the traditional practice exercises and tests. Students will inevitably need guidance in applying these concepts during revision and editing.

Most of these lessons I have taught with students in various classes at the college level, but particularly with the preservice and inservice teachers in my Grammar and Teaching Grammar class. In working with those enrolled in this course, I have usually had a dual or triple aim: to teach something that could benefit them as writers themselves; to suggest and exemplify something that they might profitably teach to their students, at least in simplified form; and to model possible ways of teaching grammar in context. Here, these suggestions often look like rather formal lesson plans, with goals indicated and the reader addressed as "you." But to emphasize the fact that these lessons represent ongoing experimentation, some lessons or parts of them have been written in a more conversational tone — to share what I have done as a teacher at the college level and sometimes to make suggestions for how my experiments might be modified to achieve goals at other levels. This, I hope, will also emphasize the fact that adaptations will usually be necessary as well as desirable: that we must all to some extent reinvent the wheel of effective instruction in our own classrooms, even while we share our efforts with each other, collaborate with one another, and benefit from others' experiences.

1. Introducing Participial Phrases

GOALS   To help writers see the effectiveness of using present participle phrases, when used as free modifiers. In addition, to help writers see that they can sometimes move such phrases for greater effectiveness, as they revise. Such lessons are most appropriate for writers who provide few narrative and descriptive details in their writing, or writers who provide such details in separate sentences, instead of appropriately subordinating some details in modifying phrases.

BACKGROUND   One of the constructions that most distinguishes professional writers from student writers is the participial phrase used as a free modifier — that is, as a modifier that is not absolutely essential to the sentence and therefore is set off by punctuation — usually by commas in prose, but sometimes just by line divisions in poetry (Christensen and Christensen, 1978). The present participle phrase commonly conveys action, whether it is used in poetry, fiction, or nonfiction. Such free modifiers most commonly occur at the end of the clause, even if they modify the subject of that clause. The second most common position is before the subject-predicate unit. Least common is a participial free modifier occurring between the subject and the predicate.

Possible Procedures

1. Put some examples on transparencies and discuss them with the students. For example:

I watched the flashing past of cotton fields and cabins, *feeling that I was moving into the unknown.*   — Ralph Ellison, *Invisible Man* (1952)

"I wish we could get wet," said Lily, *watching a boy ride his bicycle through rain puddles.*   — Amy Tan, *The Moon Lady* (1992)

Father,
All these he has made me own,
The trees and the forests
Standing in their places.
         — Teton Sioux, *The Trees Stand Shining* (H. Jones, 1993)

Still laughing, Mama bustled about the kitchen until her masterpiece was complete.   — Phil Mendez, *The Black Snowman* (1989)

Far below, a sea of purple and orange clouds churned, *dashing like waves in slow motion against the mountain's green forests and reddish-brown volcanic rock.*
         — Tom Minehart, "On Top of Mount Fuji, People Hope for Change"
         (July 17, 1993)

The river that used to surge into the Gulf of California, *depositing ruddy-colored silt that fanned out into a broad delta of new land at its mouth,* hardly ever makes it to the sea anymore.
         — Paul Gray, "A Fight over Liquid Gold" (1991)

2. Discuss the placement of the participial phrases. In most cases, the participial phrase is probably most effective as is. However, what about putting the participial phrase before the subject in the second example?

Watching a boy ride his bicycle through rain puddles, Lily said, "I wish we could get wet."

Is this order perhaps as good as the original, even though the focus has changed? By thus discussing the effects and effectiveness of placing modifiers differently, students develop a sense of style and an ability to suit the grammar to the sense of what they are writing.

3. You might also discuss examples like the following sentences from Richard Wright's poem "Between the World and Me" (1935), wherein two past tense verbs are followed by a present participle phrase:

The dry bones stirred, rattled, lifted, *melting themselves into my bones.*

And then they had me, stripped me, *battering my teeth into my throat till I swallowed my own blood.*

Why might the poet have switched from past tense verbs to present participle phrases at the ends of these sentences? How is the effect different?

ADDITIONAL MINI-LESSONS   Students may benefit from follow-up lessons in which they listen to or read more literary excerpts making effective use of present participle phrases. The teacher can encourage the students to find and share examples themselves. Another kind of mini-lesson can involve taking a bare-bones sentence from a student's paper and brainstorming together about details that might be added in free modifying -ING phrases. Similarly, one can demonstrate how to combine already written sentences during revision. See also the following lessons in this category.

2. Using Present Participle Phrases as Free Modifiers

POSSIBLE PROCEDURE   Suggest to writers the option of writing "I am" poems (see Figure 1) in which they equate themselves metaphorically with things that reflect their interests, suit their personalities, suggest their goals. Emphasize the possibility of using present participle free modifiers by sharing examples in which the writer has used them effectively.

3. Creating Participial Phrases and Absolutes through Sentence Combining

GOAL   To encourage writers to use participial phrases (both present and past) and absolute constructions in their writing. Also, to consider the stylistically effective placement of these free modifiers.

Possible Procedures

1. Put the sets of sentences shown in Figure 2 on transparencies, leaving plenty of room to write the changes that the students suggest. It may be helpful to provide a copy of the activity for each student, so that students can more easily focus on the task and keep a record of the sentences they have created. Adapted from Allyn & Bacon's *The*

Figure 1. Example of an "I am" poem, in which the writer uses participial phrases as free modifiers.

I am "Four Strong Winds" and the "Moonlight Sonata,"
    melancholy yet serene.
I am a Bilbo's pizza with whole wheat crust,
    tomato bubbly and cheese gooey.
I am 5 A.M., a nun
    greeting the morning solitude,
    grateful for the absolution of a new day.
I am a midnight lover,
    cherishing and tender,
    tracing a smile in the dark
    with my fingertips.
I am a whitewater raft,
    sturdy yet flexible,
    bouncing over hidden rocks
    to rest beyond the whirlpool.

Connie Weaver

Writing Process, Book 9 (1982), the sentences describe a short nonverbal motion picture titled *Dream of the Wild Horses.*

2. Explain that, for now, you want the sentences in each set combined into a single sentence, with the sentence in capitals remaining untouched and the others reduced to parts of sentences (free modifiers), but kept in the same order. Do the first two or three with the students. If the students reorder the parts of the resultant sentence or choose a different original sentence to leave unchanged (which is common), you can accept these variations but, whenever possible, discuss which version works better in the flow of the narrative. Don't worry, for now, about examining the structure of the newly created parts of sentences; that can be done after the narrative is created.

3. After creating a satisfying narrative, you can call students' attention to the three kinds of free modifiers they have created:

Running dreamily, the herd fades into the distance, *leaving sea and shore undisturbed.* [present participle phrase. The *-ing* in these free modifiers shows that the phrases are present participles. They are verb phrases functioning as modifiers.]

The herd stampedes, *panicked by an inferno.* [past participle phrase] *Singed by the flames and choked by the smoke,* the herd plunges desperately into the sea. [past participle phrase. The *-ed* forms in these free modifiers show that the phrases are past participles. They, too, are verb phrases functioning as modifiers.]

Figure 2. Sentences for creating participial phrases and absolutes.

1. A HERD OF WILD HORSES RACES ALONG A BEACH.
   Their hoofbeats carve patterns in the sand.
   Their hoofbeats churn the surf.
   [A herd of wild horses races along a beach, their hoofbeats carving patterns in the sand and churning the surf.]

2. Manes are flying
   Legs are flailing
   THE HORSES SURGE FORWARD INTO A DEEPENING MIST.
   [Manes flying, legs flailing, the horses surge forward into a deepening mist.]

3. THE THUNDERING HERD ALMOST DISAPPEARS.
   The herd is veiled by a blue haze.
   [The thundering herd almost disappears, veiled by a blue haze.]

4. Two stallions emerge suddenly.
   TWO STALLIONS BEGIN TO FIGHT.
   [Suddenly emerging, two stallions begin to fight.]

5. THEY REAR ON THEIR POWERFUL HIND LEGS.
   They circle each other in a deadly dance.
   [They rear on their powerful hind legs, circling each other in a deadly dance.]

6. The stallions have fought to a stalemate.
   THE STALLIONS RACE TO THE FRONT OF THE HERD.
   [Having fought to a stalemate, the stallions race to the front of the herd.]

7. THE HERD STAMPEDES.
   The herd is panicked by an inferno.
   [The herd stampedes, panicked by an inferno.]

8. The herd is singed by the flames.
   The herd is choked by the smoke.
   THE HERD PLUNGES DESPERATELY INTO THE SEA.
   [Singed by the flames and choked by the smoke, the herd plunges desperately into the sea.]

9. Their fears are forgotten.
   THE HORSES FROLIC IN THE WAVES.
   They dive into the depths.
   They surface again.
   [Their fears forgotten, the horses frolic in the waves, diving into the depths, then surfacing again.]

10. The horses are restored.
    THE HORSES MOVE BACK TOWARD THE SHORE.
    [Restored, the horses move back toward the shore.]

11. THE SHORE IS NOW SOFTENED BY TWILIGHT.
    The shore is tinted with muted pinks and lavenders.
    [The shore is now softened by twilight, tinted with muted pinks and lavenders.]

Figure 2.   (continued)

12. THE HORSES GALLOP IN SLOW MOTION.
    Their manes are suspended in twilight.
    Their hooves trace deliberate patterns in the sand.
       [The horses gallop in slow motion, their manes suspended in twilight, their hooves tracing deliberate patterns in the sand.]

13. The herd runs dreamily.
    THE HERD FADES INTO THE DISTANCE.
    The herd leaves sea and shore undisturbed.
       [Running dreamily, the herd fades into the distance, leaving sea and shore undisturbed.]

Their fears forgotten, the horses frolic in the waves. [absolute phrase. The absolute has a subject and retains the essence of the verb phrase. Often, the absolute can be restored to a complete sentence by adding *am, is, are, was,* or *were,* as in *Their fears were forgotten.*]

The horses gallop in slow motion, *their manes suspended in twilight, their hooves tracing deliberate patterns in the sand.* [The first absolute consists, in effect, of a subject plus a past participle phrase. The second absolute has a subject followed by a present participle phrase. The addition of *were* would restore each absolute to a complete sentence.]

As these examples illustrate, the participial phrase is essentially a verb phrase functioning like an adjective, to modify a noun. The present participle phrase typically connotes present action, while the past participle phrase connotes completed action or description. The absolute construction is effective for conveying descriptive detail, without giving it the full weight of a grammatically complete sentence.

Teacher Resources

Christensen, F., and B. Christensen. *Notes toward a New Rhetoric: Nine Essays for Teachers.* 2nd ed. New York: Harper & Row, 1978. These essays by Francis Christensen are valuable in helping us understand some of the characteristics of today's prose style.

Daiker, D. A., A. Kerek, and M. Morenberg. *The Writer's Options: Combining to Composing.* 4th ed. New York: Harper & Row, 1990. Intended as a text at the college level, this book is also especially valuable to teachers interested in implementing sentence-combining activities that draw upon the research of Christensen and others.

Killgallon, D. *Sentence Composing: The Complete Course.* Portsmouth, NH: Boynton/Cook, 1987. Excellent book for students, especially at the high school level. . . .

4. Appreciating and Using Absolute Constructions

GOALS   To help writers appreciate the absolute construction as a means of conveying descriptive detail, and to help them become sufficiently aware of the absolute construction to use it in their writing.

NOTE   . . . Technically the absolute is a phrase, because it's not quite grammatically complete as a sentence. Because the absolute has a "subject" and the *essence* of a verb, it can also be described as a near-clause.

Possible Procedures

1. Locate some effective absolutes from literature. The references cited in the lesson immediately above are good resources, as is Scott Rice's *Right Words, Right Places* (1993). The absolute construction is particularly common in narrative fiction and poetry — even in many picture books for children. Here are some further examples:

> I saw the giant bend and clutch the posts at the top of the stairs with both hands, bracing himself, *his body gleaming bare in his white shorts.*
> — Ralph Ellison, *Invisible Man* (1952)

> Before me, in the panel where a mirror is usually placed, I could see a scene from a bullfight, *the bull charging close to the man and the man swinging the red cape in sculptured folds so close to his body that man and bull seemed to blend in one swirl of calm, pure motion.*
> — Ralph Ellison, *Invisible Man* (1952)

> A sudden blow: *the great wings beating still*
> *Above the staggering girl, her thighs caressed*
> *By the dark webs, her nape caught in his bill,*
> He holds her helpless breast upon his breast.
> — W. B. Yeats, "Leda and the Swan" (1924)

Notice how the three absolutes in the Yeats excerpt keep the reader suspended before the main clause, as Zeus in the form of a swan approaches and then claims the girl.

2. As a follow-up, encourage students to experiment with absolutes in their own writing. As a preparatory activity, you might encourage "boast" poems like this:

> My car is a sleek gray cat,
> its paws leaping forward the instant I accelerate,
> its engine purring contentedly.

3. Often in students' narrative writing, one finds simple sentences like *My car is a sleek gray cat*, sentences that could benefit from including more descriptive detail in absolute phrases. When writers are ready to revise at the sentence level, the teacher can help them consider ways

of expanding some sentences through absolutes that convey descriptive detail. Past participle phrases can also add descriptive detail, while present participle phrases are often effective in conveying narrative detail.

Classroom Activities

At the end of the mini-lesson on introducing participial phrases, Weaver suggests: "Students may benefit from follow-up lessons in which they listen to or read more literary excerpts making effective use of present participle phrases. The teacher can encourage the students to find and share examples themselves." Have students locate interesting examples from texts that you are reading in class. Then ask students, working individually or in small groups, to find as many phrases as they can. Have students write their favorite examples on the board; then, as a class, try moving the participial phrases around to experiment with word order. Does the placement of the participial phrase make a difference to the sense of the sentence, or to the power of the language?

Thinking about Teaching

In Figure 1, Weaver provides yet another inventive example of using participial phrases in context, the "I am" poem. Consider beginning a meeting or writing workshop for teachers by having each person write his or her own version of an "I am" poem. You can decide as a group which particular version of the participial phrase you would like to try. Share the poems in small groups or with the whole group, or publish them in a small booklet or electronically. You may also wish to try this activity with students, writing along with them in class and reading the results aloud. Weaver asks us as teachers of writing to pay attention to the many ways language can work so that we can experience the benefits of teaching and studying grammar in the context of reading and writing. The "I am" poems are a creative means of working toward this end.

6

Learning Differences

D eveloping writers arrive in our classrooms with complex sets of needs generated by their varied learning differences, learning styles, previous education, and current educational support systems. In a fruitful learning environment, varied teaching methods can work to support both the individual and collective needs of our students.

The selections in this chapter offer diverse strategies and suggestions for teaching students with complex needs. Linda S. Houston presents a case study of a student with diagnosed learning disabilities and discusses how she and the student worked together to find appropriate strategies for completing writing assignments. Linda Feldmeier White argues that "we can be more effective teachers and advocates for students with LD if we separate the idea of learning disability [. . .] from the positivistic discourse that dominates LD research and pedagogy." She further examines the implications of her position for the composition classroom. Both of these writers offer methods for teaching and empowering students with diagnosed learning disabilities. Furthermore, both suggest that all students, whatever their needs, may benefit from instruction that addresses a variety of learning differences.

Accommodations for Learning Differences in the English Classroom

Linda S. Houston

In the article that follows, originally published in 1994 in Teaching English in the Two-Year College, *Linda S. Houston presents a case study of John, a thirty-one-year-old student with dyslexia who graduated with honors from his two-year college program. Although the accommodations John requested may seem unusual (taping his entire composing process rather than handing in a written rough draft, for instance), Houston suggests that such strategies helped him create a successful environment for his own learning.*

You may not be aware that college teachers are required by law to make accommodations for students with learning disabilities. Once a student identifies himself or herself, the teacher is responsible for "equaliz[ing] . . . opportunity" for a meaningful learning experience. Houston provides a helpful list of accommodations for students with learning disabilities as well as many other concrete and inspiring suggestions.

Introduction

In 1973, Congress passed Section 504 of the Rehabilitation Act. The law prohibits discrimination on the basis of physical or mental handicap. It states:

> No otherwise qualified handicapped individual in the United States . . . shall, solely by reason of (his) handicap, be excluded from the participation in, be denied the benefits of, or be subjected to discrimination under any program or activity receiving federal financial assistance.

The handicapped individual identified in the Rehabilitation Act of 1973 includes the learning disabled student.

According to the United States Office of Education's *Definition and Criteria for Defining Students as Learning Disabled* (1977), a specific learning disability means "a disorder in one or more of the basic psychological processes involved in understanding or in using language, spoken or written, which may manifest itself in an imperfect ability to listen, speak, read, write, spell, or do mathematical calculations."

When working with students who have been documented as learning disabled in the English classroom, it is essential to teach the whole individual. To do this, faculty must know the responsibilities of the college, of the individual faculty members teaching the student, and of the disabled student in order to meet the specifications of Section 504 of the Rehabilitation Act. This article discusses the legal responsibilities and the specific accommodations made by a two-year technical college for an adult student with learning disabilities (called John for the purposes of this article), who was able to identify and meet his own needs through the Learning Assistance Center at my college.

Responsibilities

Educational institutions must provide auxiliary aids for a student who identifies herself or himself with handicaps. Postsecondary students with handicaps must notify the college they attend about the type of handicap condition and the appropriate and required aids for learning. John took responsibility for his own needs by identifying a college appropriate for those needs and constantly identifying and improving upon his required aids during his two-year college career.

John was thirty-one years old when he began college in a program designed to prepare him for the job of golf course superintendent on a family owned public course. John's disability falls under the broad dyslexic classification although, as will be explained later, it manifested itself in many forms. This serious student was in my technical writing course, and while he and I spent many hours working together outside of class, he always attended class and often asked questions I believe other students wanted to ask but did not.

Accommodations

According to the publication *Auxiliary Aids and Services for Postsecondary Students with Handicaps: Higher Education's Obligations Under Section 504*, auxiliary aids and services for students may include taped texts, note takers, interpreters, readers, student tutors, talking calculators, and electronic readers, to list just a few. Whatever aids are chosen, they must equalize the opportunity to the student with the disability. While the college has an extended accommodations list (Figure 1), aids are not limited to this particular list. John chose to tape lectures and discussions so that he could listen in class without being forced to take notes, though he often tried to do both. He took advantage of study tables, professional tutors (as opposed to student tutors), direct conferences with his teachers as well as voice taping his written assignments, punctuation and all, which his wife readily transcribed for him. John found peer tutoring disappointing because he came to believe the younger student tutors did not understand his frustrations. Whether or not that was the situation, he was free to develop his own repertoire of accommodations to best meet his individual needs.

In a first-year composition course, John detailed his own learning differences in a written assignment. Through the assignment, the scholar John, as I came to think of him, processed his own accommodations. While reading, he said, he might lose his place and then start in a different place and thus lose his train of thought. Sometimes a learning disabled individual sees the printed page as a jumble of information (Figure 2) or, as John described it, just like lines with all the let-

Figure 1. Accommodations List for Students with Disabilities.[1]

ACCOMMODATIONS LIST

Dear _____ of _____
           (instructor)   (course)

This form verifies that _____ has a documented specific learning disability or handicapping condition. This student is entitled, but not limited, to the below listed accommodations:

For examinations, in-class writings, labs, etc., the student is entitled to:

_____ Extended time on tests in the form of _____ time

_____ Distraction free environment

_____ Reader

_____ Scribe

_____ Word processor with spell checker

_____ Spell checker or dictionary

_____ Not to be penalized for spelling disability

_____ Calculator

_____ Other

For lectures, field experiences, etc., the student is entitled to:

_____ Tape record lectures

_____ Assistance in obtaining notes

_____ Priority seating

_____ Other_____

_____

_____

---

[1] Prepared by Tanya Kunze, Learning Disability Specialist, Agricultural Technical Institute, The Ohio State University, Wooster, Ohio.

ters the same. His requested accommodation for help with this problem, then, was to have larger printing which was double spaced. He also found that well-written summaries or condensed versions of the material helped him sort out major concepts.

Another particular area of concern for John was following along in a class where a teacher used the chalkboard frequently, especially if the teacher used a chalkboard to express her or his interpretation of information. Listening and following lectures alone were not a problem for him, but having to take notes required immense concentration, thus interfering with his ability to learn. However, a class without notes would have been difficult for him to pass since he needed study materi-

Figure 2. How a learning disabled individual sees the printed page.[1]

Learning Disabilities Quiz
What do you know about learning disabilities
and learning differences?
(Watch out for your b's, d's, p's, and q's!!)

per th alearninddis   asa verage oradovea   tellipence?
1. A sonwi   adility h   verage in
                              True or False
              sons   ar   ninddis   lett   kwards   qqed?
2. Allder   withle   adilitiessee ers dac   or fli
                              True or False
        lea   ability is   otib   child co   struddle
3. I   fa   minddis   n   entified a nda   ntin uesto
    d   feeldumd,   chi ldha s   anceof   lodind
an   the nthat   a95% ch   deve
–   em   de 12?
sec   on bary   otion alqro   blems by a
                              True or False
        ith Att   ent   icit Biso   re   way shyder
4. Deoplew   ionDe f   rder(APP)   a   al   active
      asy to   sqot   our cl   as
    anba   ree   in y   sroom?
                              True or False
5. aminddis   ad   c   ively ef fect   ocial in t
    Le   ilities ann eqat   yours   eractions
              ea   s anb   ficanto the
w   ith   col que   sig   ni   rs?
                              True or False

[1] Prepared by Tanya Kunze, Learning Disability Specialist, Agricultural Technical Institute, The Ohio State University, Wooster, Ohio.

als. Prewritten notes, outlines of chapters, the use of his tape recorder, and textbooks on tape helped him deal with these difficulties.

A final concern for John was he trouble he had comprehending technical writing such as articles and manuals. He found he had to read the article, or have it read to him, several times. Therefore, extended time for reading assignments was another accommodation. He found that his ability to think logically, without paper and pencil (or computer), gave him an advantage. He could visualize material from his texts and even his own thoughts, including punctuation.

These accommodations were not without their frustrations for John and the faculty. In the technical writing class, I questioned the arrival of an almost perfectly structured report done entirely away from the classroom, the Writing Lab, and the Learning Assistance Center. Disturbed at my concern, John offered to tape the sessions where he dictated his thoughts to his wife, who transcribed them to the computer.

One assignment, a proposal, filled four ninety-minute tapes. Those tapes were then transferred to a script which enabled me to view the process that John used. Generating ideas, writing a first draft, verbal revision, and rewriting were evident. It was clear from the tapes that, by his own account as mentioned earlier, John could think clearly without paper and pencil.

John fulfilled his responsibility as delineated in Section 504 of the Rehabilitation Act of 1973 by notifying the college about the nature of his disability and the effective auxiliary aids he required. As a postsecondary school, my college fulfilled its responsibility by providing the aids and services needed by the student.

Discussion

Some faculty at my college question the fairness of accommodations to the disabled student as well as to the student who does not receive special provisions. What happens, they say, if a student, for example, has an exam read to him or her and that student then receives a higher grade than an individual in the class who reads his or her own exam? The unspoken implication by the faculty member may be that those students with learning differences are not as bright as those without the difference. Aside from the legal requirement that no longer gives faculty an option of supplying or not supplying services, faculty must have a clearer understanding that learning disabled does not mean less capable.

John graduated from college with honors and received the Outstanding Student of the Year Award. He is currently a superintendent at his own public golf course and has just recently published his first article, written in the method described earlier, in a trade journal. Clearly, providing John with accommodations enabled him to succeed academically and move into a productive career.

Conclusion

How should a teacher work with students identified as learning disabled? The answer to that question is found in the law described earlier. There is no option; there is only a requirement. When a college, its faculty, and the learning disabled student identify and fulfill their responsibilities, success is inevitable.

Works Cited

United States Department of Education. *Auxiliary Aids and Services for Postsecondary Students with Handicaps.* Washington: GPO, 1991.

United States Office of Education. *Definition and Criteria for Defining Students as Learning Disabled.* Federal Register 42:250 P. 65083. 1977.

Classroom Activities

Students with learning disabilities can be invited to participate in creating an accommodating environment. In addition to the items on the accommodations list she provides, Houston cites other strategies that John employed to complete his composition courses: using study tables and professional tutors, audiotaping writing assignments (including punctuation), and audiotaping conferences, lectures, and discussions. In individual conferences with students with learning disabilities, you may wish to discuss which particular strategies will work best for each student.

Thinking about Teaching

The politics of special education and mainstreaming may be particularly volatile at your institution. Meanwhile, students have immediate needs that must be dealt with within the contexts of the composition classroom and the institution in general. Collaborate with colleagues to find out not only what accommodations your institution offers students but also how students are diagnosed with learning disabilities. Other useful questions for investigation and discussion could be: What are the specific categories of learning disabilities? What are the characteristic learning behaviors associated with each category? How do learning disabilities translate into retention and attrition rates at your school? At many schools, "including" and "accommodating" mean spending precious resources and making tough choices; how is your institution dealing with these difficult issues?

From Learning Disability, Pedagogies, and Public Discourse

Linda Feldmeier White

In these excerpts from a longer article first published in College Composition and Communication *(CCC) in 2002, Linda Feldmeier White analyzes the social construction of learning disabilities research and teaching methods "from the perspective of disability studies." In particular, she interrogates the notion of "overcoming" used to support a behaviorist pedagogy of remediation and the teaching of "fragmented skills." In addition, White examines the implications of social class and race in the diagnosis of learning disabilities as she argues for a constructivist pedagogy that will address the needs of all students.*

I n a 1995 speech titled "Disabling Education: The Culture Wars Go to School," Boston University (BU) historian Jon Westling told a story about a student he called "Somnolent Samantha." Samantha approached him on the first day of class with a letter from the disability services office requesting accommodation for a learning disability (LD) involving "auditory processing": she would need extra time on tests, a separate room for testing, a seat in the front row, and help from her professor if she missed information because she could not help falling asleep during his lectures. Though Samantha is clearly a parody of students with LD, the satire is pointed and the intent is serious. Samantha represents Westling's argument, expounded in several speeches, that the LD movement, and egregious instance of political correctness, tries to replace academic rigor with excuses ("We are taught not that mathematics is difficult for us but worth pursuing, but that we are ill.") and common sense with double talk ("LDU [Learning Disabled University] is trying to keep LD philosophy students safe from the perplexities of Aristotle, to accommodate foreign language majors who have foreign language phobia, and to comfort physics students who suffer from dyscalculia, which is, of course, the particular learning disablement that prevents one from learning math" [Strosnider A38; Westling, "Government"]). To challenge these "myths," Westling, as provost, began to deny accommodations to students at BU. He enforced policies requiring students to have disabilities recertified every three years, denied requests for services, and refused to allow course substitutions for foreign language requirements. Ten students with LDs brought a class-action suit against the university, arguing that Westling violated their civil rights and was guilty of discrimination.

Westling's anti-LD salvos misfired. When Judge Patti Saris ruled on the case in 1997, by which time Westling was BU's president, six students were awarded damages, more stringent requirements for recertifying disabilities were removed, and BU was instructed to establish a committee to examine its policy on course substitutions. Saris's ruling focused on the Samantha speech as evidence of Westling's bias, an indication that he had made decisions about students on the basis of stereotypes — a violation since the law requires that decisions be "based on actual risks and not on speculation, stereotypes, or generalizations about disabilities." Saris noted that Westling had admitted that Samantha was not a real student, and that both Westling and his assistant, Craig Klafter, had

> expressed certain biases about the learning disabilities movement and stereotypes about learning disabled students. Westling and Klafter indicated repeatedly that many students who sought accommodations on the basis of a learning disability were lazy or fakers (e.g., "Somnolent Samantha"), and Klafter labeled learning disabilities evaluators "snake oil salesmen." If not invidiousness, at the very least, these comments reflect misinforced stereotypes. . . . (*Guckenberger et al. v. Boston University*)

Saris also faulted Westling for becoming involved in reviewing accommodation requests, since he had "no expertise in learning disabilities and no training in fashioning reasonable accommodations for the learning disabled."[1]

The story of Samantha, Westling, and Saris raises issues that are not often discussed in composition studies.[2] Like Saris, most composition specialists see LD as the province of experts whose special training enables them to diagnose and treat the condition and whose judgments should not be questioned. I find this deference to medical constructions of learning problematic: If we think that students with LD are beyond our expertise, then we marginalize them as essentially different from "normal" students. The current public discourse on LD offers only two positions: either LD is a neurological condition that only experts understand, or LD is a myth, a euphemism for lack of intelligence. Questioning the first view allies one with the second. But there are other ways to look at LD — new ways to see problems are emerging, among both LD professionals and their critics, that composition specialists should be aware of. In this article, I examine LD from the perspective of disability studies. Though my reading of the LD literature has led me, like Westling, to question the concept of LD, my position is different from his. I critique LD, but not because I want to exclude students with LD from higher education. My argument is that we can be more effective teachers and advocates for students with LD if we separate the idea of learning disability — that school failure subjects students to the same kinds of oppression that characterize other disabilities — from the positivist discourse that dominates LD research and pedagogy.

Historically, the LD movement won support for some students who have difficulty with schooling by establishing LD as a neurological impairment. According to this argument, it is because their learning problems are biologically based that LD students deserve accommodation; without neurological impairment, they would be no different from other poor students. Within this framework, arguments about the social construction of LD are easily conflated with arguments that LD is a fraud. But it is important to recognize that LD, like all disabilities, is socially constructed. Further, it is possible to do so without aligning oneself with Westling's campaign to keep students with LD out of higher education — indeed, as I discuss later, LD professionals who focus on neurological impairment are more closely allied with conservatives like Westling than with supporters of inclusive admissions policies, in both epistemology and pedagogical theory. If we bracket the question of whether a physical impairment exists, LD is no less real. Its growth as a diagnosis since the mid-1960s is inarguable. For LD to have gained its current popular, disciplinary, and legal status in only a few decades, our culture must have been primed to understand learning problems as "an invisible handicap," perhaps because the consequences and the stigma of school failure are so similar to those attached to physical impairments. A school child discovered to have "congenital word blindness" who, therefore, changes status from "dunce" to "cripple-brained" (an early twentieth-century term for LD) or from "slow learner" to "learning disabled" or "dyslexic" is not taking a very big step.[3] [. . .]

Epistemology and Pedagogy

In this section, I use spelling instruction as an illustration of the differences between LD pedagogy and holistic models of language teaching. Spelling pedagogies are revealing because spelling appears to be one of the most unambiguously mechanical literate behaviors but is actually heavily influenced by semantic knowledge. Comparing LD spelling pedagogy with whole-language spelling pedagogy provides clear examples of the limitations of behaviorist theory in explaining the perception of language.

Cognitive psychologists outside of special education are exploring relationships between culture and perception. Indeed, in "Shared Cognition: Thinking as Social Practice," Lauren Resnick maintains that constructivism is now "a pervasive assumption" of cognitive psychology. Research into "situated cognition" or "shared cognition" is based on the premise that knowledge is always an interpretation of experience. Conclusions drawn from earlier experiments are being revised by researchers aware that laboratory learning experiments can be misleading if the lab setting is assumed to be neutral, since no setting is neutral. Perception is affected by schema: "The empiricist assumption that what we know is a direct reflection of what we can perceive in the physical world has largely disappeared" (1). The collection of conference papers in which Resnick's statement appears, which includes work by Jean Lave, James Wertsch, Shirley Brice Heath, Barbara Rogoff, and Michael Cole, we published in 1991 by the American Psychological Association and is in its third printing. But, as Mike Rose notes in a 1988 *CCC* article, "cognitive reductionism," the tendency "to see singular, unitary cognitive explanations for broad ranges of poor school performance," though it is often challenged, is "surprisingly resilient" and re-emerges (267). Nowhere is this resiliency more evident than in learning disability research and pedagogy.

The dominant paradigm of the LD field is summarized by one of its founding fathers, William Cruickshank: "Neurological dysfunction leads to perceptual processing deficits which, in turn, result in a variety and complexity of learning disabilities" (xiv). In Cruickshank's scheme, there is no space between deficit and disability, no mediation that needs to be accounted for. Learning is acquiring knowledge through repetition and practice, and teaching is placing information in the brain, where knowledge and ability are quantities most reliably measured by standardized tests. Thus, in *Learning Disabilities and Brain Function*, William Gaddes analyzes learning to spell as a matter of creating engrams (altering neural tissue to constitute a memory). The causes of spelling deficit are "brain lesions in the language circuits." Spelling disability is an "impaired or undeveloped behavioral skill" and remediation requires "the exercise of neuromuscular *movement*" (410, emphasis in original). Gaddes directs the diagnostician who wants to help a learning disabled child learn to spell to conduct a series of forty-two tests in order to discover deficits so that the appropriate remedial drills can be selected. There are seventeen questions about "auditory processes and aphasic signs in oral speech" (e.g., "Is hearing normal on an audiometric test?"); thirteen questions about "visual processes" (e.g., "Can the child look at pictures of common objects and match them with a similar picture?"); six questions about "tactile processes" ("Can the child write while blindfolded or with his hand obscured?"); and six questions about "motor-expressive processes" (e.g., "What is the child's finger-tapping speed for each hand? Are they both normal?") (411–13). Multisensory teaching methods (writing letters on the child's back or asking him to write the letters in damp sand while sounding them phonetically) are recommended in order to "build engrams linking the occipital, temporal, parietal, and motor strip areas that are crucial to correct writing." But despite his assertion that this diagnostic battery is needed to plan remediation, Gaddes devotes little space to making connections between diagnosis and teaching: "Once a clearly defined diagnostic understanding of the child's strengths and weaknesses is made available to the special teacher, a suitable battery of remedial techniques can be selected. Any experienced teacher already has an armamentarium of teaching skills to draw from" (413).

Disciplinary isolation is evident here, as it is in most LD pedagogy. Though the text, published in 1994, is in its third edition (the first was in 1980), there is no recognition of the limits of behaviorism. LD specialists are determined to keep meaning making out of their tent, as they must be, since paying attention to meaning would turn the enterprise of manipulating and measuring behavior into a much different field of investigation. The diagnostic questions Gaddes asks keep him from seeing others. He is uninterested in questions about language, a variable whose nature he assumes he understands. When he asserts that "the phonetic inaccuracy of a person's spelling is a reliable measure that discriminates LD from normal groups" (413–14), Gaddes is unaware that our ideas about phonetic accuracy are constructions. He is not thinking of phonetically (in)accurate correct spellings like "jumped" or "gives" or "sign" or "neuropsychological" or of the phonetic (in)accuracy of these children's misspellings: "groceriss," "mistiufus," "emidietly," "pachont," "feachure," "plesher," "nolage," "marvales" (Hughes and Searle 98, 115).

Even when empirical evidence fails to confirm the effectiveness of behaviorist teaching strategies, LD researchers often seem unaware that there might be relevant research in other disciplines. Thomas Oakland and his colleagues report a controlled experiment with the Dyslexia Training Program (DTP), an adaptation of the Orton-Gillingham Alphabetic Phonics method of multisensory instruction. In the DTP, the lessons begin with letter recognition and "extend sequentially to sophisticated levels of linguistic knowledge," like the syllabication of polysyllabic words. "As they progress through the curriculum, students are taught an extensive vocabulary to apply to their language learning, code marks that indicate speech sounds, symbols plus abbreviations related to word decoding, and formulas for syllable division and spelling" (141). The experimental program the researchers studied consisted of 350 one-hour lessons, five days a week, for ten months a year, for two years. (In some cases, the DTP was delivered via videotape, to test the feasibility of using the curriculum with students whose teachers lack the training to administer the program. Videotape was equally effective.) At the end of the program, DTP students had made "clinically significant" gains in reading ability, which the researchers note were "relatively modest . . . given the intensity and duration of the intervention." Students' spelling performance had not improved, and the researchers note that the failure of the DTP to improve spelling had already been well documented in "more than 2,000 children using the DTP in Texas schools." In explaining this result, although they notice that spelling is a complex skill requiring "morphological and semantic" knowledge, they don't question their methods. Their explanation is that spelling is complex and "rarely mastered by individuals with severe reading disability" (Oakland et al. 146).

If they looked at research in other fields, LD specialists would find a richer and more useful picture of language and learners. Margaret Hughes and Dennis Searle's work provides a good contrast. Theirs is an eight-year longitudinal study of children from three elementary schools, from kindergarten to sixth grade. They do not attempt to prove that one and not the other of the methods used by the teachers whose students they followed produce uniformly good spellers. Their research produces a different kind of knowledge, a narrative about how correct spelling develops from presound logic, to phonemic spelling, to the use of nonsound features characteristic of correct spelling. Among their findings are that children who reached correct spelling did so in different ways; that some whose development stalled in an early grade made progress later on; that good spellers approached spelling with the assumption that it had order that they could make sense of, while poor spellers saw it as arbitrary; that poor spellers judged correctness by assessing the act of production rather than the appearance of the word — if they found a word difficult to produce, they weren't certain it was correct, but they were adamant that words they found easy to spell were correct, even when they were wrong (Hughes and Searle, 103, 125). [. . .]

Overcoming and Maintaining Standards

While Westling was battling LD, other proponents of "academic standards" were publishing arguments that attacked a different group of students similarly judged to be illiterate and recipients of undeserved accommodation in open admissions programs. The opponents of remediation at CUNY have been more successful (see Sternglass 296–

302; Healy). Arguments like Traub's *City on a Hill* accomplish what Westling failed to achieve: a convincing representation of students whose differences matter so much that their presence compromises higher education. Though we recognize students with LD as different from basic writers, it is important to notice that the same person can have both identities. Westling recognizes the similarity of the LD and basic writer identities when he attacks LD as political correctness. As recipients of legal protection on college campuses, the students of "LDU" are tainted by their association with other minorities who refuse to stay in their places. But there are problems with the fit between LD and political correctness. Westling can't pursue his criticism of LD diagnosis too seriously without challenging philosophies congenial to conservative views. Problems with LD diagnosis are too closely tied to problems with IQ and standardized tests to be explored. The attack on LD has been less successful than the attack on basic writing because conservatives and LD researchers share key beliefs in the certainty and objectivity of empirically produced knowledge and in the inevitability of hierarchical structures.

Both the learning disabled and the basic writer occupy sites at the intersection of conflicting stories about learning and schooling. Bruce Horner has analyzed ways that the texts constituting basic writing, in responding to the dominant public discourse on open admissions without challenging its binaries, established an academic field as it also reinscribed basic writers as marginal to the university (201–02). Writers with LD are more privileged than basic writers; "learning disabled" is a middle-class, white identity. But writers with LD are marginalized; their presence in higher education is always a concession, recognized as privilege and not invisible as normal. For students with LD, marginalization is maintained by the trope of overcoming.[4] When Westling focused on Samantha's somnolence, he made it easy for Judge Saris to accuse him of misrepresentation. Being a hard worker is a crucial part of the LD identity. Dudley-Marling and Dippo hypothesize that the concept of LD supplements the conventional beliefs about schooling that are needed to justify inequality in a democratic society: that public education allows everyone who works hard to succeed, in proportion to their genetic endowment of intelligence. LD provides an explanation for failure, failure that is "unexpected" and, therefore, doesn't require social change. In the LD narrative, school failure is always an anomaly and always a prelude to later success — often extraordinary success. The metaphors of discrepancy and reversal are crystallized in another element of LD culture, the idea that LD is the "affliction of geniuses." Lists of famous people who have been diagnosed or retrospectively diagnosed (Einstein, Edison, Hans Christian Anderson, William Butler Yeats, among others) grow ever longer. But if, as Westling notes, LD provides "comforting illusions," these are not without a price. It is cold comfort to a student who is not doing well that her disability is the affliction of geniuses. She might doubt that she is a genius; the burden of failure remains with the individual.

This focus on overcoming is, in fact, pervasive. LD is a media staple, and the conservative jeremiad is less common (and perhaps less harmful) than the interlocking narratives of scientific progress and overcoming that organize this discourse. A recent feature story on LD in Newsweek, whose cover announces "New Hope for Kids Who Can't Read," is similar to many others. The story of revolutionary new discoveries is familiar:

> Until recently, dyslexia and other reading problems were a mystery to most teachers and parents. As a result, too many kids passed through school without mastering the printed page. Some were treated as mentally deficient; many were left functionally illiterate, unable to ever meet their potential. But in the last several years, says Yale researcher Sally Shaywitz, "there's been a revolution in what we've learned about reading and dyslexia." Scientists like Shaywitz and Berninger are using a variety of new imaging techniques to watch the brain at work. Their experiments have shown that reading disorders are most likely the result of what is, in effect, faulty wiring in the brain — not laziness, stupidity, or a poor home environment. (Kantrowitz and Underwood 74)

No mention is made in the article of alternative views of emergent literacy.

Accompanying this narrative is a series of then-and-now case studies. Eleven-year-old Jason Nicholas was assigned in first grade "to special education classes with three mildly retarded children." Now, after a summer program for dyslexic boys at the University of Washington, "he'll never be a great speller. He still stumbles over new words in a text. But he's an honors student in his sixth-grade class" (74). Jean Urban (pictured examining MRI images of her own brain) couldn't grasp phonics in the first grade. "With special training Urban, now ten and in fifth grade, is making progress and says she's 'pretty good at reading.' She is part of a study at Yale that will see whether the special training is actually changing how her brain works" (73). Matthew Schafir "finally got help, thanks to his mother, Peggy." They lived in a tent in order for him to receive "intensive intervention" at a reading clinic seven hours away from their home. "His reading level went from second to fifth grade in six weeks" (74). "Discount broker Charles Schwab struggled in school with reading. At Stanford, he flunked English 'once or twice' and failed French. He never knew his problem was dyslexia, though, until his son was diagnosed with it" (75). John Corcoran was a social studies teacher but couldn't read. "At forty-eight, he registered for a public library literacy program. That was a start, but the real improvement came when he began treating the dyslexia explicitly" (78). Harvard MBA Susan Hall quit her job in order to help her son Brandon, who "finally made a breakthrough" when she took him to the Lindamood clinic in California (78). A full page is devoted to Stephen J. Cannell, who is "so dyslexic he barely made it through school" but now "one of TV's most prolific writer-producers and a successful novelist" (79).

The emphasis is relentless. Overcoming is so necessary a part of the LD story we are willing to make public, that, after I had read research studies and popular accounts of LD for many years, my perceptions of LD changed dramatically when I read Gerber and Reiff's *Speaking for Themselves: Ethnographic Interviews with Adults with Learning Disabilities*. Gerber and Reiff chose nine subjects for their study, to represent a range of adult outcomes. Of their three least successful subjects, none finished high school. Even the most successful adults — a dentist, a lawyer, and a counselor — have less than glowing stories to tell. The longitudinal studies Gerber and Reiff review, from 1968 as well as from 1985, indicate that successful adults with LD are those with less severe impairments, from affluent families, who had a positive educational experience (often in private schools) (Gerber and Reiff 5–12). Within the narrative of scientific progress, there is no place for this story or, for that matter, for stories about mothers who don't solve their children's problems.[5]

Implications for the College Writing Classroom

The research that I have done on LD was first motivated by my questions about how to work with students with LD. That research led to a second question: I then wanted to know why teaching fragmented skills was so often recommended for students with LD, when all that I knew about teaching writing had led me away from these methods. I think that the foregoing discussion answers the second question and also suggests how to answer the first. The answers to questions about teaching given by "learning disability" — those that have evolved from trying to tie pedagogy directly to empirical research on neurological dysfunction — offer false hope that scientific progress will cure what is wrong. But the broader field of learning disability — the insights and strategies that have evolved as education has become more inclusive — has much to offer. As Brueggemann, Cheu, Dunn, Heifferon, and I have argued in an earlier *CCC* article, disability provides a better position than (temporarily) able ones from which to question what is normal. The accommodations that have developed for students with LD often reveal features of schooling that serve to invent or increase differences among students. We can create better assignments and assessments if we use the lens provided by LD to examine whether teaching practices that require accommodations are really necessary.[6]

In working with students with LD, it is important to try to create a classroom that offers the pleasures of academic writing (getting to explain and having others listen to one's explanations) and reading (the joy of changing one's mind). Teaching that attempts to "remediate" by focusing on what is wrong with the way students are reading and writing only emphasizes their disability. When Rosalie Fink interviews successful adults with dyslexia, she finds that they have been able to learn to read. All are professionals who have careers that require sophisticated reading and writing abilities. Despite continuing difficulty with phonetic decoding, they all as children became avid readers but at a later age than usual, often when they were ten or eleven. They started to read because there were things that they wanted to know. Reading in a particular area of interest (e.g., chemistry, airplanes, love stories), they developed enough knowledge to be able to make sense of words they couldn't decode. When Fink administered a battery of tests to her study's participants, they all scored well on reading comprehension. Some were also able to read quickly, and some had also developed subskills (like oral reading accuracy, spelling, and word recognition), while others had not. Their experiences parallel those of Christopher Lee. He says that when his teachers worked hard to teach him how to decode, he never did get past "first base." It was only later that he realized he could get to home plate (comprehension) without necessarily touching all the bases. He finally began to understand reading in his sophomore English class in college, when he had a teacher who was good at making the readings she assigned interesting. She didn't confine reading to just working with print; she played music, showed films, had students role play: "Although there were pages of reading requirements, the class was never about reading; it was about meaning — transporting ourselves from the classroom right into the story. . . . Even the most complex material would come clear to me. For the first time, I was able to talk intelligently about these stories" (Lee and Jackson 30–31). Lee learned the basics of writing in a high school English class by observing fellow students' reactions to his and others' weekly papers; he developed confidence in his sense of audience and that strength led to the practice and discipline he needed to become a writer (52–53). For teachers who work with students with LD, the most important teaching skills are those that work with all students.

I end with a story to counter Westling's. I was teaching a first-year writing class in which my attempts to enact critical pedagogy were more successful than they usually are. This class had become a community of learners in which my role was important but no longer central. At about mid-semester, a student who had been turning in very carefully edited papers turned in an essay that had noticeable mistakes in spelling and punctuation. He came to me after class to explain why. His girlfriend had edited the other papers, and this was the first one he hadn't asked her to do for him. He turned in what he was able to do on his own because he decided it was worthwhile to work on editing, and he wanted to know how well he was doing. I wish that I had more stories like this to tell. Students become skilled at dealing with the classrooms they have lived in, where not learning is often a better, safer bet than learning. I have met — at times I have been — the student Westling remembered when he represented her as "Somnolent Samantha." I don't believe that Samantha is just a fiction but that a better reader of classrooms and students would see that she learned to sleepwalk in school.

Notes

1. Westling claimed during the trial that he had been misunderstood and "was not attacking individuals who have or believe they have disabilities" — a disingenuous defense. It is clear that he was looking for politically correct excesses to attack. In a speech to the Heritage Foundation, he joked that having denied students accommodations, he was waiting to be sued, "as intrepidly as a brewer of hot coffee" ("Getting Government Out of Higher Education"). Though Saris ruled against BU on the most significant issues, the damage awards were not large — they ranged from $1 in nominal damages to $13,000, and totaled $30,000 (Wolinsky and Whelan 290). BU eventually prevailed on the course substitution issue. When the BU committee that Saris instructed to study course substitutions met, it recommended that foreign language requirements not be waived. In a subsequent ruling in 1998, Saris then upheld the university's right to refuse course substitutions, since the university could now demonstrate that it had considered the accommodation but had a legitimate curricular reason for denying it (Selingo "Judge Says Boston U. Can Require Learning Disabled to Meet Language Requirement"; Sparks and Ganschow 285). Accounts of the trial are available in *The Chronicle of Higher Education*, which reprints the judge's ruling at its Web site. (See *Guckenberger et al. v. Boston University et al.*; Kim Strosnider "Boston U. Chief Admits He Made Up Story of Disabled Student"; Jeffrey Selingo "Judge Says Boston U. Violated Rights of Learning Disabled.") Most national newsmagazines also covered the trial, e.g., Joseph Shapiro "The Strange Case of Somnolent Samantha." The *Journal of Learning Disabilities* devotes its July 1999 issue to the BU case with articles by BU attorneys Lawrence Elswit, Erika Geetter, and Judith Goldberg; and plaintiffs' attorneys Sid Wolinsky and Amy Whelan as well as LD specialists' reflections on the implications of the decision. A more recent (1999) Supreme Court decision on the ADA curtails protections for those whose disabilities have been mitigated by treatment. This decision makes LD students' rights to accommodations in higher education less certain. After making its ruling, the Supreme Court directed a federal appeals court to reconsider its judgment in favor of Marilyn Bartlett, who is learning disabled but has a Ph.D. in educational administration, had sued the New York bar examination board when they refused her request for accommodations in the administration of the bar exam. The law board argued that Bartlett was no longer disabled since she had learned to compensate for her deficits. (Hebel; *Bartlett v. NY State Board of Law Examiners*).

2. Patricia Dunn's *Learning Re-Abled*, which provides an extensive review of LD research and critiques of that research, is the only extended treatment of the relationship between LD and composition studies. Dunn reviews the small amount of previous literature on LD in composition studies, noting that "the LD field is a bottomless ocean into which composition specialists have rarely ventured" (48–57). She points out that theories underlying the discourse of LD and the discourse of composition studies are incompatible. Making the leap means negotiating different paradigms, with different language, common knowledge, and assumptions — at times, it has seemed to me, different realities. Dunn's resolution of these conflicts is more sympathetic to LD theory than mine is. *Learning Re-Abled* and her more recent *Talking, Sketching, Moving: Multiple Literacies in the Teaching of Writing* describe ways of teaching composition that recognize and build upon diversity.

3. Eileen Simpson, author of a well-known autobiography about dyslexia, recognized the connection long before she was diagnosed. Speculating on why one of her elementary school teachers chastises other students for reading poorly but doesn't punish her when she cannot read at all, she recognizes her kinship with another disabled body:

> It must be that whatever was the matter with me — and surely it was something grave if all the others could make words out of the letters, and, even more remarkable, string the words together so that they told a story — it must be that whatever was the matter with me was beyond punishment. I searched for an explanation, and found one. Often when we had gone on outings to the nearby village, we had seen an ill-tempered dwarf who made rude and incomprehensible remarks as we passed by the bench where he sat. The nuns had taught us not to stare at him. We were to avert our eyes and say silently, "God bless the mark!" Mother Cecilia had averted her eyes. She must silently have said the prayer for me. (8)

4. Simi Linton explains the implications of overcoming: "The ideas imbedded in the *overcoming* rhetoric are of personal triumph over a personal condition. The idea that someone can *overcome* a disability has not been generated within the community; it is a wish fulfillment from the outside" (18).

5. The NIMH brochure, in its "case studies" of Susan, Dennis, and Wallace, does recount a story in which difficulties in school are predictive of later failure. Wallace had problems in school, dropped out in the tenth grade, and "spent the next twenty-five years working as a janitor" (15). Significantly, Wallace went to school during the early 1960s, so his LD went undiagnosed. Susan and Dennis are doing well because someone diagnosed their problem and they were able to get help. "Wallace, sadly, was a product of his time, when learning disabilities were more of a mystery and often went unrecognized" (16). In order for diagnosis to be hopeful, being undiagnosed is the only possibility for failure that can be recognized.

6. The controversy over whether students with LD should be allowed to have extra time on tests is a good example. Stanovich ("Sociopsychometrics" 358) and Kelman and Lester (161–80) examine this issue and conclude that there is usually no or very little explicit rationale for making tests speeded. They argue that if speed is genuinely important for some real-world performance, then speed should be a factor for everyone who takes the test, even if he or she has dyslexia. If it isn't, then speed shouldn't be a requirement for anyone.

Works Cited

American Psychiatric Association. *Diagnostic and Statistical Manual of Mental Disorders*. 4th ed. Washington, DC: American Psychiatric Association, 1995.

Bartlett v. NY State Board of Law Examiners. U.S. Court of Appeals. Docket No. 97-9162. 14 September 1998. Rpt. in *U.S. Court of Appeals for the Second Circuit Decisions* 27 May 2000 <http://www.law.pace.edu/lawlib/legal/us-legal/judiciary/search-second.html>.

Brueggemann, Brenda Jo, Linda Feldmeier White, Patricia A. Dunn, Barbara A. Heifferon, and Johnson Cheu. "Becoming Visible: Lessons in Disability." *CCC* 52 (2001): 368–98.

Cruickshank, William. Foreword to the First Edition. *Learning Disabilities and Brain Function: A Neuropsychological Approach.* 3rd ed. By William H. Gaddes and Dorothy Edgell. New York: Springer-Verlag, 1994. xii–xv.

Dudley-Marling, Curt, and Don Dippo. "What Learning Disability Does: Sustaining the Ideology of Schooling." *Journal of Learning Disabilities* 28 (1995): 408–14.

Dunn, Patricia. *Learning Re-Abled: The Learning Disability Controversy and Composition Studies.* Portsmouth: Boynton/Cook, 1995.

———. *Talking, Sketching, Moving: Multiple Literacies in the Teaching of Writing.* Portsmouth: Boynton/Cook, 2001.

Fink, Rosalie. "Literacy Development in Successful Men and Women with Dyslexia." *Annals of Dyslexia* 48 (1998): 311–46.

Gaddes, William H., and Dorothy Edgell. *Learning Disabilities and Brain Function: A Neuropsychological Approach.* 3rd ed. New York: Springer-Verlag, 1994.

Gerber, Paul J., and Henry B. Reiff. *Speaking for Themselves: Ethnographic Interviews with Adults with Learning Disabilities.* Ann Arbor: U of Michigan P, 1991.

Hebel, Sara. "New Supreme Court Rulings Could Impede Disability-Bias Suits against Colleges." *Chronicle of Higher Education* 2 July 1999: A31.

Horner, Bruce. "Discoursing Basic Writing." *CCC* 47 (1996): 199–222.

Hughes, Margaret, and Dennis Searle. *The Violent E and Other Tricky Sounds: Learning to Spell from Kindergarten through Grade 6.* York: Stenhouse, 1997.

Kantrowitz, Barbara, and Anne Underwood. "Dyslexia and the New Science of Reading." *Newsweek* 22 November 1999: 72–78.

Kelman, Mark, and Gillian Lester. *Jumping the Queue: An Inquiry into the Legal Treatment of Students with Learning Disabilities.* Cambridge: Harvard UP, 1997.

Lee, Christopher, and Rosemary Jackson. *What About Me? Strategies for Teaching Misunderstood Learners.* Portsmouth: Heinemann, 2001.

Linton, Simi. *Claiming Disability: Knowledge and Identity.* New York: New York UP, 1998.

National Institute of Mental Health (NIMH). *Learning Disabilities.* By Sharon Neuwirth. Washington, DC: GPO, 1993.

Oakland, Thomas, et al. "An Evaluation of the Dyslexia Training Program: A Multisensory Method for Promoting Reading in Students with Reading Disabilities." *Journal of Learning Disabilities* 31 (1998): 140–47.

Resnick, Lauren. "Shared Cognition: Thinking as Social Practice." *Perspectives on Socially Shared Cognition.* Ed. Lauren B. Resnick, John M. Levine, and Stephanie D. Teasley. Washington, DC: American Psychological Association, 1991. 1–20.

Rose, Mike. "Narrowing the Mind and Page: Remedial Writers and Cognitive Reductionism." *CCC* 39 (1988): 267–302.

Selingo, Jeffrey. "Judge Says Boston U. Can Require Learning Disabled to Meet Language Requirement." *Chronicle of Higher Education* 12 June 1998: A42.

———. "Judge Says Boston U. Violated Rights of Learning Disabled." *Chronicle of Higher Education* 5 September 1997: A65.

Shapiro, Joseph. "The Strange Case of Somnolent Samantha." *U.S. News & World Report* 14 April 1997: 31.

Simpson, Eileen. *Reversals: A Personal Account of Victory over Dyslexia.* 1979. Rev. ed. New York: Noonday–Farrar, Straus and Giroux, 1991.

Sparks, Richard L., and Leonore Ganschow. "The Boston University Lawsuit: Introduction to the Special Series." *Journal of Learning Disabilities* 32 (1999): 284–85.

Spear-Swerling, Louise, and Robert J. Sternberg. "The Sociopsychometrics of Learning Disabilities." *Journal of Learning Disabilities* 32 (1999): 350–61.

Sternglass, Marilyn S. *Time to Know Them: A Longitudinal Study of Writing and Learning at the College Level.* Mahwah: Lawrence Erlbaum, 1997.

Strosnider, Kim. "Boston U. Chief Admits He Made Up Story of Disabled Student." *Chronicle of Higher Education* 18 April 1997: A38.

Traub, James. *City on a Hill: Testing the American Dream at City College.* Reading: Addison-Wesley, 1995.

Westling, Jon. "Getting Government Out of Higher Education." The Heritage Foundation Lectures and Seminars 3 May 1995 and 6 July 1998 <http://www.heritage.org/library/categories/education/lect533.html>.

Wolinsky, Sid, and Amy Whelan. "Federal Law and the Accommodation of Students with LD: The Lawyers Look at the BU Decision." *Journal of Learning Disabilities* 32 (1999): 286–91.

Classroom Activities

White suggests: "In working with students with LD, it is important to try to create a classroom that offers the pleasures of academic writing (getting to explain and having others listen to one's explanations) and reading (the joy of changing one's mind)." She also cites studies that indicate that struggling students make the most significant gains when they find a subject of critical interest to them and are given the chance to study it in depth.

In this regard, consider giving students the opportunity to complete extended study of a topic or issue that they find particularly compelling. At the beginning of the semester, work with the class to come up with a list of topics that they would like to examine in depth over the course of the semester. Have each student choose the topic or issue that most interests him or her and then organize the class into small groups according to their choices. Work with each group to develop appropriate reading and writing assignments for the semester.

Thinking about Teaching

White argues that "comparing LD spelling pedagogy with whole-language pedagogy provides clear examples of the limitations of behaviorist theory in explaining the perception of language." Behaviorist theory, White further suggests, can be linked to the standards movement in education and to the emphasis on phonics (as opposed to meaning-making) in reading instruction.

With this in mind, consider familiarizing yourself with the No Child Left Behind Act of 2001 (see < http://www.ed.gov/offices/OESE/esea/>). The act mandates that all states implement accountability systems relying on annual standardized tests in reading and math. In light of White's article, how do you feel about the act's emphasis on standardized tests and "programs that use scientifically proven ways of teaching children to read," including phonics instruction as a key component of reading pedagogy? (No Child Left Behind stresses mastery of five key components of reading: phonemic awareness, phonics, fluency, vocabulary, and comprehension.) Does this emphasis on teaching and assessing fragmented reading skills shape K–12 accountability tests in your state? Does your state also require successful completion of standardized tests in order to matriculate to or graduate from a college or university? As you investigate these questions, consider your own perspectives on the issues involved, as well as the implications for access to higher education for students with learning differences. You may wish to share White's article with colleagues and discuss how it affected your views on standardized testing, whole-language pedagogy, and strategies for teaching students with learning disabilities.

7

Writing and Adult Learners

As more adult learners and students of "nontraditional" ages (beyond the usual demographic of eighteen- to- twenty-four-year-olds) decide to begin or return to college, many of us will see a shifting population in our basic writing classrooms. Such adult learners may well have different needs and purposes for attending college than their younger counterparts. Balancing child care and other family responsibilities with full-time jobs and college course work can be a critical concern for this population. At the same time, many adult learners, as well as their teachers, report a more pronounced sense of commitment to their education and a more direct sense of purpose than they see in younger students. The presence of adult learners in the classroom can certainly enhance the learning environment for all of our students, as the following arguments demonstrate, often using the writing of returning adult students as evidence.

Many of us have wondered how to create a stronger connection between our course and the lives of our students. The voices of adult learners that speak in the following selections reinforce the notion of the writing process as an everyday problem-solving activity. Sarah Nixon, Mary Kay Jackman, and Barbara Gleason describe pedagogies that grow out of the real-world experiences of adult learners. Throughout this section, each of the writers offers suggestions that can stimulate the learning environment (both in the classroom and beyond) for all of our students.

Using Problem-Posing Dialogue in Adult Literacy Education

Sarah Nixon

In the following article, first published in 1995 in the journal Adult Learning, *Sarah Nixon considers the needs of adult learners as she presents the activity of problem-posing, which "begins by listening for students' issues" and which "can build confidence and self-esteem in [students'] abilities to think critically." This student-centered classroom structure provides opportunities for even the most reticent students to begin to speak. Nixon proposes a set of discrete steps that engage "adult learners [who] need the initial structure." Not only do these steps create a real-world framework; they also reflect aspects of the writing process. Students work collaboratively to "describe the content" of a given text, dialogue, picture, or orally presented story, to "define the problem," to "personalize the problem," to "discuss the problem," and to "discuss alternatives (solutions) to the problem." Such collaborative work strengthens real-world skills in solving problems and imagining alternative solutions — skills implicit in the writing process.*

A group of women are gathered around a table, deep in discussion. Spreadsheets with schedules, open notebooks with lists, copies of government documents, and a diagram with measurements of a living space are spread before them. The women are discussing several options, looking earnestly at the pros and cons of each, and speaking in detail on specific aspects of one option. While two women are searching for a specific reference in the government documents, another is rapidly taking notes on the discussion at hand. In all aspects this appears to be a professional business planning meeting, right? Close, but not quite. This is a group of women in an adult literacy class who have arrived at a solution to their childcare situation by using a process called problem-posing dialogue.

Problem-posing is a tool for developing and strengthening critical thinking skills. It is an inductive questioning process that structures dialogue in the classroom. Problem-posing dialogue is noted in the works of Dewey and Piaget who were strong advocates for active, inquiring, hands-on education that resulted in student-centered curricula (Shor, 1992). Freire expanded on the idea of active, participatory education through problem-posing dialogue, a method that transforms the students into "critical co-investigators in dialogue with the teacher."

Learners bring to adult education programs a wealth of knowledge from their personal experiences, and the problem-posing method builds on these shared experiences. By introducing specific questions, the teacher encourages the students to make their own conclusions about the values and pressures of society. Freire (1970) refers to this as an "emergence of consciousness and *critical intervention* in reality."

So how is this done? What does it look like? What is the final outcome? Let's take a look at these questions as we walk through the process of problem-posing.

How to Conduct Problem-Posing Dialogue

Problem-posing begins by listening for students' issues. During breaks, instructors should listen to students' conversations with one another and make notes about recurring topics. Based on notes from these investigations, teachers then select and bring the familiar situations back to the students in a codified form: a photograph, a written dialogue, a story, or a drawing. Each situation contains personal and social conflicts that are of deep importance to the students.

Teachers begin by asking a series of inductive questions (listed below) that moves the discussion of the situation from the concrete to the analytical. The problem-posing process directs students to name the problem, understand how it applies to them, determine the causes of the problem, generalize to others, and finally suggest alternatives or solutions to the problem. The "responsibility of the problem-posing teacher is to diversify subject matter and to use students' thought and speech as the base for developing critical understanding of personal experience, unequal conditions in society, and existing knowledge" (Shor, 1992).

Five Steps of Problem-Posing

Auerbach (1990) has simplified the steps of problem-posing. Problem-posing is a means for teaching critical thinking skills, and many adult learners need the initial structure these steps provide in order to build confidence and esteem in their ability to think critically. When beginning to problem-pose, it is important to spend time on each step, for these are all essential components in learning how to critically think about one's world.

Describe the Content

The teacher presents the students with a *code*. Codes are a vital aspect of problem-posing. They *must* originate from the students' concerns and experiences, which makes them important to the students and their daily lives. According to Wallerstein (1983), codes can be

- written dialogues, taken from a variety of reading materials, that directly pertain to the problem being posed.

- role-plays adapted from written or oral dialogues.

- stories taken from the participants' lives and experiences.

- text from newspapers, magazines, community leaflets, signs, phone books, welfare or food stamp forms, housing leases, insurance forms, school bulletins.

- pictures, slides, photographs, collages, drawings, photo-stories, or cartoons.

After the students have studied the code, the teacher begins by asking questions, such as: What do you see in the picture (photograph, drawing, etc.)? What is happening in the picture (photograph, drawing, etc.)? or What is this dialogue (story, article, message) about? What is happening in the dialogue (story, article, message)?

Define the Problem

The students uncover the issue(s) or problem(s) in the code. Teachers may need to repeat the following questions: What is happening in the picture (photograph, drawing, etc.)? What is happening in the dialogue (story, article, message)? Students may identify more than one problem. If this occurs, the teacher should ask the students to focus on just one problem (especially with beginning problem-posers), using the other problem(s) for a future problem-posing idea. Students may identify two problems or issues that cannot be separated and must be dealt with together. This, too, is acceptable just as long as it is the students' decision to work with the two problems together.

Personalize the Problem

At this point, the teacher becomes the facilitator of the discussion, thus guiding the students to talk about how this problem makes them feel and what the problem makes them think about, so that they can internalize the problem. Through discussion, the students will relate the issue(s) or problem(s) to their own lives and cultures. The facilitator should assure that all students are given the chance to share their experiences, understanding as well that some may choose not to share. No one should be made to speak if she/he does not feel comfortable doing so. Learning that others have been in similar situations is very important; this experience will serve as an affirmation to their experiences, lives, and cultures; as an esteem builder; and as a means for bonding with other learners and the facilitator.

Discuss the Problem

The facilitator guides the students toward a discussion on the social/economic reasons for the problem by asking them to talk about why there is a problem and how it has affected them. During this step, it is critical for the facilitator *not* to expound upon personal and political beliefs. This temptation may be very strong during problem-posing dialogue, but resistance to do so is absolutely vital to the growth of the students. Because students' beliefs may differ greatly from those of the facilitator's, students will be more apt to take risks and openly share their beliefs if they believe that this is *their* dialogue and they have ownership in its process.

Discuss Alternatives to the Problem

The facilitator should coach the students into suggesting possible solutions to the problem, and discuss the consequences of the various courses of action. Through discussion, adult students become aware that they have the answers to their problems, especially when they approach their problems and concerns through a cooperative, group effort. Facilitators need to urge the students to search for several alternatives to the problem or issue at hand; the solutions need to be those that can be achieved.

Problem-posing delves deeply into any issue or problem, demonstrating the extent of its social and personal connections. Problem-posing "focuses on power relations in the classroom, in the institution, in the formation of standard canons of knowledge, and in society at large" (Shor, 1992). It challenges the relationship between teacher and student and offers students a forum for validating their life experiences, their cultures, and their personal knowledge of how their world works. Problem-posing is dynamic, participatory, and empowering.

Problem-posing is more than a technique that teaches critical thinking; it is a philosophy, a way of thinking about students and their ability to think critically and to reflect analytically on their lives. Eduard Lindeman, one of America's founding fathers of adult education, firmly believed that the responsibility of adult education was to teach learners how to think analytically and critically; this, too, is the role of problem-posing.

Problem-Posing in Action: Two Case Studies

So what does this look like in an adult literacy education (ABE) program? Let's take a look at two examples from actual literacy programs.

Case 1: An ABE Literacy Class

As an ABE instructor, I was always on the lookout for methods that would promote critical thinking in my class. The students in the program were bright and resourceful adults, and I felt the need to challenge their abilities and push them to question the surrounding world view. I spent many hours listening to my students talk about their lives, experiences, and cultures. Living in the Southwest and being an Anglo woman (many times the only Anglo) among the Latinas/Latinos and Native Americans made me very aware of our differing cultures and lifestyles, but more importantly, it made me see the similar problems that all of us encountered and experienced as people and as women. This awareness made me seek out the problem-posing method.

In one class, in particular, the subject of childcare was always on the women's minds; they discussed the topic before, during, and after class. I introduced this issue in "codes" for problem-posing. Because the topic was extremely relevant to their everyday lives and came from them, not me (as I informed them), it was emotionally charged and personal. They worked through the first three steps quickly and with ease. They related to the pictures I brought in, the short story and newspaper articles that we read, and the story that I shared about my divorced sister and her two children. They brought in relevant reading materials and shared their own stories on the problem of childcare — some of them funny and happy, most of them full of frustration and sadness. Their discussions on the reasons for this lack of good afford-able childcare ranged from money issues, to unreliable (or no) trans-portation, to physical isolation from others, to cultural beliefs about who is qualified to care for someone else's children.

For weeks we worked on this topic. Writing assignments arose natu-rally as the women wrote their feelings about the discussions in dia-logue journals, sharing these with others, and their oral histories be-came written testaments of their lives. They researched different laws on childcare facilities and they learned about co-operatives, thus read-ing materials on varying levels of difficulty. They answered their prob-lem by taking this issue into their own hands — into their own con-trol — and discussed reasonable alternatives to this overwhelming problem. Their solution was to organize a system for childcare on their own by sharing their resources. They planned schedules for taking care of each others' children, and those with reliable transportation arranged for carpools. They planned meals for their children and the care keeper(s) using arithmetic to figure amount of food and cost. They dis-cussed discipline problems, and they organized a system for funding their project. They had a problem, and they found the solution for it.

This is problem-posing in action. It is exciting and educational; it is cross-cultural and multicultural because it draws from all of the stu-dents' cultures. Additionally, problem-posing builds confidence and com-munity among learners. When I initiated problem-posing dialogue into my ABE class, I had no idea exactly where it would take us. But I believed that my students were able to work through this process and arrive at tangible solutions to their childcare dilemma. All of the basic skills were used. They read different types of materials on different reading levels; they wrote journal entries, oral histories, and letters; they planned schedules, organized carpools, and figured budgets. They learned that they had the answers to their problems, and they learned the steps to take in order to arrive at solutions.

Case 2: A GED Writing & Social Studies Class

In *Empowering Education: Critical Teaching for Social Change,* Ira Shor (1992) discusses different ways to tie problem-posing into all classes: science, health, computers, writing, literature, media, engineering, ar-chitecture, and sociology. He begins each class "in a participatory and critical way by posing the subject matter itself as a problem." He asks his students to investigate their knowledge about the subject matter and to think critically about it in an active and reflective way. So, how is this achieved?

I practiced this form of problem-posing in my GED classes. I began by asking the students to think about a specific issue (e.g., What is correct writing? Who sets the standards for correct writing? or What is history? Why should history be studied?). Then I would ask them to write their feelings about this issue, keeping in mind the following questions: What do you think about it? How does it make you feel? Why do you feel this way? What are your personal experiences with this? After the students had time to reflect, we began discussing the topic. If no one volunteered to be the first to share with the class, I would start by talking about my experiences. This would get the dialogue flowing, and others soon willingly volunteered to talk about their feelings and experiences.

Next, I asked small groups of students to compare their responses and explore the similarities or differences in each other's experiences. As a class, we talked about the differences or similarities, what we could learn from them, and how their beliefs could be applied to the class. We tried to figure out ways to make the class materials relevant and meaningful to their studies and their lives. We brought outside materials into the class. We talked about how to make the class theirs — how the curriculum, materials, and instruction could reflect their interests and preferences.

Problem-Posing as a New Concept

This was a new concept for most of my students. Some students had a difficult time with the nontraditional format of the class structure. Most were not used to being asked their opinions or beliefs. They did not believe in themselves; they did not believe that they were capable of helping to build the curriculum of a class, of their class. And of course, a few grasped this idea wholeheartedly and ran with it from the beginning. They became leaders, and they accepted the challenge to change their education. They also helped the others to see the benefits of problem-posing dialogue and the importance of learning to think critically.

As the instructor, I had to learn the art of facilitating the discussions and the cooperative groups. I had to learn to let go of power and control and turn it over to my students, thus becoming a facilitator who guides, shares, and coaches. Problem-posing taught me to trust students, to trust in their abilities, to rely on their resourcefulness and experiences, and to make learning meaningful to them.

Problem-posing enables students to bring to the program their experiences, cultures, stories, and life lessons. Their lives are reflected in the thoughtful, determined, and purposeful action that defines problem-posing dialogue. Moreover, problem-posing is a dynamic, participatory, and empowering philosophy that teaches students how to think critically and examine analytically the world in which they live.

Works Cited

Auerbach, Elsa R. *Making Meaning, Making Change: Participatory Curriculum Development for Adult ESL and Family Literacy.* Boston: University of Massachusetts, 1990.

Freire, Paulo. *Pedagogy of the Oppressed.* New York: Seabury, 1970.

Shor, Ira. *Empowering Education: Critical Teaching for Social Change.* Chicago: University of Chicago Press, 1992.

Wallerstein, Nina. *Language and Culture in Conflict: Problem-Posing in the ESL Classroom.* Reading, MA: Addison-Wesley, 1983.

Classroom Activities

Adult learners have a variety of concerns that connect their lived experiences to the world of the classroom. Students can work through the process that Nixon describes by selecting a reading or working on a community problem that captures their collective interest, and then following the steps of problem-posing to create connections between the classroom and the "real world." Such an approach may also work as the first step of a research project. For instance, students concerned about welfare reform might consult an article in a local newspaper or from the Internet. Following Nixon's steps, students would work together to "describe the content" of the article, "define the problem" suggested by the article, "personalize the problem" in terms of their own communities, "discuss the problem," and "discuss alternatives to the problem." While each step suggests a writing assignment (personalizing a problem, for instance, could lead to a narrative essay), students could work through the entire process collaboratively to gain a fuller perspective of the problem. Each student could then write his or her own researched essay exploring the proposed alternatives. Which solutions are feasible? Which solutions probably will not work? As they complete their research and compose their essays, students should be encouraged to evaluate solutions in terms of the needs and concerns in their communities. This sort of approach creates a realistic purpose for writing, since students use problem-posing to confront problems and to propose action concerning issues that are crucial in their own lives and in the world outside their classroom.

Thinking about Teaching

Adult learners approach the study of writing and reading with varying expectations about education and from the perspective of many different learning styles. Problem-posing dialogue depends on active class discussion to consider the issues at hand. Nixon suggests that during the problem-posing process "it is critical for the facilitator not to expound on personal and political beliefs." However, as Nixon acknowledges, even the most fascinating lesson plan may not generate significant discussion. You may wish to discuss with colleagues the appropriateness of presenting personal experiences and opinions as part of the classroom conversation. Consider how students might respond. Will some students automatically accept the teacher's position? Will others automatically rebel against it? Will students think that their own opinions are being stifled and become afraid to speak? Or, in conveying your own ideas to students, is it possible to demonstrate respect for all opinions presented in the classroom, even if they are significantly different from your own? Try using problem-posing dialogue as a way to discuss these issues and to create alternative solutions to the problem. This discussion might take place within an electronic discussion group for a broader geographic representation. You may also wish to pose this problem to students as part of class discussion.

When the Personal Becomes Professional: Stories from Reentry Adult Women Learners about Family, Work, and School

Mary Kay Jackman

Originally published in Composition Studies *in 1999, Mary Kay Jackman's essay reminds us that a majority of the adult learners in our classrooms will be women students. Citing research by hooks, Belenky, and others, Jackman discusses the critical needs and issues of this group of students. What makes Jackman's article particularly unique, however, is that she tells the stories of several women and their discoveries upon encountering the writing classroom: Margie, a thirty-three-year-old white woman who finds that "pressures arise" not only from her studies, but "from the multiple roles she must play in her family: wife, mother, sister, daughter"; Ann, a twenty-seven-year-old Hispanic woman who lives with her parents and, "returning to college after a seven-year hiatus, . . . juggles two jobs and four classes"; and Sophie, their teacher, a white woman and a "reentry adult woman learner" herself (and master's degree candidate), who "tell[s] personal stories in class to teach writing" and uses extensive conferencing as a way of "mentoring" her students. As Jackman concludes: "The stories from Margie, Ann, and Sophie — three out of the hundreds of adult women now returning to colleges and universities — suggest the power of the personal to bring about academic transformations, indeed, to (re)create professional academic realities." Indeed, the strong voices of these adult women learners as they tell their stories can be a motivating force and an inspiration for all our students, as well as for ourselves as teachers.*

During the fall semester of 1995, I conducted an ethnographic study of a first-year writing classroom focusing on narrative's role in that particular classroom culture at a mid-size state university. The writing instructor in the classroom I studied engaged in personal narrative as one of her principal teaching techniques, and all nine student volunteer research participants responded to her stories in various ways to build their identities as writers and to accomplish their writing assignments. Thus, in writing the results of my study, I argued for narrative's constitutive and epistemic value in a writing classroom and for the autobiographical anecdote in particular as a bridge between teaching and learning.

In sorting through the mountain of data generated by this project, including all the papers each volunteer wrote for class and the transcripts of each of their three interviews with me, I began to hear another argument about the function and value of narrative taking shape, this one more specifically voiced by three reentry adult women participating in the project: students Margie and Ann, and their instructor, Sophie.[1] That argument centers on adult women learners' necessary and workable narrative negotiation of the personal and professional aspects of their lives in order to reach their academic goals. More so than the younger, traditional students in the study, Margie, Ann, and Sophie relied on stories from their lived experience to make learning and teaching sites both inside and outside the classroom useful and valuable to them.

Unlike younger students, whether men or women, for whom college is an anticipated "next step" after high school, older adult women who reenter college have made a conscious choice to do so, expecting the experience to radically change their lives (Goldsmith and Archambault 12). As a reentry adult woman learner myself, I recognize the truth of that claim. My dissertation research came five years after I had returned to graduate school for the third time, almost thirty years after I had earned my bachelor's degree. Like Sophie and similar to Ann, I anticipated a career change after completing the academic program I had entered; like Margie, I was hoping to feel better about myself when the academic journey was over.

Margie, Ann, Sophie, and I, as nontraditional, reentry adult women learners, constitute the fastest growing segment of the student population in higher learning and continuing education programs (Hayes and Flannery 2). The state university we attended, New Mexico State University, had a total student population in fall 1995 of 15,127, of which 7,479 were men and 7,648 were women. Three years later, fall 1998, the population had increased slightly to 15,409, of which 7,274 were men (a slight decrease) and 8,135 were women (a moderate increase). At New Mexico State women outnumbered men in all age brackets except ages twenty to twenty-four and twenty-five to twenty-nine during 1995, 1996, 1997, and 1998.[2] This is only one institution and one study, but the increase in women students corresponds with research findings that indicate a trend of adult women returning to the academy in increasing numbers (see also Nixon-Ponder; Stoffel; Goldsmith and Archambault; Kiskis).

The point of my going into such detail here is that as more and more adult women return to school, notions about the academy's role in the community, about acceptable academic discourse, and about effective teaching practices in higher education may all be challenged. That is, as the material characteristics of the student body change, the material structure and function of the academy itself become susceptible to change. I make this claim based on the stories I hear from Margie, Ann, and Sophie; from the stories I read in recent studies of returning women students; and from my own experience, in which the personal is often inseparable from the professional, a life-state that traditional academic environments not only devalue but attempt to displace (see hooks, *Teaching*; Kiskis). As you will see, Margie and Ann draw on their lived experiences at home and at work to satisfy writing course requirements, and their instructor, Sophie, turns her lived experiences into autobiographical anecdotes that she purposefully uses to teach writing.

Margie

> *I like writing. . . . I keep a journal at home. . . . The nice thing about a journal is that you don't have to make sense. It's just your thing. . . . It's mostly . . . therapy when I write. . . .* (Personal interview)

> *I've come to realize now that I'm over thirty it's not what you do or what you have that counts in life, it's who you are.* (Unpublished essay)

At thirty-three, Margie is the oldest first-year student participating in the research project. A slender woman with curly, medium-brown hair, dark brown eyes, and an easy smile, she is the only married student in the study and the only mother, aside from the instructor, Sophie.

Margie sees herself as a devoted family woman who is now "gonna do something for [herself]" by returning to school. Working within this self-conception,[3] Margie likes to write in her journal at home, but doesn't consider herself a writer when she enters the first-year writing course. As she explains in her first interview, "A writer is somebody who writes a book." Even though Margie's self-image as a writer is limited to her journaling, she believes writing in her journal "does help [her] with the pressures of everyday," pressures that arise from the multiple roles she must play in her family: wife, mother, sister, daughter.

She made her decision to return to school after almost fifteen years of marriage and after discussions with her husband in which Margie says he told her, "'You can go to college. . . . I know you're smart enough.' And [she] would say, 'Oh, I'm not, I'm not. I didn't learn anything in high school.'" She remembers herself as a lackluster student: "[M]y grades weren't the greatest. I was average always." Unmotivated to learn, Margie remembers being placed in the "lower class" in high school with other students who weren't interested in learning. Unsupported by her parents, Margie says, "I think I ended up just giving up."

Margie's history of giving up in high school, marrying and having children early, and living for her family is common to many women, as is her current desire to learn and live for herself (see Belenky, Clinchy, Goldberger, and Tarule; Goldsmith and Archambault). Margie tells me:

> [N]ow that I'm older, I wish I could go back and really absorb all that stuff that they were trying to teach . . . really have listened so that I could have known more. . . . Now that I've come to college, it's really broadened my way of thinking, and it's boosted up my confidence. It's really made me feel good about myself. I'm thinking of [becoming] a counselor . . . because I really like to talk with children. . . . [A]nd I'm really into health. I like to exercise, so it's kinda like something physical versus . . . counseling, psychology, or something.

She negotiates her desire to be a learner among her family's demands for her to function as wife and mother and among the demands of a university classroom in which she must operate effectively as writer and student. While she has operated as a writer within her family, keeping her private journal for over ten years, Margie must somehow learn to operate as a student there, adding that role to her family-sanctioned roles as mother and wife. In the classroom, Margie assesses her roles and positions as student/writer in relation to the expectations of her instructor, Sophie, and to the abilities of the other students. Reflecting the sense of isolation Mary Miritello identifies among returning adult learners (1–3), Margie laughs as she remarks, "[S]ometimes you think that the person next to you is doing so much better than you are and that they understand so much more than you do, and it makes you feel like, 'Well, am I the dummy here or what?'"

Recognizing the multiple roles she must perform effectively at home *and* at school if she is to attain the success she wants for herself and still keep her family functioning, Margie says,

> [M]y mind is sometimes there with the family, but yet it's [pause] split in the middle. You feel like there's two of you, and one of you has to be this good student and the other one has to be a good, understanding mom. And that makes it a little hard . . . to try to be everything for everybody and make the grade. . . . [Keeping my family together] is like [having] two jobs. You have to juggle everything. You have your kids . . . and the attention that they want, and you can't give it because you're so busy doing this or that for your classes. . . . But . . . I've learned to juggle a little bit of everything at once.

C. M. Greenwood points out that adult women learners are much more likely than men learners to sacrifice their studies for family obligations (4), implying that a woman's familial roles are much stronger than her role as student. Margie, however, has learned to play multiple roles simultaneously. She does this by taking the classroom home with her and by bringing her family into the classroom and into her writing. She turns her experiences into stories that help her analyze problems, explain concepts, and evaluate circumstances.

Virtually all of Margie's writing in the first-year writing course grows out of her life experiences in some way. For example, in responding to the assignment which asks her to identify a problem and propose a solution to it, Margie chooses the problem of alcoholism in a family and writes about a weekend visit by her sister and brother-in-law and his drunken behavior. Before she decided on that as her topic, however, she discussed it with her husband. He not only helped her decide to write on her brother-in-law's drinking problem, he also helped her remember things that had happened during her sister and brother-in-law's weekend visit, even "the words they used here and there."

Margie's inclusion of her husband as collaborator in her writing and studenting roles seems to be both voluntary and involuntary. Sometime during the year after she returns to school with his apparent encouragement, Margie's husband begins reading her journal. His intrusion into her private space, a place separate and apart from her other positions within the family, causes her to abandon the journal writing for a time. Margie tells me, "I can't really write in it anymore because I know he read it. . . . It's hard for me to get back into that little book and start writing . . . I feel like I gotta be real careful what I write. I can't just let the pen flow." He also periodically looks through Margie's school books and notebooks without asking her permission. When she asks him why, he tells her it's "to see what you're doing at school." Rather than argue with him, Margie shrugs, "Whatever. Let him look if he wants to look. But it's no privacy, and it bugs me; it bothers me." Margie's frustration in negotiating her student/writer roles within her family shows when she comments ironically: "I wish I could just tell him to stop, but what can you do? He's your husband and the father of your three children, so . . . [laughs]."

Margie's painful recounting of the way her husband monitors both her private journal writing and her student writing calls to mind Belenky, Clinchy, Goldberger, and Tarule's work with women whom they identify as "subjective" knowers, some of whom, similar to Margie, are attempting to redefine some of their conventionally assigned family roles. In transition, having moved from silence into a state of received knowledge, such adult women knowers are searching for a "self" of their own within and without the family. As Belenky et al. point out, and as Margie's experiences illumine, a family very often does not recognize or nurture "the budding subjectivist's impetus toward change, redefinition, and application of her new ways of knowing and learning" (79).

Margie, however, finds ways to negotiate and compromise these family and school positionings with her husband, her children, her instructor, her classroom peers, and herself. Her ongoing but largely unacknowledged writer role at home has already evoked some changes among family members. Margie's husband read about himself in her journal; "[He] started making changes on the way he treated me, and he started paying more attention to the kids, so I guess by writing in my journal, it helped my marriage in a way." Thus, at home Margie's writing as wife and mother paves the way for her new role writing as student in the family. In the first-year writing classroom, Margie links writer and student through her family roles, creating a working balance for herself by writing stories about her lived experiences to satisfy course assignments.

In doing so, Margie actively seeks collaboration and feedback on her student writing from family members. Their collaboration and feedback, while acknowledging Margie's writer and student roles and the self-images they evoke, ultimately validate her self-conception as a family woman. The feedback that most strongly influences Margie's self-images as writer and student, however, is the feedback she receives from her instructor, Sophie. Margie remembers Sophie's comments to her: "'I can tell you're a writer.' That made me feel really good when she said that; that made my day." Margie believes Sophie genuinely cares about her students, a teacher quality Margie values highly, since to Margie, it leads to successful learning. She writes in her final, reflective essay,

> I have learned so much this semester and feel I'm leaving this class a better writer and feeling good about myself as a writer. I have always liked to write, but never felt I was any good until I took this class. I know that you Sophie made me feel this way about my writing. I only heard good things come out of you to all of us. You were always encouraging us telling us we were all good writers and I could tell you meant it.

From Sophie, Margie the student-writer receives the encouragement she didn't receive from her parents in high school. Margie says Sophie motivates her to "put out some to learn," just as Margie encourages and challenges her children: "I really make sure my kids apply themselves." Once again, Margie seeks to mesh home and school, family and classroom, breaking the boundaries between them. Her self-conception as devoted family woman remains largely unchanged during the semester; she simply stretches it through her autobiographical writings to accommodate her revised and strengthened self-images as student and writer. Testifying to her self-perceived success as both, Margie says:

> I'm not as dumb as I thought I was. [Laughs] I can honestly say I feel like I'm a pretty good writer, that I'm okay. Before I never thought I was, but now I can. . . . I'm just proud of myself that I can do these things. Sometimes I even think of maybe writing a book, you know?

Ann

I've never really cared for English. . . . Even before I started [the English course], I was already panicking. . . . I didn't want to be there . . . because I knew that English is not my subject. . . . And, now that I'm done with it, I don't feel like that anymore. (Personal interview)

Tall, plump, and pretty with short, curly, brown hair, Ann is twenty-seven years old, unmarried, and living at home with her parents again after staying with a boyfriend for a while. Returning to college after a seven-year hiatus, Ann juggles two jobs and four classes. She is determined to stay in school this time around and earn her marketing degree. In her first interview with me, Ann states, "I decided I better go back. I feel like I'm getting older, and I don't want to regret it later." Ann values independence and seeks a career that will provide a good income so that she can support herself: "I don't want to rely on somebody else to help me with the rent or any other expenses like I did before." She also wants a career that will provide her with a variety of tasks and responsibilities (so she will not be bored) and physical activity rather than desk work (so she will not feel confined).

Ann refers to herself as an impatient person, anxious to complete tasks in a hurry. While acknowledging her reserve and occasional shyness, Ann writes in an early essay that she "get[s] along with people" like her Hispanic grandfather did. In fact, when Ann describes herself, she writes that she is very much like her grandfather: stubborn and sociable with a sense of humor. By specifically linking herself to her grandfather, Ann implies other traits within her self-conception that she attributes to him but that she values in and for herself: a stable, versatile, hard-working, physical laborer. Ann's grandfather "followed his father's footsteps" and worked for a large, local farm for thirty-eight years; he later worked as a school custodian for ten years. Ann's first job, when she was fourteen years old, was in the office of the same agribusiness her grandfather labored for. Ann worked with her mother on that job, where she learned that she didn't like being confined to an office. One of Ann's present jobs is painting schools for the same school district for which her grandfather worked before he died; some of her coworkers were also his. Ann's other job is painting houses with her father and working with him in construction. Thus, Ann's self-conception is located within an established, respected family and community of physical laborers, becoming for Ann what Pierre Bourdieu calls a "habitus," a collection of habits of mind and body, "durable, transposable dispositions" (72) that she has absorbed from childhood.

Within her strong self-conception as a working woman, Ann's image of herself as both student and writer at the start of her first school semester in seven years remains pale and unfocused. Ann doesn't return to school to learn to write; she returns *despite* having to take a writing course. Her self-conception as a single working woman who seeks to better her economic position within her habitus brings her back to the writing classroom and carries her past her initial panic at being there. To Ann, then, taking and passing the first-year writing course is an economic necessity, even though she enters it with the self-image of a fearful, uninterested student and failed writer.

Ann failed an English class in high school after a teacher, ignoring Ann's objecting voice, enrolled her in a literature course. Ann told the teacher she had no background for nor interest in the course, but the teacher put her in it anyway. Ann says, "I had no idea what was going on in [that class]. It just didn't interest me enough, . . . [and] I flunked it." The teacher, who refused to listen to Ann's reasons for not wanting to be in the course, then blamed Ann when she failed. Ann remembers the teacher telling her, "'You didn't put enough effort into it.'" Ann, whose well-established and respected position within her habitus of laborers assures that her voice will be listened to, found her position in high school unsettling and her voice largely ignored.

Ann chose the noncollege track in high school because she didn't think she would ever attend college. She didn't take courses then that would satisfy college entrance requirements later when, at her aunt's insistence and with her aunt's financial support, she did decide to go for an associate's degree in architecture. Switching positions from noncollege laborer to college student for Ann meant taking the precollege courses, or their equivalents, that she hadn't taken in high school, one of which was a basic writing course that Ann remembers as "English 111."

Ann thought she was "doing pretty good" in the writing course; all her papers had come back to her marked "satisfactory" or "revise," which she did. On the final paper, however, "that decided if we pass or fail," Ann failed. Once again, Ann's position and voice as student seemed to work against her; she had no inkling prior to the exit essay that she would fail the course.

Seven years later, after Ann decided to return to college to obtain a marketing degree that will elevate her economic position within her habitus, she realizes that she will have to retake a first-year writing course. She tells me, "I just didn't think I was going to get through that class because I knew that English is not my subject." Ann chuckles as she remembers and voices her initial thoughts: "I am going to take English 111 for the rest of my life!"

Ann acknowledges her fears and discomfort as a reentry adult learner in a clear, strong voice on the opening day of the semester. After she is introduced by another student, Ann speaks for herself from her habitus of laborers, smiling and chuckling with a pleasant, open expression as she lets the whole class know that she doesn't like writing, doesn't like English, and would rather be at work painting schools. Other than this opening vocal performance and her oral report later in the semester, Ann remains virtually silent in the classroom. "I never really participate in class," she tells me. "I'm the type of person that won't say anything. I'll just sit there." While Ann's voice as a working woman can speak confidently on the first class day, her student voice remains mute, perhaps because it has failed her in the past.

Even with her reluctance to speak up in class discussions, Ann, like Margie, successfully completes the required writing course by calling upon her experiences in her family and work environments to help her make sense out of her experiences in the classroom. As Malcolm Knowles reminds us, adult learners are life-centered rather than subject-centered; they generally want to enrich their experiences through learning, not simply satisfy academic requirements (33). Further, unlike children, who perceive experience as something that happens to them, adult learners look at their experiences as *"who they are"* (60). Ann, then, seeing herself as a competent, respected member of her laboring family and habitus, uses that self-conception and the experiences constituting it to work for her as student/writer in the classroom. Like Margie, she tells stories from her lived experience to satisfy course assignments.

She includes stories about her grandfather in her first in-class essay assignment, and in the revised essay portion of her portfolio. She asks her coworkers to tell her stories about her grandfather, and she includes some of them in her revised essay. She uses an anecdote about her grandmother to support some of her claims concerning elderly drivers in her problem/solution paper, and she includes her grandmother in her portfolio's revised essay. Her father and cousins appear in these papers as well, and her mother helps her with ideas for the problem/solution paper. Her own experience of miscarrying a child whose father was a heavy cocaine user acts as the impetus for her research paper on the effect of drugs on pregnant women and the fetuses they carry.

Writing these autobiographical accounts helps Ann negotiate and voice her worker, family-member, and student-writer positions. Doing so allows her to perform effectively as a working woman *and* as a student-writer in the classroom (she ultimately earns a "B" in the course). Consciously carrying her habitus into the classroom, Ann seems to have discovered her student-writer voice among her coworkers. She smiles as she tells me in our final interview:

> I always tell [this one man that I work with], "Oooooh, you're so full of it." And I always tell him, "Oh, I owe it all to you." And he goes, "What are you talking about?" And I go, "In my English class — I just learn from you; you're so full of it, and you keep rambling on and on. So, I learned from you, and that's how I can write my papers now."

Using a voice from her habitus and operating from a temporary position as student-writer, Ann successfully completes the first-year writing course, and, thus, takes a step in an upward economic direction. Ann believes that she probably will not be writing much in her career, but knows she will have to write in one more required writing course before she can attain her degree goals. By semester's end, Ann feels writing is "not so bad after all" and believes she is no longer "hopeless at writing papers." She faces the next writing course with more confidence than she had coming into the first-year course:

I don't feel like I could just pick something up and start writing about it and it would come out great. But I feel comfortable enough to where if I was asked to write something, that it might take a while, but I could get through it. I just feel a lot more confident than I did before.

Sophie

Ann attributes her newfound confidence in herself as a practical, working writer to her instructor, Sophie. Like Margie, Ann likes the way Sophie "explain[s] everything" and "shows more" than her past English teachers about how to do the assignments. A reentry adult learner herself, Sophie has returned to the university to earn a master's degree in technical writing after raising four sons and working in the automobile industry for more than ten years. She is a graduate assistant in New Mexico State's English department. One of the terms of her assistantship is that she teach a section of writing for the department each semester in which she is enrolled in its master's program.

Sophie characterizes herself to me in our first interview as a writing "mentor" who uses "storytelling teaching" in her classroom. She uses stories from her lived experience to introduce the course's required, sequenced assignments and to model various writing techniques, particularly invention and arrangement. For example, when introducing the first writing exercise of the semester, which is to describe a place important to the writer, Sophie tells two stories about her experiences at Yosemite Park: seeing her first waterfall and being chased by a bear. She tells me later that she uses the stories to teach invention by modeling her invention process — "meditation, listing, and freewriting," and the ways these processes help her recall the experience and help her understand why Yosemite is an important place to her. Engaging the class in discussions about the stories, Sophie also uses them to illustrate description that touches the five senses as well as description that sometimes omits details. As she does with virtually all the autobiographical anecdotes she tells, Sophie asks the students to offer feedback on some aspect(s) of the story. In the case of the Yosemite stories, she asks students to provide more detail and to speculate about different details she could have provided or left out. Sophie's storytelling does not go unnoticed by Margie and Ann; they both respond favorably to the way she "explains."

In addition to telling personal stories in class to teach writing, Sophie also holds conferences regularly and privately with each student to discuss his or her specific writing projects. Sophie says "[my students] talk to me a lot. . . . [I'm] personally involved . . . mostly because I do all of this conferencing. I know a lot about them, so it's not as though they're just people out there in desks. . . . [T]hey know me, too." Like storytelling, Sophie's conferencing helps her "become connected" to her students; it's a teaching method she wouldn't give up, even if she were to teach a four-or-five-course load. "I don't think that I could not be conferencing," she says.

As noted earlier, Margie interprets Sophie's classroom and conference demeanor as a personal expression of care and concern for her students. However, Margie also notices Sophie's commitment to her professional obligations as a writing mentor who comes to the classroom prepared to address specific writing tasks. Margie points out:

> You could tell that she plans what she's gonna come in with, and she doesn't all of a sudden just think of something to say or do. She knows what she's gonna do and then, that's that. . . . She's serious about everything she assigns. That to me is a good instructor. And I like the fact [that] she's not mean, but she means what she says.

Sophie's classroom management, as perceived by the two reentry adult women learners discussed here, demonstrates characteristics of what Wendy Luttrell refers to as "maternal authority" (124), a way of managing classroom dynamics through "love, care, protection, and acceptance" that promotes "mutual, egalitarian, and respectful relationships" and has a positive impact on students (124, 125). Her classroom management also reflects characteristics of the "connected teaching" that Belenky et al. believe is most conducive to women's learning (214–229). Such a teaching method combines the personal with the professional: telling and listening to each other's stories in interactive learning, expressing concern for learners (students *and* their instructor) as individuals with complicated lives, and working within a predictable, intentional structure of task analysis and problem solving. As Margie noticed and Belenky et al. point out, most women want some structure in their learning environments (204). Yet, within that structure, they respond to a dialogic exchange of experience, an "antihierarchical" system in which the learning facilitator is unafraid of bringing personal issues and uncertainty into the classroom (Rich 145). Sophie says,

> I'm not really sure that we do any teaching. Maybe we're just there to encourage them. I'm not sure about that. I'm not sure that any teaching technique has been very helpful. I'm more personal about it [in my classroom]. I suppose I come at it from [knowing] what it's like to be a writer. It's hard. "This is what I do to try to solve the problem for myself. This is a way for you to get started." I hope I'm not telling them this is the *only* way to do it. . . . My main goal is to give them some tools so that they can fly a little bit — get off the ground, so that later on they can do whatever they want. Since I'm such an ordinary person, I'm not a great scholar or a great writer or anything else, . . . I think that if I can do it, they can [chuckles]. That's my attitude. And I *like* teaching. I like [the students]. They surprise me. I learn a lot.

Summary and Implications

As older, returning students, Margie and Ann are nontraditional adult women learners who must pass the required, first-year writing course with a "C" or better if they are to realize their goals: increased self-esteem and confidence as a writer for Margie, with perhaps a career; a marketing degree, greater personal and financial independence, a higher economic position, and a business career for Ann. Their instructor Sophie, herself a nontraditional, returning adult learner, must effectively teach the required writing course if she is to retain her graduate assistantship and complete her master's degree. As Malcolm Knowles points out, adult learners want to see practical gains; they need to see how what they are learning can be applied to their lives (61), a concept echoed in the connected teaching that Belenky et al. describe (219) and demonstrated by the storytelling teaching that Sophie practices.

Michael Kiskis, who has worked extensively with adult learners, an increasing number of whom are women (57), believes that "most adult students . . . seek out and find material within their studies that can be transported back to their home or work environments to help them make better sense out of experiences they face" (60). Margie and Ann, however, in addition to carrying classroom experiences into their home and work, also transport their family and work environments back to the first-year writing classroom to help them make sense out of the experiences they face *there* as students-writers, just as a "mid-wife teacher" in a "connected class" might encourage them to do (Belenky et al. 219) and just as Sophie *does* encourage them to do. Sophie, while relying on autobiographical anecdotes to teach writing in the classroom, also discusses her teaching with her husband at home. He, too, is an educator, conducting classes on interrogation and interview techniques for law enforcement officers. Sophie has observed his classes and has noticed the way "he makes [the police officers] feel valuable . . . important" by inviting them to "bring their real cases [into the classroom] to talk about." Thus, all three women call upon their families and upon the larger habitus in which they find themselves (Bourdieu 81). They locate usable voices in the classroom that emerge from family and habitus by telling stories from their lived experience to learn more about writing.

Earlier this century, John Dewey recognized the "organic connection between education and personal experience" (25) in any effective learning site. Reflecting over our experiences, reviewing and interpreting their meaning, Dewey believed, is the way we learn (86–87), whether in youth or in adulthood, whether male or female. Malcolm Knowles also emphasizes the importance of including personal, lived experience in formal learning situations, particularly when working with adult learners. Since adults perceive their experience as their identity, according to Knowles, denigrating or denying its inclusion in their classroom learning is often interpreted by an adult learner as a personal affront.

The stories told by the reentry adult women learners discussed here seem to exemplify Dewey's notion of learning through reflection and interpretation of experience and Knowles's notion of learning as an adult as opposed to learning as a youth. That is, Margie, Ann, and Sophie have come to the learning environment (the first-year writing classroom) with widely varied experience compared to the somewhat limited experience of the younger student participants. All three women apply what they are learning to their lives in and out of the classroom. Further, they are responding to both internal and external motivations (Knowles 59–63) in that Margie is looking for self-esteem, a higher quality of life; Ann is looking for career advancement, more money; Sophie is looking for satisfaction as an educator/learner, a master's degree.

Neither Margie, even though she writes in her journal, nor Ann considered herself a writer when she entered Sophie's classroom. By semester's end, both Margie and Ann see themselves as writers. In Ann's case, the role may be a temporary one, but Margie is thinking of writing a book. Both women believe they have learned that they can write, that they are learners, that they are not dumb. In Wendy Luttrell's terms, both women are well on their way to "becoming somebody" (1–3). In terms provided by Belenky et al., both women have moved from a state of silence, through states of received and subjective knowledge, to at least some level of procedural knowledge, in the sense of feeling more in control of their own lives (99).

Margie and Ann believe that they have made this move not only by way of their own motivations but also by way of Sophie's connected teaching, which includes the telling of autobiographical stories by all classroom participants, personal concern for students as manifest in one-on-one conferencing throughout the semester, and professional structuring of classroom activities. Through her use of personal stories that she asks the class to critique and sometimes complete, Sophie becomes a "co-inquirer," an interactive learner with her students, and a mentor who facilitates rather than dominates class discussion — attributes Knowles believes work effectively in adult education (Knowles 31).

The importance of personal, lived experience in adult education cannot be ignored in these women's stories nor in established theories of how learning happens. Both Margie and Ann draw on their lived experience to address writing tasks, to fulfill writing assignments, and to function effectively as writers and students. Sophie routinely uses her own personal experience as part of the "objective conditions" (Dewey 45) of the classroom through her storytelling and through her encouragement of storytelling by her students.

As interactive learners and storytellers, bringing their personal lives into the classroom and carrying the classroom into their homes and jobs, Margie, Ann, and Sophie are challenging boundaries between university and community, between personal writing and academic discourse, and between traditional and "co-intentional education" (Freire 56). Dissolving boundaries between the community surrounding the university and the university itself is something Adrienne Rich believes a university should encourage. Rich believes the academy, to be an effective learning center, must address local issues and must listen to the stories of people who live around it (152–153), people like Margie, Ann, and Sophie. Dissolving boundaries between personal writing and academic discourse by using personal experiences to explain and fulfill required writing assignments exemplifies what Ruth Behar recognizes as "a sustained effort to democratize the academy" (1). This is a movement bell hooks would characterize as one of "transgression" (*Teaching* 12) beyond conventional educational and epistemic bounds. Such a movement dissolves boundaries between traditional educational practices, whose historical and theoretical bases rest largely on the teaching of children and youth by teacher-experts, and educational practices in which teacher-student and student-teacher come to know and (re)create reality "through common reflection and action" (Freire 56) as learning equals. With boundaries gone, interactive learning is more likely to occur for *all* learners within the academy, and interactive learners are more likely to discover themselves as "[reality's] permanent re-creators" (Freire 56).

Thus, the stories from Margie, Ann, and Sophie — three out of hundreds of adult women now returning to colleges and universities — suggest the power of the personal to bring about academic transformations, indeed, to (re)create professional academic realities.

Notes

1. These are their chosen research names.
2. These figures are from the office of Institutional Research, Planning and Outcomes Assessment at New Mexico State University, and they came to me through personal e-mail correspondence with research analysts and by way of the office's web site: <http://www.nmsu.edu/research/iresearc/>.
3. This term and the term *self-image* are borrowed from social psychologist Ralph H. Turner. For Turner, *self-conception* refers to "the picture an individual has of himself [*sic*]" (93). One's self-conception, then, according to Turner, is usually perceived by a telling self as being relatively consistent compared to the instability and mutability of various, simultaneously held, self-images.

Works Cited

Behar, Ruth. "Dare We Say 'I'? Bringing the Personal into Scholarship." *The Chronicle of Higher Education* 29 (1994): B1–2.

Belenky, Mary Field, Blythe McVicker Clinchy, Nancy Rule Goldberger, and Jill Mattuck Tarule. *Women's Ways of Knowing: The Development of Self, Voice, and Mind.* New York: HarperCollins, 1986.

Bourdieu, Pierre. "Structures and the Habitus." *Outline of a Theory of Practice.* Trans. Richard Nice. Cambridge: Cambridge UP, 1977. 72–95.

Dewey, John. *Experience and Education.* The Kappa Delta Pi Lecture Series. 1938. New York and London: Macmillan, 1963.

Freire, Paulo. *Pedagogy of the Oppressed.* Trans. Myra Bergman Ramos. New York: Seabury P, 1970.

Goldsmith, Diane J., and Francis X. Archambault. "Persistence of Adult Women in a Community College Re-Entry Program." Research Study. 1997. ERIC ED 409 958.

Greenwood, C. M. "'It's Scary at First': Reentry Women in College Composition Classes." *Teaching English in the Two-Year College* 17 (1990).

Hayes, Elisabeth, and Daniele D. Flannery. "Adult Women's Learning in Higher Education: A Critical Review of Scholarship." Annual Meeting of American Educational Research Association. San Francisco. Apr. 1995. ERIC ED 382 838.

hooks, bell. *Talking Back: Thinking Feminist, Thinking Black*. Boston: South End P, 1989.

———. *Teaching to Transgress: Education as the Practice of Freedom*. New York: Routledge, 1994.

Kiskis, Michael J. "Adult Learners, Autobiography, and Educational Planning: Reflections of Pedagogy, Andragogy, and Power." *Pedagogy in the Age of Politics: Writing and Reading (in) the Academy*. Ed. Patricia A. Sullivan and Donna J. Qualley. Urbana: NCTE, 1994. 56–72.

Knowles, Malcolm. *The Adult Learner: A Neglected Species*. 4th ed. Houston: Gulf, 1990.

Luttrell, Wendy. *Schoolsmart and Motherwise: Working-Class Women's Identity and Schooling*. New York: Routledge, 1997.

Miritello, Mary. "Teaching Writing to Adults: Examining Assumptions and Revising Expectations for Adult Learners in the Writing Class." *Composition Chronicle: Newsletter for Writing Teachers*. 9.2 (1996).

Nixon-Ponder, Sarah. "Determining the Characteristics of Successful Women in an Adult Literacy Program." Research Study. Kent State University. 1996. ERIC ED 392 988.

Rich, Adrienne. *On Lies, Secrets, and Silence: Selected Prose 1996–1978*. New York: Norton, 1979.

Stoffel, Judith. "So, You're a Woman, 38, Back in School, and Writing the 'Research Paper.'" Conference on College Composition and Communication. Cincinnati. 19 Mar. 1992. ERIC ED 345 267.

Turner, Ralph H. "The Self-Conception in Social Interaction." *The Self in Social Interaction*. Ed. Chad Gordon and Kenneth J. Gergen. Vol. I. New York: John Wiley, 1968. 93–106.

Classroom Activities

An important part of Sophie's pedagogy is to "mode[l] her invention process — 'meditation, listing, and freewriting.'" Sophie uses these stories of real-life experiences from beyond the classroom to teach such basics as how "to illustrate description," as well as to revise for details. But the stories also seem to demonstrate how personal narrative can be connected to students' own struggles with the writing process, a potentially critical connection for women adult learners, according to Jackman. As Jackman notes, "Sophie's storytelling does not go unnoticed by Margie and Ann; they both respond favorably to the way she 'explains.'" Several suggestions follow from such pedagogy. Of course, you can tell your own stories orally to your students and have students suggest different details for invention and revision. Students can also relate their own narratives to the class.

However, another effective teaching tool would be to have students write a narrative about a significant experience in their lives outside the classroom, such as Sophie's being chased by a bear at Yosemite Park. As a next step, have students read each other's stories. Then, have students suggest what these personal narratives seem to represent about the writing process. For instance, does Sophie's apparent escape from the bear indicate her ingenuity and her ability to take risks in writing, as well as in real life? Do Ann's experiences as a house painter indicate her perseverance? Do Margie's abilities to motivate her children to "apply themselves" to their schoolwork suggest that she would be a careful reader and thoughtful member of a peer review group? What do students' personal stories seem to suggest about their potential abilities as adult learners? Try discussing these stories in small groups and then as a whole class, in order to compare notes.

Thinking about Teaching

One of the most interesting aspects of Jackman's article is that she uses the technique of narrative herself to emphasize its importance as a pedagogical technique for reentry adult women in the writing classroom. Consider writing for publication a narrative case study similar to Jackman's article. Some researchers have described such a style as a "feminist" approach to research, which considers women's particular cultural concerns as primary. Jackman's bibliography includes germinal texts by bell hooks, Adrienne Rich, Mary Field Belenky, and others who have written about feminist approaches to teaching, learning, and research. (Note that Chapter 1 includes an excerpt from one of these texts — Rich's *On Lies, Secrets, and Silence.*)

Take a look at some of the books and articles by these writers listed in Jackman's bibliography, and write down your responses to their ideas in your teaching journal. Do you see immediate applications to your own classroom — and in particular, to students who are adult learners? What suggestions about pedagogy seem helpful? What suggestions about pedagogy seem limited to particular times and places? What ideas do these writers inspire in your own classroom teaching? Share your ideas with other teachers, and consider how they might apply as you craft a case study based on your observations of your own students and their progress as writers.

Returning Adults to the Mainstream: Toward a Curriculum for Diverse Student Writers

Barbara Gleason

In the following article, Barbara Gleason writes:

> *I endorse the position that remediation is inappropriate for adults who are returning to college after a five-, ten-, or even twenty-year hiatus. Far preferable are courses that have been designed to meet the specific needs of working adults, needs that are best understood not by analyzing placement test scores but by understanding these students' diversity in areas such as age, gender, family, educational history, culture, social class, sexual orientation, and employment.*

To further articulate her position, Gleason describes such a course, provides examples of student writing, and includes sample case studies of two very different adult students. These case studies are particularly effective in demonstrating how Gleason translates theory into practice. By studying the progress of these two students throughout the course, Gleason illustrates the success of a particular assignment sequence — "(1) a language / literacy autobiography, (2) a storytelling and story writing multitask project, (3) a student interview report, and (4) an ethnographic research writing project" — and suggests the necessity of a specialized curriculum that builds on the diverse strengths that adult students bring to the classroom. Although Gleason argues for mainstreaming adult writers and draws on her experiences teaching a full-credit-bearing, mainstreamed course, the pedagogy she describes can certainly benefit students in a basic writing classroom as well.

The phenomenon of working adults returning to college has generated a great deal of interest and curricular experimentation since the 1970s. In *Second Shift: Teaching Writing to Working Adults*, Kelly Belanger and Linda Strom describe innovative approaches to writing instruction in five worker education programs affiliated with colleges or universities. Issues associated with remediation must inevitably be confronted by such programs, where the prevailing view is that non-credit remedial courses are inappropriate for mature adults returning to college. At Youngstown State University and Swingshift College, for example, Kelly Belanger and Linda Strom developed a mixed ability writing course addressing the needs of the working students who belong to a steelworkers' union (72–84).

I endorse the position that remediation is inappropriate for adults who are returning to college after a five-, ten-, or even twenty-year hiatus. Far preferable are courses that have been designed to meet the specific needs of working adults, needs that are best understood not by analyzing placement test scores but by understanding these students' diversity in areas such as age, gender, family, educational history, culture, social class, sexual orientation, and employment. By reading students' personal narratives and autoethnographies of home, neighborhood, and work communities, teachers can learn about their students to better assist them in entering the culture of college. Similarly, students' analyses of their own home and community languages can help pave the way for their acquisition of academic literacies (Groden, Kutz, and Zamel; Kutz, Groden, and Zamel). As Terry Dean argues in "Multicultural Classrooms," composition courses offer a valuable and much-needed space in which students can focus on learning academic culture and, in many cases, "mainstream" culture as well.[1]

For the past three years, I have been teaching "remedial" and "college-level" returning adult students in one introductory writing course offered by a worker education bachelor's degree program within the City College of New York (CCNY).[2] Since its inception in 1981, this program — The Center for Worker Education (CWE) — has offered only full-credit college courses in its regular curriculum: the program's founders believed that all CWE students should enroll in full-credit bearing courses, regardless of placement test scores. As a teacher of writing in this program, I have been learning about how the particular needs and interests of these students can dovetail with a curriculum for a mainstreamed writing course.

Understanding the "Diversity" of Returning Adults

To encourage students to become acquainted, I ask that they introduce themselves to one other student during the first class meeting. The homework assignment for that week is for each student to write a letter to a peer about the challenges, joys, and fears of returning to college. By following up on initial introductions in class with an exchange of letters, each student learns about the cultural background, educational history, and special concerns of one other person in the class. As they develop friendships, these older adult students often form support networks and encourage each other academically. In addition, this initial assignment enables me to begin to know my students, for I read these letters as well.

I also ask my students to complete a questionnaire about their educational, language, and cultural backgrounds. By learning about my students' educational histories, I am far better equipped to assist them in entering an academic community with specialized forms of communication. I view my role as one of intervening in a lifelong process of literacy development, a conceptual frame for writing instruction best articulated by Louise Wetherbee Phelps:

> But what is it, then, that teaching teaches? Not literally writing as a discursive practice. . . . *Teaching teaches writing to developing persons within concrete life situations* [emphasis added]. Thus it teaches the development of literacy, addressing itself not simply to particular

> discourse events and texts but to the whole life process by which
> literacy — and reflection — become habitual, skilled, mature, and
> subject to self-understanding. . . . (71)

With each passing semester, I learn more about the "concrete life situations" of these students and, as a result, more fully appreciate the issues that are likely to concern them. For example, I only recently realized that earning a General Equivalency Diploma (rather than completing high school) may represent an important accomplishment or a sense of educational failure — or both. Reading students' commentaries on their literacies and educational histories allows me to begin assisting them individually early in the semester.

The completed questionnaires of the twenty-four students who had registered for my spring 1999 CWE writing class reveal the high level of diversity common to introductory CWE classes. As has been true of all my CWE classes, this group was highly heterogeneous in every way except for one: gender. Twenty-one students (86 percent) were women and three were men — a proportion that has remained constant throughout the six semesters that I have taught in this program. In all other respects, this class was notable for its diversity. Students' ages ranged from twenty to fifty, with an average age of thirty-six. Ten of these twenty-four students were immigrants, all but one coming from countries in the Caribbean, Central America, or South America. English was the primary language of sixteen students, six were bilingual in Spanish and English, and two were actively learning English as a second language. Eight of the fourteen U.S.-born students were African-American women.

These students were just as diverse academically as they were culturally. Ten had earned a General Equivalency Diploma and fourteen, a high school diploma. Of these fourteen, five had earned a high school diploma in a country outside the U.S.; that means that only nine in a class of twenty-four students had earned a high school diploma within the U.S.[3] This variability in high school backgrounds is matched by these students' City University of New York (CUNY) skills test scores and their college grade point averages. Of the twenty-two students who completed the course, twelve had no test scores listed in the CCNY student database, either because they had not taken the tests or because their scores had not yet been recorded. Of the ten students whose test scores were recorded, four had failed either the reading or the writing test, and six had passed both the reading and the writing test. As for their grade point averages, four students' transcripts indicate that they had GPAs below 2.0 and seven students had GPAs of 3.0 or higher.

From the standpoint of curriculum, there are two ways in which these students' cultural and educational diversity is important. First, these students have a great deal to teach me and each other about their social and cultural worlds; and second, nearly all of these students are struggling at some level to enter into an unfamiliar world of expectations, attitudes, ways of knowing, and styles of communicating.

This is even more likely to be true for students enrolled in an elective writing class due to educational insecurities, low grades, or failing test scores. Unlike many middle class, native English-speaking people, these students do not usually experience college as a natural extension of their home communities or even of high school.

Jacqueline Jones Royster refers to this home-school culture gap in an analysis of her own experiences as an African-American woman who routinely crosses discourse boundaries: "Like [W. E. B.] Du Bois, I've accepted the idea that what I call my 'home place' is a cultural community that exists still quite significantly beyond the confines of a well-insulated community that we call the 'mainstream'" (34). One important consequence of this gap, Royster goes on to explain, is that it "narrows the ability [of educators] to recognize human potential" (34). Those of us who function as gatekeepers, however reluctantly, by virtue of teaching entry-level writing courses understand that academic styles of communicating are generally only partially familiar — if familiar at all — to "nonmainstream" students (Bartholomae; Bizzell).

The older adult students who enter CWE have often been observed by their teachers to be remarkably capable conversationalists and oral presenters whose writing skills frequently belie their intellectual and verbal capacities. These students — most of them women — are likely to have raised families and held full-time jobs while maintaining close ties to extended families, which is to say that they have been negotiating complex verbal exchanges for many years. However, many of these students begin learning in college classes before having acquired "essayist literacy" — the generalized academic style of communicating that is characterized by "straightforward, objective, specially organized representations of reality rather than personally authored, socially embedded discourse" (Farr 9). Despite this, many of these students are expert communicators in the oral traditions of their home cultures, a phenomenon that presents special opportunities for teachers in multicultural classrooms.

A Curriculum for Mainstreaming

My CWE writing curriculum comprises a sequence of four assignments that move students from an initially inward focus on their own literacies and languages to a progressively outward focus on the literacies and communication practices of others.[4] The four assignments are (1) a language/literacy autobiography, (2) a storytelling and story writing multitask project, (3) a student interview report, and (4) an ethnographic research writing project. All of these assignments involve students in practicing academic forms of knowing, persuading, and communicating while reflecting on their own literacy experiences and examining the languages and literacies of other people.

The first formal essay assignment is a language/literacy autobiography, which students prepare for by writing a letter to a classmate about combining work with school and returning to college at a mature age. These letters are followed by a more formal autobiographical essay assignment that invites students to examine their formal and informal literacy learning as children, adolescents, and younger adults. Very often, recalling these memories and recording them in writing is painful, for the very events being remembered may account for students' having decided not to pursue higher education earlier. On the other hand, most have successful work histories that bolster their self-esteem and provide the self-discipline and everyday habits necessary to succeed in college. These positive aspects of students' lives can be usefully examined in self-reflective, autobiographical writing.

The second assignment involves a sequence of four successive tasks. Students begin by telling each other brief conversational stories during class and then writing down these same stories. They later transcribe their audiotaped recordings, producing a transcript of an oral story that can then be compared to the written story. In the final phase of the project, students write a comparative analysis of the oral story and the written story, examining differences in story structure, content, and language. At the end of the project, students generally report that they prefer their written stories, and that these stories benefited from the absence of pressure associated with conversational situations and from the opportunity to revise. With this finding comes a new respect for their own writing and a resolve on the part of most students to improve their speaking and storytelling competencies (Gleason "Something of Great Constancy").

Students then move on to writing reports on interviews they conduct with one another about writing. This interview assignment, which I explain more fully below, functions to prepare students for the ethnographic research project — which I view as the capstone assignment of this course. A key value of the ethnographic writing project is its multitask feature: it offers such a wide array of reading, speaking, research, and writing activities that every student can experience some forms of success while stronger writers are always challenged by the analytical and rhetorical demands of writing an ethnographic essay.

In the remainder of this chapter, I will describe the interview assignment and the ethnographic research project, and establish a rationale for their use in a mainstreamed writing course for returning adults.

Capitalizing on Conversational Competencies

To introduce students to ethnographic research strategies, I begin with a student–student interview on the subject of writing outlined by Peter Elbow and Pat Belanoff in *A Community of Writers* (153–65). The two stated purposes of this interview are (1) for students to learn about writing and writers in a general sense, and (2) for each student to inquire about the specific experiences, attitudes, and aspirations of one writer. An unstated goal of this assignment is for students to get to know each other and form mutually supportive bonds that are sorely needed by commuter students who work full time while attending college. Well over one half of these students reported to me later in the semester that they have formed new friendships during the course of their initial and follow-up interviews (on the phone and in class).

To prepare students for interviewing, I distribute a short written explanation of the importance of scripting a list of questions before-hand, remaining flexible during the interview, audiotaping, and note-taking. We talk in class about the value of ice-breaker questions, being sensitive to privacy issues, and staying focused as an interviewer.[5] For nearly all students, this is the first interview they have ever conducted, it is anticipated with some trepidation, and it turns out to be a surpris-ingly pleasurable and memorable learning experience. One fall 1999 student succinctly sums up her perception of this assignment's value: "My best work is my interview with Maria. This is the exercise that taught me the most new skills. I interviewed, recorded, transcribed, summarized, and analyzed. I was very pleased with the final draft." Others report listening, asking questions, and incorporating quotes into their writing as particularly important skills that they practiced while interviewing and writing the interview report.

Most students say they value the relationships formed with their peers as well as the research and writing skills they practiced, often for the first time, while working on their interview projects. As much as I value these two dimensions of this project, I prize even more its use of conversational expertise as a resource for developing writers. Many of these students' communication styles differ from the topic-centered, "get-to-the-point" styles common to mainstream American speakers, and their language (oral and written) may therefore be sub-ject to negative evaluation by teachers; nonetheless, these students' communication styles tend to serve them well in conversational situa-tions. Moreover, as Peter Elbow reminds us, we teach to strength by "capitalizing on the oral language skills students already possess and helping students apply those skills immediately and effortlessly to writing" ("The Shifting Relationships" 290).

By inviting them to conduct interviews with one another during class, I encourage students to use their existing language forms as a bridge to acquiring academic styles of thinking, talking, and writing. Students may, for example, speak to one another in both Spanish and English; or they may use a narrative style that seems to "meander from the point and take on episodic frames" — suggested by Akua Duku Anokye as the preferred narrative style of some African Americans (48); others make particularly effective use of humor and joke-telling while conversing with each other. These culturally and personally preferred communication styles are then folded into the student interviewer's written report to illustrate an interviewee's particular style of speak-ing and as evidence for the student writer's claims. Two features cen-tral to academic writing are "the giving of reasons and evidence rather than just opinions, feelings, [and] experience" and the ability to "step outside one's own narrow vision" (Elbow "Reflections on Academic Dis-course" 140). Reporting on an interview requires a writer to consider and represent an interviewee's point of view by means of summary, paraphrase, and quotes in a prose style that blends narrative and exposition as well as personal and public forms of writing.

Presenting Ethnographic Research Strategies to Student Writers

In *The Professional Stranger*, Michael H. Agar explains that ethnography refers to both a research process and a written product (1–2). Agar describes ethnographic research as a process that "involves long-term association with some group, to some extent in their own territory, with the purpose of learning from them their ways of doing things and viewing reality" (6). With this general definition in mind, I present ethnography to students as a process that initially entails gaining entry to a community of people and then observing that group's daily routines, rituals, traditional customs, and communicative practices. I go on to explain that an ethnographer records these observations by writing descriptive "fieldnotes" and soon begins searching for recurring themes or topics that will form the basis of an analysis. To further introduce ethnography to students, I rely on *Fieldworking*, an innovative textbook that builds an entire curriculum on the foundation of reading and writing strategies commonly employed by ethnographers (Chiseri-Strater and Sunstein).

To illustrate the forms of writing that I am assigning, I distribute samples of former students' ethnographic essays along with excerpts from a professionally written ethnography. By reading good examples of ethnographic writing, students gain substantial insight into the task they are now being asked to undertake. When we discuss these writing samples in class, I elicit their explanations for why these texts exemplify successful writing: not surprisingly, there are some in every group who already know "what makes writing good" (Coles and Vopat). Such discussions also allow me to demystify the approach I take to evaluating and grading students' final products.

I frequently hand out in class copies of a student's ethnographic essay entitled "You Wanna Play with Me?" The author, Marthe, created a title that gives voice to the children in the Head Start program she was studying and at the same time alludes to her thesis: that children learn through playing.[6] This thesis appears in her introduction, is developed with examples of children's behaviors all through her essay, and reappears quite persuasively in Marthe's conclusion. After describing the classrooms, the teachers, and the children in this Head Start program, Marthe begins building her argument by presenting and commenting on children playing:

> Everything young children do is a learning experience. In one of my observations of this classroom, I observed how Jade, a happy, confident, assertive little girl took some building blocks and asked me "you wanna play with me?" I explained to her that I came to watch the children play

and I asked her if she mind. She answered, "No, but you gonna play with me after?" I answered, "Maybe, if I had time." She then said, "Can you make me a box?" I asked her to try. "I can't try," she whined. As I continued my observation she began to stack the blocks and join them together. After a while she said, "Look, I made a box." From this one attempt Jade did not only strengthen her problem solving skills and develop language, but she also learned how to make a box which in turn helped her develop her self esteem and made her confident in her abilities. Since Jade is very verbal, she also developed her reasoning skills and her social interaction with adults.

A major strength of Marthe's essay is her successful use of narrative and descriptive writing to construct an argument. Her essay exemplifies two points made by Donna Dunbar-Odom: ethnographic research methods offer students the opportunity (1) to "'own' their research," and (2) to learn that constructing an argument is far more complex than "merely taking and supporting one side of a binary argument" (20).

Because of her enthusiasm for working with small children, Marthe was highly motivated by her research, as she explains in her portfolio cover letter:

> The one assignment I enjoyed the most was my ethnographic research, "You Wanna Play with Me?" I enjoyed this the most because I studied and observed a group of individuals I hold dear to my heart, *children*. Not only are children unique and remarkable individuals, but they are also the group of individuals that society has put at the end of their list.

Marthe's testimonial on her engagement as a writer aligns closely with the feelings of many other student ethnographers: selecting a community for their research generally allows students to spend time with people they want to know better or to study a place of special interest to them. A woman with an emerging awareness of animal rights produced a remarkably fine report on an animal shelter; another woman interviewed several co-workers in her office and analyzed the reasons for a pervasive morale problem; and an immigrant from the Dominican Republic wrote about one of the family-owned stores, or *botanicas*, that sells products associated with *Santería*, which she describes as a "system of common belief among Dominican and other Caribbean people" that "mixes African and Catholic religions." As their teacher, I am continuously learning about the special interests, workplaces, and cultural communities that my students report on, just as they learn from one another by reading their work-in-progress and discussing these research projects with each other in class.

In addition to distributing samples of other students' ethnographic writing, I usually invite students to read an excerpt from Barbara Myerhoff's *Number Our Days*, after which we view her thirty-minute film by the same name. Through her descriptive and narrative writing about a community of elderly Jewish immigrants, Myerhoff develops an argument that agism is a pervasive problem in contemporary U.S. society. An unusual feature of her writing is her hybrid style: literary language is combined with a social scientist's purpose. Developing a writing style is not a prominent feature of most introductory writing classes; however, more advanced students often take pleasure in noticing and imitating other writers' styles. In every writing course I have taught, there are some students, usually the most proficient writers, who want to focus on stylistic issues. By closely reading the prose of authors such as Barbara Myerhoff, these students can pursue their interests in developing their own prose styles.

To illustrate the potential that this project holds for diverse student writers, I will describe the cases of two returning adults — one classified as "remedial" and the other as "college-level" by their scores on the City University of New York (CUNY) Writing Assessment Test. I have chosen to underscore the mainstreaming challenge to teachers by selecting two extreme examples of students who are enrolled in the same class. The two students whose cases I cite as "Joan" (age thirty-three) and "Liam" (age thirty-six).

Joan and Liam both withdrew from high school without graduating and later earned their GEDs. Not surprisingly, these two students recall early school failures in the literacy autobiographies that they wrote at the beginning of our course. Educational insecurities and writing anxieties had led both Joan and Liam to register for my elective introductory writing course. But here is where their similarities end. Joan's writing efforts are significantly burdened by a complex learning disorder — a diagnosis she received while enrolled in my writing class. Liam, on the other hand, brings to his college education nineteen years of avid reading and a substantial history of political activism that includes crafting political messages for publication in the broadcast and print media.

Joan

Having left her Brooklyn high school without graduating, Joan had had "to go on public assistance" to support her infant daughter. While her daughter was still very young, Joan worked as a waitress and then as a file clerk in a car wash company. Reflecting back on that period of her life, Joan recalled that she enjoyed working as a file clerk because there was "little reading and no writing" required of her.

At the age of eighteen, Joan first attempted to earn her General Equivalency Diploma. She was to fail the exam four times before passing on her fifth attempt six years later. Knowing that many others would have given up after failing, one, two, or possibly three times, I asked Joan what had induced her to persist in taking and retaking her GED exam until she finally passed. "I wanted to go to college," she explained. "I wanted to better myself," she continued, going on to say that being on public assistance had motivated her to consider attending college. Joan married at twenty-two and gave birth to a second daughter two years later. Childcare responsibilities would further delay Joan's pursuit of a college education.

At thirty-two, Joan began her college career at the Center for Worker Education. One semester later, she enrolled in the mainstreamed college writing course that I was teaching. When Joan was casting about for a community to focus on for her field research project, I asked her what she particularly wanted to learn about. Joan replied that she was interested in college and in learning about being a college student. I suggested that she focus her research on her own college environment. For Joan, this interest in college was no small matter; it represented her struggle to overcome substantial obstacles to learning, literacy, and formal education.

Despite the obvious difficulties Joan experienced with reading and writing on her GED exams and in a chef's school that she attended for eighteen months, and despite her deliberate avoidance of jobs that required reading and writing, Joan did not believe that she had problems with reading and writing. Thus, when she failed her CUNY writing assessment test, Joan attributed her poor performance to "test-taking anxiety."

In August of 1998, Joan passed the CUNY reading assessment test but failed the math and writing tests. Had she registered at our college's main campus, or at any of CUNY's other sixteen colleges, Joan would have been placed into remedial writing — which in most colleges would have prevented her from being eligible for college composition or for core curriculum courses. However, Joan chose to enter the City College Center for Worker Education, where there are no remedial courses.

Joan's Writing

I first encountered Joan's writing when she responded to a questionnaire that I distributed during the second week of class. Here are four of the questions and her written answers:

- **Why did you enroll in this writing course?**
  So I can learn how to ~~right~~ writing better
  How to use better words. I Drop out of H.S.

- **What concerns do you have about your writing?**
  That Sometimes I loose my train of thought.
  What I want to say does not come out on papper.

- **Do you feel comfortable speaking during class discussions? Please explain your answer.**
  Sometime I do and sometime I don't. depends on what is discuss.

- **Do you have any concerns about your language use (speaking or writing)?**
  My *Fear* is when people see my writing they may not understand what I am talking about

These four written responses, as well as the other comments Joan wrote on this questionnaire, portray a student with a history of difficulties in school as well as severe frustrations with writing. Joan's difficulties as a writer were expressed both by the content of her messages and by the forms of her language: sentence fragments, misspelled words, and punctuation errors appeared in nearly every statement she wrote, diminishing only slightly after she acquired some proofreading strategies. However, unlike the writing of most "basic writers" I have encountered, Joan frequently embeds metaphors in her prose, as she does in this passage from her literacy autobiography: "Diaries, stories, letters and poems: I have them all. I enjoy writing, because it lets me be me. I enjoy free writing a lot more. It is like letting the pen and paper do their dance." All through the semester, Joan continued to employ metaphorical language in her expository prose, exhibiting a verbal competency that seemed oddly out of sync with her other competencies as a writer.

While enrolled in her humanities course the previous semester, Joan had learned from her instructor that she would have to improve her writing significantly to remain in college. In an interview conducted after our writing class had ended, she talked about her experiences in that humanities course:

> My first professor . . . pulled me aside the second week of class and told me to drop out before 'cause . . . she thought I had PROBLEMS and she wanted me to get tested [for dyslexia] . . . she came up to me and said "your work is the last work I read out of everybody in all my classes" and I asked her why and she said "I dread reading your work — It's really painful" — and I asked her why — she goes "your fragments your sentence structure" um she says "your writing is atrocious" and those were her exact words and it was like a dagger in my heart and in my pride and I held them back and I bit my lip and I said "ok — I'm still not dropping your class — I'm going to do my best."

Joan did complete her humanities class, earning a passing grade at the end of the term. She also took her instructor's advice to heart and enrolled in my elective college writing course the following semester. As for the passing grade she had earned for the humanities course, Joan believed it to be a "sympathy grade" — a gift from her teacher because her mother had passed away that semester.

The number of spelling errors that I observed in Joan's writing was unusually high, even in the context of a basic writing class. In fact, Joan's unedited writing closely resembles that of a person who is "dysgraphic," that is, a person who has a great deal of trouble producing written language (McAlexander et al. 25–26). A high frequency of errors and unusual errors are two indications of dysgraphia (McAlexander et al. 26). A third signal is writing in which letters are frequently missing/dropped from words, a condition that suggests an "inability to related sounds to spelling" (28). All three of these conditions apply to Joan's writing. As it turned out, I was the fourth CWE teacher to recommend that Joan be tested for dyslexia. This she did arrange to do.

At midsemester, Joan learned for the first time, at the age of thirty-three, that she had a learning disorder. It is described in her evaluation report as "a combination of inattentiveness, auditory processing, organizational delays and emotional factors" — all of which are "contributing to Joan's short-term memory deficits and delays in language processing."[7] Almost as soon as she learned of this herself, Joan called me at home to inform me of the diagnosis. From this point on, I read and evaluated Joan's writing with this newly diagnosed learning disorder in mind.

Joan's Ethnographic Research Writing

In the seventh week of our fifteen-week semester, Joan began her ethnographic research project. She had decided to study her own college community to further her goal of becoming a successful college student. The first assignment Joan completed for this project was a short research proposal.

In a one-page essay, Joan describes the community she will study and several questions she plans to use to frame her observations and interviews. An early draft (labeled "second draft") that she turned in to me begins with the following paragraph:

> As a student at CWE I got the change to observe the students, professors and the receptionists. How the students and professors inter act with the receptionists. How the receptionists get any work done? What is there a different between the day shift and the night shift? Do they realized that the students and Staffs depend on them for the information and services. How do they feel about their job?

In this draft, Joan conveyed the direction her research would take and posed several useful questions. I encouraged Joan to begin proofreading. With the assistance of writing tutors and her computer's software program toolbox, Joan was able to produce a third draft that more closely aligns with the expectations of college teachers. Here is her revision of the paragraph cited above:

> As a student at Center for Worker Education I have the chance to observe the students, professors, the receptionists. I will observe how the students and professors deal with the receptionists. How the receptionists interact with the high demand of students and professors. I wonder if the receptionists get any work done? Is there a different between the day shift and the night shift? How do they do their job? These are some of the questions that I seek answers for as I observed the desk for several weeks.

In this proposal essay, Joan succeeds in identifying the place and the people that she will investigate while posing several questions that she will use to guide her observations. Joan had developed these questions during a conference in which she and I discussed her research plans.

By learning to revise, to proofread, and to request responses from readers, Joan made substantial progress in overcoming her writing anxieties and began to function far more effectively as a student writer. Her newly acquired writing process allowed Joan to stay afloat in class and to manage an intensive six-week project that entailed writing a research proposal, writing descriptive fieldnotes, interviewing at least one person, and writing a final research report. In addition to talking to me about her learning and her writing, Joan talked to CWE writing tutors, sometimes two or three times per week.

Joan wrote her descriptive fieldnotes during the course of three days. She focused her observations on the reception desk, where students, advisors, administrators, and faculty all approach CWE receptionists to request assistance. Once she got home, Joan wrote out and typed her notes, producing ten double-spaced pages of writing — in itself a substantial accomplishment for an insecure and inexperienced writer. Here is an excerpt from the notes Joan wrote on her second day of observing:

> Friday, April 16, 1999
> 4:30pm
> Wow! They must be at least 50 students here this is too much for me. Z, Mr. O, Mr. L, Mr. H, and J W working for their pay to day. So many student. Some look good and some are wearing jean and dress and suits. Some of the students have the hair done nice. I wonder what they are all here for. I can not hear to much anymore., because all the student are talking to each other and my bench is now filled with people sitting on it. There is so much happening around here today
>
> 4:45pm
> There is a student talking to Z not so nice, but Z is smiling and been nice to her. Z is now telling student to put there name on the list and they will be call next. Wow! She control all those students and put them in there place. . . .

Her observations on this day, in conjunction with interviews she conducted with receptionists and a program administrator, led Joan to conclude that these receptionists respond very effectively to the many requests that come their way. In addition, Joan began noticing the heavy demands placed on CWE receptionists, particularly during evening hours when classes are in session. In her ethnographic essay, Joan concluded that the CWE receptionists play a centrally important though sometimes underrecognized role in maintaining a smooth flow of communications among students, teachers, advisors, and administrators. By reading Joan's report and fieldnotes, I found myself developing a new respect for these receptionists and for their roles in this college community.

When writing her ethnographic essay, Joan successfully narrowed the focus of her research to these CWE workers' experiences and the reception desk as a central gathering place for students and staff. Although the five-page essay that Joan ultimately wrote would not be considered a good example of successful college writing by most of my colleagues, I concluded that, for Joan, the act of completing a five-page written report of her own research was a highly significant achievement in her development as a writer. Moreover, this essay clearly documents Joan's learning about academic culture generally and, more specifically, about the Center for Worker Education receptionists and the reception area as a central meeting place. Equally important, Joan's essay demonstrates her newly acquired abilities to segment discourse into paragraphs, to ask and answer research questions, to write an essay introduction, and to use quotes to support general assertions and observations. Joan's collected ethnographic writing includes a total of sixteen (typed) final draft pages: a one-page research proposal, ten pages of fieldnotes, and a five-page ethnographic essay. The sheer volume of writing that Joan produced during the six weeks that she worked on this project represented a milestone in her writing life.

Liam

Liam grew up in a rural Irish farming community that lacked electricity and television in his early years. On winter nights, Liam and his family would visit neighbors, playing cards and telling stories for entertainment. In his literacy autobiography, Liam describes his father as a man with "a flare for storytelling" and his mother as an avid letter writer. Liam's mother corresponded regularly with relatives overseas, reading the letters she received to her family "aided by only a single gaslight hanging from the ceiling." When he wasn't farming, Liam's father wrote local news for community publications.

Liam recalls learning to read both English and Gaelic in a "small two-room country school." Between the ages of eight and twelve, he often missed classes to help his aging father with farmwork. When Liam entered secondary school at the age of twelve, he left a class of only three students for a class of sixty. He learned right away that his primary school education had not prepared him to compete academically: "It hit me that I was indeed in at the deep end. I did not recognize many of the subjects the teachers were talking about, nor did I have any knowledge of them." After three years of lagging behind his contemporaries and earning low exam grades, Liam left high school without graduating. Today, he looks back on his secondary school experience as a "bad dream."

When he emigrated to England as a young man, Liam hungrily read the *Irish Post*, a newspaper that reported the news from Ireland and addressed topics of interest to Irish immigrants. It was then that

Liam developed a keen interest in learning about Ireland and, perhaps as a consequence, he became a voracious reader. A political awakening accompanied Liam's newly acquired reading habit. But writing was another matter. Liam continued to feel deeply insecure about his writing abilities.

In November of 1997, Liam took and passed the three CUNY skills tests in reading, writing, and math. During his first semester at CWE, Liam enrolled in an introductory humanities course that I happened to be teaching. Liam's performance in the class was impressive: in addition to earning an A for his coursework, he ultimately published a literacy autobiography entitled "A Reading Road: From Mayo to Manhattan" in a CWE student journal, *City at the Center*. However, Liam felt extremely anxious about writing and believed himself underprepared as a college writer. I advised Liam to address his concerns by enrolling in a college composition course, but instead he chose to enroll in a remedial writing course at another college. Liam believed that the low stress and low stakes of a remedial course would best serve his needs. After completing this remedial writing class, Liam expressed to me his satisfaction with his progress. He then enrolled in the mainstreamed writing course that I was teaching.

Liam's Writing

I had first seen Liam's writing in the humanities course he had enrolled in one year earlier. I knew Liam to be a proficient student writer who could one day publish his essays or stories. In addition to being an avid reader, Liam is an easy conversationalist and a good listener. And, like his father, Liam is a good storyteller. Having tried many different lines of work, Liam had discovered bartending to best suit his temperament and his talents. Bartending has allowed Liam to meet a wide range of people, from compulsive gamblers to "the Romeos, who conquered Beauty Queens from Manhattan to Miami but end up looking for an invitation to someone's house for Christmas or Thanksgiving." Liam is also a sharp observer of people.

When asked to complete a questionnaire at the beginning of his writing class, Liam expressed confidence about his oral communication skills but insecurities about his writing:

- **What concerns do you have about your writing?**
  Writers Block, Critical Writing, Essays, Grammar

- **Do you feel comfortable speaking during class discussions? Please explain your answer.**
  Yes Very Comfortable, Lots of Encouragement from my Professor

- **Do you have any concerns about your language use (speaking or writing)?**
  Not any about Speaking. Writing — (Grammar is a task)

Unlike Joan, who reported being told by a former teacher that her writing was "atrocious" and "painful" for her teacher to read, Liam recalls being encouraged and cites that encouragement as a reason for enrolling in this writing course. In fact, I had found Liam an easy student to encourage; and he had received similarly positive responses from the three teachers who had selected his writing for publication in the CWE student journal.

Liam's Ethnographic Research Writing

As an immigrant from Ireland, Liam takes a particularly strong interest in Irish-American organizations and publications. At the conclusion of our humanities course, Liam had given me a gift subscription to a magazine called *Irish America* and a book on the recent Irish peace accords. It came as no surprise, then, that Liam would want to focus his research on the Union Students of Ireland Travel, an organization that provides services for Irish and U.S. students who are traveling back and forth between these two countries.

In the opening of his research proposal, Liam asserts his view that Ireland should create a "national service of sorts": a program that would bring Ireland's youth to the United States to "broaden their horizons." He goes on to describe an organization that facilitates travel between the U.S. and Ireland for college students of both countries. Here is the second half of that proposal:

> The U.S. work and travel program which is sponsored by USIT has been in operation for over thirty years. Every year, students from third level colleges in Ireland travel to the U.S. to be part of this program. USIT helps Irish students to spend up to four months living, working, and traveling throughout the United States. For those students who come here, if only for a short summer stay, it gives them an opportunity to learn about the American way of life.

> The staff at the USIT office has already given me the approval to visit one day and monitor their office procedures. The following is information that I would like to find out. How do USIT select what students are accepted into their program, and what students are rejected? How much does it cost a participant? Must all participants be currently in the third level education? How is the program administered here, and in Ireland? How many students come to the U.S. each year? Is employment pre arranged, is this a major task? Is there a support network on the ground here for the students when they arrive, and for the summer? What are the student's opinion of USIT, and the U.S.A.?

> I am looking forward to this research assignment, not just because I am Irish immigrant. I was always interested in Irish immigration issues, and I successfully campaigned for a change in the 1965 Immigration Act, as it had unfairly discriminated against Immigrants from Western Europe. I will see first hand how USIT prepares students for America.

A clear strength of Liam's writing is his ability to inform and also persuade his readers with an ethical appeal. In this proposal, Liam establishes his credibility as a writer by making three claims: (1) that he himself is an Irish immigrant, which means he can draw on personal experiences as a source of knowledge; (2) that he strongly advocates travel by Irish youth to the U.S., indicating a sincere interest in an organization that provides services to U.S.-Irish travelers; and (3) that he already understands international travel and immigrants' experiences well enough to ask informed questions. Finally, Liam asserts a type of moral authority by referring to his successful efforts at participating in a campaign against unjust laws affecting immigrants.

Liam conducted his research during the week of his spring break, spending several days at the American Youth Hostel in Manhattan — where the USIT offices are housed. In the course of his research, Liam recorded his observations of people's movements and communications, he interviewed employees and student travelers, and he collected the brochures and pamphlets that USIT provides. By interviewing employees, Liam gained access to the results of a survey questionnaire designed to gauge student travelers' satisfaction with USIT's services. USIT employees also shared with Liam the unsolicited letters that they had received from Irish students.

At the end of the semester, Liam reported on the pleasure he had taken from his observations of the people who worked at USIT and of those passing through the offices of this Irish-American organization. I had distributed a list of questions about field research experiences and asked students to respond in writing. Here is Liam's response to one question:

> **Question: How easy or difficult was this assignment for you?**
>
> **Liam:** This assignment was not as difficult as it seemed to be, when first I read the assignment. I enjoyed observing and writing the field notes. Spending mornings and afternoons at the American Youth Hostel (AYH) was exciting. Interviewing was easy for me as the students were in New York during my research. I felt the notes were very helpful when I was writing my report. My notes were essential to my report.

At the conclusion of his fieldwork experience, Liam had gathered enough specific information to write a substantive ethnographic essay. As is often true of more and less proficient writers, Liam produced a ten-page essay, twice the length of Joan's.

The report that Liam completed portrays the USIT offices, the USIT workers, and the student travelers who come looking for assistance. Embedded in Liam's descriptions are telling details that are informative but also suggestive of more than has been told:

> A three-foot high black gridiron rail separates the general public from the American Youth Hostel (AYH) property. Between the gridiron and the AYH building there are a number of benches, round tables and

chairs. The tables have umbrellas to provide shade from the morning sun. Most of the seats are occupied by people in their late teens or early 20's, who are sitting around smoking cigarettes, drinking coffee, and bottles of water. It is a scene reminiscent of a Paris sidewalk café. These young people are speaking foreign languages, with the occasional American voice rising above the others. The luggage they have with them tells a geographic story of its own. One tall young man with his hair down to his shoulders, has a travel bag that promotes Argentina, while a young lady, with a punk style hair do and some tattoos, has Norway stamped in bold lettering on her backpack. The T-shirts being worn by these travelers tell a story of where they have been traveling, from the Hard Rock Café in Los Angeles to Miami Beach Florida.

In this passage, Liam uses his descriptions to portray people and also to imply questions about where they have come from and where they are going. One of the more challenging aspects of ethnographic writing is to learn how to use descriptive writing purposefully — to communicate an idea or present an argument. It is usually the stronger student writers who manage to use description for a rhetorical purpose.

On the sixth page of his essay, Liam sums up an experience common to many of the young Irish travelers: "Homesickness and loneliness are two of the most frequent problems the students suffer from when they are in the U.S." With this general assertion, Liam introduces the contents of many thank-you letters that Irish students have mailed to the USIT employees after returning home. Liam cites the volume of this mail and quotes from one such letter as evidence of the positive response of Irish students to USIT and the importance of the services it provides:

> It is obvious from the amount of thank you mail that the staff at the USIT office receive each year from students when they return to Ireland, that their support role means a lot to the visiting students. One of the many letters Maire has on file is from a student who went through a period of loneliness while in New York last year. The thank you letter, which is almost two pages in length, states "Your concern and help took a massive weight off my shoulders. The time taken by you and the manner in which you dealt with me will not be forgotten." So wrote Mary Walsh from County Kerry in Ireland.

Liam's use of textual sources sets him apart from the majority of these student ethnographers. Using printed documents as primary or secondary sources involves transcending the fundamental requirements of the ethnographic writing assignment that I have conceived for an introductory writing class. For more advanced writers, however, citing sources is often a desirable challenge. Marthe, whose work I use to model a student's ethnographic writing, has integrated a secondary source into her text and appended a bibliography to her report.

The ethnographic essay that Liam completed bears many of the hallmarks of "good writing" noted by contributors to Coles and Vopat's

What Makes Writing Good. Liam's text is a narrative that has a sense of being complete (143); his writing exhibits his commitment to his writing task, and his willingness to share his values with his readers (137). Liam creates an interplay between the particular and the general, reaching from concrete details toward abstract ideas (137); he knows how to create artful beginnings and how to use "attention-getting introductory tactics" (131); he uses a conversational tone that he knows how to translate into writing, avoiding a dull, institutional voice (126). In short, Liam's ethnographic essay exhibits many of the qualities that well-known writing teachers value.

Conclusion

Conventional college writing assignments generally fall under one of four categories: (1) personal narrative, (2) expository essay, (3) textual analysis, and (4) library research. For assignments that involve textual analysis and library research, students must first engage in critically reading new and unfamiliar types of texts and then write in a style that relies on logical reasoning and the use of evidence. For inexperienced or "basic" writers, this entire process involves a sudden immersion in academic forms of knowing and communicating and therefore a daunting challenge. As Marilyn Sternglass points out in *Time to Know Them*, these students will acquire academic language forms and writing abilities over time, especially when provided with appropriate instruction. However, they are unlikely to experience success as college writers when they begin by writing textual analyses and library research reports. Instead, they may fail to complete their assignments adequately or, when they do complete them, receive negative evaluations of their writing from teachers. This happened to Joan, who enrolled in Humanities 1 (an introductory literature course) during her first semester of college, and learned from her teacher that her writing was "atrocious" and "painful" to read.

The curriculum that I have outlined here offers one primary advantage to inexperienced writers: it enables them use "the oral [to] sustain the literate" (Brandt 7). Students begin their interviewing and ethnographic projects by using oral language in conversational situations to create two types of primary sources: transcripts of spoken language and fieldnotes. These are forms of writing that the most inexperienced and hesitant writer can dive into without fear of failure or negative evaluation from teachers: although I do comment on the content of these texts — and, very occasionally, make suggestions on how to improve them, I do not grade students' transcripts or fieldnotes. They function primarily as resources for more formal writing assignments.

More experienced student writers, such as Liam — who had passed a placement test prior to entering my writing class, still need to practice analytical thinking, research writing, and many other cognitive and rhetorical skills. All of the assignments in this curriculum require students to go beyond descriptive and narrative writing toward interpretation, inferencing, and analysis. When writing the ethnographic essay, students may choose to cite sources with in-text referencing and a bibliography. This is an appropriate challenge for the more proficient writers and one they frequently accept.

There are many possible avenues toward successful curricula for mainstreamed writing courses. The one I have been experimenting with relies on assignments with two key features: (1) the use of oral language and conversational competencies as resources for developing writers, and (2) sequenced multitask assignments comprising more and less difficult tasks. In addition to well-constructed assignments, there are still many other issues that must be addressed for mainstreamed writing classes: grading practices, support for teachers (for example, workshops and meetings), and support for students (for example, classroom tutors and class size).

In worker education classes, successfully mainstreamed writing courses take on a special significance. Slowing down student progress with noncredit remedial courses runs counter to a primary aim of these programs: they generally accelerate students' academic progress with classes conveniently scheduled in the evenings and on weekends, long class meetings that are held once a week, full-credit bearing courses, and the offer of college credits for life experiences. At the Center for Worker Education, students' academic progress is even further accelerated by four-credit courses in place of the three-credit courses commonly offered in the regular City College curriculum.

Most of the working adult students I have met in my classes are highly motivated to learn and to perform well in their college classes. They bring with them many resources that strengthen their chances of academic success, for example, workplace literacies, conversational competencies, bilingualism, self-discipline, determination, and the confidence so often born of maturity. They nevertheless enter college filled with the anxiety of this being their "last chance saloon."

Returning adult students can increase their odds for success in college by using their existing languages and literacies to negotiate their learning of new discourses and literacies. However, "students in basic writing classes . . . should not be treated differently from students in so-called regular composition courses" (Sternglass 296–97). All students entering college, regardless of writing placement test scores, benefit from immediate engagement with assignments that foster critical reasoning, interpretive reading, analytical as well as narrative writing, and persuasion. A well-designed writing course curriculum for students of highly mixed abilities will meet the dual challenge of allowing underprepared students to experience success while encouraging stronger students to expand the limits of their existing literacies.

Acknowledgments

I would like to thank Edward Quinn for many useful responses to several drafts of this essay, Karl Malkoff and Barbara Comen for their suggestions and support, and Gerri McNenny for her insightful editing.

Notes

1. As Terry Dean points out in "Multicultural Classrooms, Monocultural Teachers," various different theoretical models explain how students can mediate home and school cultures. Shirley Brice Heath is particularly well known for advocating ethnography as a venue for classroom learning about home and school cultures. This interactive, reciprocal approach to pedagogy allows for developing shared understanding and negotiation of the various languages and literacies that appear in a classroom community. In contrast to Heath's negotiation model, Paulo Freire calls for students from nonmainstream cultural enclaves to transform mainstream culture rather than being absorbed into it (*Pedagogy* 28). These issues are also addressed extensively in *Writing in the Multicultural Settings* (Severino, Guerra, and Butler).

2. The City College of New York (CCNY) is one of seventeen junior and senior colleges that comprise the City University of New York (CUNY).

3. For a useful discussion of the issues faced by immigrants who are attending college, see Hirvela.

4. This writing curriculum is one I first used as a teacher in a mainstreamed writing course for younger adult students on City College's main campus. The course formed the heart of a pilot project supported by the Fund for Improvement in Post-Secondary Education. For overviews of this program's curriculum and its evaluation, see Soliday and Gleason, and see Gleason, "Evaluating Writing Programs in Real Time."

5. Two useful resources for learning about interviewing are *People Studying People* by Robert A. Georges and Michael O. Jones and "Ch. 7: Interviewing," in *Fieldworking* by Bruce Jackson.

6. The names of all students whose writing appears in this essay have been changed. Their writing is presented here with their permission and in the form in which I received it as their teacher.

7. Joan included her evaluation report in her writing portfolio and has granted permission for its use here.

Works Cited

Agar, Michael H. *The Professional Stranger: An Informal Introduction to Ethnography.* New York: Academic Press, 1980.

Anoke, Akua Duku. "Oral Connections to Literacy: The Narrative." *Journal of Basic Writing* 13.2 (1994): 46–60.

Bartholomae, David. "Inventing the University." *When a Writer Can't Write.* Ed. Mike Rose. New York: Guilford, 1985. 134–65.

Belanger, Kelly, and Linda Strom. *Second Shift: Teaching Writing to Working Adults.* Portsmouth, NH: Boynton/Cook Heinemann, 1999.

Bizzell, Patricia. "What Happens When Basic Writers Come to College?" *College Composition and Communication* 37 (1986): 294–301.

Brandt, Deborah. *Literacy as Involvement: The Acts of Readers, Writers, and Texts.* Carbondale: Southern Illinois UP, 1990.

Chiseri-Strater, Elizabeth, and Bonnie Stone Sunstein. *Fieldworking: Reading and Writing Research.* Upper Saddle River, NJ: Prentice Hall, 1997.

Coles, William E., Jr., and James Vopat. *What Makes Writing Good: A Multiperspective.* Lexington, MA: D.C. Heath and Co., 1985.

Dean, Terry. "Multicultural Classrooms, Monocultural Teachers." *College Composition and Communication* 40 (1989): 23–37.

Dunbar-Odom, Donna. "Speaking Back with Authority: Students as Ethnographers in the Research Writing Class." *Attending to the Margins: Writing, Researching, and Teaching on the Front Lines*. Ed. Michelle Hall Kells and Valerie Balester. Portsmouth, NH: Boynton/Cook Heinemann, 1999. 7–22.

Elbow, Peter. "Reflections on Academic Discourse: How It Relates to Freshmen and Colleagues." *College English* 53.2 (1991): 135–56.

———. "The Shifting Relationships Between Speech and Writing." *College Composition and Communication* 36.3 (1985): 283–303.

Elbow, Peter, and Pat Belanoff. *A Community of Writers: A Workshop Course in Writing*. 2nd ed. New York: McGraw-Hill, 1995.

Farr, Marcia. "Essayist Literacy and Other Verbal Performances." *Written Communication* 10 (1993): 4–38.

Freire, Paulo. *Pedagogy of the Oppressed*. New York: Continuum, 1982.

Georges, Robert A., and Michael O. Jones. *People Studying People: The Human Element in Fieldwork*. Berkeley: U of California P, 1980.

Gleason, Barbara. "Evaluating Writing Programs in Real Time: The Politics of Remediation." *College Composition and Communication* 51.4 (2000): 560–88.

———. "Something of Great Constancy: Storytelling, Story Writing, and Academic Literacy." *Attending to the Margins: Writing, Researching, and Teaching on the Front Lines*. Ed. Michelle Hall Kells and Valerie Balester. Portsmouth, NH: Boynton/Cook Heinemann, 1999. 97–113.

Groden, Suzy, Eleanor Kutz, and Vivian Zamel. "Students as Ethnographers: Investigating Language Use as a Way to Learn Language." *The Writing Instructor* 6 (1987): 132–40.

Heath, Shirley Brice. *Ways with Words: Language, Life, and Work in Communities and Classrooms*. New York: Cambridge UP, 1983.

Hirvela, Alan. "Teaching Immigrant Students in the College Writing Classroom." *Attending to the Margins: Writing, Researching, and Teaching on the Front Lines*. Portsmouth, NH: Boynton/Cook Heinemann, 1999. 150–64.

Jackson, Bruce. "Ch. 7: Interviewing." *Fieldworking*. Urbana: U of Illinois P, 1987. 70–102.

Kutz, Eleanor, Suzy Q. Groden, and Vivian Zamel. *The Discovery of Competence: Teaching and Learning with Diverse Student Writers*. Portsmouth, NH: Boynton/Cook Heinemann, 1993.

McAlexander, Patricia J., Ann B. Dobie, and Noel Gregg. *Beyond the "SP" Label: Improving the Spelling of Learning Disabled and Basic Writers*. Urbana: NCTE, 1992.

Myerhoff, Barbara. *Number Our Days*. New York: Simon and Schuster, 1978.

Phelps, Louise Wetherbee. *Composition as a Human Science: Contributions to the Self-Understanding of a Discipline*. New York: Oxford UP, 1988.

Royster, Jacqueline Jones. "When the First Voice You Hear Is Not Your Own." *College Composition and Communication* 47 (1996): 29–40.

Severino, Carol, Juan C. Guerra, and Johnnella E. Butler, eds. *Writing in Multicultural Settings*. New York: MLA, 1997.

Soliday, Mary, and Barbara Gleason. "From Remediation to Enrichment: Evaluating a Mainstreaming Project." *Journal of Basic Writing* 16.1 (1997): 64–78.

Sternglass, Marilyn S. *Time to Know Them: A Longitudinal Study of Writing and Learning at the College Level*. Mahwah, NJ: Lawrence Erlbaum, 1997.

Classroom Activities

Developing writers often encounter many challenges as they learn how to incorporate quotations into their academic writing. One of the advantages of the interview assignment that Gleason presents as part of her four-assignment sequence is the opportunity for students to practice citing interview sources as part of their writing. Students also have a chance to create critical thinking questions and to practice note taking. Most significantly, as Gleason suggests, "I prize even more its use of conversational expertise as a resource for developing writers." Consider presenting this assignment to students in your basic writing class, perhaps as an introduction to an additional ethnographic assignment later in the term.

Thinking about Teaching

Gleason's article is particularly helpful in that it demonstrates ethnographic methods (by presenting case studies of students, for instance) as it describes ethnographic writing assignments for returning adult students. Take a closer look at Gleason's ethnographic approach and consider writing an ethnographic study of your own. As Gleason suggests, the late anthropologist Barbara Myerhoff's *Number Our Days* (New York: Simon and Schuster, 1980) is a fine example of an ethnographic study that would be worth reading as you consider an appropriate subject and approach for your own ethnographic work.

8

Critical Thinking

M any developing writers enter our classrooms with little awareness of their own thinking and learning processes. With practice,
however, developmental students can improve their evaluative and analytic skills, and the writers in this chapter show that the basic writing
classroom affords a wide array of opportunities for such practice. Nancy
Lawson Remler urges teachers to consider active learning strategies,
reasoning that students who are actively involved in a lesson will develop stronger critical thinking skills than those who passively absorb
information; Stephen D. Brookfield breaks down the learning process
into individual critical incidents that students use to build profiles of
themselves as active, critical learners; and Glynda Hull and Mike Rose
take a close look at the critical thinking processes of Robert, a basic
writing student at UCLA. Collectively, these writers help demystify
the teaching of critical thinking by providing strategies that take into
account the needs — and build on the strengths — that students bring
to the basic writing classroom.

The More Active the Better: Engaging College English Students with Active Learning Strategies

Nancy Lawson Remler

Using Charles Bonwell and James Eison's definition of active learning and Benjamin S. Bloom's taxonomy of educational objectives, among other theories of critical thinking, Nancy Lawson Remler illustrates her own means of encouraging student engagement in college English courses. In Remler's suggestions for providing students with leadership roles in the classroom, developmental writing instructors will find many useful applications for their classrooms. Remler's strategies — which will attract developing writers' interests and build on their skills — are designed to foster critical thinking, writing, and reading. This article originally appeared in Teaching English in the Two-Year College *in 2002.*

Among Arthur Chickering and Zelda Gamson's "seven principles of good practice" in undergraduate education are "active learning techniques" (3). These instructional strategies are popular, and evidence supporting the benefits of active learning is "too compelling to ignore" (Sutherland and Bonwell 5). In fact, Sutherland and Bonwell go so far as to say that "active learning is necessary for achieving many college course objectives" and that "all faculty can and should use it in their teaching" (83). I do. In fact, I believe that active learning not only helps students meet course objectives and grasp important concepts; it also helps students "*become aware* of strategies for learning and problem solving" (McKeachie, Pintrich, Lin, and Smith 1). Moreover, active learning facilitates enthusiasm in the classroom, enthusiasm that possibly reaps other, long-term benefits: with active learning "students may be more likely to view their college experience as personally rewarding" (Braxton, Milem, and Sullivan).

Even though active learning reinforces students' understanding of course concepts, the varied types of active learning strategies differ in how actively students participate in the learning process. Charles Bonwell and James Eison define active learning as "anything that involves students in doing things and thinking about the things they are doing" (2). They further narrow the definition by attributing to it these characteristics:

- students are involved in more than listening

- less emphasis is placed on transmitting information and more on developing students' skills

- students are involved in higher-order thinking (analysis, synthesis, evaluation)

- students are engaged in activities (reading, discussing, writing)
- greater emphasis is placed on students' exploration of their own attitudes and values (2)

Even with such characteristics in mind, active learning strategies could vary in the extent to which students engage in the learning process. Class discussion, for instance, may allow some of the more verbose students to dominate the conversation while quieter students remain in the background. Minute papers, lecture summaries, and other short writing assignments do engage students in more than listening, and they facilitate exploration of attitudes and values (Bonwell and Eison 13–19). However, they could still allow the professor to dominate classroom activity.

My preference is that student work dominate class activities. Students are, after all, the people having to grasp the concepts. I also want *all* students to participate in class activities, not just those with more vivacious personalities. My assumption is that the more active students are in the lesson (with appropriate scaffolding, of course), the more engaged they will be in the subject matter and the better opportunity they will have to learn and apply course concepts. My experiences, as well as student reactions to class activities, seem to validate this assumption.

Active Learning in College English Classrooms

Many English classes have revolved around active learning strategies since the 1960s, as the process approach gained popularity and inspired workshop composition classes (Villanueva 1). However, process writing isn't the only means of fostering students' active participation in composition and literature courses. They can also learn actively as they analyze their peers' writing, examine reading selections, and practice concepts of Standard English. In my composition and literature courses, I facilitate active learning by switching places with my students, a technique invoking Jeanne Gerlach's collaborative learning and Bonwell and Eison's peer-teaching theories, as well as Lois Rubin and Catherine Herbert's collaborative peer-teaching method. As students take the teacher's role by generating questions and guiding discussions, they not only have the most active role in the classroom, but they also boost their enthusiasm and confidence by revealing to the class (and themselves) their knowledge of the concepts they're studying. They also act responsibly as they realize the intellectual investment (as well as the time investment) required to lead a class. Several active learning strategies facilitate this student-as-teacher role.

Generating Questions for Discussion

Questioning is a good technique for fostering students' participation in class discussion. Bonwell and Eison provide several helpful guidelines for composing and asking such discussion questions. However, some professors find the technique challenging because they might ultimately be unable to avoid dominating the discussion, either from enthusiasm about the topic or because students do not discuss as actively as professors had hoped. I also value the questioning method but have modified it so that students generate their own discussion questions. Often they find this task daunting at first and ask questions inviting recall of facts. To help them in the question-writing process, I use what many scholars of active learning propose: Bloom's Taxonomy, a categorization of thinking skills ranging from factual knowledge at the lower end to evaluative thinking at the higher end. Together the class reads a children's text (or several) and compose questions about that text, working at all six of Bloom's levels of thinking. Then, also using Bloom's Taxonomy, we generate questions about a work of literature commonly taught in college classes. During subsequent literary discussion, I have students write questions about what they've read, stipulating that questions generate critical thinking above the knowledge level. Usually students' questions generate hearty discussions of the assigned reading because they have an intellectual investment not only in the assignment but also in the class plan. They can also discuss issues they find important rather than focusing on ideas the teacher wants to talk about.

A great example of this strategy is a recent discussion of W. E. B. Du Bois's *The Souls of Black Folk*. Students had read the introductory note and the forethought to that book. Before our discussion, I gave students the following instructions: "Pretend that you are teaching the class. You want to give your students a quiz on today's assigned material. Write three questions you would include on that quiz. The questions should generate thinking above the knowledge level, and they should indicate that you have read and understand these selections." Examples of students' questions were, "What does Du Bois mean by 'the problem of the Color Line'?" "What does Du Bois mean by 'the Veil'?" and "How is Du Bois's ancestry important to the purpose of this book?" The questions were the same ones I would have asked them had I led the class. But I didn't tell them that; instead, we discussed the questions enthusiastically, and students seemed to acquire a firm understanding of those concepts before reading subsequent chapters in the book. By forming the questions themselves, students established ownership in the class and were able to plan the class discussion.

Group Work in Discussing Standard English

When teaching usage of Standard English, I always fear the glazed look in my students' eyes. Even though they recognize the importance of making subjects and verbs agree or avoiding comma splices and fused sentences, the traditional mode of teaching such concepts — an explanation and subsequent drill exercise — bores them. What's more, drill exercises are often so irrelevant to students' own writing that they rarely transfer such concepts to their own essays. To get my students involved in learning these concepts, I trade places with them by putting them in small groups and assigning them a concept to explain to the class. For instance, if the day's lesson is avoiding run-ons when combining independent clauses, I'll have one group explain how to join two independent clauses using the semicolon and conjunctive adverb, while another group explains subordination of one clause, and another group explains using the period or the semicolon. As each group explains its technique, the students in the group must refer to guidelines in the textbook; they must also demonstrate the technique to the class with their own examples instead of those provided in the textbook. Leading the class makes students responsible for knowing one portion of the chapter thoroughly and referring to other portions for guidance as they write. My students corroborate John Bargh and Yaacov Schul's finding that teaching results in "an increase in the organization and/or elaboration of the specific subject matter that was taught" (594). By composing their own examples, students not only apply their knowledge, but they also make the concepts relevant to their own work, thereby increasing the likelihood of retaining those concepts. Leading the class motivates teamwork in ascertaining accuracy of examples and explanations.

As each group conducts its lesson, I sit in a student's desk and take a student's role. If I notice an omitted concept, I'll raise my hand and ask questions students usually ask me: "Is a conjunctive adverb the same kind of word that starts a dependent clause?" "Do you always put a semicolon before *however*?" If the students leading the lesson can answer my questions correctly, they've grasped the concept.

Some concepts of Standard English are more difficult than others, and students often hesitate to lead the class if they're uncertain of their assigned content. To relieve pressure, I assure students before they present their lessons that they're free to admit, "This is the part we didn't understand." When they identify their trouble spots, I step back into my teacher role and help them out. If students inadvertently explain a concept incorrectly, I also revert to my teacher role to redirect the group's thinking or to explain the concept to them. These small-group activities facilitate a learning community as we all take leadership and learner roles. Furthermore, learning processes are explicit as students demonstrate publicly what they do and do not comprehend. Finally, as they identify confusing concepts and ask for my assistance, they exhibit the necessity of making mistakes as they learn.

Group Work in Teaching Literature

In literature classes, students generally appreciate some choice of the works they read. With active learning strategies, I give them that choice. Students work in groups of four or five. Each group chooses a work of literature, subject to my approval, and they work during the semester on a lesson plan about that work. I provide guidelines for this assignment, and I confer with them during the planning process, advising them to consider their objective: what is it they want the class (me included) to learn? I also require their lesson to facilitate class discussion. Again, they use Bloom's Taxonomy as a guide, and they consult secondary sources to support their claims about their chosen work. At the same time, they use their creativity to plan an informative and engaging lesson. Recently one group taught a lesson on oral versus written poetry; another group arranged the classroom as a coffee house (juice and doughnuts included) to discuss various ways to interpret poetry. With appropriate scaffolding, these student groups led provocative discussions about literature of their choice, thereby claiming some ownership in the course. Simultaneously, they exhibited their constructed knowledge culminating from mostly independent work.

Conclusion

Although active learning strategies are numerous, one effective way to engage students and foster enthusiasm — for the course and possibly for college overall (Braxton, Milem, and Sullivan) — is to give them a leadership role in the class. Although such a strategy may not work for every class in higher education, it certainly works well in my first-year composition and sophomore literature classes. I believe these strategies could also work in other humanities or social science courses. Not only do students apply their new skills; they also participate in a learning community as they and I interchange roles. Furthermore, as students engage in the concepts of composition and literature, they simultaneously work as teams. The more active students are in the learning process, the better.

Works Cited

Bargh, John A., and Yaacov Schul. "On the Cognitive Benefits of Teaching." *Journal of Educational Psychology* 72 (1980): 593–604.

Bloom, Benjamin S., ed. *Taxonomy of Educational Objectives: The Classification of Educational Goals.* New York: Longman, 1956.

Bonwell, Charles C., and James A. Eison. *Active Learning: Creating Excitement in the Classroom.* ASHE-ERIC Higher Education Report 1. Washington: George Washington U, School of Education and Human Development, 1991.

Braxton, John M., Jeffrey F. Milem, and Anna Shaw Sullivan. "The Influence of Active Learning on the College Student Departure Process." *Journal of Higher Education* 7.5 (2000): 569–90. Education Full Text. Wilson Web. 30 Oct. 2001 http://vweb.hwwilsonweb.com.

Chickering, Arthur W., and Zelda Gamson. "Seven Principles for Good Practice in Undergraduate Education." *AAHE Bulletin* 39 (1987): 3–7.

Du Bois, W. E. B. *The Souls of Black Folk.* New York: Dover, 1994.

Gerlach, Jeanne M. "Is This Collaboration?" *Collaborative Learning: Underlying Processes and Effective Techniques.* Ed. K. Bosworth and S. Hamilton. San Francisco: Jossey, 1994. 5–14.

McKeachie, Wilbert J., Paul R. Pintrich, Lin Yi-Guang, and David A. F. Smith. *Teaching and Learning in the College Classroom: A Review of the Research Literature.* Ann Arbor: U of Michigan, 1986.

Rubin, Lois, and Catherine Herbert. "Model for Active Learning: Collaborative Peer Teaching." *College Teaching* 46.4 (1998): 26–30. Education Full Text. Wilson Web. 1 Nov. 2001 http://vweb.hwwilsonweb.com.

Sutherland, Tracey E., and Charles C. Bonwell, eds. *Using Active Learning in College Classes: A Range of Options for Faculty.* San Francisco: Jossey, 1996.

Villanueva, Victor. "The 'Given' in Our Conversations: The Writing Process." *Cross-Talk in Comp Theory: A Reader.* Ed. Victor Villanueva. Urbana, IL: NCTE, 1997. 1–2.

Classroom Activities

Remler's suggestions in the section "Group Work in Teaching Literature" help to foster students' critical literacy skills by demonstrating "their constructed knowledge culminating from mostly independent work." Consider creating a project for developing writers based on Remler's suggestions. Provide students with a list of books (or textbook readings) that they are assigned to teach to the class. As Remler indicates, choice is a key component of active learning, so student groups should have some degree of choice in their reading for this project. Remler asks students, as a second step, to decide "what [. . .] they want the class (me included) to learn." Have students plan and teach a lesson and lead a class discussion.

Thinking about Teaching

Throughout her article, Remler frequently refers to Bloom's taxonomy of educational objectives. In order to create, revise, and refresh your classroom assignments for developing writers, consider using Bloom's taxonomy to plan your own assignment sequence. A helpful web site that presents key terms for Bloom's taxonomy can be found on the University of Minnesota's Center for Teaching and Learning Services Web site at <http://www1.umn.edu/ohr/teachlearn/syllabus/bloom .html>. Consider how Bloom's "scaffolding" of intellectual development in the cognitive domain (in ascending order: knowledge, comprehension, application, synthesis, and evaluation) is an appropriate model of critical thinking for your own writing classroom.

Understanding Classroom Dynamics: The Critical Incident Questionnaire

Stephen D. Brookfield

This article, from Stephen D. Brookfield's Becoming a Critically Reflective Teacher *(1995), encourages instructors to think critically about their own teaching so that they can, in turn, encourage students to think critically about their own learning. Brookfield offers a practical instrument: a student questionnaire. Asking students to reflect on their learning experiences on a weekly basis, Brookfield argues, gets them "in the habit of hovering above themselves and studying the ways they react to different (learning) situations." Students identify "critical incidents" from each week's happenings, noting their own level of engagement in or distance from learning activities and their responses to the teacher's and other students' actions during class. As a semester-end assignment, students write a summary and analysis of their weekly responses. For the instructor, reading, analyzing, and responding to the questionnaire each week offers ongoing opportunities for rethinking pedagogy and content and for clarifying goals and expectations. Brookfield's critical incident questionnaire provides a practical starting point for charting the teaching and learning process.*

In this [article], I want to describe in detail one particular method for finding out how students are experiencing their learning and your teaching. . . . [T]his one approach — the critical incident questionnaire (CIQ) — . . . is the one that has most helped me see my practice through students' eyes. Critical incidents are vivid happenings that for some reason people remember as being significant (Tripp, 1993; Woods, 1993). For students, every class contains such moments, and teachers need to know what these are. The CIQ helps us embed our teaching in accurate information about students' learning that is regularly solicited and anonymously given. It is a quick and revealing way to ascertain the effects your actions are having on students and to discover the emotional highs and lows of their learning. The CIQ provides you with a running commentary on the emotional tenor of each class you deal with.

How the Critical Incident Questionnaire Works

The CIQ is a single-page form that is handed out to students at the end of the last class you have with them each week. It comprises five questions, each of which asks students to write down some details about events that happened in the class that week. Its purpose is not to determine what students liked or didn't like about the class. Instead, it gets them to focus on specific, concrete happenings that were significant to them.

The form that students receive has two sheets separated by carbon paper. This allows the student to keep a carbon copy of whatever she has written. Five questions are asked on the form, with space beneath each question for the student to write a response:

The Classroom Critical Incident Questionnaire

Please take about five minutes to respond to each of the questions below about this week's class(es). Don't put your name on the form — your responses are anonymous. When you have finished writing, put one copy of the form on the table by the door and keep the other copy for yourself. At the start of next week's class, I will be sharing the responses with the group. Thanks for taking the time to do this. What you write will help me make the class more responsive to your concerns.

1. At what moment in the class this week did you feel most engaged with what was happening?
2. At what moment in the class this week did you feel most distanced from what was happening?
3. What action that anyone (teacher or student) took in class this week did you find most affirming and helpful?
4. What action that anyone (teacher or student) took in class this week did you find most puzzling or confusing?
5. What about the class this week surprised you the most? (This could be something about your own reactions to what went on, or something that someone did, or anything else that occurs to you.)

Students are given the last five to ten minutes of the last class of the week to complete this form. As they leave the room, I ask them to drop the top sheet of the critical incident form on a chair or table by the door, face down, and to take the carbon copy with them. The reason I ask them to keep a copy is that at the end of the semester, they are expected, as part of their assigned course work, to hand in a summary of their responses. This summary is part of . . . [a] participant learning portfolio . . . , which documents what and how students have learned during the semester. The portfolio item dealing with the CIQ asks for a content analysis of major themes that emerged in students' responses over the semester. It also asks for a discussion of the directions for future learning that these responses suggested. Consequently, students know that it's in their own best interests to complete these questionnaires as fully as possible each week because they will gain credit for an analysis of them later in the term.

For CIQs to be taken seriously by students, it is crucial that a convincing case be made for using them. In my course outlines, I describe how the method works and justify its use by saying that it will make the course a better experience for learners. As students read the syllabus, they see that inquiry into, and public discussion of, their experiences as learners will be a regular part of the course. At the first class, I explain why I use critical incidents and how they help me make the class more responsive to students' concerns. I also mention how much students will find out about themselves as learners by completing the form.

I try to give convincing examples from earlier courses of how critical incident responses alerted me to confusions or ambiguities that otherwise could have caused serious problems for students. I let them know that what I found out caused me to change my teaching. I also point out that completing the CIQs each week helps students build up important material for the assessed participant learning portfolio. If possible, at the first class meeting, I assemble a panel of former students to talk about their experiences when they took the course. One theme I ask panel members to address is their perceptions of the advantages and drawbacks of the CIQ.

Analyzing and Responding to Data from the CIQ

After I have collected the CIQ responses at the end of the last class each week, I read through them looking for common themes. This activity usually takes no more than twenty minutes. The bus ride from the campus to my house takes about seventeen minutes, and usually, between getting on the bus and arriving at my stop, I have made a reasonably accurate analysis of the chief clusters of responses. I look for comments that indicate problems or confusions, particularly if they are caused by my actions. Anything contentious is highlighted, as is anything that needs further clarification. These comments become the basis for the questions and issues I address publicly the next time we're together.

At the start of the first class of the next week, I debrief students on the main themes that emerged in their responses. Sometimes I type up a one- or two-page summary and leave copies of this on students' chairs for them to read as they come in. At other times, I take two or three minutes to present an opening oral report. If students have made comments that have caused me to change how I teach, I acknowledge this and explain why the change seems worth making. I try also to clarify any actions, ideas, requirements, or exercises that seem to be causing confusion. Criticisms of my actions are reported and discussed. If contentious issues have emerged, we talk about how these can be negotiated so that everyone feels heard and respected. Quite often, students write down comments expressing their dislike of something I am insisting they do. When this happens, I know that I must take some time to reemphasize why I believe the activity is so important and to make the best case I can about how it contributes to students' long-term interests. Even if I have said this before, and written it in the syllabus, the critical incident responses alert me to the need to make my rationale explicit once again.

Using the CIQ doesn't mean that I constantly change everything that students tell me they don't like. We all have nonnegotiable elements to our agendas that define who we are and what we stand for. To throw them away as a result of students' opinions would undercut our identities as teachers. For example, I won't give up my agenda to get students to think critically, even if they all tell me that they want me to stop doing this. I will be as flexible as I can in negotiating how this agenda is realized, but I won't abandon it. I'll ask students to suggest different ways in which they might show me that they're thinking critically. I'll also vary the pace at which I introduce certain activities and exercises, to take account of students' hostility, inexperience, or unfamiliarity with this process. But to abandon the activity that defines who I am as a teacher would mean that I ceased to have the right to call myself a teacher. So if students use their CIQ responses to express a strong opinion that challenges what you're trying to do or how you're trying to do it, you owe it to them to acknowledge this criticism. In doing so, you need to make your own position known, justify it, and negotiate alternative ways of realizing your aims. But you don't owe it to them to abandon entirely your rationale for teaching.

Advantages of Critical Incident Questionnaires

I am a strong advocate of CIQs because of the clear benefits their use confers. Let me describe these briefly.

They Alert Us to Problems before a Disaster Develops

I have always prided myself on my conscientious use of the troubleshooting period to create a safe opportunity for students to make public anything that is troubling them. I regularly invite them to speak up during these periods about anything they find problematic, unfair, ambiguous, confusing, or unethical about the course or about my teaching. These invitations are frequently met with silence and by serried ranks of benign, smiling faces. Not surprisingly, I used to interpret this to mean that things were going along just fine. Indeed, it seemed at times that students were a little tired of this heavy-handed attempt by yours truly to appear fair and responsive. So you can imagine my surprise, hurt, and anger when I would receive end-of-course written evaluations from students saying that my course was of no real use to them, was uninspiringly taught, and was a waste of their time! I had given them ample opportunity to say these things to me earlier and had assured them I wanted to know about any problems they had so that we could work on fixing them. Why had no one spoken out?

This scenario of silent, smiling faces during troubleshooting periods followed by "take no prisoners" final evaluations repeated itself so often that I resolved to find a way to detect early on in a course any smoldering resentments students felt. If I knew about them soon enough, I could address them before they built to volcanic proportions. Using CIQs has helped me do this very effectively. My teaching has certainly not been without its problems, some of them very serious, but I have ceased to be taken by surprise when these emerge.

Behind those silent, smiling faces lies a recognition by students of the power differential that exists between themselves and their teachers. Students are understandably reluctant to voice misgivings and criticisms to people who exercise substantial influence (through the awarding of grades) over their career destinies and their self-concepts. This is as true for teachers who make repeated avowals of their commitment to democratic practice as it is for those who seem more traditionally authoritarian. However, if anonymity is assured, students may be willing to put their concerns in writing. Without anonymity, they are not comfortable voicing their misgivings, fears, and criticisms: they know the risks involved, and most of them have learned to keep quiet for fear of upsetting someone who has power over them.

Using CIQs helps teachers detect early on in a course any serious problems that need addressing before they get out of hand. The CIQ provides a direct, unfiltered account of students' experiences that is free of the distortions usually caused by the power dynamic between teacher and taught. CIQs are particularly helpful in providing teachers with accurate information about the extent and causes of resistance to learning. They also make us aware of situations in which our expectations about appropriate teaching methods and content are not meshing with those held by students. In my own teaching, CIQs give me good information about students' readiness for a particular learning activity. This, in turn, helps me pace the course. CIQs also help me curb my tendency to equate silence with mental inertia. Let me explain.

Many times in the middle of giving a lecture, I have one of those "Beam me up, Scotty" moments. This usually happens when I sense from students' body language that I've lost them. They're looking at the table, at the ceiling, out of the window — anywhere else but at me. Faced with this lack of eye contact, I feel a rising sense of panic. So I stop and ask students if there's anything I can clarify or if they have any questions about what I've just said. When my invitation is met with silence, I feel demoralized and glumly conclude that the session has been wasted. After all, didn't their blank expressions and muteness prove that they had no idea what I was talking about? Yet often after such occasions, I have been surprised and relieved to read in students' critical incident responses how moments in the lecture had been the most engaging moments of the class or how comments I had made during the presentation had been particularly affirming.

They Encourage Students to Be Reflective Learners

A second advantage of the CIQ lies in its encouragement of student reflection. When the instrument is first introduced into a class, students sometimes find the activity of completing the five questions on the form to be somewhat artificial; they feel they are going through some not very convincing motions. Over time, however, they start to notice patterns emerging in their own emotional responses to learning. They tell me that as they go through a course, they have pedagogic "out of body" experiences: by weeks five or six of the course, they are in the habit of hovering above themselves and studying the ways they react to different situations. They begin to jot down notes about critical class-room events and their reactions to them as they occur so that the infor-mation is not missed when the CIQs are completed at the end of class.

They Build a Case for Diversity in Teaching

When teachers report back to students the spread of responses to the previous week's classes, a predictable diversity emerges. One cluster of students writes that the most engaging moments for them were dur-ing the small group activity. Typical comments are: "I could recognize what others were saying," "I learned something important from a group member," "I felt my voice was being listened to." This same group of people often reports that the most distancing moments were experi-enced during my presentation. They write: "I couldn't see the point of the lecture," "What you said did not seem to make sense to me," "I'd had a long day and was fighting to stay awake."

Another cluster of responses says exactly the opposite. To these students, the most engaging moments in class were experienced dur-ing the instructor's presentation. Typical comments are: "What you spoke about related directly to me," "I enjoy hearing what you think about this," "I really benefit from having things laid out in front of me." This same group usually reports that for them the most distancing moments happened in the small group exercise: "We got off task," "An egomaniac dominated our discussion," "One man felt it was the duty of the rest of us to solve his problems." Again, in picking out affirming actions, one cluster of responses might refer favorably to a teacher's self-disclosure, while another might report this as irritating or irrel-evant. One student wrote, about a recent class of mine: "Your willing-ness to be open with us is wonderful. It makes me feel like being open in return." Another wrote, "Too much psychoanalysis, not enough con-tent — 90 percent of our class is personal disclosure and only 10 per-cent is critical rigor."

As I read out these responses at the beginning of each new week, students often comment on their diversity. They laugh as they hear how eight people picked out the small group experience as the most engaging moment and how another eight reported the same activity as the most distancing or confusing episode in the class. They tell me that they hadn't realized how the same things could be experienced so dif-ferently. Then we talk about the concept of learning styles or situated cognition and about the ways that culture, history, and personality de-termine how events are experienced. Seeing a diversity of responses emerge every week gives a drama and reality to the idea that different people learn differently.

Each week, I emphasize that my recognition of this diversity lies behind my own efforts to use a range of teaching methods and materials. The important thing about this is that I ground my use of different methods in students' reports of their own experiences as learners in my courses. I could write in my syllabus, and explain at the opening class, that because different people learn differently, I intend to use different approaches. But saying this would mean little to students who believe that everyone else learns the way they do. However, when they hear, week after week, how people sitting next to them have a completely different reaction to what goes on in class, the reason why I use a variety of approaches starts to make sense.

They Build Trust

The CIQ can play an important role in building trust between students and teachers. Students say that the experience of having their opinions, reactions, and feelings solicited regularly, and addressed publicly, is one that is crucial to their coming to trust a teacher. They say they are used to filling out evaluations at the end of courses, but that they view that activity as artificial and meaningless, since they never see any benefits from their efforts. They know that their comments might change what a teacher does with another group in the future, but this is of little importance to them.

However, with the weekly CIQs, students wait expectantly at the start of each new week for the report on the responses to the previous week's classes. They know that during this report, and in the discussion that follows it, the teacher will be talking about what she feels she needs to do and change in her own teaching as a result of what she has learned from the responses. Students say that hearing their own anonymous comments reported back to them as part of a commonly articulated class concern somehow legitimizes what had formerly been felt as a purely private and personal reaction. When they see teachers consistently making changes in their practice, and explicitly demonstrating that they are doing so in response to students' CIQ responses, the feeling develops that the teachers can be trusted.

Sometimes teachers quite legitimately feel that they can't change their practice to accommodate students' wishes as expressed in their CIQ responses. But the very fact that teachers acknowledge that they know what those wishes are, and the fact that they take the time and trouble to explain why they feel they can't, in good conscience, do what a group of students wants them to do, builds a sense that the class is one in which open and honest disclosure is encouraged.

Works Cited

Tripp, David. *Critical Incidents in Teaching: Developing Professional Judgment.* New York: Routledge, 1993.
Woods, Peter. *Critical Events in Teaching and Learning.* Bristol, PA: Falmer Press, 1993.

Classroom Activities

Brookfield suggests that an important purpose of the critical incident questionnaire is to allow students a safely anonymous position from which to articulate what they are learning from the course. Anonymity allows teachers to gauge how students perceive the progress of the course and the processes of their own learning. Students who may feel reticent about speaking up in class are given the opportunity to provide the teacher with crucial information about how the methods and goals of the course are being perceived and enacted.

For Brookfield, critical thinking involves sustained reflection on the process. As students complete the questionnaire each week, they discover patterns in their own learning; connections between critical incidents and ideas may begin to seem less random. With this in mind, devote ten minutes of each class period to writing a critical incident questionnaire. (The students keep a copy, and the instructor sees the anonymous weekly responses.) Students may wish to share these entries in small groups throughout the semester to compare and contrast experiences. At the end of the course, when you ask them to use their critical thinking skills to summarize and analyze a semester's worth of responses, students will have concrete and significant information at their disposal concerning their own learning styles and thinking and writing processes.

Thinking about Teaching

As instructors, we may not feel comfortable with student evaluations that come at the end of the term and offer only numerical ratings or cryptic comments that do not refer to specific course activities. It seems difficult, if not impossible, to learn very much about how students respond to our teaching from these often vague documents. The critical incident questionnaire is one means of ameliorating this process, giving teachers access to student perceptions of the course and of themselves as learners from the very beginning.

Yet Brookfield makes clear that teachers can also participate in the CIQ process by reflecting on their own methods and on their perceptions of critical incidents in the course. Later in his book, Brookfield recommends that teachers also keep their own learning journal as well as fill out the weekly CIQ — and that they share the results with students. Such activities may well demystify the teaching process for students. Further, such a process allows us to continue to learn about what works well for our students and ourselves and what we may consider changing. Engage in this form of teacher research with interested colleagues; meet as often as possible to share responses and exchange ideas.

"This Wooden Shack Place":
The Logic of an Unconventional Reading

Glynda Hull and Mike Rose

Glynda Hull and Mike Rose bring unique perspectives to basic writing and to the American system of education in general. Their search for solutions to systemic problems leads them to value the unconventional in the processes of reading, interpreting, and critical thinking. Yet these teachers also understand the necessity of student and teacher working together to arrive at shared meaning, as they demonstrate in the case of one student named Robert. "Robert's interpretation" of a poem he is studying "will cause his teacher to modify his reading, and the teacher's presentation of his interpretation will help Robert acquire an additional approach to the poem." In this article, first published in College Composition and Communication *in 1990, Hull and Rose examine Robert's "unconventional" reading in detail, allowing the reader to follow along as Robert reveals how social class and cultural background affect his critical thinking and close reading.*

This is a paper about student interpretations of literature that strike the teacher as unusual, a little off, not on the mark. When we teachers enter classrooms with particular poems or stories in hand, we also enter with expectations about the kind of student responses that would be most fruitful, and these expectations have been shaped, for the most part, in literature departments in American universities. We value some readings more than others — even, in our experience, those teachers who advocate a reader's free play. One inevitable result of this situation is that there will be moments of mismatch between what a teacher expects and what students do. What interests us about this mismatch is the possibility that our particular orientations and readings might blind us to the logic of a student's interpretation and the ways that interpretation might be sensibly influenced by the student's history.

The two of us have been involved for several years in a study of remedial writing instruction in American higher education, attempting to integrate social-cultural and cognitive approaches to better understand the institutional and classroom practices that contribute to students being designated remedial (Hull and Rose). One of the interesting things that has emerged as we've been conducting this research is the place of reading in the remedial writing classroom, particularly at a time when composition professionals are calling for the integration of reading and writing while affirming, as well, the place of literature in remedial instruction (Bartholomae and Petrosky; Salvatori, "Reading and Writing"). As this integration of reading, and particularly the reading of literature, into the remedial writing classroom continues, composition teachers will increasingly be called on to explore questions of interpretation, expectation, and background knowledge — particularly given the rich mix of class and culture found in most remedial programs. We would like to consider these issues by examining a discussion of a poem that was part of a writing assignment. Specifically, we will analyze a brief stretch of discourse, one in which a student's personal history and cultural background shape a somewhat unconventional reading of a section of a poem. We will note the way the mismatch plays itself out in conversation, the logic of the student's reading and the coherent things it reveals about his history, and the pedagogical implications of conducting a conversation that encourages that logic to unfold.

The stretch of discourse we're going to analyze comes from a conference that immediately followed a classroom discussion of a poem by the contemporary Japanese-American writer Garrett Kaoru Hongo. The class is designated as the most remedial composition class at the University of California; it is part of a special program on the Los Angeles campus (the Freshman Preparatory Program) for students determined by test scores to be significantly at risk. (The SAT verbal scores of this particular section, for example, ranged from 220 to 400.) Mike Rose taught the class at the time he was collecting data on remedial writing instruction at the university level, and though his class was not the focus of his research, he did keep a teaching log, photocopy all work produced by the class, and collect sociohistorical and process-tracing data on several students and tape record selected conferences and tutorial sessions with them. For reasons that will shortly be apparent, a student named Robert was one of those Rose followed: he will be the focus of this paper. Let us begin this analysis with the poem Robert and the others in the class read; the discussion took place during the third week of the fall quarter:

And Your Soul Shall Dance

for Wakako Yamauchi

Walking to school beside fields
of tomatoes and summer squash,
alone and humming a Japanese love song,
you've concealed a copy of *Photoplay*
between your algebra and English texts.
Your knee socks, saddle shoes, plaid dress,
and blouse, long-sleeved and white
with ruffles down the front,
come from a Sears catalogue
and neatly complement your new Toni curls.
All of this sets you apart from the landscape:
flat valley grooved with irrigation ditches,
a tractor grinding through alkaline earth,
the short stands of windbreak eucalyptus
shuttering the desert wind
from a small cluster of wooden shacks
where your mother hangs the wash.
You want to go somewhere.
Somewhere far away from all the dust

and sorting machines and acres of lettuce.
Someplace where you might be kissed
by someone with smooth, artistic hands.
When you turn into the schoolyard,
the flagpole gleams like a knife blade in the sun,
and classmates scatter like chickens,
shooed by the storm brooding on your horizon.

— Garrett Kaoru Hongo

The class did pretty well with "And Your Soul Shall Dance." They followed the narrative line, pictured the girl, and understood the tension between her desires (and her dress) and the setting she's in. The ending, with its compressed set of similes and metaphors, understandably gave them some trouble — many at first took it literally, pictured it cinematically. But, collaboratively, the class came to the understanding that the storm meant something powerful and disquieting was brewing, and that the girl — the way she looks, her yearning for a different life — was somehow central to the meaning of the storm. The class was not able, however, to fit all the pieces together into one or more unified readings. And during the discussion — as members of the class focused on particular lines — some students offered observations or answers to questions or responses to classmates that seemed to be a little off the mark, unusual, as though the students weren't reading the lines carefully. Rose wondered if these "misreadings" were keeping the students from a fuller understanding of the way the storm could be integrated into the preceding events of the poem. One of these students was Robert.

A brief introduction. Robert is engaging, polite, style-conscious, intellectually curious. His father is from Trinidad, his mother from Jamaica, though he was born in Los Angeles and bears no easily discernible signs of island culture. His parents are divorced, and while he spends time with both, he currently lives with his mother in a well-kept, apartment-dense area on the western edge of central Los Angeles. Robert's family, and many of their neighbors, fall in the lower-middle-class SES bracket. He was bused to middle and high school in the more affluent San Fernando Valley. His high-school GPA was 3.35; his quantitative SAT was 410, and his verbal score was 270. In class he is outgoing and well-spoken — if with a tinge of shyness — and though his demeanor suggests he is a bit unsure of himself, he volunteers answers and responds thoughtfully to his classmates.

During the last half hour of the class on the Hongo poem, the students began rough drafts of an interpretive essay, and in his paper Robert noted that his "interpretation of this poem is that this girl seems to want to be different from society." (And later, he would tell his teacher that Hongo's poem "talked about change.") Robert clearly had a sense of the poem, was formulating an interpretation, but he, like the others, couldn't unify the poem's elements, and Rose assumed Robert's inability was caused by his misreading of sections of the poem. Here is Rose's entry in his teacher's log:

Robert was ok on the 1st third of the poem, but seemed to miss the point of the central section. Talk with the tutor — does he need help with close reading?

Rose decided to get a better look, so he moved his regularly scheduled conference with Robert up a week and tape-recorded it. In the three-minute excerpt from that conference that follows, Robert is discussing the storm at the poem's conclusion — the foreboding he senses — but is having some trouble figuring out exactly what the source of this impending disruption is. Rose asks Robert if — given the contrast between the farming community and the girl's dreams and appearance — he could imagine a possible disruption in her not-too-distant future. We pick up the conversation at this point. To help clarify his own expectations, Rose replayed the stretch of tape as soon as Robert left, trying to recall what he intended in asking each of his questions.

1a *Rose:* What do you think . . . what, you know, on the one hand what might the reaction of her parents be, if she comes in one day and says, "I, I don't like it here, I want to leave here, I want to be different from this, I want to go to the city and . . ." [*Expectation:* Robert will say the parents will be resistant, angry — something rooted in the conservative values associated with poor, traditional families.]

1b *Robert:* Um, that would basically depend on the wealth of her family. You'd wanna know if her parents are poor . . . [*mumbling*] . . . they might not have enough money, whereas they can't go out and improve, you know . . . [Responds with a *qualification* that complicates the question by suggesting we need to know more. This further knowledge concerns the family's economic status, something Rose had assumed was evident.]

2a *Rose:* OK. OK. [*Acknowledges with hesitation*] From what we see about the background here and the times and the look, what can . . . can we surmise, can we imagine, do you think her parents are wealthy or poor? [*Focuses* on the poem, asking for a conjecture. *Expectation:* Robert's attention will be drawn to the shacks, the hand laundering, the indications of farm labor.]

2b *Robert:* I wouldn't say that they're wealthy but, again, I wouldn't say that they are poor either. [Responds with a *qualification*]

3a Rose: OK. [*Acknowledges with hesitation*] And why not? [Requests *elaboration. Expectation:* Robert will provide something from the poem, some line that explains the ambiguity in his answer.]

3b *Robert:* Because typical farm life is, you know, that's the way that you see yourself, you know, wear jeans, just some old jeans, you know, some old saddle shoes, boots or something, some old kinda shirt, you know, with some weird design on the shoulder pad . . . [Responds by creating a *scenario*]

3c *Rose:* Uh huh . . . [*Unsure about direction*, but *acknowledges*]

3d *Robert:* . . . for the guys. And then girls, probably wear some kind of plain cloth skirt, you know, with some weird designs on it and a weird shirt. I couldn't really . . . you really wouldn't know if they're . . . whether they were rich or not. Cause mainly everyone would dress the same way . . . [Continues *scenario* leading to an observation]

4a   *Rose:*   Yeah. [Sees the purpose of the scenario] That's right, so you wouldn't be able to tell what the background is, right? [*Confirms* Robert's observation and *reflects back*] Let's see if there's anything in the poem that helps us out. (pause) "All of this sets you apart . . ." this is about line twelve in the poem, "All of this sets you apart from the landscape: / flat valley grooved with irrigation ditches, / a tractor grinding through alkaline earth, / the short stands of windbreak eucalyptus / shuttering the desert wind / from a small cluster of wooden shacks / where your mother hangs the wash." [*Focuses* on poem] Now if she lives with her mother in a wooden shack, a shack . . . [*Begins line of reasoning*]

4b   *Robert:*   OK. OK. Oh! [*interrupts*] Right here — is it saying that she lives with her mother, or that she just goes to this wooden shack place to *hang* her clothes? [*Challenges* teacher's line of reasoning]

4c   *Rose:*   Oh, I see. So you think that it's possible then that her mother . . . [*Reflects back*]

4d   *Robert:*   [*picks up thought*] washes her clothes probably at home somewhere and then walks down to this place where the wind . . . the wind . . . so the eucalyptus trees block this wind, you know, from . . . [*Elaborates*]

4e   *Rose:*   [*picks up thought*] so that the clothes can dry.

4f   *Robert:*   Right. [*Confirms*]

5a   *Rose:*   Well, that's certainly possible. That's certainly possible. [*Confirms*] Um, the only thing I would say if I wanted to argue with you on that would be that that's possible, but it's also the only time that this writer lets us know anything about where she might live, etc. . . . [*Begins to explain his interpretation* — an interpretation, we'd argue, that is fairly conventional: that the family is poor, and that poverty is signaled by the shacks, the place, most likely, where the family lives]

Certainly not all of Robert's exchanges — in classroom or conference — are so packed with qualification and interruption and are so much at cross purposes with teacher expectation. Still, this stretch of discourse is representative of the characteristics that make Robert's talk about texts interesting to us. Let us begin by taking a closer look at the reasoning Robert exhibits as he discusses "And Your Soul Shall Dance." To conduct this analysis, we'll be intersecting socioeconomic, cognitive, and textual information, bringing these disparate sources of information together to help us understand Robert's interpretation of sections of "And Your Soul Shall Dance," explicating not the poem, but a particular reading of it in a particular social-textual setting.

Here are a few brief comments on method:

Our data comes from the stretch of discourse we just examined, from other sections of the same conference, from a stimulated-recall session (on an essay Robert was writing for class) conducted one week prior to the conference,[1] and from a follow-up interview conducted four months after the conference to collect further sociohistorical information.

To confirm our sense of what a "conventional" reading of this section of the poem would be, we asked six people to interpret the lines in question. Though our readers represented a mix of ages and cultural backgrounds, all had been socialized in American literature departments: two senior English majors — one of whom is Japanese-American — two graduate students — one of whom is African-American — and two English professors — one of whom is Mexican-American. Regardless of age or cultural background, all quickly offered the same interpretation we will be suggesting is conventional.[2]

Analysis

1a–1b

1a *Rose:* What do you think . . . what, you know, on the one hand what might the reaction of her parents be, if she comes in one day and says, "I, I don't like it here, I want to leave here, I want to be different from this, I want to go to the city and . . ."

1b *Robert:* Um, that would basically depend on the wealth of her family. You'd wanna know if her parents are poor . . . (*mumbling*) . . . they might not have enough money, whereas they can't go out and improve, you know . . .

Robert claims that the reaction of the girl's parents to "I want to leave here . . . [and] go to the city . . ." would "depend on the wealth of her family." This qualification is legitimate, though the reasoning behind it is not quickly discernible. In the follow-up interview Robert elaborates: "[If she goes to the city] she's gonna need support . . . and if they're on a low budget they won't have that much money to be giving to her all the time to support her." The social context of Robert's reasoning becomes clearer here. He comes from a large family (eleven siblings and half-siblings), some members of which have moved (and continue to move) across cultures and, to a degree, across class lines. It is the parents' obligation to help children as they make such moves, and Robert is aware of the strains on finances such movement brings — he is in the middle of such tension himself.

2a–4f

This segment includes Robert's qualified response to "do you think her parents are wealthy or poor?" his farm fashion scenario, and his perception of the "small cluster of wooden shacks." As we've seen, we need to understand Robert's perception of the shacks in order to understand his uncertainty about the parents' economic status, so we'll reverse the order of events on the transcript and deal first with the shacks.

> 4a *Rose:* Yeah. That's right, so you wouldn't be able to tell what the background is, right? Let's see if there's anything in the poem that helps us out. (pause) "All of this sets you apart . . ." this is about line twelve in the poem, "All of this sets you apart from the landscape: / flat valley grooved with irrigation ditches, / a tractor grinding through alkaline earth, / the short stands of windbreak eucalyptus / shuttering the desert wind / from a small cluster of wooden shacks / where your mother hangs the wash." Now if she lives with her mother in a wooden shack, a shack . . .

> 4b *Robert:* OK. OK. Oh! Right here — is it saying that she lives with her mother, or that she just goes to this wooden shack place to *hang* her clothes?

Those of us educated in a traditional literature curriculum, and especially those of us trained in an English graduate program, are schooled to comprehend the significance of the shacks. We understand, even if we can't readily articulate them, the principles of compression and imagistic resonance that underlie Hongo's presentation of a single image to convey information about economic and historical background. Robert, however, isn't socialized to such conventions, or is only partly socialized, and so he relies on a model of interpretation Rose had seen him rely on in class and in the stimulated-recall session: an almost legalistic model, a careful, qualifying reasoning that defers quick judgment, that demands multiple sources of verification. The kind of reasoning we see here, then, is not inadequate. In fact, it's pretty sophisticated — though it is perhaps inappropriately invoked in a poetic world, as Rose begins to suggest to Robert in 5a. We'll come back to this momentarily, but first we want to address one more issue related to Robert's uncertainty about the income level of the girl's parents.

We would like to raise the possibility that Robert's background makes it unlikely that he is going to respond to "a small cluster of wooden shacks" in quite the same way — with quite the same emotional reaction — as would a conventional (and most likely middle-class) reader for whom the shacks might function as a quickly discernible, emblematic literary device. Some of Robert's relatives in Trinidad still live in houses like those described in the poem, and his early housing in Los Angeles — further into central Los Angeles than where he now lives — was quite modest. We would suggest that Robert's "social distance" from the economic reality of poor landscapes isn't as marked as that of the conventional/middle-class reader, and this might make certain images less foreign to him, and, therefore, less emotionally striking. This is certainly *not* to say that Robert is naive about his current position in American society, but simply to say that the wooden shacks might not spark the same dramatic response in him as in a conventional/middle-class reader. The same holds true for another of Hongo's indicators of economic status — the hanging of the wash — for Robert's mother still "likes to wash her clothes by hand." Paradoxically, familiarity might work against certain kinds of dramatic response to aspects of working-class life.

In line with the above assertion, we would like to consider one last indicator of the girl's economic status — the mention of the Sears catalogue. The Sears catalogue, we believe, cuts two ways in the poem: it suggests lower-income-level shopping ("thrifty," as one of our readers put it) and, as well, the importing of another culture's garments. But the catalogue also carries with it an ironic twist: it's not likely that conventional readers would consider a Sears catalogue to be a source of fashion, so there's a touch of irony — perhaps pity mixed with humor — in this girl fulfilling her romantic dreams via Sears and Roebuck. We suggest that Robert's position in the society makes it difficult for him to see things this way, to comply with this conventional reading. He knows merchandise from Sears is "economical" and "affordable," and, to him, there's nothing ironic, pitiable, or humorous about that. When asked if he sees anything sad or ironic about the girl buying there he responds, "Oh, no, no," pointing out that "some of the items they sell in Sears, they sell in other stores." He then goes on to uncover an interesting problem in the poem. He uses the Sears catalogue to support his assertion that the family isn't all that poor (and thus doesn't necessarily live in those shacks): "She couldn't be really poor because she has clothes from the Sears catalogue." Robert knows what real poverty is, and he knows that if you have enough money to buy at Sears, you're doing OK. He goes on to speculate — again with his careful, qualifying logic — that if she is as poor as the shacks suggest, then maybe the Sears clothes could be second-hand and sent to her by relatives, in the way his family sends clothes and shoes to his relatives in Trinidad. Hongo's use of the Sears catalogue is, in some ways, undercut by other elements in his poem.

3b *Robert:* Because typical farm life is, you know, that's the way that you see yourself, you know, wear jeans, just some old jeans, you know, some old saddle shoes, boots or something, some old kinda shirt, you know, with some weird design on the shoulder pad . . .

3c *Rose:* Uh huh . . .

3d *Robert:* . . . for the guys. And then girls, probably wear some kind of plain cloth skirt, you know, with some weird designs on it and a weird shirt. I couldn't really . . . you really wouldn't know if they're . . . whether they were rich or not. Cause mainly everyone would dress the same way . . .

Now we can turn to the farm fashion scenario. Given that the "small cluster of wooden shacks" doesn't seem to function for Robert as it might for the conventional reader, he is left more to his own devices when asked: "do you think her parents are wealthy or poor?" What begins as a seeming non sequitur — and a concrete one at that — does reveal its purpose as Robert plays it out. Though Robert has a frame of reference to understand the economics of the scene in "And Your Soul Shall Dance" and the longing of its main character, he is, after all, a city boy, born and raised in central Los Angeles. What he does, then, when asked a question about how one determines the economic background of people moving across a farm landscape is to access what knowledge he does have about farm life — things he's read or heard, images he's gleaned from movies and television shows (e.g., *Little House on the Prairie*) — and create a scenario, focusing on one indicator of socioeconomic status: fashion. (And fashion is a sensible criterion to use here, given the poem's emblematic use of clothing.) Classroom-observational and stimulated-recall data suggest that Robert makes particularly good use of visual imagery in his thinking — e.g., he draws pictures and charts to help him comprehend difficult readings; he rehearses sentences by visualizing them before he writes them out — and here we see him reasoning through the use of scenario, concluding that in certain kinds of communities, distinctions by readily discernible indicators like dress might not be all that easy to make.

> 4d *Robert:* washes her clothes probably at home somewhere and then walks down to this place where the wind . . . the wind . . . so the eucalyptus trees block this wind, you know, from . . .
>
> 4e *Rose:* so that the clothes can dry.
>
> 4f *Robert:* Right.

This section also involves the wooden shacks, though the concern here is Robert's assertion that the mother doesn't have to live in the shacks to hang the wash there. Robert's reasoning, again, seems inappropriately legalistic. Yes, the mother could walk down to this place to hang her clothes; the poem doesn't specify "that [the girl] lives with her mother, or that [the mother] just goes to this wooden shack place to *hang* her clothes." But to Rose during the conference this seemed like a jurisprudential rather than a poetic reading. In the follow-up interview, however, Robert elaborated in a way that made Rose realize that Robert might have had a better imagistic case than his teacher first thought — for Rose missed the full visual particulars of the scene, did not see the importance of the "tractors grinding through the alkaline earth." Robert elaborates on "this place where . . . the eucalyptus trees block this wind." He describes this "little shack area where the clothes can dry without being bothered by the wind and dust . . . with all this . . . the tractor grinding through the earth. That brings up dust." Robert had pictured the surrounding landscape — machines stirring up grit and dust — and saw the necessity of trees to break the dust-laden wind so that wash could dry clean in the sun. The conventional reader could point out that such a windbreak would be necessary as well to protect residents, but given Robert's other interpretations, it makes sense, is coherent, to see the shacks — sheds of some kind perhaps or abandoned housing — as part of this eucalyptus-protected place where women hang the wash. What's important to note here is that Robert was able to visualize the scene — animate it, actually — in a way that Rose was not, for Rose was focusing on the dramatic significance of the shacks. Robert's reading may be unconventional and inappropriately jurisprudential, but it is coherent, and it allows us — in these lines — to animate the full landscape in a way that enhances our reading of the poem.

Conclusion

We hope we have demonstrated the logic and coherence of one student's unconventional reading. What we haven't addressed — and it could certainly now be raised — is the pedagogical wisdom of encouraging in a writing classroom the playing out of such unconventional readings. Reviewing the brief stretch of Rose's and Robert's discourse, we see how often teacher talk is qualified, challenged, and interrupted (though not harshly), and how rarely teacher expectations are fulfilled. If the teacher's goals are to run an efficient classroom, cover a set body of material, and convey certain conventional reading and writing strategies to students who are on the margin of the academic community, then all these conversational disjunctions are troubling.

What we would like to suggest, though, is that the laudable goal of facilitating underprepared students' entry into the academic community is actually compromised by a conversational pattern that channels students like Robert into a more "efficient" discourse. The desire for efficiency and coverage can cut short numerous possibilities for students to explore issues, articulate concerns, formulate and revise problems — all necessary for good writing to emerge — and can lead to conversational patterns that socialize students into a mode of interaction that will limit rather than enhance their participation in intellectual work.[3] We would further suggest that streamlined conversational patterns (like the Initiation-Comment-Response pattern described by Mehan) are often reinforced by a set of deficit-oriented assumptions about the linguistic and cognitive abilities of remedial students, assumptions that are much in need of examination (Hull et al.; Rose, *Lives*).

We would pose instead a pedagogical model that places knowledge-making at its center. The conversational techniques attending such a model are not necessarily that demanding — Robert benefits from simple expressions of encouragement, focusing, and reflecting back — but the difference in assumptions is profound: that the real stuff of belonging to an academic community is dynamic involvement in generating and questioning knowledge, that students desperately need immersion and encouragement to involve themselves in such activity, and that underprepared students are capable — given the right conditions — of engaging in such activity. We would also underscore the fact that Robert's reading (a) does bring to light the problem with the Sears catalogue and (b) animates the landscape as his teacher's reading did not do. Finally, we would suggest that engaging in a kind of "social-textual" reading of Robert's reading moves us toward deeper under-standing of the social base of literary interpretation (cf. Salvatori, "Peda-gogy").

In calling for a richer, more transactive model of classroom dis-course, we want to acknowledge that such a model removes some of the control of teacher-centered instruction and can create moments of hesi-tance and uncertainty (as was the case with Rose through the first half of the transcript). But hesitancy and uncertainty — as we all know from our own intellectual struggles — are central to knowledge-making. Fur-thermore, we are not asking teachers to abandon structure, goals, and accountability. A good deal of engineering still goes on in the transactive classroom: the teacher focusing discussion, helping students better ar-ticulate their ideas, involving others, pointing out connections, keep-ing an eye on the clock. Even in conference, Rose's interaction with Robert is clearly goal-driven, thus Rose's reliance on focusing and re-flecting back. Rose operates with a conventional reading in mind and begins moving toward it in 5a — and does so out loud to reveal to Rob-ert the line of such reasoning. Robert's interpretation, though, will cause his teacher to modify his reading, and the teacher's presentation of his interpretation will help Robert acquire an additional approach to the poem. (In fact, the very tension between academic convention and stu-dent experience could then become the focus of discussion.) This, we think, is the way talk and thought should go when a student seems to falter, when readings seem a little off the mark.[4]

Notes

1. In stimulated recall, a student's writing is videotaped and, upon comple-tion, replayed to cue recall of mental processes occurring during compos-ing. For further discussion of the procedure and its advantages and limita-tions, see Rose, *Writer's Block*.

2. Frankly, we had trouble arriving at a way to designate the readings we're calling conventional and unconventional. And we're not satisfied yet. Cer-tain of Robert's responses seem to be influenced by class (e.g., his reaction to the wooden shacks and Sears), and we note that, but with reluctance. We don't want to imply that class is the primary determiner of Robert's read-ing (vs., say, socialization into an English department — which, we realize, would correlate with class). We also don't want to imply that middle-class readers would, by virtue of class, automatically see things in a certain way, would have no trouble understanding particular images and allusions. One of the people who read this paper for us, Dennis Lynch, suggested that we use Wayne Booth's notion of "intended audience" — that Robert is simply not a member of the audience for whom the poem was written, thus he offers a reading that differs from the reading we're calling conventional. The notion of intended audience makes sense here, and fits with our dis-cussion of socialization. Hongo, like most younger American poets, honed his craft in an English department and an MFA program, places where one's work is influenced by particular audiences — fellow poets, faculty, jour-nal editors, etc. But, finally, we decided not to use the notion of intended audience, for it carries with it a theoretical framework we're not sure does

Robert or Hongo full justice here. We use words like "conventional" and "middle-class," then, with reserve and invite our readers to help us think through this problem.

3. For two different but compatible perspectives on this claim see Shor; Tharp and Gallimore.

4. We would like to thank Linda Flower, Kay Fraser, Marisa Garrett, Jonathan Lovell, Dennis Lynch, Sandra Mano, Cheryl Pfoff, Mariolina Salvatori, Melanie Sperling, and Susan Thompson-Lowry for their comments on this paper. We benefited from a discussion at a meeting of the directors of the California Writing Project, and we would also like to acknowledge three anonymous *CCC* reviewers who gently guided us toward an understanding of the gaps and blunders in the essay. This work has been supported by grants from the McDonnell Foundation Program in Cognitive Studies for Educational Practice and the Research Foundation of the National Council of Teachers of English.

Works Cited

Bartholomae, David, and Anthony Petrosky, eds. *Facts, Counterfacts and Artifacts: Theory and Method for a Reading and Writing Course.* Upper Montclair: Boynton, 1986.

Hongo, Garrett Kaoru. "And Your Soul Shall Dance." *Yellow Light*. Middletown: Wesleyan UP, 1982. 69.

Hull, Glynda, and Mike Rose. "Rethinking Remediation: Toward a Social-Cognitive Understanding of Problematic Reading and Writing." *Written Communication* 6 (Apr. 1989): 139–154.

Hull, Glynda, Mike Rose, Kay Losey Fraser, and Marisa Garrett. "The Social Construction of Remediation." The Tenth Annual Ethnography in Education Forum. Univ. of Pennsylvania, Feb. 1989.

Mehan, Hugh. *Learning Lessons*. Cambridge: Harvard UP, 1979.

Rose, Mike. *Lives on the Boundary: The Struggles and Achievements of America's Underprepared*. New York: Free Press, 1989.

———. *Writer's Block: The Cognitive Dimension*. Carbondale: Southern Illinois UP, 1984.

Salvatori, Mariolina. "Pedagogy: From the Periphery to the Center." *Reclaiming Pedagogy: The Rhetoric of the Classroom*. Ed. Patricia Donahue and Ellen Quandahl. Carbondale: Southern Illinois UP, 1989. 17–34.

———. "Reading and Writing a Text: Correlations between Reading and Writing Patterns." *College English* 45 (Nov. 1983): 657–666.

Shor, Ira. *Empowering Education: Critical Teaching for Social Change*. Chicago: Chicago UP, 1992.

Tharp, Roland G., and Ronald Gallimore. Rousing Minds to Life. New York: Oxford UP, 1989.

Classroom Activities

Hull and Rose ask readers to think critically about the class and cultural backgrounds of their students. Extend this inquiry by asking students to think critically about the class and cultural backgrounds of their audience for a specific writing task. Focusing on the audience will help them answer such questions as the following: What does my audience already know about this topic? What is the attitude of my audience toward this topic? What background information do I need to supply to help the audience to understand my point of view? Such an activity can help students frame their purposes more concisely; it can also serve as a journal entry or prewriting exercise.

Thinking about Teaching

Hull and Rose discuss how their interpretation of Garrett Hongo's poem is influenced by what they call a "conventional middle-class reading." It might be interesting to spend some time discussing what constitutes a conventional middle-class reader or writer. Such an activity could lead to a better understanding of how class differences may play out in the classroom. Recall, for example, an assignment that you presented in class that elicited a very different response from what you had expected, with varied responses among the students themselves. Perhaps differences in social class conventions or expectations account for the variety of interpretations, as Hull and Rose maintain. Discussing such incidents with other teachers may help you draw connections between classroom experiences and real life and could provide insights into teaching the processes of critical thinking and writing.

9

Collaborative Learning

M any of us have attempted to use collaborative learning strategies in our classes and have been discouraged or dissatisfied with the results. In the revision stage of the writing process, for example, students often seem afraid to critique their peers and are not willing to trust other students to critique their writing, since they see this task as belonging strictly to the teacher. Group members may fall off task or have difficulty communicating with each other because of cultural or other differences. Yet many teachers continue to revise their strategies and expectations because they see the potential benefits: increased communication among students, better problem solving, and better critical thinking skills. The selections in this chapter highlight the use of teamwork as part of a comprehensive plan for the writing classroom and present two interesting experiments.

Peter Elbow provides step-by-step collaborative learning activities that may appeal to students who are not normally comfortable working in groups. His collage activity will be helpful to instructors interested in trying out new approaches to collaborative learning. Richard Raymond writes about a collaborative learning community he helped create with teachers of Speech Communications and Anthropology at the University of Arkansas–Little Rock. A class of entering first-year students took linked courses in these disciplines, as well as Raymond's course in composition. Raymond documents the collaboration that took place as teachers and students came together as a community of learners.

Using the Collage for Collaborative Writing

Peter Elbow

Peter Elbow, whose work on freewriting has heavily influenced today's process-oriented basic writing courses, presents in this article the metaphor of collage as a means for practicing a variety of collaborative writing activities. He begins by outlining the strengths and weaknesses of collaborative writing, and then presents the notion of collage as a way of building on the strengths of collaboration and addressing its weaknesses. In addition, Elbow suggests how collaborative writing can incorporate both individual and group work. The collage, as Elbow shows, helps students understand the benefits of collaborative work, while facilitating an opportunity for them to strengthen their individual writing. This article was originally published in Composition Studies *(formerly* Freshman English News) *in 1999.*

Plenty of people have celebrated collaborative writing (e.g., Ede and Lunsford; LeFevre), so I can invoke the medieval trope of *occupatio*: I will *not* give all the reasons why collaborative writing is a good thing; I will *not* talk about how frequently it occurs in the world and therefore how our students should learn to use it; nor about the collaborative dimension of writing we think of as private; nor about how collaborative writing helps students learn better because of all the pooling of information, ideas, and points of view; nor about the students who have hated writing because it makes them feel lonely and helpless but who come to *like* it when they write with others; nor will I cite the much-cited Harvard research showing how students who study together get better grades (Light).

But I will mention in passing one interesting benefit of collaborative writing that I've noticed but found undercelebrated. When people write alone, they make countless simple and complex writerly decisions *tacitly*, instinctively — without articulating the reasons for them (e.g., to start with this idea, or to move that point later in the paper, or to change a word or phrase to modify the voice or the relationship to the reader). And that's as it should be: tacit decisions are quicker and the writer is going by feel, by ear. As Polanyi reminds us, our tacit knowledge always outstrips our conscious and articulate knowledge. But the process of writing with someone else forces us to put many of these decisions into words. If I say to my partner, "Let's start with this point," I usually have to say why — especially if I am proposing a change. And if my partner disagrees with me, he or she will naturally give reasons for the resistance. In short, the process of collaborative writing forces students to become more conscious and articulate about rhetorical decision making.

But when I find underrepresented in our professional literature about collaborative writing are the *problems*. First, collaborative writing is difficult and often unpleasant. When I used to force students to write pieces in pairs of groups, at least half of them would say at the end that it was the worst experience of the semester. And when I gave them the choice, relatively few took it. Collaborative writing may be jolly and social, but it takes a long time and leads to disagreements. Is there anyone who has not vowed never again to engage in a piece of committee writing?

Second, the writing that results from collaboration is often pretty bad. It is likely to be bland because the parties have to agree and they can only agree on lowest-common-denominator thinking. And there is often a dead, "committee" voice — no energy or presence. The surest proof of the existence of God is the King James translation of the Bible: only divine intervention could have permitted a committee to produce such wonderful prose.

Third, the collaborative process often silences weaker, minority, or marginal voices. The assertive and entitled tend to carry the day. Whenever there is a need for consensus in group work, there is great danger of silencing weaker voices (see Clark and Ede; Trimbur).

In order to deal with this perplexity — that collaborative writing is at once so valuable, so important, and yet so problematic — I've come to use the collaborative collage. Where the solo collage can serve as a bridge to regular essays, the collaborative collage can serve as a bridge to full collaboration. But like the solo collage, the collaborative collage is valuable in its own right. It can be as nice to stand on the bridge as on the other shore. (Readers not familiar with written collages will probably get a pretty good picture from what follows. But for a full and direct description of written collages, see "Collage: Your Cheatin' Art" in this volume,* and also the first workshop in Elbow and Belanoff.)

The procedure for creating a collaborative collage is so easy and simple that it will make some people nervous. Let me lay out the directions I give to pairs or small groups working together.

- Individually, write as much as you can about the topic. Write your own thoughts. It's fine to use rough, exploratory writing. Try to exploit the insights, language, and energy that come from moving fast and getting caught up in your thinking and feeling.

- There is an alternative first step you can use if you prefer. Each person writes for ten or fifteen minutes — however he or she wants to start. Then people switch papers for the next piece of writing so that what is written is some kind of response to what the first person wrote. And so on. This method adds more of the quality of dialogue — thought answering thought. But by the same taken, it can reduce the amount of sheer diversity in the collage, because the writers are much in touch with each other. In

---

*Peter Elbow. *Everyone Can Write: Essays Toward a Hopeful Theory of Writing and Teaching Writing.* New York: Oxford UP, 2000. [Editor's note]

the first, nondialogical method, writers might well be in entirely different ball parks — which can be a genuine advantage.

- Individually, go back over what you yourself have written and choose the bits and sections you like most. Some might be a page or more, others very short. Choose at least twice as much material as you'll need for your contribution to the finished collage. Clean them up enough to share, but there's no need to spend too much time on the job.

- Together in your pair or group, read your individual pieces to each other. (Or share them through silent reading.)

- Together, agree on which pieces should be chosen for the collage. (Ground rule: no fair leaving anyone out — or letting anyone dominate the final version.)

- Together, give some feedback and suggestions in response to those pieces you have chosen. But there's no need for agreement in your responses. Just let everyone throw in their two cents. (You'll also have to agree on whether the final revising and polishing of bits should be done by the original authors or by means of trading pieces with each other.)

- Together, decide on a sequence for all the pieces you've chosen.

- Together, as part of this discussion about sequence, you may well decide you need some new pieces. Good new ideas might have come up in discussion; or you might realize that something important is missing.

- Individually, write any necessary new pieces; and revise and polish the chosen pieces.

- Together, look at what you have produced and decide whether to call if finished or to carry on with more work: for example, reordering of parts; revising of parts; writing new parts. This decision is collaborative, but further work can be individual.

Note that some of these tasks require agreement, but many do not. That is, there is genuine collaboration going on here — but only to a limited degree. This makes it much easier on participants than full collaboration and gives them a good bridge from individual work to group work. That is, participants *don't* have to agree on their ideas, thinking, conclusion, or thesis. They *don't* have to agree on language, wording, or phrasing. There are none of those awful tippy-toe discussions or time wasting arguments about how to phrase something. Nor about the voice or tone. At every moment, individuals are entirely in charge of every piece of writing with respect to thinking, wording, and voice — though of course these decisions are often influenced by comments and feedback from others.

Yet genuine collaboration is also going on — in fact two levels of collaboration:

- *Weak collaboration:* members read their writing to each other and give and receive individual responses from each other, and thereby *influence* each others' thinking and writing; this collaboration has a substantive effect on the final outcome. Yet this degree of collaboration is easy and nonstressful because participants don't have to agree.

- *Strong collaboration:* participants have to agree on which blips to use; they have to agree on what order to put them in; they have to agree on who does the revising; they have to agree on whether more revising is needed or whether to call it finished. Strong collaboration is harder because it requires agreement or consensus. But the scope of what people have to agree on is pretty limited.

Thus the collaborative collage speaks to the first problem of collaboration: difficulty or unpleasantness. But can it deal with the other two problems — weak or bland writing and the stifling of minority ideas and voices? Obviously, it can.

The collaborative collage invites all participants to stay entirely in charge of their own writing, and as a result, the final product is richer and more complex than most collaborative writing. (Even if members decide to revise each others' pieces, single individuals are in charge of thinking and language at any given moment.) The final product contains multiple points of view, multiple voices, multiple styles — and as a result, more tension and energy. Minority ideas and thinking have not been left out. In a collage, contrasts are a benefit, a source of energy that stimulates thinking in readers. The collaborative collage is a gathering of pieces each written from an "I" point of view — for the sake of a "we" enterprise.

The process I've described so far usually results in an *open* collage — a collage with multiple and conflicting points of view. If the students need to produce a *focused* collage, they must carry their partial collaboration a few steps further. They needn't leave out any of the conflicting material, but they need to spend additional time discussing the thinking in their open collage and find a way to agree on a conclusion or at least a common point of view. And then they need to write, add, arrange, or revise bits — again not taking away any of the contradictory material — in order to make the whole collage end up saying or implying their collaborative conclusion or point of view. They can even stop short of full agreement if they can agree on where they disagree and articulate that meta-agreement — further spelling out the implications of the various views and explaining what would need to be decided in order to settle their disagreement. But it's important for students to realize that even though they reach ultimate agreement on a conclusion or point of view, the focused collage still can and really ought to contain wildly divergent and contradictory pieces.

Learning to Make Space for Other Voices

Let me briefly suggest three additional methods for helping solo writers begin to get comfortable collaborating with other writers. These activities can serve as a bridge or introduction even to the mild collaboration I've already described.

1. The student writes a draft alone, but then shares that draft with one or more others and invites them to write out some of their own thoughts in response: new thoughts on the topic itself or thoughts about what the writer has said — perhaps even how it was said. These responses go to the original writer who then gets to incorporate some passages from them into his or her piece. The writer can put these passages in quotation marks, or in a different typeface, or even in a separate column running alongside the writer's own text. Thus the single writer stays in complete charge of his or her text — but incorporates the voices of others.

2. The student is writing about a topic while also doing lots of reading or interviewing about it. The student is asked to produce not a conventional, connected research or documented essay, but a collage that contains extensive and extended quotations from the reading or interviews. Again, the interjected material might be in long block quotations, in separate typefaces, or in a parallel column or two. The goal here is to help students "place" their own thoughts and voices in authoritative dialogue with the voices of others, especially of published writers. That is, this procedure can help prevent two common problems in research or documented essays by students: (a) essays where the writer says almost nothing and merely wholesales the ideas and voices of others; (b) essays where the writer brings in nothing but perfunctory "quotes" to back up what is essentially his or her own monologue.

3. Students work in pairs (or trios) and start by writing a "real time" dialogue: they simply pass a sheet of paper back and forth to each other so each can write a response to the previous turn. (The process is even easier in an online classroom.) If they want to avoid one writer having to wait while the other one is writing, they can get two dialogues going on two different topics. This procedure can seem odd and artificial at first, but students get comfortable pretty quickly if we help them see that they are simply putting on paper what they do naturally and comfortably in spoken conversation. They usually benefit from being encouraged to let the dialogue go where it wants to go, even if it wanders. It's a voyage of thinking and discovery. Then the students read over what they have created, and they collaborate on revising it

into a satisfying and coherent dialogue. This doesn't mean the organization or sequence of ideas has to be neat and tidy. Think about Plato! Thus the students have to agree about what the main line or direction should be, which parts to keep and discard, and how to arrange or rearrange. But they each get to revise their own contributions.

These three processes help students get used to making good texts out of multiple thoughts and voices.

Using the Collaborative Collage as a Bridge Back to Better Solo Writing

The collaborative collage can guide students not only toward better full collaboration, but also toward better solo writing. That is, the experience of writing and sharing collaborative collages — and seeing the unexpected virtues of them — can help students learn to get into their solo pieces some qualities that are rare and precious in writing: conflicting ideas, multiple points of view, perplexity, tension, and complexity of structure. The larger principle of learning that operates here (as articulated by Vygotsky and Mead) is that we eventually learn to do by ourselves what we first learned to do socially in interaction with others. We internalize the social process.

That is, much *solo* writing suffers from the same weakness that is found in much collaborative writing. Many student writers, feeling a pressure always to have a clear "thesis," end up settling for the lowest-common-denominator point that the various parts of the self can agree on. They are tempted to stop writing when they feel perplexed or come across conflicting feelings and ideas — nervously sweeping complications under the rug. Students have somehow been led to think that writing should always "flow" — a favorite word of praise — and thus that the texture should be seamless. They don't realize the pleasure and energy that comes from *bumps*. In truth, most good solo writing represents a single writer having some internal dialogue with herself — having more than one point of view and using more than one voice. Writing needs the drama of thinking and the performance of voices.

All these virtues can be summed up in the catchword that we've taken from Bakhtin's mouth: "dialogic." Fair enough. But it's fruitful to encourage some notes of overt *dialogue* into solo writing: passages where the writer actually breaks out into a different voice and point of view. It's not hard to create such passages by using launching pads like these: "Notice the complications we must consider, however, when we listen to the thoughts of someone who disagrees: '. . .'" or, "There are some serious objections, however, to what I have just been saying: '. . .'" Or, "But wait a minute. Let's look at this issue from a contrasting point of view: '. . .'" In each case, the writer can carry on for a paragraph or longer speaking in a different voice from a different point of view. Of course it's hard to get full rhetorical control over multiple voices and points of view, but even when students don't handle the richness and complexity so well, they almost always gain powerful benefits to their thinking. (Teachers have often found ways to give better grades to papers that fall down — when their downfall stems from the attempt to deal with complex thinking — than to seamless papers that settle for simple, obvious thinking.)

I'm fascinated by the literal ability to talk to oneself — to give voice to the multiple views and consciousnesses that inhabit us. The ability to have thoughtful dialogues with oneself may be one of the most important goals of schooling. It is surely the mark of educated or developed persons to be able to engage in thinking and dialogue when there are no others around who are interested in their topic or interested in talking to them. One of the biggest difficulties for adolescents, in particular, is that they feel so vulnerable to their peers and therefore find it hard to delve very far into issues or feelings or points of view that their peers ignore or scorn as weird. One of the main things I want to teach my students is that they can pursue their ideas, even when they feel alone and can't get others to listen.

To sum up. My goal in this teaching activity is to make collaborative writing not only easier and more inviting, but also more complex and conflicted. And in the end, the most lasting goal may be to get richer thinking and more voices into solo writing as well.

Works Cited

Clark, Suzanne, and Lisa Ede. "Collaboration, Resistance, and the Teaching of Writing." *The Right to Literacy.* Ed. Andrea Lunsford, Helene Moglen, and James Slevin. NY: Modern Language Association, 1990. 276–87.

Ede, Lisa, and Andrea Lunsford. *Singular Texts/Plural Authors: Perspectives on Collaborative Writing.* Carbondale IL: Southern Illinois UP, 1990.

Elbow, Peter, and Pat Belanoff. *A Community of Writers: A Workshop Course in Writing.* 3rd ed. NY: McGraw-Hill, 1999.

LeFevre, Karen Burke. *Invention as a Social Act.* Carbondale IL: Southern Illinois UP, 1987.

Light, Richard J. *Harvard Assessment Seminar: Explorations with Students and Faculty about Teaching and Learning and Student Life.* Cambridge: Harvard Graduate School of Education, 1990.

Mead, George H. *Mind, Self, and Society.* Chicago: U of Chicago P, 1934.

Polanyi, Michael. *Personal Knowledge: Toward a Post-Critical Philosophy.* New York: Harper and Row, 1958.

Trimbur, John. "Consensus and Difference in Collaborative Learning." *College English* 51 (Oct 1989): 602–16.

Vygotsky, Lev. *Mind in Society: The Development of Higher Psychological Processes.* Ed. M. Cole, V. John-Steiner, S. Scribner, and E. Souberman. Cambridge: Harvard UP, 1978.

Classroom Activities

Elbow provides a variety of activities for teaching collage and for facilitating collaborative learning among students. Consider choosing one or more of these activities based on student need and level of development in the writing process. As Elbow suggests, one of the most important benefits of collaborative writing may be "better solo writing. That is, the experience of writing and sharing collaborative collages — and seeing the unexpected virtues of them — can help students learn to get into their solo pieces some qualities that are rare and precious in writing: conflicting ideas, multiple points of view, perplexity, tension, and complexity of structure."

In particular, Elbow focuses on the need for multiple points of view in solo writing, a strategy that may be especially tricky for developing writers to negotiate. Building on the benefits of the collage activities, Elbow lists several "launching pad" sentence openers that students can employ to acknowledge multiple voices, including: "Notice the complications we must consider, however, when we listen to the thoughts of someone who disagrees: '. . .'" You may want to create and distribute a handout of such openers and invite students to use them in their writing. After students have worked on collaborative learning activities with peers and are experimenting with this method of engaging multiple voices in their solo writing, remind them of the connections between the conversations of collaborative learning and the dialogue that the individual writer conducts with his or her own thoughts.

Thinking about Teaching

To illustrate the problems of collaborative writing, Peter Elbow asks the rhetorical question: "Is there anyone who has not vowed never again to engage in a piece of committee writing?" Although Elbow presents collage exercises as a way of mitigating collaborative writing problems for students, clearly these activities have applications for instructors as well. Elbow provides ten bullet-point steps for creating a collaborative collage that he believes are "so easy and simple that it will make some people nervous." With a colleague or other writing partner, follow the ten steps that Elbow suggests. To reflect further on this activity, write in your teaching journal about your own process of completing the steps, and decide whether Elbow's activity would be worth using at a committee meeting to stimulate the group's thinking.

Building Learning Communities on Nonresidential Campuses

Richard Raymond

In the following article, which won TETYC's nineteenth annual best article award for 1999, readers will find a clearly written narrative of how three teachers at Richard Raymond's institution created a successful learning community at a primarily nonresidential campus. In addition, Raymond offers pragmatic suggestions and assignments for fostering collaborative learning and critical thinking in the writing classroom — and for drawing connections among a linked, interdisciplinary series of three courses that his entering first-year students were required to take. With help from a university grant and support from the administration and from teachers of composition, speech communication, and anthropology, they all worked together inside and outside of the classroom to create an innovative collaborative learning environment for students. Raymond also includes entries from his teaching journal, comments from a student assessment of the program conducted outside the classroom, and an excerpt from a student paper in order to document the progress that students made throughout the semester.

Introduction

Over the last three decades, I have taught in a rural two-year college and in two urban universities; all three schools have been dormless or nearly so. In each of these institutions, I have worked with writing teachers who shared my dismay when we learned of a first- or second-year student transferring elsewhere, having found no community, no place to live and learn, no core as she accumulated credits in the "core." We grieved, too, over students lost not to other schools but to learning. Sometimes, these students dropped out; others stayed, writing just well enough to pass the state Regents' essay, but not well enough to connect ideas in and among other disciplines.

Over these same years, "learning communities" have emerged, with program designers and administrators hoping that clustered classes would shore up enrollment, the first concern described above. But they have claimed a more high-minded motive as well: to help students form a site where — through writing — they feel connected even as they connect what they learn. According to recent comprehensive studies of learning communities, promises of enduring friendships and enriched learning have been kept (Matthews et al.; Tinto, Goodsell-Love, and Russo). Major universities — including BYU, Wisconsin, Washington, UC Berkeley, and SUNY — have kept these promises with interdisciplinary explorations of a common theme such as "World Hunger." Four-year and two-year colleges, notably Evergreen State in Washington and La Guardia Community College in New York, have done likewise, "clustering" courses in composition, social science, and humanities around topics like "Work, Labor, and Business in American Life" (Matthews et al. 460). Assessment of these programs consistently confirms that students have found not only a place to stay but also a way to learn, constructing knowledge through reading and writing, listening and speaking (Matthews et al. 469).

In fall semester 1997, encouraged by this history of success, I joined two colleagues in starting a learning community at the University of Arkansas at Little Rock (UALR). Our community linked my section of Comp I with Carol Thompson's section of speech communication and Julie Flinn's section of cultural anthropology. Naturally, we hoped to help solve the retention problem at UALR, where 59 percent of the first-year students never see a second year, having dropped out or having transferred to the cheaper Pulaski Technical College, to the residential, less urban University of Central Arkansas thirty miles away, or to the more fashionable University of Arkansas at Fayettville, the state system's flagship institution. We also wanted to help twenty-five students to connect these core courses by exploring themes of acculturation, the role of language in finding one's place.

In addition to the studies mentioned above, we found decades of literature on structuring learning communities to help us set up the thematically linked courses. However, we quickly saw an obstacle faced only by the nonresidential schools mentioned in the literature: lack of student residents. UALR, an urban university of some eleven thousand students, has just one five-story dormitory; most of the nonresident students, averaging twenty-seven years of age, work part- or full-time off campus. Such students — even the traditional eighteen-year-olds — come to campus for back-to-back classes and then leave for work. With this student profile, we could not promise the bonding that would come with living as a community in a dorm, nor could we promise regular student-faculty meals, a selling point in some programs.

Below I describe a solution to this problem, one that roots in demographics but that finds solutions in expressivist, cognitive, and social constructionist pedagogies (White 59). The narrative, I hope, will honestly expose the errors — strategic and pedagogical — as well as ground our feelings of success. I hope, too, that this story will encourage the many four- and two-year colleges whose non-residential campuses make learning communities seem improbable consider developing them.

This story begins with crucial preliminaries: letter-writing, securing the help of administrators and registrars, coordinating schedules, and linking syllabi thematically. Moving then to the teaching of the community, the narrative relates first-day activities, the linking of assignments and communal learning, then discusses assessment.

Preliminaries

Julie, Carol, and I wanted to see if a learning community could help average students connect core curriculum courses and, in so doing, help them find their place as learners. Therefore, in collaboration with the dean, we decided to aim the promotional letter at *all* entering first-year students eligible for Composition 1, that is, those who had scored a quite modest 19 or higher on the ACT, a pool of some seven hundred students. The letter stressed communal learning, even though we had no dormitory and regular meals to offer (see Appendix A).

Stressing connected, communal learning, the letter apparently addressed a need that both students and parents recognized. Within five working days, we had accepted thirty students, begun a waiting list, and mailed a follow-up letter inviting the students to one of the advising and registration sessions.

Prior to mailing the letters, we three teachers met twice with Dr. Thea Hoeft, Director of Undergraduate Advisement, deans, the head registrar, and the vice-chancellor for student activities, all of whom we needed to make the community happen:

- The vice-chancellor, head of UALR's First-Year Experience program, promoted the learning community in his oral and written recruiting efforts.

- The registrar approved listing the three courses as "restricted" to ensure that we would have only volunteers in the community. He also approved cross-listings in the university course schedule, including a "comment line" instructing the students to call any of the three instructors for further information.

- The dean of the College of Arts, Humanities, and Social Sciences, Deborah Baldwin, agreed to pay for mailing the letters and to receive all the response cards. She also has taken every opportunity to promote this and subsequent learning communities before the college faculty.

- Thea Hoeft gave up five hours of her time to conduct the two advisement sessions.

Such collaboration between faculty and administrators builds a professional community that doesn't exist on every campus; more to the point here, this teamwork proved critical to starting and sustaining the learning community.

We also received help from the associate vice-chancellor, whose committee on curriculum development grants approved our proposal for financial support. The grant provided each teacher $1,950 as compensation for developing the courses over the summer. We also happily accepted an additional $400 to pay for assessment materials and for food we would share with the students on the first day and during assessment sessions (see discussion below).

As each teacher developed a syllabus over the summer, we met three times — twice over coffee, once over lunch — to find and synchronize the thematic links, a process made possible by reading each other's texts. Eventually, we settled on the following interrelated anthropological themes, each taken up at approximately the same time in each class:

- Coming into a Culture,
- Making Words and Making a Living,
- Gender and Marriage,
- Social Ranking and Stratification, and
- Government, Religion, and Justice.

Using Jack Selzer's thematic reader *Conversations* in a Comp I class, I easily found selections that would help the students explore the concepts they were learning in anthropology.[1] While they learned about ethnocentrism in anthropology, for example, the students read Alice Walker's "Everyday Use" in Comp I to find distinctions between ethnocentrism and legitimate racial pride. Similarly, the students read and discussed Sizer's "Horace's Compromise" to understand the difference between teaching that produces conformists and teaching that acculturates thinkers. They explored Rodriguez's "Aria" and Darrow's "Address to the Prisoners" to contemplate the causes of exclusion from cultures, Glaspell's "Trifles" to learn what happens when marriage stifles individualism, Orwell's "A Hanging" and Koch's "Death and Justice" to understand the causes and effects of capital punishment, and King's "Birmingham Jail" to see the roles of government and churches in making justice a dream deferred.

Speaking, Reading, and Writing in the Learning Community

With the syllabi thematically linked, we teachers met one more time to plan strategy for the first day of class. Wanting to assess the learning that occurred in the community, we thought of devoting the first session to an in-class essay on a "Doonesbury" cartoon depicting a jaded lecturer and his mindless students (Selzer 95). We would then ask for another essay on this same cartoon on the last day, hoping to see not only better writing but also better understanding of the traditional classroom as a potentially destructive site of acculturation.

The need for assessment data notwithstanding, we quickly realized the deadening effect of such an opener, one that would intimidate most students and do nothing to establish community. We therefore moved the "Doonesbury" essay to a first homework assignment (see discussion of assessment below), focusing instead on community-building activities. First, we decided that all three teachers as well as the assessment expert, Dr. Kathy Franklin, should attend my 8:00 A.M. composition class, where we would reintroduce ourselves as their learning community teachers — we had already met at the advisement sessions mentioned above — and invite the students to enjoy the donuts and coffee provided by the grant budget.

Wanting learning as well as pastries to characterize the first day, we also borrowed a "birth order" workshop from the National Writing Project to stimulate thought on the influence of early discourse communities in shaping the ways we learn and interact. Appendix B displays the guidelines we distributed to move from pleasantries to active learning for all the Older Children, Middle Kids, Babies, and Onlies in the class.

As each student stood by his or her birth order poster and reported the group's findings, predictably celebrating the group's virtues — leadership, flexibility, patience — while playfully demonizing the Other, the Bossy Big Sisters, the Spoiled Little Brothers, we quickly saw the value of this one-hour workshop.

- First, we had broken the ice, with instructors participating in the appropriate birth order group, underscoring implicitly the idea of students and teachers as peers in learning.

- We also moved from conversation to writing (posters), then to public speaking and listening, modeling thereby the interconnectedness of speech and composition.

- We introduced the role of family in acculturating students, a central theme in the anthropology class.

- We bonded with laughter, a far stronger glue than donuts when it comes to holding communities together.

Having bonded on day one, we devoted the next two weeks to readings and writings on families and education to explore further the anthropological theme of "coming into a culture" (header in Comp I syllabus, weekly schedule). To help the students read anthropologically, I first assigned Alice Walker's story "Everyday Use" and asked them to answer the questions in Figure 1 in their journal.

Questions one through six introduced the students to close reading and helped them understand the term "ethnocentrism," the first word they would learn in anthropology; question seven helped them to understand journaling as a reflective process, a way of moving from "what happened?" to "what does the text mean?" At the same time, answering these questions prepared the students for class discussion and for writing their first papers on one of the ethnocentrism topics in Appendix C.

While the essay assignment does restrict students to the "conversation" started by Walker — thereby fostering responsible reading — it also encourages the students to find their own topics (Murray; Graves). In addition, the assignment allows students to interpret Walker's text in anthropological terms or to respond to her story with an anthropological story of their own.

Figure 1. Questions on Walker's "Everyday Use"

Walker, "Everyday Use," pp. 74–82

1. In paragraphs 1–6, what actions and details reveal the narrator's (mother's) view of Dee?

2. How has the fire (2, 10) affected Maggie's personality?

3. How does Dee's education affect her view and her treatment of her mother and her sister Maggie (11, 22, 25–27, 36)? What is the nature of her **ethnocentrism?**

4. Why does Dee want the churn top and the quilts (53, 66)?

5. Why does the mother return the quilts to Maggie?

6. Find five similes (or metaphors) in the narrative and explain what each comparison reveals about the character described.

7. What inference can you draw from this narrative that will answer the question at the top of p. 74, "What's college for?"

Reinforcing the concept of community, I scheduled a writing group day, when each student shared her first draft with two peers, who then responded orally and in writing, using guidelines I provided. After this community-building experience, the students conferred individually with me, then revised their papers and submitted the draft and the revision. Having received my written responses to the second draft, the students revised a second time, then submitted the piece again for further comment and a grade (see discussion below on further revision in portfolio assignment). Then to underscore the *ongoing* nature of dialogue in any learning community, I scheduled a reading day, when four volunteers read their papers to the whole class and invited responses.

During the two-and-a-half-week period devoted to the writing of this paper in response to Walker, the students continued their reading and journaling on the anthropological theme of "coming into a culture." Focusing now on nonfiction pieces — Gardner's "A Nation at Risk," Rich's "Claiming an Education," and others — students examined the roles of schools and teachers in effecting — or stifling — healthy acculturation.

Moving next to a related theme concurrently studied in the anthropology class, "making words and making a living," the students continued these same rhythms of study — reading, journaling, discussing — exploring such pieces as Smitherman's "White English in Blackface, or Who Do I Be?" and Rodriguez's "Aria: a Memoir of a Bilingual Childhood." Such work led to a second essay (Appendix D), one asking students to narrate their experiences being brought into their cultures by teachers.

Having moved through the drafting-responding-revising process on this assignment, I held a second communal reading day, then broke new anthropological ground with the themes "gender and marriage" and "social ranking and stratification," featuring not only Glaspell's "Trifles," as mentioned above, but also Steele's "A Negative Vote on Affirmative Action" and Wilkins's "Racism Has Its Privileges."

To help students probe more deeply into the connection between these readings and the textbook material in anthropology, all three teachers periodically asked students to write in class in their reflective journals (a journal separate from the one they kept for Comp I), noting points of anger, confusion, or enthusiasm as they learned of placement and displacement in cultures, both American and Other. Also, Kathy Franklin, the assessment expert, began meeting with a student focus group. Having lured volunteers with pizza (paid for by the grant) to meet with her outside of class, Kathy asked them to practice the collaborative techniques they learned in speech to examine their experiences — negative as well as positive — learning in a community. They spoke of teachers allowing too little time for journaling, of students having no time to meet as study groups outside of class, of peers who seem unprepared for response sessions, of students and teachers who talk too much; they also admitted — now — to seeing their peers as friends, their teachers as fellow learners, and the classroom far less stratified than those they had experienced in high school or in college.

Having received this midterm assessment from Dr. Franklin, we resolved to allow more writing/reflecting time in class and to draw out the less talkative students by inviting them to read from their journals. We also resolved to bite our lips more often, sharing our views as community members but not dominating any conversation. Though duly chastened by the students' negative remarks, we teachers enjoyed hearing that the students shared our perception of a growing community that had learned how to learn.

Buoyed by a shared sense of community, we continued reading, talking, and writing, focusing now on the themes that would round out the students' course in cultural anthropology: "Government, Religion, and Justice." In addition to the pieces by Orwell, Koch, and Dr. King noted above, we read Weisberg's "This Is Your Death." The students journaled as always to monitor their responses to these controversial texts; in so doing, they also prepared for class, where I asked them to mediate arguments on crime and punishment, on order and justice. These discussions, usually quite lively, generated healthy peer exchanges over drafts and mainly successful essays.

In helping the students find their topics, I did not require them to confront an adversary, to strike the militant Aristotelian stance of one who seeks to vanquish a foe rather than to build community (Lamb). Instead, I asked them to enter an ongoing conversation, using the text — whether the fictional text of Glaspell, the nonfiction texts of Steele, Koch, or King, or the "text" of the learning community — to present readings designed to keep readers talking, encouraging healthy dissensus as well as mediated consensus (Bruffee; Trimbur).

As the end of the semester approached, I wanted to give the students a chance to position themselves as individuals within the community. To facilitate this finding of place, I asked each student to focus on a text(s) and a conversation she or he had found most compelling. Appendix E shows this invitation to critical analysis.

The first topic invited students to respond to an ethnographic text read in anthropology, either the exotic story of Eskimo life recorded in *Never in Anger* or the story of RVing in America, *Over the Next Hill*. The second topic encouraged students to return to a conversation in Comp I, choosing a text worthy of response and of rhetorical analysis; the third offered the same encouragement but took students beyond the texts we had read in the community. Whatever the student's choice, each wrote on the nature of living in communities and the challenge of doing so as an individual, as one voice responding to many voices.

Assessing the Nonresidential Learning Community

Naturally, we will need to accumulate years of data to show conclusively that the learning communities have performed as well as their predecessors on other campuses in achieving the two objectives: to retain students and to improve learning. However, we have been encouraged by the early results, as generated by the following instruments of assessment (Franklin):

- Pretest: The "Doonesbury" essay, given as the first night's homework, showed some understanding of learning theory and the potentially stupefying effect of lecturing. However, nearly all the essays lacked development, offering little or no textual support for the inferences drawn. I returned the papers, with comments but no grade, and asked the students to file them in their journals. They did so and promptly forgot the exercise.

- Posttest: We asked the students to write about the same cartoon again, this time as a final exam, counting ten percent of the grade in Comp I. Many complained loudly, a reaction I anticipated, given their weariness by the end of the semester. Their objections notwithstanding, I stuck with the requirement, not wanting to sabotage the assessment plan. In addition, I saw the analysis of the cartoon as a way to see what they had learned about its imbedded anthropological themes. Of course, in assessing the results, we factored in their low motivation on the pretest (no grade) and the high motivation on the posttest (grade). Nevertheless, we were pleased by the papers: they showed more sophisticated understanding of the cartoon as an example of misacculturation; also, unlike the pretests, all but two of the essays showed facility in using examples to support generalizations.

- Attitude Survey: This lengthy questionnaire, prepared by Dr. Franklin, provided qualitative data suggesting that students generally endorse the idea of learning communities. However, they more frequently praised the linked courses for increasing their number of friends rather than for helping them learn anthropology, failing to see the connection between the "fun, comfortable environment" of the community and the depth and range of their learning. Predictably, too, some said that "learning community" means "more work, less credit."

- Focus Group: This group of eight students echoed the voices in the survey, praising the "comfort," the new friendships, wishing for more time to meet outside of class, objecting to having to do "more work" than other first-year students do in unlinked classes. As mentioned above, they also complained of too little time for journal writing in class and of too much teacher talk. Having purged these complaints, they recognized, too, the connectedness of writing and speaking as ways to learn anthropology; consequently, they hoped to take more linked courses at higher levels in and beyond the core curriculum.

- Portfolio: The students' sense of "belonging" to the learning community — and the learning generated, at least in part, by that sense of connectedness — were born out in most of the portfolios. Determining forty percent of the course grade in Comp I, the portfolio included a piece from Comp I, from speech (an outline or text of a speech), and from cultural anthropology; it also included an artifact symbolizing their work in the learning community (or their life in the family), their reflective journal (not graded, just required), and the metacognitive cover essay.

- Grades on the Portfolio: Seven of the students earned an *A* on the portfolio, twelve a *B*, three a *C*, one a *D*. No one received an *F*. These high grades resulted primarily from cover essays that showed the metacognitive ability to analyze the strengths and weaknesses of a piece of writing and to place each piece in a larger picture of struggle and growth.

- Faculty Reflective Journals: All three faculty kept a reflective journal, as did the students. For both students and teachers, the reflective journal provided a place to complain without fear of penalty of too little time, of annoying or uncooperative peers, of having to meet unrealistic expectations. More important, this journal also invited a healthy looking back, attempting to see where and how learning happened or collapsed.

To provide admittedly selective evidence of these claims of partial success, I share some remarks from my reflective journal, then move to a sample of student writing strong enough — particularly in contrast to writing in recent unlinked writing classes — to motivate me to try the learning community again.

Reflective Journal Entries

September 18

Before class begins each day, the students grow ever more rowdy. I complimented them today for their noise: they seem comfortable with one another, joking as well as talking — quite a contrast to the beginning of the semester.

September 25

Class got off to a rocky start today; sleepy faces, no show of interest. But Heather Rainey read from her thoughtful journal; her remarks challenging Darrow's view of the causes of crime led to some rich discussion, some honest talk about access to the American Dream.

December 9

Just finished reading the portfolios. I'm pleased. After all their stewing about artifacts, they came through with photos of family members, pictures of the tools of our community, ritual necklaces made in anthropology. My favorite portfolio is that of Sarah Martin. Using her photographic skills, she composed a 9"x12" portrait of the ethnographies, The Easy Access Handbook, a CD, and owl candles — all really quite striking. Sarah's cover piece offers sophisticated reflection on her growth as writer and learner. While Sarah's cover piece may be the best, it is not atypical. As far as I'm concerned, these portfolios tell us what we need to know to assess the educational value of learning communities. The case of Zhang Bing-wen confirms this view. In the beginning, Zhang, as Asian student, begged to drop the LC. He just knew he would fail anthropology and lose "face" at school and at home. His older sister phoned me to beg for his release. Instead of granting their request, I urged Zhang to give us three teachers a chance; I also referred him to Carol and Julie, invoking our "talk first" policy. It worked. He stayed, earned a *B* on the first anthro test. With his head no longer bowed in silence, he went on to become one of the most talkative students in the class. He earned a *B* in Comp and *B*s in the other courses as well. In short, he learned and we retained him!

Excerpt from Student Writing

This excerpt comes from a student who early in the course confessed her American ethnocentrism. In this passage, written near the end of the semester, she expresses tolerance, even appreciation, for the Other, suggesting that she has achieved an objective of the community: to value difference:

From a Comp I essay on the anthropological ethnography, *Never In Anger*: [The Utku Eskimos] show a great amount of affection to a child before he or she acquires *ihmuma*, reason. . . . *Ihuma* is developing

when a child begins to respond to the social world, to recognize people
. . . to understand and talk . . . to participate in useful social games . . .
used to tease the child into doing what is right. In America, we have do's
and don'ts for our children, but the Utku just wait for the child to
conform. One example occurs when Saarak had to quit nursing from her
mother because a new baby was born. Saarak screamed and slapped at
her mother and sister, but Saarak's mother only said, "Don't hurt her"
. . . Many Americans believe the best way to get a child to conform to
society is by using strict discipline. The Utku culture has showed,
however, that a child without discipline can decide his or her own
progress without spoiling society.

— Heather Rainey,
"The Utka Acculturation"

Impressions

While we lack sufficient data to make any conclusive claims about the
value of learning communities on a primarily nonresidential campus, I
can describe two strong impressions shared by me and my two colleagues, as well as by Dr. Franklin, the assessment chief.

- Having spent hours together in designing and teaching the
  linked courses, we teachers have transformed ourselves from
  professional acquaintances to professional friends. Clearly, we
  should expect our students to experience the hollowness of the
  curricular core if we work in isolation from our colleagues across
  campus. A fragmented faculty will almost certainly teach a
  fragmented curriculum.

- Most first-year students can write and think metacognitively in
  thematically linked courses.

Two-thirds of the students shared these impressions, valuing their
deeper capacities for independent thought as well as their new friends.
The following comment from a student's reflective journal speaks for
many in the group:

The connections of these courses taught me not only the use of the
skills, but also how to use those skills to connect smaller things in my
life to form a larger picture, a broader spectrum, of what the world
actually looks like. . . . [The teachers have] taught me to take off my
ethnocentric lenses and to look at the world in a new light.

Such sentiments bode well for using learning communities not only to
facilitate this connected learning but also to retain students. Though
five withdrew before the semester began, the result of conflicts with
work or family responsibilities, only one student dropped the learning
community after it had formed. Typically, core composition classes lose
at least five students over the course of the semester.

Teaching in this learning community has also convinced me that we can overcome the inherent obstacles to linked courses on nonresidential campuses. True, we have far less time to meet, eat, and talk outside of class, compared to that time available on residential campuses. But we knit the students together by relying on social constructionist theory in all three classes, using small group work to interpret texts and to respond to writers, collaborating in the making of community knowledge. We also encouraged the students to develop and heed individual voices in the community. We did so by using the reader-response journal as a cognitive prewriting activity; by encouraging expressivist writing — freewrites, narratives — and by holding reading days that celebrate individual voices.

Last fall I taught a Comp I linked to courses in ethics and in personal awareness — the newest learning community. This spring, my colleagues offered communities linking Comp II with ethics and religious world views, Comp I with earth science, and Comp II with Civilization II. As other ideas for linkages percolate across campus, we have begun to see the campus's single dorm as the reason why we must build learning communities, not as the reason why we can't.

Appendix A

Invitation Letter

Dear _____:

Congratulations on your admission to UALR! We're looking forward to your studying here with us. We're also eager to help you make those choices that will shape your life — socially, academically, and professionally — during and after your years at UALR.

With this letter, we invite you to make that first choice: to consider enrolling in our **Learning Community,** a new program for eligible first-year students. And you're eligible!

Here's how the Learning Community works: You will enroll in a "block" of **three core courses: Rhetoric 1311.19, Composition I,** 8:00–9:15, Tuesday and Thursday; **Speech Communication 1300.17,** 9:25–10:40, Tuesday and Thursday; **Cultural Anthropology 2316.02,** 10:50–12:05, Tuesday and Thursday.

Consider the advantages of enrolling in this block of back-to-back courses:

- Preferred Scheduling: You'll be first to register. Also you'll have Tuesday and Thursday afternoons free for study, for part-time work on or off campus, or for other courses.

- Study Groups: You'll be part of a Community of Learners studying and working together in all three courses. Such support from trusted peers will help you do well in these three courses and foster habits of collaborative learning that will carry you far in your academic and professional lives. And study partners often become good friends!

- Making Connections: You will reinforce your learning by connecting each class to the other two. For example, some of your compositions and speeches will ask you to respond to readings from cultural anthropology. In turn, your anthropology class will give you further practice in writing and speaking as means of learning the material.

Please let us know if you're interested in joining our Learning Community by returning the enclosed card. We will select twenty-five students, filling the slots as we receive the cards, so please don't delay!

After we have chosen our Community members, we will invite you to campus to get acquainted and to complete your academic advisement for fall semester. We look forward to hearing from you!

Dr. Juliana Flinn, Professor of Anthropology
Dr. Carol Thompson, Associate Professor of Speech
Dr. Rich Raymond, Professor of Rhetoric and Writing

Appendix B

Collaborative Learning Task: Birth Order

Directions:

1. Pull your chairs together with others of your birth order group.

2. Appoint a person to read through the task before you go any further.

3. Agree on another person to record the views expressed by the group and the decisions the group makes collectively.

4. Choose a person to speak for the group.

5. Read and discuss the following questions:

   a. How did your position in the family affect your behavior in the family?

   b. How might that family history affect your behavior in a group within the learning community?

6. Review the recorder's notes to see that they accurately express the views of the group. List your findings on the poster paper provided; tape your paper to the wall.

Source: Pat Fox and the Coastal Georgia Writing Project; the Little Rock Writing Project.

Appendix C

Essay Assignment on "Ethnocentrism"

First Essay: Ethnocentrism

Please write an essay on one of the following topics. Be sure that your paper presents a **thesis** that addresses your **purpose** and your **audience.** Because you must present **examples and explanations** to support your thesis, your essay will probably be 2–3 pages long (double-spaced, 12 point type). Your final draft, **due Tuesday, September 2,** must be word processed. I will return your essay on Thursday, September 4; the **revision** will be due on **September 9.**

1. Use Wangeroo Leewanike (Dee) in Walker's story: "Everyday Use," to illustrate the meaning of "ethnocentrism." *Audience:* Parents or friends who have heard you use the term "ethnocentrism" but aren't sure what you mean. *Purpose:* to make sure that your audience understands the difference between healthy ethnic pride and ethnocentrism.

2. Describe two or three artifacts cherished by your family. *Audience:* Members of your learning community. *Purpose:* to explain the "everyday use" of each artifact (it need not be valuable in monetary terms) and the reasons for cherishing each object.

3. Devise your own topic in response to Walker's story. You might focus on brother/sister rivalries as students, or on the role of parents as teachers, or on your reasons for attending college. *Audience:* Members of your writing group and, potentially, the whole class. *Purpose:* to introduce yourself as an individual shaped as a learner by your experience as a family member.

Appendix D

Narrative Assignment

Your essay should explore at least three episodes in your life in which a teacher or teachers have shaped your attitudes toward learning, toward formal education, and toward your local, state, or national culture. Your essay should reach a conclusion on what conditions foster — and stifle — your sense of place, of belonging in American culture.

Appendix E

Critical Analysis

For your fourth assignment, please compose a critical essay on a text or texts that have some anthropological significance. The word "critical" does not mean "to find fault"; rather, it means to analyze and interpret your chosen text(s).

Suggested Topics

1. Focusing on *Never in Anger* or on *Over the Next Hill,* discuss one of the author's conclusions about the subculture examined in the ethnography. The possibilities are endless: sources of entertainment, distribution of work, gender roles, attitudes toward the Other (outsiders, dominant culture), methods of subsistence, language, contributions to dominant culture. Audience: Members of the learning community for spring semester, all of whom dread having to read an ethnography.

2. The title of your reader, *Conversations,* implies that reading and writing involve an **exchange,** a "conversation" between writer and reader. Focusing on one of the essays (five pages or longer) that we have read,

discuss the **techniques** the author uses to draw us into the conversation on the anthropological issue at hand (education and acculturation, gender roles, ethnocentricity, capital punishment, social justice, and the roles of church and state). Your essay should explain to what extent the author made you respond, lured you into conversation. Your **audience** doubts that any "freshman reader" is worth the paper it's printed on.

3. Design your own topic. *Guidelines:* Your topic must relate to one of the anthropological themes printed in your Comp I syllabus. Your paper must also respond to a "text" — a book, a novel, an essay, a film. You must aim your paper at a particular audience, people who need to hear what you have to say.

Note

1. For a copy of the Comp I syllabus — and any other pedagogical or assessment tool mentioned in this article — send an e-mail message to rcraymond @ualr.edu.

Works Cited

Bruffee, Kenneth. "Collaborative Learning and the 'Conversation of Mankind.'" Villanueva 393–414.

Franklin, Kathy K. "Making Connections: Evaluation of the 1997 Learning Community Pilot." Univ. of Arkansas at Little Rock, July 10, 1998.

Graves, Richard L. "What I Learned from Verle Barnes: The Exploratory Self in Writing." *Rhetoric and Composition: A Sourcebook for Teachers and Writers.* 3rd ed. Ed. Richard L. Graves. Portsmouth: Heinemann, 1990. 132–136.

Lamb, Catherine E. "Beyond Argument in Feminist Composition." *College Composition and Communication* 42 (1991): 11–24.

Matthews, Roberta S., Barbara Leigh Smith, Jean MacGregor, and Faith Babelnick. "Creating Learning Communities." *Handbook of the Undergraduate Curriculum.* Ed. J. G. Gaff and J. L. Ratcliff. San Francisco: Jossey, 1997. 457–475.

Murray, Donald. "Teach Writing as a Process Not Product." Villanueva 3–6.

Selzer, Jack. *Conversations.* 3rd ed. New York: St. Martin's, 1997.

Tinto, Vincent, Anne Goodsell-Love, and Pat Russo. "Freshman Interest Groups and the First-Year Experience: Constructing Student Communities in a Large University." *Journal of the Freshman Year Experience* 6.1 (1994): 7–28.

Trimbur, John. "Consensus and Difference in Collaborative Learning." Villanueva 439–456.

White, Charles R. "Placing Community-Building at the Center of the Curriculum." *Metropolitan Universities: An International Forum.* Baltimore: Towson U, 1998. 55–62.

Villanueva, Victor. ed. *Cross-Talk in Comp Theory: A Reader.* Urbana: NCTE, 1997.

Classroom Activities

In Appendix B, Raymond provides a collaborative learning task on birth order (from Pat Fox and the Georgia Coastal Writing Project and the Little Rock Writing Project) that was used as a first-day icebreaker for students in the composition course and was a key element of the collaborative learning community. An important purpose of this activity was to build community in the classroom from the very beginning as students divided themselves into groups and followed a set of directions based on birth order ("Older Children, Middle Kids, Babies, and Onlies"). Teachers also participated in this activity, "underscoring implicitly the idea of students and teachers as peers in student learning." Consider participating in this collaborative learning task with your own students, either as a first-day exercise or later in the term when the class may need support and continued focus in the benefits of creating a learning community. You may want to give more emphasis to writing by changing steps 5a and 5b to include an in-class writing component that students can then read aloud to other members of their group. Another way to build writing into this task would be to assign students to write a journal entry or short summary that evaluates the success of this collaborative learning task on birth order.

Thinking about Teaching

Although the learning community that Raymond helped to build was designed for students who were eligible for first-year composition, successful learning communities have also been created for students in developmental studies. To find out more about how these collaborative learning groups work at other colleges and universities, consult an Internet search engine such as <www.google.com> and do a search using the term *learning communities.* You will then have access to several web pages that describe learning communities for colleges and universities that serve a variety of populations, including "virtual" learning communities located on the World Wide Web. From this selection, and from the details included in Raymond's article, you can begin to create your own idea of what a learning community for developmental learners might look like at your own institution. Consult with other teachers across disciplines to discern interest, and share your thoughts with administrators.

10

Technology

Teachers of composition help students become better communicators, more skillful problem solvers, and more engaged members of their community. Many now recognize the advantages of electronic technology in teaching and developing these skills. However, access to technology for the composition classroom can be a volatile political issue, stirring up problems of institutional privilege and financial solvency. Moreover, whereas some students arrive in our classrooms already acquainted with the Internet and have access to computers at home or at work, others can barely afford the bus fare to campus. Limited access to computers at educational institutions may seem an inconvenience to the first group of students; to the second, it is a serious liability.*

In this chapter, Jeffrey T. Grabill and Virginia Crank provide important insights for this discussion. Grabill analyzes the efforts of one English department to redefine the relationship of basic writing to technology as a means of initiating institutional change. As the title of her essay suggests, Crank examines the outcome of using asynchronous electronic peer response in a hybrid composition course — a class that combines face-to-face meetings with an online component. She is careful to explain how such a course can work with community college students who "may have limited access to computers off campus and/or difficulty coming to campus to use the computers there." Whether or not our students and we ourselves have access to technology now, it is important to begin considering the benefits of and issues related to computer-mediated instruction in our classrooms.

*For a critical perspective on access to technology, see Cynthia Selfe's *Technology and Literacy in the Twenty-First Century: The Perils of Not Paying Attention* (Carbondale, Ill.: Southern Illinois University Press, 1999).

Technology, Basic Writing, and Change

Jeffrey T. Grabill

In the following article, first published in the Journal of Basic Writing *in 1998, Jeffrey T. Grabill argues for the necessity of demonstrating to institutional stakeholders that basic writing courses should not be defined as stand-alone "remedial" classes for so-called marginal students but instead as an integral part of the composition program as a whole. Grabill believes that linking basic writing to technology is key to formulating this argument. Facility with technology, he holds, is critical to overall student success at the university and therefore a compelling necessity for the basic writing curriculum. He contends that "writing technologies matter so much to the identity of writing programs (and therefore what is possible in the classroom) that we must participate in the design of the technological systems available to basic writing. Technological design, in other words, is an avenue for agency, for changing basic writing." By relating the transformation of basic writing and its relationship to technology at his own large research university, Grabill demonstrates how technology design can serve as an "institutional wedge" for raising the status of basic writing within the university.*

As writing teachers, we are accustomed to thinking of change within classrooms and with our students. We like to think that our classrooms are dynamic, that we have some control over them, and that every now and then, we make a difference in the lives of a few of our students. Writing teachers, in my experience, are most likely to say that we never teach the same course the same way twice and that students, the real "subject" of a writing course, make each class new. I talk about my classroom this way, and I hope that my characterization is true, that as teachers we have the power and ability to change what happens in our classrooms. I want to talk about teaching writing and change, but I will do so by looking "outside" the classroom at systems that affect the classroom. In fact, to be argumentative, I suggest that real change cannot happen exclusively within the classroom but must also take place on "larger" institutional levels.

To engage these larger institutional levels, I draw on my own experience and focus on one aspect of program design that has been an effective lever for effecting institutional change — technology design. In this respect, I look at technology not in terms of specific classroom uses or ways technology can be used to foster particular pedagogies or means of text production. I look at technology as an integral and necessary part of the institutional space occupied by a writing program. My purpose is to explore a method for local change that first is attentive to the institutional space that basic writing occupies and second develops tools — institutional wedges — to change that space. The institutional wedges in this case are technological in nature — the ways in which technologies can be designed to change a basic writing program by altering the place that program occupies in the larger institution (like an English Department or college). Basic writing, like all writing programs, has always been institutionally situated, so I'm exploring a way to see basic writing that allows us strategically to change and reposition it within the university and English department. My hope is to develop tools that enable the continued existence — the active creation and recreation — of sophisticated, dynamic basic writing programs within the shifting structures of colleges and universities. Participating in the design of the technologies utilized by a basic writing program constitutes one such tool for changing the institutional space basic writing occupies, for changing basic writing.

Technology Matters

I should disclose from the outset my fundamental feeling about technology and writing instruction: we can't choose to write without technology, so our choice as writing teachers and program administrators is not whether basic writing uses technologies in the classroom but rather which technologies we use and how we use them. As Stuart Blythe has discussed, we are surrounded by technologies that we use but rarely think about. We sit at desks and use pens or pencils and paper; we write on black or white boards; and every now and then we flip on the overhead projector. Most importantly, when we decide to move the desks into a new configuration, when we decide to use the white board in a new way, we are participating in subtle ways in the design of those technologies. The answers to questions about which technologies we use and why can have a significant impact on the identity of a writing program.

The connections between technology and writing are deeper. Christina Haas argues that "technology and writing are not distinct phenomena; that is, writing has never been and cannot be separate from technology" (x). Haas writes that while her statement strikes many as "common sense" on one level, the implications of such a position aren't immediately clear. Haas notes, as do Sullivan and Dautermann, that technologies often become transparent in our lives and in the research we conduct on writing, which can be good (if technologies seamlessly aid production) and can be bad (if we fail to consider how technologies affect our lives). It is this last point, the possibility that the transparency of technology can be harmful, that is my point of departure here. If we don't consciously choose to write in certain ways with certain technologies, then those decisions will be made for us, both actively (in the sense that we may be given access to certain writing technologies and not others) and passively (in the sense that writing technologies may never be made available to our programs, to our students).

But the connections between technology and writing are deeper still. As Nancy Kaplan writes, "each tool brings into the classroom embedded conceptions of what exists, what is good or useful or profitable, and what is possible with its help" (77). Her statement is remarkable in at least two ways. The first is the way in which she connects tools to ideology, to the ways in which the choices of writing technologies govern to a significant degree who we are and what we can do as writing teachers. The second sense in which her statement is remarkable is what Feenberg would call its "ambivalence," or the sense in which every technology brings with it both constraint and possibility. In other words, the choice to use technologies in a basic writing program changes things, but importantly, the technology itself is not an autonomous agent. Rather, the choice of a writing technology opens up possibilities, and some of these potential changes may be useful, some harmful; some possibilities will be actualized, and others will go unrealized.

This brings me to the core of why technology matters — we can change it. Somebody (usually somebodies) is making the choice (or not) to make available certain writing technologies (and not others) to basic writing students, teachers, and programs. Do we, as basic writing teachers and administrators, take part in these decision-making processes? If not, why not? As I'm trying to argue here, we cannot simply see technology as one isolated variable among others that can be included or separated from the ways in which we design our writing programs. In fact, I think we can see technology as a "wedge" for active change. As Feenberg has continually argued, cultural systems from the most local to the most global are always already technological, and the only way we can create a "good" system, even to decide on the definition of a "good" system, is if people who are affected by that system participate in its design. According to Feenberg's critical theory view of technology, technological systems matter a great deal, and if they remain invisible to those most affected by those systems, they will be designed to meet certain needs and not others because while technological systems may be invisible to some (perhaps many), they aren't invisible to everyone.

In basic writing, if we talk about writing technologies at all (Stan and Collins note the lack of work on computers and basic writing), we talk about them in terms of the classroom or how individual students may or may not use computers. I think this work is important, but I want to push us beyond the classroom. I see choices of writing technologies as part of the institutional systems we call writing programs, English departments, and universities and therefore integral to the identities of those systems. Writing is always already technological, and institutional systems (like writing programs) are dynamic and continually shape how we conduct our lives as writing teachers; institutional systems continually shape what is possible for our students. Simply put, we can't choose to ignore writing technologies, and furthermore, writing technologies matter so much to the identity of writing programs (and therefore what is possible in the classroom) that we must participate in the design of the technological systems available to basic writing. Technological design, in other words, is an avenue for agency, for changing basic writing.

Institutions Matter

My sense of technological design and the role of instructional technology in changing basic writing is dependent upon another concept — a particular view of institutions. I have used the term "institutions" and the phrase "institutional systems," yet I think it is important to understand what I mean by these terms and how they facilitate a view of basic writing as an institutional system that is open to change.

During my time as co-director of Developmental (or basic) Writing, my colleagues and I began to think about its position within the university.[1] Like many in basic writing, we had been developing curricula over a number of years that were as challenging as any "normal" composition course, and we felt our students needed to be acknowledged for their efforts. We faced three local challenges related to Developmental Writing:

- the need to introduce sophisticated writing technologies to our students for reasons of access — students could not be successful at our university without access to these technologies.

- the need to make the course credit bearing — in nearly each case, Developmental Writing does not fulfill any part of the composition requirement. After our course, most students must then take the "normal" two courses in the composition sequence. Thus students earn credits in Developmental Writing that don't count, a problem with the status of the course.

- the need to develop a *way* to change both the course and its relation to the larger institution (the department and the university as a whole) — our problems were larger than those we were used to addressing (e.g., classroom issues), and so how to change Developmental Writing became, itself, a challenge.

But what does it mean to talk of a program as part of an "institutional system"? And how can writing teachers change institutions? My view is that we must see basic writing programs as part of much larger institutional systems and that these systems can be changed. Both stances — seeing the institution as specific and concrete and seeing it as malleable — are uncommon. That is, many readers may be thinking that viewing basic writing as part of larger institutional systems is so commonplace as to be unworthy of comment — nothing new here. But I disagree. We don't talk concretely and meaningfully about institutions because we don't know how to see them. Thus we don't see how something like technology design could change an institution.[2] In most uses of the term, "institution" is either abstract or unmanageably large (and sometimes both). In the abstract, we refer to Religion, English Studies, or The Law as institutions. We know what they are, and we even have an idea of how they operate, but it is tough to *see* them concretely, to see places to interact with and perhaps change such institutions. Similarly, the schools where we teach may seem more concrete, but they also appear hopelessly large, seemingly operated by invisible hands (or more powerful hands), certainly not ours. David Harvey writes that institutions are composed of "semiotic systems" (e.g., writing) that organize practices that affect people subject to or active through a particular institution. Institutions are the universities where we teach, the schools our children attend, and the locations of a great number of public interactions (the department of motor vehicles; social service agencies; parent-teacher groups; neighborhood committees). Institutions, then, are local systems of decision-making within which people act (rhetorically) in ways that powerfully affect the lives of others.

Conceptualizing institutions as I have is a first step toward change. To conceptualize institutional change, I draw on the concept of "institutional critique," a pragmatic mechanism for change that "insists that institutions, as unchangeable as they may seem (and indeed, often are), do contain spaces for reflection, resistance, revision, and productive action" (Porter et al., 3). The claim that institutions can be changed rests on the definition of institutions as local rhetorical systems of decision-making (17). As is likely apparent, "space" is an important term for me as well. While the concept of "space" has metaphorical or symbolic connotations, space is also quite concrete and inhabitable. The space I am talking about with respect to institutions is very "real": it is concrete and material as well as rhetorical/discursive (both the concrete and rhetorical refer to different, though often related, ways to conceptualize "reality"). For geographer Doreen Massey, space is constructed. Space is *produced* by interrelations and interactions between people — like the systems of decision-making that are institutions. The "space" of basic writing, then, is produced by people within university institutional systems. Basic writing is a set of interrelations (a system, like decision-making processes) with both discursive and material attributes and effects. My position is that because space is produced, it can be reproduced (changed), thereby changing the institution itself.

Both the university and the English department create rhetorical and material space for basic writing through processes like placement procedures, course number designations, administrative and teaching lines devoted to the course, and classrooms reserved for the course (those who have had difficulty scheduling a computer classroom for a writing class [a *discursive* act] can attest to the importance of such acts and the value of the *material* space attached to them). That is, the "space" of basic writing is a function of these processes. This space is both discursive (e.g., curriculum, budget lines, listings in course catalogs) and material (e.g., desks, teachers, classrooms). It is important to see that practices such as assessment and placement of students, allotting teaching lines, and curriculum and technology design are linked. They are part of a system of decision-making that connects specific courses and programs with the seemingly "larger" practices of the department, the college, the university. The key to changing institutions is to find the spaces within these institutional systems where change is possible;

that is, to participate in decision-making about how we do our work in locations within the institution that we may not normally be. For us, the practices of technology and curriculum design (they are inextricably linked) were locations where we could act — they were spaces of reflection, resistance, revision, and productive action that affected the classroom, and most importantly, intersected with and affected the larger institution as well. Therefore, technology and curriculum became our "wedges" for changing the institutional space of basic writing.

Changing Basic Writing

We turned to technology and curriculum as an institutional wedge for changing the position of Developmental Writing for three reasons: (1) we were committed to teaching writing with computers for intellectual and pedagogical reasons;[3] (2) we were committed to introducing sophisticated writing technologies to our students (access); and (3) instructional technology and its necessary intersection with curriculum also intersected with the larger institution and was an area over which we had some control. In effect, technology and curriculum design was one part of the institutional system that affected basic writing — it was our "institutional wedge" for effecting change. An "institutional wedge" is a process or an issue that can be used to "pry open" other institutional systems or processes that might otherwise be closed. Technology design was a way for us to interact with other systems of decision-making within the university — instructional technology support, for example. In this case, technology and curriculum design became the wedges of choice because they were two of the few options available to us. Technology/curriculum design was one way in which we could change the course and make the course visible and accountable to others in the university. In the case of Developmental Writing, the course was "remedial" and didn't "count." By extension, so were the students and the work they produced. Most importantly, those affected by the exclusionary boundary between "basic" and "normal" writing had little say in its construction. The course had been defined *for* students and teachers (even if for good reasons). Developmental Writing, then, was an institutional space within which work was of little value, and historically, a space over which those most affected had little control.

The first space over which we did have some control was the curriculum of Developmental Writing. The process of changing that curriculum began long before I started teaching, and so from the perspective of those within the program, there had been nothing "basic" about Developmental Writing for a long time. The curriculum used in Developmental Writing when I first joined the program as a teacher had two important characteristics. It was designed to introduce students to a range of research and writing practices that were valued by the university (although not necessarily by "English"). The curriculum was also designed with a theory of Developmental Writing students that saw them deficient (if deficient at all) in terms of possessing effective strategies for accomplishing writing tasks. Thus the curriculum began with a paper on "observing culture" that introduced students to observation-based research and writing practices, a second paper on "culture and personal experience" that explicitly built on the first by asking students to write their way into the culture they had been observing, a third paper that asked students to analyze the public discourse surrounding an issue of concern to them in any number of local communities that intersected on campus (e.g., the town or within a residence hall), and a fourth paper that asked students to enter the public discourse they analyzed in the third paper. To aid students with these writing and research tasks, the curriculum was built around analytical strategies to guide their writing processes (e.g., observational research guides, audience strategies, possible organizational plans).[4] In subsequent years, we revised the curriculum to make writing technologies themselves objects of critique (in addition to "culture" and/or "public issues"), thereby linking the class to technology in a way that refused to allow it transparency.[5] The new curriculum was theoretically and pedagogically similar to the previous curriculum. What changed were the issues/objects we examined and a few of the methods.

The normal first year writing sequence consists of one course that is largely personal narrative (with wide variety) and one course that has a research writing component (almost exclusively writing the English research paper). In Developmental Writing, students are exposed to narrative techniques and a range of research writing techniques. The traditional English research paper — either about literature or utilizing the library to show proficiency with textual sources and MLA citation styles — is only *part* of the discourse of the university. In Developmental Writing, we introduce students to a range of research practices (e.g., observation-based and online research) and diverse ways of writing up their research (largely taken from the social sciences). In addition, Developmental Writing students are asked to analyze the cultures from which they come and those into which they are moving (e.g., "the university"). In short, the course, like many if not most basic writing courses, is intellectually challenging and meets our institutional responsibilities to prepare students both for the first year writing sequence and to introduce them to the research and writing practices of the university as a whole.

While curriculum design was important for our sense of the course — we knew it was no longer "remedial" — it becomes a method of institutional critique when those responsible for a class like Developmental Writing make this argument to others — and use the curriculum as evidence. In our case, we began with the department (which wasn't difficult) and then began to have conversations with academic advisors on campus who were still recommending the class as a place for remedial grammatical work. Interacting with program stakeholders is a key move because it allows us as teachers and administrators to expand our "space" in order to begin the process of changing the identity of basic writing. Thus, over time, arguments must be made at multiple levels that (1) the class is no longer "remedial" or a "support program" (pick your negative construction), but that (2) it is a sophisticated, challenging course that better meets the needs of its students and/or its institutional reasons for existence. Our work with curriculum is serious work, and one way that we can put it to serious use is as a technique for program revision, a tactic that can facilitate conversations within the institution that can carve a place in decision-making about the work we do. In short, we tried to use new curricula as a wedge for institutional change by constructing new relationships with stakeholders and hopefully altering the ways they make decisions about the program.

The second space over which we had some control was technology design. One of the best traditions within basic writing, I think, is the commitment to "put marginal students immediately within representative academic projects . . ." (Bartholomae "Writing" 70). The commitment to expose students to sophisticated literacies and ideas prevents basic writing from becoming (or being labeled as) "remedial," a label that can have dire institutional consequences.[6] What is rarely a part of discussions about teaching the best a university has to offer is teaching *with the best technologies* the university has to offer. Given the argument that writing is a technology and that the act or processes of writing cannot be separated from technologies, this absence is striking. Inseparable from the writing and thinking of the academy are the technologies the academy writes and thinks with. At this university in particular, understanding the role of writing technologies was crucial for envisioning our students' success. It was technologically a relatively rich university, and if our students were to be successful writers, they needed to be able to research and write successfully with computer technologies.

Pedagogically, we moved writing classes into computer classrooms because our classes became more like workshops, and in these workshops, students actually wrote in-class where peers, the teacher, and the writing tutor were present for assistance. But our move to computer classrooms was never meant to rest with word processing. Networked and internetworked technologies were central to our developing notions of writing and the curriculum revisions that followed.[7] Networked writing was another way to facilitate both in-class and more distant communication and collaboration between students and between students and their teacher. But technology was just as important for larger institutional reasons, in particular the access a computer-based writing program allowed our students. Access to computers for writing is an extremely important issue, and one that has occupied the computers and writing community for some time (see Hawisher et al.). Porter argues that access is perhaps the number one justice issue in computers and writing, and in his book on ethics and electronic writing, he provides a useful framework for understanding the complexity of access. In his framework, access is three-fold, encompassing infrastructural access (money and machines), literacy (education and training), and community acceptance (freedom to speak online). In a technologically rich environment, the borders between basic and normal writing were far more than textual — they were technological. During the Spring 1994 semester, for example, approximately 200 bulletin boards or newsgroups were set up for courses, and many more classes used electronic mail (Yagelski and Grabill). So even if courses were not taught in dedicated computer classrooms, many university classes were utilizing sophisticated communication technologies, and nearly everyone on campus required written material to be word processed. Since 1994 (ages ago technologically), those numbers have only increased. In order to be successful writers at the university, students needed to be able to write with computer technologies. We felt strongly that Developmental Writing needed to provide the access to these technologies, especially for our students, and we provided all three types of access — to the machines, to literacies, and to community acceptance through the use of electronic communities in the classroom. In effect, we provided our students with an advantage.

The fact that Developmental Writing was a computer-based course may have added to its image as a "sophisticated" course — I think it did based on my conversations with stakeholders inside and outside the English department. But like changes in the curriculum, changes in technologies are only important as institutional levers if we use them outside the program. Technology design allowed us significant interaction with the university community outside English. Because we were involved with the design of our own instructional technologies, we were involved with technology support services on campus in a way that gave the program some status with that segment of the university community. Here as well we had to struggle with the perception that our students were "remedial" and therefore didn't need the best technologies the university had to offer. Through conversations about the design of software, systems access for students, and the classrooms in which we wanted to teach, we were not only able to have significant control over the design of our courses, but we were able to legitimize our technology use to that portion of the university community who controlled it. Quickly, those of us associated with Developmental Writing became one of the primary contacts between instructional technology support and the English department, and just as importantly, our classrooms often served as test sites for new technologies. The move from a "remedial" program that needed to argue for why it needed computer technologies to a program with status and ethos as a technologically-based writing program was an important move and a piece of the larger argument necessary for changing Developmental Writing.

A New Developmental Writing?

I claim that our processes of curricular and technology design were intended to change the institutional positioning of Developmental Writing.[8] But what has changed? My goal for Developmental Writing was to see it in a new way and to get others to see it differently as well.

Institutions are dynamic, not static, and thus some change is inevitable. The key is to develop tactics for effecting *positive* institutional change. In the case of Developmental Writing, the most significant change has yet to take place — giving students credit for the work they do in the class — but I feel strongly that the groundwork has been laid for such a move. Collectively, over a number of years, we have changed the space of Developmental Writing because we have begun to change the nature of the differences between "basic" and "normal" classes and programs.

Changing basic writing is difficult work. Donna Dunbar-Odom, discussing basic writing textbooks, writes

> There is no perfect textbook that will liberate or empower its readers on its own. However, authors and publishers of textbooks need to move away from practices and attitudes that predate the Dartmouth Seminar and begin to serve an avant garde function, testing and "transcending the boundaries" of the field of basic writing, re-imagining their audience as a consequence. In other words, basic writing courses and textbooks need to be designed and written so that they produce a narrative of the intellectually, developmentally, cognitively, and emotionally capable, and most importantly, literate adult (7).

Changing textbooks and changing local curricula have a long history as attempts to change the nature and identity of writing courses and programs. What I am suggesting here is that these attempts absent a sense of institutional power and space may not work well because they often fail to move beyond the isolated classroom itself. As Robin McTaggart argues, "Clearly the development of educational work [i.e., change through participatory action research] cannot be achieved by looking at 'teaching' practice alone" (32). The problems we faced demanded that we see Developmental Writing as more than a set of students or classrooms. Indeed, we needed to see it as more than a single isolated course. We needed to see Developmental Writing as part of larger institutional systems of decision-making about what courses existed, their value, and their relation to the curriculum as a whole. Finally, we needed to use something over which we had some control and power as our "wedge" into these larger institutional systems. Technology and curriculum design (and not, for example, assessment and placement practices) served as such a wedge.

So what is Developmental Writing (for us, locally)? It is not a location for fixing remedial texts but is rather the institutional location where students designated as "developmental" by the university can be given their own space to grow as writers. This is not necessarily a textual or psychological space (although it can be); this space is institutional. Our purpose is improved writing and high rates of student retention, and to achieve this purpose, we provide them with small classes, significant contact with instructors, tutors, and peers, a challenging curricula, and access to the best writing technologies the university has to offer. No longer a "remedial" class in the minds of those responsible for the program and some within the university community as a whole, Developmental Writing is a sophisticated, challenging course that grants its students exceptional access to the writing and writing technologies necessary to be successful in the university.

As an institutional system, basic writing can fulfill important needs for students within the university. My purpose here has been to think about the continued existence of basic writing by exploring ways of changing institutional systems. While only the partial story of one program — and a story with ambiguous results at that — the linked tactics of technology and curriculum design can facilitate the institutional change that enables basic writing teachers (and perhaps students) to participate in the construction of their own borders. The key is to find those spaces within local institutional systems that allow students, faculty, and administrators room for the reflection necessary to develop tools for resistance and institutional change.

Notes

1. Developmental writing at Purdue is a relatively small program within the larger first year writing program. Offered only during the Fall semester, typically there are between twelve and fifteen sections taught at a time. With the cap at fifteen students per section (a real benefit of the program), Developmental Writing serves about 125 students each year. Students in this program benefit from small class sizes and a close relationship with the university writing center. A staff of undergraduate tutors is recruited and trained specifically for the program. One tutor is assigned to each section of Developmental Writing, and that tutor attends at least one class per week and meets with each student once a week for a writing tutorial.

   The program is administered and taught exclusively by graduate students. Advanced graduate students work with the director of composition, but are generally responsible for curricula, instructional technology, and training new teachers (through a semester long mentoring program). While a wonderful opportunity for graduate students, the staffing of Developmental Writing is an indication of its status within the department and the university. My association with the program began as a new teacher and continued through two years as co-director and teacher. The narrative of this article and many of my arguments are the result of this direct and indirect collaboration.

2. Furthermore, we relegate such institutional work to the silence of service and therefore minimize this work and its effects. Most composition teachers and program administrators engage in some form of institutional action every day — fighting for writing programs is part of the history and *ethos* of rhetoric and composition. Yet we don't often think about this work beyond the framework of our own institutions, and we certainly don't frame such institutional action as "research" or write about it, even though these institutional actions are important to understand and share with others. This framework for understanding institutions and seeing them as a site for action and reflection is an attempt to value this work outside narrow local contexts.

3. The directors of Developmental Writing at the time that I began teaching in the program were Joanne Addison and Karin Evans. It was their decision to begin moving classes into computer classrooms because they saw the computer classroom as pedagogically beneficial and the technologies as likely to enhance the writing practices (if not abilities) of our students. My subsequent work was self-consciously an extension of their work.

4. The curriculum was modeled theoretically on the invention strategies in the textbook *Four Worlds of Writing* by Janice Lauer, Gene Montague, Andrea Lunsford, and Janet Emig.

5. The "we" I refer to here is Barb L'Eplattenier and I. Together we undertook a revision of the curriculum to include computer technologies as objects of critique.

6. At Georgia State, for example, all "remedial" programs must be eliminated as part of a university system realignment that will equalize standards across the state's four research universities. The rhetoric used to construct and maintain writing programs is meaningful — it can mean the elimination of programs and the good they can do for students. If basic writing wants to survive in a situation like this, its existence must be institutionally positioned differently from "remedial" work even though it might serve the same students.

7. One problem voiced by many teachers is the need to teach technology as well as writing, a need that consumes too much class time and energy. Teaching some technology will always be a "problem," but there are ways to lessen the burden of this. One way we have always done this is through the use of "mini-projects." These small, collaborative projects have a dual purpose: (1) to introduce students to collaborative work, and (2) to collaborate on learning the technologies necessary for success in the class. The class might decide, for instance, that it is necessary to be able to open and save a new document in the word processor, to know how to cut and paste, and to use the spell checker. In addition, it also might be necessary to know how to read and send email messages. Small groups of students can volunteer or be assigned to learn and teach these discrete technologies to the class. But the larger point I want to make is that learning writing technologies cannot be seen as an "add-on" or "extra work" in a writing classroom. If writing technologies are important — either at the university or in the workplace — then they are curricular not extracurricular.

8. I think it is important to point out that it may not have been the intent of everyone involved with Developmental Writing to "change the institution." In fact, early in my time with the program, it wasn't my intention either — we were trying to put together a darn good course for our students. But during my second year as co-director of Developmental Writing, I began explicitly to think about the issues of identity and institutional change. The language I am using to describe it — institutional and border critique, for instance — has come later in an attempt to make sense of what I/we were trying to do and to help frame future institutional action.

Works Cited

Bartholomae, David. "Writing on the Margins: The Concept of Literacy in Higher Education." *A Sourcebook for Basic Writing Teachers.* Ed. Theresa Enos. New York: Random House, 1987. 66–83.

Blythe, Stuart. "Technologies and Writing Center Practices: A Critical Approach." Diss. Purdue University, 1997.

Dunbar-Odom, Donna. "And They Wrote Happily Ever After: The Nature of Basic Writing as Portrayed in Textbooks." *Composition Chronicle* 9 (1996): 4–7.

Feenberg, Andrew. *Critical Theory of Technology.* Oxford: Oxford UP, 1991.

Haas, Christina. *Writing Technology: Studies on the Materiality of Literacy.* Mahwah, NJ: Lawrence Erlbaum, 1996.

Harvey, David. *Justice, Nature & the Geography of Difference.* Cambridge, MA: Blackwell, 1996.

Hawisher, Gail E., Paul LeBlanc, Charles Moran, and Cynthia L. Selfe. *Computers and the Teaching of Writing in American Higher Education, 1979–1994: A History.* New Directions in Computers and Composition Studies. Ed. Gail E. Hawisher and Cynthia L. Selfe. Greenwich, CT: Ablex, 1996.

Kaplan, Nancy. "Ideology, Technology, and the Future of Writing Instruction." Evolving Perspectives on Computers and Composition Studies: Questions for the 1990s. Ed. Gail E. Hawisher and Cynthia L. Selfe. Urbana: NCTE and Computers and Composition, 1991.

Lauer, Janice M., Gene Montague, Andrea Lunsford, and Janet Emig. *Four Worlds of Writing.* 3rd ed. New York: HarperCollins, 1991.

Massey, Doreen. "Politics and Space/Time." *Place and the Politics of Identity.* Ed. Michael Keith and Steve Pile. London: Routledge, 1993. 141–161.

McTaggart, Robin. "Guiding Principles for Participatory Action Research." *Participatory Action Research: International Contexts and Consequences.* Ed. Robin McTaggart. Albany: State University of New York Press, 1997. 25–44.

Porter, James. E. *A Rhetorical Ethics for Internetworked Writing.* New Directions in Computers and Composition Studies. Ed. Gail E. Hawisher and Cynthia L. Selfe. Greenwich, CT: Ablex, 1998.

Porter, James E., Patricia Sullivan, Stuart Blythe, Jeffrey T. Grabill, and Libby Miles. "(Re)writing Institutions: Spatial Analysis and Institutional Critique." Unpublished (1998).

Stan, Susan, and Terence G. Collins. "Basic Writing: Curricular Interactions with New Technology." *JBW* 17 (1998): 18–41.

Sullivan, Patricia, and Jennie Dautermann, eds. *Electronic Literacies in the Workplace: Technologies of Writing.* Urbana: NCTE and Computers and Composition, 1996.

Yagelski, Robert P., and Jeffrey T. Grabill. "Computer-Mediated Communication in the Undergraduate Writing Classroom: A Study of the Relationship of Online Discourse and Classroom Discourse in Two Writing Classes." *Computers and Composition* 15 (1998): 11–40.

Classroom Activities

In an endnote, Grabill acknowledges that "one problem voiced by many teachers is the need to teach technology as well as writing, a need that consumes too much class time and energy." Grabill addresses this problem by suggesting that students work collaboratively to learn the facets of technology that may be new to them. In other words, by turning potential stumbling blocks into collaborative learning and critical thinking activities, students can formalize the learning processes that often happen informally in computer-mediated classrooms.

Try to make sure that each group mixes students with different levels of technological experience. As with other collaborative activities, each group can be assigned a different computer skill (word processing, searching for online sources, evaluating those sources, or e-mailing, for example), to learn and then teach to the class as a whole. You might want to ask each group to create a "help" document to distribute as a handout. As a follow-up activity, students can write about their classroom learning/teaching processes with electronic technology in a formal essay, a journal entry, or an online conversation.

Thinking about Teaching

Grabill suggests: "If we don't consciously choose to write in certain ways with certain technologies, then those decisions will be made for us, both actively (in the sense that we may be given access to certain writing technologies and not to others) and passively (in the sense that writing technologies may never be made available to our programs, to our students)." In your teaching journal, respond to Grabill's statement. Have you been a participant in or a witness to any aspect of the decision-making process at your institution (whether at a program, department, or schoolwide level)? If so, what kinds of decisions were made and what were the reasons behind them? What attitudes regarding the links between basic writing courses and technology seem prevalent among teachers and administrators at your institution?

You might also want to reflect on the issue of access to technology. Does everyone at your institution (including part-time and commuting students and contingent faculty) have equal access to computer use and to computer-mediated instruction? If not, what barriers to access seem to be in place? How can those barriers be changed, or at least ameliorated? Compare notes with other teachers to broaden your perspective and to decide on a course of action as necessary.

Asynchronous Electronic Peer Response in a Hybrid Basic Writing Classroom

Virginia Crank

Like the preceding selection by Jeffrey T. Grabill, this essay suggests that technology is not merely an "add-on" to the basic writing course but rather a means of shaping basic writing pedagogy, thereby addressing the learning process for all students. As she investigates how computers can facilitate collaborative learning and peer response, Virginia Crank examines the differences between face-to-face peer response and asynchronous electronic peer response. She has found that when students posted peer response comments online, "they began taking more time and thinking of more specific things to say." The article, first published in Teaching English in the Two-Year College *in 2002, relates the implications and practices that evolve from Crank's observations.*

While observing in-class peer-response sessions in both my own and my colleagues' basic writing classes, I've overhead comments we've probably all heard dozens of times; one exchange I recently heard in a colleague's class went like this:

"Yours is perfect."

"Is it good, though?"

"Yeah."

After watching students read one another's drafts silently, I then heard a student say, "I thought it was good. I mean, I'm not an English teacher, but I thought it was good," as she handed the essay back to her classmate and then sat quietly waiting for the same sort of affirmation of her own essay. Other bits of conversation revealed similarly cursory reactions: "Mine was true; was yours true?" and "He wants dialogue, which you didn't know about. Use 'he said,' 'she said'" and "You made a lot of sentence mistakes" and "You were supposed to write about standing up for yourself."

As instructors, we strive and contrive to get our students to offer clear, specific, constructive peer response, which will help writers with revision. In 1999, I started using asynchronous electronic peer response, which has helped my students become better responders by

- promoting a written interchange,
- giving them practice using writing to express their thoughts,
- forcing them to articulate their expectations and reactions,
- giving them the time and distance to think carefully about what their reactions to a text are,
- giving them the flexibility to read and reread when they have time and attention, and
- making exchanges more student-centered (because the students are writing to one another, not to or for me).

This peer-response experiment began when I converted my traditional composition classes to online/traditional hybrids.

Hybrid Composition Classes

I began teaching hybrid composition through a convergence of weekly class sessions in the computer lab and the introduction of a networking software system to our campus. Instead of simply designing word-processing assignments for our lab days, I began to design activities that would use the conference system. One day in lab, as my students were chatting online about an assigned reading, I overheard a student say, "Why are we using these computers to talk to someone we're sitting next to?" The next semester, I made the weekly lab session (either a Friday or a Monday, depending on room scheduling) an online class day with attendance optional. After five weeks of meeting in the lab together to learn to use the software, the students were then "set free" to complete the weekly online assignment when and where they wished. Changing the attendance policy for lab day guaranteed students access to the computers and software during our class time even if they didn't have it at any other time in the week.

The necessity of access was the "mother" of my hybrid class format; community college students, particularly basic writing students, may have very limited access to computers off campus and/or difficulty coming to campus to use the computers there. This weekly online class needed to be fully integrated into what we did during the rest of the week, not to seem like "homework" or "extra work" that was difficult to do; giving them their assigned lab time to use as they determined seemed the best way to create that feeling.

Patterns of Communication in Asynchronous Discussion

In examining the general discussions that took place over our asynchronous conference network, I noticed the students responding to one another in at least ten ways:

1. Affirmation and repetition ("I agree. This is a scary trend.")

2. Disagreement ("I think living to 100 would be terrible!")

3. Correction ("I think you missed the author's main point; he does say that medical tests have been done.")

4. Piggybacking or taking a thread in a new direction ("I agree that melatonin sounds good. I worry, however, about the consequences for pregnant women.")

5. Questioning to promote further thought ("I see your point about animal testing; are there any other ways to determine if something is safe for humans?")

6. Relating personal experience ("My grandmother also had Alzheimer's, and we would have done anything to prevent it.")

7. Rethinking original position ("I hadn't really thought about that aspect of it; I think I might be a little less enthusiastic about melatonin now.")

8. Offering similar examples ("I agree. We thought that diet drug was safe, too.")

9. Prediction ("I think they're going to figure out that this stuff isn't all that safe.")

10. Praise ("What an excellent point! You really write clearly; you said what I think I was trying to say, only better.")

Certainly, some of these same patterns of discussion take place in face-to-face classes, but not as carefully, clearly, or extensively. In the particular asynchronous discussion from which some of the above examples were taken, about an essay they'd all read for homework, I heard from every student, and every student heard from several other students, comments directed specifically at their own contributions to the discussion. A traditional classroom, no matter how we arrange the chairs, still inherently places the teacher at the center of all discussions, as moderator, validator, authority. Perhaps some discussion elements, such as praise for another's comments, even go unspoken during face-to-face discussion; students leave that to the teacher, unless prompted to evaluate.

Peer Response in the Hybrid Basic Writing Class

Other than general discussion, some of the activities due online by midnight on Monday (or Friday) are rough drafts, homework exercises from our text, brainstorming, group essays, polished essays, and peer response. It is with the peer response in the basic writing classes that I found the greatest improvements when moving into the hybrid asynchronous environment. By making the textual interaction more "real," more directed at actual tasks and purposes, a new kind of composing community was created within my basic writing classes. Basic writers could see the immediate effect of their writing on an audience beyond the "teacher/evaluator."

When the weekly online assignment was peer response, the instructions were limited to, "Post your draft to the conference and then read and respond to your classmates' drafts." I gave them no training in peer response, no worksheets to follow, and only a one-sentence guideline: "Make your response at least fifteen lines long, and make sure you offer advice that will help your classmate improve his or her writing." I was, without knowing it, following the advice of Sandy Varone in her observations of computer-mediated peer response in her basic writing classes, that we create peer-response environments that are "spontaneous yet planned, guided yet unrestrained by the authority of predetermined questions and procedures" (218). I suspected that these basic writing students would begin to use both their internalized guidelines for good writing and those we had been discussing during our regular class sessions and that they would echo the kinds of responses they had received from past teachers and me. Basic writers sometimes feel that their writing has been a series of mistakes and "don't"s; my own practice was to praise those things in their drafts which were strong and ignore mechanical and grammatical errors until later in the writing process. I hoped they would see the value of this practice and implement it in their peer response, but I didn't push that idea on them before they began the process. Their responses to my limited directions did come in the form of a self-initiated set of criteria based, beautifully, on the things we had discussed in class and the comments I'd made on their previous papers. They offered praise for specific strengths, suggestions for specific revisions/additions, questions to prompt further thinking and detail, agreement with and expansion of ideas, and contradictions of or challenges to ideas.

The resulting peer-critique letters, which Michael Stephen Marx's study of e-mail peer response describes as "text itself, rather than a step in the writing process," pleased me more than any in-class peer exercises ever had. The students engaged with the text as genuine readers, describing their reactions to one another's stories. When I asked them to read and respond to one another's writings in class, what I mostly overhead was, "I liked it," "That's really good," "Yeah, that same thing happened to me." But when I began requiring them to respond asynchronously, posting their responses to our class conference, they began taking more time and thinking of more specific things to say. Tiffany, in response to Yvonne's story about a boy complimenting her "big backyard" (a euphemism about her body) wrote a very letter to her peer, beginning with a great compliment: "I couldn't help but laugh out loud in the quiet computer room." She goes on to relate the elements of the story to her own experience and to ask her peer some questions about the text that might help the writer revise and clarify her draft. Her response strays into some personal reflection, but then she returns to the text with a compliment ("Your writing was definitely funny"), a suggestion ("Maybe putting more describing words could make it longer and more funnier"), and one final question that indicates something she, as a reader, sees as missing from the draft ("Did you laugh when he told you what that meant or were you upset or did you even care?").

In her response to the same story, Amelia gives Yvonne the response of a genuine, interested reader, saying, "When I was reading I thought you may tell a story about your first boyfriend or something like that but we found a very different story[;] he used different words to mean a totally different thing you know." By describing her reading process, Amelia has adapted a sophisticated technique of reader response, one I saw modeled by my graduate professors. This kind of prediction, which teaches the writer about audience expectations and how to manipulate them to her own ends, doesn't happen explicitly in face-to-face interaction, unless the student is prompted by a teacher's instructions.

There are, of course, still responses that don't seem very instructive for the writer, such as Lisa's response to her classmate's slang dictionary:

> I think you had a good dictionary then you stop with this. I think you could go into much greater detail about why where and when this would help your reader understand better because it is a little unclear. i realized that I know almost all of the words you used and use some of them in my everyday talk. it just made me realize how much slang is a part of my everyday life.

Lisa praises the writer, relates her own experience with the subject (slang), but doesn't offer specific suggestions for revision (just "go into greater detail") nor any specific strengths of the essay. Still, even this response (which, granted, was early in the semester — their first time to do electronic peer response, in fact) offers more feedback than just "It was good." The writer still gets a well-developed reaction to her writing.

The necessity of text in the asynchronous environment forces students to compose answers more carefully. A "That was good" can be tossed off in a brief, face-to-face class group but seems silly and inefficient in an e-mail message. Even those inclined never to criticize will expand on their "That was good" by noting specific strengths and points of interest or by adding the perspective of their own experience with the same issue, which is the kind of "real-reader" interaction that Karen Spear's *Sharing Writing* says is the essential benefit of peer response. Most e-mail programs allow students to very easily select portions of the original essay to include in their replies, and students will occasionally do that in order to illustrate their specific response to the paper.

The performance pressure (respond *now*, in class!) that so often stifles basic writers may also be relieved by the electronic part of the peer response, which offers some partial anonymity. Although the students do know one another and they know that the writer will see each respondent's name on the reply e-mail, they seem to feel more comfortable being honest about their reactions when writing them.

The necessity and anonymity of text in e-mail peer response are supplemented by the expanded time available for students to read one another's texts and think about how to respond. In a regular fifty-minute class session, a student may have three to four minutes to read a paper and another three to five minutes to compose a response. Often, in consideration of time, I'll have students read their papers aloud to their groups rather than exchanging papers to read quietly. While there are certain advantages to reading aloud, one thing that is lost is the peer reader's ability to closely examine, to reread, to decipher text without the idiosyncrasies of accent, pace, and speaking style. In a situation where specific comments and suggestions are desired, reading at one's own pace, even with the disadvantage of reading from a computer screen, beats hearing a nervous writer read his own draft. Marx's study of e-mail response confirms that students can compose "honest and thorough critiques" when they escape the pressure of in-class peer response (par. 29).

My basic writers' peer responses demonstrate some of the same patterns of communication earlier noted in general asynchronous electronic discussion. Most responses fall within the categories of praising, offering similar examples, questioning to promote further thought, relating personal experience, and affirming and repeating, which is probably not that different from what happens in traditional, face-to-face peer response. The significant differences are the specificity of the e-mail responses, their fuller development, and their focus on global issues in the text rather than on editing issues or the author.

The praise response, for example, may be what Geoffrey Sirc and Tom Reynolds, in their study of networked collaboration, describe as a social function, but, if specific enough, it can also serve a rhetorical function, reinforcing for writers the audience-generated qualities of good writing. Writing the following comment, the student allows her peer to see some specific ways in which her text conforms to the idea that good writing is vivid and descriptive:

> I really enjoyed reading your paper about your top three values. I liked how you added vivid words and details in the paper that allowed us to visualize your experience at the pool. [. . .] What really caught my attention is the descriptiveness that you added when you talked about your neighbor kids playing in the pool, and how this reminded you of learning your lesson of honesty. I also really liked where you talked about jumping off the diving board, and the sweat that was pouring out of your forehead, and how your heart was pounding. I also like where you described your legs as limp licorice sticks. This really allowed me to imagine how nervous you were.

Pointing out the effectiveness of such images as "sweating pouring out of your forehead" and "legs as limp licorice sticks" allows this reader to reinforce the writer's strengths in description.

Similarly, affirmation and repetition serve social and rhetorical functions, offering specific feedback about the writer's strengths, as this example illustrates:

> i think that you are correct in what you said in your paper about everybody having the right to their own opinion and that's why I like your paper. You weren't afraid to say what your own experience was and that you believe in these traits.

While at once coming from what Spear calls "a need to preserve harmony" (25) and what Sirc and Reynolds call "face-saving," both of these response styles also focus on the text, the writer's position in it, and the reader's interaction with it.

Offering similar examples and relating personal experience could be considered less productive peer response, if we judge the value of peer response by its rigorous focus on the writer's text. However, even setting aside its valuable social and community-building functions, relating personal experience can serve rhetorically to reinforce lessons about audience and about the value of finding common ground with the reader. The following example shows how this connection to personal experience allowed the reader also to make a connection with the writer's ideas, linking the reader's personal experience to "new" concepts introduced by the writer:

> I liked your values essay. I totally agree with the idea of ambition and setting goals. I set goals all the time. If you don't set goals for yourself then you really don't have an idea of what you're working for. Success is another good value. I like how you linked it back to ambition and setting goals again to make yourself successful.

Students using this response style enact their knowledge (both innate and recently learned) that rhetoric is, as Aristotle said, "an ability, in each case, to see the available means of persuasion" (36), beginning by seeing areas of common interest and agreement.

The last most common category of electronic asynchronous peer response involves making suggestions for revision; basic writing students tended to make these suggestions most often in the form of questioning to promote further thought. A peer reader's questioning, which is a rather mature "teacherly" interaction with text in the basic writing class, encourages the writer to consider other concepts or problems raised by her writing. The following student response, whether consciously or not, imitates my own style of response early in the writing process, when my goal is to demonstrate where ideas need development:

> I strongly agree with your statement that parent's have more obligations then the child. In your third paragraph I was a little confused. You said once you have children of your own then the parents don't have responsibility. What if you don't have children? Is there an age that that would relieve the parents of the responsibility?

Far from simply maintaining harmony or keeping a safe distance from her classmate's text by staying on the local, word/sentence level, this reader engages on the global level of idea.

As these examples demonstrate, asynchronous responses rarely fall neatly into one category. In addition to whatever else they do, students almost always include praise, affirmation, and repetition, and at least one or two specific suggestions for revision. This level of specificity is what leads me to assert that asynchronous electronic peer response offers strengths often lacking in traditional face-to-face peer response or synchronous electronic peer response. The asynchronicity and the flexibility, along with the formality of e-mail (as compared to either real or virtual chat), compel students to write more specific and constructive comments. Marx describes this phenomenon as "the burden of providing reasons for any revisions the critic suggests (par. 30)."

Another positive result of the e-mail format, and one that is probably also influenced by the intimidation factor, is that the students know they are writing this e-mail directly to their classmates, not to me. This response is not a paper that I collect, check, and then, eventually, give to the writer; this is a direct letter to the writer about his or her text. Having that real audience reinforces the audience awareness lessons I've been teaching in class while it teaches students to look at texts critically for their strengths and weaknesses. Since the e-mail has a specific purpose as well as a specific audience, the peer responses tend to be more focused on the text rather than the student or the process, and the responses tend to be more global. Since the writer's text is only available in electronic form, the reader has less opportunity to "red-ink" it or zero in on editing and proofreading errors. The reader focuses, therefore, on the content and organization of the draft.

Perspectives on Electronic Peer Response

Some of my colleagues were a bit skeptical when I first started teaching my basic writing classes as hybrids; they feared, I think, that the students' lack of fluency with writing would be compounded by their limited experience with computers, that the entirely text-centered nature of the computer would intimidate students who already felt underprepared in dealing with text. My feeling, however, was that developmental writers might find the new medium enjoyable and that we would be doing them a great service by introducing them to electronic communication. My experience further allayed my fears as I saw that students who spoke very little in class, even during small-group peer work, would freely exchange ideas over our class conference.

This phenomenon in connection with electronic peer response has been studied by Mark Mabrito, who analyzed the differences between e-mail and face-to-face peer-response groups for low- and high-apprehensive writers. He reasoned that the asynchronous environment of e-mail might make high-apprehensive writers more comfortable because of the less threatening environment. Mabrito studied four low- and four high-apprehensive writers and had them do group peer-response both face-to-face and through e-mail. Among his findings was that "high apprehensives devoted more of their idea units to offering directions for revising texts during e-mail meetings than they did during face-to-face meetings" and "high apprehensives reported that revision decisions were influenced more by group comments received during e-mail sessions than by group comments received during face-to-face sessions" (521). Mabrito concluded that the "productive and apparently nonthreatening nature of e-mail allowed high-apprehensive writers to participate in a "collaborative venture" they would have avoided in a traditional class setting (529).

While other thought-provoking research on electronic peer response has been done by Marx, Sirc and Reynolds, Michael Palmquist, Irvin Peckham, and Varone, most of the work has concentrated on group response done using some sort of *synchronous* chat function and has demonstrated very mixed results. A more recent article by Lee Honeycutt, however, takes a step beyond comparing electronic and nonelectronic peer response to compare e-mail peer response with synchronous peer response. Honeycutt's findings support my own contentions: he found that students make more specific references to text when they are doing peer response in an e-mail format than in a synchronous chat environment, and that they "used a significantly greater number of words to reference both documents and their contents than they did when using chats" (45).

Some of the weaknesses of the synchronous chat protocol that Honeycutt describes are the same as those found in more traditional, face-to-face peer-response groups: off-task discussion, vague comments, a rush to read, digest, and respond in a short time, and the confusion of sorting out multiple voices. Honeycutt notes, "In e-mail response sessions [. . .] students do not have to worry about patterns of conversational turn-taking and therefore independently self-select and initiate the processes by which they provide evaluations to their peers" (32). He recommends e-mail also because it "is more like traditional forms of text, containing greater coherence and unity of thought" (33). The specificity and coherence of the e-mail response are of great help to both the writer and the reviewer as practice in writing to a specific audience and for a specific purpose. That clearer sense of the purpose for the peer interaction might also explain why less social talk occurs, less "group maintenance." Honeycutt states, "When students used e-mail, they may have focused more on the document under review and thus devoted a significantly greater amount of their comments to document, content, and rhetorical context references" (41).

One of the limitations of Honeycutt's study is that the e-mail responders had the same amount of time and the same physical setup as the synchronous responders; they were seated in a computer lab for a period of two hours; without that limitation, the freedom to think and compose carefully is even greater. With that extra time, basic writing students are even more capable of what Honeycutt describes as a "deeper processing of documents under revision" (51).

Hybrid: "The Best of Both Worlds"

One point of contention in the ongoing discussion of electronic peer response is the debate between those who favor synchronicity and those who vouch for asynchronicity. Some early users of computer-mediated peer response found it unsatisfactory because of their attempts to preserve synchronicity, and this concern continues to inhibit some composition instructors. Joel Haefner, in "The Importance of Being Synchronous," contends that "computer-aided instruction that is solely asynchronous cannot possibly convey any kind of immediacy." As Peckham urges in "If It Ain't Broke, Why Fix it? Disruptive and Constructive Computer-Mediated Response Group Practices," Haefner wishes to preserve the "energy and earnestness" of face-to-face communication, encouraging teachers to question the value of asynchronous writing components. The hybrid class, nonetheless, which allows for all the advantages of asynchronous electronic peer response as well as the dynamic interaction and reinforcement of the more traditional classroom, offers a chance to guide basic writing students into conversation and contemplation, to encourage them to "try out" the lessons they're learning in the classroom, and to demonstrate to them that the process of writing, indeed, of learning, extends beyond the four walls of the college buildings and beyond the confining traditions of writing instruction. In the process of guiding them to online peer response, we activate their learning, calling upon them to demonstrate and trust both their innate and their recently acquired standards for good writing. We create a more fully integrated writing community, in which peer response is a natural extension of writing rather than "busywork" or "class filler" or even a teacher-driven exercise.

Works Cited

Aristotle. *On Rhetoric.* Trans. George A. Kennedy. New York: Oxford UP, 1991.

Haefner, Joel. "Opinion: The Importance of Being Synchronous." *Academic Writing: Interdisciplinary Perspectives on Communication across the Curriculum.* 9 Apr. 2000. 10 Jan. 2002 http://aw.colostate.edu/teaching/haefner2000.htm.

Honeycutt, Lee. "Comparing E-Mail and Synchronous Conferencing in Online Peer Response." *Written Communication* 18.1 (Jan. 2001): 26–60.

Mabrito, Mark. "Electronic Mail as a Vehicle for Peer Response: Conversations of High- and Low-Apprehensive Writers." *Written Communication* 8.4 (Oct. 1991): 509–32.

Marx, Michael Steven. "Distant Writers, Distnat Critics, and Close Readings: Linking Composition Classes through a Peer-Critiquing Network." *Computers and Composition* 8.1 (Nov. 199): 23–39. 10 Jan. 2002 http://corax.cwrl.utexas.edu/cac/archives/v8/8_1_html/8_1_2_Marx.html.

Palmquist, Michael E. "Network-Supported Interaction in Two Writing Classrooms." *Computers and Composition* 9.4 (Nov. 1993): 25–57. Mar. http://10_4_3_Palmquist.html.

Peckham, Irvin. "If It Ain't Broke, Why Fix It? Disruptive and Constructive Computer-Mediated Response Group Practices." *Computers and Composition* 13 (1996): 327–39.

Sirc, Geoffrey, and Tom Reynolds. "The Face of Collaboration in the Networked Writing Classroom." *Computers and Composition* 7 (Apr. 1990): 53–70. 10 Jan. 2002 http://corax.cwrl.utexas.edu/cac/archives/v7/7_spec_html/7_spec_4_Sirc.html.

Spear, Karen. *Sharing Writing: Peer Response Groups in English Classes.* Portsmouth, NH: Boynton, 1988.

Varone, Sandy. "Voices from the Computer Classroom: Novice Writers and Peer Response to Writing." *TETYC* 23.3 (Oct. 1996): 213–18.

Classroom Activities

If your students have regular access to computers at home or on campus, consider assigning a peer-response exercise similar to the one described in this essay. Before students exchange papers, hold a class discussion on the categories of peer-response comments that Crank lists. It might be useful to create some example comments and, as a class, decide which category or categories each comment fits into. This exercise will help students think critically about their roles as peer reviewers, and it will show them the broad range of directions that their discussions might take. You could also discuss with students why certain types of responses are especially helpful—and others could be made more helpful.

Crank acknowledges that some instructors prefer face-to-face peer response for its "energy and earnestness." Consider initiating a discussion with students on the positive and negative consequences of communicating via e-mail. You may want to pose the following questions: How is e-mail similar to and different from other modes of communication? Are audience expectations different for e-mail and face-to-face peer response? How can you convey in an e-mail the tone you would use when responding in person to a peer's writing? If your students have regular access to computers, consider posing these questions as part of an electronic conversation.

Thinking about Teaching

If you are able to assign electronic peer-response sessions, take notes in your teaching journal on your students' experiences with the assignments. If you have also observed face-to-face peer-response sessions, note the differences in quality between the in-person comments and the electronic comments. Crank notes that in asynchronous electronic response, some types of comments may not differ substantially from those in face-to-face conversations. Nonetheless, she found that the longer response time available with electronic asynchronous response allowed students to write with more "specificity" and "fuller development," as well as with a greater "focus on global issues in the text rather than on editing issues or the author." Do your observations of your own students corroborate Crank's?

11

Writing and Race, Class, and Gender

How do we meet the challenges of a culturally diverse classroom? Often the classroom is a microcosm of the community outside its doors — where race, social class, gender, sexual orientation, age, ethnicity, and language differences create fear and conflict rather than understanding and harmony among our students. Moreover, based on past experiences with those who openly displayed prejudices or held inappropriate stereotypes, students may perceive teachers as representatives of alien cultures. How can we facilitate a classroom in which differences are not denied but mediated? The challenge is to create a learning environment in which all students feel valued and appreciated for who they are and who they are becoming.

By demonstrating the interconnections of language and culture, the writers in this chapter document the persistence of racism, classism, and sexism and the challenges of working for social justice through teaching and writing. Gloria Anzaldúa reflects on how childhood experiences with language (Spanish and English) and education in South Texas continue to impact her adult views of cross-cultural relations. June Jordan presents a teaching narrative that argues for the power and persistence of Black English in a society committed to the cultural practices of standard ("white") English. Kay Thurston writes about challenges facing students at Navajo Community College. In describing the cultural background of her students, she also challenges white composition teachers to confront their own Western ethnocentrism and to begin to envision a more inclusive course design. The purpose of such a redesign would be to "mitigate barriers" between Eurocentric ideas of education and a Navajo approach. Confronting the reader with real-life situations in school and beyond, Anzaldúa, Jordan, and Thurston provide thoughtful explorations of potentially transforming cultural practices that have critical implications for our students and for ourselves.

How to Tame a Wild Tongue

Gloria Anzaldúa

Gloria Anzaldúa writes, "So, if you really want to hurt me, talk badly about my language. Ethnic identity is twin skin to linguistic identity — I am my language. Until I take pride in my language, I cannot take pride in myself." As a Chicana / tejana lesbian feminist poet, fiction writer, and teacher, she explores the implications of growing up on the "borderlands" of the Mexican and American cultures in Texas. In her preface to Borderlands/La Frontera *(1987), Anzaldúa clarifies her terms: "[B]orderlands are not particular to the Southwest. In fact, borderlands are physically present when two or more cultures edge each other, where people of different races occupy the same territory, where under, lower, middle, and upper classes touch, where the space between two individuals shrinks with intimacy." Such cultural space sounds not unlike many of our classrooms.*

In this selection, a chapter from Borderlands/La Frontera, *Anzaldúa recounts how growing up Chicana continues to shape her life, especially in terms of language. She writes in "Spanglish," a combination of Spanish and English, both to help the reader understand the rich cultural conditions of the borderlands and to demonstrate to Anglo and non-Spanish-speaking readers what it means to be the "other" — outside of so-called mainstream language and culture. Certainly, many ESL students may have shared Anzaldúa's childhood experience of the teacher who did not care to understand how Anzaldúa pronounced her name. "If you want to be American, speak 'American,'" her teacher tells her. In this essay, Anzaldúa reminds us that there are many ways of speaking American.*

"We're going to have to control your tongue," the dentist says, pulling out all the metal from my mouth. Silver bits plop and tinkle into the basin. My mouth is a motherlode.

The dentist is cleaning out my roots. I get a whiff of the stench when I gasp. "I can't cap that tooth yet, you're still draining," he says.

"We're going to have to do something about your tongue," I hear the anger rising in his voice. My tongue keeps pushing out the wads of cotton, pushing back the drills, the long thin needles. "I've never seen anything as strong or as stubborn," he says. And I think, how do you tame a wild tongue, train it to be quiet, how do you bridle and saddle it? How do you make it lie down?

> Who is to say that robbing a people of
> its language is less violent than war?
>
> — Ray Gwyn Smith[1]

I remember being caught speaking Spanish at recess — that was good for three licks on the knuckles with a sharp ruler. I remember being sent to the corner of the classroom for "talking back" to the Anglo teacher when all I was trying to do was tell her how to pronounce my name. "If you want to be American, speak 'American.' If you don't like it, go back to Mexico where you belong."

"I want you to speak English. *Pa'hallar buen trabajo tienes que saber hablar el inglés bien. Qué vale toda tu educación si todavía hablas inglés con un* 'accent,'" my mother would say, mortified that I spoke English like a Mexican. At Pan American University, I and all Chicano students were required to take two speech classes. Their purpose: to get rid of our accents.

Attacks on one's form of expression with the intent to censor are a violation of the First Amendment. *El Anglo con cara de inocente nos arrancó la lengua.* Wild tongues can't be tamed, they can only be cut out.

Overcoming the Tradition of Silence

> *Abogadas, escupimos el oscuro,*
> *Peleando con nuestra propia sombra*
> *el silencio nos sepulta.*

En boca cerrada no entran moscas. "Flies don't enter a closed mouth" is a saying I kept hearing when I was a child. *Ser habladora* was to be a gossip and a liar, to talk too much. *Muchachitas bien criadas,* well-bred girls don't answer back. *Es una falta de respeto* to talk back to one's mother or father. I remember one of the sins I'd recite to the priest in the confession box the few times I went to confession: talking back to my mother, *hablar pa' 'tras, repelar. Hocicona, repelona, chismosa,* having a big mouth, questioning, carrying tales are all signs of being *mal criada.* In my culture they are all words that are derogatory if applied to women — I've never heard them applied to men.

The first time I heard two women, a Puerto Rican and a Cuban, say the word *"nosotras,"* I was shocked. I had not known the word existed. Chicanas use *nosotros* whether we're male or female. We are robbed of our female being by the masculine plural. Language is a male discourse.

> And our tongues have become
> dry   the wilderness has
> dried out our tongues   and
> we have forgotten speech.
>
> — Irena Klepfisz[2]

Even our own people, other Spanish speakers *nos quieren poner candados en la boca.* They would hold us back with their bag of *reglas de academia.*

Oyé como ladra: el lenguaje de la frontera

Quien tiene boca se equivoca.

— Mexican saying

"*Pocho,* cultural traitor, you're speaking the oppressor's language by speaking English, you're ruining the Spanish language," I have been accused by various Latinos and Latinas. Chicano Spanish is considered by the purist and by most Latinos deficient, a mutilation of Spanish.

But Chicano Spanish is a border tongue which developed naturally. Change, *evolución, enriquecimiento de palabras nuevas por invención o adopción* have created variants of Chicano Spanish, *un nuevo lenguaje. Un lenguaje que corresponde a un modo de vivir.* Chicano Spanish is not incorrect, it is a living language.

For a people who are neither Spanish nor live in a country in which Spanish is the first language; for a people who live in a country in which English is the reigning tongue but who are not Anglo; for a people who cannot entirely identify with either standard (formal, Castillian) Spanish nor standard English, what recourse is left to them but to create their own language? A language which they can connect their identity to, one capable of communicating the realities and values true to themselves — a language with terms that are neither *español ni inglés,* but both. We speak a patois, a forked tongue, a variation of two languages.

Chicano Spanish sprang out of the Chicanos' need to identify ourselves as a distinct people. We needed a language with which we could communicate with ourselves, a secret language. For some of us, language is a homeland closer than the Southwest — for many Chicanos today live in the Midwest and the East. And because we are a complex, heterogeneous people, we speak many languages. Some of the languages we speak are:

1. Standard English

2. Working class and slang English

3. Standard Spanish

4. Standard Mexican Spanish

5. North Mexican Spanish dialect

6. Chicano Spanish (Texas, New Mexico, Arizona and California have regional variations)

7. Tex-Mex

8. *Pachuco* (called *caló*)

My "home" tongues are the languages I speak with my sister and brothers, with my friends. They are the last five listed, with 6 and 7 being closest to my heart. From school, the media, and job situations, I've picked up standard and working class English. From Mamagrande Locha and from reading Spanish and Mexican literature, I've picked up Standard Spanish and Standard Mexican Spanish. From *los recién llegados*, Mexican immigrants, and *braceros*, I learned the North Mexican dialect. With Mexicans I'll try to speak either Standard Mexican Spanish or the North Mexican dialect. From my parents and Chicanos living in the Valley, I picked up Chicano Texas Spanish, and I speak it with my mom, younger brother (who married a Mexican and who rarely mixes Spanish with English), aunts, and older relatives.

With Chicanas from *Nuevo México* or *Arizona* I will speak Chicano Spanish a little, but often they don't understand what I'm saying. With most California Chicanas I speak entirely in English (unless I forget). When I first moved to San Francisco, I'd rattle off something in Spanish, unintentionally embarrassing them. Often it is only with another Chicana *tejana* that I can talk freely.

Words distorted by English are known as anglicisms or *pochismos*. The *pocho* is an anglicized Mexican or American of Mexican origin who speaks Spanish with an accent characteristic of North Americans and who distorts and reconstructs the language according to the influence of English.[3] Tex-Mex, or Spanglish, comes most naturally to me. I may switch back and forth from English to Spanish in the same sentence or in the same word. With my sister and my brother Nune and with Chicano *tejano* contemporaries I speak in Tex-Mex.

From kids and people my own age I picked up *Pachuco*. *Pachuco* (the language of the zoot suiters) is a language of rebellion, both against Standard Spanish and Standard English. It is a secret language. Adults of the culture and outsiders cannot understand it. It is made up of slang words from both English and Spanish. *Ruca* means girl or woman, *vato* means guy or dude, *chale* means no, *simón* means yes, *churro* is sure, talk is *periquiar*, *pigionear* means petting, *que gacho* means how nerdy, *ponte águila* means watch out, death is called *la pelona*. Through lack of practice and not having others who can speak it, I've lost most of the *Pachuco* tongue.

Chicano Spanish

Chicanos, after 250 years of Spanish/Anglo colonization, have developed significant differences in the Spanish we speak. We collapse two adjacent vowels into a single syllable and sometimes shift the stress in certain words such as *maíz/maiz, cohete/cuete*. We leave out certain consonants when they appear between vowels: *lado/lao, mojado/mojao*. Chicanos from South Texas pronounce *f* as *j* as in *jue (fue)*. Chicanos use "archaisms," words that are no longer in the Spanish language, words that have been evolved out. We say *semos, truje, haiga, ansina*, and *naiden*. We retain the "archaic" *j*, as in *jalar*, that derives from an earlier *h* (the French *halar* or the Germanic *halon* which was lost to standard Spanish in the sixteenth century), but which is still found in several regional dialects such as the one spoken in South Texas. (Due to geography, Chicanos from the Valley of South Texas were cut off linguistically from other Spanish speakers. We tend to use words that the Spaniards brought over from Medieval Spain. The majority of the Spanish colonizers in Mexico and the Southwest came from Extremadura — Hernán Cortés was one of them — and Andalucía. Andalucians pronounce *ll* like a *y*, and their *d*'s tend to be absorbed by adjacent vowels: *tirado* becomes *tirao*. They brought *el lenguaje popular, dialectos y regionalismos.*)[4]

Chicanos and other Spanish speakers also shift *ll* to *y* and *z* to *s*.[5] We leave out initial syllables, saying *tar* for *estar, toy* for *estoy, hora* for *ahora* (*cubanos* and *puertorriqueños* also leave out initial letters of some words). We also leave out the final syllable such as *pa* for *para*. The intervocalic *y*, the *ll* as in *tortilla, ella, botella*, gets replaced by *tortia* or *tortiya, ea, botea*. We add an additional syllable at the beginning of certain words: *atocar* for *tocar, agastar* for *gastar*. Sometimes we'll say *lavaste las vacijas*, other times *lavates* (substituting the *ates* verb endings for the *aste*).

We use anglicisms, words borrowed from English: *bola* from ball, *carpeta* from carpet, *máchina de lavar* (instead of *lavadora*) from washing machine. Tex-Mex argot, created by adding a Spanish sound at the beginning or end of an English word such as *cookiar* for cook, *watchar* for watch, *parkiar* for park, and *rapiar* for rape, is the result of the pressures on Spanish speakers to adapt to English.

We don't use the word *vosotros/as* or its accompanying verb form. We don't say *claro* (to mean yes), *imagínate*, or *me emociona*, unless we picked up Spanish from Latinas, out of a book, or in a classroom. Other Spanish-speaking groups are going through the same, or similar, development in their Spanish.

Linguistic Terrorism

> *Deslenguadas. Somos los del español deficiente.* We are your linguistic nightmare, your linguistic aberration, your linguistic *mestisaje*, the subject of your *burla*. Because we speak with tongues of fire we are culturally crucified. Racially, culturally, and linguistically *somos huérfanos* — we speak an orphan tongue.

Chicanas who grew up speaking Chicano Spanish have internalized the belief that we speak poor Spanish. It is illegitimate, a bastard language. And because we internalize how our language has been used against us by the dominant culture, we use our language differences against each other.

Chicana feminists often skirt around each other with suspicion and hesitation. For the longest time I couldn't figure it out. Then it dawned on me. To be close to another Chicana is like looking into the mirror.

We are afraid of what we'll see there. *Pena.* Shame. Low estimation of self. In childhood we are told that our language is wrong. Repeated attacks on our native tongue diminish our sense of self. The attacks continue throughout our lives.

Chicanas feel uncomfortable talking in Spanish to Latinas, afraid of their censure. Their language was not outlawed in their countries. They had a whole lifetime of being immersed in their native tongue; generations, centuries in which Spanish was a first language, taught in school, heard on radio and TV, and read in the newspaper.

If a person, Chicana or Latina, has a low estimation of my native tongue, she also has a low estimation of me. Often with *mexicanas y latinas* we'll speak English as a neutral language. Even among Chicanas we tend to speak English at parties or conferences. Yet, at the same time, we're afraid the other will think we're *agringadas* because we don't speak Chicano Spanish. We oppress each other trying to out-Chicano each other, vying to be the "real" Chicanas, to speak like Chicanos. There is no one Chicano language just as there is no one Chicano experience. A monolingual Chicana whose first language is English or Spanish is just as much a Chicana as one who speaks several variants of Spanish. A Chicana from Michigan or Chicago or Detroit is just as much a Chicana as one from the Southwest. Chicano Spanish is as diverse linguistically as it is regionally.

By the end of this century, Spanish speakers will comprise the biggest minority group in the U.S., a country where students in high schools and colleges are encouraged to take French classes because French is considered more "cultured." But for a language to remain alive it must be used.[6] By the end of this century English, and not Spanish, will be the mother tongue of most Chicanos and Latinos.

So, if you want to really hurt me, talk badly about my language. Ethnic identity is twin skin to linguistic identity — I am my language. Until I can take pride in my language, I cannot take pride in myself. Until I can accept as legitimate Chicano Texas Spanish, Tex-Mex, and all the other languages I speak, I cannot accept the legitimacy of myself. Until I am free to write bilingually and to switch codes without having always to translate, while I still have to speak English or Spanish when I would rather speak Spanglish, and as long as I have to accommodate the English speakers rather than having them accommodate me, my tongue will be illegitimate.

I will no longer be made to feel ashamed of existing. I will have my voice: Indian, Spanish, white. I will have my serpent's tongue — my woman's voice, my sexual voice, my poet's voice. I will overcome the tradition of silence.

My fingers
move sly against your palm
Like women everywhere, we speak in code . . .
— Melanie Kaye/Kantrowitz[7]

"Vistas," corridos, y comida: My Native Tongue

In the 1960s, I read my first Chicano novel. It was *City of Night* by John Rechy, a gay Texan, son of a Scottish father and a Mexican mother. For days I walked around in stunned amazement that a Chicano could write and could get published. When I read *I Am Joaquín,*[8] I was surprised to see a bilingual book by a Chicano in print. When I saw poetry written in Tex-Mex for the first time, a feeling of pure joy flashed through me. I felt like we really existed as a people. In 1971, when I started teaching High School English to Chicano students, I tried to supplement the required texts with works by Chicanos, only to be reprimanded and forbidden to do so by the principal. He claimed that I was supposed to teach "American" and English literature. At the risk of being fired, I swore my students to secrecy and slipped in Chicano short stories, poems, a play. In graduate school, while working toward a Ph.D., I had to "argue" with one advisor after the other, semester after semester, before I was allowed to make Chicano literature an area of focus.

Even before I read books by Chicanos or Mexicans, it was the Mexican movies I saw at the drive-in — the Thursday night special of $1.00 a carload — that gave me a sense of belonging. *"Vámonos a las vistas,"* my mother would call out and we'd all — grandmother, brothers, sister, and cousins — squeeze into the car. We'd wolf down cheese and bologna white bread sandwiches while watching Pedro Infante in melodramatic tearjerkers like *Nosotros los pobres,* the first "real" Mexican movie (that was not an imitation of European movies). I remember seeing *Cuando los hijos se van* and surmising that all Mexican movies played up the love a mother has for her children and what ungrateful sons and daughters suffer when they are not devoted to their mothers. I remember the singing-type "westerns" of Jorge Negrete and Miquel Aceves Mejía. When watching Mexican movies, I felt a sense of homecoming as well as alienation. People who were to amount to something didn't go to Mexican movies, or *bailes* or tune their radios to *bolero, rancherita,* and *corrido* music.

The whole time I was growing up, there was *norteño* music sometimes called North Mexican border music, or Tex-Mex music, or Chicano music, or *cantina* (bar) music. I grew up listening to *conjuntos,* three- or four-piece bands made up of folk musicians playing guitar, *bajo sexto,* drums and button accordion, which Chicanos had borrowed from the German immigrants who had come to Central Texas and Mexico to farm and build breweries. In the Rio Grande Valley, Steve Jordan and Little Joe Hernández were popular, and Flaco Jiménez was the accordian king. The rhythms of Tex-Mex music are those of the polka, also adapted from the Germans, who in turn had borrowed the polka from the Czechs and Bohemians.

I remember the hot, sultry evenings when *corridos* — songs of love and death on the Texas-Mexican borderlands — reverberated out of cheap amplifiers from the local *cantinas* and wafted in through my bedroom window.

Corridos first became widely used along the South Texas/Mexican border during the early conflict between Chicanos and Anglos. The *corridos* are usually about Mexican heroes who do valiant deeds against the Anglo oppressors. Pancho Villa's song, *"La cucaracha,"* is the most famous one. *Corridos* of John F. Kennedy and his death are still very popular in the Valley. Older Chicanos remember Lydia Mendoza, one of the great border *corrido* singers who was called *la Gloria de Tejas.* Her *"El tango negro,"* sung during the Great Depression, made her a singer of the people. The everpresent *corridos* narrated one hundred years of border history, bringing news of events as well as entertaining. These folk musicians and folk songs are our chief cultural mythmakers, and they made our hard lives seem bearable.

I grew up feeling ambivalent about our music. Country-western and rock-and-roll had more status. In the fifties and sixties, for the slightly educated and *agringado* Chicanos, there existed a sense of shame at being caught listening to our music. Yet I couldn't stop my feet from thumping to the music, could not stop humming the words, nor hide from myself the exhilaration I felt when I heard it.

There are more subtle ways that we internalize identification, especially in the forms of images and emotions. For me food and certain smells are tied to my identity, to my homeland. Woodsmoke curling up to an immense blue sky; woodsmoke perfuming my grandmother's clothes, her skin. The stench of cow manure and the yellow patches on the ground; the crack of a .22 rifle and the reek of cordite. Homemade white cheese sizzling in a pan, melting inside a folded *tortilla.* My sister Hilda's hot, spicy *menudo, chile colorado* making it deep red, pieces of *panza* and hominy floating on top. My brother Carito barbequing *fajitas* in the backyard. Even now and three thousand miles away, I can see my mother spicing the ground beef, pork, and venison with *chile.* My mouth salivates at the thought of the hot steaming *tamales* I would be eating if I were home.

Si le preguntas a mi mamá, "¿Qué eres?"

> Identity is the essential core of who
> we are as individuals, the conscious
> experience of the self inside.
>
> — Kaufman[9]

Nosotros los Chicanos straddle the borderlands. On one side of us, we are constantly exposed to the Spanish of the Mexicans, on the other side we hear the Anglos' incessant clamoring so that we forget our language. Among ourselves we don't say *nosotros los americanos, o nosotros los españoles, o nosotros los hispanos.* We say *nosotros los mexicanos* (by *mexicanos* we do not mean citizens of Mexico; we do not mean a national identity, but a racial one). We distinguish between *mexicanos del otro lado* and *mexicanos de este lado.* Deep in our hearts we believe that being Mexican has nothing to do with which country one lives in. Being Mexican is a state of soul — not one of mind, not one of citizenship. Neither eagle nor serpent, but both. And like the ocean, neither animal respects borders.

Dime con quien andas y te diré quien eres.
(Tell me who your friends are and I'll tell you who you are.)

— Mexican saying

*Si le preguntas a mi mamá, "¿Qué eres?" te dirá, "Soy mexicana." My brothers and sister say the same. I sometimes will answer "soy mexicana" and at others will say "soy Chicana" o "soy tejana." But I identified as "Raza" before I ever identified as "mexicana" or "Chicana."

As a culture, we call ourselves Spanish when referring to ourselves as a linguistic group and when copping out. It is then that we forget our predominant Indian genes. We are seventy to eighty percent Indian.[10] We call ourselves Hispanic[11] or Spanish-American or Latin American or Latin when linking ourselves to other Spanish-speaking peoples of the Western hemisphere and when copping out. We call ourselves Mexican-American[12] to signify we are neither Mexican nor American, but more the noun "American" than the adjective "Mexican" (and when copping out).

Chicanos and other people of color suffer economically for not acculturating. This voluntary (yet forced) alienation makes for psychological conflict, a kind of dual identity — we don't identify with the Anglo-American cultural values and we don't totally identify with the Mexican cultural values. We are a synergy of two cultures with various degrees of Mexicanness or Angloness. I have so internalized the borderland conflict that sometimes I feel like one cancels out the other and we are zero, nothing, no one. *A veces no soy nada ni nadie. Pero hasta cuando no lo soy, lo soy.*

When not copping out, when we know we are more than nothing, we call ourselves Mexican, referring to race and ancestry; *mestizo* when affirming both our Indian and Spanish (but we hardly ever own our black ancestry); Chicano when referring to a politically aware people born and/or raised in the U.S.; *Raza* when referring to Chicanos; *tejanos* when we are Chicanos from Texas.

Chicanos did not know we were a people until 1965 when Cesar Chavez and the farmworkers united and *I Am Joaquín* was published and *la Raza Unida* party was formed in Texas. With that recognition, we became a distinct people. Something momentous happened to the Chicano soul — we became aware of our reality and acquired a name and a language (Chicano Spanish) that reflected that reality. Now that we had a name, some of the fragmented pieces began to fall together — who we were, what we were, how we had evolved. We began to get glimpses of what we might eventually become.

Yet the struggle of identities continues, the struggle of borders is our reality still. One day the inner struggle will cease and a true integration take place. In the meantime, *tenémos que hacer la lucha. ¿Quién está protegiendo los ranchos de mi gente? ¿Quién está tratando de cerrar la fisura entre la india y el blanco en nuestra sangre? El Chicano, si, el Chicano que anda como un ladrón en su propia casa.*

Los Chicanos, how patient we seem, how very patient. There is the quiet of the Indian about us.[13] We know how to survive. When other races have given up their tongue, we've kept ours. We know what it is to live under the hammer blow of the dominant *norteamericano* culture. But more than we count the blows, we count the days the weeks the years the centuries the eons until the white laws and commerce and customs will rot in the deserts they've created, lie bleached. *Humildes* yet proud, *quietos* yet wild, *nosotros los mexicanos-Chicanos* will walk by the crumbling ashes as we go about our business. Stubborn, persevering, impenetrable as stone, yet possessing a malleability that renders us unbreakable, we, the *mestizas* and *mestizos,* will remain.

Notes

1. Ray Gwyn Smith, *Moorland Is Cold Country,* unpublished book.
2. Irene Klepfisz, "*Di rayze aheym*/The Journey Home," in *The Tribe of Dina: A Jewish Women's Anthology.* Melanie Kaye/Kantrowitz and Irena Klepfisz, eds. (Montpelier, VT: Sinister Wisdom Books, 1986), 49.
3. R. C. Ortega, *Dialectologia Del Barrio,* trans. Hortencia S. Alwan (Los Angeles, CA: R. C. Ortega Publisher & Bookseller, 1977), 132.
4. Eduardo Hernandéz-Chávez, Andrew D. Cohen, and Anthony F. Beltramo, *El Lenguaje de los Chicanos: Regional and Social Characteristics of Language Used by Mexican Americans* (Arlington, VA: Center for Applied Linguistics, 1975), 39.
5. Hernandéz-Chávez, xvii.
6. Irena Klepfisz, "Secular Jewish Identity: Yidishkayt in America," in *The Tribe of Dina,* Kaye/Kantrowitz and Klepfisz, eds., 43.
7. Melanie Kaye/Kantrowitz, "Sign," in *We Speak in Code: Poems and Other Writings* (Pittsburgh, PA: Motheroot Publications, Inc., 1980), 85.
8. Rodolfo Gonzales, *I Am Joaquin / Yo Soy Joaquin* (New York, NY: Bantam Books, 1972). It was first published in 1967.
9. Gershen Kaufman, *Shame: The Power of Caring* (Cambridge, MA: Schenkman Books, Inc., 1980), 68.
10. John R. Chávez, *The Lost Land: The Chicano Images of the Southwest* (Albuquerque, NM: University of New Mexico Press, 1984), 88–90.
11. "Hispanic" is derived from *Hispanis (España,* a name given to the Iberian Peninsula in ancient times when it was a part of the Roman Empire) and is a term designated by the U.S. government to make it easier to handle us on paper.
12. The Treaty of Guadalupe Hidalgo created the Mexican-American in 1848.
13. Anglos, in order to alleviate their guilt for dispossessing the Chicano, stressed the Spanish part of us and perpetrated the myth of the Spanish Southwest. We have accepted the fiction that we are Hispanic, that is Spanish, in order to accommodate ourselves to the dominant culture and its abhorrence of Indians. Chávez, 88–91.

Classroom Activities

Anzaldúa suggests that there are many languages that Chicanos speak; she lists them as follows:

1. Standard English

2. Working class and slang English

3. Standard Spanish

4. Standard Mexican Spanish

5. North Mexican Spanish dialect

6. Chicano Spanish (Texas, New Mexico, Arizona, and California have regional variations)

7. Tex-Mex

8. *Pachuco* (called *caló*)

Like Anzaldúa, students can also list the languages they speak and write as well as discuss how language usage may change depending on such variables as audience, purpose, and occasion. We as teachers might use Anzaldúa's work to help us think about what it means to "speak American"; furthermore, what does it mean for our students? Do these definitions continue to change in relation to cultural shifts?

Thinking about Teaching

The cultural conflicts between students, and between teachers and students, often mirror the actual problems in our communities — and sometimes the difficulties seem insurmountable. Yet Anzaldúa's work offers a vision of how change might be enacted. With other teachers, you may wish to read and discuss the issues Anzaldúa presents in *Borderlands / La Frontera,* including how language is implicated in the formation of identity and culture. How do Anzaldúa's ideas figure in your teaching? What are the social and political implications for basic writing and ESL courses, at your school and across the country?

Nobody Mean More to Me Than You[1] and the Future Life of Willie Jordan

June Jordan

For the late writer and teacher June Jordan, language and literacy issues remained inseparable from social justice work. In the following essay, first published in her collection On Call: Political Essays *(1985), Jordan chronicles her experiences with teaching Black English to undergraduates at SUNY–Stony Brook. Intertwined with Jordan's narrative is the story of her student Willie Jordan, who struggles with events surrounding the murder of his brother by New York City police officers. Throughout the essay, Jordan intersperses examples of student writing, such as the "Guidelines to Black English" on which her class collaborated, and Willie Jordan's end-of-semester essay on "racism, poverty, and the abuse of power." Noting that "Willie's writing needed the kind of improvement only intense practice will yield," Jordan looked forward "to see[ing] what happened when he could catch up with himself, entirely, and talk back to the world." The story of Willie's progress — as well as the stories of the writing processes of Jordan's students in the Black English course as they struggled with questions of audience and purpose — make for compelling reading and pose many questions about the political and cultural implications of language.*

Black English is not exactly a linguistic buffalo; as children, most of the thirty-five million Afro-Americans living here depend on this language for our discovery of the world. But then we approach our maturity inside a larger social body that will not support our efforts to become anything other than the clones of those who are neither our mothers nor our fathers. We begin to grow up in a house where every true mirror shows us the face of somebody who does not belong there, whose walk and whose talk will never look or sound "right," because that house was meant to shelter a family that is alien and hostile to us. As we learn our way around this environment, either we hide our original word habits, or we completely surrender our own voice, hoping to please those who will never respect anyone different from themselves: Black English is not exactly a linguistic buffalo, but we should understand its status as an endangered species, as a perishing, irreplaceable system of community intelligence, or we should expect its extinction, and, along with that, the extinguishing of much that constitutes our own proud, and singular identity.

What we casually call "English," less and less defers to England and its "gentlemen." "English" is no longer a specific matter of geography or an element of class privilege; more than thirty-three countries use this tool as a means of "intranational communication."[2] Countries as disparate as Zimbabwe and Malaysia, or Israel and Uganda, use it as their non-native currency of convenience. Obviously, this tool, this "English," cannot function inside thirty-three discrete societies on the basis of rules and values absolutely determined somewhere else, in a thirty-fourth other country, for example.

In addition to that staggering congeries of non-native users of English, there are five countries, or 333,746,000 people, for whom this thing called "English" serves as a native tongue.[3] Approximately 10 percent of these native speakers of "English" are Afro-American citizens of the U.S.A. I cite these numbers and varieties of human beings dependent on "English" in order, quickly, to suggest how strange and how tenuous is any concept of "Standard English." Obviously, numerous forms of English now operate inside a natural, an uncontrollable, continuum of development. I would suppose "the standard" for English in Malaysia is not the same as "the standard" in Zimbabwe. I know that standard forms of English for Black people in this country do not copy that of whites. And, in fact, the structural differences between these two kinds of English have intensified, becoming more Black, or less white, despite the expected homogenizing effects of television[4] and other mass media.

Nonetheless, white standards of English persist, supreme and unquestioned, in these United States. Despite our multi-lingual population, and despite the deepening Black and white cleavage within that conglomerate, white standards control our official and popular judgments of verbal proficiency and correct, or incorrect, language skills, including speech. In contrast to India, where at least fourteen languages co-exist as legitimate Indian languages, in contrast to Nicaragua, where all citizens are legally entitled to formal school instruction in their regional or tribal languages, compulsory education in America compels accommodation to exclusively white forms of "English." White English, in America, is "Standard English."

This story begins two years ago. I was teaching a new course, "In Search of the Invisible Black Woman," and my rather large class seemed evenly divided between young Black women and men. Five or six white students also sat in attendance. With unexpected speed and enthusiasm we had moved through historical narratives of the nineteenth century to literature by and about Black women, in the twentieth. I had assigned the first forty pages of Alice Walker's *The Color Purple,* and I came, eagerly, to class that morning:

"So!" I exclaimed, aloud. "What did you think? How did you like it?"

The students studied their hands, or the floor. There was no response. The tense, resistant feeling in the room fairly astounded me.

At last, one student, a young woman still not meeting my eyes, muttered something in my direction:

"What did you say?" I prompted her.

"Why she have them talk so funny. It don't sound right."

"You mean the language?"

Another student lifted his head: "It don't look right, neither. I couldn't hardly read it."

At this, several students dumped on the book. Just about unanimously, their criticisms targeted the language. I listened to what they wanted to say and silently marvelled at the similarities between their casual speech patterns and Alice Walker's written version of Black English.

But I decided against pointing to these identical traits of syntax; I wanted not to make them self-conscious about their own spoken language — not while they clearly felt it was "wrong." Instead I decided to swallow my astonishment. Here was a negative Black reaction to a prize-winning accomplishment of Black literature that white readers across the country had selected as a best seller. Black rejection was aimed at the one irreducibly Black element of Walker's work: the language — Celie's Black English. I wrote the opening lines of *The Color Purple* on the blackboard and asked the students to help me translate these sentences into Standard English:

> *You better not never tell nobody but God. It'd kill your mammy.*
> Dear God,
>   I am fourteen years old. I have always been a good girl. Maybe you can give me a sign letting me know what is happening to me.
>   Last spring after Little Lucious come I heard them fussing. He was pulling on her arm. She say it too soon, Fonso. I aint well. Finally he leave her alone. A week go by, he pulling on her arm again. She say, Naw, I ain't gonna. Can't you see I'm already half dead, an all of the children.[5]

Our process of translation exploded with hilarity and even hysterical, shocked laughter: The Black writer, Alice Walker, knew what she was doing! If rudimentary criteria for good fiction include the manipulation of language so that the syntax and diction of sentences will tell you the identity of speakers, the probable age and sex and class of speakers, and even the locale — urban/rural/southern/western — then Walker had written, perfectly. This is the translation into Standard English that our class produced:

> *Absolutely, one should never confide in anybody besides God. Your secrets could prove devastating to your mother.*
> Dear God,
>   I am fourteen years old. I have always been good. But now, could you help me to understand what is happening to me?
>   Last spring, after my little brother, Lucious, was born, I heard my parents fighting. My father kept pulling at my mother's arm. But she told him, "It's too soon for sex, Alfonso. I am still not feeling well." Finally, my father left her alone. A week went by, and then he began bothering my mother, again: Pulling her arm. She told him, "No, I won't! Can't you see I'm already exhausted from all of these children?"

(Our favorite line was "It's too soon for sex, Alfonso.")

Once we could stop laughing, once we could stop our exponentially wild improvisations on the theme of Translated Black English, the students pushed me to explain their own negative first reactions to their spoken language on the printed page. I thought it was probably akin to the shock of seeing yourself in a photograph for the first time. Most of the students had never before seen a written facsimile of the way they talk. None of the students had ever learned how to read and write their own verbal system of communication: Black English. Alternatively, this fact began to baffle or else bemuse and then infuriate my students. Why not? Was it too late? Could they learn how to do it, now? And, ultimately, the final test question, the one testing my sincerity: Could I teach them? Because I had never taught anyone Black English and, as far as I knew, no one, anywhere in the United States, had ever offered such a course, the best I could say was "I'll try."

He looked like a wrestler.

He sat dead center in the packed room and, every time our eyes met, he quickly nodded his head as though anxious to reassure, and encourage, me.

Shirt, with strikingly broad shoulders and long arms, he spoke with a surprisingly high, soft voice that matched the soft bright movement of his eyes. His name was Willie Jordan. He would have seemed even more unlikely in the context of Contemporary Women's Poetry, except that ten or twelve other Black men were taking the course, as well. Still, Willie was conspicuous. His extreme fitness, the muscular density of his presence underscored the riveted, gentle attention that he gave to anything anyone said. Generally, he did not join the loud and rowdy dialogue flying back and forth, but there could be no doubt about his interest in our discussions. And, when he stood to present an argument he'd prepared, overnight, that nervous smile of his vanished and an irregular stammering replaced it, as he spoke with visceral sincerity, word by word.

That was how I met Willie Jordan. It was in between "In Search of the Invisible Black Woman" and "The Art of Black English." I was waiting for Departmental approval and I supposed that Willie might be, so to speak, killing time until he, too, could study Black English. But Willie really did want to explore Contemporary Women's poetry and, to that end, volunteered for extra research and never missed a class.

Towards the end of that semester, Willie approached me for an independent study project on South Africa. It would commence the next semester. I thought Willie's writing needed the kind of improvement only intense practice will yield. I knew his intelligence was outstanding. But he'd wholeheartedly opted for "Standard English" at a rather late age, and the results were stilted and frequently polysyllabic, simply for the sake of having more syllables. Willie's unnatural formality of language seemed to me consistent with the formality of his research into South African apartheid. As he projected his studies, he would have little time, indeed, for newspapers. Instead, more than 90 percent of his research would mean saturation in strictly historical, if not archival, material. I was certainly interested. It would be tricky to guide him into a more confident and spontaneous relationship both with language and apartheid. It was going to be wonderful to see what happened when he could catch up with himself, entirely, and talk back to the world.

September, 1984: Breezy fall weather and much excitement! My class, "The Art of Black English," was full to the limit of the fire laws. And, in Independent Study, Willie Jordan showed up, weekly, fifteen minutes early for each of our sessions. I was pretty happy to be teaching, altogether!

I remember an early class when a young brother, replete with his ever present pork-pie hat, raised his hand and then told us that most of what he'd heard was "all right" except it was "too clean." "The brothers on the street," he continued, "they mix it up more. Like 'fuck' and 'motherfuck.' Or like 'shit.'" He waited. I waited. Then all of us laughed a good while, and we got into a brawl about "correct" and "realistic" Black English that led to Rule 1.

Rule 1: *Black English is about a whole lot more than mothafuckin.*

As a criterion, we decided, "realistic" could take you anywhere you want to go. Artful places. Angry places. Eloquent and sweettalkin places. Polemical places. Church. And the local Bar & Grill. We were checking out a language, not a mood or a scene or one guy's forgettable mouthing off.

It was hard. For most of the students, learning Black English required a fallback to patterns and rhythms of speech that many of their parents had beaten out of them. I mean *beaten.* And, in a majority of cases, correct Black English could be achieved only by striving for *incorrect* Standard English, something they were still pushing at, quite uncertainly. This state of affairs led to Rule 2.

Rule 2: *If it's wrong in Standard English it's probably right in Black English, or, at least, you're hot.*

It was hard. Roommates and family members ridiculed their studies, or remained incredulous, "You *studying* that shit? At school?" But we were beginning to feel the companionship of pioneers. And we decided that we needed another rule that would establish each one of us as equally important to our success. This was Rule 3.

Rule 3: *If it don't sound like something that come out somebody mouth then it don't sound right. If it don't sound right then it ain't hardly right. Period.*

This rule produced two weeks of compositions in which the students agonizingly tried to spell the sound of the Black English sentence they wanted to convey. But Black English is, pre-eminently, an oral/spoken means of communication. *And spelling don't talk.* So we needed Rule 4.

Rule 4: *Forget about the spelling. Let the syntax carry you.*

Once we arrived at Rule 4 we started by fly because syntax, the structure of an idea, leads you to the worldview of the speaker and reveals her values. The syntax of a sentence equals the structure of your consciousness. If we insisted that the language of Black English adheres to a distinctive Black syntax, then we were postulating a profound difference between white and Black people, *per se*. Was it a difference to prize or to obliterate?

There are three qualities of Black English — the presence of life, voice, and clarity — that testify to a distinctive Black value system that we became excited about and self-consciously tried to maintain.

1. Black English has been produced by a pre-technocratic, if not anti-technological, culture. More, our culture has been constantly threatened by annihilation or, at least, the swallowed blurring of assimilation. Therefore, our language is a system constructed by people constantly needing to insist that we exist, that we are present. Our language devolves from a culture that abhors all abstraction, or anything tending to obscure or delete the fact of the human being who is here and now/the truth of the person who is speaking or listening. Consequently, *there is no passive voice construction possible in Black English*. For example, you cannot say, "Black English is being eliminated." You must say, instead, "White people eliminating Black English." The assumption of the presence of life governs all of Black English. Therefore, overwhelmingly, *all action takes place in the language of the present indicative*. And every sentence assumes the living and active participation of at least two human beings, the speaker and the listener.

2. A primary consequence of the person-centered values of Black English is the delivery of voice. If you speak or write Black English, your ideas will necessarily possess that otherwise elusive attribute, *voice*.

3. One main benefit following from the person-centered values of Black English is that of *clarity*. If your idea, you sentence, assumes the presence of at least two living and active people, you will make it understandable because the motivation behind every sentence is the wish to say something real to somebody real.

As the weeks piled up, translation from Standard English into Black English or vice versa occupied a hefty part of our course work.

Standard English (hereafter S.E.): "In considering the idea of studying Black English those questioned suggested — "

(What's the subject? Where's the person? Is anybody alive in there, in that idea?)

Black English (hereafter B.E.): "I been asking people what you think about somebody studying Black English and they answer me like this:"

But there were interesting limits. You cannot "translate" instances of Standard English preoccupied with abstraction or with nothing/nobody evidently alive, into Black English. That would warp the language into uses antithetical to the guiding perspective of its community of users. Rather you must first change those Standard English sentences, themselves, into ideas consistent with the person-centered assumptions of Black English.

Guidelines for Black English

1. Minimal number of words for every idea: This is the source for the aphoristic and/or poetic force of the language; eliminate every possible word.

2. Clarity: If the sentence is not clear it's not Black English.

3. Eliminate use of the verb *to be* whenever possible. This leads to the deployment of more descriptive and therefore, more precise verbs.

4. Use *be* or *been* only when you want to describe a chronic, ongoing state of things.

    He *be* at the office, by 9. (He is always at the office by 9.)
    He *been* with her since forever.

5. Zero copula: Always eliminate the verb to be whenever it would combine with another verb, in Standard English.

    S.E.: She is going out with him.
    B.E.: She going out with him.

6. Eliminate *do* as in:

    S.E.: What do you think? What do you want?
    B.E.: What you think? What you want?

    Rules number 3, 4, 5, and 6 provide for the use of the minimal number of verbs per idea and, therefore, greater accuracy in the choice of verb.

7. In general, if you wish to say something really positive, try to formulate the idea using emphatic negative structure.

    S.E.: He's fabulous.
    B.E.: He bad.

8. Use double or triple negatives for dramatic emphasis.

    S.E.: Tina Turner sings out of this world.
    B.E.: Ain nobody sing like Tina.

9. Never use the *–ed* suffix to indicate the past tense of a verb.

    S.E.: She closed the door.
    B.E.: She close the door. Or, she have close the door.

10. Regardless of intentional verb time, only use the third person singular, present indicative, for use of the verb *to have*, as an auxiliary.

> S.E.: He had his wallet then he lost it.
> B.E.: He have him wallet then he lose it.
> S.E.: He had seen that movie.
> B.E.: We seen that movie. Or, we have see that movie.

11. Observe a minimal inflection of verbs. Particularly, never change from the first person singular forms to the third person singular.

> S.E.: Present Tense Forms: He goes to the store.
> B.E.: He go to the store.
> S.E.: Past Tense Forms: He went to the store.
> B.E.: He go to the store. Or, he gone to the store. Or, he been to the store.

12. The possessive case scarcely ever appears in Black English. Never use an apostrophe ('s) construction. If you wander into a possessive case component of an idea, then keep logically consistent: *ours, his, theirs, mines*. But, most likely, if you bump into such a component, you have wandered outside the underlying worldview of Black English.

> S.E.: He will take their car tomorrow.
> B.E.: He taking they car tomorrow.

13. Plurality: Logical consistency, continued: If the modifier indicates plurality then the noun remains in the singular case.

> S.E.: He ate twelve doughnuts.
> B.E.: He eat twelve doughnut.
> S.E.: She has many books.
> B.E.: She have many book.

14. Listen for, or invent, special Black English forms of the past tense, such as "He losted it. That what she felted." If they are clear and readily understood, then use them.

15. Do not hesitate to play with words, sometimes inventing them: e.g. "astropotomous" means huge like a hippo plus astronomical and, therefore, signifies real big.

16. In Black English, unless you keenly want to underscore the past tense nature of an action, stay in the present tense and rely on the overall context of your ideas for the conveyance of time and sequence.

17. Never use the suffix *–ly* form of an adverb in Black English.

> S.E.: The rain came down rather quickly.
> B.E.: The rain come down pretty quick.

18. Never use the indefinite article *an* in Black English.

> S.E.: He wanted to ride an elephant.
> B.E.: He want to ride him a elephant.

19. Invariant syntax: in correct Black English it is possible to formulate an imperative, an interrogative, and a simple declarative idea with the same syntax:

> B.E.: You going to the store?
> You going to the store.
> You going to the store!

Where was Willie Jordan? We'd reach the mid-term of the semester. Students had formulated Black English guidelines, by consensus, and they were now writing with remarkable beauty, purpose, and enjoyment:

I ain hardly speakin for everybody but myself so understan that."
— Kim Parks

Samples from student writings:

"Janie have a great big ole hole inside her. Tea Cake the only thing that fit that hole . . .
"That pear tree beautiful to Janie, especial when bees fiddlin with the blossomin pear there growin large and lovely. But personal speakin, the love she get from starin at that tree ain the love what starin back at her in them relationship." (Monica Morris)

"Love is a big theme in, *They Eye Was Watching God.* Love show people new corners inside theyself. It pull out good stuff and stuff back bad stuff . . . Joe worship the doing uh his own hand and need other people to worship him too. But he ain't think about Janie that she a person and ought to live like anybody common do. Queen life not for Janie." (Monica Morris)

"In both life and writin, Black womens have varietous experience of love that be cold like a iceberg or fiery like a inferno. Passion got for the other partner involve, man or woman, seem as shallow, ankle-deep water or the most profoundest abyss." (Constance Evans)
"Family love another bond that ain't never break under no pressure." (Constance Evans)

"You know it really cold/When the friend you/Always get out the fire/Act like they don't know you/When you in the heat." (Constance Evans)

"Big classroom discussion bout love at this time. I never take no class where us have any long arguin for and against for two or three day. New to me and great. I find the class time talkin a million time more interestin than detail bout the book." (Kathy Esseks)

As these examples suggest, Black English no longer limited the students, in any way. In fact, one of them, Philip Garfield, would shortly "translate" a pivotal scene from Ibsen's *Doll House,* as his final term paper.

Nora: I didn't gived no shit. I thinked you a asshole back then, too, you make it so hard for me save mines husband life.

Krogstad: Girl, it clear you ain't any idea what you done. You dont exact what I once done, and I losed my reputation over it.

Nora: You asks me believe you once act brave save you wife life?

Krogstad: Law care less why you done it.

Nora: Law must suck.

Krogstad: Suck or no, if I wants, judge screw you wid dis paper.

Nora: No way, man. (Philip Garfield)

But where was Willie? Compulsively punctual, and always thoroughly prepared with neatly typed compositions, he had disappeared. He failed to show up for our regularly scheduled conference, and I received neither a note nor a phone call of explanation. A whole week went by. I wondered if Willie had finally been captured by the extremely current happenings in South Africa: passage of a new constitution that did not enfranchise the Black majority, and militant Black South African reaction to that affront. I wondered if he'd been hurt, somewhere. I wondered if the serious workload of weekly readings and writings had overwhelmed him and changed his mind about independent study. Where was Willie Jordan?

One week after the first conference that Willie missed, he called: "Hello, Professor Jordan? This is Willie. I'm sorry I wasn't there last week. But something has come up and I'm pretty upset. I'm sorry but I really can't deal right now."

I asked Willie to drop by my office and just let me see that he was okay. He agreed to do that. When I saw him I knew something hideous had happened. Something had hurt him and scared him to the marrow. He was all agitated and stammering and terse and incoherent. At last, his sadly jumbled account let me surmise, as follows: Brooklyn police had murdered his unarmed, twenty-five-year-old brother, Reggie Jordan. Neither Willie nor his elderly parents knew what to do about it. Nobody from the press was interested. His folks had no money. Police ran his family around and around, to no point. And Reggie was really dead. And Willie wanted to fight, but he felt helpless.

With Willie's permission I began to try to secure legal counsel for the Jordan family. Unfortunately Black victims of police violence are truly numerous while the resources available to prosecute their killers are truly scarce. A friend of mine at the Center for Constitutional Rights estimated that just the preparatory costs for bring the cops into court normally approaches $180,000. Unless the execution of Reggie Jordan became a major community cause for organizing, and protest, his murder would simply become a statistical item.

Again, with Willie's permission, I contacted every newspaper and media person I could think of. But the William Bastone feature article in *The Village Voice* was the only result from that canvassing.

Again, with Willie's permission, I presented the case to my class in Black English. We had talked about the politics of language. We had talked about love and sex and child abuse and men and women. But the murder of Reggie Jordan broke like a hurricane across the room.

There are few "issues" as endemic to Black Life as police violence. Most of the students knew and respected and liked Jordan. Many of them were from the very neighborhood where the murder had occurred. All of the students had known somebody close to them who had been killed by police, or had known frightening moments of gratuitous confrontation with the cops. They wanted to do everything at once to avenge death. Number One: They decided to compose personal statements of condolence to Willie Jordan and his family written in Black English. Number Two: They decided to compose individual messages to the police, in Black English. These should be prefaced by an explanatory paragraph composed by the entire group. Number Three: These individual messages, with their lead paragraph, should be sent to *Newsday*.

The morning after we agreed on these objectives, one of the young women students appeared with an unidentified visitor, who sat through the class, smiling in a peculiar, comfortable way.

Now we had to make more tactical decisions. Because we wanted the messages published, and because we thought it imperative that our outrage be known by the police, the tactical question was this: Should the opening, group paragraph be written in Black English or Standard English?

I have seldom been privy to a discussion with so much heart at the dead heat of it. I will never forget the eloquence, the sudden haltings of speech, the fierce struggle against tears, the furious throwaway, and useless explosions that this question elicited.

That one question contained several others, each of them extraordinarily painful to even contemplate. How best to serve the memory of Reggie Jordan? Should we use the language of the killers — Standard English — in order to make our ideas acceptable to those controlling the killers? But wouldn't what we had to say be rejected, summarily, if we said it in our own language, the language of the victim, Reggie Jordan? But if we sought to express ourselves by abandoning our language wouldn't that mean our suicide on top of Reggie's murder? But if we expressed ourselves in our own language wouldn't that be suicidal to the wish to communicate with those who, evidently, did not give a damn about us/Reggie/police violence in the Black community?

At the end of one of the longest, most difficult hours of my own life, the students voted, unanimously, to preface their individual messages with a paragraph composed in the language of Reggie Jordan. *"At least we don't give up nothing else. At least we stick to the truth: Be who we been. And stay all the way with Reggie."*

It was heartbreaking to proceed, from that point. Everyone in the room realized that our decision in favor of Black English had doomed our writings, even as the distinctive reality of our Black lives always has doomed our efforts to "be who we been" in this country.

I went to the blackboard and took down this paragraph, dictated by the class:

"... You cops!

We the brother and sister of Willie Jordan, a fellow Stony Brook student who the brother of the dead Reggie Jordan. Reggie, like many brother and sister, he a victim of brutal racist police, October 25, 1984. Us appall, fed up, because that another senseless death what occur in our community. This what we feel, this, from our heart, for we ain't stayin' silent no more:"

With the completion of this introduction, nobody said anything. I asked for comments. At this invitation, the unidentified visitor, a young Black man, ceaselessly smiling, raised his hand. He was, it so happens, a rookie cop. He had just joined the force in September and, he said, he thought he should clarify a few things. So he came forward and sprawled easily into a posture of barroom, or fireside, nostalgia:

"See," Officer Charles enlightened us, "Most times when you out on the street and something come down you do one of two things. Over-react or under-react. Now, if you under-react then you can get yourself kilt. And if you over-react then maybe you kill somebody. Fortunately it's about nine times out of ten and you will over-react. So the brother got kilt. And I'm sorry about that, believe me. But what you have to understand is what kilt him: Over-reaction. That's all. Now you talk about Black people and white police but see, now, I'm a cop myself. And (big smile) I'm Black. And just a couple months ago I was on the other side. But see it's the same for me. You a cop, you the ultimate authority: the Ultimate Authority. And you on the street, most of the time you can only do one of two things: over-react or under-react. That's all it is with the brother: Over-reaction. Didn't have nothing to do with race."

That morning Officer Charles had the good fortune to escape without being boiled alive. But barely. And I remember the pride of his smile when I read about the fate of Black policemen and other collaborators, in South Africa. I remember him, and I remember the shock and palpable feeling of shame that filled the room. It was as though that foolish, and deadly, young man had just relieved himself of his foolish, and deadly, explanation, face to face with the grief of Reggie Jordan's father and Reggie Jordan's mother. Class ended quietly. I copied the paragraph from the blackboard, collected the individual messages and left to type them up.

Newsday rejected the piece.

The Village Voice could not find room in their "Letters" section to print the individual messages from the students to the police.

None of the tv news reporters picked up the story.

Nobody raised $180,000 to prosecute the murder of Reggie Jordan.

Reggie Jordan is really dead.

I asked Willie Jordan to write an essay pulling together everything important to him from that semester. He was still deeply beside himself with frustration and amazement and loss. This is what he wrote, un-edited, and in its entirety:

"Throughout the course of this semester I have been researching the effects of oppression and exploitation along racial lines in South Africa and its neighboring countries. I have become aware of South African police brutalization of native Africans beyond the extent of the law, even though the laws themselves are catalyst affliction upon Black men, women and children. Many Africans die each year as a result of the deliberate use of police force to protect the white power structure.

"Social control agents in South Africa, such as policemen, are also used to force compliance among citizens through both overt and covert tactics. It is not uncommon to find bold-faced coercion and cold-blooded killings of Blacks by South African police for undetermined and/or inadequate reasons. Perhaps the truth is that the only reasons for this heinous treatment of Blacks rests in racial differences. We should also understand that what is conveyed through the media is not always accurate and may sometimes be construed as the tip of the iceberg at best.

"I recently received a painful reminder that racism, poverty, and the abuse of power are global problems which are by no means unique to South Africa. On October 25, 1984, at approximately 3:00 p.m. my brother, Mr. Reginald Jordan, was shot and killed by two New York City policemen from the 75th precinct in the East New York section of Brooklyn. His life ended at the age of twenty-five. Even up to this current point in time the Police Department has failed to provide my family, which consists of five brothers, eight sisters, and two parents, with a plausible reason for Reggie's death. Out of the many stories that were given to my family by the Police Department, not one of them seems to hold water. In fact, I honestly believe that the Police Department's assessment of my brother's murder is nothing short of ABSOLUTE BULLSHIT, and thus far no evidence had been produced to alter perception of the situation.

"Furthermore, I believe that one of three cases may have occurred in this incident. First, Reggie's death may have been the desired outcome of the police officer's action, in which case the killing was premeditated. Or, it was a case of mistaken identity, which clarifies the fact that the two officers who killed my brother and their commanding parties are all grossly incompetent. Or, both of the above cases are correct, i.e., Reggie's murderers intended to kill him and the Police Department behaved insubordinately.

"Part of the argument of the officers who shot Reggie was that he had attacked one of them and took his gun. This was their major claim. They also said that only one of them had actually shot Reggie. The facts, however, speak for themselves. According to the Death Certificate and autopsy report, Reggie was shot eight times from point-blank range. The Doctor who performed the autopsy told me himself that two bullets entered the side of my brother's head, four bullets were sprayed into his back, and two bullets struck him in the back of his legs. It is obvious that unnecessary force was used by the police and that it is extremely difficult to shoot someone in his back when he is attacking or approaching you.

"After experiencing a situation like this and researching South Africa I believe that to a large degree, justice may only exist as rhetoric. I find it difficult to talk of true justice when the oppression of my people both at home and abroad attests to the fact that inequality and injustice are serious problems whereby Blacks and Third World people are perpetually short-changed by society. Something has to be done about the way in which this world is set up. Although it is a difficult task, we do have the power to make a change."

> — Willie J. Jordan Jr.
> EGL 487, Section 58, November 14, 1984

It is my privilege to dedicate this book to the future life of Willie J. Jordan Jr.
August 8, 1985

Notes

1. Black English aphorism crafted by Monica Morris, a Junior at S.U.N.Y. at Stony Brook, October 1984.
2. *English Is Spreading, But What Is English?* A presentation by Professor S. N. Sridahr, Dept. of Linguistics, S.U.N.Y. at Stony Brook, April 9, 1985: Dean's Conversation Among the Disciplines.
3. Ibid.
4. *New York Times*, March 15, 1985, Section One, p. 14: Report on study by Linguistics at the University of Pennsylvania.
5. Alice Walker, *The Color Purple* (1982), p. 11, Harcourt Brace, N.Y.

Classroom Activities

Developing writers of all cultural backgrounds can benefit substantially from reading teaching and literacy narratives, especially stories that deal with social justice and struggles with the languages of community and school. In this regard, consider reading "Nobody Mean More to Me Than You and the Future Life of Willie Jordan" with your students. Invite your students to create critical thinking questions for discussion that focus on language, writing, and rhetoric.

Example questions to stimulate students' thinking might include the following: How would you explain this statement: "The syntax of a sentence equals the structure of your consciousness" (Rule 4 in "Guidelines for Black English")? How would you describe the three qualities of Black English that Jordan lists ("the presence of life, voice, and clarity")? What struggles with audience did Jordan's students face, and how did they address those struggles? Who was Jordan's audience for this essay, and what were her purposes for telling these particular stories about her teaching? Give students the opportunity to discuss their questions in small groups and to develop their responses in their journals or in a longer paper. You might also ask students to write a literacy narrative — an essay in which they reflect on their own experiences with language and explore how various communities have shaped the way they speak, write, and read.

Thinking about Teaching

Jordan's essay, first published in the mid-1980s, presents compelling insights into the intersections of teaching writing and issues of social justice. Consider your reading of Jordan's essay as an opportunity to reflect on such issues both locally and globally in your teaching journal — and perhaps in an essay of your own. Jordan's work also can be a catalyst for a group discussion with other teachers. This discussion could be a starting point in considering the implications of education for social justice as it pertains to basic writing programs at the local, regional, or national level. Faculty may have questions or suggestions about how or whether to include social justice content in a writing course. Moreover, a forum for sharing ideas may lead to curricular and institutional changes. Faculty across the curriculum may want to share syllabi and assignments; guest speakers could also be arranged.

Mitigating Barriers to Navajo Students' Success in English Courses

Kay Thurston

Kay Thurston won TETYC's 1998 Best Article Award for this description of "the tremendous barriers to success in colleges and universities" that Navajo students face. She draws on her experiences teaching writing and literature at Navajo Community College, a two-year tribal college in the center of the Navajo, or Diné, nation. Ninety-six percent of the students are Navajo, the majority of whom live in poverty. Thurston does a thorough job of describing the geographic isolation of her students and the rich cultural heritage with which they arrive in the composition classroom. Rather than blaming the victim or the culture for "the high failure rate" experienced by her students, Thurston suggests that we look at more global factors, which she sees as applicable to "students from radically different cultures." Thurston describes in detail five major barriers that her students encounter: "financial difficulty, family obligations, prescriptive attitudes toward Standard American English, instructor/faculty ethnocentrism, and ambivalence toward Western education." Thurston also presents thoughtful solutions that challenge the reader to examine his or her own values and prejudices.

Introduction

Navajos, or the Diné, are one of four hundred Native American tribes currently recognized by the U.S. government. Of the 150,000 people living on the Navajo reservation despite its isolation and intense poverty, many are struggling to retain their traditional ways — their language, spiritual beliefs and ceremonies, and a culture completely unlike that of white, middle-class Americans.

Navajo Community College (NCC), the first tribally controlled college, was built in 1968 by tribal leaders and medicine men on a sacred site between the Chuska Mountains, Tsaile Lake, and Canyon de Chelly in northeastern Arizona. NCC is located in the center of the Navajo Nation, which is, in many ways, like a third-world country, about the size of West Virginia. To buy groceries, NCC staff, faculty, and students make a 60-mile round trip to Chinle, Arizona, a town of seven thousand. To shop at K-Mart, a hardware store, or to see a movie, they make a 180-mile round trip past pine-covered mountains, red-orange Navajo sandstone towering above rugged piñon and juniper, and sheep, cows, and horses scattered among clumps of sage to Gallup, New Mexico.

Of the 550 students who attend NCC's main campus annually, 96 percent are Navajo. NCC's mission is to take these Navajo students, most of whom grew up on the reservation (some in very traditional families, and others in families that have been influenced, to varying degrees, by dominant society), and make them bicultural so that they can function effectively in both the Western and Navajo worlds. NCC succeeds because it focuses on Navajo culture, tradition, and beliefs; it addresses Navajo students' unique needs; and its faculty, knowing that most Navajo dropouts are not academic failures, accept part of the blame for the high Navajo failure and attrition rate. Still, these students face tremendous barriers to success in colleges and universities, and it seems to me that the barriers take five major forms: financial difficulty, family obligations, prescriptive attitudes toward Standard American English, instructor/faculty ethnocentrism, and ambivalence toward Western education.

Financial Difficulty

Probably the number one reason for the high attrition rate of Navajo students is financial. While it would, of course, be incorrect to suggest that every Navajo student struggles financially, the fact is that poverty on the Navajo reservation is so widespread it's the norm. According to the Navajo Nation's 1990 Census Report, only 44.8 percent of those over sixteen are employed in the labor force — for males sixteen and over, the unemployment rate is 30.3 percent. In 1989, the Navajo Nation's median household income was $10,433, and per capita income was $4,106, putting 56.1 percent of the Navajos living on the reservation below the poverty level. Half the homes are without water and electricity — it is disconcerting to see hogans (traditional round dwellings made of wood and earth) without power standing beneath massive systems of power lines strung from the reservation's coal-generating plants to meet energy consumption needs in distant cities in California. Many commuting students live in traditional hogans with earthen floors and can't make it to class after heavy rains that turn their roads into slippery mud. Most cannot call for a missed assignment, either, as 77.5 percent of the homes on the Navajo Nation are without telephone service.

For me, the reality of the students' extreme level of poverty was hammered home recently when I required students to use the college's computers to type their writing assignments. Two weeks later, two students were still turning in handwritten assignments because they had been unable to find one dollar for a disk. To ameliorate students' financial burdens, I allowed some class time each semester for a student services or financial aid representative to counsel students. I also considered the cost of the textbooks I selected, put texts and articles on reserve in the library, and remained flexible about requiring typed assignments. I learned to ask questions and then to make exceptions, for example, for the single parent who has returned to school and is trying to feed four children on food stamps. Though computer and typewriter use may be free, child care is not. To middle-class faculty, this level of poverty may seem inconceivable, but I assure you it is real, and it is a factor with which many, if not most, Navajo students struggle continuously.

Family Obligations

A second serious obstacle the Navajo student faces is the faculty member who doesn't understand or won't acknowledge the importance and time-consuming nature of family responsibilities. Many of us, probably, would raise an eyebrow at a student who tells us that she missed a week of classes because her grandfather had a stroke, but to a traditional Navajo's way of thinking, this problem is not only legitimate but imperative. The student and her family would first take the stroke victim to a diagnostician to determine what healing ceremony (or ceremonies) needed to be performed. If the diagnostician calls for a Lightning Way or Wind Way ceremony, the student's presence will be required for four or five days; if the grandfather should pass on, then for four days, her presence would be required to help her grandfather's spirit travel on to the fifth world. Since most reservations are located far from urban centers and universities, and since most ceremonies last from two to nine days, the student is likely to be out of town for seven to ten days. If her English teacher's absence policy drops students after three or four absences, but the student's family requires her presence for a ceremony that will enable her grandfather to walk again, chances are high that the student will drop the class, especially if the family needs the grandfather out of the nursing home as quickly as possible to care for the livestock that constitute the economic base for the entire extended family.

The family ties of Native American students are usually strong and can never be underestimated. Navajo students, for example, introduce themselves not by telling what they do for work, but by naming their four clans. When, in developmental writing courses, I ask students to write a paragraph describing their best friend, most describe a parent, grandparent, uncle, aunt, brother, sister, or cousin. In the Navajo kinship system, cousins are more akin to brothers and sisters, and aunts and uncles more like mothers and fathers. The Navajo word for paternal uncle, in fact, means "little father," and for maternal aunt, "little mother": these terms reflect the Navajo relatives' assumption of far more responsibility than Anglos for the welfare of their nieces and nephews. Such relationships lend an urgency that an Anglo instructor may not understand to a student's attendance at his niece's Kinaaldá — a female puberty ceremony lasting four days, held when a niece begins menstruation — a family duty that cannot be put off, for example, until spring break. A traditional Navajo student with strong family ties, when forced to choose between honoring a teacher's absence policy and his "little daughter's" entrance into womanhood, will probably choose the latter. Other ceremonies require the participation of the entire community: the Jemez Pueblo people of New Mexico, for example, have feast days and dances, most lasting about a week. For instance, late in November, Jemez Pueblo students attending the University of New Mexico return home for three to five days to pray and fast, clean the Pueblo village, replaster houses, prepare food for the guests, and perform ceremonial dances.

The holidays scheduled at mainstream institutions — Columbus Day, the Fourth of July, President's Day, and Christmas — do not hold special significance for Navajos. Therefore, Anglo instructors follow the lead of Native American instructors who, because they are more likely to understand and respect Native American students' need for family contact and involvement, are generally more flexible with absence policies and more willing to accommodate students with family responsibilities.

Prescriptive Attitude toward Standard American English

A third problem that Navajo students encounter in the English classroom is that an Anglo instructor often has little or no knowledge of Native American language conventions. Such instructors (1) assume in students a level of familiarity with Standard American English (SAE) that a middle class Euro-American would have; (2) are untrained and unaware of dialect or second language difficulties, regarding conventional Indian English as "wrong," and expecting students to "clean up" the English they have spoken and heard their entire lives; and (3) expect students to replace their Navajo English dialect with SAE in fifteen to sixteen weeks.

When 82 percent of the adults on the Navajo reservation speak Navajo, and only 21 percent of the 131,229 Navajos five years and older speak English only, it's unreasonable to expect Navajo students to be as familiar with SAE as Anglo students.[1] Navajo English is quite different from SAE. Let me illustrate with three examples. Navajo students, in general, have difficulty with plural formation, verb tenses, and rhetorical style. In Navajo, animate nouns are made plural not by adding an *"-s"* but by adding a variety of other endings. "Boy," in Navajo, is *ashkii;* "boys" is *ashiike.* No affix is attached to inanimate nouns; instead, the plural is indicated by changes in the verb associated with the noun in question. As a result, Navajo students will write that they have one ball, "two ball," and "many ball scattered about the field." Or "Many of my relative live in Shiprock." Navajo English forms plurals by adding "-*s,*" but also contains words such as "elderlies," "sheeps," "cattles," "firewoods," "mens," "womens," and "childrens." Another example illustrates the special difficulties of bilingual or nonstandard dialect. In Navajo, verb tense is shown by the position of the verb in a sentence, not by a change in its ending. In Navajo English, although the position of the verb does not change, past tense endings are often omitted, as in "I hear him sing yesterday." Irregular verbs pose problems as well — often, after learning to form the regular past tense, students create words like "hurted" and "eated."

Recognition that Native American students are often bilingual and speak a nonstandard American English dialect has led to two strategies at NCC:[2] first, ESL, bilingual, and nonstandard American English speakers, as well as students from historically oral cultural backgrounds require more than one or two semesters to establish and refine college-level writing skills. For this reason, NCC instructors offer three developmental English courses. About 96 percent of the students complete at least one of them before moving on to first-year composition, and many work their way through all three. In the first level are students who cannot write a complete, coherent sentence. The second and third levels of developmental English deal not only with the nuts and bolts of English usage and Western rhetorical styles, but also with problems specific to Navajo and Navajo English speakers. NCC faculty members are in the process of designing a textbook for these classes — an English textbook specifically for Navajo students, one that uses Navajo themes in its sample writings and exercises and that addresses the kinds of errors bilingual Navajo students are most likely to make.

In addition, maximum enrollment in developmental English courses at NCC is limited to fifteen so that students can receive the individual attention and the specific instruction they require to become proficient in written SAE. Finally, composition instructors at NCC approach SAE as one dialect, not superior to Navajo English, but the one required for success in the world beyond the Navajo Nation's four sacred mountains.

Instructor/Faculty Ethnocentrism

Anglo instructors' (often unconscious) ethnocentrism and almost total ignorance about Native American cultures constitute a fourth barrier to Navajo students' success in English courses. I believe this ethnocentrism is caused primarily by gaps in our education: even though we understand that to be effective teachers, in Hap Gilliland's words, we "must understand and accept as equally valid, values and ways of life different from our own," we know little about others' cultures, histories, and educational philosophies. Gilliland adds that when "the teacher does not know, understand, and respect the culture of the students, then the students are at a disadvantage *in that teacher's class*" (4).

Such ethnocentrism or ignorance causes us to lose far more Native American students than we realize. During the second week of teaching a composition course at the University of New Mexico, I used an essay by Jessica Mitford on embalming; the next day, the three Navajos enrolled in the class dropped it. Later, I discovered that in Navajo culture, talking or writing about death is taboo. By requiring the students to discuss death and then write about it, I had offended and alienated them. Patricia Clark Smith had a similar experience teaching on the Navajo reservation. When she once brought an owl she'd fashioned out of scrap cloth to a class, the students "literally recoiled." "I learned too late," she writes, "that owls and images of owls are just something you do not mess with if you are Navajo" (287). Owls, in Navajo culture, are messengers warning a person to be alert and careful, especially for the next four days.

But instructor ethnocentrism does more than cause instructors inadvertently to alienate Native American students; it also leads to failure to acknowledge and validate different rhetorical styles. The Navajo rhetorical style differs considerably from the European linear style. In an unpublished paper, Navajo English instructor Della Toadlena writes that "Navajo is an oral language in which much story telling takes place," and that this tradition explains why Navajo students do better with narrative essays that follow chronological order than with expository essays (5). "An English speaker wastes no time in stating his argument right off and then brings in details to support his idea. Unlike his Anglo counterpart, a Navajo brings out detail after detail and eventually arrives at the point he wants to make" (Toadlena 13). For Navajos, it is important not to offend the audience they are addressing by coming right to the point. To illustrate the more indirect communication style of Navajo people, Toadlena discusses a typical visit from relatives. First, greetings are exchanged, and then the welfare of each family and its members is discussed. Next, food is served while weather, livestock, and crops are discussed. Only after all this exchange is the real reason for the visit brought out by the visitors — the relatives, in this case, were sponsoring an Enemy Way Ceremony and needed some help (13–14).

Use of the Western rhetorical style is, therefore, awkward and difficult for some Navajo students. When Anglo instructors ask students to state their thesis at the beginning of an essay, they're asking students to go against their cultural conventions — and asking them to be bad storytellers. Most composition instructors fail "thesis-less" papers, or papers that make their point in a roundabout or indirect way near the conclusion, when instead, we should be learning, promoting, and assigning equal value and legitimacy to the various rhetorical styles of all cultures. Here in the Southwest, then, effective instructors would teach both the Western and the Navajo rhetorical styles, privileging neither, and would explain the necessity of taking audience and purpose into account when choosing a particular rhetorical strategy.

Instructor ethnocentrism also manifests itself in the tendency to gear courses and methods toward the Anglo student, with little or no consideration for others. Navajo educators criticize Western education for its lack of relevance, saying that it fails to tie schoolwork to anything real; that course content is not connected to everyday life — to family, community, and nation. This criticism is legitimate. Too often, the texts in the composition classroom speak only to the experiences and cultural backgrounds of Anglo students. Textbook publishers' efforts to include multicultural readings in texts have not gone unnoticed at tribal colleges. Still, instructors must supplement those texts with others and explore issues impacting students' lives today, such as the Navajo/Hopi land dispute, Anglo appropriation of Native American rituals and spirituality, the American Indian Religious Freedom Act, the use of peyote in the Native American Church, and autobiographical narratives. And here at NCC, some instructors are successfully experimenting with portfolios that include community projects like writing letters for illiterate community members, making videos, recording oral histories, and so forth.

Although the traditional Navajo way of life is based on sharing and cooperation, and not on acquiring and competing, English instructors often expect work to be performed individually, with little (if any) collaboration. Those teaching Navajos need to place less focus on the individual and more on community — to lecture less, plan more collaborative and small group work, and try to build "learning communities."

Finally, I've noticed that the discussion styles of Navajo and Anglo students are a bit different. Navajo students typically take more time to consider a response to a question — a few seconds longer than most Anglo instructors are willing to wait. The Navajo method of discussion takes more time, is more thorough, and more in depth. I expect students to be open and expressive — and some are — but, as Toadlena writes, "that is not the proper way Navajos are taught to deal with strangers" (8). I like the way Northern Cheyenne elder Grover Wolf Voice explains the "delay" in responding. He says, "Even if I had a quick answer to your question, I would never answer immediately. That would be saying that your question was not worth thinking about" (Gilliland 32).

Patricia Clark Smith's experience teaching on the reservation illustrates the Navajo discussion style. She writes:

> I had to get used to the fact that when I asked a question, I would not see several hands waving competitively in the air. Instead, there'd usually be a silence — sometimes a long silence. Then someone might say something. And after a while, someone else. And then another

person. It wasn't that there were never heated exchanges and wild laughter; there were, especially as the class came to trust me and one another more. But for the most part the class felt not so much like a tennis match with questions and answers volleyed back and forth from the teacher's side to the students' side as like a circle slowly drawing together in consensus. The actual result was that a larger percentage of the people in that class eventually spoke up than during an average class on campus, where the most persistent handwavers often shut down other students. (286)

In order to eradicate ethnocentrism and ignorance about Navajo cultures, Navajo Community College formally educates its instructors so that they become familiar with Navajo students' cultural backgrounds and the historical context within which they teach. In two mandatory semester-long courses, faculty learn about the Navajo creation stories — or at least the first of twelve levels of understanding the stories. The first level seems like a fairy tale, myth, or religion, with Holy People and insect people, Father Sky and Mother Earth, monsters, and the Twins who slay the monsters. Instructors learn that the stories represent a historical charter between the Holy People and the Diné and that relating course material to traditional creation stories will inspire and motivate traditional Navajo students. Instructors also learn about Navajo history, for example, that the United States government paid fifty dollars for each scalp (or, sometimes, an ear) of a dead Navajo. They learn that the Diné — as well as Native Americans of almost every tribe — were "relocated" or forced from their homelands and contained within reservations on less desirable land. They learn that Kit Carson, who is portrayed as an American hero in Anglo school books, led the United States Army in hunting down resisting Navajos and forcing their surrender by destroying their shelters, livestock, and crops. After four years' incarceration in Ft. Sumner, New Mexico, a location so barren that self-sufficiency was impossible, the Diné were allowed to return to their traditional homeland, only to find that 90 percent had been taken by settlers, ranchers, and mining interests. In return for the loss of land, and for agreeing to accept reservations, tribes were offered annuities and education. Navajo leaders thought they were agreeing to an education that would combine the best of both the Navajo and Western worlds — one that would allow the Diné to keep their own traditional ways and values. What they got was something very different.

Often well-meaning educators (both Anglo and Navajo) saw Native Americans' cultural customs as "stumbling blocks" and set out to destroy them. They tried to eradicate Navajos' language, dress, and traditions, including their complex healing ceremonies. Educators went to reservations also determined to negate Navajo ways of knowing, such as crystal-gazing and hand trembling; and to negate Navajo ways of doing — it is said, for example, that before white people came and the knowledge was lost, Navajos could travel from one place to another by means of prayer. Navajos had, too, an advanced judicial system in which perpetrators of crimes, rather than being locked up or banished, were brought back into balance through participation in certain ceremonies and by making restitution to the victim or victim's family. White educators tried to eradicate the Navajos' completely different way of viewing the world, one that, rather than being based on separation and difference, is circular and cyclic, one that sees things in terms of patterns in nature.

To "civilize" Indians, the United States government created off-reservation boarding schools designed not to provide a real education, but to assimilate Native Americans into the dominant culture and to train them for menial positions in the labor force. A 1950s Bureau of Indian Affairs (BIA) program report from Riverside, California, for example, describes in glowing terms the successful training of four bus boys. Anglo educators considered that a laudable achievement. Navajo leaders did not agree and were also deeply troubled that Navajo children placed in BIA boarding schools were separated from their parents for three to five years, even throughout the summers, when they were placed with area families; were paddled or forced to clean toilets for speaking Navajo instead of English; were punished for refusing to worship a Christian god or for participating in traditional Navajo religious practices like praying with corn pollen to the Holy People at dawn; and were one hundred times more likely to commit suicide than white teenagers. Most Navajo students at any institution have either attended BIA boarding schools or have close relatives who did, and today, many traditional Navajos blame the rise in domestic violence and alcoholism on the trauma experienced by students at BIA boarding schools. Knowing the history of Navajo experience of Western education helps NCC faculty understand why some students' grandparents discourage them from attending college (among traditional people, some students tell me, education still has a "bad, bad name").

Ambivalence toward Western Education

Often what instructors interpret as poor or lackluster performance, lack of ability, or lack of motivation by Navajo students is actually ambivalence toward Western education. Historical, philosophical, and practical reasons for this ambivalence toward Western education exist that have far more to do with failure and attrition rates than have been acknowledged. In teaching English, we deny or negate the students' own tribal languages. Toadlena writes that for Navajo students, "English often represents more than the usual freshman irritant. It is a symbol of oppression and, as such, is a formidable stumbling block" (1). "Even today," she adds,

> there is no choice about learning English. While for most Americans learning a second language is not a requirement for economic survival, for the Navajo student, it is a must. It is not a cultural imposition

suggesting that the individual give up something of who he is in order to survive. For the Navajo students, surviving has to do with being able to operate adequately within a different value system foreign to them. (1)

The goals of Navajo education are actually broader than our own: they include a deeper understanding of and appreciation for Western as well as Navajo history, culture, language, and literacy; an understanding of the importance of the Navajo values of equality, balance, sharing, cooperation, kinship, and high ethical standards; and the building of students' self-confidence and inner strength. Self-confidence and inner strength are important to Navajo people because they believe that before individuals can go out and build or contribute to their community, they must build their own centers. Only after building a strong personal foundation can they focus on livelihood, and only then on building community or nation. Also considered absolutely essential to a quality education is the application of knowledge. Clearly, Navajos raised to believe that this is the nature of a quality education will be disillusioned when they enter institutions of higher education that negate, deny, or exclude their native values and beliefs.

Navajo students may be ambivalent about Western education for practical reasons, too. Success in college can cost the student a great deal in terms of family and culture, and it is not hard to understand why they might not be especially eager to pay the price. Success in a Western institution, too often, means leaving home and traditional ways behind. It means assimilation into a dominant culture that values materialism, and that, to many Navajos' way of thinking, focuses on technological development at the expense of other equally or more important ends.

How should educators address students' ambivalence toward Western education? I'm not sure, but it is my opinion that as long as the ambivalence remains hidden or unstated, it constitutes an obstacle to students' success. It helps when the instructor understands his or her place in the larger historical context and when the instructor understands the reasons for his or her students' ambivalence. Perhaps if we acknowledge up front that the United States education system has been used as a tool for all-out assimilation and affirm that that is not our purpose, emphasize that SAE can be used as a tool to resist assimilation and preserve Navajo tradition, and show students how writing skills can help students meet the needs of their families, communities, and nations, we can make a difference. On a practical level, this might mean having Navajo students use reading skills to analyze and interpret government documents for community members at Chapter Houses and then use their Navajo literacy skills to translate government documents from English into Navajo. Students could also be taught to use their English skills to write letters to newspaper editors, members of Congress, and other public officials to express their views. If we can make English writing skills relevant, perhaps we can retain more Navajo students.

Conclusion

Navajos and other Native Americans have a great deal to contribute to their own communities and to the larger society.[3] But are we doing enough to mitigate the barriers between Navajos and a college degree? Statistics indicate that we are not: five years ago, the Native American high school student dropout rate, at 35.5 percent, was over twice that of Euro-American students and higher than that of any other United States ethnic or racial group; and according to the Navajo Nation's 1990 Census Report, 56.5 percent of the adults living on the reservation do not have high school degrees, and only 5.5 percent have a bachelor's degree or higher. In 1993, an unpublished study of composition courses at the University of New Mexico conducted by the Orality/Literacy Committees[4] found that Native Americans are two and a half times more likely to drop or fail those courses than their Anglo counterparts — and because it is the only course required of all college graduates at many institutions, failure to pass composition means failure to attain a degree.

It is time for English instructors, when faced with students from radically different cultural backgrounds and whose needs differ from those of mainstream students, to stop blaming the high failure and attrition rates solely on bilingualism, substandard schooling, low self-esteem, lack of familiarity with SAE, and/or lack of motivation — it is time to look beyond these factors and work to mitigate all the barriers that all minority culture students face.

Notes

1. This situation is not unique to the Navajo people: 221 different Indian languages are known today, and before European colonization, the number was as high as 2,000 (Snipp 41).

2. Mainstream institutions in the Southwest (including the University of New Mexico, Northern Arizona University, and Arizona State University, where the Native American student populations are relatively high), have established composition sections specifically for Native American students. Typically taught by instructors familiar with Native American students' cultures and their dialects, most of these sections use readings and create assignments geared toward Indians and issues that affect them. Problems associated with this strategy include first the assumption of the existence of the "Native American," when the term actually refers to four hundred different Native American peoples in the United States alone, each with different customs, beliefs, languages, and English dialects. Second, each student comes to college with different levels of traditionalism and assimilation into dominant culture, and the more assimilated often don't need or want to enroll in a special section of composition.

3. What impact, for example, would the Native American belief that before a decision is made, its impact on the next seven generations must be considered have on, say, the development of use of nuclear power? The federal deficit? The stockpiling of nuclear weapons?

4. An interdisciplinary group of interested University of New Mexico faculty and graduate students organized the Orality/Literacy Committee in 1992 to explore the causes and to devise appropriate responses to a perceived high failure rate for Native Americans in UNM composition courses.

Works Cited

Gilliland, Hap. *Teaching the Native American*. 2nd ed. Dubuque: Kendall, 1992.

Navajo Nation Government. 1990 Census: Population and Housing Characteristics of the Navajo Nation. Scottsdale: Printing, 1993.

Smith, Patricia Clark. "Icons in the Canyon." *The New Criticism and Contemporary Literary Theory: Connections and Continuities.* Ed. William J. Spurlin and Michael Fischer. New York: Garland, 1995. 275–95.

Snipp, C. Matthew. *American Indians: The First of This Land*. New York: Sage, 1989.

Toadlena, Della. "Why Navajo Students Have Problems with Writing." Unpublished manuscript, 1989.

Classroom Activities

Many developing writers from a variety of cultural backgrounds have had to deal with cultural issues and concerns about assimilation in regard to learning Standard American English. Thurston suggests that instructors "acknowledge up front that the United States education system has been used as a tool for all-out assimilation." In this way, instructors can begin to recognize their students' concerns and "ambivalence toward Western education." However, Thurston advises, we need to go even further, to "show students how writing skills can help students meet the needs of their families, communities, and nations. . . ." Classroom activities that inspired Thurston's pedagogy include translating government documents for those who cannot read or write in English (which uses both Navajo and English literacy skills) and writing "letters to newspaper editors, members of Congress, and other public officials to express their views." Most communities have immediate, if often hidden needs, for those with literacy skills, and opportunities exist for developing writers to intervene in purposeful ways. Ask students to research what kinds of literacy issues exist in their home communities. Students can work together to make lists and brainstorm ideas for service learning projects. If your college or university also has a service learning or volunteer services office, invite a representative from that office to speak to your class on the literacy needs in your community — and on how students can help. Students can keep journals of their service learning work and can complete research-oriented tasks related to their service learning projects. Thurston's letter-writing project would also work well in conjunction with this activity.

Thinking about Teaching

Thurston suggests that teachers need to confront their own "often unconscious" ethnocentrism, which may include the privileged Eurocentric and Western notions of the teaching of writing and reading. One means of doing this work is to learn as much as you can about your students' cultural backgrounds. Students should not be expected to do this work for their teachers (especially since many students are still engaged in the lifelong process of learning more about their own cultural heritage); rather, teachers can take on this task themselves, either individually or in groups. In addition, you and your colleagues may wish to examine your views concerning stereotypes. What can be done to help us face our fears, intolerance, impatience, or lack of understanding of students from cultural, racial, religious, or class backgrounds different from our own — and to create an environment in which we internalize and then model tolerance, cultural appreciation, and community?* All of these goals, Thurston offers, go a long way toward promoting a positive learning climate for students and for increasing retention. Reflect on these issues in your teaching journal, and share your ideas with other instructors and students.

*I am indebted to Susan Peterson and Lynne Shivers, English department faculty at the Community College of Philadelphia, who ran workshops on confronting stereotypes for students and instructors when I was a junior faculty member at the College in the mid-1990s. Participating in forums that gave people of many backgrounds the opportunity to speak and listen openly with each other is an experience that has inspired my teaching ever since. [Editor's note]

Teaching ESL

E SL students come from a great diversity of backgrounds, including but not limited to: international students choosing to study abroad; refugees who are forced to flee for their lives from their countries of origin; and students who were born and raised in the United States but whose native language is not English. This chapter accounts for this diversity by focusing on pedagogies that value this wide range of student voices and experiences. Readers will have encountered many of the concerns in this chapter when they read about combining reading and writing, collaborative learning and peer review, and writing and race, class, and gender elsewhere in this ancillary. The writers in this chapter are aware of the need to understand their students' cultural differences. Clearly, the focus here is not on the "grammatical correctness" of ESL students' writing. Instead, readers will encounter a pedagogy that emphasizes student-centered learning and writing as a means of gaining fluency in English. Although such a pedagogy may now be a commonplace in courses for developing writers who learned English as their first language, traditional approaches to ESL have focused on teacher-centered classrooms, with an emphasis on the "basics" of English.

In contrast, the articles in this section emphasize a student-centered approach in which understanding the writing process (including peer review and small-group discussion) is a primary goal. Loretta Frances Kasper examines her work with ESL students in a process-based classroom. Yu Ren Dong asks students to write literacy narratives about their experiences with writing and reading in their first language so that they can understand the continuum of the writing process. Linda Lonon Blanton argues for the importance of a curriculum focused on critical literacy for language minority students, whom she defines as graduates of "U.S. urban high schools [. . .] whose home language is not English." Together, these essays demonstrate a pedagogy that focuses on English language fluency and that values the whole student. The student voices represented in these selections help to tell an important part of the story.

ESL Writing and the Principle of Nonjudgmental Awareness: Rationale and Implementation

Loretta Frances Kasper

In the following article, first published in 1998 in Teaching English in the Two-Year College, *Loretta Frances Kasper clearly articulates the differences between emerging basic writing pedagogy and traditional ESL pedagogy: "Basic writing programs generally apply a process approach to writing, emphasizing development of ideas and gradually placing a greater responsibility on the students as they go through the writing process. . . . In contrast, many ESL programs still maintain a product approach to writing in which grammar is explicitly taught and in which the final product becomes more important than the process which it was created by." Kasper suggests that the emphasis on product creates anxiety for ESL students, especially in placement examination situations. She found that when she switched to a process-based pedagogical model, her students not only improved their fluency but also achieved better results on their final writing examination, which "was cross-graded by two other ESL instructors."*

R ecent statistics show that ESL students enrolled in community colleges are steadily increasing. In fact, Crandall reports that ESL is the fastest growing area of study in community colleges in the United States. In community colleges within the City University of New York system (CUNY), dubbed by Crandall a "microcosm of the United States as a whole" (4), 25 percent of entering students now need instruction in English as a Second Language (Nunez-Wormack). By 2000, estimates are that more than 50 percent of full-time first-year students in the CUNY system will be ESL students (Professional Staff Congress). College ESL students must demonstrate writing proficiency for full entry into the mainstream curriculum. However, developing this proficiency presents an especially difficult problem for such students.

Studies of both basic and ESL writers have shown that instructor feedback plays a significant role in students' progress as writers (Bass; Zak) and that the priorities of the instructor become the priorities of the student. Therefore, when responding to ESL students' writing, instructors must be aware of the priorities they communicate to their students and should provide evaluative feedback that decreases writing anxiety as it increases writing satisfaction. I have found that implementing Gallwey's principle of nonjudgmental awareness with a process approach that emphasizes fluency and clarity of expression and deemphasizes correctness has improved the performance of intermediate-level (TOEFL score of approximately 350) ESL students.

The Principle of Nonjudgmental Awareness

The principle of nonjudgmental awareness was first advanced by W. Timothy Gallwey in his book, *The Inner Game of Tennis*. Gallwey believes that learning proceeds most effectively and effortlessly when the learners allow themselves to move naturally through the learning process, aware of relevant aspects of performance without making excessive critical judgments about that performance.

Although initially advanced as a means of learning a physical skill such as tennis, the principle of nonjudgmental awareness has been applied to learning skills in academic domains. For example, Ploger and Carlock successfully used this principle to teach students to construct computer programs designed to represent ideas from biology. They found that implementation of the principle of nonjudgmental awareness made it easier for students to learn how to write programs that were both meaningful and accurate, and then, to revise those programs to explain the problem-solving strategy step-by-step. Ploger and Carlock believe that the nonjudgmental instructional technique lessened the anxiety students felt about the task of writing a computer program and ultimately enabled these students to gain a deeper overall understanding of the principles of biology.

Task anxiety and insufficient understanding of the writing process also plague and inhibit the writing performance of ESL students. For this reason, I decided to adopt a nonjudgmental instructional approach in an attempt to lessen my intermediate-level ESL students' writing anxiety and to improve their writing performance. As I use the term, "nonjudgmental instructional approach" refers to an approach to writing instruction that is process- rather than product-oriented, is student-centered, and one in which the chief goal of instruction is to help students attain fluency and clarity of expression. I do not explicitly teach grammar in the ESL writing class; rather, students acquire and improve their use of the grammatical structures they need to express ideas most effectively through a series of progressive attempts to refine and clarify those ideas. Thus, mechanical accuracy is not the means to achieving fluency and clarity of expression; rather, mechanical accuracy is the result of having worked to express ideas most fluently and clearly.

To evaluate the effectiveness of this approach, I conducted an informal three-semester study. My students come from a number of diverse linguistic, ethnic, and cultural backgrounds, including Russian, Hispanic, Haitian, and Asian. Over a period of three semesters, I gradually adopted a less error- and more expression-oriented response approach in which I moved from correcting virtually all student errors to simply identifying those errors and requiring that the students themselves correct them. The results of my informal analyses indicated that over the course of the three semesters a progressively greater percentage (61 percent, 82 percent, 89 percent) of the students passed the final writing examination. This writing final required students to plan, write, and revise a persuasive essay on their choice of three assigned topics based on the work done during the semester and was cross-graded by two other ESL instructors in the department.

Rationale for the Nonjudgmental Approach

Although basic writing instructors may find nonjudgmental response not a radical departure from traditional pedagogy, the approach to teaching writing in many ESL programs is quite different from that in most basic writing programs. Basic writing programs generally apply a process approach to writing, emphasizing the development of ideas and gradually placing greater responsibility on the students as they go through the writing process. In this approach, writing becomes a process of discovery in which "ideas are generated and not just transcribed" (Susser 35).

In contrast, many ESL programs still maintain a product approach to writing in which grammar is explicitly taught and in which the final product becomes more important than the process by which it was created. In product-driven ESL writing programs, instructors continually provide students with accurate models of language, the assumption being that, with more grammar and more correction, students will be able to produce fluent and clear compositions.

One of the rationales offered for product-driven ESL writing programs is that ESL students are required to pass college assessment examinations that often judge writing on the basis of grammatical accuracy. In one study, Sweedler-Brown found that "sentence-level error was . . . the crucial factor in pass/fail decisions in ESL essays" (12), and she concludes that "we may be doing our ESL students a disservice if we are not willing to become language teachers as well as writing teachers" (15). The problem with this approach is that too often the priority becomes teaching students sufficient language rules so they can write accurately enough to pass an examination, rather than helping them develop their potential to discover and express their ideas.

Furthermore, a study conducted by MacGowan-Gilhooly demonstrated that when the ESL writing course focused on producing grammatical correctness for the purpose of preparing students to pass a college writing assessment test, they did not progress as well, and some actually regressed from former performance levels. Of course, this regression may have been the result of students' attempts to produce more sophisticated linguistic structures: however, MacGowan-Gilhooly attributes it to the pressure produced by writing for evaluation where that evaluation depends upon correctness of language rather than upon quality of content. Like MacGowan-Gilhooly, Bass has also found that, in general, students' progress is often inhibited when they anticipate that their writing will be evaluated for its correctness.

Implementing the Principle of Nonjudgmental Awareness

On the very first day of classes, I describe the nonjudgmental instructional approach to my ESL student writers. I explain that I want them to focus on expressing ideas in their essays, and we discuss the purpose of writing as the communication of those ideas to another person. I tell students not to worry about correctness in their initial drafts, to allow their ideas to flow freely onto the paper. I explain that they will receive both instructor and peer feedback on each essay. I then announce that when I respond to their essays, I will not be correcting errors in grammar. Instead, I will point out where the errors are, but that they will be responsible for correcting those errors. I tell them that if they have any problems, they should discuss those problems with me, and we will solve them together.

Some students do express anxiety when they first hear about this approach; however, after only a few assignments, they discover that as they work through several drafts of each essay, increasing the fluency and clarity of each subsequent draft, they gradually become aware of the mechanical errors and rhetorical features which obscure meaning in their writing. With their continued practice, my support, and the suggestions of their peer partners, the students learn how to reduce their errors. Successfully assuming this responsibility not only gives ESL students the confidence they need to continue to improve their writing skills, but also helps them to view good writing as clear communication rather than merely as accurate grammar.

Because priorities communicated through instructor feedback have such a great impact on the progress of student writers, it is important to adopt response styles that will be most facilitative to this progress and which will lessen students' anxiety and increase their confidence. We can help students gain confidence in their writing abilities by asking them to gradually assume more responsibility for their growth as writers, while at the same time providing them with the instructional support they need to achieve their writing goals. Implementing a nonjudgmental approach in an ESL writing class does just that by creating a climate in which students are acknowledged for their successes and, at the same time, are taught specific strategies for dealing with their deficiencies in writing. Moreover, a nonjudgmental instructional approach asks students to assume a more active role in their own learning as they critique both their own and their classmates' work. Feedback from both the instructor and their peers encourages students to express ideas more clearly and more fluently. As Connors and Lunsford's research demonstrates, the more student writers focus on clarifying meaning, the fewer the number of errors they make.

Nonjudgmental Techniques

The pedagogical techniques used in a nonjudgmental writing class are, for the most part, student — rather than instructor — centered. Students assume greater responsibility for their progress and learn instructional techniques to help them assume this responsibility. Below I describe some of the nonjudgmental techniques that I have found effective. These techniques include providing instructor feedback via task-oriented questions, guiding students in providing peer evaluation, teaching students to vocalize thoughts when they have trouble writing, and obtaining student feedback through writing evaluation questionnaires and writing autobiographies.

Providing Instructor Feedback via Task-Oriented Questions

While error correction is instructor-centered, task-oriented questions are student-centered. Task-oriented questions direct students' attention to ways they may improve the content and the clarity of their ideas. Task-oriented questions may request more information, reflect on students' thoughts, and/or share experiences similar to those expressed by the student (Beaven). These are some of the task-oriented questions I have used: "Could you be more specific, provide more details, about this point?" "Could you open up the essay with a more general statement?" "How does this example relate to the main point of your essay?" These task-oriented questions have helped ESL students improve and expand the content of their essays and increase the clarity of their ideas.

Using Peer Evaluation

According to Stanley, "peer evaluation can provide student writers with a wide range of benefits, including reduced writing anxiety, increased sense of audience, and increased fluency" (217). Moreover, Stanley asserts that peer evaluation "facilitates the transition from what Flower and Hayes term 'writer-based prose' to 'reader-based prose'" (218). In the process of critiquing their classmates' writings, students take the stance of the reader; they learn what works and what does not work and develop an increased awareness of the elements of fluent and clear writing. However, Stanley has found that for peer evaluation to be effective, students need to be coached "to be specific in their responses, . . . to point to problematic portions of text, to alert writers to lapses in coherence, to offer specific advice for solving these problems, and to collaborate with the writer on more suitable phrases" (226–227).

Following Stanley's recommendations, I offered ESL students such coaching. Then I divided the class into several groups of two or three students each, with the only restriction that, whenever possible, students within the same group not speak the same native language because they might tend to use (and so not recognize) the same inaccurate English language structures which would obscure the clarity of their writing. I then asked the students to exchange and read the drafts of the others in their group and to fill out a peer evaluation questionnaire for each paper they read. This peer evaluation questionnaire asked the students to evaluate how clearly ideas were expressed as they answered the following eight questions: (1) What was the topic of the essay? (2) What was the writer's opinion about this topic? (3) Where in the essay was this opinion stated? (4) What did you like best about this essay? (5) List any places where you did not understand the writer's meaning. He/she will need to clarify these things in the next draft. (6) What would you like to know more about when the writer revises this essay? (7) Reread the first paragraph of the essay. Do you think this is a good beginning? Does it make you feel like reading on? Explain; and (8) How could the writer improve this paper when he/she revises it? Make only one suggestion.

Some researchers have reported that ESL students are often recalcitrant when asked to evaluate the writing of their peers (Nelson and Murphy); however, I found that, after some initial hesitation, students enjoyed the peer evaluation process and said that it was very helpful. This activity made writing "a task of communicating" (Stanley 217), and in their interactions with peers, students developed increased confidence and were more willing to take risks in their writing. In addition, these partnerships helped to promote interpersonal relationships among students, leading them to an increased understanding and tolerance of cultural differences.

Teaching Students to Vocalize Thoughts

Another effective nonjudgmental technique is teaching students to vocalize thoughts to help them get past writing blocks. Students can do this alone or within the context of their peer evaluation group. Peter Elbow has pointed out the value of vocalizing thoughts: "If you are stuck writing . . . , there is nothing better than finding one person, or more, to talk to. . . . I write a paper; it's not very good; I discuss it with someone: after fifteen minutes of back-and-forth I say something in response to a question . . . of his and he says, 'But why didn't you say that? That's good. That's clear'"(49).

When my ESL students are doing in-class writing or interacting in their peer evaluation groups, I circulate around the room to check work or offer assistance. If I notice an inaccuracy or a confusion in writing, I ask the student, "What did you want to say here?" I then suggest that the student write down what he or she has just told me. I also tell students that if they get stuck in the writing process, they should think of how they would express the idea if they were speaking to someone. More often than not, my intermediate level ESL students, even those with somewhat limited fluency in the spoken language, are able to tell me or their writing partners in relatively correct English what they wanted to say: On those occasions when students are not able to vocalize their ideas completely, they usually can communicate enough of the idea so that either I or their peer partners can provide assistance. Thus, asking students to vocalize thoughts can help them to improve both written and spoken English.

If we can get students to think of how they would communicate their ideas orally and then transfer that oral communication to the written form, we may be able to demystify the writing process and help students to improve their writing. I have found that when ESL students vocalize their thoughts when writing, the result is a decrease in the number of structural and grammatical errors and an increase in the clarity of expression.

Student Feedback: Writing Evaluation Questionnaires

This questionnaire, designed to elucidate the kinds of teacher responses that students perceived as helpful, asked them to identify the specific instructor feedback techniques they found most useful when revising their writing. A majority of the students found instructor feedback in the form of task-oriented questions useful in revision, stating that these questions directed attention to exactly what needed to be improved in the essay. Some of the other responses indicated that feedback on how to organize the essay and on how to write a good introduction and conclusion was helpful. Many of the students also said that although at first they were uncomfortable about correcting their own grammatical errors, as the semester went on, they were able to find and correct many of their errors. This discovery went a long way toward helping students become better writers. As many of them indicated in their feedback questionnaires, being able to find and correct their own errors gave them confidence in their ability to write English.

Student Feedback: Writing Autobiographies

The writing autobiography was the last essay students wrote before taking their writing final. The writing autobiography question sheet was adapted from one used by Sandman and Weiser (19) and asked students to describe positive and negative experiences in writing English and their strengths and weaknesses as writers. In addition to the three questions suggested by Sandman and Weiser, I also asked students the following question, "What have you learned this semester about your ability as a writer? How, specifically, do *you* think your writing has improved? What areas of your writing do you think still need work?" This writing autobiography had several objectives — to elucidate students' attitudes toward writing, to help them monitor their development as writers, and to assist them in developing sound criteria for assessing their writing performance. Moreover, by increasing students' awareness of their own writing experiences and knowledge, the writing autobiography encouraged them to think of themselves as writers.

Their responses to the writing autobiography activity indicated that students had developed a clearer understanding of their personal involvement in the writing task. The students all said that writing was a positive experience when they were writing about something that they enjoyed because then they were able to express their ideas on a subject of interest. They each noted that a negative experience was when they had to write an essay for the writing assessment test upon entrance to the college. Many of them said that they lost confidence and felt unable to write because of the pressure. They knew that they had to write correctly to pass the test and that the result of the test would determine which courses they would be required or allowed to take in college. As a result, some said that the pressure of the test "had made their minds go blank." These responses support the claims of both MacGowan-Gilhooly and Bass that writing for evaluation can inhibit students' progress.

Their responses to the writing autobiographies indicated that when these ESL students focused on expressing their ideas, they found writing to be a positive experience. In contrast, when students focused on producing correct language, they concentrated on their perceived weaknesses, their ideas were stifled, and writing became a negative experience.

After being exposed to the nonjudgmental approach, when asked to describe their strengths and weaknesses, students generally focused on their strengths. A common response was, "I have good ideas, and it's interesting to tell other people about those ideas." Furthermore, few of these students cited grammar as a weakness; in fact, their responses illustrated that they had come to view mistakes as a means to improving writing. Rather than weaknesses in grammar, their responses now focused on weaknesses in conveying meaning, such as difficulty organizing their thoughts or writing an effective introduction or conclusion.

For a nonjudgmental approach to enhance writing proficiency, it must result in students' experiencing increased confidence and decreased anxiety when writing English. The students' feedback on the question of what they had learned that semester about their ability as writers demonstrated that the nonjudgmental approach had achieved this goal. One response predominated in each of the essays; the students had learned that they were able to communicate their ideas in written English. They expressed an increased confidence in their ability to write, so that they were more willing to take risks in their writing. Moreover, they had learned that if they made mistakes, they were not only able to find and correct those mistakes, but they were able to learn from them.

Here are some students' responses: "I learned I could make my writing better if I tried areas that I still need work in"; "I saw that after every writing task, I could express my ideas better and fully"; "I learned how to check my work by myself. I was really surprised when I saw that I could find a lot of mistakes without any help"; "I realized that I can break down a subject in my own words without much difficulty"; "I learned that I have the ability to write more than I used to"; and "I got more confidence in my writing. It is my firm belief that in the future I will know how to write English better if I practice it every day."

The focus on fluency and clarity of expression in the nonjudgmental, process-oriented approach also helped ESL students to learn the value of revision. I encouraged students to refine ideas, not just to correct language in their revisions, and many commented that writing an essay several times had taught them how to clarify meaning by adding new information and by rearranging sections of the essay.

In his research on second language writing, Krashen (19) has found that developmental writers usually do not understand that revision can help them generate new ideas. In fact, they usually think that their first draft contains all their ideas, and they believe that revising an essay simply means making the first draft neater by correcting language errors. In the process of revision for clarity of expression, my students discovered not only that they could write English, but also that writing itself became easier and more satisfying with each subsequent revision.

Conclusion and Implications for Instruction

Bernard Susser has noted the concern of some ESL researchers that process-based approaches emphasize fluency at the expense of accuracy. However, my experience indicates that a process-based, nonjudgmental instructional approach can help intermediate-level ESL students improve both the fluency and the accuracy with which they express their ideas in written English. Like the students in Sweedler-Brown's study, my students had to improve grammatical accuracy to pass the writing final. Nevertheless, in contrast to Sweedler-Brown's contention that we should become "language teachers as well as writing teachers" (15), I found that the number of students who passed the final rose as I provided less grammatical feedback. In fact, the students made the greatest progress in expressing themselves fluently, clearly, and correctly when they themselves assumed the most responsibility for their own learning.

As my ESL students shifted their focus from correctness of form to fluency and clarity of expression, they discovered that they had something to say and that they were able to say it fluently, clearly, and, for the most part, correctly. Writing became a more positive experience as they gained confidence in their ability to express themselves in written English. The students became aware of their strengths and weaknesses as writers, and when given the time and the opportunity to develop their strengths, they were able to minimize their weaknesses.

Most importantly, they got their priorities straight as they came to realize that the primary goal of writing is the communication of ideas and that through the process of writing we discover and refine those ideas. They also learned that in the process of clarifying ideas, they could minimize language errors. As a result, they became less intimidated by their mistakes.

For years, basic writing programs have focused on refining writing skills through a step-by-step process in which the writer is encouraged to develop and expand upon ideas, and is ultimately responsible for his or her own progress. It is time for ESL writing programs to follow suit. If the goal of ESL composition instruction is to help students become proficient writers of English, it must provide a learning environment which both allows students to gain confidence in their ability as writers and transfers the ultimate responsibility for their development as writers from teachers to students. Implementing the principle of nonjudgmental awareness in the ESL writing class achieves this goal by making communicative competence, rather than grammatical accuracy, the primary focus of instruction.

Note

I thank Dr. Don Ploger for sharing his ideas and insights on learning and awareness during my research.

Works Cited

Bass, Barbara Kaplan. "The Mathematics of Writing: Shaping Attitude in Composition Classes." *Teaching English in the Two-Year College* 20 (1993): 109–14.

Beaven, Mary. "Individualized Goal Setting, Self-Evaluation, and Peer Evaluation." *Evaluating Writing.* Ed. Charles R. Copper and Lee Odell. Urbana: NCTE. 135–56.

Connors, Robert J., and Andrea A. Lunsford. "Frequency of Formal Errors in Current Writing, or Ma and Pa Kettle Do Research." *College Composition and Communication* 39 (1988): 395–409.

Crandall, JoAnn. "Diversity as Challenge and Resource." *Conference Proceedings ESL Students in the CUNY Classroom: Faculty Strategies for Success.* 5 Feb. 1993. Manhattan Community College/CUNY. 1–2.

Elbow, Peter. *Writing without Teachers.* New York: Oxford UP, 1973.

Flower, Linda S., and John R. Hayes. "A Cognitive Process Theory of Writing." *College Composition and Communication* 32 (1981): 365–88.

Gallwey, W. Timothy. *The Inner Game of Tennis.* New York: Random, 1974.

Krashen, Stephen. *Fundamentals of Language Education.* Torrence: Laredo, 1992.

MacGowan-Gilhooly, Adele. "Fluency before Correctness: A Whole-Language Experiment in College ESL." *College ESL* 1.1 (1991): 37–47.

Nelson, Gayle L., and John M. Murphy. "An L2 Writing Group: Task and Social Dimensions. *Journal of Second Language Writing* 1.3 (1992): 171–93.

Nunez-Wormack, Elsa. "Remarks." *Conference Proceedings ESL Students in the CUNY Classroom: Faculty Strategies for Success*. 5 Feb. 1993. Manhattan Community College/CUNY. 1–2.

Ploger, Don, and Margaret Carlock. "Programming and Problem Solving: Implications for Biology Education." *Journal of Artificial Intelligence in Education* 2.4 (1991): 15–31.

Professional Staff Congress/City University of New York. "CUNY Plans Language Immersion Institute." *Clarion* 24.4 (1994): 1–3.

Sandman, John, and Michael Weiser. "The Writing Autobiography: How to Begin a Two-Year College Writing Course." *Teaching English in the Two-Year College* 20 (1993): 18–22.

Stanley, Jane. "Coaching Student Writers to Be Effective Peer Evaluators." *Journal of Second Language Writing* 1.3 (1992): 217–33.

Susser, Bernard. "Process Approaches in ESL/EFL Writing Instruction." *Journal of Second Language Writing* 3.1 (1994): 31–47.

Sweedler-Brown, Carol O. "ESL Essay Evaluation: The Influence of Sentence-Level and Rhetorical Features." *Journal of Second Language Writing* 2.1 (1993): 3–17.

Zak, Frances. "Exclusively Positive Responses to Student Writing." *Journal of Basic Writing* 9.2 (1990): 40–53.

Classroom Activities

Kasper provides a list of eight questions from a peer review questionnaire that she distributes during rough draft workshops. The questions range from descriptive ("What was the topic of the essay?") to evaluative ("How could the writer improve this paper when he/she revises it? Make only one suggestion.") Give a copy of this questionnaire to your students, and work together with students to make the questionnaire more specific to their own paper assignments. Questions can be revised based on concepts that the students are learning. For example, students could ask: "Does this paper have a thesis statement? If so, what is it? If not, where would the reader expect to see the thesis statement?" and so forth. In addition, when considering how students are to be divided into peer groups, Kasper suggests only one restriction: "whenever possible, students within the same group must not speak the same native language because they might tend to use (and so not recognize) the same inaccurate English structures which would obscure the clarity of their writing." Notice again that the emphasis for Kasper is not on grammatical correctness but on the fluency and clarity of student writing.

Thinking about Teaching

Kasper bases her definition of nonjudgmental awareness on the principles presented in W. Timothy Gallwey's book *The Inner Game of Tennis*. Gallwey believes that learners are most effective when they "allow themselves to move through the learning process, aware of relevant aspects of performance without making excessive critical judgments about that performance." In your teaching journal, reflect on your own response to Gallwey's principles. How might these principles be related to second language learning? Reflect on Noguchi's idea about how "grammatical incorrectness" often seems to violate "socially approved" norms. Is there a connection between such social approval and approaches to grammatical correctness in traditional ESL pedagogy? What might social class or race have to do with how "correctness" is determined? Are some errors made by ESL students traditionally considered to be less acceptable than others? What has usually been the criteria for determining which errors are more or less acceptable? Discuss your findings with other teachers and students, as appropriate.

The Need to Understand ESL Students' Native Language Writing Experiences

Yu Ren Dong

"Teachers are quick to recognize ESL students' grammatical errors in their writing," writes Yu Ren Dong, "but often they are slow to get to know these students, who differ widely in their expectations of schooling, their views of the roles of teacher and student, their reading and writing experiences back home, their learning preferences, and how all of these impact their learning to read and write in English." To ameliorate this situation in her own classroom, Dong invites students to write about "how they learned to write in their native language . . . and about the differences they perceived when comparing writing in their native language to writing in English." Her article, first published in Teaching English in the Two-Year College *in 1999, documents her study of twenty-six first-year students at a four-year university who had come from a wide variety of backgrounds, had had extensive training in reading and writing in their first language, and had also attended New York City public high schools. Throughout the article, the voices of Dong's students speak clearly and poignantly about their experiences with literacy in their native countries. For instance, a student from Russia writes: "I had one great teacher. . . . She gave us such nice topics to write about that everyone wanted to write. The teacher told us: 'You think you are students? No! You are writers!'" Dong's strategies for understanding students' literacy histories will certainly benefit native English speakers as well as ESL students.*

Introduction

I remember a high school assignment that I dreaded. I had to write about my experiences in life and how they influenced my life. I thought to myself "What real experience did I have in my life?" I sat down for days without anything. But a week later I started to write a list of things that I did when I was young back in my home country, and soon I began to see that there were a lot of things on the list. I began to write my paper and was surprised to see how wonderfully it turned out. This was the most satisfying assignment that I had ever done. This was because I found out something about myself that influenced me tremendously in my life. From that I learned that when writing you can find out more about yourself.

Like the above first-year ESL student, many non-English-speaking students come to college composition with rich home cultural, educational, language, and literacy backgrounds. In particular, some have acquired sophisticated literacy skills in their native languages. Research on second language acquisition in academic settings done by Cummins and Collier has shown that students with native literacy skills often acquire English language skills faster than those without native literacy skills. Unfortunately, these students' native language and literacy learning experiences are often not considered when planning instruction.

Teachers are quick to recognize ESL students' grammatical errors in their writing, but often they are slow to get to know these students, who differ widely in their expectations of schooling, their views of the roles of teacher and students, their prior schooling, their reading and writing experiences back home, their learning style preferences, and how all of these impact their learning to read and write in English. As composition instructors encounter more and more linguistically and culturally diverse students in their classrooms, they must attempt to learn about these students' literacy backgrounds and to develop strategies to make good use of what the students learned back home in order to accelerate their learning of English reading and writing skills. Such knowledge is particularly important not only for these students to succeed in American schools, but also for building a classroom environment where diverse educational, cultural, and literacy backgrounds are valued and become resources rather than problems.

Method

In order to investigate ESL students' native literacy learning experiences, I invited twenty-six first-year college students at a four-year college in New York City to write autobiographies describing how they learned to write in their native language. I wanted to find out how these students learned to read and write in their native countries, what writing assignments they liked, and what the differences in writing were between their native language and English. The twenty-six students who participated in the research project had all had extensive schooling in their home countries before coming to America. Most of them had acquired a high level of native language literacy skills and, therefore, were competent readers and writers in their native languages, which included Chinese, Korean, French/Creole, Hebrew, Italian, Russian, Polish, and Spanish. The majority of them also attended and graduated from New York City public high schools. Their average American educational experience was about two and half years. Therefore, they were able to compare two educational systems and two sets of language and literacy learning experiences, native and United States.

In order to elicit students' responses, I wrote a letter to these students with a series of probing questions (see Appendix). I asked them specifically about how they learned to write in their native language, about the first things they remember writing, about the most satisfying piece of writing in their native language, and about the differences they perceived when comparing writing in their native language to writing in English.

Students were more responsive about their learning experiences with writing in the following three major areas:

- writing instruction in their native languages,

- most satisfying writing assignments in their native languages,

- differences between writing in their native language and in English.

Writing Instruction in Native Languages

Despite a wide range of native literacy learning experiences noted by these twenty-six students, a common theme emerged: students all had had some kind of native language writing instruction before coming to the United States. Very often this instruction began in the elementary school, as one student wrote:

> I was only four year old when I started to go to school in my country, Peru. When I went to the first grade, my teacher began to teach us the vowels and then the consonants of the alphabet. Then the teacher proceeded to teach the class how to form simple words like: mama and papa and then Mi mama me mima, which means my mother cares for me. In the second grade, I was taught to read simple stories and later my teacher taught the class components of a sentence. We learned about the verb, the subject, and the predicate. It was a bit hard for most seven year old, including me to learn these grammar rules. . . . By the time I finished the third grade, I knew how to form complicated sentences and how to construct paragraphs that made sense. I was also able to read books that were more complex, the newspapers and signs in the street that once I wondered what they meant. In my fourth grade, my teacher taught the class words that were similar in meanings and I learned a variety of words quickly and also learned how to use them in sentences too.

Reflecting on their native literacy learning experiences, many students revealed the distinctive ways that their teachers back home used to teach them how to write in their native languages. For example, the student from Haiti recalled writing instruction in his schooling like this:

I learned speak Creole first, but went to school learning French. Some of the first things that I remember writing were about my family. I was about five year old then. The teacher asked us to describe my family and the games that I played. . . . The teachers in my country (Haiti) would have me recite what I had written for homework. Haitian teachers are also very strict. Some would have me rewrite word-for-word what I had to read the previous day. If I could not write and remember, I would be beaten or be sent to detention. Sometimes a teacher would sent a student to stand in the corner on one foot for fifteen minutes in order to get students to do their work.

Several Russian students revealed a strong focus on language and structure in native writing instruction, for example:

Usually teachers in Russia paid more attention to the grammar mistakes. Therefore they helped us how to use correct words. We had some special orthographic rules. Teachers helped us to combine sentences and spelling. . . . At school back in Russia, we had a lot of homework and sometimes the teachers gave us the permission so that we could stay behind and study in the afternoon. The classmates who had excellent marks helped us to do better work by tutoring. . . . Some of the teachers who didn't have families stayed with us and gave extra help.

One Russian student noted the excitement of learning to write in Russian and the high expectations that her teacher maintained for the students:

In Russia, students write a lot. In my middle school years, we used to write compositions for ten to fifteen pages. I had one great teacher. She did not give us any unusual techniques, but she explained to each and every student any mistakes he or she made, and told us how to write better. She gave us such nice topics that everyone wanted to write. The teacher told us: "You think you are students? No! You are writers!"

Students also described a range of writing tasks assigned by their teachers back home. These assignments included: diary/journal, literature responses, research papers, aesthetic prose, and essays. A Korean student recalled a progression from diary writing to writing a book report in her schooling back in Korea and how the teacher motivated the students to write:

I began to write in Korean when I was about nine year old. I had to write my diary as homework. I wrote almost everyday, and my teacher looked over and gave me some comments. When I was a middle school student, I used to write about my impression of certain books that we read. There were two or three contests about this type of writing on certain books every month. The teacher gave a prize to a student who was the best writer of the month.

A Polish student wrote about a variety of writing assignments given by her teachers and the expectation of how to write a literary analysis in her high school:

I started to learn how to write in Polish, my native language, during the last few years in the elementary school. The teacher gave us a lot of freedom in our writing. Our assignments could be a letter, a dialogue, a monologue, or defending a position. Later we had to write what the authors point in the writing the book was and what the main characters and ideas in the book were and how we could compare it to our lives and our experiences and what our personal opinion was about the book.

A Russian student described a kind of research-oriented essay assignment in his high school experience:

In my high school days back home, we were assigned to write essays. The essays in Russian were usually much longer and complicated. For example, we wrote a book about the life of Tolstoy, a famous Russian writer. It was about twenty-one pages long and very complicated. I had to say a lot of different information from different sources like encyclopedias.

A Chinese student confirmed the similar writing assignments that she had back home and in the United States. However, she mentioned a different type of writing that she was taught to write:

Back in China at middle school and high school, we learned how to write a kind of prose, we called san wen, an interpretation of a natural scenery using your own voice. This was a literary genre created by classical Chinese writer Zhu Zi Qing. Reading his writing, for example his masterpiece "The moonlight over the lotus pond," I had this (transactional) feeling with the writer and enjoyed the way the writer put the words on the paper. It was beautiful.

Several students noted a close connection between reading and writing when talking about their progression in learning how to write in their native language. These students said that they were taught to use literature for vocabulary development and imitating certain styles of writing. A strong emphasis on reading to write was shown in these students' reflections as shown in the following Chinese student's autobiography:

Reading is important because it lets you know how a nice piece should be like. You can't write down something nice without knowing what is nice. It's easy to read some stories as entertainment, but it's not easy to catch the ways that how these good writers wrote. My teachers back in China helped us know how these writers wrote by explaining their ideas and how they chose words with similar meanings.

Reading was closely related to writing. Several students noted the importance of reading to write and imitating the style of the writers:

When I was more proficient in Spanish, my native language, I was taught to read the famous authors' works like Miguel de Cervantes and other famous Spanish novelists works. They influenced me a lot in my style of writing. I fell in love with the way they used the words in their novels. Since then, I started to use complex sentence structures in Spanish with a great many fancy words. Thanks to them I gained a vast knowledge of the Spanish vocabulary.

A Bangladeshi student recalled how he took trouble to bring books to America to use reading to refresh his reading and writing skills:

> Now I write letters to my friends back home and I also read novels in my native language. The best writing practice of my language is to read novels. When I came over here, I brought about two hundred books with me and now I am rereading them again and again since I don't have more books to read. By doing that, I can still feel about my country and keep up with my writing.

Most Satisfying Writing Assignments in Their Native Languages

Reading through these students' writing autobiographies, I noticed a consistency. Though many of these students might not be verbal in class or perform well in English, they were already successful writers in their native languages. Many of them continued writing in their native languages after coming to the United States. Students told stories of how the most satisfying piece of writing that they wrote made a difference in their perception of writing and motivated them to become successful writers. For example, a Polish student recalled:

> I still remember my first favorite book on love and the assignment based on that book back home in Poland. It was an old Celtic myth "Tristan and Tholdo" and "Tristan 1964". My writing was read in front of the class, that made me feel like a really good writer. When I finished elementary school, I already knew that I liked to write and my papers were pretty good. According to that I chose a high school with a special writing program. I wrote a lot, especially poetry. One of my poems "Angel" got the first award in school poetry contest.

A Russian student wrote about competing in a writing contest:

> When I was twelve, I read a story and I hated the end of it. So, I rewrote the end of the story and made it a happy one. There was a writing contest among all the school students of the Soviet Union. I sent in my story. I was not among the first winners, but I still got a prize of one hundred rubles. It was big money for me, a small girl who have never had more than a ruble.

A Chinese student revealed how he used writing to express his feelings and passion to win his girlfriend back:

> I love to write a lyric prose. My most satisfying school assignment came when I was in the secondary school back in Hong Kong. I had a girlfriend back then and we had wonderful days together. But we broke up

after a while. I was so hurt. One day, my Chinese teacher asked us to write a letter to someone we love. I wrote about my ex-girlfriend and I didn't know how to stop or did not even want to stop. I said all the words that I wanted to say to her and I listened to my feelings from my heart. Finally this composition was marked a highest grade in class and my teacher encouraged me to send it to the newspaper and I did. A few weeks later, my writing was printed on the prose section of the newspaper. My girlfriend was so touched by all this that we went back together. From writing that piece I learned how powerful writing is and I liked to express myself in writing.

The most satisfying writing assignment was also remembered by many students as the most challenging assignment. The challenge stimulated their interest and motivated them to achieve, as shown in the following:

The most satisfying school assignment that I can remember was when I had to do a research project in my high school back home. The project was about some of the pre-Inca cultures in my country. In the field research I had to go to some ruins in the mountains with my fellow students. The trip was fun and the ruins were a nice place to visit with lots of tourists around. In my group I had to be the leader because I was the one with more background about the subject. At the end our research paper was about forty pages long, full of graphs and pictures.

Differences between Writing in a Native Language and Writing in English

Home literacy stories told by these students also revealed their struggles with writing in English. Besides learning a different language and writing system, students indicated that often the differences between their native language and English baffled them and created more barriers in learning to write in English. For example, comparing her writing in Korean and writing in English, Kim talked about her struggle with the whole process of writing in English:

It is quite different to write in Korean and in English. When I write in Korean, I do not worry about my grammar or vocabularies. I just write in papers what I think in my head. Some grammar makes me confused, but I don't think it twice because I know that I can express my thought anyway. However, writing in English takes long time because I have to think about grammar and vocabulary. Every time I write, I have trouble with some sentences because I can't express my thoughts in well organized sentences. So I rewrite three or four times. Also grammar in Korea and in English is different. For example, in Korea, a verb comes after an object. There isn't a subject-verb agreement.

In addition to language differences and rhetorical and stylistic differences in writing, especially the impact of writing instruction on students' perceptions of what was judged as a piece of good writing, teacher expectations varied from culture to culture. For example, a Polish student wrote:

> There are a lot of things similar but there are a lot of things different too between the two languages. Sometimes when I write, I like to write it in general not specific. . . . In Polish, we wrote papers, we didn't have to give statistics or write sentences specific, what happened first and then the next, and examples. We were supposed to just give clues rather than being specific in Polish. A lot of times we had to write about our own opinions in Polish. So our own opinions should be counted as good too. But here I had to write about in more specific ways, especially when I don't know how to pick examples from a lot of things. I didn't think of it when I first came to America, because I thought Americans should write the same way as Polish people do. What can be different? But right now I am really seeing the difference.

A Chinese student recalled something considered in American schools as taboo but in her culture a common practice for developing writing skills:

> In my high school years, my Chinese teacher used to talking about three parts of essay writing, my opinion, proving it and the conclusion. It looked like writing in English, but it doesn't require a lot of examples or details and we can use other's words without stating where they come from because they are something everyone knows.

Another Chinese student further commented on writing instruction she received in China and how that influenced her learning to write in Chinese:

> My Chinese teachers back in high school asked us to use strong supporting details from old times. For example, if you want to write: The soldiers who are not ambitious are not good soldiers. This topic demands you give historical examples to show your point, such as Napoleon and many Chinese historical figures to illustrate that those who did not have high goals in their lives, cannot succeed anything. Very often you don't remember the exact words such as what Napoleon said, but the teacher did not look for those details. In Chinese, good writing often begins with a historical background information from the past to the present. Then the writer leads the reader into the thesis.

Conclusion/Implications

Even though the scale of this native literacy investigation was small, the findings reveal something worth noticing and exploring. Stories coming from students' own voices were telling. They offered a glimpse into the educational systems and cultural values from these students' perspectives. The findings, especially in cross-cultural writing differences, confirmed some results obtained from second language writing research done by Ballard and Clanchy, Carson, and Matalene. The students' insights into their native writing instruction, such as the use of sources for learning to write, the methods used in teaching students how to write, and the ways of motivating students to write, give composition teachers information about different ways of learning and viewing literacy in different cultures. Instead of treating these different ways of knowing as deficient or ignoring the impact of these ways of knowing on students' learning to write in English, we need to, as Matalene suggests, "try to understand and appreciate, to admit the relativity of our own rhetoric, and to realize that logics different from our own are not necessarily illogical" (806). It is only by doing so that we can begin to understand ESL students and to design instruction that is responsive to their needs.

First, in dealing with nonnative students, composition instructors need information about students' native literacy learning in order to tailor their instruction. In getting to know the students and their home literacy backgrounds, teachers send the message that ESL students' home literacy backgrounds are acknowledged and valued rather than dismissed or ignored. This sharing can be used as an activity of cross-cultural literacy awareness for both the teacher and the students in the classroom. Such sharing is crucial in building a community of learners so that students who are outsiders can play the roles of insiders whose native literacy and native cultural backgrounds are considered rich resources and not obstacles.

Second, differences in writing and in writing instruction across languages and cultures challenge teachers to expand their teaching repertoire and to diversify teaching strategies when dealing with diverse students. Composition instructors can pinpoint areas for more focused and individualized instruction according to each individual student's needs and background. For example, the Polish student's native literacy instruction is different from the Chinese student's. As Matalene argues, composition teachers need to be aware of not only students' ways of knowing, but also the social, cultural, historical, and educational contexts where students' schooling has been situated. In doing so, teachers can gain deeper understanding of the students' worlds of learning to write, such as their perceptions of the role of memory, the nature of writing, and the issues of authenticity and ownership of the text. Teachers need to incorporate such knowledge into their teaching, helping students to be consciously aware of the differences in writing between their native language and English and to understand the need to adapt to a new discourse in the new culture.

Third, students from different educational and cultural systems often bring with them a whole set of expectations, including anticipated teacher behaviors and preferences for literacy learning in the new culture. Therefore, teachers need to find ways to accommodate students' needs and make good use of students' strengths. For example, giving students choices in reading and writing assignments and allowing students to use their native language in writing at the initial stage can ease the transition and build confidence on the part of learners.

Fourth, one difficulty identified by these ESL students in their autobiographies was their lack of basic working vocabulary and knowledge about the English language. This points to the need for providing ESL students the time and the opportunity to learn new English vocabulary and to use it in their writing. Effective ways of teaching vocabulary might be keeping a reading vocabulary journal, teaching reading for contextual clues, designing language awareness activities focusing on major language points in reading and writing, and training in dictionary and thesaurus skills. All these provide the language assistance which ESL students desperately need.

Fifth, in the reading and literature oriented curriculum, the purposes and functions of reading need to be expanded to address a wide range of demands and needs, such as reading for pleasure, reading for aesthetic appreciation, reading for comprehension, reading for learning and critical thinking, and reading for writing. Writing needs to be brought into the reading curriculum. Teachers need to make explicit connections between reading and writing.

As indicated by the majority of these ESL students' autobiographies, the students would like their American teachers to understand their struggle with learning the new language, literacy skills, and academic content at the same time. One way of building the understanding is for teachers to learn about the students' native language and literacy backgrounds. The more teachers know, the better they can serve ESL students.[1]

Appendix

Writing Prompt for Native Writing Experience

Dear Student,
Thank you very much for having written a composition on your journey to become a writer in English at the beginning of this semester. I was impressed by your achievement in English, especially in learning to write in a language that is not your native language. Your writing makes me want to know more about your writing, specifically, about your native language writing. In your writing, please try to answer the following questions:

What is your native language?

How did you learn to write in your native language?

What writing assignments did your teacher back home assign to you?

How did your teacher go about teaching you how to write in your native language?

What are the differences in writing in English and in your native language?

Do you write in your native language now? If so, what do you write about and to whom?

Note

1. I would like to thank Kevin Birth, Sue L. Goldhaber, and Norman Lewis for their help with this project, and the students who participated in the study. I am also grateful for valuable input from Judith Summerfield in the course of the research process and to Myra Zarnowski in the course of writing this article.

Works Cited

Ballard, Brigid, and John Clanchy. "Assessment by Misconception: Cultural Influences and Intellectual Traditions." *Assessing Second Language Writing in Academic Contexts*. Ed. Liz Hamp-Lyons. Norwood: Ablex, 1990. 19–36.

Carson, Joan G. "Becoming Biliterate: First Language Influences." *Second Language Writing* 1 (1992): 37–60.

Collier, Virginia Patricia. "Age and Rate of Acquisition of Second Language for Academic Purposes." *TESOL Quarterly* 21 (1987): 617–41.

Cummins, James. "The Role of Primary Language Development in Promoting Education Success for Language Minority Students." *Schooling and Language Minority Students: A Theoretical Framework*. Ed. California State Department of Education. Los Angeles: California State University, Evaluation, Dissemination, and Assessment Center. 1981. 3–49.

Matalene, Carolyn. "Contrastive Rhetoric: An American Writing Teacher in China." *College English* 47 (1985): 789–808.

Classroom Activities

Have students write a narrative on "their native learning literacy experiences." First they can brainstorm a list of important features of their first language (Does their first language include articles? How many letters does the alphabet have? Are there masculine and feminine forms of words?) and of their cultural background (political situations in their homelands, celebration of holidays and rites of passage, favorite foods and activities). In discussing these lists, ask students to describe the relationships they see between language and culture and to explain how language is a medium of expression for culture. After reflecting on these ideas, students can begin to draw connections between language as a form of identity and how they learned to write in their native language.

Thinking about Teaching

Not all ESL students have attained written fluency in their language of origin. This concern may be especially important for students who have experienced interruptions in their education, for a variety of reasons. Students in this situation may share a great deal with native speakers of English who have not attained written fluency in English and who are often enrolled in classes for developing writers. If you already teach native speakers of English, note in your teaching journal the similarities and differences that you see as these students grapple with written fluency in English. If you teach exclusively in an ESL program, consider initiating discussions with teachers in a basic writing program. Similarly, basic writing teachers may want to begin speaking on a regular basis with teachers of ESL students. Work together to create shared conversations on issues of common concern. Keep track of similarities and differences in approaches to pedagogy. Make sure to hold the literacy narratives of your students clearly in mind as you work together to discuss solutions. Share the results of these conversations with students so that you can have their input as well.

From Classroom Instruction and Language Minority Students: On Teaching to "Smarter" Readers and Writers

Linda Lonon Blanton

The following excerpts from Linda Lonon Blanton's longer article, which first appeared in Generation 1.5 Meets College Composition *(1999), advocate for a systemic approach to preparatory college courses that include language minority students. Blanton defines language minority students as U.S. citizens or residents who "receive most, if not all, of their secondary schooling here [in the United States], although their home language is not English." Although these students are often more proficient in English than in their home language, they are often placed in ESL courses with international students or in basic writing classes where they may still be labeled "ESL" (and consequently written off as beyond the reach of the teacher's capabilities). Blanton argues that the needs of language minority students are not well served by traditional curricula in either ESL or basic writing that teach isolated skills such as grammar, vocabulary, and rhetorical modes. Instead, Blanton recommends a focus on critical literacy, or "ways of interacting with texts." This concentration on writing instruction, and its intersections with reading, more clearly addresses the issues faced by language minority students, as well as "the needs of all students preparing for college writing."*

Language Minority Students: Who Are They?

Armed with diplomas from U.S. urban high schools, thousands of students whose home language is not English enroll in urban colleges across the country every year. Many of these students immigrated to the United States with their families some years back, when they were in the elementary grades. Others arrived more recently but in enough time to receive most, if not all, of their secondary schooling here. Some, of course, may have been born here.

Many young immigrants or children of immigrants acculturate and assimilate well. And by the time *they* leave high school, their language and literacy capabilities and their academic records place them in a strong position for the most competitive of U.S. colleges. Students like these went to my daughter's high school — immigrants from India, Argentina, Korea, Vietnam, China, and other places — and they had their pick of postsecondary schools. As noted in her school's roster of graduating seniors, these particular classmates of hers chose Georgia Tech, Carnegie Mellon, Vanderbilt, Emory, LSU, Dartmouth, NYU, UT/Austin, UCLA, Rice, Wake Forest, Tulane, and Texas A&M. And given their accomplishments in high school, they are almost certain to be stars in college. These are the success stories, however, and are definitely *not* the students in need of remediation or any other preparatory services as they enter college.

For reasons not always clear to us, other students, whose home language is also not English, tell different stories. They too graduate from U.S. high schools, but then find their educational possibilities limited by their high school experience and records, by their failure to perform well on entry exams or placement tests, or by all of these. Students fitting this latter profile crowd into urban community colleges and city/state universities and are shunted into preparatory programs. These students are ones I have worked with for several decades and have written about (Blanton, 1992a, 1992b, 1993, 1994), ones I refer to here as *language minority* students.

When these students reach college, they may feel strongly that they shouldn't be placed differently from other U.S. high school graduates, and are offended when labeled *ESL*. They are, after all, not *foreign*. In most cases, they either hold green cards and are official residents, or they are U.S. citizens. They and their families are also likely be taxpayers in the locale where they attend college. They probably dress and look like other American students.

Many language minority students speak English with fluency, whether or not it is accented with the imprint of their home language. Some may even sound native-like. Others, for reasons not always in accord with the number of years in the country or length of schooling, may have gotten stuck in a sort of interlanguage. These latter students have difficulty being understood, their pronunciation is "flawed," and their grammar is nonstandard. They may have received the same amount of schooling as the former students, but, for reasons perhaps more related to personal identity or to learning style, it has had little effect on their speech (Ioup, 1996).

Regardless of the state of their spoken English, language minority students, as defined in this discussion, write below par and are designated ESL or basic/developmental/remedial in their college placement. Yet these students are often more literate and schooled in English than in their home language, leading to their unfortunate characterization by some teachers as remedial in two languages.

Problems with Placement

If administrative procedures, placement exams, and particularities of their writing preclude language minority students from being main-streamed,[1] where do we place them? It is not always a solution for them to be placed with basic/remedial writers whose home language *is* English, in part because teachers of these classes often throw up their hands, claiming they are not trained or equipped to work with ESL problems. And, in fact, the writing of language minority students often does show evidence that English is not their mother tongue. A reasonable programmatic response is to train basic writing teachers to integrate language minority students into their classes, but reason does not always prevail.

To complicate matters further, it is also problematic for language minority students to be placed in ESL programs, in part because they take it as an act of discrimination. Why *should* they be separated from other U.S. high school graduates and not allowed to take regular courses, they reason. They assume that writing courses enrolled in by students whose home language is English are more legitimate and will move them toward their major courses more quickly. This, in fact, may be so, because the writing of students in ESL programs is often held to a standard of grammatical perfection not applied to the writing of non-ESL-enrolled students.

Language minority students are also uncomfortable, they say, when placed in ESL classes with "foreigners," that is, international students with F-1 visas who arrive in the United States to complete their higher education and then return home. Not surprisingly, language minority students have little in common with international students, either in terms of future plans, prior school experience, or degree of familiarity with the surrounding community. To add insult to injury, they may be given textbooks that require them, for example, to compare aspects of life in "their" countries to those in the United States. And they may suffer the indignities of being introduced to instructional details, such as which side of their notebook paper to write on, or to cultural aspects of U.S. life, such as, say, the frequent use of first names among casual acquaintances, as if they were newcomers to the country. (See Harklau, in press, for a detailed discussion of the cultural orientation, common-place in ESL instruction, that is inappropriate for language minority students.)

---

[1]Although I use *mainstream* to refer to the curriculum that language minority students are not permitted to enter on arriving at college, I see the metaphor as problematic. It sets these students apart, as if their writing and reading needs represent *differences of kind*. Rather, I assume along with Farr and Daniels (1986) that the teaching of writing/reading to students of all linguistic backgrounds must be guided by the same general principles.

When placed in preparatory classes with "internationals," language minority students naturally assume that they are mistaken for foreign. Their membership in the community is challenged. Their status as residents or citizens is ignored. And their right not to be treated differently from other U.S. high school graduates is denied. With such resentment — submerged as it may be — draining away their energies, no wonder some language minority students have difficulty concentrating on learning. They are insulted. They have lost face.

Ill-Suited Instructional Designs

Whether language minority students are placed in ESL programs with internationals or in basic/remedial writing classes with (other) Americans, classroom instruction is often ill-suited to their literacy needs. Let's take ESL instruction first. Traditional pedagogy in ESL classes assumes a focus on linguistic structures, understood as part of the language acquisition process. As such, classwork targets language forms, such as modals and verb tenses, if sentence-oriented. If discourse-oriented, instruction targets more global elements such as, say, connectors as part of paragraph cohesion or introduction-body-conclusion essay development. Either way, grammatical, syntactic, and rhetorical elements — that is, language structures — form the pedagogical focus.

More advanced instruction, in tradition ESL pedagogy, translates into students' presumed need to acquire *more* English, which may indeed be the case for international students with prior limited exposure to the language. Even with the pedagogical focus shifted away from speaking English to reading and writing it, ESL teachers, relying "almost exclusively on linguistics for their conception of literacy" (Rodby, 1992, p. 2), teach reading and writing as language structure/form. When not concentrated on comprehension exercises and vocabulary work, reading activities may focus on unraveling syntax that readers might stumble over, or on analyzing an essay writer's use of discourse elements to achieve a particular rhetorical effect. In writing class — and reading and writing continue to be handled separately — students write on assigned topics in order to practice using language correctly. Because, in a traditional paradigm, writing improvement is assumed to result from correction, student writing is turned in to the teacher, who corrects it and hands it back, thereby providing necessary feedback for better writing on the next assignment.

Conflating literacy acquisition with language acquisition, ESL instruction marches ahead, teaching "more" English to students, some of whom have spent much of their schooling, if not most of their lives, in the United States. Evaluated in their ESL classes according to the norms of a discourse community that marginalizes them, even threatens to exclude them (Harklau, in press), language minority students' frustrations mount.

The problems then are these. To begin with, the administrative practice of placing internationals and language minority students in the same classes, without regard to individual circumstance or instructional need, ignores the assault of that practice on the identity and pride of language minority students. Worse, program decisions in those joint classes usually privilege the internationals: teaching goals, textbook choices, and instructional talk are all founded on everyone's "newness" to things "American" and to everyone's need for greater English-language fluency.

Next, let's discuss basic/remedial writing instruction, which is often on an institutionally parallel track with ESL writing instruction. When placed in basic/remedial writing courses with non-ESL students, language minority students don't always fare much better than in ESL courses with internationals. Traditionally, basic/remedial courses are designed for native English speakers, primarily nonmainstream dialect speakers who have experienced little success with school writing. The institutional crux of the matter is that while traditional writing pedagogy presumes that basic/remedial students have little need for language development — and, if they did, teachers of basic writing generally have little linguistic training — basic writing programs, traditionally taught, demonstrate little understanding of literacy either.

Shaughnessey's (1977) and Rose's (1989) insights to the contrary, eradicating the nonstandardness of students' written English remains the paramount goal of most basic/remedial programs today. Get their writing cleaned up and get them through the proficiency test that stands between them and further college study: that's the pressure placed on basic writing teachers by administrators, who don't want noncredit-bearing programs siphoning off scarce resources, and state legislators, who oppose appropriating funds for remedial education.

Akin to the recent congressional debate on welfare, the debate on remedial education is a blame game. If secondary schools were doing their jobs, if parents were taking proper responsibility for their children's learning, if students were more serious about school, then we wouldn't have students, particularly immigrant students, entering college in need of remedial English (and math). So we must take a stand against all that permissiveness and personal irresponsibility — *us* paying for *them* — and either cut off funds for remedial programs altogether, or give students a small window of opportunity — one to two semesters, at most — to get up to speed. Move them on or move them out.

No wonder that teachers, like drill sergeants, march students through training in standardizing the forms they use in writing. But even before heightened anti-immigrant sentiments and new funding pressures, basic writing textbooks were written according to a traditional pedagogy that made them little more than grammar exercise books. The focus was almost exclusively on the most frequent and "egregious" errors basic writers make in using English-language forms: lack of subject–verb agreement, sentence fragments, run-on sentences, spelling and punctuation mistakes, and nonstandard verb tenses.

Even when traditional basic/remedial writing instruction takes a more rhetorical slant, it, like traditional ESL writing instruction, sticks to a form-centered pedagogy (Blanton, 1995), simply shifting the focus to overall paragraph or essay structure. Writing practice then centers on matters such as, say, thesis statements, topic sentences, or supporting examples. Infused with an antiquated perception of English discourse as "fitting" rhetorical modes (Bain, 1866), like muffins in a tin, remedial writing lessons model, say, expository essay structure or cause–effect arrangement. With little concern for reading, except for analyzing texts as models of rhetorical modes, traditional pedagogy gets students operating in conceptual frames that, true, can manifest themselves in English discourse (whether academic or not), but — herein lies the fundamental instructional problem — with form externally imposed on writerly efforts, effectively stifling a writer's possibility to generate thoughtful prose.

Before discussing further the literacy needs of language minority students — and, I would add, the needs of all students preparing for college writing — I want to briefly outline some of the unsuccessful instructional practices that are commonplace in ESL and basic/remedial writing programs today. For ease of expression, I often use the term *preparatory* to refer to both ESL and basic/remedial programs, because language minority students may be institutionally tracked along either route. . . .

Critical Literacy and Classroom Instruction

As discussed elsewhere (Blanton, 1994), my experience with language minority readers is of treating texts as "dead on the page." As readers, they are not aware of the possibility of interacting with texts, yet this is the very behavior that researchers put at the heart of formal learning and academic success (Bartholomae & Petrosky, 1986; Carson, 1993; Heath & Mangiola, 1991; Leki, 1993; Salvatori, 1996; Spack, 1993; Wall, 1986; Zamel, 1996). Being unaware of textual interaction does not make language minority students "illiterate." Not at all. But their literacy is functional, not critical.[2]

Functional and critical literacy are different behaviors. Briefly, functionally, but not academically, literate readers decode texts, but seem

---

[2]Throughout, I discuss the absence of what I call critical literacy as an educational problem for language minority students; and, indeed, I believe it is, given academic expectations in postsecondary U.S. schools. I do not, however, see the absence of critical literacy as an intellectual failure on students' part. Critical literacy, despite its privileged status in U.S. academia, is a way of being/knowing in the world, and, like all ways, it is socially constructed and culturally derived. If we knew more about the social and linguistic backgrounds of language minority students, we might well discover that, like Heath's (1983) Roadville and Trackton children, these students' literate ways simply do not synchronize with school ways; and *that* is the point of failure.

unaware they can and should (from the academy's perspective) bring their own perspectives to bear in creating a reading. When the last word on the last page is decoded, the reading is finished. To functionally literate readers, "poor" reading, then, is failing to remember the words of a text.

If remembering the words were possible, even a decoding relationship to texts would be difficult with poor writing of the sort discussed earlier, with texts written by and to no one in particular. When a reader's mind "hydroplanes" over the surface of a page because it doesn't connect with anything *on* the page (Hairston, 1986), then even functional reading becomes undoable.

So students' failure becomes multilayered. They can't remember the words of a text because no one can. Even if it were possible, they couldn't remember poorly written texts because their minds wouldn't connect with anything on the page. And, with better-written texts, where a connection — and an interaction — is theoretically possible, these readers have no experience connecting and interacting. Unlike Alice, they don't know there *is* a looking glass to step through, into a world of "talking reading and writing" (Heath & Branscombe, 1985, p. 15).

Students who have no experience talking reading and writing claim no individualized perspective on texts. They don't factor themselves into the picture. And they reduce textual and intellectual complexity to a reductive simplicity. If you ask them questions that can be answered from a reasonably accessible text, you'll get answers. If you ask questions that can't be answered from the text, you'll still get answers from the text, or you'll get silence. A while back, I realized that I, too, had once been that kind of reader, the result of years of schooling where all my answers to others' questions were either right or wrong. And I am aware that at times I still have to stop myself from attempting to commit to memory the words of a text, as if I can't trust myself to assign significance.

Whatever else teachers do with language minority students to prepare them for academic study, we must create opportunities for them to interact with texts: Create opportunities to know that a text can function as a fulcrum to bring reader and writer together; to know that the reader has the responsibility of giving voice to the writer's argument, in the writer's absence, and then engaging in conversation with that voice; to have the confidence to match voices with the text's author; and to recognize, as in poorly written academic texts, when an author has failed to make a conversation possible (Salvatori, 1996).

In reading-writing classrooms, creating opportunities to interact with texts means engaging in tasks that require talking and writing about them. In particular, classroom activities need to engage students in questioning texts, linking them to each other, connecting them to their readers' experience, using them to support or explain their readers' ideas, using texts to illuminate their readers' experience, and using their experience to illuminate texts (Heath & Mangiola, 1991). These are the practices that accomplish critical literacy.

According to Heath and Mangiola (1991), these practices can be independent of any particular academic discipline, but underlie success in all fields of study. This idea accords with Spack's contention (1988) that language minority students should not work with ESL or basic writing teachers in the various disciplines. Rather, they need from preparatory teachers the kind of instructional work that can transfer to all disciplines.

Critical literacy needs to be distinguished from literacy *skills*, which lie outside of texts as wholes. Literacy skills are "mechanistic abilities that focus on separating out and manipulating discrete elements of a text — such as spelling, vocabulary, grammar, topic sentences, and outlines" (Heath & Mangiola, 1991, p. 40). Literacy skills can be learned from lessons and workbook exercises on, say, commas and verb agreement, but they do not accomplish critical literacy.

Critical literacy is more than learning to read and write, and more than know-how in using language conventions. Readers and writers achieve it through textual interaction because that, in fact, is what *it* is: ways of interacting with texts. Although literacy skills undoubtedly transfer to students' future coursework — especially in enabling them to offer up acceptable-looking assignments — critical literacy practices, and not skills, make the crucial difference in academic success. [. . .]

Acknowledgments

I am indebted to my colleague Elizabeth Penfield and to Linda Harklau, for critical readings of earlier drafts of this chapter.

References

Bain, A. (1866). *English composition and rhetoric: A manual.* (American edition, revised.) New York: D. Appleton.

Bartholomae, D., & Petrosky, A. (1986). Facts, artifacts and counterfacts: A basic reading and writing course for the college curriculum. In D. Bartholomae & A. Petrosky (Eds.), *Facts, artifacts and counterfacts: Theory and method for a reading and writing course* (pp. 3–43). Upper Montclair, NJ: Boynton/Cook.

Blanton, L. L. (1992a). A holistic approach to college ESL: Integrating language and content. *ELT Journal, 46*(3), 285–293.

Blanton, L. L. (1992b). Reading, writing, and authority: Issues in developmental ESL. *College ESL, 2*(1), 11–19.

Blanton, L. L. (1993). Reading as performance: Reframing the function of reading. In J. G. Carson & I. Leki (Eds.), *Reading in the composition classroom: Second language perspectives* (pp. 234–246). Boston: Heinle & Heinle.

Blanton, L. L. (1994). Discourse, artifacts, and the Ozarks: Understanding academic literacy. *Journal of Second Language Writing, 3*(1), 1–16.

Blanton, L. L. (1995). Elephants and paradigms: Conversations about teaching L2 writing. *College ESL, 5*(1), 1–21.

Carson, J. G. (1993). Reading for writing: Cognitive perspectives. In J. G. Carson & I. Leki (Eds.), *Reading in the composition classroom: Second language perspectives* (pp. 85–104). Boston: Heinle & Heinle.

Farr, M., & Daniels, H. (1986). *Language diversity and writing instruction.* New York: ERIC and Urbana, IL: National Council of Teachers of English.

Hairston, M. (1986). *Successful writing* (2nd ed.), New York: W. W. Norton.

Harklau, L. (1999). Representing culture in the ESL writing classroom. In E. Hinkel (Ed.), *Culture in second language teaching and learning.* New York: Cambridge University Press.

Heath, S. B. (1983). *Ways with words: Language, life, and work in communities and classrooms.* Cambridge, England: Cambridge University Press.

Heath, S. B., & Branscombe, A. (1985). "Intelligent writing" in an audience community: Teacher, students, and researcher. In S. W. Freedman (Ed.), *The acquisition of written language: Response and revision* (pp. 3–32). Norwood, NJ: Ablex.

Heath, S. B., & Mangiola, L. (1991). *Children of promise: Literate activity in linguistically and culturally diverse classrooms.* Washington, DC: National Education Association.

Ioup, G. (1996). *Can form-focused instruction have an effect on fossilized grammatical rules?* Unpublished manuscript.

Leki, I. (1995). Good writing: I know it when I see it. In D. Belcher & G. Braine (Eds.), *Academic writing in a second language* (pp. 23–46). Norwood, NJ: Ablex.

Rodby, J. (1992). *Appropriating literacy: Writing and reading English as a second language.* Portsmouth, NH: Boynton/Cook Heinemann.

Rose, M. (1989). *Lives on the boundry.* New York: Penguin.

Salvatori, M. (1996). Conversations with texts: Reading in the teaching of composition. *College English, 58*(4), 440–454.

Shaughnessy, M. (1977). *Errors and expectations.* New York: Oxford University Press.

Spack, R. (1993). Student meets text, text meets student: Finding a way into academic discourse. In J. G. Carson & I. Leki (Eds.), *Reading in the composition classroom: Second language perspectives* (pp. 183–196). Boston: Heinle & Heinle.

Spack, R. (1988). Initiating ESL students into the academic discourse community: How far should we go? *TESOL Quarterly, 22,* 29–51.

Wall, S. V. (1986). Writing, reading and authority: A case study. In D. Bartholomae & A. Petrosky (Eds.), *Facts, artifacts and counterfacts: Theory and method for a reading and writing course* (pp. 105–136). Upper Montclair, NJ: Boynton/Cook.

Zamel, V. (1996). Transcending boundaries: Complicating the scene of teaching language. *College ESL, 6*(2), 1–11.

Classroom Activities

Citing Salvatori (1996), Blanton maintains that critical literacy for language minority students must focus on engagement and interaction with texts, including "learning to recognize, as in poorly written academic texts, when an author has failed to make a conversation possible." Invite students to bring to class samples from at least two academic texts that they have read in other courses. One text should clearly demonstrate the possibilities of "engaging in conversation" with the reader; the other should demonstrate difficulties in creating such a conversation. Have students read aloud excerpts from each type of text and then describe in writing the differences that they find in the texts' voices and presentations. Students can work to identify the criteria that constitute a successful academic text, as well as what preparation a reader should bring to the text to sustain continued engagement and critical thinking.

Thinking about Teaching

Blanton articulates the political issues that can have a critical impact on, and often serve as unstated assumptions for, programs that serve large populations of language minority students. In particular, she notes "heightened anti-immigrant sentiments and new funding pressures." Blanton's argument seems prescient, given that it was written well before the September 11, 2001, attacks and the 2003 war against Iraq. Considering these recent historical developments, as well as the continued funding cutbacks for public colleges and universities, what are the implications for language minority students in your community or region? How have these events impacted particular student populations or programs? Has your teaching changed as a result, and if so, in what ways? Reflect on these issues in your teaching journal and consider developing your ideas in an article for publication.

13

Placement and Assessment

More than many issues within the field of composition," write the authors of the Conference on College Composition and Communication position statement, "writing assessment evokes strong passions." Most likely you have struggled at some point to define and refine your own assessment strategies. As a discipline, we continue to search for the most effective ways of assessing — that is, measuring, judging, evaluating — our students' writing proficiency. Too often *effective* becomes confused with *efficient*. The three articles in this chapter revisit many of the issues that evoke debate, including placement and exit testing, proficiency criteria, the writing process, and portfolio review. The CCCC document presents assessment in hypothetical (if not utopian) terms. The two other selections, by Daniel J. Royer and Roger Gilles, and by Kay Harley and Sally I. Cannon, document actual institutional practice in placing and assessing basic writing students and in defining the parameters of the basic writing course. In addition to practical suggestions, these articles offer teachers an opportunity to contemplate their own individual notions about and definitions of assessment.

CCCC Position Statement

For several years, the Conference on College Composition and Communication Committee on Assessment worked to create "an official position statement . . . that would help [writing teachers] explain writing assessment to colleagues and administrators and secure the best assessment options for students." Because teachers and administrators often seem to be at cross-purposes in defining the means and ends of writing assessment, the CCCC position statement attempts to help all parties involved reach some sort of consensus. The statement lists ten assumptions regarding writing assessment that should be considered when creating new policies and implementing new classroom practices. The rest of the document illustrates these assumptions, as the writers list how assessment implicates students, faculty, administrators, and legislators. The CCCC Committee on Assessment is forceful in its argument that institutional assessment measures should involve neither an exploitation of students and faculty nor a compromise of pedagogical integrity.

I n 1993, the CCCC Executive Committee charged the CCCC Committee on Assessment with developing an official position statement on assessment. Prior to that time, members of CCCC had expressed keen interest in having a document available that would help them explain writing assessment to colleagues and administrators and secure the best assessment options for students.

Beginning in 1990 at NCTE in Atlanta, Georgia, open forums were held at both NCTE and CCCC conventions to discuss the possibility of a position statement: its nature, forms, and the philosophies and practices it might espouse. At these forums, at regular meetings, and through correspondence, over one hundred people helped develop the current document.

An initial draft of the statement was submitted to the CCCC Executive Committee at its March 1994 meeting, where it was approved in substance. The Executive Committee also reviewed a revised statement at its November 1994 meeting. An announcement in the February 1995 issue of CCC invited all CCCC members to obtain a draft of the statement and to submit their responses to the Assessment Committee. Copies of the draft statement were mailed to all 1995 CCCC Convention preregistrants, and the final draft was presented in a forum at the 1995 CCCC Convention in Washington, D.C. Changes based on discussions at that session, and at a later workshop, were incorporated into the position statement, which was subsequently approved for publication by the CCCC Executive Committee.

The CCCC Committee on Assessment acknowledges the contributions of the cochairs of the previous [1994] CCCC Committee on Assessment, Edward Nolte and Sandra Murphy. In addition, Donald Daiker provided substantial assistance as a former member of the committee.

Members of the [1995] CCCC Committee on Assessment [were]: Kathleen Blake Yancey, Chair; Arnetha Ball, Pat Belanoff, Kathleen Bell, Renee Betz, Emily Decker, Christine Farris, Thomas Hilgers, Audrey Roth, Lew Sayers, and Fred Thomas.

More than many issues within the field of composition studies, writing assessment evokes strong passions. It can be used for a variety of appropriate purposes, both inside the classroom and outside: providing assistance to students; awarding a grade; placing students in appropriate courses; allowing them to exit a course or sequence of courses;

and certifying proficiency, to name some of the more obvious. But writing assessment can be abused as well: used to exploit graduate students, for instance, or to reward or punish faculty members. We begin our position statement, therefore, with a foundational claim upon which all else is built; it is axiomatic that in all situations calling for writing assessment in both two-year and four-year institutions, the primary purpose of the specific assessment should govern its design, its implementation, and the generation and dissemination of its results.

It is also axiomatic that in spite of the diverse uses to which writing assessment is put, the general principles undergirding writing assessment are similar:

> Assessments of written literacy should be designed and evaluated by well-informed current or future teachers of the students being assessed, for purposes clearly understood by all the participants; should elicit from student writers a variety of pieces, preferably over a period of time; should encourage and reinforce good teaching practices; and should be solidly grounded in the latest research on language learning.

These assumptions are explained fully in the first section below; after that, we list the rights and responsibilities generated by these assumptions; and in the third section we provide selected references that furnish a point of departure for literature in the discipline.

Assumptions

All writing assessments — and thus all policy statements about writing assessment — make assumptions about the nature of what is being assessed. Our assumptions include the following.

First, *language is always learned and used most effectively in environments where it accomplishes something the user wants to accomplish for particular listeners or readers within that environment.* The assessment of written literacy must strive to set up writing tasks, therefore, that identify purposes appropriate to and appealing to the particular students being tested. Additionally, assessment must be contextualized in terms of why, where, and for what purpose it is being undertaken; this context must also be clear to the students being assessed and to all others (i.e., stakeholders/participants) involved.

Accordingly, there is no test which can be used in all environments for all purposes, and the best "test" for any group of students may well be locally designed. The definition of "local" is also contextual; schools with common goals and similar student populations and teaching philosophies and outcomes might well form consortia for the design, implementation, and evaluation of assessment instruments even though the schools themselves are geographically separated from each other.

Second, *language by definition is social.* Assessment which isolates students and forbids discussion and feedback from others conflicts with current cognitive and psychological research about language use and the benefits of social interaction during the writing process; it also is out of step with much classroom practice.

Third, *reading — and thus, evaluation, since it is a variety of reading — is as socially contextualized as all other forms of language use.* What any reader draws out of a particular text and uses as a basis of evaluation is dependent upon how that reader's own language use has been shaped and what his or her specific purpose for reading is. It seems appropriate, therefore, to recognize the individual writing program, institution, consortium, and so forth as a community of interpreters who can function fairly — that is, assess fairly — with knowledge of that community.

Fourth, *any individual's writing "ability" is a sum of a variety of skills employed in a diversity of contexts, and individual ability fluctuates unevenly among these varieties.* Consequently, one piece of writing — even if it is generated under the most desirable conditions — can never serve as an indicator of overall literacy, particularly for high stakes decisions. Ideally, such literacy must be assessed by more than one piece of writing, in more than one genre, written on different occasions, for different audiences, and evaluated by multiple readers. This realization has led many institutions and programs across the country to use portfolio assessment.

Fifth, *writing assessment is useful primarily as a means of improving learning.* Both teachers and students must have access to the results in order to be able to use them to revise existing curricula and/or plan programs for individual students. And, obviously, if results are to be used to improve the teaching-learning environment, human and financial resources for the implementation of improvements must be in place in advance of the assessment. If resources are not available, institutions should postpone these types of assessment until they are. Furthermore, when assessment is being conducted solely for program evaluation, all students should not be tested, since a representative group can provide the desired results. Neither should faculty merit increases hinge on their students' performance on any test.

Sixth, *assessment tends to drive pedagogy.* Assessment thus must demonstrate "systemic validity"; it must encourage classroom practices that harmonize with what practice and research have demonstrated to be effective ways of teaching writing and of becoming a writer. What is easiest to measure — often by means of a multiple choice test — may correspond least to good writing, and that in part is an important point: *choosing a correct response from a set of possible answers is not composing.* As important, just because students are asked to write does not mean that the "assessment instrument" is a "good" one. Essay tests that ask students to form and articulate opinions about some important issue, for instance, without time to reflect, to talk to others, to read on the subject, to revise and so forth — that is, without taking into account through either appropriate classroom practice or the assessment process itself — encourage distorted notions of what writing is. They also encourage poor teaching and little learning. Even teachers who recognize and employ the methods used by real writers in working with students can find their best efforts undercut by assessments such as these.

Seventh, *standardized tests, usually developed by large testing organizations, tend to be for accountability purposes, and when used to make statements about student learning, misrepresent disproportionately the skills and abilities of students of color.* This imbalance tends to decrease when tests are directly related to specific contexts and purposes, in contrast to tests that purport to differentiate between "good" and "bad" writing in a general sense. Furthermore, standardized tests tend to focus on readily accessed features of the language — on grammatical correctness and stylistic choice — and on error, on what is wrong rather than on the appropriate rhetorical choices that have been made. Consequently, the outcome of such assessments is negative: students are said to demonstrate what they do "wrong" with language rather than what they do well.

Eighth, *the means used to test students' writing ability shapes what they, too, consider writing to be.* If students are asked to produce "good" writing within a given period of time, they often conclude that all good writing is generated within those constraints. If students are asked to select — in a multiple choice format — the best grammatical and stylistic choices, they will conclude that good writing is "correct" writing. They will see writing erroneously, as the avoidance of error; they will think that grammar and style exist apart from overall purpose and discourse design.

Ninth, *financial resources available for designing and implementing assessment instruments should be used for that purpose and not to pay for assessment instruments outside the context within which they are used.* Large amounts of money are currently spent on assessments that have little pedagogical value for students or teachers. However, money spent to compensate teachers for involvement in assessment is also money spent on faculty development and curriculum reform since inevitably both occur when teachers begin to discuss assessment which relates directly to their classrooms and to their students.

Tenth, and finally, *there is a large and growing body of research on language learning, language use, and language assessment that must be used to improve assessment on a systematic and regular basis.* Our assumptions are based on this scholarship. Anyone charged with the responsibility of designing an assessment program must be cognizant of this body of research and must stay abreast of developments in the field. Thus, assessment programs must always be under review and subject to change by well-informed faculty, administrators, and legislators.

Assessment of writing is a legitimate undertaking. But by its very nature it is a complex task, involving two competing tendencies: first, the impulse to measure writing as a general construct; and second, the impulse to measure writing as a contextualized, site and genre-specific ability. There are times when re-creating or simulating a context (as in the case of assessment for placement, for instance) is limited. Even in this case, however, assessment — when conducted sensitively and purposefully — can have a positive impact on teaching, learning, curricular design, and student attitudes. Writing assessment can serve to inform both the individual and the public about the achievements of students and the effectiveness of teaching. On the other hand, poorly designed assessments, and poorly implemented assessments, can be enormously harmful because of the power of language: personally, for our students as human beings; and academically, for our students as learners, since learning is mediated through language.

Students who take pleasure and pride in using written language effectively are increasingly valuable in a world in which communication across space and a variety of cultures has become routine. Writing assessment that alienates students from writing is counterproductive, and writing assessment that fails to take an accurate and valid measure of their writing even more so. But writing assessment that encourages students to improve their facility with the written word, to appreciate their power with that word and the responsibilities that accompany such power, and that salutes students' achievements as well as guides them, should serve as a crucially important educational force.

Students should:

1. demonstrate their accomplishments and/or development in writing by means of composing, preferably in more than one sample written on more than one occasion, with sufficient time to plan, draft, rewrite, and edit each product or performance.

2. write on prompts developed from the curriculum and grounded in "real-world" practice.

3. be informed about the purposes of the assessment they are writing for, the ways the results will be used, and avenues of appeal.

4. have their writing evaluated by more than one reader, particularly in "high stakes" situations (e.g., involving major institutional consequences such as getting credit for a course, moving from one context to another, or graduating from college).

5. receive response, from readers, intended to help them improve as writers attempting to reach multiple kinds of audiences.

Faculty should:

1. play key roles in the design of writing assessments, including creating writing tasks and scoring guides, for which they should receive support in honoraria and/or release time; and should appreciate and be responsive to the idea that assessment tasks and procedures must be sensitive to cultural, racial, class, and

gender differences, and to disabilities, and must be valid for and not penalize any group of students.

2. participate in the readings and evaluations of student work, supported by honoraria and/or release time.

3. assure that assessment measures and supports what is taught in the classroom.

4. make themselves aware of the difficulty of constructing fair and motivating prompts for writing, the need for field testing and revising of prompts, the range of appropriate and inappropriate uses of various kinds of writing assessments, and the norming, reliability, and validity standards employed by internal and external test-makers, as well as share their understanding of these issues with administrators and legislators.

5. help students to prepare for writing assessments and to interpret assessment results in ways that are meaningful to students.

6. use results from writing assessments to review and (when necessary) to revise curriculum.

7. encourage policy makers to take a more qualitative view toward assessment, encouraging the use of multiple measures, infrequent large-scale assessment, and large-scale assessment by sampling of a population rather than by individual work whenever appropriate.

8. continue conducting research on writing assessment, particularly as it is used to help students learn and to understand what they have achieved.

Administrators and higher education governing boards should:

1. educate themselves and consult with rhetoricians and composition specialists teaching at their own institutions, about the most recent research on teaching and assessing writing and how they relate to their particular environment and to already established programs and procedures, understanding that generally student learning is best demonstrated by performances assessed over time and sponsored by all faculty members, not just those in English.

2. announce to stakeholders the purposes of all assessments, the results to be obtained, and the ways that results will be used.

3. assure that the assessments serve the needs of students, not just the needs of an institution, and that resources for necessary courses linked to the assessments are therefore available before the assessments are mandated.

4. assure opportunities for teachers to come together to discuss all aspects of assessments; the design of the instruments; the standards to be employed; the interpretation of the results; possible changes in curriculum suggested by the process and results.

5. assure that all decisions are made by more than one reader.

6. not use any assessment results as the primary basis for evaluating the performance of or rewards due a teacher; they should recognize that student learning is influenced by many factors such as cognitive development, personality type, personal motivation, physical and psychological health, emotional upheavals, socio-economic background, family successes and difficulties which are neither taught in the classroom nor appropriately measured by writing assessment.

Legislators should:

1. not mandate a specific instrument (test) for use in any assessment; although they may choose to answer their responsibility to the public by mandating assessment in general or at specific points in student careers, they should allow professional educators to choose the types and ranges of assessments that reflect the educational goals of their curricula and the nature of the student populations they serve.

2. understand that mandating assessments also means providing funding to underwrite those assessments, including resources to assist students and to bring teachers together to design and implement assessments, to review curriculum, and to amend the assessment and/or curriculum when necessary.

3. become knowledgeable about writing assessment issues, particularly by consulting with rhetoricians and composition specialists engaged in teaching, on the most recent research on the teaching of writing and assessment.

4. understand that different purposes require different assessments and that qualitative forms of assessment can be more powerful and meaningful for some purposes than quantitative measures are, and that assessment is a means to help students learn better, not a way of unfairly comparing student populations, teachers or schools.

5. include teachers in the drafting of legislation concerning assessments.

6. recognize that legislation needs to be reviewed continually for possible improvement in light of actual results and ongoing developments in writing assessment theory and research.

Selected References

Belanoff, Pat, and Marcia Dickson, eds. *Portfolios: Process and Product*. Portsmouth: Boynton, 1991.

Black, Laurel, Donald Daiker, Jeffrey Sommers, and Gail Stygall, eds. *New Directions in Portfolio Assessment: Reflective Practice, Critical Theory, and Large Scale Scoring*. Portsmouth: Boynton, 1994.

Cooper, Charles, and Lee Odell, eds. *Evaluating Writing: Describing, Measuring, Judging*. Urbana: NCTE, 1977.

CCCC Committee on Assessment. "A Selected Bibliography on Postsecondary Writing Assessment, 1979–91." *College Composition and Communication* 43 (1992): 244–55.

Elbow, Peter. "Ranking, Evaluating, and Liking: Sorting Out Three Forms of Judgment." *College English* 55 (1993): 187–206.

Gordon, Barbara. "Another Look: Standardized Tests for Placement in College Composition Courses." *WPA: Writing Program Administration* 10 (1987): 29–38.

Greenberg, Karen. "Validity and Reliability: Issues in the Direct Assessment of Writing." *WPA: Writing Program Administration* 16.1–2 (1992): 7–22.

Greenberg, Karen, Harvey Wiener, and Richard Donovan, eds. *Writing Assessment: Issues and Strategies*. New York: Longman, 1986.

Huot, Brian. "Reliability, Validity, and Holistic Scoring: What We Know and What We Need to Know." *College Composition and Communication* 41 (1990): 201–13.

Moss, Pamela. "Can There Be Validity without Reliability?" *Educational Researcher* 23.2 (1994): 5–12.

———. "Validity in High Stakes Writing Assessment: Problems and Possibilities." *Assessing Writing* 1.1 (1994): 109–28.

Odell, Lee. "Defining and Assessing Competence in Writing." *The Nature and Measurement of Competency in English*. Ed. Charles Cooper. Urbana: NCTE, 1981: 95–139.

White, Edward. "Issues and Problems in Writing Assessment." *Assessing Writing* 1.1 (1994): 11–29.

———. *Teaching and Assessing Writing*. 2nd ed. San Francisco: Jossey, 1994.

Wiggins, Grant. *Assessing Student Performance: Exploring the Purpose and Limits of Testing*. San Francisco: Jossey, 1993.

———. "Assessment: Authenticity, Context, and Validity." *Phi Delta Kappan* 75.3 (1993): 200–14.

Williamson, Michael, and Brian Huot, eds. *Validating Holistic Scoring for Writing Assessment*. Cresskill: Hampton, 1993.

Yancey, Kathleen Blake, ed. *Portfolios in the Writing Classroom: An Introduction*. Urbana: NCTE, 1992.

Classroom Activities

The writers of the CCCC document argue that "the means used to test students' writing ability shape what they, too, consider writing to be." Consider this assumption in the context of your basic writing curriculum. Near the beginning of the course, ask students to reflect in their journals about how their placement test seems to define writing ability. Then, near the end of the course (and especially if the writing program includes an end-of-course assessment measure), have students reflect on what they have learned about writing ability. How do students define *good writing?* Have their assumptions changed or remained the same? Why? How are these ideas implicated in the end-of-term assessment? Asking students to reflect on the content of the course, the assessment process, and their own success as learners further encourages them to use their critical thinking skills.

Thinking about Teaching

The sixth assumption of the CCCC document states: "assessment tends to drive pedagogy." With this statement in mind, examine the assessments used in your writing program; what is driving your pedagogy? With other teachers, consider evaluating your institution's assessment strategy in light of the CCCC recommendations. Determine which guidelines your program already includes and which aspects of your program are in need of reevaluation and revision. Also consider how the assessment of basic writing students may be driven by institutional or legislative goals. Are such goals congruent with your goals for the course? With students' goals?

You may wish to suggest faculty review of assessment tools and processes, if such a review does not already exist. The CCCC position statement suggests that faculty affected by (but not responsible for designing) an assessment should demand an explication of its theoretical base.

Directed Self-Placement: An Attitude of Orientation

Daniel J. Royer and Roger Gilles

In this selection, which originally appeared in College Composition and Communication *in 1998, Daniel J. Royer and Roger Gilles offer a solution to the dilemmas of placement testing which they call "directed self-placement," a system that enables students to choose the writing course that they think is most appropriate for them. Although students make this decision independently, they are given input from the director of composition as well as from their academic advisers. As students choose their courses, they examine course descriptions for both basic writing and college writing and are asked to assess their own experiences with reading and writing. Such a system, Royer and Gilles suggest, allows students to focus on those aspects of their education that need the most attention and creates an environment conducive to student-centered, self-directed learning. It also opens up possibilities for course design.*

> No particular results then, so far, but only an attitude of orientation, is
> what the pragmatic method means. *The attitude of looking away from
> first things, principles, "categories," supposed necessities; and of looking
> towards last things, fruits, consequences, facts.*
> — William James (27)

Dan stands at the front of a buzzing lecture hall, a yellow trifold
brochure in hand, watching about a sixth of next year's 2400 "seats"
find a seat. New students are seats; that's the kind of talk one hears as
director of composition at a university that breaks its own enrollment
record every year, doubling in size to nearly 16,000 students over the
last decade. What Dan has to say to these 400 new seats invites an
interesting irony: the administrators love what he's about to say precisely because they think of students as "seats," while Dan is eager to
talk because, in Deweyan fashion, he is eager to upset the prevailing
student/teacher power relations by presenting the students with an
authentic educative choice.

The buzzing subsides, and after brief speeches by the Dean of Students and a counselor from the Financial Aid office, Dan steps forward,
holding up the yellow brochure, and introduces himself as the director
of composition. "In the next few minutes I'm going to ask you to make
the first of many important choices you'll make as a student at this
university — so please listen carefully.

"The Admissions people have placed a yellow trifold brochure, like
this one, in your folder. Let's take a look at it. It says on the front,
English 098 or 150: Which Course is Right for You? Before you register
for classes this afternoon, you'll need to select one of these two courses
to begin with as you begin your freshman year.

"Before I get to the specifics, let me explain why it is we want you
to make this decision and why we aren't going to make it for you. At
many schools, in fact at this school until very recently, people like me
'place' you into a writing course by looking at your ACT or SAT score,
your high-school GPA, and perhaps by having you step into another
room and return to us two hours later with a 'sample' of your writing.
But it turns out that this is not a very valid or reliable way to find out
which first-year writing course is best for you. Writing ability, at least
as we conceive of it, is far too complex to measure so quickly and easily.

"The fact is, we just don't know very much about you as writers.
Perhaps the *best* way to measure your writing ability would be for us to
sit down with each one of you for an hour or so and talk with you about
writing. If I had an hour with each of you, I'd ask you to show me samples
of your best writing from high school. I'd ask you to describe your
strengths and weaknesses as a writer. I'd ask you to tell me how much
you read, and how well you read. If your GPA or standardized test
score didn't look too impressive, I'd ask you if anything much has
changed in your image of yourself or in your habits as a student since
you started your last year of high school. I know that many students
arrive as college freshmen very different people — and become very

different students — from what they were just a few months earlier. Some of you here today must know what I mean.

"I'd ask you how motivated you are. I'd ask you how much you like to write. I'd ask you how well you type. I'd ask you many things. I think you get my point: to find out which first-year writing course is really right for you, I would need to know more than a single test score, and I'd need to see more than a single sample of how you write under pressure or even a portfolio of your high school writing — which has probably gotten pretty stale over the summer.

"Instead, I'm going to ask you to make a responsible choice about which course to take. The question you face is: Should I take English 098 or English 150? Let me explain the difference. English 098 is a preparatory course that helps you write more confidently and purposefully, and it helps you develop ways to clarify and edit your writing for a college-level audience. You will get a letter grade in English 098, and it figures into your GPA, but it doesn't count as one of the 120 credits you need to graduate. English 150, on the other hand, is a four-credit course that prepares you for the variety of writing experiences you will have as a university student in the coming years. The focus is on source-based writing in a variety of genres. All students must eventually get a C or better in English 150 in order to satisfy the freshman composition requirement. The decision you face is whether to go ahead and begin with English 150, or to take a two-semester sequence by starting with English 098 in the first semester and taking English 150 the second.

"Before you make up your mind too quickly, hear me out. Many schools offer a two-semester sequence of first-year writing anyway, so don't feel that you are going to get behind if you begin with 098. You don't want to enroll in 098 if 150 is best for you, and you don't want to enroll in 150 if 098 is best for you. The university has no interest in making you start with either course — that's why *you* are deciding. What we do have an interest in is your success as a student. There is no advantage to beginning with English 150 if you fail or struggle in the course because it's not the right course for you. People do fail that course, and you don't want that to happen to you.

"Generally speaking, you are well prepared for English 150 if you have done quite a bit of reading and writing in high school. English 150 instructors will assume that you can summarize and analyze published material from magazines, newspapers, books, and scholarly journals. They will also assume that you have written a variety of essays in a variety of forms, including narrative, descriptive, and persuasive writing. Look at the checklist on the center panel inside the brochure. These are some of the characteristics that we faculty look for in solid writing students. Do any of these statements describe you?

I read newspapers and magazines regularly.

In the past year, I have read books for my own enjoyment.

In high school, I wrote several essays per year.

My high school GPA placed me in the top third of my class.

I have used computers for drafting and revising essays.

My ACT-English score was above 20.

I consider myself a good reader and writer.

"Perhaps you do see yourself in at least some of those statements. If many of the statements don't describe you or if you just don't consider yourself a strong reader or writer, you might consider taking English 098. In 098 you will focus on writing in specific ways to reach specific audiences. You will write a lot in order to develop comfort and fluency. You will get lots of practice, including many hours with our Writing Center tutors, and you will work on understanding the conventions of standard written English — spelling, grammar, punctuation, and usage. Let's look at the list of general characteristics that may indicate that English 098 is best for you.

Generally I don't read when I don't have to.

In high school, I did not do much writing.

My high school GPA was about average.

I'm unsure about the rules of writing — commas, apostrophes, and so forth.

I've used computers, but not often for writing and revising.

My ACT-English score was below 20.

I don't think of myself as a strong writer.

"In English 098 you will read successful samples of essays written by professionals and by other students. In a typical class, you will complete five or six short essays — two or three pages each. You may cite some of the essays you have read or people you have interviewed, but generally you will not write research-based essays. Indeed, the purpose of English 098 is to give you the confidence, organization, and command necessary to write the research-based essays demanded in English 150 and beyond. English 098 will get you ready to do well in English 150 the next semester.

"Many of you will see statements that describe you in both lists. Others may clearly see that one or the other course is the right one to begin with. If after thinking about it you still can't decide, I'll be glad to talk with you — even to spend an hour and look at some of your writing as I talked about a minute ago — but I think most of you can make the right choice on your own. You all have advisers, and they can help you as well. You'll be meeting with them later today.

"I said before that we don't know much about you. About all I *do* know is that before you earn a 'C' or better in English 150, you'll become a pretty solid college writer. Today you simply have to decide if that will take you one semester or two.

"You may be wondering if you can squeeze your way through English 150 if you aren't really ready for it. Probably not. We use a portfolio-based grading system that requires each student to submit a folder of final work that is graded by a total of three faculty members from a larger group of English 150 teachers who have met all semester to discuss their own and our university's expectations about college writing. Your final portfolio accounts for the majority of your final course grade, and because we 'team grade,' we're confident that an 'A' in one class matches up pretty well with an 'A' in another. Our grading system is described in more detail in the brochure. For now, I just want you to realize that your decision today should not be taken lightly. You really do have to write well in order to move beyond English 150.

"There's other important information in this brochure. Look at the back page under the heading, 'What to Expect the First Day.' Go ahead and read those paragraphs while you listen to me talk for another minute or so. Notice that in both 098 and 150, on the first day of class your teacher will ask you to write a brief essay. Your teacher will read the essay as a simple indication of your writing abilities and let you know what he or she thinks. During this first week of class, you will have the opportunity to switch from one class to the other if you wish. But remember, the decision is yours, not your teacher's. Note too that the brochure includes information about the Writing Center, the Library Skills program, our junior-level writing requirement, and our Writing Across the Curriculum program. We value writing a lot, and in your time as a student here you'll be doing quite a bit of it, so we want you to be as ready as you can be.

"English 098 and 150 are both very good courses. English 150 is a course you will share in common with every freshman. You will all take it. And many of our very best instructors teach English 098. Believe me, we will have many full sections of 098 and every student in that class with you, if that's the one you take, will be there because he or she chose to take it. Nobody will be in 098 against their will, and for this reason many students find the atmosphere there encouraging and helpful. For many, it is a way to brush up, get some practice, and prepare themselves for the challenge of English 150.

"Finally, before I leave, I'd like to see a show of hands, not to indicate which course you will take, but to indicate whether or not you have made a choice. OK. If you're still not sure which course you should enroll in, please talk with me or your adviser later today. Thanks for your time, and I wish you all the best of luck."

Why Directed Self-Placement?

During the summer of 1996, either Dan or Roger, the previous composition director, gave a version of this ten-minute speech to five other groups — and in the end over 22 percent of the students placed themselves into ENG 098. What compels 500 students to place themselves in a course that doesn't count as college credit? Are these the same students that we would have placed in ENG 098 had we used our old method of ACT-English score plus writing sample? We don't yet fully know the answers to these questions, but after our second full year of using what we're calling "directed self-placement," we feel that we've found a placement method that works very well for all of us — teachers, students, and administrators alike.

Our decision to give directed self-placement a try originated with widespread frustration over our traditional placement method. We knew of the well-documented limitations of placement tests — the artificiality of direct writing and the questionable reliability and validity of traditional direct assessment (see, for instance, Elbow). And we'd never liked using ACT-English scores, but we'd resorted to them as a preliminary screen when our freshman-orientation groups got so big we had trouble scoring all the essays in the brief turnaround time available to us. The Admissions people who ran orientation didn't like our method much, either; they had to schedule an hour for writing, then wait for the results before they could help the students register.

Our ENG 098 students weren't very fond of the system, either. They started the class with a chip on their shoulder after having been told during orientation that, despite their "B" average in high school, they were *required* to take a no-credit English class. We surveyed our students in the Fall of 1995 and found that only 38 percent of the ENG 098 students felt they were properly placed in the course. There were quite a few negative comments about both the placement procedure and the course itself.

Finally, the teachers themselves were frustrated. Not only did they have to deal with unhappy students, but they also had to replicate the placement essay during the first week of classes and shift students to the appropriate course, often against the students' will. By January of 1996, it became clear that we were kidding ourselves if we believed that these "supposed necessities" were fair to anyone involved. We decided to rethink our approach.

We first considered trying to improve traditional placement-test procedures. Schools such as the University of Pittsburgh and Washington State have "contextualized" placement decisions by shifting their focus from how student writing matches up against general and fixed criteria to how it fits with the actual curriculum (Huot 553–54). In other words, they place students into *courses* rather than into categories. This alternative does involve some looking away from what William James would call "first things, principles, and 'categories,'" but it seemed to us not to make the full pragmatic turn toward "last things, fruits, consequences, facts." Indeed, we had already been using a version of this method to place our students. But we realized that no matter how site-specific and contextualized we made our reading of placement essays, we might side-step some reliability concerns and finesse our notion of validity, but we would inevitably wind up making decisions based on the inadequate data of a single writing sample. We were beginning to feel that our old placement engine could not, once again, be retuned or rebuilt.

We toyed with the idea of entrance portfolios — which would move us beyond the single piece of writing — but the Admissions directors balked. "This isn't Stanford," they told us. "If we make students put together an entrance portfolio and the next school doesn't, the students will simply pick the next school." Besides, we knew that asking for entrance portfolios would place quite a burden on our already overburdened summer faculty. How would we read over two thousand portfolios? And even if we could do this, we would still be mired in the interrater-reliability fix, even if it was transformed into a question of reliability among those rater/teachers who would be teaching the course. The only real way around this last problem would be to insure that raters taught just those students whose portfolios they assessed, and this would be impossible in the context we faced.

We were stuck. In the meantime, at our administration's prompting, our "institutional analyst" evaluated the placement data and composition grades over the past several years. His conclusion was bleak: statistically speaking, neither of our two placement devices bore much relationship to student success in composition classes, if "success" could be defined as earning credit for the course (earning a "C" or better). High ACT scores did correlate somewhat with *high* grades in our ENG 150 course, but students on all levels of the ACT appeared to have about the same chance of getting a "C" or better. From an administrative point of view, we couldn't very well keep students out of a course they could earn a "B–" or "C+" in.

Of more concern to us within the writing program was the fact that fully one-fifth of our ENG 150 students were either withdrawing or earning below a "C" — that is, failing to earn credit for the course — but according to our analyst these students did not show any particular ACT-score tendencies. That is, ACT scores alone could not predict who would fail or struggle in ENG 150.

Our placement-essay system didn't fare much better, according to the analyst. Over the past few years, enough students had either not taken a placement test or simply ignored our placement decision that he could conclude again that not much relationship existed between "placement" and "success" in composition classes. Students who'd been placed into ENG 150, students who'd skipped the placement test, and even students who'd been placed into ENG 098 but taken ENG 150 instead all had about the same chance of earning credit in our ENG 150 course.

From the students' point of view, they had little to lose in giving ENG 150 a try, for ACT score or placement-essay results had very little predictive value. Statistically, about 80 percent of them — regardless of test scores — would get a "C" or better. Finally, at a meeting between upper-administration and writing-program administrators, the statistician remarked that, given all the time, effort, and money we put into placing students in composition courses, a random placement would make as much sense and that we might just as well let the students place themselves. At first we chuckled. Then we looked again at our options. In the end, we decided to take the man seriously.

Our statistician had lifted a veil from before our eyes: all of our efforts had been directed toward finding a better way for *us* to place our students — for us to assess our students' writing abilities quickly and effectively, preferably in an hour or two. Before this nudge from the statistician, we lacked what Peter Elbow calls the "utopian or visionary impulse," which kept us "blinded by what seems normal" (83). Normally, the placement universe revolves around teachers; we choose the methods, we score the essays, we tell students what courses to take. Now we began to envision students at the center, and for the first time we turned our attention to the people who knew our students best: the students themselves.

We have not regretted our decision. Our ENG 098 "placement rate" has dropped from 33 percent to 22 percent, but for the first time we feel the right students are taking our developmental writing class. All in all, we believe there are several good reasons to adopt directed self-placement.

Directed Self-Placement Feels Right

Directed self-placement possesses what computer programmers call elegance, what philosophers might call the shine of Ockham's razor. It has a pleasing feel about it with influence stretching in every direction: from a simple brochure at the hub, its vectors point to students, local high schools, teachers, and administrators. Its simplicity recommends it over the unreliability of test scores. Its honesty calls out to students and lures them in the right direction. Its focus is on the future and each student's self-determined advance. This alternative placement strategy is a consummate movement toward what Patricia Mann terms "familial unmooring," a concept that Grego and Thompson use to urge compositionists and their academic institutions to break nostalgia's hold on students and their writing and enable students to "remember themselves as whole people (not just a number or a grade)" (74). In this manner, directed self-placement involves the restoration of interpersonal agency — but not without some cost. Grego and Thompson remind us:

> Nostalgic views of student writing would rather hold on to ways of assessing and teaching students writing which make the institution's job predictable and containable, neat and tidy. To do otherwise is to get pretty messy, to engage in the struggle to make sense of the complexities of student writing not "organized" by the traditional assessments and curriculum of a particular academic site. (75)

And it's not just students who are encouraged to change. Directed self-placement is an attitude, James's pragmatic attitude. We feel very differently about our jobs, about students, and about writing after our ten-minute speech, much differently from the way we felt after several hours of reading placement essays. Our old concerns about validity and reliability are now replaced with something akin to "rightness." And the rightness of the choice now lies with the student, where we feel it belongs.

We surveyed our Fall 1996 students, and they told an altogether different story from the previous group. Their written comments repeatedly stressed that when the two courses were explained to them at orientation, the students who chose ENG 098 simply felt that it was the course for them. Because of their past experiences with writing, they felt they needed to "brush up" before tackling ENG 150. Interestingly, the reasons students cited most frequently for choosing ENG 098 centered on behavior and self-image — not test scores or grades. Our ENG 098 students saw *themselves* as poor readers and writers. In the past, we had done the seeing for them.

We asked students to tell us which of the seven potential indicators most strongly influenced them to take ENG 098. These were the indicators that we faculty had designed as we thought about our own composition classes. The indicators reveal what we saw, and continue to see, as the main prerequisites for success in our first-year composition program: solid reading habits, writing confidence, familiarity with the mechanical aspects of writing, and experience with computers. They are analogous to the "contextualized" placement practices that Huot cites (553–54), but instead of measuring sample student writing against our contextualized expectations, we have asked the students to measure their own perceptions of themselves against our expectations. We added ACT scores and high-school grades to our list primarily as a possible anchor for students not used to assessing their abilities qualitatively.

We were pleasantly surprised by what we found. Of the 230 responses, barely a quarter cited test scores and grades:

1. 24 percent said "Generally I don't read when I don't have to."

2. 23 percent said "I don't think of myself as a strong writer."

3. 15 percent said "My ACT-English score was below 20."

4. 12 percent said "My high school GPA was about average."

5. 12 percent said "I'm unsure about the rules of writing."

6. 9 percent said "In high school, I did not do much writing."

7. 6 percent said "I've used computers, but not often for writing and revising."

Notice that items 1, 2, and 5 (59 percent) reflect self-image and self-assessment, items 3 and 4 (27 percent) reflect external judgments, and items 6 and 7 (15 percent) reflect high-school or other past educational experience. It seems right to us that our students are selecting

ENG 098 because of their own view of themselves. And indeed, we hope that the course will help them change that view and give them confidence as they move on in the curriculum.

In retrospect, we believe that our discomfort with traditional placement methods arose from an uneasy feeling of impropriety. In the space of an hour or two, we had been trying to make a major decision for hundreds of students. At ten o'clock we didn't know their names, but by noon we "knew" what first-semester course they should take. No matter how careful we tried to be, we felt that any decision would be hasty. The "emergent" placement procedures cited by Huot, which view placement either as "a teaching decision" or as "a screening process," share an assumption that simply doesn't sit well with us — that whatever decision made is to be made by teachers, not students (556).

But what of reliability? Obviously two of the items listed in our brochure, ACT-English scores and high-school GPA, are extremely "reliable" data, even if they are problematic measures of writing ability per se. But we have come to view the other indicators as very reliable as well. First, there is no "interrater-reliability" problem since there is only one rater. More importantly, a student is unlikely to respond to a statement like "I don't read when I don't have to" differently from one week to the next. Leaving aside for a moment the question of validity, we are convinced that student responses to our brochure prompts are very reliable — more reliable, we believe, than summer faculty's holistic responses to anonymous and impromptu student writing.

Directed Self-Placement Works

What does it mean to say that directed self-placement works? First, we might admit failure if *no one* chose our developmental writing course, although even then we might chalk it up as a victory for mainstreaming first-year writing students. Along with those who, with some important cautions, advocate mainstreaming (Elbow and Soliday), we agree that students should not be marginalized, but we think the most practical reconception of remediation does not involve eliminating basic writing courses, but rather thinking very differently about placement. Indeed, conventional notions of "remediation" may not apply to students who in effect *ask* for the extra course. Elbow anticipates this development when he concedes that some students may "*want* to be held apart in a separate and protected situation . . . , so perhaps it would make sense to have a conventional basic writing course for those who want it. But let us ask them and give them a choice instead of deciding for them" (93).

In practice, we observe that many students decide for themselves that they need a basic or conventional writing course, "a sheltered educational pocket" (Soliday 85). For us, reconceiving remediation begins by taking student choice seriously — that is, to heed Elbow's wise concession. Our 22 percent placement rate has held steady for two years, so we feel that we are reaching a significant population of students. In a sense, our new placement method "works" no matter how many students choose ENG 098; we simply want to make the course available to those who want or need it.

We also might say that self-placement works if it manages to locate the same group of ENG 098 students that our more traditional (and labor-intensive) methods located. In 1995, our method was to screen with ACT-English scores and then to look at a timed writing sample. In 1996 and 1997 we used directed self-placement. We compared two of the most easily measured characteristics of the two populations and found that the groups shared very similar high-school GPAs (just under 3.0, compared to our freshman class's overall average of just over 3.2) and ACT-English scores (17.8 in 1995, 18.6 in 1996 and 1997, compared to our overall average of 22). This suggests that the students took their high-school GPAs and ACT-English scores into account: we didn't need to do it for them. So as a "replacement" of the old system, directed self-placement worked, though as we have begun to discover, there may be good reasons to dismiss these general indicators of academic ability as unable to predict success in writing courses.

We also looked at grades in ENG 098 and ENG 150. The overall GPA in ENG 098 was significantly lower in 1996 (2.56) than it was in 1995 (2.90), but then it jumped back up to 2.82 in 1997. We hesitate to conclude too much from these three years, but one possible explanation for the general drop in GPA in ENG 098 is that directed self-placement did a better job of locating genuinely struggling writers — that is, the very writers we hope to assist in ENG 098 — within the larger group with below-average ACT scores and high-school GPAs. On the other hand, perhaps our grading has simply fluctuated.

If our overall goal is to help students succeed in ENG 150 (so that they can go on and succeed in other classes and in their careers), then perhaps it's too early to say whether our directed self-placement system really works. We do know that about 66 percent of our 1995 ENG 098 students went on to earn credit for ENG 150 by the end of the next semester, while just 55 percent of the 1996 group did the same. The difference seemed to be that while in 1995 about 87 percent of the ENG 098 students went on to take ENG 150 the next semester, in 1996 only 75 percent of our ENG 098 students took ENG 150 the next semester. There could be several reasons for this, and we're still looking into it. Did they drop out of school? Did they feel overwhelmed by writing and choose to stay away from the next course? Or did they feel well-prepared for their other classes and simply decide to delay ENG 150 until a more convenient time?

Even with questions like these unanswered, we are convinced that directed self-placement is working at our school. We continue to locate hundreds of students each year that feel they need additional help with their writing, and we do it very efficiently and on terms the students understand and appreciate.

Directed Self-Placement Pleases Everyone Involved

To analyze numbers is, to some extent, to fall back into the thinking that what's most important about placing students in developmental or regular first-year writing courses is a quantifiable assessment of their writing ability. Teachers assess students' ability at the end of every term, but placement ought to be a student's own choice. Traditional placement procedures, as well as those procedures that Huot calls "emergent writing assessment" (556), assume that students don't know enough about what lies before them to make an intelligent choice. Or perhaps they cynically hold that students don't want to make wise choices and that they want to take as few writing courses as possible. We are careful to address the former assumption with our talk and our brochure. We address the latter concern by assuming ourselves that students will live, for better or for worse, with the choices they make, and by teaching each class at the level described in our brochure and course catalog.

Huot indicates that notions of assessment validity are evolving. Beyond measuring what they purport to measure, valid assessment procedures "must have positive impact and consequences for the teaching and learning of writing" (551). We tell students that their education — and this first decision about ENG 098 or ENG 150 — is their responsibility. We can offer direction, we can outline the purposes and expectations of each course, but we simply can't make the decision as intelligently as they can. It pleases students to know that they are in charge of their learning. It may be the most important message they receive at freshman orientation. It also puts some pressure on them — pressure that rightly belongs to them. When we place students, we take away from them a critical component in their educational lives. If we choose for them, they may think that the right thing is being done, but it is understandable that many take our choosing for them as an excuse to become either angry or defeated. The sense of rightness comes to students who make their own decisions in a matter like this and when they vow to affirm through hard work that the right decision has been made.

Students who appraise their ability too highly have a challenge before them. On the other hand, students who believe that ENG 098 is the best course for them are happy to have the opportunity to improve themselves and pleased to possess the dignity of making such a choice for themselves.

To illustrate this, we'll describe the experiences of two students — not to prove that directed self-placement works in the same way for everyone, but to show how it *can* work for individual students.

Kristen and Jacob were both traditional freshmen, a month or two past their 1997 high-school graduation ceremonies, when they attended summer orientation and selected their first composition courses. Based on sheer numbers (3.68 high-school GPA, ranked in the top 12 percent of her class, ACT-English score of 19), we might have expected Kristen to place herself into ENG 150, but she selected ENG 098. And we might have expected Jacob (3.16 high-school GPA, ranked in the top 46 percent of his class, ACT-English score of 15) to place himself into ENG 098, but he selected ENG 150.

What went into their decisions? Kristen, who made her decision while looking over the two lists of "characteristics" in the brochure, felt unsure of her ability to step right into college-level writing. "I was just being cautious," she says now. "I was just starting college and didn't know what to expect. I figured that English 098 would get me back into the writing mode. I'd been out of school all summer." Kristen's parents supported her decision, but she told them about it afterwards, after she'd already registered. "I made the decision during orientation," she recalls. "I was on my own."

Jacob, on the other hand, sought advice from others before making his final decision. He registered for ENG 150 during orientation, but then he spoke with his parents and high-school English teacher over the next several days. "When I was back home after orientation, I gave my advanced-comp teacher a call and read the class description of both classes, and both she and I decided that 150 was a good choice." His parents, though, disagreed. "My parents wanted me to take 098 because they didn't want me to screw up my first semester. But I wanted to take 150 to show them I wouldn't screw up."

Both Kristen's caution and Jacob's determination seem to us excellent reasons for selecting the courses they chose. Kristen did well in ENG 098 (she earned a B+) and enjoyed the class. "It was flexible, and everyone wrote at their own pace. It was not very stressful. We mostly wrote on things that interested us." She also says that she improved her writing: "We went to a tutor once a week. During the semester, I learned that there are different ways to write a paper. There are different emotions and audiences that a person must consider. You must also deal with many drafts before a final draft. You have to make enough time to get everything done."

Now that she is in ENG 150, Kristen feels well-prepared and well-situated as a college writer. "ENG 150 is more of an 'on-your-own' class. We use computers, and we do a lot of reading and research. Overall, I think I'm doing pretty well."

Jacob also looks back on his decision as a good one. He says that he took the decision very seriously — more seriously than he might have back in high school: "In high school you're just taking classes, but in college you've got money involved." Like Kristen, he feels that he learned a lot in the course. "My final paper was a work of art compared to my high-school papers. The most important thing I gained from the class was to simply make my paper flow much better than I could before, not jumping from thought to thought."

Jacob earned a "C" in ENG 150, and he feels content with the experience. "Now I feel like I'm writing at a proficient college level. In my opinion, that's the goal of a freshman course."

In the responses of these students, we see a welcome shift in attitude, a merging of our goals and theirs. Where there might have been conflict, there is now cooperation. And we can say that as teachers, we adopt a very different attitude toward students who place themselves in ENG 098 or ENG 150. Teachers in ENG 098 know that the students, by their own admission, are asking for some help to get ready for college writing. No developmental writing teacher begins class with the view that the first order of business is to prove to the student that he or she was indeed placed correctly. Our best students are the ones that ask us to help them learn, and now in no other class on campus can a teacher assume with as much confidence that this is precisely what every student in the ENG 098 class wants. In fact, the ENG 098 class is becoming a favorite choice among writing faculty because of this positive attitude of orientation. This class fulfills no college requirement and doesn't count as credit toward graduation, yet the students are there and this pleases anyone with teaching instincts.

Those of us teaching ENG 150 know that each student has accepted the challenge of the course. The students have another option, but they feel ready to begin the required first-year writing course. Although occasionally the first-day writing sample indicates there is a student or two that might be better off in ENG 098, the teacher now faces a student, not an ACT score or the evidence of a one-shot writing sample. If the student knows what is expected and accepts the challenge, who are we to tell them they can't take this course? If a student fails ENG 150, that student must recur to his or her own self-placement, not a writing sample or the inflated high-school transcript. Teachers are pleased when the placement responsibility lies with the student, for the relationship is thus cleaner, less muddied with the interference of test scores and with predictions for success or failure from everyone *except* the student.

Finally, we have discovered that administrators are also pleased with directed self-placement. Admissions directors don't have to help organize placement exams or explain to students why they need to begin their college career with a not-for-college-credit course. They are pleased to invite potential students to compare the way we and other schools treat their incoming students: we provide options, while other schools take them away. And of course, unlike placement exams, directed self-placement costs nothing.

Like Huot, we want a placement procedure that focuses "inward toward the needs of students, teachers, and programs rather than outward toward standardized norms or generalizable criteria" (555). With directed self-placement we've found a way to place the focus first and foremost on students and their own self-understanding, capabilities, and purposes. Our teachers have been freed from an uncomfortably hasty kind of assessment so that they can focus entirely on the more authentic kinds of assessment that go on over the course of an entire semester. And the integrity of our program has benefited from the honest challenge presented by our promise to stick to our advertised course standards and objectives and to offer help and preparation to those who believe they need it.

A Pragmatist Theory of Writing Assessment

As we've indicated above, we believe that the assumptions and practices that Huot describes as "new, emergent writing assessment" are not yet deeply enough contextualized in the students' own personal and educational lives. The placement method we are advocating has its theoretical roots in John Dewey's democratic and pragmatist philosophy of education. Pragmatist understanding of experience, particularly Dewey's instrumentalism, supplies the soundest theory in support of directed self-placement. Dewey supplies us with these principles of learning: educational growth should be directed; inquiry begins in uncertainty and moves toward transformation; instrumental intelligence requires the freedom and power to choose.

Dewey says that "it is the office of the social medium," which includes schools, "to direct growth through putting powers to the best possible use" (*Democracy* 114). We direct our students' growth in part by establishing and communicating the goals of ENG 150 and the abilities required to succeed in the course. The *power* that directed self-placement taps is the desire among new college students to get started on the right foot and to finally make some personal choices about their education. Freshmen come to the university hyper-aware of their educational background, their capabilities, and the promise of success. They generally have a good sense of where they stack up in comparison to their peers. Where there is indetermination and uncertainty — uncertainty about preparation, about writing, and about one's ability to fit in to the new discourse community — there is a need for what Dewey calls transformation.

The *instrumental* function involves the way inquiry is used as a tool to intelligently direct one's experience. For Dewey, inquiry "is the controlled or directed transformation of an indeterminate situation into one that is so determinate in its constituent distinctions and relations as to convert the elements of the original situation into a unified whole" ("Pattern" 320). Instrumentalism replaces static understanding ("you are a basic writer") with an emphasis on the dynamic relation between the student and the possibilities waiting in his or her environment ("perhaps I should take a developmental writing course").

Our placement program thus relies on honest student inquiry and interactive participation. Our orientation talk offers direction: it is a critical first moment in four years of communication. We tell students where they need to end up, and they tell us how they want to get there. Dewey writes in *Democracy and Education:* "The communication which insures participation in a common understanding is one which secures similar emotional and intellectual dispositions — like ways of responding to expectations and requirements" (4). Our invitation to satisfy the first-year writing requirement in two semesters or one, by beginning with either ENG 098 or ENG 150, fosters the disposition characteristic of genuine learning and offers an invitation to academic community as opposed to establishing from the get-go that teachers are going to take over control of student learning.

Other theories of assessment define too narrowly what placement is all about. Edward White maintains that essay tests are "perfectly appropriate" if all we seek is "information that will help students enroll in courses for which they are ready" (33). But placement is not about *our* discovery of information; it is about getting a student's higher education started in the best possible way. If we want to communicate to students the dispositions characteristic of all inquirers, then most decidedly an essay test is *not* perfectly appropriate. To think so is to take on the mindset of administrators, who often view students merely as "seats" in a classroom. Finding the right "seat" for a student is not enough.

A pragmatist theory of assessment situates placement with regard to each student's aims and dispositions. The power relations that are violated by taking away choices are not repaired by mainstreaming, which simply eliminates options, or by updating methods of administering and scoring placement-essays, which continues to tell students that they are not ready to make their own decisions. Dewey remarks that "aims, beliefs, aspirations, knowledge — a common understanding — . . . cannot be passed physically from one to another like bricks" (4). What is required is communication — and every placement method communicates something important to students. Perhaps this is why traditional placement into remedial courses has not proven to equip students to succeed in the regular writing course. Perhaps those students are still waiting for someone to fix what ails them. We hope that we are encouraging in our new students, in pragmatist fashion, an intelligent way of responding to expectations and requirements.

If proper placement is a matter of guiding students into the course that is best suited to their educational background and current writing ability, directed self-placement may be the most *valid* procedure we can use. If the clarity of criteria and their consistent application is the standard of *reliability*, directed self-placement ranks high as long as we use current course goals and standards for success to inform and guide students in their choice.

Directed self-placement is no panacea. It does not address the problem of how to teach, how to bring students in from the margins, or how to deal with all of the politics of institutional change. Soliday, Grego and Thompson, Bartholomae and others address many of these concerns that would take us far beyond the limited scope of placement alternatives. But our placement alternative does lay the ground work for much that these authors recommend.

And so to conclude this essay, we return finally to a practical concern we confronted when we turned an important choice over to students — the risk. The "risk" of directed self-placement is peculiar. We imagined, for example, that, left to make the final decision on their own, no students would enroll in ENG 098. There we would be with twenty empty sections. If this were to happen, who would we blame? How bad would it really be? Who would be hurt? The peculiar feature of directed self-placement is that, in one sense, it can't really fail. If nobody took our developmental writing class, it could be a choice that each student made with his or her eyes open; our brochure and our orientation talk would make sure of that much. And if ill-prepared students take ENG 150, the teacher's complaint about unprepared students would have to be directed back toward the students. If they pass the course, who can blame them for taking the chance? If they fail, they will, we hope, learn that a college education is a serious endeavor and that success often begins with a proper estimation of one's abilities.

Acknowledgments

We would like to thank Peter Elbow for his generous encouragement and for his thoughtful comments on the early drafts of this article. We also want to acknowledge our indebtedness to Thomas Newkirk's "Roots of the Writing Process" for its clear exposition of several key concepts in Dewey's philosophy as they relate to writing instruction.

Works Cited

Bartholomae, David. "Inventing the University." *Perspectives on Literacy.* Ed. Eugene R. Kintgen, Barry M. Kroll, and Mike Rose. Carbondale: Southern Illinois UP, 1988. 273–85.

Dewey, John. *Democracy and Education.* 1916. New York: Free P, 1966.

———. "The Pattern of Inquiry." *Logic: The Theory of Inquiry.* New York: Holt, 1938. 101–19. Rpt. in *Pragmatism: The Classic Writings.* Ed. H. S. Thayer. Indianapolis: Hacket, 1982. 316–34.

Elbow, Peter. "Writing Assessment in the Twenty-First Century: A Utopian View." *Composition in the Twenty-First Century: Crisis and Change.* Ed. Lynn Bloom, Donald Daiker, and Edward White. Carbondale: Southern Illinois UP, 1996.

Grego, Rhonda, and Nancy Thompson. "Repositioning Remediation: Renegotiating Composition's Work in the Academy." *CCC* 47 (1996): 62–84.

Huot, Brian. "Toward a New Theory of Writing Assessment." *CCC* 47 (1996): 549–66.

James, William. "What Pragmatism Means." *Pragmatism.* 1907. Cleveland: World, 1955.

Newkirk, Thomas. "Roots of the Writing Process." *More than Stories: The Range of Children's Writing.* Portsmouth: Heinemann, 1989. 177–208.

Soliday, Mary. "From the Margins to the Mainstream: Reconceiving Remediation." *CCC* 47 (1996): 85–100.

White, Edward M. "An Apologia for the Timed Impromptu Essay Test." *CCC* 46 (1995): 30–45.

Classroom Activities

Royer and Gilles in "Directed Self-Placement" present educational issues of interest to students who may be questioning the goals and purposes of a basic writing course. Students may be interested in reading and discussing this article and may find it useful as a writing prompt.

Of particular concern to students may be the criteria used for directed self-placement into basic writing and college writing. Students may also be interested in the description of how first-year orientation works at Grand Valley State University and in the profiles of the two students who selected different first-year writing courses for very different reasons. Students could compare and contrast their own experiences with the events described in the article. What are some of the assumptions made about students and writing courses in the Royer and Gilles article? How is placement in writing courses at your own institution different from or similar to the approach at Grand Valley State University? Do students have access to academic advisers before classes begin? What do they say about their experiences of new-student orientation? What aspects of orientation work well? What would students like to see changed or improved? Students may then wish to work in small groups to create a description of the basic writing course(s) at their own institution; based on this description, they could develop a set of criteria for directed self-placement. What are the unstated assumptions behind placement in a basic writing course? How could students' descriptions and criteria address those assumptions and help future students understand the goals and purposes of the course?

Thinking about Teaching

To create a more student-centered environment, take notes on your students' discussions of basic writing course descriptions and placement issues. Which of their ideas can be readily implemented? Which ideas seem unfeasible or would require a great deal of institutional change? To test out your ideas, share the Royer and Gilles article, and your students' responses, with other teachers of developing writers — and pose questions similar to those asked by your students. What are Royer and Gilles's unstated assumptions about placement systems and writing courses? Do those assumptions apply to the realities of your institution? How would a system of directed self-placement work at your institution? What conditions would have to be present to make such a system feasible? Moreover, what implications does the notion of directed self-placement hold for ideas of student agency? What does it mean to ask a student to place himself or herself in a course, as opposed to the skills-based model of placement tests described in the article? Finally, how are placement systems linked to course design? Examine the pragmatic aspects of Royer and Gilles's argument to determine how placement criteria can be applied to the practical issues of syllabus construction and course content.

Failure: The Student's or the Assessment's?

Kay Harley and Sally I. Cannon

First published in 1996 in the Journal of Basic Writing, *the following article by Kay Harley and Sally I. Cannon is powerful and poignant. Both a "good read" and pedagogically provocative, the article presents a case study of Mica, a student in a pilot program at Saginaw Valley State University that combined basic and first-year English courses. Harley and Cannon use this study to explore the notion of assessment.*

The writers acknowledge the ongoing struggle to define and redefine academic discourse related to assessment. For instance, most assessment instruments look at a sample as an isolated text instead of reading a piece of writing contextually and intertextually. That is, much assessment deals with what a writer doesn't do, how his or her writing doesn't measure up. Such criteria often fail to recognize current controversies in composition studies, such as the role of personal voice in academic writing. After considering these and other controversial issues, Harley and Cannon conclude that assessment practices need further evolution. Moreover, Mica's voice resonates throughout this article, arguing for a reconsideration of what it means to be a basic writing student.

> The issue, then, is not who misses the mark but whose misses matter and why.
>
> — Bartholomae ("Margins" 68)

> Being in an college english class I felt I was final going to learn something about this word call english. . . . I knew I was going to learn everything I always want to learn it made me feel good.
>
> — Mica

Overview

In some ways, Mica was like other underprepared, basic writers who enrolled in the pilot program for developmental writers at our midwestern state university. Acknowledging her checkered academic past and resolved to start afresh, Mica was attracted to our pilot program. Instead of taking the traditional sequence of a three-hour, non-credit, basic writing course followed by a two-semester freshman writing course, students like Mica, whose placement essay exam indicated the need for developmental work in writing, could enroll in our program, which combined the developmental and the first semester freshman English courses. The pilot provided intensive support through increased contact time with faculty, collaboration with peers, and tutoring from upper class students who focused on improving students' writing and on assisting the freshmen in negotiating their ways into the university community. We used Mike Rose's *Lives on the Boundary* as a focal text to foreground issues of language and learning, access and denial, power and education, supplemented by brief articles from local and national sources.

The pilot program gave another option to students like Mica, a young African American, nineteen years old, and a single mother of a young child. Her high school performance garnered a 2.7 GPA but was interrupted by the emotional and physical demands of a pregnancy during her junior year. She scored in the fourth percentile on the Nelson-Denny reading test (equivalent to an upper elementary student) which placed her in the university's developmental reading course. She felt unsure about herself and her writing, and, in her own words, went through high school worried that "someone knew my secret and they were calling me dumb behind my back." She was a student "at risk" whose success at the university was a gamble. In addition, Mica found herself at a preponderantly white university, where 300 African American students often feel isolated in a university population of about 7,000. The university's demographics were mirrored in our pilot population; Mica was one of three African Americans out of a total of forty-five enrolled in the Fall 1992 pilot.

However, Mica stood apart from her peers because she was a student whom our best teaching and assessment strategies did not serve. She forced us to rethink just about everything we did. Her writing continually challenged our expectations and ways of reading. Mica was also often vocal and forthright, letting us know what she was thinking, and not afraid of challenging us: "Why are you teaching us this?"; "What do you mean?"; "You said this yesterday and today you're telling us this!" Then, increasingly as the semester wore on, she became sullen and silent, defensive about our response to her writing. We had often praised her writing for its strong content and lively voice. At the same time, however, we would note the structural and grammatical problems that plagued every draft. She seemed confused about what she perceived as our ambivalence toward her writing.[1]

At the end of the semester, Mica failed the pilot program. We, however, asked ourselves how we had failed Mica, specifically in our assessment of her work. With over 80 percent of the students passing the combined course with a "C" or better, it became particularly important to analyze reasons for Mica's failure.

The assessment practice we used is widely considered one of the best to date in the discipline: a holistically scored portfolio, judged pass/fail by English faculty both within and external to the pilot. Nonetheless, as we've reflected upon our assessment of Mica, we have come to believe that a mismatch exists between our portfolio criteria and the texts Mica produced, even texts that had been revised over the semester with our criteria in mind. We now doubt that current assessment criteria and practices can "read" Mica's work adequately, or the work of other culturally diverse students whom our institutions are publicly committed to educating. Jay Robinson and Patti Stock in "The Politics of Literacy" have written, "if we would be literate, and help others to become so, it is time for thoughtful listening to those voices that come from the margins; it is time for reflective reading of texts that inscribe those voices as centrally human ones" (313). While many of us have made progress in learning to listen to others' voices, this progress is not embodied adequately in our assessments.

While the profession discusses writing as embedded in a context, we represent writing in our assessments as uniform and monolithic. We may call for multiple samples by which to evaluate performance, but during the portfolio evaluation itself, we read each paper largely as an isolated text, not contextually or intertextually. And while we may specify different genres, the criteria we use for evaluation fail to acknowledge the blurring of genres that is evident in much writing both within and outside the academy today. Further, our criteria fail to recognize the current controversies over the role of personal voice in academic writing and argument. They also privilege linear forms of organization. In short, our assessments penalize students for "missing the mark" in ways that may be incompatible with our profession's evolving notions of the socially contextualized nature of writing and discourse.

This paper, then, explores what we now see as our failure in assessing Mica's work and speculates on how we might reconceptualize the assessment of writing, particularly the writing of culturally diverse students.

Assessment and the Pilot Program

Briefly, our assessment required the students to submit a portfolio of four pieces selected from writing they had done during the course. While we urged students to incorporate ideas or examples from early papers in later ones or revise versions of early ones as their thinking on issues was deepened by the reading, writing, and discussions in the course, the requirements for the portfolio didn't describe or reflect this. Rather they read quite conventionally:

a. Personal Reflective piece: This essay should demonstrate your ability to use details effectively to narrate/describe; it should have a focus, a point.

b. Expository piece: This essay should demonstrate your ability to create a thesis and support it with evidence — personal examples, examples of others, material from the coursepack or Rose.

c. Synthesis paper: This essay should demonstrate your ability to synthesize (make connections between) ideas from the coursepack, Rose, and your own thinking about education and work, to focus them in a thesis, and to present them in an organized and coherent fashion.

d. In-class/Impromptu paper: This essay should demonstrate your ability to write a clear and organized essay under timed conditions and without the opportunity to revise.

The criteria we shared with students and used as a department in the pass/fail evaluations of student portfolios also reflected traditional rubrics.

A Pass portfolio should demonstrate the ability to:

a. write fluently

b. grapple with a topic; develop and explore the implications of ideas and insights

c. provide a focus, generally through an explicit thesis statement

d. support ideas with reasons and/or examples from personal experience and/or outside sources

e. organize ideas into clear paragraphs

f. avoid multiple grammatical mistakes, particularly sentence boundary problems.

Challenges of Reading and Assessing Mica's Writing

The following essay, Mica's first of the semester, illustrates the difficulty we had in assessing her writing. The assignment asked the students to describe an experience or moment in their lives in which they learned something. By establishing a clear focus and drawing upon sensory details, they were to narrate the experience so that their readers could relive the moment with them and reflect upon what that experience taught them. Mica decided to write about the birth of her child. The first two paragraphs of her essay, entitled "Ready or Not," are reprinted below:

> Waking up saying good-bye to everyone "Bye Mama, Beebee, and Chris". Oh well I'm left here in this empty house again no one to talk to. Don't anybody care that I'm 9-1/2 months pregnant and my stomach is as big as a beach ball, and that I wobble like a weeble when I walk.
>
> I remember whimpering as if I was a two years old. Mica get a whole to yourself stop whimpering for your eyes get puffy. Baby, why don't you come out. All my friend have had their babies. What are you waiting on to come out of there; sweetie your mama is tired of being pregnant. I can remember being so angry that if anybody would have came over here I would have chewed them up alive. Oh! I got to get out of here before I go crazy. Running up and down the stairs, I figure if I jiggle you up then maybe you will come out. Doing this for five minutes and nothing happen. Just huffing and puffing like a dog sitting in the hot summer sun. Well, I guess I'll take me a shower. Getting undress and guess what the telephone rang, Oh, Oh, somebody cares about me. The Mrs. Know-it-all-mother-in-law, the bat. Hello, "Mica what are you doing?" "I replied," nothing, I was about to get into the shower, can you call me back?" Yeah, bye bye. Wicked witch I never thought she cared. Oh well back to the shower. In the shower the water running on my stomach I

can feel you in there come out of there my stomach began making the gesture like the baby was trying to really come out.

For most readers of freshman English essays, this paper misses the mark. It isn't "correct." Yet, we want to argue, these notions of "correctness" — correctness not only in terms of surface features but also of acceptable styles, genres and organization — though deeply embedded in our thinking and assessment criteria are often unstated and not fully examined. Mica's paper jars and challenges, yet it handles language in complex ways. It shifts from direct to indirect discourse; from Mica as narrator, to Mica as a character thinking aloud, to Mica speaking directly to other characters or her unborn child. But we dismiss this complexity and judge through the lens of "error." The direct discourse is often unmarked. Sentences are sometimes fragmented or fused. Tense shifts occur seemingly at random. The missing tense markers, particularly "d" or "ed," and copula ("to be") deletions reflect Black English Vernacular (BEV). Further, her organization contains nothing explicit.

Mica's writing did not include any of the distancing and reflecting that were part of our expectations for a personal reflective essay. In "Reflections on Academic Discourse: How It Relates to Freshmen and Colleagues," Peter Elbow explores how academic discourse assumes "that we can separate the ideas and reasons and arguments from the person who holds them" (140).[2] Mica was unable or refused to squelch the personal — to separate the message from the messenger — to adopt a disinterested, objective stance. Her preference for situating her ideas in personal terms is seen in several other essays discussed later in this paper.

Rather than reading Mica's text for what it doesn't do, it can be read for what it is achieving. Robert Yagelski, for example, suggested in his 1994 CCCC presentation that we might evaluate a student text like this as personal testimony. Mica's writing does render the immediacy of her experience of labor with her first child. It is filled with strong details. The storying patterns, oral resonances, and rich rhythm give the piece its poignancy and power. These reflect a mode of discourse prevalent in Black English that Geneva Smitherman in *Talkin and Testifyin: The Language of Black America* defines as tonal semantics. One feature of tonal semantics, Smitherman notes, is the use of repetition, alliterative word play, and a striking and sustained use of metaphor, something seen throughout Mica's work (134). Mica writes about a jumbled, chaotic, and intensely personal time that demands a strong emotive voice. That Mica has achieved such a voice is a mark, not of a basic writer, but of an accomplished one.

Features similar to those in Mica's personal essay appeared in all of her subsequent writing in the course, including her summaries and explanatory essays. More clearly in those papers did we see how personal anecdotes are acceptable in academic discourse only when framed by generalizations. It is the framing that appears indispensable, for if a student like Mica offers a personal example without a corresponding generalization, the personal doesn't qualify as support.

David Bartholomae has noted that all errors are not created equal.

> The errors that count in the work of basic writers have no clear and absolute value but gain value only in the ways that they put pressure on what we take to be correct, in the ways that these errors are different from acceptable errors. The work that remains for the profession is to determine the place of those unacceptable styles within an institutional setting, within an institution with its own styles of being right, its own habitual ways of thinking and writing ("Margins" 68–69).

Mica's paper challenged our habitual ways of assessing writing and left us questioning whether the "unacceptable" in Mica's writing might have a rightful place in a freshman writing course and in academic discourse more generally. Can the boundaries of academic discourse be broadened so that "personal testimony" or an "emotive voice" or "tonal semantics" might find a place? In suggesting this, we are not suggesting that a student like Mica cannot or should not learn the dominant academic discourse, including what some describe as the "superficial features" of grammar, style, and mechanics. Nor are we suggesting that our job as teachers is not to help all students to do so, giving them access to many voices and styles. Nonetheless, we are suggesting that the writing of students like Mica may also call us to transform academic discourse and the assessment practices which support it.

Unpacking Metaphors of Exclusion: Deficiency, Foreignness, and Monogeneric Papers

Bartholomae demonstrates that we sort out and label "on the assumption that basic writers are defined by what they don't do (rather than by what they do), by the absence of whatever is present in literate discourse: cognitive maturity, reason, orderliness, conscious strategy, correctness" ("Margins" 67). While we immediately recognized a power and immediacy in Mica's writing, our early diagnoses of her work focused on deficits — the lack of reason, orderliness, conscious strategy, and correctness that Bartholomae (and our assessment guides) enumerate. These quick notes made for ourselves, for example, focus on what Mica failed to do in an expository essay exploring the distinction between child abuse and discipline, a paper that drew upon a time when she was accused of abusing a toddler at a day care center at which she worked:

> — problems framing the experience and/or moving between her frames/generalizations and her examples — movement is a key problem, transitions — abruptly inserts dictionary definitions of discipline and child abuse — moves directly into 1st person narrative example with no lead in and a complete shift in style — ends with question posed to

reader rather than restatement (or even direct statement) of main point of paper — multiple tense marker errors and other BEV features —

While these notes exemplify error analysis and try to move beyond a simple recording of errors ("her moves show an awareness of what is needed"), they nonetheless show that we read Mica's essay primarily in terms of its deficits: it lacks conventional features of academic prose.

Here is the opening of the essay:

Ten years ago if you told your child "don't do that," and they did it any way you would spank them for not listening to you. Back then the way you discipline your child was your business. Now days its everybodys business the way you discipline your child.

Child Abuse vs. Discipline

When do you know its child abuse? And when do you know it simply discipline.

DISCIPLINE is defined as training especially training of the mind.

CHILD ABUSE is defined as mistreatment of a child by parents or guardians.

It's Thursday, I said to myself, I have one more day before I can rest, rest, rest. Dealing with 20-5 kids a day really takes a lot out of you. . . .

It was 10:05 and all the kids had arrived. We sang good morning to each other then split up in groups. We had a full load and that was about 25 kids so that made us have five kids a piece. As the day went along it was time for coloring. I caught one of my kids putting crayons in his mouth. "David get the crayons out of your mouth. They're not to eat, but to color," I said. He didn't have anything to say back. But as soon as I turned my head he had them back in his mouth. We went through this about four times. The fourth time I got up and tapped him on his hand — Not hit, or smack but tapped him on his hand. He didn't cry, he just took the crayons out of his mouth and continued coloring.

If, instead of assessing Mica's essay in terms of its deficits, we set it alongside some of the reading we were doing and asked students to do, Mica's style does not look so foreign or lacking. Her abrupt shifts and lack of transitions are not altogether dissimilar to those of Mike Rose in his opening of *Lives on the Boundary,* the book used in our course.

Rose moves from description of students and of the university campus, to a carefully recorded observation of a teacher drawing out students' knowledge about the renaissance, to a pictorial image of the medieval goddess Grammatica which then functions metaphorically, to statistics about changing enrollment patterns in American universities — all of which create a rich and multifaceted collage. No explicit transitions mark the movements, only white space on the page.

Rose's style is quite different from directly stated thesis and support pattern that guides much of our instruction and assessment of basic writers. He interweaves precise objective description, vivid image, significant anecdote, personal experience, quotes from official documents, general statement, and reflection. Mica's child abuse paper parallels Rose in significant ways. Her essay is full of ideas and passion as she explores the damaging consequences of mistaking discipline for child abuse and the difficulties of clearing your name, particularly if you are a single mother from a minority group, when charges of abuse have been leveled. She offers personal testimony, clearly conveys the events/examples, includes detail and dialogue to place the reader in the scene, and writes with a strong sense of conviction. While not using many of the devices of academic argument, she is nonetheless making a claim: that discipline should not be mistaken for child abuse. She elaborates upon her points and shows the harm that mistaking discipline for child abuse can cause. She writes to effect change.[3]

To take another example, David Bartholomae has demonstrated how a careful look at the writing of Patricia Williams, an African American legal scholar and author of *The Alchemy of Race and Rights,* can cause us to question the way we read the prose of basic writers. Williams, like Rose, upsets our conventional expectations of academic prose. "Williams' writing is disunified: it mixes genres; it willfully forgets the distinctions between formal and colloquial, public and private; it makes unseemly comparisons. In many ways, her prose has the features we associate with basic writing, although here those features mark her achievement as a writer, not her failure" ("Tidy House" 11). We do not, Bartholomae suggests,

> read "basic writing" the way we read Patricia Williams' prose, where the surprising texture of the prose stands as evidence of an attempt to negotiate the problems of language . . . She is trying to do something that can't be conventionally done. To say that our basic writers are less intentional, less skilled, is to say the obvious . . . It is possible . . . that when we define Williams-like student writing as less developed or less finished . . . we are letting metaphors of development or process hide value-laden assumptions about thought, form, the writer, and the social world ("Tidy House" 19).

Errors in Our Expectations

Two papers Mica wrote later in the course again show her defying our expectations about the appropriate form and content. In one, we had asked students to select an article, summarize it, and respond. Mica chose a collection of brief interviews concerning women and work entitled "Is Success Dangerous to Your Health?" She opens as follows:

> In reading the interview article, "Is Success Dangerous to your Health," none of the three interviewees in their interview explain or answer the question ask in the title of the interview, Is Success Dangerous to your Health? I couldn't grasp what the author was try to do however, what I did find in the article is "RESPECT". All of the three interviewees felt

they were not respect. The title of the article pull me right into the paper. However, I was very disapointed not to find what I was looking for. Will my career affect my health in anyway.

Mica had written guidelines, model opening sentences, and class assistance on how to write a summary and response. However, she sets these aside (perhaps largely unconsciously) to pursue her own frustration with the title, a point she returns to in her conclusion where she unabashedly makes suggestions to the author about how to answer the question the title posed. Her "back talk" to the author is a significant rhetorical move, yet it and her use of first person belie the expectations for an objective summary. Again, our immediate response to Mica's summary/response is to dismiss it as not meeting the terms of the assignment. And, indeed, it does not. However, her gutsy move in challenging the author surely demonstrates critical thinking as well as a critical engagement with the text, something our assessment practices sometimes overlook in favor of acceptable genre features. Consider, for example, the "safe" and predictable but totally unengaged five paragraph theme that passes without question. The paper passes, no doubt, because it can demonstrate the surface features and stylistic conventions of academic discourse: the clear structure, the explicit signposting, etc. But content — which we continually maintain is the most important feature when assessing any kind of prose — is often overlooked. Is this a "fair" and accurate assessment of either writer?

The last assignment of the semester was a synthesis paper which asked students to bring together their thinking about education or work, the two themes of the class. Students were to create a fresh look at the topic by making connections among the different readings from the course and integrating those with their views, experience, and writing done in earlier papers and in their journal.

Mica chose to write about education, specifically her experience in the pilot project. Our initial assessment of Mica's paper was that it failed to do what was expected. In our minds it did not "read" as a synthesis. The paper never established a focus in the form of a thesis statement, it failed to smoothly link specific examples and personal experience to generalizations, and it made little use of quotations from the reading as support. Instead, Mica recounted her experience from the beginning of the semester to the end with no immediately apparent synthesis or reflection, as these first two paragraphs suggest:

> It's first day in college, and I'm excited I drove around the hold campus to find a policeman so, I can get direction to my class. Finally I found one he and looked like he was hiding behind the trees waiting to give someone a ticket. I drove over to him, and rolled down my window. "Can I help you?," He said, Yes you can I need help trying to find my class the room number z204. "O.K. young lady you keep straight on this street we one and turn right, Then you see this building a lot of people will be coming in and out of it." Thank you very much sir. I seen this big building about as half big as a major hotel like the Marriot Hotel. I

entered the building, Everyone was walking so fast like they were in a marathon.

Finally, I found room z204 I walk in; it was pretty full. I sat by the window so I could look out of it since no one was talking. Being in a college English class I felt I was final going to learn something about this word call english. All through high school I felt so insure about writing, I always felt someone knew my secret and they were calling me dumb behind my back. I felt a little dumb but, I knew someday I will learn were to put a period, comma, and a semicolon without feel unsure about it. So, in college I felt this is when every thing is going to change. I knew I was going to learn everything I always want to learn it made me feel good.

The paper adopts a narrative stance from which it never departs, thus defying our expectations for a synthesis paper. However, if we temporarily put aside those expectations to read differently, the paper does synthesize Mica's experience in the pilot course. She captures the confusion and anxiety of a new student coming to a college campus for the first time, likening the campus buildings and the policeman's behavior to the closest thing she knows: the city. She compares our modern buildings to a Marriot hotel. That comparison, coupled with her admission of her "secret" about feeling "dumb," suggests how much strength it actually took to walk in the doors of our institution.

The paper shows Mica as a beginning writer, new to the university and its expectations, negotiating her way into academic discourse, just as she seeks to find her way physically into the academic campus. She explores issues of anxiety about writing, the pitfalls of peer response groups, and power relations in the classroom. This reading acknowledges a focus, which our initial reading could not because, limited by predetermined portfolio requirements and paper features, it linked focus with thesis. Now we realize that the focus was there: it was Mica's — her story of her first semester college English experience. The narrative mode was her way of shaping her experience, of telling her story.

Carolyn Heilbrun in *Writing a Woman's Life* discusses the ways female literary figures write to organize and make sense of their lives. While Heilbrun is discussing works of fiction, not academic discourse, Jane Tompkins and other scholars writing academic discourse do directly call upon their personal experience to enrich and organize their understanding of professional concepts. If Tompkins, why not Mica? Certainly the profession is expanding its notion of what is acceptable in its own academic discourse. And while Mica's writing is far from model prose, and she does not have conscious control over the strategies she uses, her writing has made us realize that the time is ripe for a reconsideration of what is "acceptable" in student discourse as well.

Locating Oneself in the Privileged Discourse of the Academic World

Clearly, Mica is a student whose style betrays her and sets her apart from the mainstream at our — and most — college campuses. Perhaps, then, we need to assess Mica's work as her attempt to locate herself in the privileged discourse of the academic community. This would lead us to view her writing problems not as internal or cognitive, but rather as ones of appropriation. Mica's work throughout the course was marked by styles that clashed with our deeply embedded notions of academic discourse represented in our assignment and evaluation constructs. In assessing her, we judged these as deficits. Consistently rich in details, we said, but she could not control them. Our assignments called for the person, the details, yet our assessments demanded that these be "controlled," that specifics be framed, that thesis and generalization be tied to example. If her status in coming to the university is deeply divided, fragmentary, how can we expect a central point, a main idea?

David Bartholomae suggests

> if we take the problem of writing to be the problem of appropriating the power and authority of a particular way of speaking, then the relationship of the writer to the institutions within which he writes becomes central (the key feature in the stylistic struggle on the page) rather than peripheral (a social or political problem external to writing and therefore something to be politely ignored) ("Margins" 70).

Our assessment criteria didn't allow us to read Mica's prose as an attempt to negotiate the problems of language. Rather, the assessment criteria were presented as objective and uniform. Such criteria may protect us and the university community at large from looking critically at the mismatch between the rhetoric of our policies and programs for ethnically underrepresented and academically underprepared students and the realities of their struggles to make sense of an unfamiliar social dialect.[4]

Grammar Is Not Neutral

Mica describes quite poignantly her purpose in voluntarily enrolling in our pilot program: "I was final going to learn something about this word call english." She suggests an academic history fraught with insecurity, afraid that someone would find out her "secret." Interestingly, Mica views that secret and the solution to her problem as a mechanical one: "I knew someday I will learn were to put a period, comma, and a semicolon." This characterization of writing in terms of grammar, of course, is not unusual. Many writers (and teachers) conflate the two. (Consider the numbers of people who, when told that you are an English teacher, respond with a comment about "watching their grammar.") As we continued to study Mica's writing and reflect upon our work with her long after the semester ended, we began to understand how strongly Mica held to her belief in the power of punctuation. We realized that learning correct grammar *was* Mica's agenda. As Mina Shaughnessy noted, "grammar still symbolizes for some students one last chance to understand what is going on with written language so that they can control it rather than be controlled by it" (11).

Carolyn Hill discusses how grammar is a political issue to basic writers: "Grammar is not a neutral 'thing' to them, rather a completely socialized representative of those authorities who *seem* to students to be outside themselves" (250). Later in her synthesis paper, Mica constructs her instructors' point of view and appears suspicious of our motives in not focusing dominantly upon grammatical issues. She writes:

> I enjoy every bit of writing I did in the class but, I felt disappoint cause I didn't learn what I want to learn in the class. . . . I really felt that we should have discuss more of what I believe she saw going on in the class. Since, she mentioned it herself that she was having a problem with grammer, fused sentence, tense sentences, and fragments. We did work on this for a couple of days but i felt it wasn't enough.

In saying "we should have discuss more of what *I believe she saw going on in the class*" Mica seems to feel that we were unjustly withholding information that she believes could solve her writing problems and eliminate her "secret." That intensive one-on-one tutoring from peers and instructors, diagnostic analyses of her patterns of error, comparisons of her own patterns to typical nonstandard patterns of Black English Vernacular, and extensive opportunities for revision did not help Mica gain greater power over spelling, punctuation, and syntax remains one of our greatest puzzles.

Mica's sentence points to power relations in the classroom. Mica frames the teacher/student relationship as a struggle between two people with two competing solutions to her writing problems. She is indignant (perhaps rightfully so) that her solution, more grammar instruction, is being ignored. In retrospect, we suspect that our actions are well described by Hill: "Ostensibly I wanted to give up authority, help students to be self-starters. Covertly, the institution and I collaborated to see to it that students be quickly notified if that start did not place them in the proper arms of Standard English, focused and controlled" (78).

Mica wanted to gain control over her writing and her errors; she wanted access to the social power identified with academic discourse. Yet neither she nor her instructors confronted this agenda centrally. Her relationship to the institution within which she wrote, her very placement in a basic writing course, the value placed by the university and those exercising influence in the society on copy editing, correctness and conventional styles were peripheral concerns. Correctness was thought of as context-free. That is something the English profession can no longer afford to assume. Perhaps that is why we saw such little change in these areas of Mica's writing.

Rethinking Assessment

Reexamining and questioning our assessment of Mica's portfolio has left us with more questions than answers. As we now critique our portfolio assessment we see that we inadvertently worked to keep intact the boundaries and borders by which basic writing is institutionally defined, ironically the very boundaries our pilot project meant to collapse.

Thus, while we endorse and encourage more courses like ours, courses which collapse borders and work to eliminate notions of basic writers as "foreigners,"[5] we realize that our assessment practices must evolve significantly as well.

First, we need to understand that assessment is complexly situated, and different audiences may require different evaluations. In reviewing our guidelines for a passing portfolio we would now ask, "For whom are we evaluating Mica's work?" During the portfolio reading, who is the primary audience? Is it Mica? Is our purpose to reveal to her where she has succeeded or failed in meeting the standards set for an introductory university writing course? Is the primary audience her future college instructors? If so, what do they need to learn about writing as a deeply embedded cultural and social act, about the time needed to acquire new discourse practices, and about current challenges to hierarchical patterns of organization if they are to determine what should constitute "passing" work in an introductory writing course which enrolls culturally diverse students? Or is the audience the local, state, or national community? The needs and interests of these groups differ; our assessments need to reflect this.

In addition, we need to devise ways to read student texts contextually and intertextually not only in the classroom setting but in evaluation sessions. Our prespecified portfolio requirements pressured us into reading each paper as an individual entity. What we now want to strive for is a more intertextual reading of the portfolios, an assessment practice that views the essays in a portfolio as interrelated and recursive. Read as a whole, Mica's papers have a surprising unity, both in content and approach. We wonder what would happen if during the portfolio evaluation we actively read Mica's work as her ongoing exploration of the issues that were central to her views of education, work, and mastery of written English. All of them contain strong narrative elements; all have a directness in confronting the issues she's chosen as her topics; all fail to clearly and explicitly link example to generalization, provide direct transitions, or follow a linear order; and all demonstrate a lack of control of surface features including spelling, word ending, person and tense inflections, and punctuation.

We need to resist (or read against) our unconscious notions of academic discourse as monolithic and standard. It's a myth that all synthesis papers will look like some imagined prototype of a synthesis paper. Yet, when evaluating portfolios holistically, we often operate under this myth. Papers that contain the expected features of a particular assignment pass without question, while quirky papers that don't easily correspond to a genre or mode — even if particularly rich in content — are often failed. Narrative strategies are undervalued, even when they are deeply reflective. In professional conferences and articles, we repeatedly remind ourselves to avoid false dichotomies, yet too often we fall back into simplistic either/or formulations in evaluation. Our assessment criteria suggest an essay is either personal reflection or exposition, either narrative or argument. The language is either academic discourse or not. The thesis/generalization is either directly stated or it cannot be credited. We need to immerse students in a variety of discourses, being careful not to limit students like Mica to only one voice. We do well to remember the frustration of feminist writer, bell hooks, with teachers who "did not recognize the need for African American students to have access to many voices" (qtd. in Delpit 291).

Finally, we need to understand errors, not as deficits, but as attempts at appropriating the discourses of other communities. This shift would allow us to recognize and extend rather than automatically penalize these attempts at appropriation. Matters of syntax and usage are not neutral as our portfolio criteria imply. We need to become sensitive to the power relationships implicit in all language use and to the political implications of judgments of error as "nonstandard," particularly as higher education opens itself to an increasingly diverse student body.

We have no clear answer to the question raised in our title. Was the failure Mica's or that of our assessment procedures? We suspect the failure rests on both sides. We did fail Mica: we failed to read her texts contextually; we failed to assess her portfolio in light of her attempts to appropriate a new discourse; we failed by oversimplifying the nature of academic discourse; we failed by setting her work against some constructed "mythical" portfolio demonstrating competence; we failed by not seeing the power relations involved in any attempts to work on nonstandard usages. The answer, however, is also complex — as complex, perhaps, as Mica's writing and as Mica herself. At times she appeared evasive and angry; at times bewildered; at times fiercely proud and determined.

Would we pass Mica's portfolio today? No. However, Mica's writing has challenged our notions of what is good and acceptable written discourse in introductory academic settings, and we think it should challenge others in the English profession, the university, and society.

Mica did not meet our expectations. Her writing continues to intrigue and frustrate us. Yet it may be the Micas — those students who do not meet our expectations — who shed the strongest light on our practices.

Notes

1. Some ambivalence was undoubtedly present, both on our part and on Mica's. In working with Mica, we probably at times exemplified "a certain sense of powerlessness and paralysis" that Lisa Delpit has described "among many sensitive and well-meaning literacy educators who appear to be caught in the throes of a dilemma. Although their job is to teach literate discourse

styles to all of their students, they question whether that is a task they can actually accomplish for poor students and students of color. Furthermore, they question whether they are acting as agents of oppression by insisting that students who are not already a part of the 'mainstream' learn that discourse" (285). Mica also may have been deeply ambivalent, caught in the conflicts between her home discourses and the discourses of the university, and feeling torn between institutions and value systems in ways that Keith Gilyard documents. Thus, she may have been choosing to resist or "not learn" as Herb Kohl describes it, rather than learn that which she perceived as denying her a sense of who she was. While issues such as these are important to our thinking, this paper looks more specifically to the implications of current assessment practices.

2. Elbow makes the good point that "it's crazy to talk about academic discourse as one thing" (140). However, we often teach and assess academic discourse as if it were. We believe that many teachers of writing (perhaps unconsciously) hold a collective, monolithic view of academic discourse, which poses problems to assessment, particularly the assessment of students at risk. This monolithic view of academic discourse is defined primarily by its stylistic and mechanical surface features, features such as mapping or signposting, explicitness, objectivity, and formal language (Elbow 144–46).

3. Smitherman discusses a characteristic use of narrative as a persuasive tool in black English: "The relating of events (real or hypothetical) becomes a black rhetorical strategy to explain a point, to persuade holders of opposing views to one's own point of view, and in general, to 'win friends and influence people'" (147–48).

4. Anne DiPardo explores this issue in *A Kind of Passport* when she examines the "patterns of tension" in an institution's commitment to educational equity, looking particularly at the "good intentions and enduring ambivalence" embedded in the language of the basic writing curricula.

5. See Bruce Horner for a recent discussion of this and other metaphors used to characterize basic writers.

Works Cited

Bartholomae, David. "The Tidy House: Basic Writing in the American Curriculum." *Journal of Basic Writing* 12.1 (1993): 4–21.

———. "Writing on the Margins: The Concept of Literacy in Higher Education." *A Sourcebook for Basic Writers.* Ed. Theresa Enos. New York: Random House, 1987. 66–83.

Delpit, Lisa D. "The Politics of Teaching Literate Discourse." *Freedom's Plow: Teaching in the Multicultural Classroom.* Ed. T. Perry and J. W. Fraser. New York: Routledge, 1995. 285–95.

DiPardo, Anne. *A Kind of Passport: A Basic Writing Adjunct Program and the Challenge of Student Diversity.* Urbana: National Council of Teachers of English, 1993.

Elbow, Peter. "Reflections on Academic Discourse: How It Relates to Freshmen and Colleagues." *College English* 53.2 (1991): 135–55.

Gilyard, Keith. *Voices of the Self.* Detroit: Wayne State UP, 1991.

Heilbrun, Carolyn. *Writing a Woman's Life.* New York: Ballantine Books, 1988.

Hill, Carolyn Ericksen. *Writing from the Margins: Power and Pedagogy for Teachers of Composition.* New York: Oxford UP, 1990.

Horner, Bruce. "Mapping Errors and Expectations for Basic Writing: From the 'Frontier Field' to 'Border Country.'" *English Education* 26.1 (Feb. 1994): 29–51.

Kohl, Herb. *I Won't Learn From You! The Role of Assent in Education.* Minneapolis, MN: Milkweed Editions, 1991.

Robinson, Jay, and Patti Stock. "The Politics of Literacy." *Conversations on the Written Word: Essays on Language and Literacy.* Ed. Jay Robinson. Portsmouth: Boynton/Cook, 1990. 271–317.

Rose, Mike. *Lives on the Boundary.* New York: Free Press, 1989.

Shaughnessy, Mina. *Errors and Expectations.* New York: Oxford UP, 1977.

Smitherman, Geneva. *Talkin and Testifyin: The Language of Black America.* Boston: Houghton Mifflin, 1977.

Williams, Patricia. *The Alchemy of Race and Rights.* Cambridge: Harvard UP, 1991.

Yagelski, Robert P. Speech. "Writing Assessment and the Challenges of Cultural Diversity." Conference on College Composition and Communication. Nashville, March 1994.

Classroom Activities

Mica writes: "I enjoy every bit of writing I did in the class but, I felt disappoint cause I didn't learn what I want to learn in the class." Harley and Cannon identify Mica's concern as wanting "to gain control over her writing and her errors; she wanted access to the social power identified with academic discourse. Yet neither she nor her instructors confronted this agenda centrally." Such an agenda seems difficult to confront; nonetheless, it may be worthwhile to stage such a confrontation with students to allow them "to gain control" over their progress in the course. The goals and reasons for institutional assessment can be presented not only to discuss these tools but also to challenge them.

Moreover, students can learn to chart their own improvement when you replicate the conditions of institutional writing assessment on a small scale. At the beginning of the semester, have students write a timed essay in response to a question or prompt. Collect the essay, but do not mark or grade it. Instead, put this writing away until the end of the semester, at which time students can complete a timed in-class essay based on a prompt or question similar to the initial assignment. Have students compare and contrast their writing from the beginning and the end of the semester. What has changed? Where do students see improvements? If you use writing portfolios in your course, this reflective response can be a valuable addition to each student's portfolio.

Thinking about Teaching

If our pedagogy continues to change to include more diverse student voices, Harley and Cannon affirm, so also must our assessment procedures and policies "evolve significantly." Harley and Cannon urge us to consider that assessment is "complexly situated" and that we need to look not only at the texts we are assessing but also at the multiple audiences for whom the assessment is intended.

Such reflection introduces the notion of standards as a political issue. Assessment practices tend to privilege correctness, orderliness, reason, distance, and formula, mirroring the value placed on these categories by administrators and employers, if not by ourselves and our students, as markers of good writing. Yet at the same time, we emphasize in our classes that rhetorical maturity, risk taking, and critical engagement are also important goals in a basic writing course. If these practices and emphases need not contradict each other in the classroom, then perhaps they also need not be at cross-purposes in assessment. Such issues may be critical starting points for an important discussion among teachers and administrators evaluating the assessment needs of their students in writing courses.

14

Basic Writing and the Writing Center

In this final chapter, Gregory Shafer and Anne DiPardo discuss the ways in which writing centers can contribute to the education of developing writers. Shafer refers to the work of Brazilian educator Paulo Freire as he articulates the purposes of the writing center as a site of democratic education and critical pedagogy. DiPardo studies the interactions of two young female students of color, a Navajo student who is enrolled in basic writing and an African American student who works as a peer tutor in the writing center. Together these two articles present the satisfactions and challenges of writing center work for developing writers and their tutors.

Negotiating Audience and Voice in the Writing Center

Gregory Shafer

"Back in the writing center," writes Gregory Shafer, "composition is too often about imposed power, about learning to write for one's teacher, about learning a prefabricated, immutable form. It is too often about following orders." In the following article, originally published in Teaching English in the Two-Year College *in 1999, Shafer attempts to negotiate basic writing students' struggles with voice, with instructors' emphases on teaching five-paragraph themes and other "basic skills" in a typical developmental writing curriculum. Included in this selection are the inspired voices of four developing writers, whose compelling stories could not be confined to the strictures of the five-paragraph essay. Using the*

ideas of Freire and hooks, as well as those of Elbow and Shaughnessy, Shafer attempts to evolve a pedagogy that values both audience and voice as he and students work together in the writing center.

Introduction

Each day they trudge into the writing center with the same familiar look of consternation and anger. Sometimes it's because their instructor has failed to address the content of their essays, but more often it's simply about voice and control. Within their classes, a kind of power struggle ensues as each writer attempts to transcend the mechanical and prescribed prose that has become a staple of the five-paragraph theme. They are developmental writers, but they want to use elements of their dialect, include their culture and diction, and pepper their narratives with the occasional obscenity when it accurately captures the heart of their story.

Marcus, a husky African American student, slides into the seat next to me and gingerly lays his paper in front of my eyes. "She says I can't use the word 'thug-ass' to describe my cousin," he says as he wipes the sweat from his forehead and lowers his backpack to the floor. Marcus's essay is a character paper about his cousin, a man who has comic aspirations to be a big-time criminal. Thus, Marcus, in his smartly sarcastic style, has given the appellation of "My Thug-Ass Cousin" to his paper. Quickly, I read it over again, only I already know the content and style. Marcus is a wonderfully fluid writer. His style is unrestrained and honest. His detailed description of his cousin chronicles both the humor and pathos in a young man who has romanticized the "gangster" image. Marcus's approach to his paper is both personal and racial. He wants to make his audience laugh while helping them to see the continuing blight of racism and the concrete way it affects real people. And yet, through all of the raw honesty and pathetic humor, he is being told to "eliminate the obscenities" because they are "inappropriate in an academic setting." "So what am I supposed to do?" he asks me with his big, undaunted smile. "She's not gonna let me use 'ass' in my paper."

Silence. I sit and contemplate the things I'd like to say to his instructor. The way she is blunting and effacing the voice of a talented young writer seems unethical, unconscionable, but I can't sacrifice his grade so I can make a statement. "Let me talk to her," I say. "Leave the paper as it is," I add with reassurance. "It's beautiful and thoughtful. It makes your audience think. I like it a lot!" Marcus smiles and shakes his head. Now the hard work begins as I think about talking to his instructor about voice and a very special talent.

Each week, my work in the writing center presents me with at least a couple of the dilemmas that I describe with Marcus. I have come to call them questions of autonomy and voice, since their implications go well beyond issues of "appropriateness" or academic format. Indeed, they touch upon the basic freedom we are willing to extend to basic and minority writers. With all of the talk about empowerment and hegemony in our profession, are we really willing to elevate genuine expression above petty, egocentric worries about academic protocol? In the same way, is our hesitance about "obscenities" more about academics or culture? Are we jittery about "nasty language" because it symbolizes an unharnessed and angry political voice? And finally, are we truly doing our job, if we censor the uninhibited writer simply because he doesn't fit into the narrow parameters of what has come to be called safe "academic discourse"? Who, in the end, are we serving when we shape and limit unconventional students? In this essay, I hope to answer some of these questions.

Another Example

Polly is twenty-five, but her experience and wisdom make her seem much older. As she strolls confidently into the writing center, she personifies bell hooks's description of the student who is adamant about receiving a "liberatory education" while feeling "terribly wounded" (19) by the dearth of true freedom she receives from her instructors. As with Marcus, Polly is engaged in a very riveting, flesh-and-blood experience concerning her ex-husband. As I read over her paper, I'm shocked and moved by her vivid description of the beatings, the verbal abuse, the cavalier use of intimidation. "This is real — right?" I ask her with an incredulous look. Quickly, she smiles and shakes her head, yes. Polly is reliving her marriage and the emotional scars it left. As I read more, the dialogue, the detail of the beatings seem more and more authentic and dramatic. I stop and take a deep breath.

It is, put simply, a paper that exposes the brutality that is lamentably a part of too many marriages. Its style is unreserved, unbridled. Polly isn't holding back: "He scratched me with his long nails. He was doing more than hurting me now. He wanted to leave a scar, to leave his mark on my face."

Finally I reach her instructor's comments and recognize the focus of Polly's frustration. The evaluation seems detached and unrelated to the paper. Somehow, the instructor has washed away the emotion and violence that oozes from the writing and has limited her observations to questions of form and usage. Her comments are professional, surgical. She has taken a personal drama and reduced it to insipid comments on rules and form: "Your form is good, but you sometimes deviate from the thesis. Remember, you're writing a comparison/contrast paper. Don't lose that focus. You might consider a review of fragments too. They pop up quite frequently. Well done!"

"What do you think of my paper?" asks Polly. "Because this doesn't tell me nothing!" she fumes with obvious anger. Again, as with Marcus's work earlier, I see what seems to be a stripping away of the meat and blood of a paper. Each instructor seems unsure or unwilling to deal with the topics that transcend the "academic community." Lost in both of their evaluations is the need for writers to be heard, to bring a piece of their lives, culture, and social context into the writing they do. The struggle, while simmering beneath the surface, is very real and raises serious questions about the role of college writing instruction. Is it our job to assist students in becoming models of academic discourse, replete with properly placed commas and standard white English, or rather, is it our job to help them unleash the clamor and discord that rumbles inside their heads, a cacophony that can enliven their papers if it is allowed to become part of their discourse?

The Practice of Academic English

Most scholarship I have read seems to suggest that we should be guardians of civilized English, that we should quiet writers by molding them into "academic scholars," into people like us. David Bartholomae's "Inventing the University" talks candidly about the cumbersome but necessary task a college student faces in trying to approximate the jargon and style of the academic community. His message is that the academy's first job is to prescribe a style that mirrors itself. Forget about individualism, our role is to make students more like us. "I am continually impressed with the patience and good will of our students," writes Bartholomae in describing the daunting task of learning academic prose. The students are "appropriated by a specialized discourse," which requires them to "speak our language," or "carry the bluff" (273). In short, then, the most difficult but important role of the college composition instructor is to help writers become more like the university, to shed their cultural personas and learn to embrace a foreign and rather stiff language, one that serves them in few ways beyond the context in which they use it.

Little is said about self-actualization, expression, or fulfillment. Indeed, it is an ironic aspect of our profession that we extol the democratic and strive for student autonomy while forcing students to write in a contrived discourse that serves to exult the academic community over the students it is supposed to empower. Is this what students would call a paradox if they were in Literature 101?

Marcus and Polly are certainly left empty and alienated by the practice. Neither have aspirations of being scholars or academics, but that doesn't prevent their instructors from compelling them to learn the specific style and expectations that academic discourse entails. Should we then wonder why students feel that college composition is less about them and their lives than the foreign register of their instructor, who stands at the front of the class loaded with answers? In the same way, should we feel surprised or upset when our students crank out the plastic, apocryphal prose that is too often a part of first-year composition? We cry for voice and power. We preach liberation. And then we require the fabricated prescriptions that embody nothing of the person behind the words.

Working with students like Marcus and Polly helps highlight the importance of a curriculum that transcends this egocentric, self-aggrandizing approach. Both demonstrate an extremely deft and vivid eye for their world and the significance of their experiences. Marcus writes about his "Thug-Ass Cousin" as both a parody on the romanticism some youths have toward a violent world and a dramatic statement on the limitations placed on African Americans:

> He sits in front of this bank, getting himself up for a big-time bank robbery that's ain't ever gonna happen. He could have and probably should have gone to work that day. But minimum wage doesn't get him out of bed the way it should. And it probably never will.

The writing is poetic, almost song-like. The wisdom and message are profound. Marcus doesn't write like any university or college professors I know, and this is perhaps one of the reasons his prose is so dramatic and riveting. The challenge for us as a scholarly community is what to do with this forever emerging and organic voice. Do we define a liberatory education as shaping our students to be like us, or do we celebrate a mosaic of new styles and voices radiating from our classrooms — voices and styles that are troubling and difficult because they are not part of our formal education? There is a kind of arrogance in Bartholomae's message, and it hasn't been lost on the academic community that enforces it. Instead of reaching out to the dialects and cultures outside the ivy-covered walls of the college, it defines success as a labor of mimicry.

Support from Freire and bell hooks

I have often felt that the sentiments of Paulo Freire and bell hooks better reflect the ideas of a truly emancipatory education. Rather than advocating an experience that exults the power and inherent goodness of the academic world, it seems clearly revolutionary and rebellious. Marcus and Polly, I am virtually certain, would be better served by their inclusive political pedagogy. In particular, bell hooks seems in touch with the power of "transgressing" and the implications of such an education. "I have been most inspired," writes hooks, "by those teachers who have had the courage to transgress those boundaries that would confine each pupil to a rote, assembly-line approach to learning" (13). She writes about the dichotomy between an education of "active participation" and one that embraces the "passive consumer" (14). In other words, students become most alive and empowered when they are personally creating, actively evaluating their world in a style that reflects and changes that world. Marcus tells his story through not only the content but the style as well. The pathos and violence of his life is reflected in his use of double negatives, in his deviations from standard English.

To eliminate this component from his essay is to rip out its viscera and leave it as little more than an assembly line replica of what too many first-year students think is effective writing. How often have I heard college instructors lament such spiritless writing? And yet, how often have I seen these same instructors practice a prescription that takes the pen out of their students' hands?

Many professors should ask themselves if they are afraid or threatened by a truly emancipatory education, one that begins with students and transcends the safe haven of the college theme. Many, I believe, are intimidated by the idea that their students might force them to think, that prose like that of Marcus's might compel them to redefine and broaden the concept of acceptable writing — forcing them into unknown territory. Indeed, when I asked Marcus's instructor why it was "wrong" or "inappropriate" to use "gonna" or a double negative, she fell safely back on the assertion that it is not part of "academic writing." Really? Would this instructor, I silently wondered, be surprised to read some of the work of Geneva Smitherman or bell hooks? Is the premise that such writing is "inappropriate" an arbitrary way of precluding new voices, as many attempt to do in the field of canonical literature? Clearly, this instructor, while seeming to want the best for Marcus, was acting as an oppressor.

Such instructors hooks calls "benevolent dictators," those who are more interested in maintaining their authority "within their mini-kingdom, the classroom" (17) than in self-actualization. Within such a system, few people grow, learn, or change, as a static and immutable form of discourse is inculcated to its passive subjects. The key, adds hooks, is to promote risk-taking and to embrace it as a part of learning for both teacher and student. "Professors must practice being vulnerable in the classroom, being wholly present in mind, body, and spirit," she contends (21). The alternative, she later adds, is a curriculum that "reinforces systems of domination," that perpetuates a smug and lifeless status quo. "Empowerment cannot happen if we refuse to be vulnerable while encouraging students to take risks" (21), she reminds us.

For Paulo Freire, such risks are key to humanistic education. In his classic *Pedagogy of the Oppressed,* he labels passive, top-down approaches to learning as a "banking system of education," one that relegates students to the role of receptacle. For Freire, true, humanistic education emanates from a pedagogy that promotes problem-posing and dialogue over transferals of information and "domestication" (71). In considering the plight of both Marcus and Polly, we can quickly see his point. In a composition class that seeks to deposit information in a linear, static way, there is simply no room for thought, dialogue, or growth. In such a scenario, students become little more than robots who obediently learn and memorize the single, instructor-endorsed way to success. Without dialogue or debate, the instruction is narrative in form, flowing from teacher to student and devoid of action and reflection. The task becomes one of pursuit, chasing the instructor and trying to unlock the keys to success.

For Polly and Marcus, the process is also demoralizing because it leaves them as something less than human. Indeed, how can we consider ourselves thinking and vital individuals when our culture and language is being expunged without critical discussion? Again Freire speaks to this in his distinction between animal and human. For Freire, the animal is primarily a being that lives without reflection, a being that adapts without considering implications or meaning. "Animals," writes Freire, "are beings in themselves" (87). They do not, in other words, step away from their lives to contemplate the significance of why and how they exist. It is not, in short, a critical, introspective life.

In contrast, truly human beings are able to step back and analyze their lives and values. They can ascribe meaning to actions and synthesize events to make conclusions about their feelings and ethics. In short, they construct reality rather than simply respond to it. They, to use Freire's words, "infuse the world with their creative presence" (88). They become active partners in their education.

Polly and Marcus both find themselves being treated as passive beings that are expected to learn the routine in much the same way a dog learns tricks. With the context being bereft of dialogue or active problem-posing, the learning is more akin to rote memorization. The students are irrelevant, voiceless. Again, Freire addresses this with eloquent prose: "Animal activity, which occurs without praxis, is not creative; man's transforming activity is" (91).

In the end, then, we must ask ourselves who is really being served in a pedagogy that elevates prescription over critical dialogue. Is it the developmental writer, who, according to many of my colleagues, needs close instruction because of a lack of experience? Or is it really the instructor, who finds it both easier and safer to disseminate rules and forms over an organic process of learning? My experience in the writing center would clearly indicate that the instructor is the main beneficiary of a top-down education. While such a pedagogy instills students with a formula for organization and usage, it negates the fundamental act of thinking, of learning through a heuristic, personal process.

After our second meeting, Marcus is ready to change his essay to "what will ever make my instructor happy," while Polly is resigned to the limited comments she receives. Both, lamentably, have come to see the context as being despotic and impersonal. "I'm just worried about my grade in the end," says Marcus later in the semester. "I'll do what makes her happy. It's her class."

Solutions and Alternatives

Writing Is Social

On Tuesday, Sally wheels herself into the writing center, surveying the room as she maneuvers her wheelchair to the computer and timidly touches the keys. She is a fifty-eight-year-old student who has returned to school to take writing classes and get out of the house.

"Think you could take a look at this?" she asks me in a deferential tone. Her essay is titled "My Old Brown Coat," and as I read it over, I'm immediately touched by the quaint voice as well as the short, simple sentences. Her paper is nostalgic and filled with a curious affection for a piece of apparel:

> The old brown coat I owned was not like any coat I owned. After it was torn, it became a disaster. It lost its shape and style. It was tattered. The coat was ten years old. It was so special.

"This is nice," I say with a smile. However, as I continue to reread, I become increasingly aware of the jerky sentences, and I wonder how her audience will respond to the lack of fluidity. I begin to think of strategies to help her connect sentences and assist her audience in reading and enjoying her paper. "You know," I say to her as I look away from the computer screen, "we could work on the flow of your prose. I like your paper, but as I read it, I want you to combine some of your sentences — so I don't have to work so hard as a reader."

My work with Sally begins to provide me with ideas for how to empower other students, students like Marcus and Polly who are struggling with demands of audience. All three, it seems to me, highlight the social character of writing. When we sit down to write a paper, we are not simply writing for ourselves but for a group of subjective people. The content and style, then, must reflect a cooperative effort to express our views without alienating readers.

In the case of Marcus and Polly, decisions must be made as a negotiation. Teachers must ask themselves what is essential in terms of diction, organization, and style, while writers must consider both their readers and the goals of their writing. For Polly and Marcus, the value of their cultural lexicon must be weighed along side audience expectations. For Sally, integrity of voice must be weighed against the demand for more melodic sentences.

Similar questions, it seems to me, must be asked in response to nonstandard dialects. Both writers and instructors must consider the transaction between reader and writer (Rosenblatt) — the social dynamic of communication — and come to a collaborative decision as to what is acceptable in a certain context. Such a democratic approach includes students and helps illuminate the realities of writing for an audience. At the same time, it eliminates a linear caveat from teacher to student, resulting in a class that stresses obedience over construction.

This vision is especially important as I begin to work with Kathy. Her essay on how she contracted a socially transmitted disease is poignant and moving. However, it is rife with the most offensive array of gratuitous obscenities I have ever read in a student paper. And then, there is the request from her teacher to place the thesis statement at the end of the introduction.

Kathy is the consummate example of why it is important to protect the integrity of the writer's voice while fulfilling the demands of one's audience. Indeed, as I read over her writing, I am plunged into the chaos of the doctor's examination table. And yet, the obscenities seem to intrude more than enhance:

> I winced as the assistant rolled in a tray of metal gadgets. There was no little speculum this time. This man was wielding what looked like a fucking shoehorn. I cried out when he shoved it between my legs. He then chided me, telling me it didn't hurt. Like he had a god damn clue [. . .].

I finish reading, take a deep breath, and smile. "This is wonderful," I assure her. "I'm wondering, however, if we could respond to your teacher's concerns about language and thesis. Do the obscene words contribute to your message or divert attention from it?"

Later, as we begin to reconsider the essay, we work together to capture the essence of this personal experience while respecting the concerns of readers. It is always a collaborative experience, a negotiation. There are ways, we find, to respect the visions of author and teacher. Writing is about more than either a monolithic model of the university essay or a personal vision of what the author has planned.

Writing Is a Process

Much has been written about alternatives to the traditional composition class. Many of these suggestions have centered on the importance of process, development, and autonomy as integral parts of learning as one writes. Little debate exists as to the need for time as one constructs and designs a piece of writing. We know, for instance, that composition is not a clean, linear act but one that is recursive, messy, social, and cooperative. While more and more instructors allow for this freedom and process in the college composition class, fewer are willing to extend this same autonomy to basic writers, who are often perceived as unable to generate prose without careful and direct instruction. This, I believe, gives rise to the benevolent despot, the instructor, who, in his/her attempt to help the basic writer, actually stymies any generative process. "These students come from deprived backgrounds," an instructor once told me. "They simply need more help from us."

That help, I would contend, begins with process and the journey of discovery that every writer experiences as he/she begins to write. It does not begin with a prescriptive, emasculating set of caveats but enough freedom so that the student has the opportunity to "cook and grow" as Peter Elbow would say. Basic writers, argued Mina Shaughnessy, must "learn by making mistakes" (5). The process, as with other writers, is one of gradual, evolutionary construction. While it is filled with errors, it is also a time of learning through direct experience. "The writer understands that writing is a process, not a rigid procedure. He continually rediscovers his subject," says Donald Murray. It is "discovery of meaning, discovery of form — and the writer works back and forth [. . .]" (7).

Conclusion

All of this would suggest that the best way to teach basic writers is through both process and a respect for the social discovery that ensues as one composes. To negate or trivialize the context in which they write is to alienate students and relegate them to a passive process of imitating others rather than learning to create and synthesize information from their own world. "Bartholomae's pedagogy," writes Richard Boyd, "sets up a kind of master/slave relationship where the student-as-mimic is relegated to a perpetually subordinate role" (41). Indeed, to reduce writing to a series of "skills" and prescriptions does not teach empowered, creative thought. Rather, it marginalizes writers, telling them their experiences are not important, that composition is not about social critique but rules and obedience. It is the antithesis of Freire's vision for a liberated, problem-posing community.

Back in the writing center, composition is too often about imposed power, about learning to write for one's teacher, about learning a prefabricated, immutable form. It is too often about following orders. For Polly and Marcus, two basic writers who show incredible insight, ideas and experiences become submerged as they are coerced into joining this "university of writers." It is a practice that needs to be changed if we are ever to be truly democratic and inclusive in the way we teach college composition.

Works Cited

Bartholomae, David. "Inventing the University." *Perspectives on Literacy*. Ed. Eugene Kintgen, Barry Kroll, and Mike Rose. Carbondale: Southern Illinois UP, 1988. 273–85.

Boyd, Richard. "Imitate Me; Don't Imitate Me: Mimeticism in David Bartholomae's 'Inventing the University.'" *Journal of Advanced Composition* 11 (1991): 335–45.

Elbow, Peter. *Writing without Teachers*. New York: Oxford UP, 1973.

Freire, Paulo. *Pedagogy of the Oppressed*. New York: Continuum, 1990.

hooks, bell. *Teaching to Transgress*. New York: Routledge, 1994.

Murray, Donald. *A Writer Teaches Writing*. Boston: Houghton, 1968.

Rosenblatt, Louise. *The Reader, the Text, the Poem*. Carbondale: Southern Illinois UP, 1978.

Shaughnessy, Mina. *Errors and Expectations*. New York: Oxford UP, 1977.

Classroom Activities

What happens when a student has a particular story to tell and needs to tell it in his or her own voice, a voice that mirrors the streets or the rural back roads, a voice with much to say, but in language often not easy to hear? Shafer poses this important problem as he describes his work as a tutor in the writing center and his discussions with teachers and students. One way to approach this issue is to discuss it directly with students. Where do students find topics for "narrative" writing assignments? What happens if their story doesn't fit the conventional five-paragraph essay format? How do students "negotiate" the need to find their own voices and tell their own stories with the need to write in "audience-appropriate" language that their instructors and tutors will accept as "correct"? This activity can be an opportunity to empower students, as Freire would have it, to begin to claim their own education. Students can learn what kinds of questions to ask of their teachers and of their writing center tutors in order to learn and grow in their writing — and to not merely produce "what the teacher wants." Moreover, teachers can see this discussion as an opportunity to examine their own views about what "counts" as acceptable prose in the basic writing course. Should the basic writing course concern itself only with survival skills, such as writing five-paragraph essays in academic discourse? Or should students new to process-based writing (as many basic writing students often are) have the opportunity to experiment with prose style and storytelling as a way to learn the variety of rhetorical choices available to writers?

Thinking about Teaching

In your teaching journal, reflect on the questions presented above and work out some of the difficult issues presented in Shafer's article. Have you or a colleague ever received a paper similar to Marcus's "My Thug-Ass Cousin"? What was the response to this writing — and on what criteria was the response based? How were those criteria constructed in relation to the course requirements of basic writing and in relation to facilitating an opportunity for students to grow as writers? Shafer frames the question as follows: "Is it our job to assist students in becoming models of academic discourse, replete with commas and standard white English or rather, is it our job to help them unleash the clamor and discord that rumbles inside their heads, a cacophony that can enliven their papers if it is allowed to become part of their discourse?" Perhaps this problem need not be posed as two diametrically opposing sides. Moreover, as Shafer suggests, "Writing is about more than either a monolithic model of the university essay or a personal vision of what the author has planned." There is, in fact, room for negotiation and for honoring process, which Shafer contends is often taken for granted more in composition courses than in the basic writing course. Consider other essays in this ancillary that refer to the problematic nature of the basic writing course, such as Linda Lonon Blanton's "Classroom Instruction and Language Minority Students: On Teaching to 'Smarter' Readers and Writers." Also take a look at Paulo Freire's germinal work, *Pedagogy of the Oppressed*, which provides an important perspective on student-centered learning. Consider facilitating an open discussion on this issue among teachers, students, and tutors. Perhaps such a discussion could be sponsored by the writing center and could involve a wide range of participants across the curriculum. Finally, consider writing an article on your own perspective on this issue, based on your ideas and experiences as a teacher in the basic writing classroom.

"Whispers of Coming and Going": Lessons from Fannie

Anne DiPardo

In the following article, first published in 1992 in The Writing Center Journal, *Anne DiPardo presents a case study of Fannie, a basic writing student who was the only Navajo at her predominantly white West Coast college. Fannie, DiPardo writes, "was still struggling to find her way both academically and socially, still working to overcome the scars of her troubled educational history." To document this struggle, DiPardo presents excerpts from transcripts of Fannie's tutoring sessions with Morgan, an African American student and writing center tutor. These young women from different economic and cultural backgrounds bring contrasting communication styles to their tutoring sessions, resulting in significant challenges for each. DiPardo chronicles these challenges and suggests implications for tutoring language minority students, as well as for training tutors.*

> *As a man with cut hair, he did not identify the rhythm of three strands, the whispers of coming and going, of twisting and tying and blending, of catching and of letting go, of braiding.*
>
> — Michael Dorris, *A Yellow Raft in Blue Water*

We all negotiate among multiple identities, moving between public and private selves, living in a present shadowed by the past, encountering periods in which time and circumstance converge to realign or even restructure our images of who we are. As increasing numbers of non-Anglo student pass through the doors of our writing centers, such knowledge of our own shape-shifting can help us begin — if *only* begin — to understand the social and linguistic challenges which inform their struggles with writing. When moved to talk about the complexities of their new situation, they so often describe a more radically chameleonic process, of living in non-contiguous worlds, of navigating between competing identities, competing loyalties. "It's like I have two cultures in me," one such student remarked to me recently, "but I can't choose." Choice becomes a moot point as boundaries blur, as formerly distinct selves become organically enmeshed, indistinguishable threads in a dynamic whole (Bakhtin 275; Cintron 24; Fischer 196).

Often placed on the front lines of efforts to provide respectful, insightful attention to these students' diverse struggles with academic discourse, writing tutors likewise occupy multiple roles, remaining learners even while emerging as teachers, perennially searching for a suitable social stance (Hawkins) — a stance existing somewhere along a continuum of detached toughness and warm empathy, and, which like all things ideal, can only be approximated, never definitively located. Even the strictly linguistic dimension of their task is rendered problematic by the continuing paucity of research on the writing of non-mainstream students (see Valdés; "Identifying Priorities"; "Language Issues") — a knowledge gap which likewise complicates our own efforts to provide effective tutor training and support. Over a decade has passed since Mina Shaughnessy eloquently advised basic writing teachers to become students, to consider what Glynda Hull and Mike Rose ("Rethinking," "Wooden Shack") have more recently called the "logic and history" of literacy events that seem at first glance inscrutable and strange. In this age of burgeoning diversity, we're still trying to meet that challenge, still struggling to encourage our tutors to appreciate its rich contours, to discover its hidden rigors, to wrestle with its endless vicissitudes.

This story is drawn from a semester-long study of a basic writing tutorial program at a west-coast university — a study which attempted to locate these tutor-led small groups within the larger contexts of a writing program and campus struggling to meet the instructional needs of non-Anglo students (see DiPardo, "Passport"). It is about one tutor and one student, both ethnic minorities at this overwhelmingly white, middle-class campus, both caught up in elusive dreams and uncertain beginnings. I tell their story not because it is either unusual or typical, but because it seems so richly revealing of the larger themes I noted again and again during my months of data collection — as unresolved tensions tugged continually at a fabric of institutional good intentions, and as tutors and students struggled, with ostensible good will and inexorable frustration, to make vital connection. I tell this story because I believe it has implications for all of us trying to be worthy students of our students, to make sense of our own responses to diversity, and to offer effective support to beginning educators entrusted to our mentorship.

"It, Like, Ruins Your Mind": Fannie's Educational History

Fannie was Navajo, and her dream was to one day teach in the reservation boarding schools she'd once so despised, to offer some of the intellectual, emotional, and linguistic support so sorely lacking in her own educational history. As a kindergartner, she had been sent to a school so far from her home that she could only visit family on weekends. Navajo was the only language spoken in her house, but at school all the teachers were Anglo, and only English was allowed. Fannie recalled that students had been punished for speaking their native language — adding with a wry smile that they'd spoken Navajo anyway, when the teachers weren't around. The elementary school curriculum had emphasized domestic skills — cooking, sewing, and especially, personal hygiene. "Boarding school taught me to be a housemaid," Fannie observed in one of her essays, "I was hardly taught how to read and write." All her literacy instruction had been in English, and she'd never become literate in Navajo. Raised in a culture that valued peer collaboration (cf. Philips 391–93), Fannie had long ago grasped that Anglo classrooms were places where teachers assume center stage, where the students are expected to perform individually: "No," her grade-school teachers had said when Fannie turned to classmates for help, "I want to hear *only* from *you*."

Estranged from her family and deeply unhappy, during fifth grade Fannie had stayed for a time with an aunt and attended a nearby public school. The experience there was much better, she recalled, but there soon followed a series of personal and educational disruptions as she moved among various relatives' homes and repeatedly switched schools. By the time she began high school, Fannie was wondering if the many friends and family members who'd dropped out had perhaps made the wiser choice. By her sophomore year, her grades had sunken "from A's and B's to D's and F's," and she was "hanging out with the wrong crowd." By mid-year, the school wrote her parents a letter indicating that she had stopped coming to class. When her family drove up to get her, it was generally assumed that Fannie's educational career was over.

Against all odds, Fannie finished high school after all. At her maternal grandmother's insistence, arrangements were made for Fannie to live with an aunt who had moved to a faraway west-coast town where the educational system was said to be much stronger. Her aunt's community was almost entirely Anglo, however, and Fannie was initially self-conscious about her English: "I had an accent really bad," she recalled, "I just couldn't communicate." But gradually, although homesick and sorely underprepared, she found that she was holding her own. Eventually, lured by the efforts of affirmative action recruiters, she took the unexpected step of enrolling in the nearby university. "I never thought I would ever graduate from high school," Fannie wrote in one of her essays, adding proudly that "I'm now on my second semester in college as a freshman." Her grandmother had died before witnessing either event, but Fannie spoke often of how pleased she would have been.[1]

Fannie was one of a handful of Native Americans on the campus, and the only Navajo. As a second-semester first-year student, she was still struggling to find her way both academically and socially, still working to overcome the scars of her troubled educational history. As she explained after listening to an audiotape of a tutorial session, chief

---

[1]"Fannie" was the actual name of this student's maternal grandmother. We decided to use it as her pseudonym to honor this lasting influence.

among these was a lingering reluctance to speak up in English, particularly in group settings:

> *Fannie:* When, when, I'm talking . . . I'm shy. Because I always think I always say something not right, with my English, you know. (Pauses, then speaks very softly.) It's hard, though. Like with my friends, I do that too. Because I'll be quiet — they'll say, "Fannie, you're quiet." Or if I meet someone, I, I don't do it, let them do it, I let that person do the talking.
>
> *A.D.:* Do you wish you were more talkative?
>
> *Fannie:* I wish! Well I am, when I go home. But when I come here, you know I always think, English is my second language and I don't know that much, you know.
>
> *A.D.:* So back home you're not a shy person?
>
> *Fannie:* (laughing uproariously) No! (continues laughing).

I had a chance to glimpse Fannie's more audacious side later that semester, when she served as a campus tour guide to a group of students visiting from a distant Navajo high school. She was uncharacteristically feisty and vocal that week, a change strikingly evident on the tutorial audiotapes. Indeed, when I played back one of that week's sessions in a final interview, Fannie didn't recognize her own voice: "Who's that talking?" she asked at first. But even as she recalled her temporary elation, she described as well her gradual sense of loss:

> Sometimes I just feel so happy when someone's here, you know, I feel happy? I just get that way. And then (pauses, begins to speak very softly), and then it just wears off. And then they're leaving — I think, oh, they're leaving, you know.

While Fannie described their week together as "a great experience," she was disturbed to find that even among themselves, the Navajo students were speaking English: "That bothered me a lot," she admitted, surmising that "they're like embarrassed . . . to speak Navajo, because back home, speaking Navajo fluently all the time, that's like lower class." "If you don't know the language," Fannie wrote in one of her essays, "then you don't know who you are. . . . It's your identity . . . the language is very important." In striking contrast to these students who refused to learn the tribal language, Fannie's grandparents had never learned to speak English: "They were really into their culture, and tradition, and all of that," she explained, "but now we're not that way anymore, hardly, and it's like we're losing it, you know." Fannie hoped to attend a program at Navajo Community College where she could learn to read and write her native language, knowledge she could then pass on to her own students.

Fannie pointed to the high drop-out rate among young Navajos as the primary reason for her people's poverty, and spoke often of the need to encourage students to finish high school and go on to college. And yet, worried as she was about the growing loss of native language and tradition, Fannie also expressed concerns about the Anglicizing effects of schooling. Education is essential, she explained, but young Navajos must also understand its dangers:

> I mean like, sometimes if you get really educated, we don't really want that. Because then, it like ruins your mind, and you use it, to like betray your people, too. . . . That's what's happening a lot now.

By her own example, Fannie hoped to one day show her students that it is possible to be both bilingual and bicultural, that one can benefit from exposure to mainstream ways without surrendering one's own identity:

> If you know the white culture over here, and then you know your own culture, you can make a good living with that . . . when I go home, you know, I know Navajo, and I know English too. They say you can get a good job with that.

Back home, Fannie's extended family was watching her progress with warm pride, happily anticipating the day when she would return to the reservation to teach. When Fannie went back for a visit over spring break, she was surprised to find that they'd already built her a house: "They sure give me a lot of attention, that's for sure," she remarked with a smile. Many hadn't seen Fannie for some time, and they were struck by the change:

> Everybody still, kind of picture me, still, um, the girl from the past. The one who quit school — and they didn't think of me going to college at all. And they were surprised, they were really surprised. And they were like proud of me too . . . 'cause none of their family is going to college.

One delighted aunt, however, was the mother of a son who was also attending a west-coast college:

> She says, "I'm so happy! I can't wait to tell him, that you're going to college too! You stick in there, Fannie, now don't goof!" I'm like, "I'll try not to!"

"I Always Write Bad Essays": Fannie's Struggles with Writing

On the first day of class, Fannie's basic writing teacher handed out a questionnaire that probed students' perceptions of their strengths and weaknesses as writers. In response to the question, "What do you think is good about your writing?" Fannie wrote, "I still don't know what is good about my writing"; in response to "What do you think is bad about your writing?" she responded, "everything."

Fannie acknowledged that her early literacy education had been neither respectful of her heritage nor sensitive to the kinds of challenges she would face in the educational mainstream. She explained in an interview that her first instruction in essay writing had come at the eleventh hour, during her senior year of high school: "I never got the technique, I guess, of writing good essays," she explained, "I always write bad essays." While she named her "sentence structure, grammar, and punctuation" as significant weaknesses, she also adds that "I have a lot to say, but I can't put it on paper . . . it's like I can't find the vocabulary." Fannie described this enduring block in an in-class essay she wrote during the first week of class.

> From my experience in writing essays were not the greatest. There were times my mind would be blank on thinking what I should write about.
>
> In high school, I learned how to write an essay during my senior year. I learned a lot from my teacher but there was still something missing about my essays. I knew I was still having problems with my essay organization.
>
> Now, I'm attending a university and having the same problems in writing essays. The university put me in basic writing, which is for students who did not pass the placement test. Of course, I did not pass it. Taking basic writing has helped me a lot on writing essays. There were times I had problems on what to write about.
>
> There was one essay I had problems in writing because I could not express my feelings on a paper. My topic was on Mixed Emotions. I knew how I felt in my mind but I could not find the words for expressing my emotions.
>
> Writing essays from my mind on to the paper is difficult for me. From this experience, I need to learn to write what I think on to a paper and expand my essays.

"Yes," her instructor wrote at the bottom of the page, "even within this essay — which is good — you need to provide specific detail, not just general statements." But what did Fannie's teacher find "good" about this essay — or was this opening praise only intended to soften the criticism that followed? Fannie had noted in an interview that she panicked when asked to produce something within forty-five minutes: "I just write anything," she'd observed, "but your mind goes blank, too." Still, while this assignment may not have been the most appropriate way to assess the ability of a student like Fannie, both she and her instructor felt it reflected her essential weakness — that is, an inability to develop her ideas in adequate detail.

At the end of the semester, her basic writing teacher confided that Fannie had just barely passed the course, and would no doubt face a considerable struggle in first-year composition. Although Fannie also worried about the next semester's challenge, she felt that her basic writing course had provided valuable opportunities. "I improved a lot," she said in a final interview, "I think I did — I know I did. 'Cause now I can know what I'm trying to say, and in an afternoon, get down to that topic." One of her later essays, entitled "Home," bears witness to Fannie's assertion:

> The day is starting out a good day. The air smells fresh as if it just rained. The sky is full with clouds, forming to rain. From the triangle mountain, the land has such a great view. Below I see hills overlapping and I see six houses few feet from each other. One of them I live in. I can also see other houses miles apart.
>
> It is so peaceful and beautiful. I can hear birds perching and dogs barking echos from long distance. I can not tell from which direction. Towards north I see eight horses grazing and towards east I hear sheep crying for their young ones. There are so many things going on at the same time.
>
> It is beginning to get dark and breezy. It is about to rain. Small drops of rain are falling. It feels good, relieving the heat. The rain is increasing and thundering at the same time. Now I am soaked, I have the chills. The clouds is moving on and clearing the sky. It is close to late afternoon. The sun is shining and drying me off. The view of the land is more beautiful and looks greener. Like a refreshment.
>
> Across from the mountain I am sitting is a mountain but then a plateau that stretches with no ending. From the side looks like a mountain but it is a long plateau. There are stores and more houses on top of the plateau.
>
> My clothes are now dry and it is getting late. I hear my sister and my brother calling me that dinner is ready. It was beautiful day. I miss home.

"Good description," her instructor wrote on this essay, "I can really 'see' this scene." But meanwhile, she remained concerned about Fannie's lack of sophistication: "Try to use longer, more complex sentences," she added, "avoid short, choppy ones." Overwhelmed by the demands of composing and lacking strategies for working on this perceived weakness, Fannie took little away from such feedback aside from the impression that her writing remained inadequate.

Although Fannie was making important strides, she needed lots of patient, insightful support if she were to overcome her lack of experience with writing and formidable block. Only beginning to feel a bit more confident in writing about personal experience, she anticipated a struggle with the expository assignments that awaited her:

> She's having us write from our experience. It'll be different if it's like in English 101, you know how the teacher tells you to write like this and that, and I find that one very hard, cause I see my other friends' papers and it's hard. I don't know if I can handle that class.

Fannie was trying to forge a sense of connection to class assignments — she wrote, for instance, about her Native American heritage, her dream of becoming a teacher, and about how her cultural background had shaped her concern for the environment. But meanwhile, as her instructor assessed Fannie's progress in an end-of-term evaluation, the focus returned to lingering weaknesses: "needs to expand ideas w/examples/description/explanation," the comments read, not specifying how or why or to whom. Somehow, Fannie had to fill in the gaps in her teacher's advice — and for the more individualized support she so sorely needed, she looked to the tutorials.

"Are You Learnin' Anything from Me?": The Tutorials

Morgan, Fannie's African American tutor, would soon be student teaching in a local high school, and she approached her work with basic writers as a trial run, a valuable opportunity to practice the various instructional strategies she'd heard about in workshops and seminars. Having grown up in the predominantly Anglo, middle-class community that surrounded the campus, Morgan met the criticisms of more politically involved ethnic students with dogged insistence: "I'm first and foremost a member of the *human* race," she often said, going on to describe her firm determination to work with students of all ethnicities, to help them see that success in the mainstream need not be regarded as cultural betrayal. During the term that I followed her — her second semester of tutoring and the first time she'd worked with non-Anglo students — this enthusiasm would be sorely tested, this ambition tempered by encounters with unforeseen obstacles.

Morgan's work with Fannie was a case in point. Although she had initially welcomed the challenge of drawing Fannie out, of helping this shy young woman overcome her apparent lack of self-confidence, by semester's end Morgan's initial compassion had been nearly overwhelmed by a sense of frustration. In an end-of-term interview, she confessed that one impression remained uppermost: "I just remember her sitting there," Morgan recalled, "and talking to her, and it's like, 'well I don't know, I don't know'... Fannie just has so many doubts, and she's such a hesitant person, she's so withdrawn, and mellow, and quiet. ... A lot of times, she'd just say, 'well I don't know what I'm supposed to write.... Well I don't like this, I don't like my writing.'"

Although Fannie seldom had much to say, her words were often rich in untapped meaning. Early in the term, for instance, when Morgan asked why she was in college, Fannie searched unsuccessfully for words that would convey her strong but somewhat conflicted feelings:

Fannie: Well ... (long pause) ... it's hard ...

Morgan: You wanna teach like, preschool? Well, as a person who wants to teach, what do you want outta your students?

Fannie: To get around in America you have to have education ... (unclear).

Morgan: And what about if a student chose not to be educated — would that be ok?

Fannie: If that's what he wants ...

At this point Morgan gave up and turned to the next student, missing the vital subtext — how Fannie's goal of becoming a teacher was enmeshed in her strong sense of connection to her people, how her belief that one needs an education "to get around" in the mainstream was tempered by insight into why some choose a different path. To understand Fannie's stance towards schooling, Morgan needed to grasp that she felt both this commitment *and* this ambivalence; but as was so often the case, Fannie's meager hints went unheeded.

A few weeks into the semester, Morgan labored one morning to move Fannie past her apparent block on a descriptive essay. Fannie said only that she was going to try to describe her grandmother, and Morgan began by asking a series of questions — about her grandmother's voice, her presence, her laugh, whatever came to Fannie's mind. Her questions greeted by long silences, Morgan admitted her gathering frustration: "Are you learnin' anything from me?" she asked. Morgan's voice sounded cordial and even a bit playful, but she was clearly concerned that Fannie didn't seem to be meeting her halfway. In the weeks that followed, Morgan would repeatedly adjust her approach, continually searching for a way to break through, "to spark something," as she often put it.

The first change — to a tougher, more demanding stance — was clearly signalled as the group brainstormed ideas for their next essays. Instead of waiting for Fannie to jump into the discussion, Morgan called upon her: "Ok, your turn in the hot seat," she announced. When Fannie noted that her essay would be about her home in Arizona, Morgan demanded to know "why it would be of possible interest to us." The ensuing exchange shed little light on the subject:

Fannie: Because it's my home!

Morgan: That's not good enough . . . that's telling me nothing.

Fannie: I was raised there.

Morgan: What's so special about it?

Fannie: (exasperated sigh) I don't know what's so special about it . . .

Morgan: So why do you want to write about it, then?

Morgan's final question still unanswered, she eventually gave up and moved to another student. Again, a wealth of valuable information remained tacit; Morgan wouldn't learn for several weeks that Fannie had grown up on a reservation, and she'd understood nothing at all about her profound bond with this other world.

Two months into the semester, Morgan had an opportunity to attend the Conference on College Composition and Communication (CCCC), and it was there that some of her early training crystallized into a more definite plan of action, her early doubts subsumed by a new sense of authoritative expertise. Morgan thought a great deal about her work with Fannie as she attended numerous sessions on peer tutoring and a half-day workshop on collaborative learning. She returned to campus infused with a clear sense of direction: the solution, Morgan had concluded, was to assume an even more low-profile approach, speaking only to ask open-ended questions or to paraphrase Fannie's statements, steadfastly avoiding the temptation to fill silences with her own ideas and asides. As she anticipated her next encounter with Fannie, she couldn't wait to try out this more emphatic version of what had been called — in conference sessions and her earlier training — a "collaborative" or "non-directive" stance.

Still struggling to produce an already past-due essay on "values," Fannie arrived at this first post-CCCC tutorial hour with only preliminary ideas and nothing in writing. Remembering the advice of Conference participants, Morgan began by trying to nudge her towards a focus, repeatedly denying that she knew more than Fannie about how to approach the piece:

> *Morgan:* What would you say your basic theme is? And sometimes if you keep that in mind, then you can always, you know, keep that as a focus for what you're writing. And the reason I say that is 'cause when you say, "well living happily wasn't . . ."
>
> *Fannie:* (pause) . . . Well, America was a beautiful country, well, but it isn't beautiful anymore.
>
> *Morgan:* Um hm. Not as beautiful.
>
> *Fannie:* So I should just say, America was a beautiful country?
>
> *Morgan:* Yeah. But I dunno — what do you think your overall theme is, that you're saying?
>
> *Fannie:* (long pause) . . . I'm really, I'm just talking about America.
>
> *Morgan:* America? So America as . . . ?
>
> *Fannie:* (pause) . . . Um . . . (pause)
>
> *Morgan:* Land of free, uh, land of natural resources? As, um a place where there's a conflict, I mean, there, if you can narrow that, "America." What is it specifically, and think about what you've written, in the rest. Know what I mean?
>
> *Fannie:* (pause) . . . The riches of America, or the country? I don't know . . .
>
> *Morgan:* I think you do. I'm not saying there's any right answer, but I, I'm — for me, the reason I'm saying this, is I see this emerging as, you know, (pause) where you're really having a hard time with dealing with the exploitation that you see, of America, you know, you think that. And you're using two groups to really illustrate, specifically, how two different attitudes toward, um the richness and beauty of America, two different, um, ways people have to approach this land. Does that, does this make any sense? Or am I just putting words in your mouth? I don't want to do that. I mean that's what I see emerge in your paper. But I could be way off base.

Fannie: I think I know what you're trying to say. And I can kind of relate it at times to what I'm trying to say.

Morgan: You know, I mean, this is like the theme I'm picking up . . . (pause) I think you know, you've got some real, you know, environmental issues here. I think you're a closet environmentalist here. Which are real true, know what I mean. (pause) And when you talk about pollution, and waste, and um, those types of things. So I mean, if you're looking at a theme of your paper, what could you pick out, of something of your underlying theme.

Fannie: (pause) . . . The resources, I guess?

Morgan: Well I mean, I don't want you to say, I want you to say, don't say "I guess," is that what you're talking about?

Fannie: Yeah.

Morgan: "Yeah?" I mean, it's your paper.

Fannie: I know, I want to talk about the land . . .

Morgan: Ok. So you want to talk about the land, and the beauty of the land . . .

Fannie: Um hm.

Morgan: . . . and then, um, and then also your topic for your, um, to spark your paper . . . what values, and morals, right? That's where you based off to write about America, and the land, you know. Maybe you can write some of these things down, as we're talking, as focusing things, you know. So you want to talk about the land, and then it's like, what do you want to say about the land?

What *did* Fannie "want to say about the land"? Whatever it was, one begins to wonder if it was perhaps lost in her tutor's inadvertent appropriation of these meanings — this despite Morgan's ostensible effort to simply elicit and reflect Fannie's thoughts. While Fannie may well have been struggling to articulate meanings which eluded clear expression in English, as Morgan worked to move her towards greater specificity, it became apparent that she was assuming the paper would express commonplace environmental concerns:

Fannie: I'll say, the country was, um, (pause), more like, I can't say perfect, I mean was, the tree was green, you know, I mean, um, it was clean. (long pause). I can't find the words for it.

Morgan: In a natural state? Um, un-, polluted, um, untouched, um, let me think, trying to get a . . .

Fannie: I mean everybody, I mean the Indians too, they didn't wear that (pointing to Morgan's clothes), they only wore buffalo clothing, you know for their clothing, they didn't wear like . . . these, you know, cotton and all that, they were so . . .

Morgan: Naturalistic.

Fannie: Yeah. "Naturalistic," I don't know if I'm gonna use that word . . . I wanna say, I wanna give a picture of the way the land was, before, you know what I'm, what I'm tryin' to say?

The Navajos' connection to the land is legendary — a spiritual nexus, many would maintain, that goes far beyond mainstream notions of what it means to be concerned about the environment. However, later in this session, Morgan observed that Fannie was writing about concerns that worry lots of people — citing recent publicity about the greenhouse effect, the hole in the ozone layer, and the growing interest in recycling. She then brought the session to a close by paraphrasing what she saw as the meat of the discussion and asking, "Is that something that you were tryin' to say, too?" Fannie replied, "Probably. I mean, I can't find the words for it, but you're finding the words for me." Morgan's rejoinder had been, "I'm just sparkin', I'm just sparkin' what you already have there, what you're sayin'. I mean I'm tryin' to tell you what I hear you sayin'."

Morgan laughed as, in an end-of-term interview, she listened again to Fannie's final comment: "I didn't *want* to find the words for her," she mused; "I wanted to show her how she could find 'em for herself." Still, she admitted, the directive impulse had been hard to resist: "I wanted to just give her ideas," Morgan observed, adding that although Fannie had some good things to say, "I wanted her to be able to articulate her ideas on a little higher level." Although it was obvious to Morgan that the ideas in Fannie's paper were of "deep-seated emotional concern," she also saw her as stuck in arid generalities: "'I don't know, it's just a beautiful country,'" Morgan echoed as she reviewed the audiotape. While Morgan emphasized that she "didn't wanna write the paper for her," she allowed that "it's difficult — it's really hard to want to take the bull by the horns and say, 'don't you see it this way?'" On the one hand, Morgan noted that she'd often asked Fannie what she was getting out of a session, "'cause sometimes I'll think I'm getting through and I'm explaining something really good, and then they won't catch it"; on the other hand, Morgan emphasized again and again that she didn't want to "give away" her own thoughts.

Although Morgan often did an almost heroic job of waiting out Fannie's lingering silences and deflecting appeals to her authority, she never really surrendered control; somehow, the message always came across that Morgan knew more than Fannie about the ideas at hand, and that if she would, she could simply turn over pre-packaged understandings. While her frustration was certainly understandable, I often had the sense that Morgan was insufficiently curious about Fannie's thoughts — insufficiently curious about how Fannie's understandings might have differed from her own, about how they had been shaped by Fannie's background and cultural orientation, or about what she stood to learn from them.

When asked about Fannie's block, a weary Morgan wrote it off to her cultural background:

You know, I would have to say it's cultural; I'd have to say it's her you know, Native American background and growing up on a reservation . . . maybe . . . she's more sensitive to male-female roles, and the female role being quiet.

On a number of occasions Morgan had speculated that Navajo women are taught to be subservient, a perception that contrasted rather strikingly with Fannie's assertion that she wasn't at all shy or quiet back home.[2] Hoping to challenge Morgan's accustomed view of Fannie as bashful and retiring, in a final interview I played back one of their sessions from the week that a group of Navajo students were visiting the campus. Fannie was uncharacteristically vocal and even aggressive that morning, talking in a loud voice, repeatedly seizing and holding the floor:

Fannie: You know what my essay's on? Different environments. Um, I'm talking, I'm not gonna talk about my relationship between my brothers, it's so boring, so I'm just gonna talked about both being raised, like my youngest brother being raised on the reservation, and the other being raised over here, and they both have very different, um, um, (Morgan starts to say something, but Fannie cuts her off and continues) characteristics or somethin' like that. You know, like their personalities, you know.

Morgan: Um. That's good. (Morgan starts to say something more, but Fannie keeps going.)

Fannie: It's funny, I'm cutting, I was totally mean to my brother here. (Morgan laughs.) Because, I called, I said that he's a wimp, you know, and my brother, my little brother's being raised on the reservation, is like, is like taught to be a man, he's brave and all that.

Luis (a student in the group): That's being a man?!

Fannie: And . . .

Luis: That's not being a man, I don't find.

Fannie: (her voice raised) I'm sorry — but that's how I wrote, Ok?! That's your opinion, I mean, and it's . . .

Luis: I think a man is sensitive, caring, and lov —

[2]Morgan's assumption is also contradicted by published accounts of life among the Navajo, which from early on have emphasized the prestige and power of female members of the tribe. Gladys Reichard, an anthropologist who lived among the Navajos in the 1920s, reported that "the Navajo woman enjoys great economic and social prestige as the head of the house and clan and as the manager of economic affairs, and she is not excluded from religious ritual or from attaining political honors" (55). Navajo women often own substantial property, and children retain the surname of the matrilineal clan; the status accorded women is further reflected in the depictions of female deities in Navajo myths (Terrell 57; 255).

Fannie: (cutting him off) No, no . . .

Luis: . . . and able to express his feelings. I don't think that if you can go kill someone, that makes you a man.

Fannie: I mean . . .

Luis: That's just my opinion (gets up and walks away for a moment).

Fannie: (watching Luis wander off) Dickhead.

Morgan listened with a widening smile to the rest of this session, obviously pleased with Fannie's sometimes combative manner and unflagging insistence that attention be directed back to her. "Ha! Fannie's *so* much more forceful," Morgan exclaimed, "And just more in control of what she wants, and what she needs." When asked what she thought might have accounted for this temporary change, Morgan sidestepped the influence of the visiting students:

> I would love to think that I made her feel safe that way. And that I really um, showed her that she had, you know, by my interactions with her, that she really had every right to be strong-willed and forceful and have her opinions and you know, say what she felt that she needed to say, and that she didn't have to be quiet, you know. People always tell me that I influence people that way. You know? (laughs). "You've been hangin' around with Morgan too much!"

Hungry for feedback that she'd influenced Fannie in a positive way, Morgan grasped this possible evidence with obvious pleasure. Fannie was not a student who offered many positive signals, and it was perhaps essential to Morgan's professional self-esteem that she find them wherever she could. In this credit-taking there was, however, a larger irony: if only she'd been encouraged to push a little farther in her own thinking, perhaps she would have found herself assisting more often in such moments of blossoming.

Conclusion: Students as Teachers, Teachers as Students

When Morgan returned from the CCCC with a vision of "collaboration" that cast it as a set of techniques rather than a new way to think about teaching and learning, the insights of panelists and workshop leaders devolved into a fossilized creed, a shield against more fundamental concerns. Morgan had somehow missed the importance of continually adjusting her approach in the light of the understandings student make available, of allowing their feedback to shape her reflections upon her own role. At semester's end, she still didn't know that Fannie was a non-native speaker of English; she didn't know the dimensions of Fannie's inexperience with academic writing, nor did she know the reasons behind Fannie's formidable block.

Even as Morgan labored to promote "collaborative" moments — making an ostensible effort to "talk less," to "sit back more," to enact an instructional mode that would seem more culturally appropriate — Fannie remembered a lifetime of classroom misadventure, and hung back, reluctant. Morgan needed to know something about this history, but she also needed to understand that much else was fluid and alive, that a revised sense of self was emerging from the dynamic interaction of Fannie's past and present. Emboldened by a few treasured days in the company of fellow Navajos, Fannie had momentarily stepped into a new stance, one that departed markedly from her accustomed behavior on reservation and campus alike; but if her confidence recalled an earlier self, her playful combativeness was, as Fannie observed in listening to the tape, a new and still-strange manifestation of something also oddly familiar, something left over from long ago.

Rather than frequent urgings to "talk less," perhaps what Morgan most needed was advice to *listen more* — for the clues students like Fannie would provide, for those moments when she might best shed her teacherly persona and become once again a learner. More than specific instructional strategies, Morgan needed the conceptual grounding that would allow her to understand that authentically collaborative learning is predicated upon fine-grained insight into individual students — of the nature of their Vygotskian "zones of proximal development," and, by association, of the sorts of instructional "scaffolding" most appropriate to their changing needs (Bruner; Langer and Applebee). So, too, did Morgan need to be encouraged toward the yet-elusive understanding that such learning is never unilateral, inevitably entailing a reciprocal influence, reciprocal advances in understanding (Dyson). As she struggled to come to terms with her own ethnic ambivalence, to defend herself against a vociferous chorus proclaiming her "not black enough," Morgan had reason to take heart in Fannie's dramatic and rather trying process of transition. Had she thought to ask, Morgan would no doubt have been fascinated by Fannie's descriptions of this other cultural and linguistic context, with its very different perspectives on education in particular and the world in general (John; Locust). Most of all, perhaps she would have been interested to know that Fannie was learning to inhabit both arenas, and in so doing enacting a negotiation of admirable complexity — a negotiation different in degree, perhaps, but certainly not in kind, from Morgan's own.

Having tutored only one semester previously, Morgan was understandably eager to abandon her lingering doubts about her effectiveness, eager for a surefooted sense that she was providing something worthwhile. Her idealism and good intentions were everywhere apparent — in her lengthy meditations on her work, in her eager enthusiasm at the CCCC, in her persistent efforts to try out new approaches, and in the reassurance she extended to me when I confessed that I'd be writing some fairly negative things about her vexed attempts to reach Fannie. Morgan had been offered relatively little by way of preparation and support: beyond a sprinkling of workshops and an occasional alliance with more experienced tutors, she was left largely on her own — alone with the substantial challenges and opportunities that students like Fannie presented, alone to deal with her frustration and occasional feelings of failure as best she could. Like all beginning educators, Morgan needed abundant support, instruction, and modeling if she were to learn to reflect critically upon her work, to question her assumptions about students like Fannie, to allow herself, even at this fledgling stage in her career, to become a reflective and therefore vulnerable practitioner. This is not to suggest that Morgan should have pried into hidden corners of Fannie's past, insisting that she reveal information about her background before she felt ready to do so; only that Morgan be respectfully curious, ever attentive to whatever clues Fannie might have been willing to offer, ever poised to revise old understandings in light of fresh evidence.

Those of us who work with linguistic minority students — and that's fast becoming all of us — must appreciate the evolving dimensions of our task, realizing that we have to reach further than ever if we're to do our jobs well. Regardless of our crowded schedules and shrinking budgets, we must also think realistically about the sorts of guidance new tutors and teachers need if they are to confront these rigors effectively, guiding them towards practical strategies informed by understandings from theory and research, and offering compelling reminders of the need to monitor one's ethnocentric biases and faulty assumptions. Most of all, we must serve as models of reflective practice — perennially inquisitive and self-critical, even as we find occasion both to bless and curse the discovery that becoming students of students means becoming students of ourselves as well.

Works Cited

Applebee, Arthur, and Judith Langer. "Reading and Writing Instruction: Toward a Theory of Teaching and Learning." *Review of Research in Education*, Vol. 13. Ed. E. Z. Rothkopf. Washington, DC: American Educational Research Association, 1986.

Bakhtin, Mikhail Mikhailovich. *The Dialogic Imagination: Four Essays by M. M. Bakhtin*. Ed. Michael Holquist, trans. Caryl Emerson and Michael Holquist. Austin: U of Texas P, 1981.

Bruner, Jerome. "The Role of Dialogue in Language Acquisition." *The Child's Conception of Language*. Ed. A. Sinclair. New York: Springer-Verlag, 1978.

Cintron, Ralph. "Reading and Writing Graffitti: A Reading." *The Quarterly Newsletter of the Laboratory of Comparative Human Cognition* 13 (1991): 21–24.

DiPardo, Anne. "Acquiring 'A Kind of Passport': The Teaching and Learning of Academic Discourse in Basic Writing Tutorials." Diss. UC Berkeley, 1991.

———. *"A Kind of Passport": A Basic Writing Adjunct Program and the Challenge of Student Diversity*. Urbana: NCTE, (1993).

Dorris, Michael. *A Yellow Raft in Blue Water*. New York: Holt, 1987.

Dyson, Anne. "Weaving Possibilities: Rethinking Metaphors for Early Literacy Development." *The Reading Teacher* 44 (1990): 202–213.

Fischer, Michael. "Ethnicity and the Postmodern Arts of Memory." *Writing Culture: The Poetics and Politics of Ethnography.* Eds. J. Clifford and G. E. Marcus. Berkeley: U of California P, 1986.

Hawkins, Thom. "Intimacy and Audience: The Relationship Between Revision and the Social Dimension of Peer Tutoring." *College English* 42 (1980): 64–68.

Hull, Glynda, and Mike Rose. "Rethinking Remediation: Toward a Social-Cognitive Understanding of Problematic Reading and Writing." *Written Communication* 6 (1989): 139–154.

———. "This Wooden Shack: The Logic of an Unconventional Reading." *College Composition and Communication* 41 (9190): 287–298.

John, Vera P. "Styles of Learning — Styles of Teaching: Reflections on the Education of Navajo Children." *Functions of Language in the Classroom.* Ed. Courtney B. Cazden and Vera P. John. 1972. Prospect Heights, IL: Waveland, 1985.

Locust, Carol. "Wounding the Spirit: Discrimination and Traditional American Indian Belief Systems." *Harvard Educational Review* 58 (1988): 315–30.

Philips, Susan U. "Participant Structures and Communicative Competence: Warm Springs Children in Community and Classroom." *Functions of Language in the Classroom.* Ed. Courtney B. Cazden and Vera P. John. 1972. Prospect Heights, IL: Waveland, 1985.

Reichard, Gladys. *Social Life of the Navajo Indians.* 1928. New York: AMS P, 1969.

Shaughnessy, Mina. "Diving In: An Introduction to Basic Writing." *College Composition and Communication* 27 (1976): 234–39.

Terrell, John Upton. *The Navajo: The Past and Present of a Great People.* 1970. New York: Perennial, 1972.

Valdés, Guadalupe. *Identifying Priorities in the Study of the Writing of Hispanic Background Students.* Grant No. OERI-G-008690004. Washington, DC: Office of Educational Research and Improvement, 1989.

———. "Language Issues in Writing: The Problem of Compartmentalization of Interest Areas Within CCCC." Paper presented at the Conference on College Composition and Communication. 21–23 March, 1991.

Vygotsky, Lev. *Mind in Society.* Cambridge: Harvard UP, 1978.

Classroom Activities

DiPardo's conclusion suggests that, despite the continuing challenges, there is much potential for developing writers and their tutors to benefit from participation in writing center activities. If your campus has a writing center, take your students on a tour or have a peer tutor or other personnel representative visit your class to talk about the writing center's services. Find out how your writing center recruits peer tutors, and be sure to recommend that interested students apply for those positions. If your campus does not have a writing center, have your students do research on other support systems that are available for developing writers and readers, both on and off campus. For instance, what kinds of tutoring services are available at public libraries or community centers? If you or your students are interested in finding more information about resources offered by writing centers at other campuses, visit the National Writing Centers Association home page at <http://iwca.syr.edu>. This site includes resources for writers, tutor stories, e-mail discussion groups, a writing center start-up kit, and more.

Thinking about Teaching

If your campus doesn't have a writing center, find out what is needed to create out-of-class support services for student writing. See, "Classroom Activities" above for appropriate Internet resources. If your campus has a learning center, rather than a writing center, ask what services are available specifically for students who need support with writing — whether there is "remedial" help or general feedback for more "advanced" students. If your campus does have a writing center, it may be possible for you to work there yourself. Some writing centers encourage faculty to hold office hours in the writing center or to work as tutors in the center. Meet with the director of your writing center to find out what his or her policy is on instructors working there. If either arrangement is viable given writing center policies and your own schedule, try spending time working there over the course of a semester. Be sure to keep a journal of your experiences. This opportunity will enable you to experience at first hand DiPardo's call for teachers to "serve as models of reflective practice — perennially inquisitive and self-critical, even as we find occasion both to bless and curse the discovery that becoming students of students means becoming students of ourselves as well."

Bibliography

Readers may wish to consult the "Basic Writing Reading List" at <http://www.gen.umn.edu/research/cbw/reading_list.html> and *The Bedford Bibliography for Teachers of Basic Writing,* edited by Linda Adler-Kassner and Gregory R. Glau for the Conference on Basic Writing (this resource is also online at <http://bedfordstmartins.com/basicbib/>.) Many of the following works were located via these excellent sources for texts on basic writing pedagogy.

1   Basic Writing: Teachers' Perspectives

Adams, Peter D. "Basic Writing Reconsidered." *Journal of Basic Writing* 12.2 (1993): 22–26.

Baker, Tracy, and Peggy Jolly. "The 'Hard Evidence': Documenting the Effectiveness of a Basic Writing Program." *Journal of Basic Writing* 18.1 (1999): 27–39.

Bartholomae, David. "Inventing the University." *When a Writer Can't Write: Studies in Writer's Block and Other Composing Problems.* Ed. Mike Rose. New York: Guilford, 1985. 134–65.

———. "The Tidy House: Basic Writing and the American Curriculum." *Journal of Basic Writing* 12.1 (1993): 4–21.

Collins, Terence G. "A Response to Ira Shor's 'Our Apartheid: Writing Instruction and Inequality.'" *Journal of Basic Writing* 16.2 (1997): 95–100.

David, Denise, Barbara Gordon, and Rita Pollard. "Seeking Common Ground: Guiding Assumptions for Writing Courses." *College Composition and Communication* 46 (1995): 522–32.

Dwinnel, Patricia L., and Jeanne L. Higbee, eds. *Developmental Education: Enhancing Student Retention.* Carol Stream, IL: National Association for Developmental Education, 1997.

Enos, Theresa, ed. *A Sourcebook for Basic Writing Teachers.* New York: Random, 1987.

Freire, Paulo. *Pedagogy of the Oppressed.* Rev. ed. New York: Continuum, 1994.

Gay, Pamela. "Rereading Shaughnessy from a Postcolonial Perspective." *Journal of Basic Writing* 12.2 (1993): 29–40.

Glau, Gregory R. "The 'Stretch' Program: Arizona State University's New Model of University-Level Basic Writing Instruction." *Writing Program Administration* 20 (1996): 79–91.

Gunner, Jeanne. "The Status of Basic Writing Teachers: Do We Need a 'Maryland Resolution'?" *Journal of Basic Writing* 12.1 (1993): 57–63.

Higbee, Jeanne L., and Patricia Dwinell, eds. *Defining Developmental Education: Theory, Research, and Pedagogy.* Carol Stream, IL: National Association for Developmental Education, 1996.

Hindman, Jane E. "Re-inventing the University: Finding the Place for Basic Writers." *Journal of Basic Writing* 12.2 (1993): 55–77.

Horner, Bruce. "Discoursing Basic Writing." *College Composition and Communication* 47 (1996): 199–222.

Lewiecki-Wilson, Cynthia, and Jeff Sommers. "Professing at the Fault Lines: Composition at Open-Admissions Institutions." *College Composition and Communication* 50 (1999): 438–62.

Maher, Jane. "Writing the Life of Mina P. Shaughnessy." *Journal of Basic Writing* 16 (1997): 51–63.

Royster, Jacqueline Jones, and Rebecca Greenberg Taylor. "Constructing Teacher Identity in the Basic Writing Classroom." *Journal of Basic Writing* 16.1 (1997): 27–50.

Shaughnessy, Mina P. Introduction. *Errors and Expectations: A Guide for the Teachers of Basic Writing.* New York: Oxford UP, 1997. 1–13.

Shor, Ira. "The First Day of Class: Passing the Text" from *Empowering Education: Critical Teaching for Social Change.* U of Chicago P 1992.

———. "Inequality (Still Rules): Reply to Collins and Greenberg." *Journal of Basic Writing* 17.1 (1998): 104–08.

Soliday, Mary. "From the Margins to the Mainstream: Reconceiving Remediation." *College Composition and Communication* 47 (1996): 85–100.

Soliday, Mary, and Barbara Gleason. "From Remediation to Enrichment: Evaluating a Mainstreaming Project." *Journal of Basic Writing* 16.1 (1997): 64–78.

2 Basic Writing: Students' Perspectives

Adler-Kassner, Linda, and Susanmarie Harrington. *Basic Writing as a Political Act: Public Conversations about Writing and Literacy.* Creskill: Hampton, 2002.

Berlin, James. *Rhetoric and Reality.* Carbondale: Southern Illinois UP, 1987.

Connors, Robert. *Composition-Rhetoric.* Pittsburgh: U of Pittsburgh P, 1997.

De Beaugrande, Robert, and Marjean Olson. "Using a 'Write-Speak-Write' Approach for Basic Writers." *Journal of Basic Writing* 10.2 (1991): 4–32.

Gray-Rosendale, Laura. "Revising the Political in Basic Writing Scholarship." *Journal of Basic Writing* 15.2 (1996): 24–49.

———. *Rethinking Basic Writing: Exploring Identity, Politics, and Community in Interaction.* Mahwah: Lawrence Erlbaum Associates, 2000.

Gray-Rosendale, Laura, and Raymona Leonard. "Demythologizing the 'Basic Writer': Identity, Power, and Other Challenges to the Discipline." *BWe: Basic Writing e-Journal* 3.1 (2001). 20 July 2001 <www.asu.edu/clas/english/composition/cbw/spring_2001_V3N1.html#laura>.

Harrington, Susanmarie. "The Representation of Basic Writing Scholarship, or Who Is Quentin Pierce?" *Journal of Basic Writing* 18.2 (1999): 91–107.

Harrington, Susanmarie and Linda Adler-Kassner. "The Dilemma That Still Counts: Basic Writing at a Political Crossroads." *Journal of Basic Writing* 17.2 (1999): 1–24.

Hull, Glynda, and Mike Rose. "This Wooden Shack Place": The Logic of an Unconventional Reading. *College Composition and Communication* 41.3 (1990): 299–329.

Mortensen, Peter. "Going Public." *College Composition and Communication* 50 (1998): 182–205.

Mutnick, Deborah. *Writing in an Alien World.* Portsmouth, NH: Boynton/Cook, 1996.

Perl, Sondra. "A Look at Basic Writers in the Process of Composing." *Basic Writing: Essays for Teachers and Administrators.* Ed. Lawrence N. Kasden and Daniel R. Hoeber. Urbana, IL: NCTE, 1980: 13–32.

Rose, Mike. "Narrowing the Mind: Cognitive Reductionism and Remedial Writers." *Cross-Talk in Comp Theory.* Ed. Victor Villanueva. Urbana, IL: NCTE, 1997.

———. *Lives on the Boundary: The Struggles and Achievements of America's Underprepared.* New York: Penguin, 1989.

Soliday, Mary. "From the Margins to the Mainstream: Reconceiving Remediation." *College Composition Communication* 47.1 (1996): 85–100.

3 Adapting the Writing Process

Anokye, Aku Duku. "Oral Connections to Literacy: The Narrative." *Journal of Basic Writing* 13.2 (1994).

Boese, Peggy, Mary Ellen Byrne, and Louise Silverman. "The Rewards of a Publication of Student Writings." *Teaching English in the Two-Year College* 24 (1997): 42–46.

Collins, James L. "Basic Writing and the Process Paradigm." *Journal of Basic Writing* 14.2 (1995): 3–18.

Davis, Mary Beth Lindley. "Revisioning the Basic Writer as Seeker and Quester: A Preparatory Course Design." *Teaching English in the Two-Year College* 17 (1990): 24–29.

Elbow, Peter. "Freewriting." *Writing with Power: Techniques for Mastering the Writing Process.* New York: Oxford UP, 1981. 13–19.

Elliot, Norbert. "Narrative Discourse and the Basic Writer." *Journal of Basic Writing* 14.2 (1995): 19–30.

Fleckenstein, Kristie S. "Writing and the Strategic Use of Metaphor." *Teaching English in the Two-Year College* 22 (1995): 110–15.

Flower, Linda, and John Hays. "Cognitive Process Theory of Writing." *College Composition and Communication* 32 (1981): 365–87.

Fulwiler, Toby. Introduction. *The Journal Book.* Ed. Toby Fulwiler. Portsmouth, NH: Boynton, 1987. 1–8.

Keithley, Zoe. "'My Own Voice': Students Say It Unlocks the Writing Process." *Journal of Basic Writing* 11.2 (1992): 82–102.

Lay, Nancy Duke S. "Response Journals in the ESL Classroom: Windows to the World." *Teaching English in the Two Year College* 22 (1995): 38–44.

Parisi, Hope A. "Involvement and Self-Awareness for the Basic Writer: Graphically Conceptualizing the Writing Process." *Journal of Basic Writing* 13.2 (1994): 33–45.

Perl, Sondra. "The Composing Processes of Unskilled College Writers." *Research in the Teaching of English* 13 (1979): 317–36.

Rico, Gabrielle. "General Principles of Clustering." *Writing the Natural Way.* Boston: Houghton, 1983. 35–39.

Robinson, William S. "On Teaching Organization: Patterns, Process, and the Nature of Writing." *Teaching English in the Two-Year College* 21 (1994): 191–98.

Schor, Sandra. "The Short Happy Life of Ms. Mystery." *Journal of Basic Writing* 10.1 (1991): 16–25.

Sills, Caryl Klein. "Arguing from First-Hand Evidence." *Journal of Basic Writing* 11.2 (1992).

Sommers, Nancy. "Revision Strategies of Student Writers." *College Composition and Communication* 31 (1980): 378–88.

Wells, Neil R. "Imitate This: Modeling Essays for Students." *Journal of Developmental Education* 3.3 (1998) 31 July 1999 <http://inet.ccp.cc.pa.us/vpacaff/divess/jde/model.htm>.

Wiener, Harvey. "Basic Writing: First Day's Thoughts on Process and Detail." *Eight Approaches to Teaching Composition*. Ed. Timothy R. Donovan and Ben W. McClelland. Urbana, IL: NCTE, 1980. 87–99.

4 Writing and Reading

Chase, Nancy, Sandra U. Gibson, and Joan G. Carson. "An Examination of Reading Demands Across Four College Courses." *Journal of Basic Writing* 18 (1994): 10–16.

Daniels, Harvey. *Literature Circles: Voice and Choice in the Student-Centered Classroom*. York, ME: Stenhouse, 1994.

Deming, Mary P. "Reading and Writing: Making the Connection for Basic Writers." *BWe: Basic Writing e-Journal* 2.2 (2000). 20 July 2001 <www.asu.edu/clas/english/composition/cbw/summer_2000_V2N2.htm#Mary>.

Dickson, Marcia. "Learning to Read/Learning to Write." *BWe: Basic Writing e-Journal* 1.1 (1999). 20 July 2001 <www.asu.edu/clas/english/composition/cbw/bwe_summer1999.htm#marcia>.

Palmer, James C. "Do College Courses Improve Basic Reading and Writing Skills?" *Community College Review* 12.2 (1984): 20–28.

Smith, Frank. *Understanding Reading: A Psycholinguistic Analysis of Reading and Learning to Read*. 5th ed. Hillsdale, NJ: Erlbaum, 1994.

Sternglass, Marilyn S. *Time to Know Them: A Longitudinal Study of Writing and Learning at the College Level*. Mahwah, NJ: Erlbaum, 1997.

Wiener, Harvey S. "The Attack on Basic Writing—And After." *Journal of Basic Writing* 17 (1998): 96–103.

5 Approaches to Grammar Instruction

Chafe, Wallace. "What Is Good Punctuation?" *Center for the Study of Writing Occasional Paper No. 2* Berkeley: Center for the Study of Writing, 1985. ERIC ED 292 120.

Dawkins, John. "Teaching Punctuation as a Rhetorical Tool." *College Composition and Communication* 46 (1995): 533–48.

Devet, Bonnie. "Errors as Discoveries: An Assignment for Prospective English Teachers." *Journal of Teaching Writing* 15.1 (1996): 129–39.

Hartwell, Patrick. "Grammar, Grammars, and the Teaching of Grammar." *College English* 47 (1985): 105–27.

Haussamen, Brock. *Revising the Rules: Traditional Grammar and Modern Linguistics.* Dubuque, IA: Kendall, 1993.

Meyer, Charles. "Functional Grammar and Its Application in the Composition Classroom." *Journal of Teaching Writing* 8 (1989): 147–67.

Newman, Michael. "Correctness and Its Conceptions: The Meaning of Language Form for Basic Writers." *Journal of Basic Writing* 15.1 (1996): 23–38.

Noguchi, Rei R. "Transformational-Generative Syntax and the Teaching of Sentence Mechanics." *Journal of Basic Writing* 6.2 (1987): 26–36.

Otte, George. "Computer-Adjusted Errors and Expectations." *Journal of Basic Writing* 10.2 (1991): 71–86.

Weaver, Constance. *Grammar for Teachers.* Urbana, IL: NCTE, 1979.

———. *Teaching Grammar in Context.* Portsmouth, NH: Boynton, 1996.

———, ed. *Lessons to Share: On Teaching Grammar in Context.* Portsmouth, NH: Boynton, 1998.

6   Learning Differences

Dunn, Patricia. *Learning Re-abled.* Portsmouth, NH: Boynton, 1995.

Emig, Janet. "Writing as a Mode of Learning." *College Composition and Communication* 28 (1977): 122–28.

Evans, Nancy J., Deanna S. Forney, and Florence Guido-DeBrito. *Student Development in College: Theory, Research, and Practice.* San Francisco: Jossey, 1998.

Gardner, Howard. *Multiple Intelligences: The Theory in Practice.* New York: Basic, 1993.

Gordon, Lawrence. *People Types and Tiger Stripes,* 2d ed. Gainesville, FL: Center for Applications of Psychological Types, 1982.

Grimes, "Targeting Academic Programs to Student Diversity Utilizing Learning Styles and Learning-Study Strategies." *Journal of College Student Development* 36 (1995): 422–30.

Houston, Linda S. "Accommodations for Learning Differences in the English Classroom." *Teaching English in the Two-Year College* (Dec. 1994).

Kalivoda, Karen S., Jeanne L. Higbee, and Debra C. Brenner. "Teaching Students with Hearing Impairments." *Journal of Developmental Education* 20.3 (1997): 10–16.

Kolb, David A. *Experiential Learning: Experience as the Source of Learning and Development.* Englewood Cliffs, NJ: Prentice, 1983.

Kutz, Eleanor, et al. *The Discovery of Competence: Teaching and Learning with Diverse Student Writers.* Portsmouth, NH: Boynton, 1993.

McAlexander, Patricia J., Ann B. Dobie, and Noel Gregg. *Beyond the SP Label: Improving the Spelling of Learning Disabled and Basic Writers.* Urbana, IL: NCTE, 1993.

O'Brien, Terrence P., and Mary J. Thompson. "Cognitive Styles and Academic Achievement in Community College Education." *Community College Journal of Research and Practice* 18 (1994): 547–56.

Rothchild, Jacqueline, and William E. Piland. "Intercorrelates of Postsecondary Students' Learning Styles and Personality Traits." *Community College Journal of Research and Practice* 18 (1994): 177–88.

Schroeder, Charles C. "New Students—New Learning Styles." *Change* Sept.–Oct. 1993: 21–26.

7 Writing and Adult Learners

Auerbach, Elsa R. *Making Meaning, Making Change: Participatory Curriculum Development for Adult ESL and Family Literacy.* Boston: U of Massachusetts P, 1990.

Greenwood, C. M. "'It's Scary at First': Reentry Women in College Composition Classes." *Teaching English in the Two-Year College* 17 (1990): 133–42.

Kiskis, Michael J. "Adult Learners, Autobiography, and Educational Planning: Reflections of Pedagogy, Adragogy, and Power." *Pedagogy in the Age of Politics: Writing and Reading (in) the Academy.* Ed. Patricia A. Sullivan and Donna J. Qualley. Urbana: NCTE, 1994. 56–72.

Knowles, Malcolm. *The Adult Learner: A Neglected Species.* 4th ed. Houston: Gulf, 1990.

Luttrell, Wendy. *Schoolsmart and Motherwise: Working-Class Women's Identity and Schooling.* New York: Routledge, 1997.

Miritello, Mary. "Teaching Writing to Adults: Examining Assumptions and Revising Expectations for Adult Learners in the Writing Class." *Composition Chronicle: Newsletter for Writing Teachers* 9.2 (1990): 6–9.

8 Critical Thinking

Blodgett-McDeavitt, Cynthia. "A Profile of Critical Thinking, Problem Solving, and Learning to Learn among Adult and Continuing Education Administrators." Amer. Assoc. for Adult and Continuing Educ. Conf. Kansas City. 1–4 Nov. 1995.

Brookfield, Stephen D. *Becoming a Critically Reflective Teacher.* San Francisco: Jossey, 1995.

———. *Developing Critical Thinkers.* San Francisco: Jossey, 1987.

Elder, Linda, and Richard Paul. "Critical Thinking: A Stage Theory of Critical Thinking." Parts 1 and 2. *Journal of Developmental Education.* 20.1–2 (1996): 34–35.

———. "Critical Thinking: Content Is Thinking/Thinking Is Content." *Journal of Developmental Education* 19.2 (1995): 34.

———. "Critical Thinking: Rethinking Content as a Mode of Thinking." *Journal of Developmental Education* 19.3 (1996): 32.

———. "Critical Thinking: Using Intellectual Standards to Assess Student Reasoning." *Journal of Developmental Education* 18.2 (1994): 32–33.

———. "Critical Thinking: Why Teach Students Intellectual Standards?" Parts 1 and 2. *Journal of Developmental Education* 18.3 (1995): 36–37 and 19.1 (1995): 34–35.

Golub, Jeff. *Classroom Practices in Teaching English.* Urbana, IL: NCTE, 1996.

McLaughlin, Margaret A., Patricia T. Price, and Mildred Pate. "Using Whole Language to Incorporate African American Literature into Developmental Reading/Writing Classes." *Teaching English in the Two-Year College* 22 (1995): 173–78.

Meyers, Chet. *Teaching Students to Think Critically.* San Francisco: Jossey, 1986.

Meyers, Chet, and Tom Jones. *Promoting Active Learning: Strategies for the College Classroom.* San Francisco: Jossey, 1993.

Middendorf, Marilyn. "Bakhtin and the Dialogic Writing Class." *Journal of Basic Writing* 11.1 (1992): 34–46.

Sirc, Geoffrey. "The Autobiography of Malcolm X as a Basic Writing Text." *Journal of Basic Writing* 13.1 (1994): 50–77.

9 Collaborative Learning

Bruffee, Kenneth A. *Collaborative Learning: Higher Education, Interdependence, and the Authority of Knowledge.* Baltimore: Johns Hopkins UP, 1994.

Clark, Milton J., and Carol Peterson Haviland. "Language and Authority: Shifting the Privilege." *Journal of Basic Writing* 14.1 (1995): 57–66.

Dale, Helen. "Collaborative Research on Collaborative Writing." *English Journal* 83.1 (1994): 66–70.

———. "The Influence of Coauthoring on the Writing Process." *Journal of Teaching Writing* 15.1 (1996): 65–79.

Grobman, Laurie. "Building Bridges to Academic Discourse: The Peer Group Leader in Basic Writing Peer Response Groups." *Journal of Basic Writing* 18.2 (1999): 47–68.

Hacker, Tim. "The Effect of Teacher Conferences on Peer Response Discourse." *Teaching English in the Two-Year College* 23 (1996): 112–26.

Holt, Mara. "The Value of Written Peer Criticism." *College Composition and Communication* 43 (1992): 384–92.

Ott, C. Ann. "Collective Research at an Urban Community College." *Teaching English in the Two-Year College* 24 (1997): 7–13.

Schaffer, Jane. "Peer Response That Works." *Journal of Teaching Writing* 15.1 (1996): 81–90.

Smagorinsky, Peter. "The Aware Audience: Role-Playing Peer-Response Groups." *English Journal* 80.5 (1991): 35–91.

Strong, Gregory. "Teaching Writing with Small Groups." *Thought Currents in English Literature* 66 (1993): 129–52.

Wallace, David. "Teaching Collaborative Planning: Creating a Social Context for Writing." *Making Thinking Visible: Writing, Collaborative Planning, and Classroom Inquiry.* Ed. Linda Flower et al. Urbana, IL: NCTE, 1994. 48–66.

10 Technology

Adler-Kassner, Linda, and Thomas Reynolds. "Computers, Reading, and Basic Writers: Online Strategies for Helping Students with Academic Texts." *Teaching English in the Two-Year College* 23 (1996): 170–78.

Conference on Basic Writing—Home Page. <http://www.asu.edu/clas/english/composition/cbw/>.

Grobman, Laurie. "'I Found It on the Web, So Why Can't I Use It in My Paper?': Authorizing Basic Writers." *Journal of Basic Writing* 18.1 (1999): 76–90.

Harris, Mark, and Jeff Hooks. "Writing in Cyberspace: Communication, Community, and the Electronic Network." *Two-Year College English: Essays for a New Century.* Ed. Mark Reynolds. Urbana, IL: NCTE, 1994. 151–62.

Hawisher, Gail E., and Cynthia L. Selfe. *Critical Perspectives on Computers and Composition Instruction.* New York: Teachers College P. 1989.

Hawisher, Gail E., Cynthia Selfe, Charles Moran, and Paul LeBlanc. *Computers and the Teaching of Writing in American Higher Education 1979–1994: A History.* Norwood, NJ: Ablex, 1996.

Hobson, Eric H., and Karen Richardson Gee. "Ten Commandments for Computer-Assisted Composition Instructors." *Teaching English in the Two-Year College* 21 (1994): 224–30.

Kish, Judith Mara. "Breaking the Block: Basic Writers in the Electronic Classroom." *Journal of Basic Writing* 19 (2000): 141–59.

Mabrito, Mark. "Electronic Mail as a Vehicle for Peer Response: Conversations of High- and Low-Apprehensive Writers." *Written Communication* 8 (1991): 509–32.

Marx, Michael Steven. "Computers and Pedagogy: Distant Writers, Distant Critics, and Close Readings: Linking Composition Through a Peer-Critiquing Network." *Computers and Composition* 8.1 (1994): 23–39.

Meem, Deborah. "The Effect of Classroom Computer Use on College Basic Writers." *Research and Teaching in Developmental Education* 8.2 (1992): 57–69.

Otte, George, and Terence Collins. "Basic Writing and New Technologies." *BWe: Basic Writing e-Journal* 1.1 (1999). 20 July 2001 <www.asu.edu/clas/english/composition/cbw/bwe_summer1999.htm#george>.

Posey, Evelyn J. "The Widening Gulf: Computer-Enhanced Instruction on the Developmental Writing Classroom." *Teaching English in the Two-Year College* 21 (1994): 231–37.

Selfe, Cynthia. "Technology and Literacy: A Story about the Perils of Not Paying Attention." *College Composition and Communication* 50 (1999): 411–36.

Stan, Susan, and Terence G. Collins. "Basic Writing: Curricular Interactions with New Technology." *Journal of Basic Writing* 17 (1998): 18–41.

Taylor, Todd. "Computers in the Composition Curriculum: An Update." *Writing Program Administration* 20 (1996): 7–18.

Thompson, Diane. "Electronic Bulletin Boards: A Timeless Place for Collaborative Writing Projects." *Computers and Composition* 7.3 (1994): 43–53.

11 Writing and Race, Class, and Gender

Annas, Pamela. "Style as Politics: A Feminist Approach to Teaching Writing." *College English* 46 (1985): 360–71.

Balester, Valerie. *Cultural Divide: A Study of African-American College-Level Writers.* Portsmouth, NH: Boynton, 1993.

Bernstein, Susan Naomi. "On Teaching, Meditations and Invitations." *Journal of Developmental Education.* 3.2 (1998). 3 August 1999 <http://inet.ccp.cc.pa.us/vpacaff/divess/jde/snb.htm>.

Blake, Francie. "Identity, Community, and the Curriculum: A Call for Multiculturalism in the Classroom." *Journal of Developmental Education* 2.2 (1997): 3–7.

Cochran, Effie Papatzikou. "Giving Voice to Women in the Basic Writing and Language Minority Classroom." *Journal of Basic Writing* 13.1 (1994): 78–91.

Cushman, Ellen. *The Struggle and the Tools: Oral and Literate Strategies in an Inner City Community.* Albany: State U of New York P, 1998.

Dean, Terry. "Multicultural Classrooms, Monocultural Teachers." *College Composition and Communication* 40 (1989): 23–37.

Delpit, Lisa. *Other People's Children: Cultural Conflict in the Classroom.* New York: New P, 1995.

DiPardo, Anne. *A Kind of Passport: A Basic Writing Adjunct Program and the Challenge of Diversity.* New York: NCTE, 1993.

———. "Narrative Discourse in the Basic Writing Class: Meeting the Challenge of Cultural Pluralism." *Teaching English in the Two-Year College* 17 (1990): 45–53.

Fox, Helen. *Listening to the World: Cultural Issues in Academic Writing.* Urbana, IL: NCTE, 1994.

Gibson, Michelle. "An All-Too-Familiar Paradox: Familial Diversity and the Composition Classroom." *Writing on the Edge* 7.2 (1996): 19–30.

Gilyard, Keith. *Voices of the Self: A Study of Language Competence.* Detroit: Wayne State UP, 1991.

Hourigan, Maureen. "Re-visioning Basic Writing." *Literacy as Social Exchange: Intersections of Class, Gender, and Culture.* Ed. Maureen Hourigan. Albany: State U of New York P, 1994.

Jordan, June. "Nobody Mean More to Me Than You and the Future Life of Willie Jordan." *On Call* Ed. June Jordan. Boston: South End P. 1985. 123–39.

Lu Min-zhan. "From Silence to Words: Writing as Struggle." *College English* 49 (1987): 437–48.

———. "Professing Multiculturalism: The Politics of Style in the Contact Zone." *College Composition and Communication* 45 (1994): 442–58.

Patthey-Chavez, G. Genevieve, and Constance Gergen. "Culture as an Instructional Resource in the Multiethnic Composition Classroom." *Journal of Basic Writing* 11.1 (1992): 75–96.

Raimes, Ann. "Out of the Woods: Emerging Traditions in the Teaching of Writing." *TESOL Quarterly* 25 (1991): 407–30.

Rich, Adrienne. "Taking Women Students Seriously." In *Lies, Secrets, and Silence: Selected Prose, 1966–1978.* Ed. Adrienne Rich. New York: Norton, 1979. 237–45.

Royster, Jacqueline Jones. "When the First Voice You Hear Is Not Your Own." *College Composition and Communication* 47 (1996): 29–40.

Sadarangani, Umeeta. "Teaching Multicultural Issues in the Composition Classroom: A Review of Recent Practice." *Journal of Teaching Writing* 13.1–2 (1994): 33–54.

Villanueva, Victor Jr. *Bootstraps: From an American Academic of Color.* Urbana, IL: NCTE, 1993.

Wallace, David, and Annissa Bell. "Being Black at a Predominantly White University." *College English* 61 (1999): 307–27.

Young, Morris. "Narratives of Identity: Theorizing the Writer and the Nation." *Journal of Basic Writing* 15.2 (1996): 50–75.

Zamel, Vivian, and Ruth Spack, eds. *Negotiating Academic Literacies Teaching and Learning across Languages and Cultures.* Mahwah: Erlbaum, 1998.

12 Teaching ESL

Benson, Beverly, Mary P. Deming, Debra Denzer, and Maria Valeri-Gold. "A Combined Basic Writing/English as a Second Language Class: Melting Pot or Mishmash?" *Journal of Basic Writing* 11.1 (1992): 58–74.

Carroll, Pamela Sissi, with Frances Blake, Rose Ann Comalo, and Smaddar Messer. "When Acceptance Isn't Enough: Helping ESL Students Become Successful Writers." *English Journal* 85 (1996): 25–33.

Ferris, Dana, and John S. Hedgcock. *Teaching ESL Composition: Purpose, Process, and Practice.* Mahwah: Erlbaum, 1998.

Harklau, Linda, Kay M. Losey, and Meryl Siegal. *Generation 1.5 Meets College Composition: Issues in the Teaching of Writing to U.S.-Educated Learners of ESL.* Mahwah: Erlbaum, 1999.

Leki, Ilona. *Understanding ESL Writers: A Guide for Teachers.* Portsmouth: Boynton/Cook, 1992.

Matsuda, Paul Kei, and Tony Silva. "Cross-Cultural Composition: Mediated Integration of U.S. and International Students." *Composition Studies* 27.1 (1999): 15–30.

Nelson, Marie Wilson. *At the Point of Need: Teaching Basic and ESL Writers.* Portsmouth, NH: Heinemann, 1991.

Ransdell, D. R., "Important Events: Second-Language Students in the Composition Classroom." *Teaching English in the Two-Year College* 21 (1994): 217–22.

Robinson, William S. "ESL and Dialect Features in the Writing of Asian-American Students." *Teaching English in the Two-Year College* 22 (1995): 303–9.

Silva, Tony, and Paul Kei Matsuda, eds. *Landmark Essays on ESL Writing.* Mahwah: Erlbaum, 2001.

———. *On Second Language Writing.* Mahwah: Erlbaum, 2001.

Smitherman, Geneva. "CCC's Role in the Struggle for Language Rights." *College Composition and Communication* 50 (1999): 349–76.

Soliday, Mary. "Towards a Consciousness of Language: A Language Pedagogy for Multicultural Classrooms." *Journal of Basic Writing* 16.2 (1997): 62–75.

Zamel, Vivian. "Engaging Students in Writing-to-Learn: Promoting Language and Literacy across the Curriculum." *Journal of Basic Writing* 19.2 (2000): 3–21.

———. "Strangers in Academia: The Experiences of Faculty and ESL Students across the Curriculum." *College Composition and Communication* 46 (1995): 506–21.

13 Placement and Assessment

Anson, Chris M. "Portfolios for Teachers: Writing Our Way to Reflective Practice." *New Directions in Portfolio Assessment: Reflective Practice, Critical Theory, and Large-Scale Scoring.* Ed. Laurel Black et al. Portsmouth, NH: Boynton, 1994. 185–200.

Bartholomae, David. "The Study of Error." *College Composition and Communication* 31 (1980): 253–69.

Belanoff, Pat. "The Myths of Assessment." *Journal of Basic Writing* 10.1 (1991): 54–66.

Cameron, Thomas D. "A Responsible Evaluation Instrument and Its Impact on a Developmental Writing Program." *Teaching English in the Two-Year College* 20 (1993): 313–23.

Gleason, Barbara. "Evaluating Writing Programs in Real Time: The Politics of Remediation." *College Composition and Communication* 51 (2000): 560–88.

Grego, Rhonda, and Nancy Thompson. "Repositioning Remediation: Renegotiating Composition's Work in the Academy." *College Composition and Communication* 47.1 (1996): 62–84.

Haswell, Richard, and Susan Wyche-Smith. "Adventuring into Writing Assessment." *College Composition and Communication* 45 (1994): 220–36.

Haviland, Carol Peterson, and J. Milton Clark. "What Our Students Tell Us about Essay Examination Designs and Practices." *Journal of Basic Writing* 11.2 (1992): 47–60.

Herter, Roberta. "Writing Portfolios: Alternative to Testing (Research and Practice)." *English Journal* 80.1 (1991): 90–91.

Hilgers, Thomas. "Basic Writing Curricula and Good Assessment Practices." *Journal of Basic Writing* 14.2 (1995): 68–74.

Hillenbrand, Lisa. "Assessment of ESL Students in Mainstream College Composition." *Teaching English in the Two-Year College* 21 (1994): 125–30.

Lindemann, Erica. "What Do Teachers Need to Know about Linguistics?" *A Rhetoric for Writing Teachers*. Ed. Erica Lindemann. New York: Oxford UP, 1987. 93–116.

Miraglia, Eric. "A Self-Diagnostic Assessment in the Basic Writing Course." *Journal of Basic Writing* 14.2 (1995): 48–67.

Sommers, Nancy. "Responding to Student Writing." *College Composition and Communication* 33 (1982): 148–56.

Sweigart, William. "Assessing Achievement in a Developmental Writing Sequence." *Research and Teaching in Developmental Education* 12.2 (1996): 5–15.

White, Edward M. "The Importance of Placement and Basic Studies: Helping Students Succeed under the New Elitism." *Journal of Basic Writing* 14.2 (1995): 75–48.

———. "Responding to and Grading Student Writing." *Assigning, Responding, Evaluating: A Writing Teacher's Guide,* 3rd ed. New York: St. Martin's, 1995. 122–48.

———. *Teaching and Assessing Writing*. San Francisco: Jossey, 1994.

Wiener, Harvey S. "Evaluating Assessment Programs on Basic Skills." *Journal of Developmental Education* 13 (1989): 24–26.

Yancey, Kathleen Blake. "Looking Back as We Look Forward: Historicizing Writing Assessment." *College Composition and Communication* 50 (1999): 483–503.

14 Basic Writing and the Writing Center

Bawarshi, Anis, and Stephanie Pelkowski. "Postcolonialism and the Idea of a Writing Center." *The Writing Center Journal* 19.2 (1999): 51–58.

Boyd, Richard. "Imitate Me; Don't Imitate Me: Mimeticism in David Bartholomae's 'Inventing the University.'" *Journal of Advanced Composition* 11 (1991): 335–45.

Harris, Muriel. "Talking in the Middle: Why Writers Need Writing Tutors." *College English* 57 (1995): 27–42.

O'Hearn, Carolyn. "Recognizing the Learning Disabled College Writer." *College English* 51 (1989): 294–302.

Tassoni, John Paul. "The Liberatory Composition Teacher's Obligation to Writing Centers at Two-Year Colleges." *Teaching English in the Two-Year College* 25 (1998): 34–43.

Supplemental Section: Teacher Research and Basic Writing

Though none of these texts fits precisely within the thematic arrangement of *Teaching Developmental Writing: Background Readings,* Second Edition, each is a useful resource for those who teach developing writers. They are included here for further reference as you plan, teach, and evaluate your basic writing course. Many of these resources draw strong links between teacher research and the problem-posing pedagogy presented in several of the articles in this volume.

Adler-Kassner, Linda, and Gregory R. Glau. *The Bedford Bibliography for Teachers of Basic Writing.* Boston: Bedford/St. Martin's, 2002.

Atwell, Nancy. *In the Middle: Writing, Reading and Learning with Adolescents.* Portsmouth, NH: Boynton, 1987.

Boylan, Hunter R., and Barbara S. Bonham. "The Impact of Developmental Education Programs." *Research in Developmental Education* 9 (1992): 1–3.

Brandt, Deborah. *Literacy as Involvement: The Acts of Writers, Readers, and Texts.* Carbondale: Southern Illinois UP, 1990.

Calkins, Lucy McCormick. *The Art of Teaching Writing.* Portsmouth, NH: Heinemann, 1994.

Croake, Edith Morris. "Toward a Mentoring Program for New Two-Year College Faculty." *Teaching English in the Two-Year College* 23 (1996): 304–11.

Daiker, Donald A., and Max Morenberg, eds. *The Writing Teacher as Researcher.* Portsmouth, NH: Boynton, 1990.

Enos, Theresa, ed. *A Sourcebook for Basic Writing Teachers.* New York: Random House, 1987.

Graves, Donald H. *A Fresh Look at Writing.* Dallas: Southern Methodist UP, 1991.

Greene, Brenda M. "Empowerment and the Problem Identification and Resolution Stratgies of Basic Writers." *Journal of Basic Writing* 11.2 (1992): 4–27.

Halasek, Kay, and Nels P. Highberg, eds. *Landmark Essays on Basic Writing.* Mahwah: Erlbaum, 2001.

Haswell, Richard. *Gaining Ground in College Writing.* Dallas: Southern Methodist UP, 1991.

Hillocks, George. *Teaching Writing as a Reflective Practice.* New York: Teacher's College P, 1995.

Horner, Bruce. "Discoursing Basic Writing." *College Composition and Communication* 47 (1996): 199–222.

Knodt, Ellen Andrews. "Taming the Hydra: The Problem of Balancing Teaching and Scholarship at a Two-Year College." *Teaching English in the Two-Year College* 15 (1988): 170–74.

Laurence, Patricia, Peter Rondinone, Barbara Gleason, Thomas J. Farrell, Paul Hunter, and Min-zhan Lu. "Symposium on Basic Writing, Conflict and Struggle, and the Legacy of Mina Shaughnessy." *College English* 55 (1993): 879–903.

Lewiecki-Wilson, Cynthia. "Professing at the Fault Lines: Composition at Open Admissions Institutions." *College Composition and Communication* 50 (1999): 438–62.

Lu, Min-zhan. "Conflict and Struggle: The Enemies or Preconditions of Basic Writing?" *College English* 54 (1992): 887–913.

Lytle, Susan L. "Living Literacy: Rethinking Development in Adulthood." *Linguistics in Education* 3 (1991): 109–38.

Maher, Jane. *Mina Shaughnessy: Her Life and Work,* Urbana, IL: NCTE, 1997.

McNenny, Gerri, ed. *Mainstreaming Basic Writers: Politics and Pedagogies of Access.* Mahwah: Erlbaum, 2001.

Minot, Walter S., and Kenneth R. Gamble. "Self-Esteem and Writing Apprehension of Basic Writers: Conflicting Evidence." *Journal of Basic Writing* 10.2 (1991): 116–24.

Neumann, Anna. *Learning from Our Lives: Women, Research, and Autobiography in Education.* New York: Teacher's College P, 1997.

Reagan, Sally Barr. "Warning: Basic Writers at Risk—The Case of Javier." *Journal of Basic Writing* 10.2 (1991): 99–115.

Stuckey, J. Elspeth. *The Violence of Literacy.* Portsmouth, NH: Boynton, 1992.

Stygall, Gail. "Resisting Privilege: Basic Writing and Foucault's Author Function." *College Composition and Communication* 45 (1994): 320–41.

Tate, Gary, Edward P. J. Corbett, and Nancy Myers. *The Writing Teacher's Source Book.* New York: Oxford UP, 1994.

About the Contributors

Linda Adler-Kassner is an assistant professor of Composition at Eastern Michigan University, where she serves as director of First-Year Writing. She has published articles in the *Journal of Basic Writing, College Composition and Communication, Teaching English in the Two-Year College,* and elsewhere. She has also edited (with Robert Crooks and Ann Watters) *Writing the Community: Concepts and Models for Service-Learning in Composition* (1997). Her article in *Teaching Developmental Writing: Background Readings* was also included in *Basic Writing as a Political Act: Public Conversations about Writing and Literacy* (2002), by Adler-Kassner and Susanmarie Harrington.

Gloria Anzaldúa is a prominent Chicana/tejana lesbian poet, essayist, and cultural theorist whose groundbreaking *Borderlands / La Frontera: The New Mestiza* (1987) combines bilingual poetry, memoir, and historical analysis to illuminate the transcultural Mexican American "borderland" experience. Her subsequent works include *Making Face, Making Soul/Haciendo Caras: Creative and Cultural Perspectives by Feminists of Color* (ed., 1990) and *Interviews / Entrevistas* (2000). The recipient of an NEA Fiction Award and the Sappho Award of Distinction, Anzaldúa writes and teaches in northern California.

Susan Naomi Bernstein has published three previous Background Readings ancillaries and the textbook *A Brief Guide to the Novel* (2002). She has also written for *Teaching English in the Two-Year College, Florida English Journal, Thirteenth Moon,* and *ATQ: American Transcendental Quarterly.* She is an assistant professor of English at the University of Houston–Downtown, where she works as a developmental writing specialist. She also serves as writer-in-residence at a Houston public elementary school for the city's Writers in the Schools program.

Linda Lonon Blanton has devoted her career to the study of second-language writing, language and literacy acquisition, and academic discourse. A professor of English at the University of New Orleans, Blanton is also full-time director of the University Honors Program. She is the author of *ESL Composition Tales: Reflections on Teaching* (2002), as well as three textbooks: *Composition Practice* (2001), *Idea Exchange: From Speaking to Writing* (2002), and *Writing Workshop: Promoting College Success* (1998).

Stephen D. Brookfield has focused his research on adult learning, teaching, and critical thinking for over thirty years. He is currently Distinguished Professor at the University of St. Thomas. He is also the author of, among other works, *Understanding and Facilitating Adult Learning* (1968), *Developed Critical Thinkers* (1989), and *Becoming a Critically Reflective Teacher* (1995). Brookfield has received the Cyrill O. Houle Award for Literature in Adult Education, as well as honorary doctorates from the University System of New Hampshire and Concordia University. In 2001, Brookfield received the Leadership Award of the Association for Continuing Higher Education. In 2002, he was Visiting Professor at the Harvard Graduate School of Education.

Irene Brosnahan teaches at Illinois State University, where she is a professor of Linguistics and the director of the ESL program. In her research with Janice Neuleib, she has promoted the integration of grammar instruction with general composition instruction and has written on the effects of personality on grammar pedagogy. Their article "Teaching Grammar Affectively: Learning to Like Grammar" appears in *The Place of Grammar in Writing Instruction* (1995), edited by Ray Wallace.

Sally I. Cannon teaches at Saginaw Valley State University. She has written about the dynamics of basic writing assessment based on her experiences as writing coordinator of the SVSU English Department.

Virginia Crank teaches courses in composition, developmental writing, and American literature as professor of English at the University of Wisconsin–La Crosse. Before that, Crank taught at Rock Valley College, Missouri Western State College, and Peru State College. She holds a Ph.D. in English from Southern Illinois University.

Anne DiPardo, a professor of Education at the University of Iowa, is a past recipient of the NCTE/CEE Richard A. Meade Award for outstanding research in English education and the NCTE Promising Researcher Award. DiPardo has published articles on observation and literacy research in such journals as *Anthropology and Education Quarterly, Review of Educational Research*, and *Theory and Research in Social Education*. She has written two books: *A Kind of Passport: A Basic Writing Adjunct Program and the Challenge of Student Diversity* (1993) and *Teaching in Common: Challenges to Joint Work in Classrooms and Schools* (1999).

Yu Ren Dong, an associate professor of English in the Department of Secondary Education and Youth Services at Queens College/CUNY, has devoted her research to the unique strengths that ESL students bring to writing classrooms and the role of teacher/student reflection in TESOL pedagogy. She has published articles in *TESOL Journal, International Journal of Bilingual Education and Bilingualism*, and *Journal of Teaching and Writing*, among others.

Peter Elbow, a professor emeritus of English at the University of Massachusetts–Amherst, has written extensively about orality, literacy, and the phenomenology of writing. In such books as *Writing without Teachers* (1998), *Writing with Power* (1998), and *Everyone Can Write: Essays toward a Hopeful Theory of Writing and Teaching Writing* (2000), Elbow sets forth an expressionist pedagogy of composition, exploring the effects of freewriting on the development of voice. During his tenure at the University of Massachusetts, Elbow directed the Writing Program for four years. He has also taught at the Massachusetts Institute of Technology, Franconia College, Evergreen State College, Wesleyan University, and SUNY–Stony Brook.

Amelia E. El-Hindi teaches in several areas, including literacy, math and science, pedagogy, multiculturalism, and the psychology of learning. An assistant professor at Transylvania University in Lexington, Kentucky, El-Hindi is currently researching the integration of literacy with math and science instruction within elementary classrooms. El-Hindi has a Ph.D. from Syracuse University.

Roger Gilles has served as director of the Department of Writing at Grand Valley State University in Allendale, Michigan. His areas of study include the rhetoric of news and politics and Richard Weaver's theory of argument. With Daniel J. Royer, Gilles has edited *Directed Self-Placement: Principles and Practices* (2002) and coauthored an article, "The Origins of the Department of Academic, Creative, and Professional Writing at Grand Valley State University," for *Field of Dreams: Independent Writing Programs* (2002).

Barbara Gleason has been an associate professor of English since 1990 at the City College of New York, where she currently administers the Masters program in Language and Literacy. She has also served as director of the composition program and teaches in the City College's Center for Worker Education. Gleason's essays on writing curricula, program evaluation, basic writing, and returning adult students appear regularly in professional journals. She has coedited *Composition in Four Keys: Inquiring into a Field* (1995) and *Cultural Tapestry* (1997). She currently serves on the Writing Instructor Advisory Board.

Jeffrey T. Grabill joined the Department of American Thought and Language at Michigan State University as associate professor in 2002. Before that, he was an assistant professor of English at Georgia State University. Grabill's research and publications reflect his wide-ranging interests in the fields of technology, technical communication, and community literacy. His award-winning articles include "Utopic Visions, the Technopoor, and Public Access: Writing Technologies in a Community Literacy Program" and "Computer-Mediated Communication in the Undergraduate Writing Classroom: A Study of the Relationship of Online Discourse and Classroom Discourse in Two Writing Classes." His book *Community Literacy Programs and the Politics of Change* was published in 2001.

Ann E. Green is the director of the writing center and an assistant professor of English at St. Joseph's University in Philadelphia. Her publications include "Difficult Stories: Service-Learning, Race, Class, and Whiteness" in *College Composition and Communication*; "Guns, Language, and Beer: Hunting for a Working-Class Language in the Academy" in *Calling Cards: Theory and Practice in Studies of Race, Gender, and Culture*, edited by Jacqueline Jones Royster and Ann Marie Simpkins (2003); and "'But You Aren't White': Racial Perceptions and Service-Learning," in *Michigan Journal of Community Service-Learning*. She teaches courses on writing, race, class, and gender.

Kay Harley, a professor of English at Saginaw Valley State University, has written about the dynamics of basic writing assessment. She has also served as director of the Saginaw Valley National Writing Project.

Linda S. Houston is an associate professor in the Arts, Science and Business Division of the Agricultural Technical Institute at Ohio State University. In addition to teaching writing and communication courses, Houston serves as director of the Writing Center. For her leadership and service to the institute's civil rights, diversity, and teaching committees, she has been honored as a student advocate inside and out of the classroom.

Glynda Hull, cochair of the Language and Literacy, Society, and Culture Area in the Graduate School of Education at the University of California–Berkeley, has been honored with the school's Distinguished Teaching Award. Her most recent book is *School's Out! Bridging Out-of-School Literacies with Classroom Practice* (2002, coedited with Katherine Schultz). Her research interests center around literacy — its definitions and acquisition.

June Jordan is a celebrated poet, novelist, essayist, and political activist. The author of twenty-six books, Jordan is the most published African American writer in history. Before her death in June 2002, she was a professor of African American Studies at the University of California–Berkeley, where she founded and directed Poetry for the People. Local high schools, churches, and prisons participated in the popular outreach program. On the strength of her poetry and books such as *June Jordan's Poetry for the People: A Blueprint for the Revolution* (1995) and *Affirmative Acts: Political Essays* (1998), Jordan received numerous grants, fellowships, and awards. Her poems have appeared in more than thirty anthologies.

Mary Kay Jackman teaches rhetoric and composition to returning and first-year students at Southern Methodist University in Dallas, Texas. Her research interests include narrative theory and the pedagogical properties of autobiography. She holds a Ph.D. from New Mexico State University.

Loretta Frances Kasper is a professor of English at Kingsborough Community College/CUNY and the author of two content-based student texts, *Teaching English through the Disciplines: Psychology* (1997) and *Interdisciplinary English* (1998). Her article "Technology as a Tool for Literacy in the Age of Information: Implications for the ESL Classroom" was named *Teaching English in the Two-Year College*'s Best Article of the Year in 2002. Kasper serves on the editorial review boards of the journals *Teaching English in the Two-Year College* and *Educational Technology and Society*. She served on the editorial review board of the journal *Reading Online* from 1997 to 2000.

William B. Lalicker is an associate professor of English at West Chester University and serves on the Board of Directors of the Volunteer English Program in Chester County, Pennsylvania. He has published on composition theory and the role of imagination in multicultural writing, and maintains that bilingual education and interdisciplinary thinking draw power from an imagination-based epistemology that makes creative use of ambivalence and dialectic. Lalicker is an advisory editor for the journal *College Literature* and was cochair of the 2003 Conference on Basic Writing.

Ilona Leki is an associate professor of English and the director of English as a Second Language at the University of Tennessee–Knoxville. She is the author of *Understanding ESL Writers: A Guide for Teachers* (1992) and *Academic Writing: Exploring Processes and Strategies* (1998), as well as the coeditor of *Academic Writing Programs: Case Studies in TESOL Practice* (2001). Leki was a member of the editorial advisory board of *TESOL Quarterly* and has served as president of Tennessee TESOL. She has shared her second-language writing pedagogy with other educators through training programs in Brazil, Colombia, Egypt, France, Turkey, and Yugoslavia.

Janice Neuleib is a professor of Linguistics and the director of Writing Programs at Illinois State University. In her work with Irene Brosnahan, she calls for the integration of grammar instruction with general composition instruction. They have also written on the effects of personality on grammar pedagogy. Neuleib and Brosnahan's "Teaching Grammar Affectively: Learning to Like Grammar" appears in *The Place of Grammar in Writing Instruction* (1995), edited by Ray Wallace.

Sarah Nixon is an associate professor at Southwest Missouri State University, where she teaches in the School of Teacher Education's Graduate Reading Program. She was formerly the assistant director of the Ohio Literacy Resource Center at Kent State University. Nixon elucidates student-centered creative problem-solving as an effective classroom practice for teachers of adult literacy and composition.

Rei R. Noguchi is a professor of English at California State University–Northridge and author of the highly influential book *Grammar and the Teaching of Writing: Limits and Possibilities* (1991). In his work, he emphasizes the need to teach the principles of grammar within the context of the student's own writing. Noguchi's other teaching and research interests include semantics, pragmatics, and historical linguistics.

Richard Raymond teaches technical communication, composition theory, and persuasive writing at the University of Arkansas–Little Rock, where he also serves as chair of the Department of Rhetoric and Writing. In 1999, Raymond won *Teaching English in the Two-Year College*'s annual Best Article Award for the selection that is included in this ancillary. Most recently he has written for *Pedagogy* and *Writing Program Administration*.

Nancy Lawson Remler is the director of the Coastal Georgia Writing Project (a local site of the National Writing Project) and is the Writing Project liaison to the Executive Board of the Georgia Council of Teachers of English. An associate professor of English at Armstrong Atlantic State University in Savannah since 1991, Remler teaches courses in composition and rhetoric.

Adrienne Rich is a prolific poet, theorist, and political activist whose influential writings have spanned more than half a century. Her commitment to social justice and the women's movement took shape during the mid-1960s, when she taught in a remedial English program for New York City's recent immigrants and other students who were underrepresented in college admissions. Her nineteen volumes of poetry and three collections of essays explore themes of linguistic privilege, sexual identity, and patriarchal systems of oppression. Rich has taught at Swarthmore College, Columbia University, Brandeis University, Rutgers University, Cornell University, San Jose State University, and Stanford University. She has been honored with the National Book Award, two Guggenheim Fellowships, and a MacArthur Fellowship, among other awards. She lives in northern California.

Mike Rose identifies literacy — its definitions and its acquisition — among his principal teaching and research interests. As a professor of Social Research Methodology at UCLA, Rose explores the cognitive, linguistic, and cultural factors that affect engagement with written language. He recounts his experiences in his autobiographical work *Lives on the Boundary* (1989) and has also written *Possible Lives: The Promise of Public Education in America* (1995).

Daniel J. Royer focuses his research on the phenomenology of writing events and the confluence of theory, history, and practice in writing instruction. He has served as the director of the Department of Writing at Grand Valley State University in Allendale, Michigan. With Roger Gilles, he edited *Directed Self-Placement: Principles and Practices* (2002) and coauthored "The Origins of the Department of Academic, Creative, and Professional Writing at Grand Valley State University" for *Field of Dreams: Independent Writing Programs* (2002).

Gregory Shafer is a professor of English at Mott Community College in Flint, Michigan, and president of the Michigan Council of Teachers of English. His publications include articles in *English Journal* and *The Humanist* and a book, *Process and Voice in the Writing Workshop* (2000). He is the former regional coordinator for the Michigan Council for the Arts and has received four Excellence in Education awards from the Kellogg Foundation.

Mina Shaughnessy began teaching composition at the City College of New York in 1967 and served as the director of the school's Basic Writing Program until her death in 1978. She founded the *Journal of Basic Writing*, and in her foundational work *Errors and Expectations* (1977) examined the question of where it is "best to begin a course in basic writing." Many thinkers and teachers in the field of developmental writing trace their roots to Shaughnessy's early inquiries about writing pedagogy, which, above all, stressed respect for students and their strengths, rather than focusing exclusively on weaknesses or deficiencies.

Kay Thurston teaches at Pima Community College in Tucson, Arizona. She formerly taught at Navajo Community College (renamed Diné College). In 1998, Thurston won *Teaching English in the Two-Year College*'s Best Article Award for "Mitigating Barriers to Navajo Students' Success in English Courses." Thurston's consciousness of the educational obstacles faced by Native Americans informs her choices as an educator, as her classes explore Native American oral and written literature in the context of that culture.

Constance Weaver, a professor of English at Western Michigan University in Kalamazoo, teaches courses in reading and writing and in language arts instruction. In addition to writing *Teaching Grammar in Context* (1996), Weaver has edited *Lessons to Share: On Teaching Grammar in Context* (1998), a collection of essays that offer a variety of perspectives and practical applications, including grammar instruction for ESL students. Weaver's other books include *Practicing What We Know: Informed Reading Instruction* (1998), *Reading Process and Practice: From Socio-Linguistics to Whole Language* (2nd ed., 2002), and *Success at Last: Helping AD(H)D Students Achieve Their Potential* (1994).

Linda Feldmeier White, a professor of English at Stephen F. Austin State University in Nacogdoches, Texas, has written and lectured on the learning disabled (LD) student experience in the college classroom and writing center. In her examination of LD pedagogy, White elucidates the educator's role in advocating for LD learners' access to higher education. Her articles have been published in *College Composition and Communication, The Writing Center Journal,* and *Children's Literature.*

Acknowledgments *(continued from page iv)*

Stephen D. Brookfield, "Understanding Classroom Dynamics: The Critical Incident Questionnaire." Originally published in *Becoming a Critically Reflective Teacher*. Copyright © 1995 by Jossey-Bass Publishers. The material is used by permission of John Wiley & Sons, Inc.

Conference on College Composition and Communication, "Writing Assessment: A Position Statement from the Conference on College Composition and Communication." From *Teaching English in the Two-Year College*, October 1995. Copyright © 1995 by the National Council of Teachers of English. Reprinted with permission.

Virginia Crank, "Asynchronous Electronic Peer Response in a Hybrid Basic Writing Classroom." From *Teaching English in the Two-Year College* 32.2, December 2002, pp. 145–55. Copyright © 2002 by the National Council of Teachers of English. Reprinted with permission.

Anne DiPardo, "'Whispers of Coming and Going': Lessons from Fannie." From *The Writing Center Journal* 12.2 (1992): 125–44. Reprinted by permission.

Yu Ren Dong, "The Need to Understand ESL Students' Native Language Writing Experiences." From *Teaching English in the Two-Year College*, March 1999. Copyright © 1999 by the National Council of Teachers of English. Reprinted with permission.

Peter Elbow, "Using the Collage for Collaborative Writing." Originally published in *Composition Studies* 27.1, Spring 1999. Copyright © 1999. Reprinted by permission.

Amelia E. El-Hindi, "Connecting Reading and Writing: College Learners' Metacognitive Awareness." Originally published in the *Journal of Developmental Education*, Volume 21 (Issue 2), published by Appalachian State University, Boone, NC 28608. Reprinted by permission of the publisher.

Barbara Gleason, "Returning Adults to the Mainstream: Toward a Curriculum for Diverse Student Writers." Originally published in *Mainstreaming Basic Writers: Politics and Pedagogies of Access*, edited by Gerri McNenny. Copyright © 2001 by Barbara Gleason. Reprinted by permission of the author.

Jeffrey T. Grabill, "Technology, Basic Writing, and Change." Copyright © 1998 by the *Journal of Basic Writing*, The City University of New York. Reprinted from Volume 17, Number 2, by permission.

Ann E. Green, "My Uncle's Guns." Originally published in *Writing on the Edge*, Volume 9, Number 1, Fall/Winter 1997/98. Reprinted by permission of the author.

Kay Harley and Sally I. Cannon, "Failure: The Student's or the Assessment's?" Copyright © 1996 by the *Journal of Basic Writing*, The City University of New York. Reprinted from Volume 15, Number 1, by permission.

Linda S. Houston, "Accommodations for Learning Differences in the English Classroom." Originally published in *Teaching English in the Two-Year College*, December 1994. Copyright © 1994 by the National Council of Teachers of English. Reprinted with permission.

Glynda Hull and Mike Rose, "'This Wooden Shack Place': The Logic of an Unconventional Reading." Originally published in *College Composition and Communication*, October 1990. Copyright © 1990 by the National Council of Teachers of English. Reprinted with permission.

Mary Kay Jackman, "When the Personal Becomes Professional: Stories from Reentry Adult Women Learners about Family, Work, and School." Originally published in *Composition Studies* 27.2, Fall 1999. Reprinted by permission.

June Jordan, "Nobody Mean More to Me Than You and the Future Life of Willie Jordan." From *On Call* by June Jordan. © 1985 by June Jordan. Reprinted by permission of the June M. Jordan Literary Estate Trusts.

Loretta Frances Kasper, "ESL Writing and the Principle of Nonjudgmental Awareness: Rationale and Implementation." From *Teaching English in the Two-Year College*, February 1998. Copyright © 1998 by the National Council of Teachers of English. Reprinted with permission.

William B. Lalicker, "A Basic Introduction to Basic Writing Program Structures: A Baseline and Five Alternatives." Originally published in *Conference on Basic Writ-*

ing: Basic Writing e-Journal (Summer 2000). Reprinted by permission of the author and *BWe*, <www.asu.edu/cls/english/composition/cbw>.

Ilona Leki, "Reciprocal Themes in ESL Reading and Writing." From *Reading in the Composition Classroom: Second Language Perspectives,* First Edition. Copyright © 1993 by Ilona Leki. Reprinted by permission of the author.

Janice Neuleib and Irene Brosnahan, "Teaching Grammar to Writers." Originally published in the *Journal of Basic Writing*, The City University of New York, Volume 6, Number 2. Copyright © 1987. Reprinted by permission of the authors.

Sarah Nixon, "Using Problem-Posing Dialogue in Adult Literacy Education." Originally published in *Adult Learning 7.2*, November/December 1995. Reprinted by permission of the author.

Rei R. Noguchi, "Teaching the Basics of a Writer's Grammar." Originally published in *Grammar and the Teaching of Writing.* Copyright © 1991 by the National Council of Teachers of English. Reprinted with permission.

Richard Raymond, "Building Learning Communities on Nonresidential Campuses." Originally published in *Teaching English in the Two-Year College*, May 1999. Copyright © 1999 by the National Council of Teachers of English. Reprinted with permission.

Nancy Lawson Remler, "The More Active the Better: Engaging College English Students with Active Learning Strategies." Originally published in *Teaching English in the Two-Year College* 30.1, September 2002. Copyright © 2002 by the National Council of Teachers of English. Reprinted with permission.

Adrienne Rich, "Teaching Language in Open Admissions." Originally published in *Harvard English Studies* #4 (1973). Copyright © 1973. Reprinted by permission of the Department of English and American Literature and Language, Harvard University.

Daniel J. Royer and Roger Gilles, "Directed Self-Placement: An Attitude of Orientation." From *College Composition and Communication* 50.1, September 1998. Copyright © 1998 by the National Council of Teachers of English. Reprinted with permission.

Gregory Shafer, "Using Letters for Process and Change in the Basic Writing Classroom." Originally published in *Teaching English in the Two-Year College*, March 2000. Copyright © 2000 by the National Council of Teachers of English. "Negotiating Audience and Voice in the Writing Center." Originally published in *Teaching English in the Two-Year College*, December 1999. Copyright © 1999 by the National Council of Teachers of English. Reprinted with permission.

Mina P. Shaughnessy, "Some New Approaches toward Teaching." Copyright © 1994 by the *Journal of Basic Writing,* The City University of New York. Reprinted from Volume 13, Number 1, by permission.

Kay Thurston, "Mitigating Barriers to Navajo Students' Success in English Courses." From *Teaching English in the Two-Year College*, September 1998. Copyright © 1998 by the National Council of Teachers of English. Reprinted with permission.

Constance Weaver, "Teaching Style through Sentence Combining and Sentence Generating." Originally published in *Teaching Grammar in Context,* by Constance Weaver. Copyright © 1996 by Constance Weaver. Published by Boynton/Cook, a subsidiary of Reed Elsevier, Inc., Portsmouth, NH. Reprinted by permission of the publisher.

Linda Feldmeier White, excerpt from "Learning Disability, Pedagogies, and Public Discourse." From *College Composition and Communication* 53.4, June 2002. Copyright © 2002 by the National Council of Teachers of English. Reprinted with permission.